NEW ENGLAND:
INDIAN SUMMER
1865-1915

NEW ENGLAND: INDIAN SUMMER 1865-1915

VAN WYCK BROOKS

THE UNIVERSITY OF CHICAGO PRESS

CHICAGO AND LONDON

Published by arrangement with E. P. Dutton, Inc.

The University of Chicago Press, Chicago 60637
The University of Chicago Press, Ltd., London

93 92 91 90 89 88 87 86 85 84   1 2 3 4 5

Library of Congress Cataloging in Publication Data

Brooks, Van Wyck, 1886–1963.
    New England: Indian summer, 1865–1915.

    Sequel to: The flowering of New England.
    Sequel: The world of Washington Irving.
    Reprint. Originally published: New York: Dutton,
1950. (Everyman's library; 641A. Essays and belles-
lettres)
    Includes index.
    1. American literature—New England—History and
criticism.   2. American literature—19th century—
History and criticism.   3. American literature—20th
century—History and criticism.   4. New England—
Civilization.   I. Title.
PS243.B72   1984   810'.9974   84–8545
ISBN 0-226-07578-8 (paper)

To

LEWIS MUMFORD

CONTENTS

CONTENTS

PREFACE

THIS book, a sequel of *The Flowering of New England,* is the second of a series in which I hope to sketch the history of American literature. It takes up the thread of the previous volume and carries it on to the present day. I am now planning, in subsequent volumes, to begin at an earlier moment than either of these and present the literary history of the rest of the country. If I am able to carry out this plan, *The Age of Washington Irving,* my next volume, will precede *The Flowering of New England* as the first of the series.

The present book requires two or three words of explanation. My choice of subjects may seem arbitrary. Which of these authors were New Englanders, and which were not? With the gradual merging of New England in the rest of the nation, it has not been easy to draw the line. I have included numbers, born outside New England, who were yet in essential ways identified with it, and I have omitted others who might well be considered New Englanders. But any sectional treatment of our literary history is bound, as it seems to me, to be arbitrary, and this question can only be judged in relation to the total effect. I have left out certain figures who might have been included here, feeling that in some future volume they could be treated to better advantage. Perhaps this is the place to add that I am not myself a New Englander, except in part by heredity and in part by adoption.

Regarding recent and living authors, except in two or three cases, I have been necessarily brief in my treatment. I have been more concerned with the background from which they emerged, and this I have tried to treat with

PREFACE

fullness. It may strike some readers that I have made too much of Boston, too much especially of Harvard, at the expense of other New England centres. But, considering that this is a literary history, I cannot feel that I have done so. Harvard has retained an extraordinarily close connection with literature in this region, if not in the nation; and Boston remains the regional capital in most things intellectual. Aside from this, my emphasis on Boston has served.to give the book a "unity of place." This was indispensable in any attempt to picture a phase of literary history so confused and complex and marked by such multifarious comings and goings. It must be added that I have not ventured to discuss philosophical writers at any length. I am not competent to do so, and, besides, I feel that these writers are related to my subject somewhat obliquely. This must be my excuse for treating so inadequately the beautiful mind and spirit of William James.

I wish to thank the Carnegie Corporation, which, through its president, Mr. Frederick P. Keppel, generously provided me with a "grant-in-aid." I am also obliged to my friends Lee Simonson and Newton Arvin, who kindly offered to read the proofs of this book.

V. W. B.

NEW ENGLAND: INDIAN SUMMER 1865-1915

CHAPTER I

DR. HOLMES'S BOSTON

IN THE early spring of 1866, a young man named William Dean Howells quietly slipped into Boston. He was twenty-nine years old, slight, with a black moustache, mild in his manner and modest in appearance. One saw that he had delicate perceptions and a shrewd gift of observation, and he gave one a marked impression of will and purpose. The brooding look in his eyes betokened a future.

This young man had realized a bold ambition. The editor of *The Atlantic Monthly*, James T. Fields, had given him a post as coadjutor. Six years before, he had come to Boston, commissioned by his paper in Ohio, with hopes that he had openly confessed. In the Western Reserve, where he had lived, Boston was a sort of holy city. The people had largely come from New England, and those who cared for letters regarded Boston as many of the Bostonians regarded London. It was the hub of the universe, as Oliver Wendell Holmes had said, and the intellectual world revolved about it. Howells, a reverent pilgrim, aspired to be the "linchpin in the hub." His only recommendation was a poem in *The Atlantic*, and Boston had nothing to offer him at the moment; but before he returned to the West, after this flying visit, an incident occurred that foreshadowed his future. Lowell invited him to dinner, to meet Holmes and Fields, in a little upper room at the Parker House. The talk lasted four hours, and Holmes said to Lowell, "Well, James, this is something like the apostolic succession. This is the laying on of hands."

The doctor's little joke was prophetic, as time was soon to show. The young man had impressed the Boston and Cambridge Olympians. "Howells is sure to be somebody if he lives," Lowell had written to Fields, who had called him back six years later; and Charles Eliot Norton, struck by the papers on Venetian life he had published in the Boston *Advertiser,* exerted himself to find and helped him to buy a house on Sacramento Street in Cambridge. There, with his wife, whom he had married in Paris,—for he had been living abroad, as consul in Venice,—Howells passed the first of the twenty years that he was to spend in New England. A sweet-brier grew over the door and pine-trees flanked the gate. There were pear-trees in the yard and tangles of grapes and blackberries. When he was not in his office, reading proofs and writing reviews, or jogging back and forth on the horse-car that ran from Harvard Square, or working on his essays and travel-sketches,—for he had scarcely begun to think of himself as a novelist,—he fed his eyes and ears with the Boston scene. Three years in Venice had not dispelled for Howells the charm of New England.

He had acted with a strategy that marked his life for fifty years. A campaign biography of Lincoln had brought him his appointment as consul at Venice, and he had set his cap at Boston as the indisputable centre of American letters. Later he was to show the same clairvoyance when the centre passed to New York, or when, as people said, he carried it with him. At present, surrounded by men who aroused his ambition, in an atmosphere that stirred his imagination, he felt his every faculty on the stretch. He had been just in time, on his earlier visit, during the two days he had spent in Concord, to see Thoreau and Hawthorne, who had passed him on to Emerson with a friendly note; and the sage had opened his door for the young man from the West and looked at him with a vague serenity. The exaltations of Concord were not for Howells, whose appetite was all for visible facts, much as he revered these luminaries, although Hawthorne, whom he adored as an artist, said what Howells felt: he longed to see an America that was free from the shadow of Europe. But he had not forgotten his excitement when, after meeting Dr. Holmes, he had walked the streets and the Common till two in the morning. He had approached New England by way of Quebec and Portland, where he had first seen the ocean, and the meadows, newly mown, and the grey stone walls, the crumbling forts, the half-deserted harbours had evoked the American past of the histories and poems, as the great square mansions of Portsmouth and Salem, withdrawing themselves in reserve from the quiet streets, suggested a more complex civilization than he had known in the West. Marblehead meant Whittier's ballad, Nahant recalled Longfellow, while the gaunt old hip-roofed houses brought back the magic of Hawthorne; and Boston had overwhelmed him at the first encounter. Was it not a legend in the West that everything noble and grand, in the national life, everything magnanimous and enlightened, had originated in Boston?* There was the "cradle of liberty," Faneuil Hall, a symbol of the days when there were giants, and there the genius of freedom had risen again in Garrison, Charles Sumner and Wendell Phillips. There King's Chapel stood, and Bunker Hill, the State House, the Old Corner Bookstore, the Hancock House, the Quincy Man-

* See the attitude of Dr. Ellison, of Eriecreek in western New York, in Howells's *A Chance Acquaintance.* Kitty, his daughter, had always heard her father and uncle "talking of some indefinite, far-off place they called Boston, in terms that commended it to her childish apprehension as very little less holy than Jerusalem, and as the home of all the good and great people outside of Palestine . . . Boston had always been Dr. Ellison's faith . . . A little formal, perhaps, a little reserved, but excellent men; polished, and certainly of sterling principles."

This was the attitude of Howells's father. It was also the attitude of Hamlin Garland's father, as reflected in *A Son of the Middle Border.*

sion, the Granary Burial Ground, renowned in poems. There Cornhill ran its crooked length, the resort of the antiquaries and the bookworms, and the back of Beacon Hill was an architectural jumble that rivalled Dr. Johnson's haunts for quaintness.* One saw the Franklin tomb, the black old gravestones of the sixteen-thirties, the Park Street Church at Brimstone Corner, the Frog Pond, the Long Path, where the Autocrat had asked a well-known question; and there whole shelves of the books of one's childhood strolled about the streets in flesh and blood. Faces rose out of the crowd, at casual moments, that one had known for years in pictures, the Autocrat's quizzical visage, or Richard Henry Dana's; or possibly one saw Emerson descending from a horse-car, or the scarcely less fabulous Dr. Howe, the husband of Julia Ward Howe, who had written the *Battle Hymn of the Republic*. The "sailors with bearded lips" sauntered about the waterfront, as if they had stepped straight out of Longfellow's poem; and even the Yankee tang and gait and accent satisfied one's thirst for recognitions. History was visible and tangible in Boston. Was it not known that Copley's daughter still lived in Beacon Street, the painter's dearest Betsy, the sister of Lord Lyndhurst, three times chancellor of England? † Mrs. Greene, born in Boston, had heard Burke's opening speech at the trial of Warren Hastings. She had known Sir Joshua Reynolds, not as a child but as a grown young lady. As her father's reader and constant companion, in the painting-room in London, she had talked with Fox and Pitt and Mrs. Siddons. She re-

* " 'I didn't suppose you Western people cared for these things,' Mr. Arbuton once said; 'I thought your minds were set on things new and square.'
" 'But how could you think so?' replied Kitty, tolerantly. 'It's because we have so many new and square things that we like the old crooked ones.' "—Howells, *A Chance Acquaintance.*

† Mrs. Greene, born Elizabeth Copley, died at the age of ninety-six in Boston in 1866, the year of Howells's arrival.

membered meeting Charlotte, the heroine of *The Sorrows of Werther*. Then, marrying a Boston man, she had
witnessed every event in the town since the year of her
return, 1800. Nor was Mrs. Greene the only person who
recalled the building of the State House. Venerable figures and things abounded in Boston. There was something harmonious and mellow, something old or odd, at
every turn of the picture, and, best of all, perhaps, the
"Boston look," a blessing for the budding man of letters.*

The aspirant from the West had arrived at the psychological moment. Ten years before, the city of light
and learning could scarcely have offered a foothold to the
stoutest invader. Dominant, abundant, efflorescent, it was
all too well supplied by its own New England, as twenty
years hence the stout invader might not have cared to
scale the Boston wall. At present, with the breach the war
had made, and with all the treasure still within the city,
Boston was ripe for invasion, and most of the younger
writers throughout the country shared Howells's feeling
about it. New England ideals and examples had a commanding influence wherever people cared for thought and
writing, and eastern Massachusetts was hallowed ground
for thousands of the rising generation. Many a pilgrim
like William Winter walked out to Cambridge in the
moonlight merely to touch the latch of Longfellow's gate.
Many walked to Concord for a glimpse of Emerson's
woodpile, wishing they had the courage to knock at the
door. Others, like Forseythe Willson, who had written
The Old Sergeant, admired and praised by Longfellow,
Lowell and Holmes, too shy to announce their presence,
installed themselves in lodgings, in order to be near these

---

* The "Boston look" was a near-sighted look, occasionally assumed or
affected, that presupposed an interest in all things intellectual. It was a
favourite subject of the comic artists, especially in New York, where it
was supposed that Boston people wore spectacles in their cradles.

6   NEW ENGLAND: INDIAN SUMMER

famous men.* Edward Rowland Sill, a student at the Divinity School in Cambridge, later well known as a poet, whose chosen themes were music and science, hungrily followed Agassiz's lectures and hovered about the music-hall, where the Boston illuminati often gathered. One felt the presence of these worthies, whom younger men revered as the Greeks of old revered their early poets,—

> old Hesiod, teaching us husbandry,
> Ploughing, and sowing, and rural affairs,
> Rural economy, rural astronomy,
> Homely morality, labour and thrift.†

They were "high priests," as *The Atlantic* was a "temple," in the eyes of Emily Dickinson, who lived at Amherst. Miss Dickinson, a lawyer's daughter, a somewhat rebellious young lady, whose friends left books for her in hiding-places, had visited during the war in Boston and Cambridge. She had dreamed of meeting Tennyson in the office of Ticknor and Fields, and Cambridge for her was rather like Westminster Abbey. In the West, the older writers were oracles and sages.‡ Meanwhile, for those who were merely romantic, the atmosphere of Boston had

* Forseythe Willson's poems, of no permanent merit, dealt with Civil War themes. Lowell read *The Old Sergeant* in a Western newspaper. He wrote to the poet and presently found that Willson was living in Cambridge, in a house facing his own.
† Aristophanes, *The Frogs.*
‡ "I stopped [about 1869] with my father over a night [at Garfield's] in Hiram, Ohio, where we found him at home from Congress for the summer. I was then living in Cambridge, in the fullness of my content with my literary circumstance, and as we were sitting with the Garfield family on the verandah that overlooked their lawn I was beginning to speak of the famous poets I knew when Garfield stopped me with 'Just a minute!' He ran down into the grassy space, first to one fence and then to the other at the sides, and waved a wild arm of invitation to the neighbours who were also sitting on their back porches. 'Come over here!' he shouted. 'He's telling about Holmes, and Longfellow, and Lowell, and Whittier!' And at his bidding dim forms began to mount the fences and follow him up to his verandah. 'Now go on,' he called to me, when we were all seated, and I went on, while the whippoorwills whirred and whistled round, and the hours drew toward midnight."—Howells, *Years of My Youth.*

much of the bookish charm of Charles Lamb's London. The auctioneers quoted Shakespeare; and, if you entered a corner grocery, perhaps to buy a codfish, the man would ask you how you liked *Lucile,* while he was tying it up. Many a queer old soul haunted the book-stalls, in quest of some ancient print or musty pamphlet, a relic of Fisher Ames's days, or the days of Benjamin Franklin, or Swift and Pope. Another young writer who had settled in Boston, in the same year as Howells, after having lived in New York, wrote to one of his friends, "The humblest man of letters has a position here which he doesn't have in New York. To be known as an able writer is to have the choicest society open to you . . . A knight of the quill here is supposed necessarily to be a gentleman. In New York—he's a Bohemian!—outside of his personal friends he has no standing." *

In short, the "American Athens" still deserved its name, seldom as one heard this any longer. In 1855, Theodore Parker had called the town the "American Dublin," which was almost more to the point, for the Irish power was rapidly rising with other strains of foreign birth.† There were signs that the building days of New England were over, and all things were ripe for change in Boston. But the Yankees were omnipotent still, in numbers, wealth and prestige, and Boston had no second as a seat of culture. In some of the country districts, where culture had less glamour, and more primitive traits of character had larger sway, the natives, whose necks were usually stiff, challenged the pretensions of their Athens. "Boston folks are full of notions" was a proverb in Rhode Island; ‡ and culture itself, in other parts, where good sense abounded, scanned with a doubtful eye

* Thomas Bailey Aldrich.

† In 1857, according to Bliss Perry, in *Park Street Papers,* Massachusetts reckoned about one-fifth of the population as either foreign-born or the children of foreign-born. In 1908, only 32% of the population was Protestant.

‡ Thomas Robinson Hazard, *The Jonny-Cake Papers.*

the cant of culture.* In New York, where nothing annoy-
ing to Boston was ever out of order, it was said that, to
enter the city, you had to pass an examination, and that
when you left it, if you passed, you were given a kind of
degree. The New Yorkers could afford to talk thus lightly,
for the goddess of Boston was none of theirs; but for
those who had to recognize the goddess,—alien writers,
artists, lecturers,—the Boston test was formidable, and
sometimes alarming. For Mark Twain, who lectured
there in 1869, a Boston audience signified "4,000 critics;" †
and a Boston man's mere presence, in many a rural household, struck terror into the heart of the local performer.‡
Some of the younger Bostonians, feeling the danger that
lurked in this, more for themselves than it lurked for the
local performer, fled the city for other parts, through fear
of being a "Boston prig," an intellectual prig, the worst
of all.§ Complacency, a pride of power that had not sufficiently tested itself, was, as it remained, the bane of Boston, a consciousness of righteousness, a consciousness of
culture that others found insufferable or funny; and many
a visitor shared the feeling expressed by one who came to
stay, when he said that a group of Bostonians with whom

* "Cousin Susan says, 'My dear, the greatest objection I have to Boston
is that there is always some word which everybody uses. When I was
there last, the word was *culture*. Every chit of a girl who came to see
Bessie talked about *culture*. I got so tired of it I forbade Bessie to use it
in my presence. In my young days we talked about *education* or *cultivation.*' Mary suggests that to say culture, after these, is to substitute guano
for the common manures."—1869, *Letters and Memorials of Thomas Wentworth Higginson.*

† "Tomorrow night I appear for the first time before a Boston audience
—4,000 critics."—Mark Twain, *Letters*, I, 168.

‡ "He asked her to play to him.
"'No,' she said, 'you are a Bostonian.'
"'But not a critic.'
"'Impossible!'"
—Elizabeth Stuart Phelps, *Doctor Zay.*

§ "I care a great deal to prevent myself from becoming what of all
things I despise, a Boston prig (the intellectual prig is the most odious of
all) . . . Anything which takes a man morally out of Beacon Street, Nahant
and Beverly Farms, Harvard College and the Boston press, must be in
itself a good."—Letter of Henry Adams, 1875.

he had talked were "simmering in their own fat and putting a nice brown on one another." * The Boston folk, who were always frank, confessed to shocking orgies, in which their favourite vices had full play, dancing while they discussed "foreknowledge" or pondered the lessons of Beethoven's symphonies, or pursuing the "holier than thou" to an *altitudo*.† These confessions were sometimes humorous, sometimes not; but in humble minds and witty minds, and minds that were also cultivated, in other regions, they left unfortunate impressions. For Boston had earned its good name; and, as for the unkind things that were said about it, one usually found some Boston man who had said them first and better. As the "little man" remarked in *The Professor,* Boston had opened, and kept open, more turnpikes leading to free thought and free speech and free deeds than any other city in the country.‡

The focus of culture in Boston was the Saturday Club, the club that Dr. Holmes would have invented if spontaneous generation had not produced it. There, once a month, the illuminati, the Autocrat and Emerson and Lowell, Longfellow, Dana, Asa Gray and Sumner, Agassiz and Charles Eliot Norton, Charles Francis Adams, on occasion, or the other diplomat, Motley, met for the talk in which the town excelled. For Boston abounded in good conversation. Experienced outsiders, guests of the club, or perhaps of *The Atlantic,* at one of its dinners, or at some private dinner for public men, were struck by the

* Henry James the elder. This trait was also described by Howells, in *The Rise of Silas Lapham,* as "the willingness Boston men often show to turn one another's good points to the light in company."

† Edward Everett Hale spoke of a dance at which Lowell, while dancing, discussed with his partner "the significance of the 5th Symphony of Beethoven in comparison with the lessons of the 2nd and the 7th, and another partner in the quadrille would reconcile for him the conflict of free will and foreknowledge."—Lilian Whiting, *Louise Chandler Moulton.*

Dr. Hale was recklessly inaccurate, and perhaps this was one of his jokes. But it is typical of the countless stories that formed the popular legend about Boston "culture."

‡ *The Professor at the Breakfast-Table.*

quality of this conversation. Sometimes, at two successive dinners, the same men talked for eight hours, without a sign of fatigue, and the conversation never fell off in interest.* If Dr. Holmes was not the centre of it, the others mostly had their centres elsewhere, in Cambridge, in Concord, in Washington or London, while the Autocrat was not only Bostonian but more than anything else a talker. His poems were versified conversation, he had Boswellized himself, and, in his airy way, he had scattered freely, more freely than the profounder minds, the ideas that had made his town a centre of culture. It was he who had named the Brahmins and described their function as leaders of learning and bringers of light. It was he who had spread the gospel of modern science. It was he who had smitten the Philistines hip and thigh and routed the tribe of the Pooh-Poohs with clouds of arrows, and, withal, as a wise old family doctor, he treated the Yankee household with a heart that was full of pity for human nature. Could one hold his incomprehensions against this lover of excellent things, who was always so bright and wide-awake? He was certainly unfair to the reformers, and there were other doctors, well instructed, who felt he was setting up the old caste-idol, who resented his assaults on rustic manners and, still more, on the Orthodox faith, the better sides of which he knew not of; for *The One-Hoss Shay* and *The Guardian Angel*, which

* Describing his first visit to Boston, in 1865, Raphael Pumpelly thus spoke of a dinner given by Anson Burlingame, the American Minister to China, to the new British Ambassador, Sir Frederic Bruce. The guests included Holmes, Longfellow, Sumner, Lowell, etc. "We stayed at table until 4 A.M. and even I was surprised at the great amount of wine that, under the influence of the brilliant talk, disappeared with only the happiest of results. The next day it was interesting to see what an impression these best representatives of American intellect produced on perhaps the ablest Englishman that had been in America. He told me later that he had never before been at a table where he had heard such a delightfully easy flow of conversation . . . Of these notable dinners I remember only that the talk never fell off in interest. What impressed me strongly, too, was the fact that at two closely successive dinners the same people could keep up an equally easy current of talk through eight hours without a sign of fatigue."—Pumpelly, *Reminiscences*, II, 551-2.

aroused the indignation of thousands, true as they were, were not the truth regarding the depths of the old religion.* Many of Dr. Holmes's constant readers found much that was hard to bear in what he said, and, in fact, he was a wit and not too wise. One had to go to Concord for the sages. But what was Voltaire, what was Erasmus? —with whom he had so much in common, as a highly intelligent man, the most intelligent man in New England. He laid trains of thought that later became abuses, as the Boston mind developed under other conditions; but whose heart, with all its foibles, was more innocent than his, or even more truly religious? His hymns were sincere, with a touch of sublimity. No one loved life more, or fought for it more gallantly, as he fought for the sports that stood for health and the poems that stood for expressive living. He loved all sorts and conditions of men, as he loved prize-fights and trotting-horses, trees, good cattle, boats and violins.

The Autocrat stood for Boston in its hour of triumph. For Boston was indeed triumphant. Its conversation bore witness to this. The town possessed authority in every sphere. If it was ripe for change, for assaults from without and within, if the Civil War perhaps had struck its hour, the war had been "Mrs. Stowe's war," in President Lincoln's phrase, and, if Mrs. Stowe was not a possession of Boston, at least she appeared at *Atlantic* dinners, wearing her wreath of laurel. Charles Francis Adams, who lived at Quincy and had always quarrelled with Boston, belonged more to Boston than to anything else, and, if Adams had not caused the war, he had certainly helped to win it: he had helped almost as much as Grant or Sherman by holding the British at bay. Motley, the Boston historian, represented his country at two important posts. Sumner, the Boston statesman, was unique in the Senate.

* See Harriet W. Preston's *Aspendale,* pp. 123-157, in which the old country doctor attacks Dr. Holmes, an interesting and powerful statement.

He was the one man there, as even his enemies said, who, during the war-years and after, kept in view the interests of thought and science; for, if Boston had power and prestige in public matters, which gave an additional tang to its conversation, much more was this the case in affairs of the mind. It set the tone of American speech.* It held in equal scales "the Yankee's 'haow,' the stammering Briton's 'haw';" † and its great new technological schools, its quarterlies, monthlies and weeklies, the Lowell Institute and other centres, not to mention the "Boston Symphony," soon to be founded, were institutions of national significance. The *North American Review* was recapturing its leading position. The supremacy of *The Atlantic* was unquestioned. To have published a poem in it, as the case of Howells showed, was to be known among writers all over the country. It was a force indeed throughout the country, setting the critical standard and spreading suggestions.‡ Boston excelled in the machinery of culture, as well as in culture itself.

In days to come, the Saturday Club, where the Boston Olympians gathered, reflected all the changes of the Yankee mind. Consisting chiefly of authors, at first, acknowledged leaders of national thought, it altered when it alteration found. Local worthies, eminent men, but eminent mainly as men of Boston, replaced the original members, who possessed an all-American sanction. As the scope of the membership altered, so did the types, and lawyers and judges, professors of science, economists, physicists,

* "[Edmund] Quincy affected me as the finest patrician type I had ever met . . . His manner was beautiful, his voice delightful, when at our first meeting he made me his reproaches in terms of lovely kindness for having used, in my *Venetian Life*, the Briticism *directly* for *as soon as*."—Howells, *Literary Friends and Acquaintance*.

† Holmes.

‡ One of its articles is said to have been the seed of Smith College. Another caused the opening of the University of Michigan to women. These instances might be multiplied in other spheres. Its authority in literary criticism is illustrated in Mark Twain's remark, thanking Howells for his review of *The Innocents Abroad*, "I felt like the woman who was so glad her baby had come white."

chemists largely supplanted the men of letters, who spoke
for the soul as well as the mind of the race. If Howells,
after his first visit, observing the Boston of 1860, felt that
he must keep himself "in cotton" till he had a chance to see
it again, one knew what he meant and understood it; and
the day had not yet come when all men said, the Bostonians most of all, "Ichabod, the glory is departed." Two
centuries lay behind the New England writers, and, if
they largely ruled the national mind, if they were *voces
populi,* there were reasons for it. They had grown in the
great tradition of the Revolution, they were closely connected with the soil, they were readers and students of the
classics,—three elements, deeply related, that explained
their power and accounted for their prestige outside the
country.* As heirs of the Revolution, they spoke for the
liberal world-community. As men who loved the land and
rural customs, they shared the popular life in its roots, at
its source. As readers and students of the classics, they
followed great patterns of behaviour, those that Europeans followed also. In short, as magnanimous men, well
seasoned, they wrote with a certain authority and not as
the scribes. If they believed in progress, and felt that
America led the way, they professed their faith in a fashion that commanded respect, for they had known doubts
and struggles, wars and vigils, and they made their profession of faith as men who had won it, not without years
in the wilderness and days of blindness. They had cultivated their gardens, they knew the country, the sea-coast
and the homestead, the lakes and mountains, where they

---

* In regard to their standing in England, Godkin ranked the American
authors as follows: "The supreme American literary reputation in England
is that of Longfellow . . . He has more readers than any living English
poet. Next in renown to Longfellow and Irving, and in about the order
given, are the names of Hawthorne, Emerson, Prescott, Lowell, Dr. Channing, Bryant and Theodore Parker."—E. L. Godkin, *Critical and Social
Essays,* 1867.
   Howells said, in *Italian Journeys,* 1867, that all cultivated Italians knew
at least four American writers, in this order: Cooper, Mrs. Stowe, Longfellow and Irving.

had wandered as boys and lived as weather-wise men, familiar with plants and animals, the ways of nature, the trades and occupations of the people. Emerson, Lowell, Holmes and Norton had their Sabine farms, and some of them, like Sumner, resembled Webster in their knowledge of common farming and all the species of cattle, domestic and foreign; and they knew ships and shipping and the forest as well as they knew men and cities. Their books were full of all these human interests, this deep sense of the local earth, a sense that was fed by their classical studies; for the Greek and Roman authors, most of whom were countrymen, had treated rural life with affectionate understanding. The reading of Virgil and Horace, who abounded in genial pictures of it, had always gone hand in hand with respect for the farmer. The decline of classical studies and the loss of respect for rural life concurred, in the age to come, with disastrous results.

The Saturday Club, as time went on, witnessed many changes. Already, more and more, with the rise of the railroads, with the growth of the factory-system, the Brahmins were going into banking, retaining their titles as Brahmins and abjuring their function; for this handsome appellation pleased the patricians, who had sometimes done little to deserve it, but who were not unwilling to appear as tinctured with the well-known Boston culture, as patrons and even protagonists of it. The acquisitive instinct that marked the Yankees, diverted into other channels, where it had produced such victories of the mind, was returning to its original channel; and trade itself was losing its wide horizons. The stately commerce of old, the India and China traffic,* had been ruined by

---

* "The grandest shipping in the world. Beautiful ships, clean as silver, manned by honest Yankee crews. There were gentlemen's sons before the mast, with their share in the venture, going out for the excitement of the thing; boys from Harvard, fellows of education and spirit. Forecastle filled with good Toms and Jims and Joes from the Cape, chaps whose aunts you knew, good stock through and through, sound to the core."—Captain Butler, in Howells's *A Woman's Reason*.

steamships and tariffs. This trade of an earlier day had connected Boston with the history of Samarcand and Venice and given it some of the splendour of Lisbon and Antwerp, and the young men who sailed before the mast, —perhaps reading Prescott in the maintop,*— or went as supercargoes to Sumatra, had lived the sort of lives that were pictured in Homer. The days were past forever when the Danas and the John Lowells roamed the world as argonauts or wrote their wills among the ruins of Thebes; and the young Boston men who were scattering westward were mostly to end their lives at desks in State Street, hugging their stocks and bonds and "standing pat." This day had not yet come, though it was coming, as alien races pressed on the native race, as new religions rose, with alien faiths. Then the city lost interest in the country, except as a field of exploitation, for business or for holiday-making, and problems of immigration and factory-problems replaced the older problems of good and evil, and men, immersed in money, ceased to read, and the "feminization of literature" was a haunting question. One could foresee a New England turned in upon itself, while Boston, sulking in its tent, refused to play with Denver and San Francisco.

At present, outside the Saturday Club lay social, financial and "earnest" Boston, three Bostons known to fame, and all represented in it, that stretched far beyond in widening circles. Nor should one forget the other Bostons, religious Boston, often earnest, musical Boston, artistic Boston, even the scholarly Boston that lived apart. Webster was dead, with Everett and Prescott. George Ticknor, in himself a circle, ignored the Saturday Club. This grand and chilly old scholar, who had written the *History of Spanish Literature* and whose handsome Geor-

* "It was in the maintop of the bark Young Turk that I read Prescott's *Ferdinand and Isabella* and Irving's *Tales of the Alhambra."*—Arthur Sherburne Hardy, *Things Remembered.*

gian mansion * faced the State House, belonged to an age
that was past and had small interest in present or future.
When Howells, venturing into his study, remarked that
the Civil War might be good for the South, Ticknor, who
was' gracious, waived the point and sighed, "Perhaps,
perhaps." The old days, slaves and all, had been good
indeed for Ticknor, and, though most of the recent writers who had made Boston famous had been trained in
modern languages in his Harvard department, he took
no interest in them, their lives, their books, their talk. A
more illustrious writer, Francis Parkman, who sometimes
appeared at the club, moved in a world of his own for
other reasons. An impetuous, active, strenuous man, vehement and reserved by turns, with keen, grey eyes and a
military figure, and a chin thrust notably forward, Parkman had wrecked his health in his Western adventures,
when he tried to live like an Indian, and he had to follow
a careful regimen. He was partially crippled by arthritis
and partially blind, and he suffered from chronic insomnia
and nervous disorders. As long ago as 1849, he had published *The Oregon Trail*. Like Dana's *Two Years Before
the Mast,* this account of his journey across the plains had
opened a new world for story-tellers; and Parkman's candid, cheerful nature, his martial tastes and his Spartan
habits suggested Dana's traits in many ways. He had
written, a few years later, *The Conspiracy of Pontiac,*
and he had been preparing ever since, when he was able
to work, for his later series of volumes on the "old
French war." His life had been broken by years of pain
and blindness; but in 1865, when he was forty-two, he had
resumed the thread of publication. A greater writer perhaps than Prescott, who had shared his physical disabili-
ties, and certainly greater than Motley, whose work,

---

* Sometimes called the "Ticknor iceberg." When someone asked "Tom"
Appleton where he had spent an afternoon, he replied, "I've been calling
on the Jungfrau, the Tête Noire and the Mère [*sic*] de Glace,"—Mr. and
Mrs. Ticknor and their daughter Anna.

since *The Rise of the Dutch Republic,* had lost itself in a
welter of documents, Parkman was the climax and the
crown of the Boston historical school, which was soon to
shift its ground and its point of view. The last romantic
historian, in a world that was turning scientific, deriving
his impulse from Scott, as he drew his design from Gibbon, Parkman was a lonely man who stood outside his
epoch, an aristocrat, a stoic and an artist.

The other Bostons, aesthetic and "earnest," were also
represented by men who left good books and better talk
behind them. The Boston Art Museum had not yet been
established, and Norton had tried in vain to interest the
town in James Jackson Jarves's Italian collection, the
Bellini, the Pollaiuolo and others that had recently found
a home at Yale. The demand for museums, however, was
rapidly rising,* and the day had passed when it required
courage to hang a painted Venus in the Athenæum.†
Even young men from the country ceased to ask, "Is this
respectable, sir?" as they opened the door of the reading-
room and beheld the casts. No one spoke for this change
of feeling better than Thomas G. Appleton, the brother
of Longfellow's wife and the son of a notable manufacturer. This early friend of Motley, with large means and
expansive tastes, was a gourmet and also a spiritualist,
and a lover of purple and gold and all things edible, visible, touchable, including Persian rugs and downy sofas.
A bachelor and a globe-trotter, a yachtsman and a book-
collector, "Tom" Appleton was the only man who could
ride over Holmes and Lowell and talk them down. There
were many who cherished him for this, although Holmes

* "The presence of twenty first-rate pictures in one of our great cities
would save a great deal of going abroad, and help to form a sincere and
intelligent standard of aesthetic judgment . . . We should have a Titian,
a Rubens, an Andrea, a Paul Veronese, and so on."—Julia Ward Howe,
From the Oak to the Olive, 1868.

† "In an early exhibition [William] Page had had the courage to hang
there a Venus—at which visitors glanced hastily, quickening their steps."
—*Later Years of the Saturday Club,* edited by M. A. De Wolfe Howe.

was not among them; for Appleton got the credit for
some of the doctor's "good things." His wit was excellent
and famous, and he loved all kinds of art and artists,
beginning with cooks and ending with Corot and Millet.
He encouraged the taste for French. t that William
Morris Hunt was also promoting. For Hunt, the painter
from Vermont, had settled in Boston recently, as the
apostolic successor of Copley and Stuart. His portrait of
Chief Justice Shaw, which hung in the Salem Court House,
had given him this position almost at once; although Hunt,
who was also a landscape-painter, a figure-painter, a
painter of horses, for which he had a passionate affection,
chafed at the time he wasted on Boston eyebrows. Somebody's fourteenth cousin was always thinking that his
eyebrows should turn up a little more. Hunt had returned
to America in 1855, after years in Barbizon and Paris,
and he had lived at Newport before he came to Boston.
In Boston, as at Newport, his "art class" was a centre of
light. He radiated an influence like Agassiz's in science
and Ticknor's in the old days at Harvard; and "what
Hunt said" passed from mouth to mouth, even when he
swore like a trooper.

In Hunt, in Tom Appleton, even in Dr. Holmes's talk,
the energy of Boston was already following new directions. The old love of learning persisted, with much of
the old religious feeling, which the doctor expressed in his
hymns; and the emphasis that was placed upon culture
was certainly stronger than ever.* But the cause of the
other-worldly and the cause of reform had lost much of
their former impulse, and the triumph of the banking interest was accompanied already by a growth of conservative feeling and all things mundane. The

* "A Greek got his civilization by talking and looking, and in some
measure a Parisian may still do it. But we, who live remote from history
and monuments, we must read or we must barbarize."—Bromfield Corey,
in Howells's *The Rise of Silas Lapham.*

solid man of Boston,
A comfortable man, with dividends,
And the first salmon, and the first green peas,

presided over an Israel at last untroubled. The days of
the great crusaders were over. The Unitarian movement
had spent its force, nor had any cause of equal strength
taken the place of Abolition. People who loved goodness
had ceased to "adore" it, with the burning heart of the
saint who lay in Mount Auburn; and, ceasing to adore,
they ceased to struggle. Emerson, it appeared, was right,
—the Unitarians, born Unitarians, had a pale, shallow
religion; * and, as Channing had been born something
else, so something else was to take his place, as the Catholics rose in power, before Phillips Brooks appeared and
the light of an Episcopalian pulpit outshone the long-
dimmed lamps of the "Boston religion." The Orthodox
faith had passed in Boston, in the minds of the more conscious classes, and no one supposed any longer that the
simple and logical creed of Channing, which had lost
Channing's genius once for all, would ever sweep the
South, as Jefferson had predicted, or even sweep Boston
in the future. But outwardly Channing's religion was still
triumphant. With Theodore Parker out of the picture,
the stirring and troublesome Parker, it was even more
respectable than ever; nor were excellent ministers wanting, admirable men, intelligent, humane, with ample
hearts. The two great divines were Dr. Clarke and Dr.
Hale, James Freeman Clarke, who had studied German
literature with Margaret Fuller, and Edward Everett
Hale, the author of *The Man Without a Country*. They
represented a liberal faith with few, if any, doctrinal elements that might have been described as ethical culture.

* "The Unitarians, born Unitarians, have a pale, shallow religion; but
the Calvinist born and reared under his vigorous, ascetic, scowling creed,
and then ripened into a Unitarian, becomes powerful, as Dr. Channing,
Dewey, Horace Mann, Wasson, Garrison and others."—Emerson, *Journals*,
IX, 408.

Both had been anti-slavery men, both were experienced writers, both applied their faith to social questions. They were "practical" theologians both. Clarke's temper was more spiritual, and he was more of a thinker than Hale; he was also more of the past, as Hale was more of the future. While his *Ten Great Religions* became, and remained, a standard book, in the field of comparative studies that was rapidly growing, his lectures on *Self-Culture* were an outgrowth of the Peabody circle, in the days of Brook Farm and the "Newness." Hale, an exuberant journalist with a touch of genius, wrote more than sixty books. With his large, cheerful, breezy mind, he was famous for his picturesqueness. In time, he became the "grand old man" of Boston.

If, in these useful characters, religious Boston showed, with whatever advances, a falling off, in zeal, in essential energy,—for neither Hale nor Clarke compared with Channing or Parker,—this was true as well in the sphere of reform. The moral passion of the old reformers, those who still survived, had largely lost its aim and its momentum. Wendell Phillips, however, continued to fight for all the new reforms; and there were others, Miss Peabody, Mrs. Howe and Dr. Howe, the well-known "Cadmus of the blind." In the good Elizabeth Peabody, the sister-in-law of Hawthorne, whose spectacles were often on her chin, whose bonnet was usually smashed, as if in some fresh encounter with the powers of darkness, while her white hair hung loose, like her opinions,—in the genius of the American kindergarten the passion for justice and progress fermented as ever, though her eyes were faded and strained by the dim lamps of lecture-halls. Miss Peabody was one of the old reformers who never lost her zest, and Julia Ward Howe and Dr. Howe resembled her in this respect. Samuel Gridley Howe had had two careers. As the surgeon-general of the Greek navy, he had played a great part in the revolution in which Byron lost his life. He had fought with the Turks hand to hand, a nineteenth-century Yankee Cervantes, sleeping under the stars with the mountaineers, dressed in snowy chemise and shaggy capote, with only his cloak for a mattress. He had risked his life in Paris, in the July revolution, and shared in a Polish revolt, and had later been imprisoned in a Prussian dungeon; and the fund he had raised for the Cretans had paid for the education of a whole generation of Cretan children. His second career, meanwhile, had made his name a household word, with the name of his famous pupil, Laura Bridgman. For Dr. Howe, as for Wendell Phillips, the cause of reform was never-ending, nor was it ever to end for Mrs. Howe. In Washington, in '61, working in the army camps, she had driven one afternoon with Dr. Clarke. The soldiers tramped beside the carriage, singing *John Brown's Body*. Her nerves and her blood were beating with the rhythm when she woke in the middle of the night, and suddenly the words came that Dr. Clarke had asked for and she wrote the *Battle Hymn* in half an hour. If she never reached this pitch again, the "good hope of humanity" was the theme of her life, and for decades and scores of years she sang it and talked it until she became a national institution.

As long as Mrs. Howe lived, there were always a few apostles left to vindicate the name of earnest Boston. A small, shapeless woman, at present, who had once been exceedingly pretty, with an air of unmistakable distinction, she radiated bonhomie and wisdom. While her hat was often askew, she abounded in wit, and her reddish hair suggested a fiery temper; but she overflowed with intelligent goodness, warmth of heart, romantic feeling, even as she excelled in common sense. Above all other jewels, she prized plain speaking. In this, she resembled another woman, also born in New York, who represented the later Boston as Mrs. Howe represented the earlier.

For Mrs. "Jack" Gardner already lived in Beacon Street, where she spent all her mornings in bed, though she was to rise betimes and gather culture in a fashion that astonished even Boston. In those days, a third woman, Mary Baker Eddy, was also to figure largely in the Boston scene, which had heard a great deal about "feminization,"—with effects, remote from the world of Holmes, that suggested an even remoter New England, the days of the evil eye and Salem witchcraft. Mrs. Eddy also, a seeress from New Hampshire, had spent seven years in bed, the victim of hysteria and depression; but she had been cured by a miracle at Swampscott and was leading a desperate life at the moment in Lynn, driven from lodging to lodging, while she toiled at a manuscript in which she hoped to reconcile her message with the teaching of the Scriptures. The doctrine of progress in the future was complicated by certain facts of which Dr. Holmes's Boston was unaware, in the days when Howells surveyed the scene, when the "American Athens" rejoiced in its strength, in its statesmen and historians, wits and poets, all in the pride of security.

At present, these complications were remote. Mrs. Stowe had called New England the "seed-bed" of the great republic, adding that its people were "called and chosen for some great work on earth." This still seemed a reasonable statement. Moreover, if New England was the seed-bed, Boston was the hothouse. There the rarer seedlings came to blossom.

CHAPTER II

CAMBRIDGE AFTER THE CIVIL WAR

CAMBRIDGE, when Howells settled there, had much of the village look of old. A low rustic fence surrounded the buildings of Harvard College. The pump stood in the square. The horses stopped to drink at the trough beside it, and cows were pastured in the vacant lots that lay beyond the Common. The agitation of one of these cows, stung by an undomesticated gadfly, was quite an event in the eyes of Howells, who knew the importance of trifles. When a large dog appeared at his gate, or two men walked up Oxford Street, or a man drove past in a trotting-buggy, Howells was really excited; and John Holmes, Dr. Holmes's brother, who lived in Appian Way, said that when two cats crossed the street all the neighbours rushed to the window. In the tranquil Cambridge atmosphere, so confident and simple, lingered still, after so many changes, the fresh morning spirit of the young republic. The Civil War had come and gone and left its tragic wreckage there as elsewhere. But the cheerful note of an earlier day survived in a timeless air of delightful studies.

The population consisted of authors, or so it was supposed in other regions. In this, the scholastic suburb resembled Concord, where, the rumour ran, in every household, they read the Rig-Veda at the breakfast-table. You could not shoot in any direction, a visitor from the West remarked,* without bringing down the writer of two or

* Bret Harte,—a little later.

three volumes; and a Cambridge lady said that, when she met a Cambridge man and found herself at a loss for conversation, she had only to ask, How is your book coming on? to receive a voluble answer. When one little girl said to another, "Your grandfather is a poet, is he not?" the natural reply could only be, "Why, yes, isn't yours?"— unless the ancestral vocation was history-writing, or editing Aristophanes or Sallust. One might be a corrector of the press, like the late "Harvard Aldus," Charles Folsom, or Ezra Abbott, son of the author of *Rollo,* the "deadly foe of error on the printed page." * There were three historic Cambridge printing-presses. But, whether as ,a scholar or a poet, an essayist on science or a story-teller, the chances were that any Cambridge stroller, on Brattle Street, the Square or the Common,—which John Holmes called the "Philosophers' Camp,"—had some connection with books and writing. The Cambridge authors were quite distinct, as Howells soon found, from the Boston authors, but there were almost as many of them. Longfellow, Lowell and Dana, popularly known as the "Duke of Cambridge," were the first of the numerous clan; but Agassiz, John Gorham Palfrey, the author of the *History of New England,* and Francis J. Child, the collector of ballads, were only less eminent than these. Nor could one forget Asa Gray, whose *Flora* and *Botanical Manual* were classical works. No one had done more than Asa Gray to spread the knowledge of natural history, and countless flower-lovers throughout the nation knew their Gray's *Manual* as they knew their Shakespeare. "Craigie House" and "Elmwood," the abodes of the poets, were the Delphian caves of Cambridge; but Dr. Holmes's gambrel-roofed birthplace still faced the Common, and even more exalted in its prestige was the dwelling of the Nortons, "Shady Hill." There, shrouded in his leafy park, the son of the "Unitarian Pope,"—so

* Horace E. Scudder.

called by Thomas Carlyle,—pursued his studies. Charles Eliot Norton, as an infant, had sat on Wordsworth's knee, and there were little boys and girls who thought the great man had written a poem about this somewhat awesome Cambridge household. For whom did he have in mind when he composed *The White Doe of Rylstone; or, The Fate of the Nortons?*

At the moment, the centre of literary Cambridge was the Dante Club that met at "Craigie House." The tragic death of Longfellow's wife had driven him to seek, for consolation, a long, laborious task; and, like Fanny Burney's father, a century before, under the same conditions, he had turned to Dante. For many years he had cherished this project, as far back as 1843, when, rising early, he had opened his day translating two or three lines of the poet, after lighting the spirit-lamp under his coffee. The exercise, he found, aroused his mind and set him in a mood for composition; and now, as age came on and his fancy flagged, this old resource was more than ever useful. One had to keep one's mental muscles working: the worn-out horse fell down the moment he stopped. Moreover, the interest in Dante studies had grown apace in Cambridge, in the years that had passed since Dr. Parsons published his *Inferno*. Norton, who had translated the *Vita Nuova,* was at work on the *Convito* at this moment. Lowell was lecturing on Dante, preparing for his essay on the poet; and a more or less Italianate circle surrounded "Craigie House," an Accademia Dantesca, however informal, suggesting King John of Saxony's, Ticknor's friend. Christopher Cranch was sometimes there, the poet who had lived in Rome and Florence and was soon to translate the *Æneid;* Dana, who later died in Rome, where he was buried near Keats and Shelley; Thomas G. Appleton, with a steamer-ticket always in his pocket, and George W. Greene of Rhode Island, who had spent twenty years abroad and served for eight years as

consul at Rome. Longfellow and Greene had met at
Naples, in the far-away days of their youth, near Virgil's
tomb and Sannazaro's ashes, and Greene was at work at
present on the admirable memoir of his grandsire, the
great Nathanael Greene of the Revolution. In Italy he
had collected materials for Prescott, and, with his gentle
manner, discreet and suave, he was rather like some old
Italian house-priest, quoting Goldoni and Manzoni with
an exquisite Roman accent. He related faded anecdotes
of the Pincio and the Corso and seemed to know all the
Italian poets by heart; and, when he visited Longfellow,
whom he adored, Howells was always invited to join the
circle. For the former consul at Venice, who had written
Venetian Life and *Italian Journeys,* was a match for any
student of things Italian. If *Venetian Life* was not what
Lowell called it, the best thing ever written on the subject, this book could only not be so described because no
book could ever deserve the description.

The object of these meetings,* soon transferred to
Norton's House, was to verify and revise Longfellow's
version. They took place in the white-panelled study,
where the father of his country had held his councils in
the anxious days of 1776. Beside the southern window, at
the upright desk, the poet stood in hours of composition;
and here and there, in the spacious room, some literary
relic caught one's fancy, George Crabbe's inkstand, the
inkstand of Coleridge, Thomas Moore's waste-paper basket, the fragment of Dante's coffin, in its little glass box,
the gifts of friends in Italy and England. It was a pleasure to bestow these trophies on one who felt so keenly the
romance of letters. Each of the visitors, ten or twelve,
held in his hand an Italian version, while Longfellow

* Strictly speaking, the Dante Society was not organized until 1880. It has
published a long series of works connected with the poet. Longfellow's
blank-verse translation follows the original line for line, and almost word
for word. It appeared in 1867. Norton's fine prose translation was published twenty-five years later, in 1891–2.

read aloud a canto from his proof-sheets, first discussing the canto of the previous evening. The poet sat at his round table, under the shaded drop-light, and he read, as Howells remembered, "with a hollow, with a mellow resonant murmur, like the note of some deep-throated horn," while the fat terrier snored at his feet. He read very slowly, pausing at doubtful passages, alert for any word of dissent from the others; and the circle debated the various readings and weighed obscure words, while Longfellow took notes and made corrections. Lowell's knowledge was accurate, Norton's even more so; but the benign poet was ready to learn even from babes and sucklings. His manner, as he looked about the table, suggested that the humblest person present was uttering the most delightful things. When the meetings and the suppers were coming to an end, Lowell expressed the general feeling. Why could not the poet translate some Indian epic, of a hundred thousand lines, to prolong the pleasure?

The Dante meetings at the Craigie house had a symbolic significance, for these post-war years were an age of translation, as the post-Revolutionary epoch, a generation before, was an age of historical writing. As a rising Boston critic observed, it was the rule for literary movements to inspire fresh translations of the major classics; * and the close of the romantic epoch, a gradual close, in America, was marked by translations, not only of Dante, but of Homer, Virgil and various others.† There was something noble and fitting in these gallant celebrations of the great of the past, this chorus of hail and farewell, in which the generation that was passing acclaimed its

* "It is curious to notice how every new literary movement inspires its supporters with the desire to make a new translation of the great classics." —Thomas Sergeant Perry, *English Literature in the Eighteenth Century*. Perry refers specifically to the age of Dryden.

† Among the American translations of these post-romantic decades were, —in addition to Longfellow's and Norton's Dante,—Bryant's Homer, Cranch's Virgil, T. W. Higginson's Epictetus, George Herbert Palmer's *Odyssey* and Bayard Taylor's *Faust*.

teachers and models, its masters and pastors, We who are about to die salute you. Other ways were coming, and other seasons, not without heights and depths of thought and feeling; but the spring days of the young republic, with all their aspirations and resolves, the Virgilian days, the Homeric days, were passing with the poets who expressed them.

In Cambridge, where Howells had settled, soon to be joined by the Jameses, where the young John Fiske was already creating a stir with his early essays, where Henry Adams taught a few years later, one saw the new age rising as nowhere else. The leaves had scarcely fallen when the buds began to form, but many of the leaves lingered late, and the sweetness of a ripe October clung to the Cambridge landscape. The sun rose there for many with healing in his wings. Some of Longfellow's finest poems, *Keramos,* for one, and the best of his sonnets, were still to come in the eighteen-sixties; and, if his more ambitious works, *Judas Maccabæus,* suggested by Handel, *Christus, Michael Angelo: A Fragment,* were inferior to the beautiful works of his prime, the story-poems *Evangeline* and *Hiawatha,* they still exhaled the personal charm, or shall one say the moral magic, that was always Longfellow's note rather than genius. This was the magic that Bret Harte felt, as he walked with the poet in the moonlight, the charm that Ruskin also found so rare.* Agassiz shared this charm, and, in fact, the two friends had much in common. Longfellow's position as a poet was at least like Agassiz's in science. The days were approaching when Longfellow's defects appeared more striking than his virtues. So it was with Agassiz, the "romantic" man of science, when he fought against the stars in their courses, opposing the theories of Darwin. His innocent

* Ruskin said to Longfellow, at their last meeting, "It's very strange, I cannot understand it. I hate Americans, and yet you and Norton, both Americans, are the only two men with whom I feel thoroughly happy, sympathetic and at ease."

vanity, then, his *réclame* and his looseness, the traits of the scientific wholesale-dealer, the jobber, the showman, the actor, who could not endure to be alone and who liked to be surrounded with admiring crowds, as he dined with a cigar in either hand or drew the long bow on the lecture-platform, talking in his large, lax fashion, abounding in anecdotes and illustrations and leaving ample spaces for applause,—all this, which had pleased the less critical world of the years before the war, offended the scrupulous minds of the age that was coming. Agassiz's pupils turned against him. They all became Darwinians at once and favoured Asa Gray, the friend of Darwin; and only the most perceptive recognized that Agassiz, with all his faults, remained the unrivalled leader. The laboratory-biologists called him superficial, but William James, for one, knew better. The time had surely come for other leaders, with other virtues, other traits and methods; but Agassiz's matchless sympathy with the living world, his temperament, his breadth of soul, his unction, made later investigators seem poor and small.* Henry Adams owed more to him than to all the rest of the Harvard instructors,—it was Agassiz's geological lectures that aroused in Adams his lifelong interest in the subject.† Through this old Humboldtian explorer, a generation had turned a

* "Agassiz came before one with such enthusiasm glowing in his countenance,—such a persuasion radiating from his person that his projects were the sole things fit to interest man as man,—that he was irresistible. He came, in Byron's words, with victory beaming from his breast, and everyone went down before him . . . The secret of it all was, that while his scientific ideals were an integral part of his being, something that he never forgot or laid aside, so that wherever he went he came forward as 'the Professor,' and talked 'shop' to every person, young or old, great or little, learned or unlearned, with whom he was thrown, he was at the same time so commanding a presence, so curious and enquiring, so responsive and expansive, and so generous and reckless of himself and his own, that everyone said immediately, 'Here is no musty *savant,* but a man, a great man, a man on the heroic scale, not to serve whom is avarice and sin.' "
—William James, *Memories and Studies.*

† "The only teaching that appealed to his imagination was a course of lectures by Louis Agassiz on the Glacial Period and Paleontology, which had more influence on his curiosity than the rest of the college instruction altogether."—*The Education of Henry Adams.*

corner; and so it was with Longfellow, Agassiz's friend. With all his defects, his flaccidity, flat and trite as he often was, Longfellow stood for poetry as no one else.* He knew it, he lived it, he taught it, he wrote it, with a joy, a breadth of learning, a devotion that caught the imagination of high and low. Was he a great poet, was Agassiz great as a man of science? One rather observed how different they were from others who were not great. They were Emersonian men, magnanimous men, speaking through poetry and science.

While science, in the coming generation, was to play a larger and larger part, the poetic impulse flagged and was flagging already. But poetry was still dominant in Cambridge, where the two most famous objects one saw on the street were Longfellow's brown overcoat and the great blue cloak-coat of Lowell. One met Lowell striding across the Common, a short, stocky, competent figure, with a slouch hat on his head and a chamois stick in his hand. He had had a great effusion of poetry during and since the war, in *The Biglow Papers*, second series, in the Harvard *Commemoration Ode*, but his interest in political writing somewhat overshadowed this, and especially his absorption in scholarly studies. He was preparing the essays that presently appeared in *Among My Books* and *My Study Windows*, the fruits of the college lectures in which he stood, and spoke, with wit and feeling, as a man of letters. These were Lowell's best years of prose, the finest critical prose that had ever appeared in the country. His radical ideas had lost their edge, and the taste for the old and the established that had marked his conservative youth reasserted itself as the poet languished within him. He lighted his pipe with flint and

---

* Much has been said about Longfellow's plagiarism, but it might be observed that Baudelaire, according to his own statement, plagiarized Longfellow in two passages of *Les Fleurs du Mal*. Baudelaire's poem, *Calumet de Paix*, was also a translation or paraphrase of a passage of *Hiawatha*.

steel, despising the new-fangled friction-matches, and an interviewer found that Lowell had forgotten he had ever written poems for *The Dial*.* He had begun to suffer from gout, the "stamp of respectability," as Norton called it, which removed him from the ranks of the dangerous writers, for gout and good investments go together; but his contagious affection for the authors of the past, the wealth of his intelligence, his gusto forestalled what Plato well described as the "hard little eye of detraction." There was much in his manner that repelled some of his ablest students, who were excellent judges of men, N. S. Shaler, for example; † but for others, Henry Adams, Barrett Wendell and George Edward Woodberry, the poet, Lowell was the incomparable teacher. He was the voice of the many-sided culture that made their vision clearer and keener in particulars, the broad, impartial view that frees the mind from specialties and brings them into relation with the rest. He represented, his pupils felt, the studies that irradiate the reason by kindling, first of all, the imagination, giving the mind repose, imparting measure and symmetry and making life noble and generous.‡

Among the friends of Lowell, and especially Norton, who appeared at the Dante Club, was Francis J. Child, the ballad-collector. "Stubby" Child, with the reddish hair that kinked and curled all over his head, a stocky little man with fresh blue eyes and skin as pink as an infant's, was the greatest living master of Anglo-Saxon. A sailmaker's son from the water-front in Boston, he had been "discovered" in his boyhood, sent through Harvard as Norton's classmate and shipped off to Göttingen to study. When Edward Tyrrel Channing died, Child had been appointed to succeed him, as the Boylston professor

* See *The Prose of Edward Rowland Sill.*
† See the *Autobiography* of Nathaniel Southgate Shaler.
‡ See Lowell's speech on the 250th anniversary of Harvard, in *Literary and Political Essays.*

of rhetoric, the chair that had once been held by John
Quincy Adams and that Charles T. Copeland held later.
Odd as a gnome and gay as a cherub, with a brain that
bubbled over with quaint conceits, he had a heart as light
and warm as if he had lived in the greenwood, as if he
were the merry man in Robin Hood's band who wrote the
ballads that he was so busy collecting. When you saw
him, with the children, in a barn, tumbling in the hay, or
sitting on the grass and telling stories, you could scarcely
believe that Child was a great professor; and, in fact, he
liked to mimic the professors, the solemn souls, with
brows bent, who strolled about with their arms in the
breasts of their waistcoats. But if you had seen him in his
class-room, you would have perceived what stores of
knowledge can exist in the crotchety mind of an erudite
angel. You might have seen an angel lose his temper,
when he sent flying through the window a costly copy of
Chaucer. The book had been bowdlerized by an unclean
hand. Evil be to him who evil thinks! Toiling over Chaucer, on whom he wrote his classic *Observations,* editing
Spenser's poems, he carried out his great work, *English
and Scottish Popular Ballads,* which reappeared in new
editions over a stretch of forty years. He had scoured the
British isles for traces of ballads; and before he died, in
1896, he examined every manuscript that was known to
exist. He printed all the variations, all the traditional
versions of all the ballads, comparing his methods, in a
long series of letters, with those of Svend Grundtvig, the
other great "ballad man" in Denmark. His final edition
of 1894 remained the definitive collection.*

---

*The "authoritative treasury" of English and Scottish ballads, the *En-
cyclopædia Britannica* calls the collection. It is said that no genuine ballad
has since been added to Child's three hundred and five. See the Child-
Grundtvig correspondence (1872–1883) in *Ballad Books and Ballad Men,*
by Sigurd S. Hustvedt.

Child's work, carried on by George Lyman Kittredge, was influential
in later efforts to collect the "vagrant" American verse of the Southern
mountaineers, the Negroes, the cowboys, the Maine lumberjacks, etc.

If Child was not a poet, he was so nearly a poet that most of the actual poets were Philistines beside him. His notes, in keeping with the ballads, were flowers of the mind, befitting one whose motto was *peu de choses, mais roses*. Child among his three hundred roses, in the garden, with its borders of box,—he was scarcely taller than the bushes,—was the most engaging sight in Cambridge. He felt about his roses as he felt about his ballads. You heard him reading Robin Hood, reciting, almost singing, with an air as shy as it was jealous. Were you certain that you felt it? Were you sure you understood it? "Do you really like it?" he asked, with an anxious glance. People flocked to see his roses, as they flocked to hear him read, but few had a call to look at roses. They were mostly good souls, Child remarked, *bonnes mères de familles probes*, as Madame Le Clerc said of the women of Cambridge, but, with respect to roses, ignorant or frivolous. Of the rose, as of love, he added, the true grand passion, all other pleasures were not worth its pains.*

Child and Lowell had memories in common. "Did you ever lick molasses on the wharves?" one of them asked the other. Lowell, as a boy, had walked in from Cambridge, just for this, and to see the ships; for Lowell had a lively palate. One felt this in his critical essays. Child, who was born and bred in the "forest of masts,"—which had ceased to be a forest, as Howells observed, and become a "gentleman's park," so great was the decline of Boston shipping,—Child had known the taste of molasses before he heard of Robin Hood. He knew the old warehouses better than any Cambridge boy, although Lowell, as well as he, had boarded the East Indiamen, and the sailors had given them both rattans and bamboos for fishing-poles. Their common friend Norton had never been

---

* See the little book, *A Scholar's Letters to a Young Lady*, edited by M. A. De Wolfe Howe. These were the letters that Child described as "affection in spray."

a boy at all. He had dreamed of editing "Father's works" when these more adventurous youngsters who had turned out poets were storing away impressions of the visible world; but Norton, as a Cambridge man, shared their interest in birds and flowers. If there, as in everything else, he was mainly the scholar, his knowledge of natural history, in certain aspects, was equally profound and precise. He proved this, years later, in *The Poet Gray as a Naturalist,* a little book designed to show Gray's prodigious learning and observation. The author of the *Elegy* had interleaved his copy of Linnæus. He had drawn, in pen and ink, on these blank pages, animals and plants, birds and insects, with notes and remarks of his own, in Latin, French, English and Italian, enough to form a whole additional volume. Ruskin had owned this copy of the *Systema naturae,* and, after Ruskin's death, it was given to Norton, whose compilation of Gray's jottings, intended as a tribute to the poet, revealed his own exactitude of habit. The grounds of "Shady Hill" were a study for a naturalist, with Norton's Irish gardener in the foreground, the gardener from the Edgeworth place who remembered "Miss Maria" in his childhood. Moreover, as if to prove that he loved the country, Norton had abandoned his summer home at Newport. He had bought an old farm at Ashfield, "Lilliput,"—Farmer Lilly's,—among the hills of western Massachusetts. He had remodelled the house, where he held his harvest festivals in after years. A trout-stream ran through the farm, with deep woods of beech and maple and rocky ledges covered with moss and fern. There, with an orchard on the sunny slope, and meadows smooth and green, one could live a luxurious life on a German professor's salary. Norton was not yet a professor. He was maturing slowly. He had scarcely opened the career that made him famous later, as Ruskin's chief apostle and, more than this, as one of the teachers of Ruskin and even a teacher of his country. At present, he was editing, with Lowell, the *North American Review*. The two friends were reviving the great days of the "old North," to meet the problems that had risen during and since the war.

No one saw Norton and Lowell in a truer light than Howells, with more affection or with more discernment. The young apprentice-novelist, who had not yet shown what he was made of, knew their foibles well, for he had a wonderful eye for character; but he also loved their magnanimous traits, Norton's simple and helpful way with students and beginners, Lowell's liberality and prodigal wit. They, in turn, found in Howells a cultivated intelligence that was both poetic and critical, steeped in all their literary interests, a fresh, perceptive, curious mind and the deferential manner that they liked. Howells faltered at Lowell's gate and walked up the path with anxious palpitations, like Bacchus at the door of Pluto's house. As a young man who knew his place, he had found his *Atlantic* post a thorny problem. He had had to play the censor over the creators of this journal, and his reverence and his literary conscience were at variance more than once. He had discovered an error in one of Sumner's Latin quotations and was obliged to endure the Sumnerian rumblings, when he could not evade the task of pointing it out. He had even had a taste of Emerson's wrath, when he placed a poem of Holmes in a position that sheared the Concord Pharos of its rightful beams. This ire in heavenly breasts had given him pause. A child among the autocrats, he was distressed and puzzled, and had finally concluded that his duty was not to diminish their self-esteem, a view that Lowell considered entirely fitting. The veteran and the aspirant had gradually formed a warm alliance. Almost every week they walked together, in the sunshine, in the rain, in the snow, exploring the unkempt outskirts of Cambridge, the Charles River flats, the Irish slums, strolling as far as the port or across to Boston. Lowell, who fed on his books for days together, was also a tireless walker, with a wholesome strain of indolence in his composition. He was a lover of whist and regularly played with his cronies, Estes Howe, John Holmes, John Bartlett of the "Familiar Quotations;" and he liked to have a younger friend to idle his time away and keep him from his work, now and then. Howells had brought him, from Venice, an inkstand in the shape of a lobster,—an object of a fearful mien, he was all too ready to think it; and Lowell, as they strolled, talked over with Howells the discoveries which the younger man had made, and stored away for future use, in the Yankee speech that Lowell knew so well. Lowell was not always pleased when Howells had observed some turn of phrase or accent that he had not remembered.

The young man himself, with his gifts of observation and perception, was a fit recruit for scholarly Cambridge; for, although he was a novelist *en herbe,* for whom scenes and persons were all-important, he was at present an essayist and poet. He was alert for impressions, and little escaped him. A Cambridge or a Boston horse-car was alive with tragi-comedy for Howells, as a battle of ants had been for Thoreau. The sight of a household moving or an auction in a mean street left lasting traces behind his eye. Nothing was too trifling for him if it exhibited character. He noted the anxious, sidelong glance that a woman gave her skirt when she shook it out. He went once or twice to the Boston police-courts, not that he felt obliged to look for life; he watched the crowds on the ferry-boats, the excursion-boats to Nantasket Beach, most of them shrewd and friendly, ready for humorous intimacies with all and sundry. Of the dramas of domestic life, in a modest suburban dwelling, Howells missed nothing,—the relations of the mistress with her maids, the stories of which one caught vistas when a pedlar appeared at the door: and he noted quite as keenly the foibles of

the Boston patricians, how they somehow proposed themselves as examples and models, as if no such examples existed elsewhere, surrounding themselves with an ether of
potential disapprobation in which they suffered strangers
to gasp and perish. For, although they had good hearts
and would have rescued a stranger, if they had known
how, from common kindness, they did not know how,—
and this was the real trouble with Boston. Howells saw
stories everywhere. He had seen them in Ohio, he had
seen them on the Hudson, he had seen them especially in
Venice. There, in his consul's office, in the shabby old palace on the Grand Canal, with the garden full of roses and
oleanders, in years of measureless leisure,—for few
Americans went abroad while the Civil War was on,—
he had studied the few Americans with a vigilant eye. He
had seen them distinctly against this alien background. He
had seen the Italians, too, as the travel-books had never
presented them; for what compares with keeping house,
on a thousand a year,—the less the better,—for introducing a foreigner behind the scenes? * He had found the
Venetians not less unique, nor less a mystery and charm,
because he saw them in a different light from that of the
old romancers. In Venice, as at home, for Howells, the
muse sang mild, domestic lays, truer, to him, than those
she had sung for Byron,—which made *Venetian Life*
something new under the sun of travel. He had an extreme aversion to melodrama. But his countrypeople, old
and especially young, and especially in their aspect as
young ladies, aroused his interest most. As the husband
of one of these young ladies, one of the Meads of Brattleboro, a family connected at various points with the public

---

* See Kipling's remark on the four years he spent in America: "I had
known a corner of the United States as a householder, which is the only
way of getting at a country. Tourists may carry away impressions, but it
is the seasonal detail of small things and doings (such as putting up fly-
screens and stove-pipes, buying yeast-cakes and being lectured by your
neighbours) that bite in the lines of mental pictures."—Kipling, *Something
of Myself.*

life of the country,* he had a good example close at hand.
Mrs. Howells knew the world better than the consul, who
felt that he had come from a simpler sphere; and, in fact,
this marriage was a canto in the great unwritten epic, the
epic of Eastern wives and Western husbands. The canto
in question was happy: one saw this in the serenity of
Howells's work. The wife was as well-informed as the
husband was observant; and she told him, in the solitude
of these years of exile, all about the New England people.
He might have lived in Brattleboro. He felt how deeply
rooted he was in American life and was desperately homesick for it, in spite of the pleasures of Italy.

In time, all these feelings and impressions emerged in
the sunny, friendly world that revealed itself in Howells's
many novels. In Venice, he had tried his hand at fiction,
but the long, quiet hours of his life there, and the pressure
of the Italian scene, had thrown him back on study as a
central interest. He might have been his own Professor
Elmore, in *A Fearful Responsibility,* who was writing a
history of Venice; † and some of the Americans he met
might well have encouraged this ambition. Motley, for
one, his chief, the Minister to Austria, deep in *The
United Netherlands,* appeared there, a "figure of worldly
splendour," as Howells recalled him later. The consul
and the minister drifted about in a gondola, and Howells
aided Motley in his work in the archives, obtaining copies
of documents for him, the relations of the Venetian am-

* Mrs. Mead's uncle, John Humphrey Noyes, was the founder of the
Oneida Community. Of her brothers, one was Rutherford G. Mead, the
architect, of the firm of McKim, Mead and White, and another, the
sculptor, Larkin G. Mead, was professor of sculpture in the school at
Florence where Michael Angelo had taught. It was through Howells's connection with President Hayes, who was Mrs. Howells's cousin, that Lowell
received his appointment as Minister to Spain.

† Howells long planned to write a history of Venice, and as late as
1900 he negotiated on the subject with the editor of *Harper's Magazine.*
The book was never written, but he drew up an outline of it. This was
printed in his *Letters,* II, 122-124. A later New England history of Venice
was written by William Roscoe Thayer.

bassadors. One of his fellow-consuls, under Motley, was the Boston historian Hildreth, at Trieste, a tired old man now, absent-minded, silent, who could not be roused from his reading of *Paradise Lost*. Howells thought vaguely that he might fit himself for a chair of modern languages at home, for he knew German, French and Spanish as well as he knew Italian. He had learned them all in Ohio, and one of his earliest projects had been to write a life of Cervantes. He sent Lowell an essay, *Modern Italian Comedy*, that appeared in the *North American Review*, and he made a careful study of the Italian poets of the years before and during the Risorgimento. He wrote the papers on Alfieri, Foscolo, Leopardi and others, who had roused the Italian people against their drowsy despots, that later formed his *Modern Italian Poets*. With competent translations, they were excellent essays, in spite of Howells's marked distaste for some of the traits of his poets, their high-flown sentiment and their vaguely aristocratic faiths. He had a temperamental suspicion of all romantic tendencies, including his own. Meanwhile, he wrote poems himself, some of which *The Atlantic* printed, poems suggesting Heine, or Whittier, or Browning. The monologue *Pordenone* was a capital piece. The most interesting of these poems were stories in hexameters, *The Movers*, an Ohio tale, *Louis Lebeau's Conversion*, *The Pilot's Story*. His mind drifted homeward, in Venice, and he saw the West again, the Mississippi, the pioneers, the boatmen and Indian hunters, incidents of the river-life, episodes and village idylls. He even wrote a novel in verse, *No Love Lost*. In all these narrative poems, his model was *Evangeline;* and one felt the originality of Longfellow's talent, seeing it thus reflected in a later writer. Howells was trying his hand at the sort of themes he was afterwards to use in his novels, and at intervals throughout his life he returned to the writing of verse.

Perhaps he wrote only one really fine poem, the lovely
In Earliest Spring,—

Tossing his mane of snows in wildest eddies and tangles,
    Lion-like, March cometh in, hoarse, with tempestuous breath.

Thus Howells had appeared in Cambridge first of all
as a student and poet. With almost no formal education,
he was prepared for the Dante Club as only a handful
were in this centre of scholars. Alone, with a sensitive
wife, for years, in Venice, he had been his own university;
and his Cambridge friends would not have received with
displeasure the statement that the Howellses, married in
Paris, had gone "at once to see the Louvre." As a child,
in a little village in southern Ohio, the son of a country
journalist and printer, he had set type before he learned
to write, and a group of neighbouring farmers, proud of
his studies, had offered to send him to Harvard. He had
chosen to stay with his family, who needed his help. They
shared his own precocious love of reading. They were
kindly, simple, gentle-hearted souls who had kept, in their
backwoods clearing, the tastes of the civilized world from
which they had come, German Pennsylvania and far-off
Wales. The father, a Swedenborgian, who had written
religious tracts and an English grammar and had published a magazine, *The Gleaner,* composed of extracts
from his favourite authors, had built with his own hands
their small brick cottage and fashioned a Welsh harp. An
anti-slavery man, who also sympathized with Robert
Owen, he dreamed of a "true state of things," in which
men would be kind, free and equal. He took over a paper-
mill, which he ran on coöperative principles;* and his
editorial articles brought him the regard of all the well-
intending politicians. He was a friend of Garfield. He
bought a Spanish grammar from a soldier of the Mexican

* Howells told the story of this venture in *New Leaf Mills.*—"turning
over a new leaf."

War, and he often read aloud from Swedenborg's *Heavenly Arcana*. His best-loved English poets were those who pictured the happy life of villagers and rustics. This elder Howells understood a boy whose day-dreams, as he toiled at the type-case, sometimes setting up his own stories, composing them over the types, were all of a great career in letters.

The family had pursued various fortunes that took them from town to town, and at last they had settled in Columbus. Howells's passion for literature had led him far. He had mastered three languages and passed through many phases, influenced by Goldsmith, Irving and Heine, Tennyson, Dickens, Cervantes. With a nature outwardly mild and inwardly humble, with a flexible mind and a will that was strong and tenacious, he loved form, he loved style and diction. Chaucer had given him a feeling for the Anglo-Saxon weft of his native language, and the grace and ease of Heine convinced him that the best writing springs from the common speech. Chaucer's cheerful temper pleased him more than the "tigerish play of sattire," as he described it; and the free and simple design of *Don Quixote,* with its large and noble lines, seemed to him the ultimate form in fiction. His work showed these influences later. At the moment, the political reporter,— for this he had become in Columbus,—had also a burning interest in human nature and a gift for "elective affinities." He met Artemus Ward and Horace Greeley, and he published with J. J. Piatt, who was afterwards consul at Cork, his first book, *Poems of Two Friends.* But he had a particular feeling for the Lilys and Julias and Sallys with whom he spent his evenings in the summer, sitting on the steps of the big brick houses that stood in their ample lawns on the wide, shady streets. For their mothers and fathers he had an eye, and even for their less enlightened brothers; for he was already writing little sketches of character. But the girls were much more

interesting in conversation. They were always waiting to
be called upon, on the front steps and piazzas, or beside
the soft-coal fire on winter evenings. They had all read
the latest novels, and they liked nothing better than to
discuss them with the only young man who had also read
them. One could spend an evening over *The Marble Faun*
and the mystery of Donatello's ears, not to mention Kenyon's studio and the spectre of the catacomb and Miriam
whose heart was as dark red as blood. Decidedly, the
young man thought, and was to think always, with a mind
that passed through other modifications, the young girl
was the most triumphant fact of American civilization.

In after years, Howells's mind drifted back to this
earlier time. Many of his books recorded the scenes of
his childhood. In some of his finest prose, he celebrated
the forest clearings, the old village life that he remembered and the people he had known in Columbus. At present, his place was in the East, where everything favoured
his budding ambitions. He had written to his father from
Venice that he could not go back to Ohio.* In this he had
shown good judgment, and, better still, when, after trying New York, he had fixed upon Boston. In New York
and elsewhere, he had met Whitman, Bayard Taylor,
John Hay, Stedman and Stoddard; but literary New
York, with Washington Irving dead and gone, was at a
low ebb in the early sixties. "Better twenty years of Boston than a cycle of New York," he thought, and he was
right, for twenty years. With his deeply affectionate nature, however, he never lost his loyalty to the places and
the persons of his youth. If they menaced his ambitions
at the moment, they occupied the centre of his heart, and
for this he was rewarded in the end; for the West rose

---

* "I do not conceal from you that I have not yet in the three years
shaken off my old morbid horror of going back . . . I must seek my fortune at the great literary centres . . . A three months' residence in Ohio
would dissipate it all."—*Life in Letters of William Dean Howells,* I,
89-90.

in his mind with a wealth of understanding that showed how profoundly he had loved it. The depth of his attach-ment to his father found utterance in his work as well. The elder Howells's vision of a "true state of things" expressed itself in the son's unworldly nature. It enlisted his interest in the Shakers and their communistic system. It drew him to Bellamy and Tolstoy. But this was in the future. His passion now was to understand New England.

It was from Columbus that he had gone to Venice, from Venice that he had come to Cambridge. He had come to venerate the luminaries who had shone so bright in his Western obscurity, and he was already a lesser star himself. He knew his own mind, he had carried the day as a journalist, and he had as much to give as to receive. He had a craftsman's hand and a friendly eye for every-thing that Boston loved and cherished. He was equipped, by aptitude and training, to share in promoting its mis-sion as a centre of culture; and, since fate had ruled the merging of New England in the nation, he was prepared to carry on the cross-fertilization with the best available seeds from other regions. He knew already half the rising authors, in New York, in Philadelphia, in the West, whom he was to attract to *The Atlantic.* With his ir-refutable talent and engaging presence, he had reason to rejoice in his good fortune. In the evening, as often as not, he went to a little party at "Elmwood," or perhaps some less exalted abode of letters, sacred or profane, but always a little profane, if it was sacred, and always a little sacred, if profane, where the dish of scalloped oysters, always present, always knew its place, and he knew his place as well as the scalloped oysters. Although he was not yet thirty, he could almost see himself as an heir apparent.

As time went on, and he rose in authority, and the novels poured from his pen, and people were forced to exclaim that, with all abatements, no one had ever scanned the country with such an all-observing eye, then, as the wonder grew, the more one saw that the "apostolic succession" was his by right. It had ceased to be anyone's gift, or in anyone's power to withhold. But this was the result of a transposition of forces that no one could foresee at the moment. One could only say that, so far as letters went, and letters went very far in Cambridge, Howells was an heir of the ages. Was he not, as Lowell observed, the living image of Chaucer, minus the beard, as anyone could see from Occleve's portrait? This was enough for Lowell, and enough for New England.

CHAPTER III

AMESBURY AND CONCORD

IN THE sea-bound region north of Boston, Essex and Middlesex counties and the tip of New Hampshire, all that was idyllic in New England found its focus after the war. In Concord, graver thoughts prevailed, and the hay-carts, decked with flowers and mosses, into which Emerson piled the children, to carry them off to Walden for a swim or a picnic, bore other invisible burdens. The trees in Concord were offshoots of Yggdrasil. In "Whittierland," they were simple pines and maples; and little more profound than the pathos of association gathered round their natural picturesqueness. The depths of human affection and religious faith underlay this pathos, but the forms they assumed in prose and verse were artless and largely impermanent. However, they marked a moment, in some respects a more than fleeting moment, in the history of the conscience and the race.

From Salem to Portsmouth and Kittery, and up the Merrimac river, where the White Mountains rose in the northern distance, the legends throve with the wild flowers that raged over the land in summer and autumn. Lake Attitash and Ramoth Hill, Ipswich, the Powow river and the Isles of Shoals, nine miles from Portsmouth out at sea, were stories in themselves and fertile mothers of stories and poems, the work of scores of writers, past and present;* for this region was an old world, em-

* A volume called *Poets of Portsmouth,* published in 1865, contained the work of forty poets who lived in Portsmouth alone.

bedded in the new world, with a depth of local history
that was scarcely paralleled elsewhere. Most of these
writers, like Whittier, never left their country. Europe
had only a vague existence for them, except when some
cause, Mazzini's cause in Italy, or Garibaldi's, or some
heroic figure, like Kossuth or Gordon, stirred a responsive chord in their bosoms. The humanitarian movement
in New England had found them all responsive. The
Abolitionist cause had flourished there, for Newburyport
was Garrison's birthplace, and Whittier lived at Amesbury, and the name of the poet Lucy Larcom, the Beverly
shipmaster's daughter, had appeared on all the petitions
in the anti-slavery days. George Edward Woodberry, the
poet of the future, who was also born at Beverly before
the war, remembered these old reformers. A touch of
their moral fervour lingered in him two generations later.
Whittier, like Lucy Larcom, never lost his interest in the
great human questions of his time, which related him to
the larger world; and, if this sympathy greatly exceeded
his care for the art of poetry, to which he was somewhat
indifferent, it kept him nevertheless, in spite of all his
peasant foibles, the reverse of selfish or petty. Except for
this, the poets of Whittier's group were local in their interests and their feelings. They lived between two horizons, the mountains and the sea, with the Merrimac flowing between. One might have seen a rose-bush in one of
their gardens, or an apple-tree perhaps, brought by the
Pilgrims from England, still bearing apples and roses.
The English pimpernel, which was not a native, grew on
the Isles of Shoals, planted there by the early settlers;
for the stream of history, in this region, which had known
few changes, flowed on serenely. The English mind of an
earlier day also lingered on there. One felt the note of
Pym and Hampden in Garrison and Whittier; and the
mayflower, the trailing arbutus, delicate, fresh and shy,
with its ineffable scent and virginal sweetness, recalled

the story of Priscilla, the Puritan *As You Like It*. Among
the youths and maidens of Whittier's country there were '
many John Aldens and Priscillas. But in this dim bond
with Shakespearian England they were wholly uncon-
nected with modern England. The ties of first and second
cousins, which even the Atlantic had not broken, had become the ghostly ties of unknown cousins of the seventh
or the eighth generation.

A line of drowsy seaports faced the ocean, northward
from Salem and Cape Ann, pervaded with salty odours
and dense grey fogs. The gables and roofs were covered
with rust, and the worm-eaten wharves, with their armour
of shells and beards of floating eel-grass, brought back
the days of the China trade that had left so many relics
in these towns. The crazy old warehouses were filled with
coils of rope and bales of sail-cloth, blocks, tar-kettles,
casks and hawsers. Here and there a mansion stood, perhaps with a Copley in the parlour, boasting a cellar large
enough to stable thirty horses. The black slate head-
stones in the graveyards, with scythes and hour-glasses
and fat-faced cherubs, symbols of the Gothic past, fed
the imagination of boys and girls who were not too young
to remember the last town-crier. With his "Hear all!"
and his bandy legs, and the bell that was almost as big as
a church-bell, he had cried auctions, funerals and mislaid
children. Little shops, kept by "dames," dotted some of
the humbler streets, and retired East India merchants,
who were sometimes oldest inhabitants, came forth to
enjoy the flowering chestnuts in May. The railroads were
destroying the reign of the "local character," but now
and then some scholarly recluse, in shabby coat of antique
cut, emerged from the Reading-room or the Athenæum,
and battered old fishermen boiled lobsters on the beach
or passed their days whittling on the wharves. Sometimes
they carved a Chinese pagoda, or even a full-rigged ship,
or perhaps they merely exercised their fingers, while the

seagulls sat in rows on the rocks or soared and screamed above them. On the calm, blue sea lay dreaming schooners, and gundalows passing with lateen sails carried one's mind to the Mediterranean; but the sea was the "dreadful sea" to the fishermen's wives, for whom the reefs were reefs of Norman's Woe. They were always watching * and waiting for those who went and came not back, and tales of lovers lost at sea, of spectre ships and mysterious beacons that lured imprudent sailors to their doom haunted the minds of the children who clambered over the granite ledges and made caves and castles of the planks and timbers. At Gloucester, on the cliffs, they listened for the roar of the devil, which Cotton Mather had heard among the rocks; and the devil was busy on stormy nights in all these angry harbours. In almost every town, some boy or girl, a poet or a story-teller later, who had played in the sparkling foam and wandered over the tops of windy headlands, had heard a knocking at the door at night that signified the presence of the devil. It was the knock of a neighbour, with sorrowful news. There was scarcely a household on this northern shore that had not given its hostage to the sea. Woodberry, the poet, remembered how he was held at his Beverly window and told that his father was somewhere "out there." This was his earliest recollection. At Newburyport, Harriet Prescott Spofford drank in this dread of the sea, where the curlews called and circled. Thomas Bailey Aldrich, who was born at Portsmouth, had lost one of his playmates, who drifted away in a rowboat and never returned. Celia Thaxter lived on the Isles of Shoals, the bleak little heaps of granite that lay on the eastern horizon. Her father, the lighthouse-keeper, who had been disappointed in his youth, had vowed he would never set foot on the main-

* In *The Madonna of the Tubs,* Elizabeth Stuart Phelps spoke of the "curious watching look" of the Gloucester women,—as if they had spent their lives "peering for the dory before dawn, or searching for the sail at dusk, or scanning the headland by moonlight."

land again, and she herself, from the age of five, had
never seen a town till she was married. Her world was
Appledore and Smutty Nose, White Island and Star Island, with its tiny stone church in the hamlet of Gosport.
The Hebrides and the Orkneys were not more lonely,
and there one knew the terror of the sea. But there, too,
as in all this region, the flowers ran riot over the rocks,
the little stars of crimson sorrel, the crowfoot blossoms
and the purple beach-pea, the goldenrod, the rose, the
spiked germander. If they were not more lavish than on
the mainland, they flourished in the salty air. They
glowed among the rocks like masses of jewels.

The wild flowers set the note of Whittier's country,
the scene and the poems that sprang from it, especially in
these post-war years, the calm that followed the storm.
The pastoral stretches along the rivers, with their long
lines of barns and sheds, blossomed with the shadbush, the
"shadblow," for April in these valleys was the time for
shadding, and the fish gave its name to flower and bird. In
Essex County, the flicker was sometimes called the shad-
spirit, for its note was thought to indicate the day when the
fish first ascended the streams. Some of these northerly valleys led to New Hampshire, where Winnepesaukee lay,
and the Pemigewasset, the mountain-encircled lake and
the silvery river, a land of sundered rocks, cascades and
pines. Crag and meadow, stream and island, this was
Whittier's world and the world of his friends; and even
Boston seemed remote in Whittier's Amesbury cottage,
with the harebells in the garden-room in spring. There he
had written *Snow-Bound,* when the death of his mother
and sister brought back his early days in the Haverhill
farmhouse, where the family had lived since 1688; and
there he liked to read his poems to Lucy Larcom and
Celia Thaxter and other ladies, gifted and less gifted;
for his women friends were as numerous as the poet Cowper's. One or two of these other ladies, with pity for his

single state, suggested themselves as partners in a closer
relation. The breezy journalle "Gail Hamilton," properly Mary Abigail Dodge,—a sort of Margaret Fuller
watered down, and also peppered up,—who was buzzing
about the country, interviewing Grant and Sherman and
others whose names were in the papers, built a little house
for a poet and his wife and hoped that her good friend
Whittier would share it with her. She was not the only
one who embroidered slippers for him, but the poet preferred to ride at anchor. He had his little vanities and
liked a mild philandering, but a game of croquet was as
far as he would go. He was the pride and joy of his neighbours. He met them in the tailor-shop, or he sat on a
sugar-barrel in the village grocery and discussed the affairs of the day for hours together; and sometimes, recalling his hair-breadth escapes, in the anti-slavery days,
he would fight the battles over again. The old man would
leap from his seat, remembering these adventures,—how
he dashed with Thompson to the carriage, through the
side-door of the hall, while the lynchers waited at the
front. He had been pelted with stones in Concord, New
Hampshire. His happiest times were the "laurel parties,"
when all the Whittier circle, old and young, visited the
laurel grounds, every year, at the end of June. They
breakfasted at Newburyport and sailed up the Merrimac
as far as the grove on the banks. There they picnicked
among the pines, surrounded with the glory of the laurels.
Speeches and songs followed the luncheon. Whittier, who
was always there, usually wrote a poem for these occasions.

In the very heart of this region, along the river, the
scenes of the laurel parties, the factory-towns, Haverhill, Lawrence and Lowell, were spewing smoke, wealth
and desolation. Thousands of immigrant working-people,
Poles, Italians, French Canadians, slaves of the "lords
of the loom" who had lured them hither, were slowly

transforming the landscape. More and more, as the factories spread, the owners ˆbandoned the region, loving it
_less the less they laboured ror it, and ruled their slaves from
Boston through the whips of agents. The whips were no
less real because nobody saw them, and the lords in no
way owned the Boston State House less because they
ruled by legal methods. The horrors of the industrial
system, visible in later days, were blighting the region
already, and poets and story-tellers, already appearing,
were soon to throw the light of truth and justice over the
ghastly scene. Who was to care for Ramoth Hill, for the
sites and scenes of Whittier's poems, when the pretty
streams were fouled with oil and the laurels werc blasted
with coal-smoke? Not the Italians and Poles, who had
their own associations; not the sons of the old inhabitants,
who had forgotten these woods and meadows. Whittier's
fame and Whittier's country were all but doomed together, so closely linked they were in a common fate; but
Whittier and his friends were scarcely aware of these
horrors. Their minds were open to social questions, and
Whittier laboured as long as he lived for pacifism, dis-
armament and penal reform; but he saw the workingman's life in the terms of an earlier age, when he had
made slippers for Boston ladies and Lucy Larcom toiled
as a Lowell mill-girl. For the rest, how many fight in two
crusades who have given all their energy to one? He had
more than earned the repose his nature needed. In the
quiet of his afternoon, he recalled the thoughts of his
early morning. Then rose from him again, transformed,
the psalms that had sanctified the Quaker household,
hymns like gentle flames, tales of devotion, memories of
the barefoot boy and the vanishing world of pasture and
meadow and cottage.

In days to come, Whittier's poems, the poems of all
the Whittier circle, found little favour in critical eyes,
even less than the poems of Cambridge. Too many were

relics of lapsed occasions, while others seemed as merely
pretty as the wild rose, the goldenrod, the laurel; and the
wintry winds of the modern mind blew them off the landscape. But the goldenrod rises again in its season, and
the folk-poem recovers its meaning when the heart of a
nation, grown old, returns to its youth. Literature abounds
in special sanctions, those that govern national anthems
and other expressions of faith,—hymns, folk-poems and
ballads,—where the only point that essentially matters is
whether the feeling, being true, is also sufficiently large
and important. Whittier possessed this immunity, and
Lucy Larcom shared it with him, as one of the glowing
moons of this mild planet. Later, when the smallest poets
were masters of their art, but few conveyed the feeling
of a world behind them, one still felt, in *Skipper Ben,* as
in her personal record, *A New England Childhood,* sincere, direct and truthful, the heroic life of an earlier day,
as of wild flowers nursed in granite.

Most luminous of these little moons, Celia Thaxter
dwelt in her far sky-parlour; or, rather, on the Isles of
Shoals, where the bells tolled on their rocking buoys, she
moved in an orbit of her own. In the vast wooden bar-
rack, with its long piazza, the Appledore hotel, kept by
her brothers, she lived with her poems, her music and her
friends, surrounded by books, ferns, flowers, shells and
seaweeds. As a child on White Island, where her father
guarded the lighthouse, she had often kindled the lamps
on the lonely rock. Her only companions were the goats
that browsed by the little stone cottage. Until she was sixteen, the fanciful girl,—the "pretty little Miranda," as
Hawthorne called her,*—ranged over the ridges and
gorges, haunted with tales of ghosts and pirates, raced
with the sandpipers, played amid the kelp and dulse, hung

---

* The account of Hawthorne's visit to the Isles of Shoals is one of the
most interesting passages in the *American Notebooks,* edited by Randall
Stewart, 256-275. At that time, 1852, the Portsmouth-Appledore boat was
called the Fanny Ellsler, after the dancer.

over the pools with their bright sea-treasures, beaten by
foam and spray, as wild and free herself as a gull or a
curlew. Then Levi Thaxter appeared, and the two were
married. Thaxter, a Harvard friend of Thomas Wentworth Higginson, and a cousin of Lowell's wife, Maria
White, who had also belonged to the "band" in the days
of the "Newness," was a teacher of elocution and a public reader. He had studied under Charles Kean, hoping
to go on the stage, and he had come to Appledore to find
a lonely spot where, like Demosthenes, he could declaim
to the waves. He was already known as a reader of
Browning.* He had joined with Celia's father in building
the hotel, for invalids, if they had to come, for poets, if
they could and would. One burst all links of habit there,
and the writers and artists came apace, Hawthorne in the
early days, and John Weiss, the Transcendentalist, the
author of the life of Theodore Parker. Then Whittier
came, and came again, at first with his sister Elizabeth,
who was also a poet. He liked to watch the pretty Celia,
with her necklaces and bracelets of seashells, reading
Dante and peeling squash, or mending her Æolian harp,
or painting on her porcelain at the window,—barberry
clusters or apple-blossoms, autumn leaves or goldenrod,
—while the wild birds on the sills twittered and fluttered.
He read his poems aloud and she read hers. The visitors
came in crowds, as the years went on, writers, musicians
and landscape-artists,† to hear Mrs. Thaxter read her
poems, in the long, light, airy room, with its glass doors
and ten windows, its tables and sofas and screens and

---

* The immense and early American vogue of Browning, as later of
Edward FitzGerald, was largely the result of Thaxter's readings. Browning wrote the inscription for Thaxter's grave, 1885.

† Childe Hassam was one of these constant visitors. A Dorchester boy,
born in 1859, Hassam painted his first landscapes in the environs of Boston,
where his studio adjoined George Fuller's. He spent many summers at
Appledore, where he painted the crags and the surf. One of his first com-
missions was to illustrate and decorate Celia Thaxter's book, *An Island
Garden*.

rugs, and the plants and the twinberry-vines in dishes of moss. Eastward lay the open sea, and westward, as the sun poured in, one saw the peaks rising, a hundred miles away.

Celia Thaxter's poems were literary water-colours, the counterparts, in theme, vein and style, of her paintings on paper and porcelain. They were graceful, touching, fragile, evanescent. The best were her verses for children, *Jack Frost* and *The Great White Owl;* but her prose was better than her poems, two or three of the tales for children and one book written to last, *Among the Isles of Shoals.* She liked to quote Keats's remark that his intensest pleasure had always been to watch the growth of flowers, and some of her delight in this expressed itself in *An Island Garden;* but *The Spray Sprite,* fresh and crisp, and *Madame Arachne* had Hans Andersen's magic in them. The child at the lighthouse window, watching the spiders, had felt herself inside the spider's mind, and the lonely girl who had roamed the rocks, among the tumbling billows with their flying spume, while the wind blew about her and the gulls rose and dropped, knew the spray-sprite well and had often seen her. No one had ever known these isles as Celia Thaxter knew them,—sad, bleak isles to others, to her enchanted,—from Captain John Smith's cairn to the farthest gorge or boulder, the rocks which the islanders thought were split at the time of the Crucifixion. A hundred men living in Portsmouth, when she was a girl, had dug for buried treasure on the islands, following their divining-rods and scraping the chests at times, they said; and some had seen "Old Bob," the ghost, with the ring about his neck and the face that was pale and dreadful. Celia Thaxter knew them, as she knew the ancient graves and ruined cellars, the church that was built from the wrecks of Spanish ships, as she knew the lean, brown old shoalers and the ballads they sang to their fiddles, the spinning-women who smoked their pipes or crept about with canes gathering herbs. She had rowed from island to island as an amateur doctor, helping at the births of children. She had watched the olive-green sea, swollen and angry, streaming with vapour from the cold, when a sudden rift in the mist revealed a vessel driving to sure destruction towards the coast; and many a night she had opened the door to shipwrecked men who had struck on a ledge, when the wharf was a mountain of ice. *Among the Isles of Shoals* was a permanent picture of all these old, unhappy, far-off things, and of much that was lovely also, and unchanging. A hooked rug in prose, one might call it, woven of pure materials, in harmonious colours.

*

*   *

If "Whittierland" was idyllic, so was Concord, though the Concord idyll had other tones. There, too, the wild grape flourished, and the hemlock and savin, the walnut, spruce and pine, and the ground was strewn in season with the kindly fruits of the earth. The quiet river, the groves and meadows, the thrifty ways of the farmer-folk, who sent their milk and firewood to Boston, suggested a tranquil happiness that knew no inordinate affections.

Concord was "without crime," in the somewhat violent phrase of one who was born there.* The only prisoner in the jail, the only one whom anyone remembered, begged,

---

* The painter Edward Simmons, one of the Ripley family, who was born in the Manse. He was a nephew of George P. Bradford, the old Brook Farmer who translated Fénelon and was Emerson's intimate friend. The limitations of Concord, from an artist's point of view, are suggested by Bradford's remark to Simmons, "Edward, anything but the physical or the material." The whimsical Edward Simmons was famous for his loquacity. When a lady begged his pardon once for interrupting him, he said, "Madam, no one can *speak* without interrupting me." It was in reference to this trait that his friend Oliver Herford posted a card by the fireplace in the Players' Club, New York. This card bore the words, "Exit, in case of Simmons."

when he was released, to be allowed to live there. He sat on the steps, on summer evenings, a great pet of the Emerson household, who was hired to play the fiddle at all the dances; and as for other odd fish, when the Concord people saw one passing, they were resigned to saying, "Oh, that's a philosopher." In Concord, as in Whittier's region, they had hidden fugitive slaves in their ovens, or built secret rooms in their attics to foil the inquisitive sheriff; and one or two Concordians had been tarred and feathered for a speech or a sermon in the South. But the tar was long since washed away, and the ovens had resumed their normal function. Bronson Alcott, building an arbour, or sitting on his rustic seat, absorbed in his Plutarch or his Plato,—or Evelyn, Donne or Cowley,—evoked the note of this later Concord. Sometimes Alcott bestirred himself to plant another row of trees, or a pleasance for his children by the brookside.

Simple as it appeared, however, Concord was very far from simple; and the wiser a visitor was the more he was puzzled. If the Sphinx was not an inhabitant, she seemed to have been a guest, at least, who had left her riddle behind her; nor had any Œdipus yet appeared, from the Theban world without, to solve or even approach the heart of the riddle. Concord was a formidable fact; and, when one tried to place one's finger on it, the fact turned out to be different from what one thought it. How was one to specify it? How was one to designate it? Most of the descriptions recoiled upon their authors. For instance, people called it the "American Weimar," as Boston had once been called the "American Athens,"—a singularly inept phrase. To have called Goethe's town the "German Concord" would not have been less appropriate; for nowhere were Goethe's claims more essentially challenged. Clever people had given up the attempt to classify Emerson. They never hit the nail on the head, and the reason for this was plain enough: Emerson was not for the

clever. Nor was Emerson or the dead Thoreau a subject
for the innocent. Whittier spoke of *Walden* as a "wicked
and heathenish book," a phrase that merely described
Whittier,—it did not describe Thoreau at all. There were
others, like the young Henry Adams, the son of Minister
Adams, who parried the riddle with irony, not attempting
to meet it; * but Adams made good his position by denying the Concord premises. Idealism, for him, was a fool-
ish thing; but, if one accepted idealism, where was the
force of the irony? The irony cheapened the ironist.
Goodness without intellect and intellect without moral
perception were helpless in the face of the Concord riddle. It was true, there were those who could read it,
though they did not bear the names of Theban princes.
Obscure as they often were, these were the children of
light, innocent as doves but wise as serpents.

Concord was deep, in other words, deeper than any
country well, and the water of life that filled it was clear
to the bottom. The difficulty was that one saw the bottom
only at fleeting moments, when the sun was high overhead
and one's own eye was quite unclouded. Three men of
genius had lived in the town, Emerson, Hawthorne, Thoreau, not to speak of the gifted Alcott and the poet Ellery Channing,—uncrystallized geniuses both, one might
have called them. If the air was full of cross-vibrations,
if it was opalescent, it shone with a clear white light,
most of the time, that signified a harmony of all these
colours; and, if there was mystery in it, the deposit of
genius, there was also a singular clarity, a clarity of per-

* "Adams approached it [Concord] in much the same spirit as he would
have entered a Gothic cathedral, for he well knew that the priests regarded him as only a worm. To the Concord church all Adamses were
minds of dust and emptiness, devoid of feeling, poetry or imagination;
little higher than the common scourings of State Street . . . He perpetually
fell back into the heresy that if anything universal was unreal, it was
himself and not the appearances; it was the poet, and not the banker; it
was his own thought, not the thing that moved it."—*The Education of
Henry Adams.*

ception and will that sprang from older sources than
Plutarch or Plato. It was this that made Goethe irrelevant in Concord. All the Concord writers knew their
Goethe. Emerson had read him from end to end, though
mainly to please Carlyle. *Wilhelm Meister* had gone the
rounds, and all the young girls were fascinated by Goethe's
correspondence with Bettina von Arnim. This appealed to
their instinct of hero-worship. It led them to form attachments for older men, naively but excessively romantic.
Louisa Alcott, under the spell of Bettina, left flowers on
Emerson's doorstep, as a young New Hampshire girl had
laid siege to Theodore Parker. Louisa, stirred again,—
she who sat in the cherry-tree, singing to the moon at
midnight,—sang Mignon's song in German under Emerson's window. Emerson had written of Goethe with sympathetic comprehension, but he stood outside him and, in
certain respects, behind him; for he judged him by an
older and deeper standard than that of nineteenth-century
culture. Mighty genius that Goethe was, mightier in genius
than any American writer, he who counted his medals and
used the world to promote his own vainglory and his personal ego, who vaunted egoism and made of this his message, while he bowed to the princes of the earth, was
small if one measured him by the wisdom of Egypt and
India; and Emerson spoke by the oldest book in the
world. The tablets of the Nile were behind him; and, as
for the Concord "criticism," if it was very deficient aesthetically, it possessed a more venerable sanction than
any modern aesthetics. Most of the classical treatises
ratified its findings. Emerson, the sage, who was only sec-
ondarily the writer, fallible in his literary judgments,
uttered first and last things on the life that underlay, as it
also transcended, all the expressions of life. He was often
astray with "phenomena," he was seldom or never astray
with "noumena,"—at least less often astray than anyone

else in his time.* Kant's "two things," the "two things" of Beethoven,—"the starry sky above me and the moral law within me,"—filled his soul and armed his words, as they had armed the words of all the prophets since the beginning of man.

This was the secret of Emerson's power. In a day when the greatest geniuses spoke for their time, he spoke for the timeless things, goodness, not in defence, the intellect, not with emotion, as one and the same; and he spoke with the calm clairvoyance of one who merely revealed a truth which the innermost mind of his hearers, responding, confirmed. For things were so and not otherwise. No doubt, the time had come for other teachers, who were not so fatalistically optimistic, for critical and reflective minds that grappled with secular problems. Too much of the Emersonian bred an indifference to the hard facts of American life,—which might come right in eternity but was certainly going wrong in time. This life had never gone so wrong as immediately after the war. Emerson's voice was lost in a babel of other voices, many of them prophesying doom. His words were overlaid, as the walls of a house are overlaid with fresh layers of paper. But what did the Ripleys find in Concord when they repapered the Manse? Stripping off layer after layer, till they reached the original paper, they found it was printed on old French journals of the time of the Revolution. It was covered with the speeches of Mirabeau and Danton. So Emerson's words were written on the walls of the nation.

* This was the point of Matthew Arnold's lecture on Emerson, in which, after saying that Emerson was "not a great writer," he observed that Emerson's essays were "the most important work done in prose . . . in our language, during the present century." This was an application of the classical law according to which the ultimate standard in writing is one that underlies the aesthetic.

It should be added that Arnold's approach to Emerson's poetry does not lead to the centre of the subject. The point is not how far Emerson fell short of Gray or Cowper, in their spheres, but how far they, in his sphere, would have fallen short of *Bacchus, Terminus* and *Give All to Love*.

Whenever, in decades to come, the house was renovated, and the old layers of paper were stripped away, these words came to light again; and America once more saw the star of promise first seen in its early morning. The Hawthornes had vanished from Concord. Thoreau was gone. At the Manse lived Mrs. Ripley, who was found in the attic once, rocking the cradle, with a Sanskrit book in her other hand, apologetic because she had to look a few words up and because she could not think in Sanskrit. Frank B. Sanborn, John Brown's friend and helper, who later wrote the lives of the Concord worthies, carried on the Concord school and contributed letters on books and authors to Samuel Bowles's paper, the *Springfield Republican*. These letters, with their news and gossip of the literary world, were a staple of conversation in the Berkshires. They kept Emily Dickinson well posted. Mrs. Hawthorne had taken her children to England. Julian, the son, who had lived as a boy in Liverpool, when his father was consul, was to pass many years in England; and there he began his life as a novelist. Before this, however, he had studied engineering in Dresden and worked for a while in New York as an engineer. One found a reminiscence of Dresden in his *Saxon Studies,* an acute but captious picture of German life, and in his later novel, *The Professor's Sister,* a spiritualistic romance with a German setting, involving hypnotic trances and astral forms. For a number of years, Julian Hawthorne reviewed books for the London *Spectator,* and for more than half a century he continued to write, as a novelist and a journalist, pursued by misfortune. His earlier novels, *Archibald Malmaison, Fortune's Fool* and *Noble Blood, Garth, Idolatry* and others suggested the later vein of the elder Hawthorne, the unfinished *Dr. Grimshawe* and *The Ancestral Footstep. Garth* was the tale of an old New Hampshire house with a gloomy legend. In *Idolatry,* an Egyptian palace rose on the banks of the

Hudson, and the story was like the dream of an opium-
eater, with hoopoe birds, enchanted rings, eccentric uncles,
mysterious murders and a vague young Dane who was
somehow descended from Thor. Others were tales of
"American claimants" in England, of whom Nathaniel
Hawthorne had met so many, in the consulate, when
Julian was a child, stories of changelings, ambiguous bar-
onets and wandering American artists, of English manor-
houses with secret panels, locked doors, dusky apartments,
towers with ghosts and faces at windows. These stories
were heavily documented as a tribute to the realism that
more and more prevailed as the years went on, but in
essence they were melodramatic; and one found less and
less in Julian Hawthorne's later stories that indicated a
personal style and vision. One saw this writer best perhaps as a rather ineffectual link between the greater Hawthorne and Henry James.

As for the Alcotts, settled at last in Orchard House,
their world was agreeably altered by Louisa's success.
For the big, bouncing, ardent girl, who was almost six
feet tall, with her "force and temerity of will,"—which
Alcott had noted in her at the age of four,—had followed her father's injunction: she was acting out her
genius with a vengeance. No longer were the neighbours,
asked to tea, obliged to bring their little baskets with
them, to fill the pot with souchong and the bowl with
sugar. "Duty's faithful child" had changed all this. Louisa
had entranced her public as a chronicler of the Alcott
household, which had cast its bread upon the waters and
found it after many days. She published *Little Women* in
1868. In the same year appeared her father's *Tablets;*
and *Concord Days* and *Table-Talk* followed, all in the
train of Louisa's good fortune. Alcott's books no longer
went a-begging; and, when he set out for the West, the
"American Plato," with his brand-new trunk and gloves
and cambric shirts, was able to count upon thousands of

auditors. His "conversational tours" were prospering as far away as Iowa, where he lectured on Webster, Garrison, Greeley and Parker. He brought New England back to the homesick minds of the exiled Yankees; and those who had never understood why Emerson thought so well of Alcott had only to read his books to solve the puzzle. They had much of the charm of Whitman's *Specimen Days*. The essay on Emerson, the "favoured of the Nine," his genius and personal influence, was a moving tribute; and the papers on gardens and orchards, their poetry and philosophy, were signs that Concord well deserved its name. Not in vain had the rural muse traversed these meadows, woodlands, fields and brooksides; and, while it sounded deeper notes in others, Alcott wrote for the future as well as Thoreau. With him the American wilderness had passed its savage and animal stage, and the gardener, not the hunter, was the man it called for.* It was finding this man in Olmsted, and Alcott was one of his prophets. He had led the way with his arbours and Virgilian woodpaths, which Olmsted translated into parks.

Louisa Alcott's life spanned all the great days of Concord, for she was born in 1832, a year before Emerson settled in the town of his forbears. She had witnessed, as an infant, her father's removal to Boston,—from Germantown, which happened to be her birthplace,—and the rise and fall of the Temple School and Fruitlands. She had built her first play-houses with diaries and dictionaries and had learned to use them both at four or five; for her father, a "child-psychologist," as people said in later years, analyzed and examined the minds of his daughters before they were able to speak and encouraged them to

---

* "I came as naturally to the spade, the plow, the scythe and sickle as to book and pen.

"The mind needs to come into tender relations with the earth and treat that most intimate of all spots with something akin to piety, since a personal pressure is diffused through every part of it, and divinity there awaits to meet us always."—*The Journals of Bronson Alcott*, edited by Odell Shepard.

shape their thoughts in diaries and stories. At Fruitlands, reading Plato with the others, she was used to discussing such subjects as "What is Man?" She liked to
watch the moon. She had good dreams. She had pleasant
times with her mind.* Moreover, she was physically
hardy. She liked cold baths at five in the morning, and she
throve on a fare of plain boiled rice, apples and Graham
meal without sugar or butter. She was a Dorian girl, if
Elizabeth Peabody wished to see one, who had undergone a training as severe as a boy's, and she knew how to
leap, run and wrestle. At six years old, in Boston, she had
driven her hoop without stopping all round the Common,
and in Concord she jumped off roofs and vaulted fences
and outplayed the boys at break-neck tag. She would have
nothing to do with any boy whom she had not outplayed.
She thought of herself as a horse, for she liked nothing
better than to race through the fields, tossing her head to
sniff the morning air. She had grown up tall, thin and
brown, with a yard and a half of chestnut hair, a towering, hoydenish, moody, stormy creature.

She had shared the Concord life in all its aspects. She
had gathered moss for Alcott's arbours and browsed in
Emerson's library, where she read Shakespeare, Dante,
Carlyle and Goethe. She had roamed the fields with
Thoreau, studying the birds and the flowers. She would
have liked to camp out with Thoreau and Ellery Channing, like Sylvia, in her first novel, *Moods,* the restless
girl who lived by "impulse,"—she had not learned to
live by "principle,"—and who joined three men on an expedition, with a cockle-shell stuck in her hat. Sylvia was
in love with the leader of this party, a tall, bronzed hero

---

* From Louisa Alcott's diary at the age of twelve:
"I wrote in my Imagination book, and enjoyed it very much. Life is
pleasanter than it used to be, and I don't care about dying any more. Had
a splendid run and got a box of cones to burn. Sat and heard the pines
sing a long time. Read Miss Bremer's *Home* in the eve. Had good dreams,
and woke now and then to think, and watch the moon. I had a pleasant
time with my mind, for it was happy."

who suggested Thoreau, as a young girl might have seen him, although Warwick usually went to the polar regions instead of Boon's Pond and Heywood's meadow. Warwick was a master of woodcraft and Indian arts, and his grip filled everyone with life and courage. Sylvia's expedition with these companions recalled the woods of Maine and Thoreau's *Week;* and Louisa, who liked to think of "affinities," and wrote this book to express her feelings, —in a Hawthornesque style that was also Goethean,— shared all of Sylvia's impulse and indifference to trifles.* She longed to be an actress, she longed to be a novelist, and she meant to live her own life, whatever the neighbours and cousins might say. She thought nothing of walking to Boston for a play or a lecture; and, when she made a "battering-ram" of her head, to force her way in the world and earn her living, she ignored the conventional notions that governed her sex. She went to the war as a nurse, or, rather, like Whitman, to amuse the wounded soldiers with games and stories; and in Boston she lived alone in boarding-houses, paying her way as a governess, a housemaid, a seamstress. Sewing sheets and pillowcases, neckties and handkerchiefs, she wrote plays and stories in her attic, lying awake and planning chapters of novels and sometimes working fourteen hours a day. One of her plays was produced at the Howard Athenæum. She was so depressed that she thought for a while of suicide. She was saved by the ministrations of Theodore Parker, who appeared as Mr. Power in her novel, *Work.*

Miss Alcott was an experienced story-teller when she finally wrote *Little Women.* Her first book was the *Flower Fables* she had told the Emerson children, in the style of Frederica Bremer or perhaps Jean Paul. But long before this she had written the melodramas and fairy-tale plays, with giants, pumpkin-coaches, harps and castles, water-

* "I like original people who speak their minds out and don't worry about trifles."—Sylvia, in *Moods.*

falls, thunder and armour, that she and her sisters had played in the barn at "Hillside,"—no doubt, the first of all the little theatres that rose in New England barns in days to come. As for *Little Women,* it was the author's high spirits that captivated the world in this charming book. She invested the Concord scheme of life with the gaiety and romance of a Robin Hood ballad.

CHAPTER IV

THE NEW ENGLAND SCENE

THE New England scene, in general, at the close of
the war, was a battle-ground of permanence and
change. The elements of change were appearing already,
but the elements of permanence, also present, were as
marked, if not equally striking. All that made New England, and was to make it, as long as New England en-
dured, was sufficiently patent; but one had to seek it in
devious ways, by a somewhat circuitous path, because the
New England mind was shy. Bold enough, aggressively
bold, in trade, in agitation, in religion, it was singularly
delicate in essence; and this delicacy, the fruit of a long
tradition of ethical culture, was more and more accentu-
ated as the years went on. Change came over the world,
and outward and material things swayed the human consciousness more and more; and then the New England
mind retreated, withdrawing into itself. The esoteric note
of the Concord authors, anomalous in earlier days, became, with Emily Dickinson, Henry Adams and many
another writer, the note of the region. The Greek phrase
"Hide thy life" was the motto of the later years. This
was a gradual process, but already the seeker of New
England found it best by a roundabout method. One had
to begin at the surface to reach the core.

One saw the surface best perhaps at Newport, for vis-
ibility there was a fact and a virtue. Besides, at this well-
known watering-place, the old and the new regime dwelt
side by side as nowhere else. While the ancient wharves

and warehouses spoke of the past, the "Avenue" spoke
of the future; and for every black old hulk that lay in the
harbour, recalling the China trade or the trade with the
Indies, there were a dozen yachts. The vast hotel with its
sweeping piazzas echoed with the strains of the waltz and
the polka; and in the afternoon, on the leafy streets, great
fragrant haycarts and loads of onions brushed the tandems and four-in-hands, the donkey-carts and goat-carts
and the basket-wagons driven by pretty girls. One saw the
ruined fort and the Mill, the tower like the tomb of
Cæcilia Metella, the mansions of the eighteenth-century
merchants, with their fine square fronts adorned and
carved, their eagles and urns and pineapples, over against
the haunts of modern fashion, rising along the sea-walk,
the mansard villas and wooden chateaus, with their crenel-
lations and turrets, cottages aspiring to be castles or castles disguising themselves as democratic. A soft yellow
haze, the breath of the Gulf Stream, lingered over the
scene.

Everything at Newport suggested leisure. The mouldering old mastyards, littered with spars and timber,
broken rudders, rusty anchors, windlasses and kettles, the
lofts, with their coils of rope and empty casks, the pigeon-
holes with faded labels bearing the names of forgotten
ships, told the tale of a past that had ceased to compete
with the present. An occasional stately bark, spreading
its sails, might have belied this impression, but the air of
the population seemed to confirm it. Everyone sauntered
in Newport, and, if one hastened one's steps, perhaps to
catch a train, curious heads appeared at the doors and
windows. Hitching-posts had been removed all over the
town, to get rid of the multitude of old men who spent
their days leaning against them. So, at least, a shrewd observer said. It was true that the yachts and four-in-hands
and tandems, the Italian opera troupes and the great
hotel referred to something else than leisure elsewhere, to

Wall Street and State Street, Western mines and oil-
wells, cotton brokers' offices and railroads, but only as
these referred to spoils and vacations. The Point was a
sort of artists' quarter; for the undulating land, the rocky
ridges, the marshy valleys opening on the sea, the picturesque decay of the wharves and the shipping, the little
dark gambrel-roofed houses, the tottering masts that
Channing had climbed as a boy, attracted the landscape-
painters. They pitched their easels along the sands where
Channing had strolled with Dana and Washington Allston. They rejoiced in the Paradise Rocks, where the
great Bishop Berkeley had written his *Minute Philosopher*. The thinker's stony seat had witnessed since many a
moonlight flirtation.

Close by the vine-clad Mill, Miss Jane Stuart lived in a
little cottage, crammed with old furniture and pictures.
The long-surviving daughter of Gilbert Stuart, who had
passed his own youth at Newport, was almost as old as
the Mill and quite as famous. A relic of the world of
1812, the world of Channing's youth and the painter
Malbone, with a headful of legends and scandals as old
and quaint as the tiles in the merchants' mansions,—the
beaux and coquettes, bewigged and hooped, the priests,
dancers and beggars of the days of Hogarth,—she had
watched the growth of the watering-place; for this old
resort of the Southern planters, whose households mingled there with the families of New York and Boston
bankers, had become a cosmopolitan centre, the unrivalled
summer seat of American fashion. As an aspiring painter,
in earlier days, she had been seen in Boston, perched on a
stool, copying her father's portraits. At present, she was
pursuing another ambition, expressed in her weekly re-
ceptions: she hoped to supply the missing link between the
world of fashion and the world of art. Miss Stuart had
to resort to desperate methods. Although she told fortunes like a gypsy and excelled in lurid stories of ghost;

and murders, she found herself obliged to stoop to conquer. She begged to be included in the humblest charades,
even in the part of a gorilla; and, as her fickle followers
fell away, she was always changing the bait with which
she hoped to win them. She would pose a pretty girl in an
oaken armchair, under a coloured window, to remind her
guests of Keats's Madeline, or she would place a bench
on the piazza, surmounted with a milkpan and a pump-
kin, intended to create a rural air. "Rusticity," Miss Stuart said, "rusticity is the dodge for me." It was old New
England's charm for modern Newport.

Rusticity was the note of Lawton's Valley, where Julia
Ward Howe and Dr. Howe, Bostonians at other seasons,
spent their summers. But Mrs. Howe was innocent of
dodges. With no pretensions to smartness, she had an
appetite for the gay and lively. She liked a whiff of fashion now and then, as she liked to rebuke its vanities, and
she "rumble-tumbled" as she chose through all the Newport circles, with a jingle or a lecture or a sermon. The
Howes had bought a farmhouse in a neighbouring glen,
with a rocky gorge, a dam and a mill, and Dr. Howe had
planted a garden, beside the little stream, and built seats
and tables under an ash-tree. A rugged knoll sheltered
the nook, where Mrs. Howe conducted her out-door
salon; and there, on summer days, as nowhere else, religion, fashion and poetry met and mingled. In the mornings, in her alfresco study, under the Norway firs, Mrs.
Howe communed with Kant and Spinoza, as if she had
never heard of Washington Square; or she organized her
"picnics with a purpose," perhaps at the Paradise Rocks,
a clambake with a seaside lecture, an hour or two of
botany, or an astronomical evening, if the stars were out.
Mrs. Howe often read a paper, on sex and education, for
example, or she spoke on the value of character and the
dangers of wealth, the ease with which money bought the
press or the folly of marrying titles, a subject that was

apropos at Newport. She and Colonel Higginson, her neighbour,—Thomas Wentworth Higginson,—formed a Town and Country Club to remind their more frivolous friends of the duties of culture. The meetings attracted many writers who lived in the town or were visiting there, the veteran George Bancroft, still working on his history, James Parton, the author of the "lives," Fanny Fern, his wife, the sister of Willis, the Reverend Charles T. Brooks, the translator of Schiller, and Katherine P. Wormeley, the translator of Balzac.* Bancroft spent every summer at his villa, "Roseclyffe." Dr. Holmes came down from Boston, and Charlotte Cushman was often there, with Thomas G. Appleton and Charles C. Perkins, whose summer home was called "Bruen Villa." Among the younger men were Alexander Agassiz, the son of the great professor, John La Farge, the painter, and Clarence King. Helen Hunt, "H. H.," who was one of Higginson's protégées, was writing her poems at Newport, where she passed the winters. Her father, an Amherst professor, had recently died in Jerusalem, whither he had gone in search of health, and her husband, an army officer, had left her a widow. She had lived for years at military posts, and she went for her summers to New Hampshire, whence she returned in October laden with chests and trunks. They were full of pressed ferns and autumn leaves, which she dispensed to her friends. Her poems were redolent of these spoils of the mountains.

* Beginning in the early eighties, Miss Wormeley translated the whole of Balzac. She lived for many years at Newport, but her later years were spent in New Hampshire.
"This year I have lost one of my dearest older friends, Miss Katherine Wormeley . . . A delightful 'great lady,'—daughter of an American mother and an English admiral, who fought in the Peninsular wars, . . . Miss Wormeley had seen much of the world all her days, but her last years were spent in a quiet house among our White Mountains, where she busied herself with French translations, Balzac, etc. . . . She lived as if she lived in London, but for months she heard few sounds beside the wind and the mountain brooks and the foxes barking on the hills."—1908, *Letters of Sarah Orne Jewett*.

Just beyond Lawton's Valley lay "Vaucluse," the stone colonial house with the large white columns, flanked by two wings, where Thomas Robinson Hazard lived, the Howes' nearest neighbour. This great grey relic of the past, surrounded with its gardens and arbours and hedges, where the rose and the myrtle ran riot, was a picture of decay and desolation. Green streaks of mould and moss covered the joints of the stones, and the long-closed shutters of most of the windows were half-hidden by creepers. From the deep-arched porch at the rear a weed-grown gravel walk led to the far-away knoll where the Hazards lay buried; and the woods stretched down to the sea, with miles of labyrinthine drives and paths. There were bowers and ruined summer-houses at the intersections, with jungles of box and ivy. The farmers still remembered the gaieties of old, when the windows of the dwelling blazed with lights and starry lanterns hung from the shrubs and the trees. All night the roses had heard the flute, as the dancers danced in tune. In those days, "Vaucluse" had been thronged with children, and scores of guests filled the paths and arbours; and even now, in June, it came to life and the soft air blew away the mouldy odours. The solitary gardener did his best to reclaim the lily-beds and the peony-bushes, and old "Shepherd Tom," on state occasions, opened his mildewed wardrobes, took out some garments of his gayer time and put them on and let them hang about him. Behind his closed shutters, most of the year, he lived among ghosts and shadows, for the old man was a spiritualist and a liberal patron of mediums. The spirits allowed him, for remembrance, to cut off locks of their hair.

Grey and thin as he was, however, "Shepherd Tom" Hazard,—so called to distinguish him from Nailer Tom, College Tom, Little Neck Tom and thirty-five other Tom Hazards, who were scattered about Narragansett, in castles, on farms,—had plenty of sap left in his veins and his bones. He had not yet written *The Jonny-Cake Papers,* a work of his eighty-third year, and he could still spin a better yarn than any of the woollen mills at Peace Dale. A rich old crotchety Quaker, he had retired from these mills, after making his fortune, and he spent his last years indulging his hobbies, reforming the asylums and the prisons and the treatment of the poor of Rhode Island. Tall, with a grizzled beard, he was a master-hand at controversy, and his two commandments were to love one's neighbour and to hate all Puritans with a perfect hatred; for, when even the dogs of Rhode Island, as strangers sometimes noted, still kept the spirit of Roger Williams,* how could he make his peace with Massachusetts? He laid about him in dozens of pamphlets, for he liked to smite the Pharisees and those who ground the faces of the poor. As a young man he had raised sheep and brought them through the snow of the bitterest winters, and for years he had ridden on horseback, all over the country, from Benny Rodman's Horsewhip to Pint Judy, vulgarly called Point Judith, delivering carded wool at the cottages of the spinners and carrying the yarn back to the mills. He rode thousands of miles through sun and storm, over bogs, stone walls, rocks and streams, till he knew every farmhouse in the state and every old wives' tale and old man's legend, from the days when Gilbert Stuart was a boy and Oliver Hazard Perry had never been heard of. He knew the Gargantuan feats of the Narragansett worthies,—Little Neck Tom, who brought down fifty-one teal with a single sweep of his duck-gun, and Stout Jeffery Hazard, who carried for several rods the sixteen-hundred-and-twenty-pound weight of the blue stone one

* "I know not whether anyone, even in New York, is so hardy as to laugh at Rhode Island, where the spirit of Roger Williams still abides in the very dogs . . . The small commonwealth, with its stronger and fuller flow of life, is more native, more typical, and therefore richer in real instruction, than the large state can ever be."—E. A. Freeman, *Impressions of the United States.*

still saw at Peace Dale. In those days, Rhode Island men lifted their barrels of cider for a drink at the bung, and a forty-pound Narragansett cheese attracted so many rats to the palace of the King of Surakarta that the king and queen had to jump out of the window. "Shepherd Tom," like Howells, knew the importance of trifles. What caused the island in the Tiber but a bull's hide lodged in the current? Did not a mighty war result from the theft of a diamond necklace? In the same way, old black Phillis also caused the French Revolution, as Shepherd Tom's readers were aware. How the Rhode Island greening was lineally descended from the Tree of Knowledge, how Commodore Perry whipped the British tars and why roasting and baking, in Phillis's kitchen, were arts the modern palate never knew,—these questions Shepherd Tom alone could answer. Although he imposed at times on the reader's patience, with his long-drawn-out parentheses and whims, *The Jonny-Cake Papers,* with its twenty-six bakings, was a classic of Rhode Island Yankee folklore.

The farmers still recalled "Shepherd Tom" driving his handsome span of buckskin horses, with his three pretty daughters grouped about him, to the old Quaker meeting-house at Portsmouth, where George Fox preached in ages past. Only the other day, he had sent the Howes a barrel of cats that almost clawed their Boston house to pieces. This "cat story No. 3," in the vein of *The Jonny-Cake Papers,* was a sample of the mediæval humour for which the old Rhode Island folk were noted. In Newport, milder ways prevailed. There one studied the Middle Ages. One did not act them out like "Shepherd Tom" and some of the Renaissance popes. Among the Newport circles, remote from the "town," and almost as remote from the world of fashion,—at least, the part that savoured of New York,—was one that knew its Florence, Rome and Venice as other Yankees knew their native duck-ponds. This was the circle of the cognoscenti who had drunk too deep of "Europe" ever to feel at home in their native pastures. For those who, having means and cultivation, had also the wandering habits of lovers of art, who wished to be in their country but not of it,—when they were not in Italy or England,—Newport was a point of reattachment that left them still detached; for the bustling American world seemed far away under the springlike sky of the Newport winter, in the soft, warm zephyrs of the Gulf Stream. There everyone had memories of the Brownings, of conversations with Landor and the haunts of Dante, and ladies who fell into reveries woke with a start and exclaimed, "Oh, I was in Italy." They lived again their days in Story's Rome. They were always "going back," with smiles of deprecation, although most of those who went returned again; for, after all, after all, there was so much to say for America! They sailed as they had sailed on the Bay of Naples, they sketched as they had sketched on the Campagna; and they gave occasional readings in the parlours of the great hotel, in which the Renaissance was often mentioned. Some of them studied with Hunt, who had settled in Boston.

Among Hunt's Newport pupils had been John La Farge and William James, the son of the theologian, Henry James, who had also come from New York; or, rather, the Jameses and La Farge had all returned from Europe, where they had lived at intervals for several years. Henry James, the elder, weary of a wanderer's life, had felt the attraction of New England, and, meeting Hunt in Paris, he had followed him to Newport so that William might have the benefit of Hunt's instruction. Turning one's back on Paris to study art in America struck his second son, the younger Henry, as a somewhat original procedure. People stared and laughed when they spoke of their plan; but the Jameses were always original, and also Irish,—they were members of a Hudson river clan. As for John La Farge, he built a hut on the Paradise Rocks that was almost as lonely and bare as Thoreau's at Walden. He liked to withdraw to this retreat, to meditate while he painted, for La Farge was a thinker and writer as well as an artist. His subtle mind, brooding and profound, was to find its best expression, perhaps, in his books, in which almost every sentence was a picture. A Catholic of French descent,—his father, a San Domingo planter, had settled in New York in 1806 and made a fortune in real estate, like Henry James's father, up the Hudson,—he had a foreign air that suggested by turns a cavalier, a priest and a dandy. There was something prelatical about him. Dressed in cool white canvas or a velvet jacket, he was always leaning forward, musing and peering, with the thick glasses and prominent eyes that were somehow vaguely Oriental. Catholic as he was, he admired Confucius and sometimes had the look of a Chinese sage, and later, in Japan, he understood the Buddhists as if he had known their doctrines in the cradle. Born and brought up in New York, in the French emigré colony, an atmosphere of wealth and cultivation, he had gone as a young man to Paris, where he lived with his mother's cousin, Paul de Saint-Victor. Among this well-known critic's friends, with whom he had been constantly thrown, were the Goncourts and Sainte-Beuve, Baudelaire and Flaubert. Like Hunt, he had studied with Couture and was drawn to the Barbizon painters, when the name of Delacroix, who was their precursor, was still a gage of battle, and he had met men who had known Greuze and hailed the dawn of David and for whom Rousseau and Millet were mere beginners. He had posed for Puvis de Chavannes and begun the study of old French glass, which he was to carry far in later years. Then, drifting into an artist's life, returning to New York, he had joined forces with Hunt and come to Newport. He and William James acted as Hunt's assistants, preparing his work, in the cool grey studio in Church Street.

In after years, La Farge, who was always an "old New York,"—he clung all his life to Washington Square,—maintained this early connection with Newport and Boston. As a boy, he had dreamed of decorating the rude, bare New York churches. Longing to renew the old alliance of all the ecclesiastical arts, he had studied mural painting in relation to architecture, sculpture and glass; and Boston was to give him, with Trinity Church, a splendid opportunity to reveal his powers. This church was the beginning of American mural decoration; and later the architect, H. H. Richardson, opened the way for La Farge's windows, for he grew more and more absorbed in the making of glass. It was he who invented opaline glass, but his mind expressed itself in many forms. Curious and versatile, as cultivated as Delacroix, he thought in colour and line, or with his senses, so that half the charm of his writing, a painter's writing, consisted in its difference from a writer's writing. Often indirect and always subtle, he expounded a philosophy of art as the love of proportions and relations, in thought, in the influences of nature, in the actions of men.* He insisted that the artist was a workman, the healthy view for himself, the healthier the more literally he held it, for it kept him out of circles where he lost his personal dignity and made him inaccessible to fashion, the destroyer of the higher taste and style. At Newport, in these early days, he devoted himself to landscape-painting, to the beauty and harmony of nature. He had brought back from France a multitude of water-colours, sketches of peasants, costumes, interiors, landscapes.

For William James and Henry James, his juniors by

---

* *An Artist's Letters from Japan* was perhaps La Farge's finest book. While his *Reminiscences of the South Seas,* composed on another journey with Henry Adams, was distinctly inferior to this, all his books were admirable,—*Great Masters, Considerations on Painting, The Higher Life in Art,*—lectures on the Barbizon painters, suggested by the memories of his youth.

almost a decade, John La Farge embodied the gospel of art. Later, he embodied it for Henry Adams also. At Newport, both the Jameses had studied with him, for William James had a passion for painting, and even the younger Henry, deep in Balzac, had worked with his brother under Hunt. He made a careful drawing of one of Michael Angelo's Captives. La Farge brought back for him the world of Paris, from which he had been so rudely snatched away,—La Farge, who had known the writers he was reading, Gautier, Baudelaire, Flaubert, as familiars in the household of his kinsfolk. At La Farge's suggestion, he translated Mérimée's *La Vénus d'Ille.* The younger Henry James never forgot these hours of art at Newport. He was always at home in the studios of painters, as many of his stories were to show; and William James,—a twelvemonth older,—might have gone far as a painter.* He returned to his first love, science, too soon for this. In the years when the Jameses were living abroad, wandering from place to place and from country to country,—in Bonn, Boulogne, Geneva and always Paris,—in school-rooms, in pensions, in hotels, William James had been constantly busy with what he called "experiments." His fingers were stained with mysterious liquids. His chosen toys were those that emitted smells. He played with galvanic batteries and chemicals and drugs and strange marine creatures that floated in jars. He had an inexhaustible interest in the possible queer effects of things. He had given all this up in a rage for painting, and the rage had passed as suddenly as it came.

* "His capacity was as extraordinary there as it has shown itself later outside. He had the promise of being a remarkable, perhaps a great painter. Even many years afterward the drawings I have seen him make to illustrate some point of anatomy have a character as a memory of Leonardo."—John La Farge, quoted in *Later Years of the Saturday Club,* edited by M. A. De Wolfe Howe.

An excellent example of William James's painting, the portrait of his cousin, Miss Katherine Temple, is reproduced in Henry James's *Notes of a Son and Brother.*

The Jameses had gone to Boston, and finally settled in Cambridge. Newport was only a halfway-house, for them, as for all the summer people and most of the artists and writers who found a perch there. The town had its own life, like all the other New England seaports, New Bedford, Salem, Gloucester, Portsmouth, Portland, and Thomas Wentworth Higginson, for one, shared this life abundantly. He was writing a novel, *Malbone,* and stories about it. But the little world of the colonists, fashionable or otherwise, touched it at few points and touched nothing else there but the somewhat exotic life they carried with them; for nowhere else did the springs and sources of American civilization, in business, politics, religion, seem vaguer or more remote than they seemed at Newport. If one saw some of the flowers there, one looked in other places for the roots and the plants. For this reason, Norton had moved his summer home to Ashfield, where the roots and plants were visible, if not the flowers; while the younger Henry James, who cared little for roots and plants, and who had scarcely seen the country elsewhere, rejoiced in his memory of Newport.

Not far away, at Providence, Sarah Helen Whitman lived, the widow of a lawyer who had practised in Boston. "Poe's Helen" had long outlived her hopes and her fame. Higginson remembered Poe. During his college days at Harvard, when all the students, deep in the *Tales,* were agog to see the author, the dark little man had appeared in Boston and given a public reading. He had recited *Al Aaraaf* in a thin, clear, tremulous voice that was somehow like the finest golden thread. Higginson and his friends had walked back to Cambridge feeling that they were under the spell of a wizard. That was in 1845, on the very trip to Boston when Poe, "on desperate seas long wont to roam," had seen this second Helen "once, once only,"—in her garden, among the roses, in the moonlight. He had seen her again at Providence, four years later, after attempting suicide in Boston, and implored her to save him from his doom; and there they were betrothed, amid cries, vows and swoons, in an atmosphere of laudanum and ether. There they had said farewell, a month before Poe's death, and Helen had remained in her scarlet parlour, with her veils and her memories and sighs, still sprinkling her garments with ether, still writing songs for the guitar that floated with Italian airs, conversing, through her medium, with the world of spirits. The time had passed for poetesses, clad in silken draperies, who wrote on locks of Mrs. Browning's hair, passing a curl about their circle and composing songs for each of its threads; but Mrs. Whitman still pursued her mission. For twenty years she devoted herself to defending her poet-lover against the attacks of Griswold and other traducers. Her *Edgar Poe and His Critics* was a skillful and generous little book, and she corresponded with Ingram, who wrote the English life of Poe, and Mallarmé, the French translator. She left no stone unturned to establish a truthful picture of Poe. Among the younger writers who had known Mrs. Whitman at Providence was Howells's friend, John Hay, the Western poet. As a student at Brown University, he owed to this romantic lady his initiation into the world of letters.

One had to look far afield, meanwhile, for the more essential Yankee traits, for the roots and the springs and sources of New England. One found them in Concord, one found them at Andover, where the old religion flourished as nowhere else. Thence, in times past, had gone forth the missionaries who made New England a power all over the world, the five apostles of 1812 who planned the Christianization of Asia and sowed the seeds of a modern China and Turkey; the founders of schools in the seven cities addressed in the Book of Revelation, in Antioch, Tarsus, Smyrna and Ur of the Chaldees, the colporteurs who had scattered the Bible up and down the

Nile, the scholars who had set up printing-presses,—the first in Bulgaria, the first on the island of Malta,—and translated the Scriptures into Tamil, into Mandarin, Burmese, Armenian, Turkish and the tongues of the Marshall and Gilbert islands. If Andover was not the mother of all these feats of the old religion, the theological seminary, of which Austin Phelps was president now, symbolized the impulse that lay behind them, the last great wave of the Puritan faith, its final crusade to redeem the world.* This faith had begotten the zeal for reform, the passion for education that marked New England, for the teaching of the black man and the red man, the education of women, the reform of prisons; and the Andover theology, with its proselytizing spirit, had spread this passion over the West as well. Many a Western college, modelled on Bowdoin, Amherst and Williams, had sprung from the inspiration of the Andover doctrines. In the strait sect of the Andoverians, the little boys played "preacher" as their chief amusement, and ecclesiastical humour was alone permitted; and Mrs. Stowe, living there, had always lived apart, for someone passed the rumour about that she had been seen in a Boston theatre. Emerson was regarded as a wicked cynic, although, when he visited the town, it was duly noted, his clear-cut, sarcastic lips assumed the well-bred curves of conformity. The Andoverians knew that Emerson was a traitor to the faith of the forbears. Even the little girls were obliged to study theology there. They listened to lectures on probation, on sanctification and eschatology, mingling with their notes hurried portraits of their favourite academy boys; and Elizabeth Stuart Phelps, the president's daugh-

---

* For a good picture of a missionary school,—at Beirut in Syria,—see John W. De Forest's novel, *Irene the Missionary*, 1879. The minister, Mr. Payson, who directs the school, says, "God has removed wisdom and knowledge from the East." He conceives it as the mission of New England to bring back God and letters to the lands that forgot God and letters after giving them to the rest of the world.

ter,* had mastered the "Andover argument." Miss Phelps, —already writing stories,—could answer most of the Andover questions, whether everlasting punishment was the same as eternal and whether one act of sin was an infinite wrong. Was the whole race responsible for the guilt of Adam? The "chemistry of heaven" was another engrossing Andover topic. Was the body after its resurrection the same as it was before, or was the blood perhaps extracted from it? The tortured conscientiousness of Miss Phelps's novels reflected the Andover atmosphere. One of her young girl friends whom a young man dared to kiss had wept in expiation for twenty-six hours.

It was true that the Andover type of thinking had already begun to lose its force, and the strength of the old religion was failing with it. For this intellectual seriousness was a firm support of the old religion. Miss Phelps's stories reflected the transformation. In her first book, *The Gates Ajar,* which she wrote as a girl of twenty in the barn and the attic, she showed the growth of aesthetic feeling in the little world of Andover, where a dish of Baldwin apples on a cold winter day was as far as one had gone in the way of entertainment. She saw this book translated into French, German, Dutch, Italian, and countless American families that had lost sons in the recent war rejoiced in the youthful heroine's meditations; for, although she too had lost a brother, she still communicated with him, and what she discovered was consoling. The life to come abounded in modern improvements. There were all sorts of things in heaven, along with the palms and the golden cities. There were flowers and trees for New England nature-lovers; and they even had pianos in the heavenly mansions. That religion should be more aesthetic was the moral of this tale; that it ought

---

* Miss Phelps's grandfather, Moses Stuart, a former president of the seminary, was the author of the first Greek lexicon prepared in America. His Hebrew grammar was republished in England by Pusey.

to be far more practical was the moral of others. *A Singular Life,* for instance, was the story of a seamen's preacher who put the theologians to shame. They were aghast at his success in saving the wrecks and the waifs at Gloucester, when they had cast him forth as unfit for the pulpit. Miss Phelps's novels were problem-stories that sprang from the Andover mind, expressing its new developments and its natural bent; for they dealt, in a missionary spirit, with dress-reform, anti-vivisection, woman's rights and other humanitarian themes and causes. Her short stories, *Fourteen to One,* were often poignant and skillful; but the tone of her work in general was too consciously righteous.

The new type of Orthodoxy was represented by Horace Bushnell, the great theologian of Hartford. Bushnell, distrusting the Andover doctrines, had evolved a fresh point of view by denying that language and logic could state religious truths exactly. An intuitive, imaginative mind, he clung to the ancient mysteries, while softening their Calvinistic rigour. He, too, stressed the aesthetics of religion; and indeed the day had already arrived when most of the Protestant doctrines were dissolved in an Emersonian ethical culture.* Even Harriet Beecher Stowe, who was also living in Hartford now, had withdrawn from the Andoverian faith of her fathers. Mrs. Stowe had gone back to Connecticut and built a spreading mansion there, with towers and gables, a fountain and a greenhouse. At this very moment, in *Old Town Folks* and *The Minister's Wooing,* she was recalling the poetry of a bygone era, the fears and sorrows of heart of the Puritans whom she had known as a child for the perfect church and state they had hoped to establish. In these books, as nowhere else, one found the roots of the

---

* In 1878, Dean Stanley told President Eliot that he had heard most of the eminent American preachers. His general impression was that the sermon was always by Emerson, no matter who the preacher happened to be.

Yankee mind, in the Hebraistic air of an earlier epoch, when all were of one blood and race and the sentiments of justice and moral indignation, in view of cruelty and crime, were uncomplicated as yet by mundane interests. In *Old Town Folks,* especially, the spirit of her grand progenitors rose in Mrs. Stowe's mind at moments, and she was often inspired and often happy; but she herself had broken with Beecherism and all its works in favour of the "insidious paw" * of the Scarlet Beast. Like others who, in former times, would have joined the Unitarians, —like the poet Lucy Larcom, for example,—she was won by the "balm of devotional liturgy" and the "shadowy indefiniteness" of the more aesthetic Episcopal form of worship. The growth of aesthetic feeling, marked in Boston, was reflected in these transformations in the sphere of religion.

Through all changes of thought and feeling, the old New England love of learning persisted in the most unlikely corners. Was not "I want to know" the Yankee watchword? No one was surprised by the mystical worship of culture that prevailed in the larger towns throughout the region, those towns that abounded in clusters of sisters who were always called "the girls" and were often also known as maiden aunts. Classes in German were universal, botany classes, French classes, led by some friend perhaps of Auguste Comte, and there were rumours of Gaelic classes, conducted by a Highland chieftain,—the last of the MacIvors or whatever,—and Sanskrit classes in charge of East Indian princes. For occasional Hindu readers of Emerson and Channing came to survey the land of these cosmic thinkers. There was a class of young girls, in the town of New Britain, as late as the middle seventies, studying Sanskrit. Their leader was the "learned blacksmith," Elihu Burritt, the

* The Episcopal Church, as the old ladies call it in Mrs. Stowe's *Poganuc People.*

former consul at Birmingham, who had organized the
first Peace Congress in Paris, in 1849, and persuaded
Victor Hugo to act as chairman. Burritt, the living and
lasting symbol of the Yankee passion for self-improvement, had retired to a farm in the evening of his days,
and there he prepared his *Sanskrit Handbook* and his
grammars of Arabic, Persian, Hindustani and Turkish.
But all this might have been taken for granted. What surprised the traveller was the learning one found on farms
and along the road. One heard all manner of anecdotes
about the rustic Yankees who confounded the wandering
scholar with their erudition. Such was Frank, in *The
Jonny-Cake Papers,* who ferried the British Minister
across to Newport. When the minister and his Newport
host, disputing over a passage of Virgil, were able to
come to no conclusion, the ragged, red-faced boatman
raised his voice and repeated the passage correctly, singing it to a camp-meeting tune. This long-dead Frank had
many successors, like the Massachusetts farmer who corrected Norton. Driving about with another professor,
Norton stopped to water his horse. As the two friends
waited, one of them said, "According to Montaigne,"
and gave a quotation, whereupon the farmer, who was
holding the bucket, remarked, "'Tweren't Montaigne.
'Twere Mon-tes-ki-ew.'" "And 'twas," said Rudyard
Kipling, to whom Norton afterwards told the story. The
day had not yet passed when country parsons tutored
bright farmers' boys in Greek, while the neophyte paid
for his tutoring by doing the chores, plucking the parson's geese and washing his sheep and helping him to
make his soap and candles. No doubt, there were other
boys like Bliss Perry's father, who left his Latin grammar
at the end of a furrow, after glancing at the declensions
and conjugations, repeating them aloud as he ploughed
the furrow down and back, then turning the page and
ploughing with another lesson. There were boys like

Charles Dudley Warner, who memorized hundreds of poems while he was milking and who named the cows after Latin numbers, Unus, Duo, Novem and Decem. There were country stores where one of the farmers related in serial form the books he was reading, so that half the young men in the village heard most of the Waverley novels. For a long generation to come, many a Western college president was drawn from this bookish world of the Yankee farm, from households that read the Bible with Josephus and cherished a Christian life in the clefts of the rock. With all this hunger for knowledge, however, one still found traces here and there of an older than mediæval superstition. In times of drought, when the wells were dry, one saw the dowser at his priestlike task, with the forked twig of hazel in his hands, moving slowly across the fields, invoking the aid of Thor,—though he may not have known the name,—in his search for water. As late as the eighties, in Vermont, the body of a woman was exhumed to prevent her from killing her family, and remedies were still used in lonely households that recalled the pharmacopæia of the Pilgrim fathers, mullein-root in cider, tansy, burdock, sowbugs tickled into a ball and swallowed before they uncurled again, dried rattlesnake-flesh, the powder of a red squirrel, baked alive, pounded in a mortar and consumed while fasting.

The pictures of rural New England that lasted best for later minds were those of Mrs. Stowe and Mrs. Cooke,—Rose Terry Cooke, who was also living in Hartford. There had been earlier writers,—Catherine M. Sedgwick, for one,—who described the humble life of the country-people, but before these admirable realists, with their homely art, no one had truly conveyed its colour and savour, its rude strength and depth of feeling. In Mrs. Stowe's books one found most of the "chestnut burrs" that became the stock-in-trade of New England fiction, the philosophical sea-captains, the stubborn farmers and wild young men, the regiment of Yankee spinsters, infinite in variegation. These types were living realities in her pages; and a young girl in Maine who was soon to write about them, with an art that Mrs. Stowe had never dreamed of, had been led to observe her world by Mrs. Stowe. For Sarah Orne Jewett, who lived at South Berwick, *The Pearl of Orr's Island* was a revelation. This was the book that opened her eyes, as she drove about the country with her father, the doctor, calling at fishermen's cottages and lonely farms. But before Mrs. Stowe wrote this novel, Mrs. Cooke was writing her short tales; and it was she who established the type of rural story that other writers developed more dexterously later.* Rose Terry Cooke was the founder of the school that produced Miss Jewett, Miss Wilkins and Alice Brown.

As one glanced in later years at this series of authors, one observed the transformation of the Yankee scene. In Mrs. Stowe one saw it in its power and fullness, before the land was sapped by the westward migration. Miss Jewett and Miss Wilkins described the Yankee ebb-tide, a world of empty houses and abandoned farms, of shuttered windows, relics, ghosts and silence. In Mrs. Cooke, the tide was still at flood, or perhaps one ought to say that one saw it turning. Between the lines of her tales one perceived already the draining and denuding of the land, the movement of the young men westward and, more evident still, the inner decay of the region. Everyone remembered the little boy in Granville who shed such bitter tears in the rocky pasture because he could not find earth to bury his seeds. Since those days, countless thousands had left their farms, in search of the fertile prairies, in Ohio, Minnesota or "Westconstant," with their clocks and spinning-wheels and covered wagons, and their studded horse-hair trunks hung on behind. They had

* One of Mrs. Cooke's stories, *Sally Parsons's Duty,* appeared in the first issue of *The Atlantic,* 1857.

cleared the forests and bridged the streams and founded cities and commonwealths, in the name of New England; and on many a Western river-bank they had reproduced their ancestral villages, the church, the school, the common, fringed with trees. For every one of their dwellings, with its white-washed fence, and its pot of baked beans on a Saturday evening, there stood some counterpart in the Yankee homeland, a weather-worn house with a maiden aunt and rooms that ached with loneliness, a mass of tumbling wood or a brick-filled hollow where the lilacs bloomed in Maytime, where

> naught remained, the saddening tale to tell,
> Save life's last wrecks—the cellar and the well.*

This world that was left behind, with its bramble-draped cellar-holes and dim trails leading through the woods, was to breed a peculiar miasma, as the years went on; and one found prefigurations of Mary Wilkins's haunted scene in the village life that Mrs. Cooke observed. How many traits of a lowered vitality were evident in this village life, how many nagging wives and sullen husbands, what covetousness and meanness with all its courage. But still, in these western New England hill-towns, straddling granite ledges covered with pines, these Stoneboros, Newfields and Wingfields, with their mountain valleys,— where the devil gave his name to glens and gorges, to bridges and punch-bowls and pulpits,—one also found youthful ambitions and romping lovers, Gargantuan feasts, high spirits and the joy of living. When a young man went to California, in one of Mrs. Cooke's tales, there was always another young man to take his place, a smart Yankee with plenty of "faculty;" and, with all that was grim and terrible in the best of these tales, the enveloping air was elastic. One heard through the night the cheerful bells of sleighing-parties; there were husk-

* Holmes.

ings, barn-dances and quilting-bees. One was never far
from the brisk little scene of the prints of Currier and Ives.

It was Mrs. Cooke's tales, perhaps, that Henry James
had in mind when he said, "I hate old New England stories—which are lean and pale and poor and ugly." Mrs.
Cooke's world was singularly charmless, and few of her
stories transcended its leanness and paleness. Her Aunt
Nancys and Miss Semanthas, her Aceldamas and Sary
Anns, her Amasas, Celestys, Philurys and Sallathiel
Bumps, with their liver-complaints and rheumatism and
their moral angles and mental spikes, had little indeed to
please the roaming fancy; and one heard too much, in
these artless narrations, about camel's-hair shawls and
black alpacas and best satin-finished black silks, about
stuffy spare bedrooms opening out of kitchens and darkened parlours smelling of ill-dried feathers. People who
will not "jaw" at table, and whose feelings and meditations are not distinguished, can expect to find few lovers
on this crowded planet. Like the deaf adder, the reader
stoppeth his ear against them and will not hearken to the
voice of charmers, charming never so wisely; and Mrs.
Cooke too often described them in terms of a provincial
scene for which all amenities were snares. But as history,
some of these tales, with their note of harsh veracity,
were never to be replaced by later authors; and as tales,
in their bleak finality, two or three,—*Too Late* and *Some
Account of Thomas Tucker,**—were all but beyond comparison. In the course of two generations, a series of
writers, Miss Jewett, Mary Wilkins and Edith Wharton,
Robinson, Frost and O'Neill, were to find their account
in this old New England, with its desperate passions and
wild regrets. They knew what volcanoes, strewn with
vines, lay under the placid hollows of its human surface.
In *Too Late,* at least, Rose Terry Cooke foreshadowed
all their stories and their plays and poems.

* In the volume called *The Sphinx's Children.*

CHAPTER V

THE POST-WAR YEARS

IN JULY, 1868, Charles Francis Adams and John Lothrop Motley returned to Boston. For many years they had lived abroad, in the diplomatic service, but Adams's mission in England had come to an end and Motley had retired from his Austrian mission. Both had reappeared to recover their bearings in the new American world. Adams's younger son, Henry Adams, who had spent the Civil War years in London, acting as his father's secretary, recorded their first impressions in words that were famous later: "Had they been Tyrian traders of the year B.C. 1000, landing from a galley fresh from Gibraltar, they could hardly have been stranger on the shore of a world, so changed from what it had been ten years before."

The adventures of Henry Adams in this world, transformed by the recent war, were to take place largely outside of New England; but no one observed his age more keenly, whether in New England or elsewhere. A shy, self-conscious little man, inordinately proud, with a restless, introspective, probing mind, he had taken it for granted, as an Adams, that he had a career before him, the sort of career that Adamses always had.* For three generations his family had had their hand on the lever of power. They had all been at home in the White House

* The Adamses were the first family that Francis Galton chose to illustrate his method in *Hereditary Genius*. Galton ended his list with Henry Adams's father.

ever since it was built, and Henry Adams had half thought he owned it. That he should some day live there was almost a matter of course with him.* It had never occurred to him, till his return, that the days of the Adamses were over.† He had had a taste of politics, the politics of the new age, that somewhat disillusioned him in London, for the British statesmen seemed to him highly disingenuous and very unlike the Adamses in this respect; but he had never supposed that America would dispense with its best-trained statesmen and cast its lot for politicians who took their orders from bankers. That statesmen could be obsolete, this was a conception the Adamses could scarcely comprehend; for, without a thought for themselves, for three generations, they had sacrificed personal interests and local interests to the welfare of the country as a whole. They had really believed in the cause of advancing mankind, and for three generations the family had fought for the country against the British and against ₀the bankers,—Downing Street, Wall Street, State Street, —and triumphed in most of their struggles; and Charles Francis Adams, as Minister to England, had foiled the British again and kept them out of the war. He had raised to its highest pitch the prestige of American policy; but the bankers had prevailed in his absence. They had won the war for the North and demanded their pound of flesh, if they had to kill the country to obtain it.

* "The Irish gardener once said to the child: 'You'll be thinkin' you'll be President too!' The casuality of the remark made so strong an impression on his mind that he never forgot it. He could not remember ever to have thought on the subject; to him, that there should be a doubt of his being President was a new idea. What had been would continue to be . . . A President was a matter of course in every respectable family."—*The Education of Henry Adams.*

† They were not as much over, politically, as Henry Adams liked to think, for he thoroughly enjoyed his disillusion. His father was at least considered for the presidency, and his brother, John Quincy Adams, was nominated for the vice-presidency. His elder brother, Charles Francis, as president of the Union Pacific railroad, was as much of a statesman as he wished to be. His nephew, the third Charles Francis Adams, was Secretary of the Navy.

John Quincy Adams, who had formed the faith of his
sons and grandsons, had had a noble vision of the country's future. He had hoped to develop the national wealth
on a collective, not a competitive, basis. He thought there
was a volume of energy stored within the Union, enough
for the prosperity of all: if this could be brought into use
in accordance with the laws of science, it would lead the
population to perfection.* For this reason, John Quincy
Adams had promoted the study of science, while he
fought with all his might against the bankers, who stood
for competition and disruption. And now it appeared that
science itself, applied in machinery and railroads, had
stimulated nothing but ambition and greed.

With some such thoughts as these, and such misgivings,
Henry Adams returned to the homestead at Quincy, the
retreat of all the Adamses for three generations in times
that called for study and meditation. Only six months before, he had been expecting to begin a career in the press
at home as the champion and the confidant of a bold and
honest American government. He had prepared in London for a publicist's life, working at financial theories and
John Stuart Mill; and his ears were still ringing with his
father's exhortations.† The fourth generation of Adamses
was to carry the Adams banner forward.‡ At moments

* See Brooks Adams's *The Degradation of the Democratic Dogma.* Henry
Adams spoke correctly when he said of himself, in the *Education,* "By
rights, he should have been also a Marxist,"—that is, as well as a Dar-
winian. John Quincy Adams's economic thought, the basis of the faith of
the family, was distinctly a form of socialism, in the voluntary pre-Marx-
ist form.

† See the letter of Charles Francis Adams to his older son, written on
June 17, 1864, the anniversary of the Battle of Bunker Hill: "The labour
of extricating us from our perils will devolve upon the young men of the
next generation who shall have passed in safety through this fiery fur-
nace . . . Great will be the responsibility that devolves upon you! May
you acquit yourselves of it with honour and success! The great anniversary has inspired me to write to you in this strain."—*A Cycle of Adams
Letters.*

‡ Henry to his brother Charles, 1862: "It will depend on the generation
to which you and I belong, whether the country is to be brought back to
its true course and the New England element is to carry the victory, or

he had dreamed the sensation of wielding unmeasured power, a sense that came like vertigo. He knew how his forbears had felt, in the spacious upstairs study, as they sat in the President's chair, at the writing-table; but he felt that he was "for sale, in the open market . . . to be bought at the price of a mechanic." The old order had passed, and his dreams of power passed with it. He would have to make his way as best he could, in a world in which his quality scarcely counted. At the moment, prepared as he was for the press, he went at once to Washington, although he foresaw already "a life of wasted energy," as he observed later in the *Education*. Grant's administration was beginning, and it had no use for reformers; but it seemed to be a law of Adams's nature to gravitate to centres of power, and all he could do was to go and try his luck there. His brother, Charles Francis the second, struck for the railroads. A brigadier-general after the war, who had studied law with Dana, he became in the end a historian; and he made of the railroad business a learned profession, in the good old Adams way. The energy and daring of New England, once devoted to foreign commerce, was turning to the developing West, and the capitalists of Boston were building railroads. The Adamses knew railroads from the cradle,* for the first line in the country was the Old Colony line, built to carry the

whether we are to be carried on from war to war and debt to debt and one military leader after another, till we lose all our landmarks and go ahead like France with a mere blind necessity to get on, without a reason or a principle."—*A Cycle of Adams Letters.*

* And felt the poetry of them. "The Chicago express glided in as gracefully and silently as though it were in quite the best society, and had run a thousand miles or so only for gentle exercise before dining at Delmonico's and passing an evening at the opera."—Henry Adams, *Esther.*

Emily Dickinson, too, felt the poetry of railroads,—*I like to see it lap the miles,* etc.

Emerson's writings abounded in references to railroads, e.g., "It is not prosaic, as people say, but highly poetic, this strong shuttle which shoots across the forest, swamp, river and arms of the sea, binding city to city. The Americans take to the little contrivance as if it were the cradle in which they were born."—Emerson's *Journals*, VI, 336.

Quincy granite for the Bunker Hill monument; and Charles Francis Adams approached this business as his grandfather had approached the career of a statesman, laying down solid blocks of knowledge, historical and financial, with which to meet the problems of the Union Pacific. The coming generation, as Henry Adams saw, was "already mortgaged to the railways," and everything they implied, capital, banks, machinery, mines, together with new ideas and habits, social and political, to fit the new scale and suit the new conditions. If the Adamses were foredoomed to failure, as they were always saying, it was largely because nothing could seem like success in the light of their family history. For the rest, they understood their generation, which Henry Adams described as a "bankers' Olympus."

Years passed before the books of the Adams brothers revealed this diagnosis of their age, an age of the utmost confusion to most of those who were living in it. To Henry Adams, in Washington, trying to understand it, both political parties were corrupt, as the public seemed indifferent. All he desired was "something to support," something that would let itself be supported; and the presidency of Grant, which opened in 1869, "outraged every rule of ordinary decency." * The Fisk-Gould "gold conspiracy," which all but involved the President's person, and about which Adams wrote an essay, was the symbol of a state of affairs with which he could not contend, and the "Crédit Mobilier" scandal seemed to prove that a similar state of affairs existed in Boston. Gone were the days when directors were also trustees; the new business men were jobbers and robbers, and no one seemed to

* "Every hope or thought which had brought Adams to Washington proved to be absurd. No one wanted him; no one wanted any of his friends in reform; the blackmailer alone was the normal product of politics as of business . . . Grant avowed from the start a policy of drift; and a policy of drift attracts only barnacles . . . Grant had no objects, wanted no help, wished for no champions."—*The Education of Henry Adams.*

care.* The Adamses wrote together, in *Chapters of Erie,*
a sharp attack on "Caesarism in business," the Drew-Fisk-
Vanderbilt war.† Then, though they did not surrender
their hopes of reform, they faded more or less from the
public picture. Failures in their own eyes, in the eyes of
others eminent successes, they carried on existences, partly
subterranean and partly broken, the real meaning of
which appeared only after both were dead. Meanwhile,
the new age, with its new symptoms, established itself in
New England. The elements of change in this long-
settled country were not as marked at first as in other
regions; nor were they ever as marked as they were in
the West. The elements of permanence were much more
firmly fixed than later writers supposed in ·New England
itself.

Such as they were, the signs of change were sufficiently
marked already, with the war, the growth of the railroads and the factory-system, the spread of wealth, the
spread of immigration; which implied the spread of poverty,—with these and the time-spirit ‡ as primary causes.
The war, in a measure, uprooted the native population,
with whom wandering habits had been growing for decades. The opening West attracted them. The gold rush
of '49 had already increased this tendency, and, after the

* Thomas G. Appleton suggested in *Windfalls* that "a gallows con-
veniently placed at either end of Wall Street might be useful."

† "Vanderbilt is but the precursor of a class of men who will wield
under the State a power created by the State, but too great for its control."—*Chapters of Erie.*

‡ Aside from local New England causes, or even the broader American
causes, one must reckon with the time-spirit of Western civilization. Bene-
detto Croce, in the following passage, describes the whole of Europe, after
1870, in terms that apply to America and, specifically, New England:
"When the great political battles were over, the new generations, and
even the old patriots and combatants, devoted themselves to business; and
competition and the struggle for markets, in their turn, helped to suggest
the primacy of energy, force, practical capacity, over ethical and national
motives. The great economic prosperity that was supposed to supply new
and plentiful gifts to the work of human ideality seemed, on the contrary,
rather to suffocate it."—Croce, *History of Europe in· the Nineteenth Century.*

war, the newly poor and those who, being poor, had never felt so, under the old conditions, went West in greater numbers for a better chance. At the same time, the rich, the newly rich, or those whom leisure filled with a taste for culture, and those who merely had the taste for culture, flocked in growing hordes to Europe. With the opening of the transcontinental railroads, the economic centre of the country gradually shifted westward; and New York, with more and more of the Western trade, increasingly drew the foreign trade from Boston. The Asiatic trade had already dropped away, and in 1868 the Cunard Line also shifted from Boston. The mail and passenger steamers from Europe made New·York the main port of entry.* Thus Boston was isolated, as compared with New York, both from the West and from Europe, although it grew richer and richer from the factory-system. It profited by the growth of the West, creating goods for the pioneers, who sent their own products to New York. Meanwhile, with these economic changes, changes took place in the population, thinned by the westward movement and the war. With the growth of machine-industry, the handicrafts were fading out. The Sandwich glass-works, for example, with its glowing chimneys and smoking forges and swarms of well-trained craftsmen, was destroyed by the war, and the cheap machine-made pressed glass replaced the beautiful glass of old. The household arts were dying. The mills supplanted the spinning-wheels and hand-looms, as photography supplanted portrait-painting, the reaper took the place of the scythe and the cradle, the village cobblers vanished, and the village tailors; and new workers were coming in to tend the machines and till the soil by methods they had learned in other countries. Everyone remembered the coming of the Irish, who had dug earthen shanties to live

* The Cunard Line and others reëstablished Boston later as a secondary port of entry.

in. The French-Canadians had crossed the border in the decade after 1840, in groups of a man and a woman, ten or a dozen children and two or three bundles. At the old "north end" of Boston, the Irish superseded the Yankees and slowly gave place to Italians and Russian Jews; and all these races, and others, spread through the smaller towns.* The factories offered some of them openings, and others took up abandoned farms. The more they swarmed, the more the "oppressed of Europe" became, in the Yankee mind, the "scum of Europe," with results that were often tragic and always fateful.

All this was to change New England appreciably. Gone was the day when foreigners were as rare as in Scotland, and poverty twice as rare, when few were rich and few produced for profit, while all but the very few produced for use, when almost every man was a craftsman, skilled in hand and brain, and everyone knew his place, on the farm, in the village, where his fathers had lived before him. The new civilization abounded in practical benefits, railroads and steamships and gaslight, telegraph-wires and friction-matches, sewing-machines and reaping-machines and what not. Its disastrous effects, however, were apparent at once. With the growth of the stock-exchanges and the corporations, the great centralized industries, the factory-owners moved to the cities and lost their connection with the country. They ceased to feel responsible for the welfare of their workers, as they had felt in the days of the little private factory, when their wealth had been anchored in the soil, when they had seen the workers and their dwellings, workers of their own race whom they knew and partially understood. As absentee directors, they ruled a foreign population. The bond between the masters and the workers, wholly ab-

---

* It was to catch the spray, as it were, from a wave of immigration that Mrs. Alcott opened an intelligence-office in Boston. As might have been expected, all the Alcotts, father, mother and daughters, caught smallpox from an immigrant family whom they invited into their garden and fed.

stract and financial, was full of the seeds of the class-war of the future, and the factory-towns became "hell-holes," in Cobbett's phrase. A similar movement followed in the rural regions. Everyone had laughed at Orestes Brownson when, about 1850, he predicted that the landlord-system was going to supplant, in New England, the universal system of local and personal ownership.* This change came slowly, it is true. As late as 1883, Matthew Arnold asked Whittier, "But where do the tenants, the working people live?" There were few visible tenants, but this condition gradually passed. The smallest towns soon had their slums, and countless farms were mortgaged: the farmers were tenants of the banks. The evils of the landlord-system rose with the evils of the factory-system; and the "summer people," the "city folks," who flocked in growing numbers to the shore and the mountains, brought with them the class-distinctions of the outside world. The rural folk became self-conscious, and the younger people, already uprooted, added the evils of the city to the evils of the country. Meanwhile, the great web of the national railroads, destroying the sectional feeling, destroyed the sectional pride that had always redeemed it; and a sharp decline of patriotic feeling accompanied the decline of sectional feeling. The war had exhausted the nation, as even Emerson felt and said. The old idealism had been burnt away, the hopes of the patriot fathers, the youthful and generous dreams of the early republic. The war, with its fearful tension, draining the national vitality, had left the mind of the people morally flabby. The indifference to the public welfare was as marked as Henry Adams thought, and a low type of "business ethics" prevailed over the old ethics, in a larger and larger measure, as time went on. Visions of sudden wealth possessed the people. Promoters and gamblers in stocks swarmed over the country, with tales of fabulous silver

*Thomas Wentworth Higginson, *Book and Heart*.

mines and coal and iron properties in the West; and war-profiteers, Jay Gould, Jay Cooke, Jim Fisk and others, set the pace for younger men whose minds were adrift among unknown forces. Wasteful and prodigal habits grew, in reaction from the past, with its parsimony and narrow frugalities, the legacy of hard early days; and a world that was used to vulgarity had scarcely seen anything more shocking than that which sprang directly from the Yankee farm-life.* The most popular New England men, in all walks of life, during these decades, Ben Butler, Beecher, Barnum, D. L. Moody, when they were not venal, were singularly coarse, as compared with the earlier leaders. Money and "numbers" governed all their thoughts, even, and even especially, in the sphere of religion. For who could imagine a greater contrast than that between Moody and Beecher and the great religious leaders of the previous age, Theodore Parker and Channing? Where Channing and Parker, learned men, had devoted themselves to advancing thought, to art, philosophy, reform, these men were political routinists, at home in Wall Street and all but devoid of intellectual interests. They thought in terms of quantity, very seldom in terms of quality, and their "publicity methods" resembled Barnum's.†

These changes in the New England scene were reflected in literature almost at once. The stories of the younger writers, whose books were already appearing, abounded in the problems of the moment, the shifting population, the abandoned farms, the evils of immigration and the

---

* E.g., the case of Jim Fisk, born and bred on a farm in Vermont.

† "Numbers is the king of our era," said Harriet Beecher Stowe, ten years before Matthew Arnold said it. "Numbers" was certainly the king of her brother and Moody, who "sold" religion as he had once sold shoes. Both were religious wholesale-dealers, and the thought of money was never out of their minds. Beecher's first thought, when he met Mark Twain, was to tell him "what to do and how to do it" in the matter of making a fortune. It was he who also manœuvred John Fiske into the hands of a lecturing-agent. As a result of this, Fiske wasted himself in giving lectures of a more and more popular type.

factory-system, the increasing corruption in politics, the rise of the newly rich, the feeling that the region was declining. Elizabeth Stuart Phelps was among the first to respond to these various problems. She had been roused to a sense of the wrongs of the factory-workers by the great mill-fire in Lawrence in 1859, when scores of New England girls were burned to death. She studied the wretched conditions that produced these horrors, the lives of hands who scarcely saw the sun, who went to the looms by gaslight and returned by moonlight, who subsisted on bread and black molasses and died of the "cotton cough." In *The Silent Partner, Hedged In* and other stories, she described the growing slums and their human wreckage. Other changes were reflected in these writers, changes in education, in religion, in family life, the relations of the sexes, alarming enough at first and significant later. One of these great changes was the surplus of women. There were fifty thousand "extra" women in Massachusetts alone,* women who were widowed by the war, or whose lovers had died in the war, or who had been left behind in the movement of the young men westward. The "glorious phalanx of old maids" that rejoiced the heart of Theodore Parker was to dominate New England for an age to come, the age of the "strong-minded women" that might have been called the age of the weak-minded men. Hawthorne had complained, years before, of the "damned mob of scribbling women" who were swarming all over America; † and the clan of women writers grew apace. The resounding success of Mrs. Stowe

---

* Census of 1870. In 1880, the number had risen to 75,000. According to the census of 1900, the surplus of women in Massachusetts was greater than in any other state.

This surplus of women was only less marked in the other New England states. In New Haven, the story was told, during the Civil War, that "a student threw a stone at a dog and, missing him, hit seven old maids."— John W. De Forest, *Miss Ravenel's Conversion.*

† "America is now wholly given over to a damned mob of scribbling women."—Letter of 1855, quoted in Caroline Ticknor's *Hawthorne and His Publisher.*

had opened the way for the women writers, with the mul-. tiplication of magazines for stories. These women writers all but outnumbered the men, with results that were far from happy; but for this who and what was most to blame? The women won their influence by default. In the new frenzy of speculation, the excitement over oil and railroads, the absorption of young men in business,—in the Hecla mine, the Buckeye Company and hundreds of other enterprises,—literary and ethical interests and those involving human rights gave place to questions of trade, finance and commerce. Gone were the days when Yankee boys aspired to be sailors or missionaries, pedlars or poets. All these occupations had stirred the imagination, and so, in its way, had the life of the farm and the forest. The farmers of old, who had known their Bible, had often been readers of Plutarch also, and most of them had read Webster's speeches. The business life was hostile to all these interests. It encouraged the reading of newspapers and occasional books on engineering, but the world of thought and feeling impeded its action; and the tendency of the younger men was more and more to withdraw from this world, which remained, with books and reading, in the hands of women.* That women were ill prepared, if only by their education, for this dominance in the world of thought and feeling, no one was better aware than a

* "Speaking generally of the mass of business men,—and the mass are business men in this country,—have they any habit of reading books? . . . Look at the drift of things. Is the feminization of the world a desirable thing for a vigorous future? Are the women, or are they not, taking all the vitality out of literature? Answer me that. All the novels are written by, for, or about women—brought to their standard . . . They write most of the newspaper correspondence—and write it for women!

"In the large cities the women's clubs, pursuing literature, art, languages, botany, history, mythology are innumerable. And there is hardly a village in the land that has not from one to six clubs of young girls who meet once a week for some intellectual purpose. What are the young men of the villages and the cities doing meantime? . . . Is it comfortable for the young man to feel that laughing eyes are sounding his ignorance"?— Charles Dudley Warner, *As We Go*.

See also the remark of the poet Stedman about the post-war period: "For ten years the new generation read nothing but newspapers."

few of themselves.* But they were not consulted. They acted on a *fait accompli*. The "feminization of literature" was a foregone conclusion.

Thus opened the somewhat dreary epoch in which the poet Whitman said, "Genuine belief seems to have left us." The decline of culture, marked throughout the country, was visible almost at once throughout New England. All that was mundane in the Yankees, already sufficiently marked, even in various leaders of culture,† came to the fore and took the helm; while Longfellow, Parkman, Norton, Higginson and many other anxious observers noted the alarming changes in the public mind. Longfellow and Norton deplored the decay in the interest in literature.‡ Higginson remarked that nine lectures in every ten were merely stump-speeches in the old Lyceums. Parkman was disturbed by the sudden debasing of standards, the disregard of cool thinking except in connection with business, the desire for sweeping statements or "something funny," the passion for amusement and excitement, in lectures and even in the pulpit. Flatulent writing, he said, was growing at the expense of pregnant writing. Was not moral and intellectual greatness the true end of man, to which material progress should be only a means? To men like Parkman, the violent activity of an age of speculation was abhorrent. It was all but fatal to their hopes and interests. Meanwhile, as the cause of culture

* "The education of our girls is extremely timorous and one-sided. Ignorance may be 'bliss,' but it is not necessarily innocence, and I doubt whether it is ever really 'folly to be wise.' "—Harriet W. Preston, *Aspendale*.

† "Horace Mann lamented that in European exhibitions the fine arts were always assigned a more conspicuous place than the useful arts. Theodore Parker complained that in Rome the studios were better than the carpenter-shops. Both exulted in the thought that in America these things were better ordered."—Thomas Wentworth Higginson, *A Plea for Culture*, 1867.

‡ "Longfellow was complaining the other day of the decline in the interest in literature and in the taste for it, nor was he mistaken,—this generation is given over to the making and spending of money, and is losing the capacity of thought. It wants to be amused, and the magazines amuse it."—Norton to Carlyle, 1873.

lost ground in New England, the region itself lost ground
in the life of the nation. Perhaps the New England statesmen were the first to feel the change, for they were un-
horsed at once and, it seemed, forever. What Henry Adams feared soon came to pass, for the West, in the person
of Grant, cared little for Boston. Did it matter that
Charles Francis Adams had also saved his country? That
Sumner, Motley and Rockwood Hoar were masters of
public affairs? These patriots of the old type, these statesmen and diplomats were "highbrows," who did not like
the methods of the cave-man. Rockwood Hoar was too
good to exist, from the point of view of Grant's friends,
and Sumner wore English clothes, and Motley "parted
his hair in the middle." * Grant disliked them one and all
at sight. Motley had been recalled from both his foreign
missions, in circumstances that almost broke his heart;
and Rockwood Hoar was marked for an early slaughter.
As for Charles Sumner, he was the last New England
statesman who played a national role for a generation.
The balance of power in politics had shifted westward,
and the tastes of the West, and its choices, won the day.

In the sphere of education, the spirit of the new age
declared itself immediately and clearly. Charles William
Eliot, an energetic chemist, had turned Harvard over
"like a flapjack." The phrase was Dr. Holmes's, and
Charles Eliot Norton's cousin turned over many flapjacks
as the years went on. The higher education of the country was largely remodelled on his ideas, for no one knew
better than he what the country desired. Harvard had
"struck bottom," he said, with a series of ineffectual presidents, who reflected the indecisiveness of the national
mind. This mind halted between two opinions, the old
classical system and the new technical system; and the

---

* "Mr. Fish afterwards told Adams, with the rather grim humour he
sometimes indulged in, that Grant took a dislike to Motley because he
parted his hair in the middle."—*The Education of Henry Adams.*

cry had been going up for instruction on special, voca-
tional lines. Technological schools were rising to meet the
new demands, with chairs of geology, engineering, mining,
schools for bridge-builders and railroad-builders, chemists
to work in the factories, geologists to develop the mineral
wealth of the West.* In the colleges, where the "man of
thought" had always ruled as a matter of course, the students debated the question, "Resolved, that the man of
action is more important." Eliot replied with a new
regime that marked the decisive change, a change that
was soon reflected in the minds of writers.†

A Channing Unitarian of the Boston-Puritan-Roman
type, serene as Cato, cheerful as a boy, Eliot was marked
by a passion for the practical and a singular grandeur of
nature. He was redeemed from Philistinism by a delicate
ethical instinct and a feeling for the values he did not
understand in others, unlike himself, whom he respected.
A daring pilot and skipper, he loved skill, as Emerson
loved it, and he shared Emerson's faith in human nature.
He was a Puritan formed on the classical model, elevated, simple, grave and patient. Abounding in all the

* The opening, in 1861, of the Massachusetts Institute of Technology
was the most notable symptom of this general movement. Eliot became
president of Harvard in 1869. At about the same moment, the "young
Yale" movement began, for college reform at New Haven. It was in 1870
that W. W. Phelps made the well-known speech that created such a furor
at Yale: "Harvard takes great poets and historians to fill its vacant pro-
fessorships—Yale takes boys who have proved their qualifications by
getting their windows broken as tutors." The modern Yale is said to date
from this hour of self-examination.

† In the mind of Henry Adams, first of all. The lesson of the Civil
War, as he saw it from London, was that the great new forces were
science and mechanics. The success of the American ironclads, the off-
spring of science, in the Battle of the Rams, caused the English to per-
ceive in three weeks that their wooden navy was antiquated and useless.
Great Britain's sea-power was "knocked in the head" by modern science.
"I tell you," Adams wrote to his brother Charles, "these are great times
. . . Man has mounted science, and is now run away with. I firmly be-
lieve that before many centuries more, science will be the master of man.
The engines he will have invented will be beyond his strength to control.
Some day science may have the existence of mankind in its power, and
the human race commit suicide by blowing up the world."—*A Cycle of
Adams Letters.*

Plutarchian virtues, which he liked to celebrate in his in-scriptions,—for his words were fit to be carved in gran-ite,*—he liked Martha better than Mary, and he served a generation that shared this taste. Eliot took for granted the Emersonian doctrine that the young should follow their stars without let or hindrance. That he himself and Emerson had only begun to follow their stars after a long immersion in the wisdom of others, in the good old Yankee way at home, in the good old classical way at col-lege,—that this immersion, in fact, was education,—did not disturb his faith that human beings instinctively knew and followed the good-for-them. They could scarcely be trusted too soon for this,—the belief that lay behind the "elective system;" and perhaps at other periods the sys-tem might have worked in the interest of a broadly human world. At the moment, the "stars" which the young were prepared to follow, the stars which they observed in the sky outside them,—and the sky offered them less and less of any other kind, as the sources of other stars grew dim-mer and dimmer, with the decline of religion, with the decline of classical studies,—were largely materialistic and often mean; and Eliot's elective system, which pre-pared them to follow these stars, worked against other objects and other causes. It was true that this system pro-moted efficiency in many socially useful professions. It opened a great new epoch in science, medicine, engineer-ing.† But one saw the total effect in time, as the other

* Among Eliot's multifarious writings, the most characteristic were his inscriptions. Towards the end of his life, it became the custom, all over the country, when a new post-office was erected, or some other public building or monument, to ask him for an inscription to be cut in the marble or granite. These inscriptions, redolent of the Roman authors, on whom he liked to dwell, and also of the Puritan tradition, in which he lived in good faith, conveyed, while often describing others, the note of Eliot's own mind.

† "We have but a halting faith in special training for high professional employments. The vulgar conceit that a Yankee can turn his hand to any-thing we insensibly carry into high places where it is preposterous and criminal. We are accustomed to seeing men leap from farm or shop to courtroom or pulpit, and we half believe that common men can safely use

universities followed Harvard and lost sight of human
ends in means. Then it became apparent that civilization
was losing its soul, as education had lost its soul already.

The first step at Harvard was to throw the classics
overboard and promote the "specialist" system the age
demanded. Thus died the old American college; the European model was discarded; the American university came
into being. The classics, not too competently taught, went
down before the new engrossing interests; * and this
marked, in literature, almost the greatest of possible
changes. The change in literary style was not the most
important, although this was sufficiently striking.† The

the seven-league boots of genius . . . This lack of faith in the prophecy
of a natural bent and in the value of a discipline concentrated upon a
single object amounts to a national danger."—Eliot's inaugural address,
1869.

In these words, the American mind turned a corner. To Eliot is largely
due the immensely increased efficiency in American professional life, along
with the efficiency of business. But this was accompanied by a sharp decline in most of the extra-mundane activities, the literary life among them.

* It is true that the study of classical philology gained greatly under
Eliot, along with everything else in the specialist system, but this con-
cerned only the special student. Eliot led the way in dropping required
Greek and Latin, and the pattern set by him was almost universally fol-
lowed. "It is a hard saying, but Mr. Eliot, more than any other man, is
responsible for the greatest educational crime of the century against
American youth,—depriving him of his classical heritage."—S. E. Morison,
Three Centuries of Harvard.

President Eliot's "five-foot shelf" was largely a realization of Emerson's theory that everything good in the classics may be gleaned from
translations. Emerson and Eliot alike were excellent classical scholars, and
one of the amusements of Emerson's old age was to compare a translation
of Plutarch with the original Greek; but it was an effect of their joint
teaching that in another fifty years one had to look far for a college man
who could read either Greek or Latin with ease or pleasure. The "five-
foot shelf" was an admission of this, and also a justification of the theory
which was the cause of this effect. It was a symbol of a social order,
materially aristocratic, that was also intellectually plebeian.

† Disregarding secondary writers, all the first-rate writers of the later
age, even those who knew the classics well, suffered, as regards their
style, from a vital indifference to the classics. Few of their books have the
authentic ring that marks the best pages of Thoreau, Dana, Hawthorne,
Motley, etc., who were steeped in Greek, Latin and the Bible. The "vices"
of their style were almost as marked as the "beauties": the thin facility
of Howells and the earlier Henry James, the obscurity of the later Henry
James, the excessive colloquialism of William James, the perversity of
Emily Dickinson, the awkward, metallic or inexpressive quality of much
of Henry Adams's writing, especially the later chapters of the *Education.*

study of the classics had always been connected with accurate linguistic training and the study of form, while
the modern tongues were loose in their construction; but,
what was even more important, the classics had made spacious men and men prepared to meet great problems.
None of the abundant cant that was uttered on this subject, both at the time and later, altered the fact. They
kept alive great patterns of behaviour, which all the
American people had seen in action in the ample minds
and characters of the earlier leaders, most of whom were
steeped in Plutarch's lives and the legends of Greece and
Rome. The close association of intimate studies had made
these patterns real, and the patterns had made great writers as they made great statesmen. They appealed to the
instinct of emulation, an instinct that in later days followed the patterns set by industrial leaders, by bankers
and by millionaires whose only ideal was the will to power
and who ruled by the blind force of money.*

Meanwhile, the coming age was represented by a number of Eliot's appointments. As William Morris Hunt
said, Cambridge was "all literature;" and whatever at
this hour spoke for Cambridge spoke for American literature also, even, and perhaps especially, when it spoke
for science. Of the new "university lecturers," Chauncey
Wright and Charles S. Peirce were influential in shaping

* "What is the American ideal of greatness?" one of the characters
asked in Howells's *A Traveller from Altruria* (1894). The banker answered: "I should say that within a generation our ideal had changed
twice. Before the war, and during all the time from the Revolution on-
ward, it was undoubtedly the great politician, the publicist, the statesman.
As we grew older and began to have an intellectual life of our own, I
think the literary fellows had a pretty good share of the honours that were
going; that is, such a man as Longfellow was popularly considered a
type of greatness. When the war came, it brought the soldier to the front,
and there was a period of ten or fifteen years when he dominated the
American imagination. That period passed, and the great era of material
prosperity set in. The big fortunes began to tower up, and heroes of
another sort began to appeal to our imagination. I don't think there is
any doubt but the millionaire is now the American ideal." If, thirty years
later still, Americans had no ideal, who was to blame for this,—which
generation?

the mind of the future. Howells stood for the modern languages, the interest in which was rapidly growing, and Eliot also appointed Emerson,—of all the older men of letters the most sympathetic to men of science.* The younger Oliver Wendell Holmes was instructor in constitutional law. But perhaps the most representative of all these teachers was the young Connecticut Yankee, John Fiske, who lectured on positivism and Darwinism, the most engrossing topics of the moment. Fiske had seen in Emerson a prophet of the new ideas that Darwin and Herbert Spencer had begun to establish.† That man had risen from inorganic matter, instead of being "specially created," that he had not fallen from perfection but had only begun his journey towards perfection, this was the notion that Fiske set out to preach; and, although he was under a cloud at first and taught in the teeth of Agassiz, the defender of "special creation," he made rapid headway with the doctrines that were universally held in later years.

This "great, simple, learned child," as one of his friends described him, was the son of a Hartford journalist who had once been Henry Clay's secretary. Fiske, whose original name was Green, had grown up at Middletown, a lanky, goggle-eyed boy with red hair and freckles who was also a prodigy of learning. Fond of sports, fonder of music, he composed a mass and an opera later, and his flowing high spirits were as marked as his deep strain of religious feeling. His zest for study was astounding. He seemed to know all about all the sciences by the time he

* This appointment, one of Eliot's first, marked the reconciliation of Emerson and Harvard. During the years in which Emerson had become a writer of world renown, the college had never forgiven him for his Divinity School address of 1838. His lectures were published as *The Natural History of Intellect*.

The subject of Howells's lectures was modern Italian literature.

† Spencer also saw in Emerson, who had read Lamarck, a herald. of the evolutionist point of view. During his visit to America, in 1882, he made a pilgrimage to Emerson's house at Concord. This is said to have been the only occasion on which Spencer paid tribute to another thinker.

entered college, and half a dozen languages as well; and
one of his classmates asked him why he had bothered to
come to Harvard. What did any college have to teach
him? He might have answered, Hebrew, Sanskrit, Gothic,
Icelandic, Roumanian, Dutch, for he presently added them
all to the rest of the list. His teachers were astonished at
the breadth of Fiske's knowledge, his grasp of history,
philology, philosophy and science, and, what was more
unusual, his gift for thinking. For with all this receptive-
ness, his mind was an active and powerful engine. His
learning was the fuel that drove it forward.

In the slight, long-legged, self-conscious student one
scarcely discerned the later Fiske, the form that became
so famous on the streets of Cambridge, the huge, hearty,
hirsute creature with the bushy beard and the gold-
rimmed spectacles who looked like a German professor.
But one had a prevision of this in his tastes and his habits,
in the long-stemmed meerschaum pipe that he smoked, for
example. He would slowly produce and assemble this pipe
from various recesses of his person, slowly fill it and
light it slowly, with a great sigh of contentment, while
he rounded up his thoughts for conversation. He was one
of William James's men who could sit over a pot of beer,
lost in the depths of his mind, for hours together; and
his first little book, *Tobacco and Alcohol,* defended his
predilections against all and sundry. On behalf of drinking and smoking and their physiological value, he mar-
shalled authorities in half the tongues he knew, Latin,
German, Spanish, Dutch, Italian; but long before this
he had shown his varied powers. He was a formidable
writer and a stormy petrel. He had studied law, en-
raptured with Blackstone, as with everything that called
for a mental tussle, and had even set up as a lawyer in
Boston; but his writing gave him little time for practice.
While he was still an undergraduate, he had written and
published several articles that aroused the attention of

readers even in England. One of these, a review of Buckle, interested Herbert Spencer and Lewes, who were soon to know much more of their youthful author. One, on the evolution of language, revealed the genius for exposition that marked Fiske's work for forty years.* Ticknor, Child, Lowell and Norton had all been struck by this model student, whose method and tone were like those of the "great reviewers;" and when Lowell and Norton took over the moribund *North American* they gave him a free hand for reviews and essays. Fiske wrote with equal competence on Longfellow's Dante, on Taine and Motley, on politics, religion, education, on philosophy, anthropology, history and music. His methodical, orderly mind moved like a stone-crusher, reducing the boulders of thought to a flow of gravel that anyone could build a mental road with. He simplified the knottiest points, he made the most difficult abstractions as lucid and easily grasped as a nursery-story, and all without any sacrifice of substance. He was supple, readable, human, direct, and, although he was seldom original and seldom suggestive, he was equally instructive and entertaining. Moreover, he was imaginative. He felt the magic power of myths, and once he saw the devil, or believed he saw him, actually sitting in his study, with hoofs, horns, fiery eyes and all. The big, warm-hearted, exuberant Fiske, whose wit was somewhat elephantine, was vehement and cheerful in manner, both in writing and in speaking. A first-rate popularizer, he was filled with the zeal of a propagandist. Evolution for him was a new religion.

His interest in this new theory dated from his college days, when his mind was full of Humboldt, Comte and Buckle. In Boston, at the Old Corner Bookstore, he had happened on a prospectus of Spencer's writings. This was

* "I never in my life read so lucid an expositor (and therefore thinker) as you are."—Letter of Darwin to Fiske, on the publication of *Outlines of Cosmic Philosophy*. Darwin further said that he had never been able to understand Spencer until Fiske elucidated Spencer's doctrines.

in 1860, when Spencer had just begun to publish the series
in which he rounded out his system. Fiske was enthralled
at once by Spencer's programme, and his interest in the
subject was confirmed when Spencer's friend Youmans
called upon him. The remarkable E. L. Youmans, who
founded the *Popular Science Monthly* and whose life
Fiske wrote in later years, was a New York farmer's boy
who had educated himself by heroic efforts and become
the American prophet of modern science. It was he who
introduced to American readers, through his *International
Scientific Series,* the writings of Darwin, Bagehot, Buckle,
Helmholtz, Huxley, Lecky and Tyndall.* Convinced that
the theory of evolution was about to remodel modern
thinking, he saw in Fiske the perfect expositor for it; and
it was Youmans who introduced Fiske to Spencer, for
whom he had raised a subscription to enable him to carry
on his work. Up to that moment, science was a mere collection of facts and rules, with no coherent body of governing truths, while the new conception of the unity of
nature bound all these facts together in a web of causa-
tion. It seemed possible to write nature's history back to
the primitive chaos, and one saw that all its phenomena,
instead of being unrelated and produced by the Creator's
personal whim, were parts of an unbroken chain of cause
and effect. Suns and stars, plants and animals had followed one law of development from a common source,
and man was also a part of this cosmic drama. Through
all the vast sweep of time, from the primordial vapour to
the multifarious world one knew today, one saw the various forms of nature evolving from previous forms. The
simile of Paley's watch was no longer valid. The simile
of the flower was a better description. For the universe

* The declining of this series by Ticknor and Fields, to whom, in 1860,
Youmans offered Spencer's *Education,* was one of the first indications of
the passing of Boston as the intellectual centre of the country. As a result
of this first refusal, all these works of science, which dominated the mind
of the coming epoch, were published by the Appletons of New York.

was not a machine,—it was an organism, with an in-
dwelling principle of life; and man had not been made,—
he had grown and developed.

Such was the great Spencerian vision that Fiske expounded at Harvard, with his own interpretations and
amplifications. Spencer had ignored previous systems, to
which Fiske related the new philosophy. To the general
notion of evolution, he contributed one idea of his own,
the effect of the prolongation of infancy in forwarding
human development; and he published his lectures presently in *Outlines of Cosmic Philosophy*. For the rest, he
found in evolution an ethical and religious meaning that
scarcely existed in Spencer's original statement. For
Spencer's Unknowable he substituted, God, as the well-
spring out of which flows the unfolding cosmos, so that
progress was not only the working out of natural laws but
a process that was controlled to beneficent ends. In this
way he reconciled science and religion, and one saw in
the end that Fiske was a religious thinker who had given
the New England faith a firmer basis. But at first he was
considered an atheist, and the feeling against him rose so
high that he was never appointed to a chair at Harvard.
He remained as assistant librarian, and he soon turned
to the writing of history, approached from the evolutionary point of view. But everyone remembered that the
great debate over evolution began, in America, at Harvard, and that Fiske had been the centre of the storm.
It was the greatest debate since the Reformation.*

While all these Harvard lecturers left their mark on
the coming age,—Fiske, Holmes, Wright, Peirce and
Howells,—none exerted a personal influence stronger
than that of another man whom Eliot's predecessor had
appointed. Raphael Pumpelly, the first professor of min-

---

* In 1869, the New York *World* reported in full Fiske's Harvard lectures. There has never been any other case in American history of such
a popular interest in a philosophical controversy.

ing, remained only two years in Cambridge; but he fired
the imagination of many a student. In a day when the
young New England men were scattering over the world,
looking for "opportunities," for mines to develop, for
the romance of travel or mere excitement, this Huguenot-
Yankee Marco Polo was a highly symptomatic figure. A
dashing, dramatic geologist, with a beard like a shower
of gold, an explorer and mystic whose life was already
a legend, Pumpelly appealed to many minds, those who
were bent upon making money, those for whom the West
and Arizona, Mongolia, China, Japan were El Dorados,
lovers of pure science and lovers of adventure who sought
their adventure now in the outer world. For the day of
the inward adventure was passing, and men who, fifty
years before, would have found their adventure in books,
like Ticknor, or, like Thoreau, in their minds,—the wildest sort of adventure,—looked for it in the physical scene
and found in Pumpelly a guide and a stimulus. There
were others, such as Howells and the brothers William
and Henry James, who found their adventure in observation, anywhere and everywhere; but, even among the perceptive, these were few. Henry Adams was only one of
the many restless younger men whose minds were touched
by Raphael Pumpelly.

Both inwardly and outwardly, Pumpelly's personality
was a striking illustration of the times. As a boy in western New York, the child of a great land-owning family,
with many farms and forests, mills and stores, a patriarchal clan of the semi-feudal type, he had found in Hugh
Miller the "wonders of geology" and gone abroad to
study in his youth. With a mind that was alive to music,
painting and poetry, as well as technology and science, he
had a zest for wild life like that of the irrepressible moufflon which he led all over Europe as a travelling com-

panion.* Between periods of study in Germany and Paris,
he spent five months in Corsica, with the bandits and the
mountaineers; and there, as later in the Rockies and the
Urals, pursuing his geological work, he fell into moods
of exaltation.† Returning to America, at the opening of
the Civil War, he went to Arizona as a mining engineer.
Thence he proceeded to Mexico, and then to Asia, to
survey Japan and China for their mineral resources; but
his great opportunity came at the end of the war. The
East buzzed with tales of the West and its iron, gold and
copper, and there were few trained experts to develop
the mines; and Pumpelly made geological surveys of the
Michigan copper and iron regions and reported on the
routes for Western railroads. Where Agassiz showed the
significance of geology for science, he showed its significance for industry and business; and, while he contributed
to scientific knowledge, he made and lost fortunes and
caused the making of larger fortunes. In the great game
of exploiting the West, Pumpelly had one of the whip
hands, the hand on the lever of power that fascinated
Henry Adams; for men who had money to invest were
obliged to rely on his judgment. As one who knew the
sources of wealth, he hobnobbed with princes and kings
and the powers of the earth. Adams's friend, Clarence
King, was another young man who discussed with Pumpelly the future of the Rockies and Asia, and John
La Farge rejoiced in his hundreds of Japanese prints and
the bronzes and bits of jade he had brought from Japan
and China. Like Washington Allston, in earlier years, he
sat where the young men passed at the cross-roads in

---

* The "moufflon story" is a lively passage in his ever-lively *Reminiscences.* Pumpelly said he had told this story in English, German, French,
Italian and Japanese.

† His excellent books, *Across America and Asia* and the later *Reminiscences,* abound in expressions of "cosmic feeling," as people used to call
it. John La Farge wrote the chapter on Japanese art in *Across America
and Asia.* This was the earliest of La Farge's published writings.

Cambridge; but he pointed towards other goals and in other directions.

If Pumpelly was not in Cambridge long, this in itself was symptomatic. He was off, he was always off, to the ends of the earth, to the "old Yuma trail" or the coalfields of China, an example for the restlessness of others. He made New England seem small; and, if it was true that this small New England had given birth to great ideas, there were many who were prepared to risk the future. What if a greater New England were to give birth to small ideas? Ideas, to them, were less important than numbers of other goods which the future promised. As for Pumpelly himself, he was far from small. His charm was his spaciousness, his feeling for horizons; and if, as another Pied Piper, he led the children up a mountain that opened and closed again and left them in the dark, it was his music that led them, and the music was real. The darkness was the cave of money to which the adventure usually led. But the music was adventure itself, the joy of a whole generation.

CHAPTER VI

THE RADICAL CLUB

THERE were other musicians, luckily, to lead the
dance of the post-war years, though their music was
relatively sombre. E. L. Godkin had founded *The Nation*
in 1865. With the prophetic eye of a sensitive alien, who
loved the old American traditions, Godkin had foreseen
the tendencies of the coming age and organized his journal to combat them. *The Nation,* a weekly review, was
one of the few periodicals that become historic, as *The
Dial* and *The Atlantic* became historic, because they focus
the mind of a new generation; and, while it was published in New York, it was closely connected with Boston
and Cambridge, where Parkman, Lowell and Norton
were its constant advisers.* Parkman made it the vehicle
of much of his occasional writing, and many of the contributors were younger Cambridge men. Howells had
worked for a time on *The Nation* before he joined *The
Atlantic,* and he and the brothers James and Henry
Adams were among the regular reviewers. Eliot had offered Godkin a professorship of history, and at various
times in the future he lived in Cambridge. It was there
he found his first editor, John Dennett, a Harvard man,
before he assumed the editor's chair himself, and his
literary editor for almost forty years was Wendell Phillips Garrison, the Liberator's son. In times that were
difficult for conscientious thinking men, with all the heavy

* Of the capital of *The Nation,* one half was raised in Boston, a fourth
in New York and a fourth in Philadelphia.

metal turned against them, at least they had an organ in
The Nation.

Godkin, an Irishman, the son of a Presbyterian minister, had settled in America in 1856. He had studied law
in England and had crossed the Atlantic, drawn by a deep
regard for the republic. A disciple of Mill and a well-
trained journalist, he had watched the disintegration of
the public life upon which he had built his faith and hope.
Educated Americans were losing all interest in public
affairs and considered them disagreeable and even repulsive, and he resolved to rally the younger generation and
revive the ideals of the country. In short, he represented
a regenerative impulse, a reaction against incompetence
and corruption. The daily press were hurried and partisan, the weekly press superficial and narrow. Thinking
men found no account in either, and Godkin, who knew
that America abounded in critical minds, proposed to
create a medium that would bring them together. *The
Nation* was modelled on the London *Spectator,* and in
certain ways Godkin's policy harmonized with President
Eliot's. Eliot preached the doctrine of special training for
special work, as against the Yankee man-of-all-trades
method. Godkin applied this doctrine to public affairs.
He championed civil-service reform, or the cause of special training in politics, as opposed to the rampant spoils
system; and he stood alone for this at first, for civil-
service reform was regarded as a "European whimsy" or
"something Prussian." The public had forgotten John
Quincy Adams, for whom the career of a statesman was
a learned profession, and Godkin made small progress at
first or later; for although the spoils system, introduced
by Jackson, had come to such a shocking head with
Grant, it was firmly fixed in the popular mind of the
country. But Godkin, who appealed to the cultivated
classes to work for the restoration of the old republic,

succeeded in winning the minds of the younger university men, for whom he was an unexampled leader.

In days to come, Godkin was the most influential American journalist, with Horace Greeley, Dana and Samuel Bowles, the editor of the *Springfield Republican*. The latter were "personal journalists" and popular spokesmen, whether for good or ill. Godkin was impersonal; he was all but unknown to the public, but he influenced the public indirectly. *The Nation* was read by other editors, and Godkin's ideas, which were seldom acknowledged, reached the general mind through a hundred channels. It was true that these ideas found little acceptance. The Jacksonian ways, upheld in the West, had saturated the mind of the masses, and Godkin, who hated the West, was hated by it. The public was indifferent to corruption because it was immersed in money-making, and money-making throve in the loose and unscrutinized system of things that Godkin brought to book in all his writings. He was called "un-American" because his mind was critical at a moment when the critical mind impeded the orgy of money-making; and it made no difference whatever that he was defending the old ideals. The mores had shifted away from the old ideals. They had even reversed these ideals,—to defend them had become "unpatriotic." *

Godkin tried to break down the system of party-organization, as the source of the worst corruption; but the party-organization had become the great American shibboleth. Godkin and *The Nation* fought against all the American shibboleths, the love of display, the love of conquest, the defence of war, the contempt for peace, the flouting of national creeds once held sacred, high tariffs, graft and greed, machine government, boss government, ostentatious wealth and shoddy thinking. Godkin's

---

* For the classic explanation of this paradox of American history, see William Graham Sumner's *Folkways*.

sympathies were narrow and his temper was harsh, but no mind of his time was more tonic. He held a unique position in American cultural history. He originated, if not a school, at least a type of American minds, the journalist-intelligentsia of the future.* *The Nation* was the parent of *The New Republic.*

Important in politics and the world of education and science, *The Nation* marked an epoch in reviewing. American reviewing, outside the *North American,* had been almost wholly personal in tone.† George Ripley, on *The Tribune,* the idol of the young, was the leading reviewer; and Ripley, except in his longer articles, devoted to established writers, was more active in heart than in mind. He was too eager to encourage those who wished to write or paint to promote the abstract welfare of art and letters. *The Nation* established at once a severe and expert standard, with no regard for persons whatsoever. It began by wiping the slate clean of the Knickerbocker school, the last decrepit relics of Irving's time. This set by the ears the literary and publishing world, which *The Nation* faced with grim determination. Merciless to private interests, it built up a staff of trained reviewers, who established its authority at once; ‡ and most of the serious writers of the coming generation owed much to its wisdom and rigour. In literary matters, Wendell Phillips Garrison was as influential as Godkin in the world of affairs. In temperament a stoic, in taste a purist, he gave *The Nation* its stamp in style and form. He translated

---

* The journalist Ford, in Howells's *The Undiscovered Country,* is an excellent early portrait of this type, so familiar in America later.

† "The great mischief has always been that whenever our reviewers deviate from the usual and popular course of panegyric, they start from and end in personality, so that the public mind is almost sure to connect unfavourable criticism with personal animosity."—Godkin, *Critical and Social Essays.*

‡ "Outside of Cambridge and Godkin, it appears to me that our literary review-writing world is only one vast Tuckerman . . . *The Nation* hasn't pronounced yet . . . Horrible, isn't it, to have only one critic for 40,000,000 of people?"—*Life in Letters of William Dean Howells,* I, 138, 144.

Petrarch and Carducci, but he wished to remain obscure and behind the scenes, upholding the standards of literature and moulding its tone. Even less known to the public than Godkin, Garrison made *The Nation* the leading literary journal of the country.*

*

*   *

In Boston, meanwhile, the reformers had lost their major impulse. The public was tired of oratory; and, while there were many new causes, they lacked the charm of the old campaigns in the days of Abolition. In an epoch of milder antagonisms, one ran no risk of tar and feathers, one could not expect to be locked in a Georgia jail; and those who had spent their youth roaming through the South, carrying the Bible to the slaves, or on platforms, in phalansteries, in conventions, running the "underground railway," in the more exciting years before the war, found all these later causes rather tame. There were no more showers of eggs: only temperance lecturers in Irish circles were ever greeted with missiles. The great days were past for the Boston crusaders. The "new truths" had no such lightning in them, and many an old reformer felt like Moorfield Storey, who regretted that he was born to ignoble times, when the devil was handcuffed and muzzled.

Earnest Boston had lost its focus, for the cause of the wage-slaves was not as simple as the cause of the chattel-slaves had been. One could not sum it up by saying to the masters, "Let my people go." When slavery was abolished, most of the Abolitionists felt that all the battles had been won for freedom. This had been Garrison's

---

* Aside from his father's life, written in collaboration with his brother, Garrison's only published work was *The New Gulliver*. This amusing satirical fable was written in defence of Darwinism. The life of William Lloyd Garrison, in four volumes, remains the standard history of the Abolition movement.

feeling, when he discontinued *The Liberator,* and Whittier had withdrawn more and more into the Quaker calm of his Amesbury cottage and the memories that he expressed in *Snow-Bound.* Edmund Quincy spoke for them when he said to Wendell Phillips, with a happy sigh, "No more picnics, Wendell." For Phillips, as it happened, the picnics never ceased. He continued with his old crusading zeal. "Welcome, new duties!" he had said, when the Abolitionist movement ended. "We will not say 'Farewell,' but 'All Hail';" and for twenty years he fought to raise the status of the workers, defending the Russian nihilists before a Harvard audience, praising the Paris Commune, the "vanguard of the Internationals of the world." To replace the profit-system by coöperation, to "crumple up wealth" by enormous taxes, to restore the old ideals of the republic was the programme of this Ishmael of Boston, whose home, as he said, was the sleeping-car, with the brakeman and porter for comrades; and men who hated his doctrines were carried away by the spell of his voice and presence. One Bostonian was observed muttering under his breath, as Phillips spoke, "The damned old liar, the damned old liar!" while he clapped his hands in violent applause. But Phillips, who represented the faith of the forties in an age that was mad for money, was a lonely man indeed and almost friendless.* Most of the old reformers were exhausted. They had no energy left for fresh campaigns, although Boston, prolific in causes, swarmed with friends of progress and new reformers rose with other movements, the cause of peace, the cause of woman's suffrage, dietary reform and Darwinism, the cause of the short-skirts league and the short-haired women who amused profane

---

* "I remember Nora Perry, the poetess, who knew him well, telling me of his meeting her once and asking her where she was going. 'To see a friend,' she replied. 'Ah,' he said, 'you remind me of the Frenchman who received the same answer and said, 'Take me along, I never saw one.' " —G. E. Woodberry, *Heart of Man and Other Papers.*

New York for a generation. Nevertheless, of the old reformers, only one was an active cynic, Charles A. Dana
of *The Sun*. Dana, for whom Brook Farm had once been
the hope of the world, was the enemy, in days to come,
of all it stood for: he ridiculed civil-service reform, opposed the control of monopolies, fought for high tariffs
and huge land-grants for railroads and defended the
banking control of the money-system. Brook Farm itself
had been used as a soldiers' camp in the war, and the
spirit it expressed had been trampled under foot with the
wild flowers that grew there in the spring. But Dana
alone, of the disillusioned farmers, seemed to take a bitter joy in reversing his former convictions.

Boston, Henry Adams thought, had ceased to believe in
itself any longer, and many a sign of the times confirmed
this feeling. The national-political element had faded out
of the Boston picture. The foreign element faded with it,
on the intellectual level, for Boston was less and less the
port of call it had been in the days of the old Cunarders.
Once every enquiring traveller had visited the town, attracted by its statesmen and its writers; while now, with
less hope of reward for the trouble, one had to make a
special journey thither. The religious element also appeared to be waning. The secularizing tendency of the
Concord writers spread rapidly in the rising generation.*
As Henry Adams said, the young men threw off Unita-
rianism and "never afterwards entered a church." † Mean-

---

* "My respect for clerical people, as such, and my faith in the utility
of their office, decreases daily."—Hawthorne, *American Notebooks,* edited
by Randall Stewart, page 165. It was very seldom indeed that Emerson
or Thoreau appeared in church.

† Many were agnostics, like Parkman and Norton.
It may be added that Howells's faith in revealed religion was destroyed
in boyhood when he read Strauss's *Life of Jesus.* "Until, in middle age,
he was walking near Florence with James Bryce and Stillman, the correspondent of the London *Times,* he had taken it for granted that no well-
read man had any faith. His happening to say so astonished his companions, and to learn that many educated men believed in God came to
him, as he described it, like a blow."—Owen Wister, *William Dean
Howells,* in *The Atlantic Monthly,* December, 1937.

while, all manner of quacks were abroad, purveying substitutes for religion. Nostrum-mongers gathered about the sincere reformers, battening on their doctrine of the "open mind." Mesmeric healers and trance-speakers throve amid waiting circles in darkened rooms, where taps were heard on the walls and tables and flowers rained from the ceiling and dim things flitted in the dusk,— a humanitarian gypsy-band to which the "new truths" often lent themselves.* The decay of the ancient faith, with its firm grasp of human realities, its feeling for values and standards, filled the air with noxious emanations; and the critical spirit gasped for breath in a world of lady-mediums and lady-preachers, of lecturers, editors, writers, mostly women; † for the age of Elizabeth Cady Stanton and Susan B. Anthony and their Boston friends and disciples was on the way, and what could one reply when Mrs. Stanton asked, "Where will you poor men stand in another fifty years? You will be crowded off the horizon." The currents of society were certainly setting in this direction, and few denied that women had a valid axe to grind. But the critical spirit was baffled in this over-feminine atmosphere. It scarcely knew where to draw the line; and even the Radical Club was not immune to the inspirations of witches and wizards. The Radical Club, in Chestnut Street, the house of the Sargent family, was the intellectual centre of earnest Boston; and to one of its members, at least, the most earnest of all, the

* The classic pictures of this phase of Boston are Howells's *The Undiscovered Country* and Henry James's *The Bostonians.*

† "The whole generation is womanized; the masculine tone is passing out of the world; it's a feminine, a nervous, hysterical, chattering, canting age, an age of hollow phrases and false delicacy and exaggerated solicitudes and coddled sensibilities, which, if we don't soon look out, will usher in the reign of mediocrity, of the feeblest and flattest and the most pretentious that has ever been."—Basil Ransome, in Henry James's *The Bostonians.*

"The talk, the social life were so completely in the hands of the ladies, the masculine note was so subordinate . . . like a country stricken by a war, where the men had all gone to the army."—Henry James, *A New England Winter.*

swans and the geese looked much alike. This was Elizabeth Peabody, who had fumbled for too many years in
her satchel for papers. She had signed too many petitions
and attended too many conventions. She longed to think
that all the frauds were heroes.

But the Radical Club did its best. As the only heir and
successor of the Peabody house of the forties, as a relic
of the Transcendental Club, it harboured the liveliest
minds in Boston. Emerson, Garrison, Wendell Phillips
were among the older frequenters, with Dr. Hedge and
Dr. and Mrs. Howe, Thomas Wentworth Higginson and
the elder Henry James, who loved a good club as he
loved his Maker. Whittier came on his visits to town,
and Frank B. Sanborn appeared from Concord. Dr.
Holmes read to the club his paper on Jonathan Edwards,
and John Tyndall spoke, fresh from London;* while
among the younger members or speakers were John Fiske
and Thomas Davidson, the peripatetic Scottish philosopher who had recently come from St. Louis.† In a spacious

* John Tyndall addressed the club in 1873, when he was giving his
Lowell lectures. He was astonished to hear that Emerson had not been
asked, and would not be asked, to lecture at the Lowell Institute. "If anyone can be said to have given the impulse to my mind," he remarked, "it
is Emerson. Whatever I have done the world owes to him."—*Sketches and
Reminiscences of the Radical Club.*

† See William James's essay on Davidson, in his *Memories and Studies,
A Knight-Errant of the Intellectual Life.* This learned and picturesque
philosopher conducted summer schools at Farmington, St. Cloud, New
Jersey, and Hurricane in the Adirondacks. Later he founded the Educational
Alliance in New York. "He denounced me," William James said, "for
the musty and mouldy and generally ignoble academicism of my character . . . The memory of Davidson will always strengthen my faith in
personal freedom and its spontaneities, and make me less unqualifiedly
respectful of 'civilization,' with its herding and branding, licensing and
degree-giving, authorizing and appointing, and in general regulating and
administering by system the lives of human beings."

"Thomas Davidson was really a remarkable man; that was clear to me
even on a first meeting . . . I came away feeling that this was the most
remarkable man, the most intensely alive man I had ever met; I am not
at all sure that I should not say so still."—Havelock Ellis, *My Life.*

Davidson established in London the Fellowship of the New Life,—with
Havelock Ellis, Edward Carpenter, etc.,—from which sprang the Fabian
Society.

closet in this house, all the remaining copies of all the
anti-slavery tracts were neatly arranged on shelves. One
drew a long breath as one opened the door, thinking of
all the thunders that lay asleep there. It was almost as
impressive as the Tower of London, Thomas Wentworth
Higginson felt,—filled with the relics of wars that were
fought for freedom. This closet, he thought, should be
kept as a sacred place, like the Old South Church and
Faneuil Hall. The meetings of the Radical Club could
hardly rise to the old heights; but, if they had an air of
Indian summer, suggesting brighter seasons of the past,
they showed that plain living and high thinking could
still exist in unheroic ages. One speaker said that Margaret Fuller in many respects resembled Sappho, a tribute to Sappho's genius, from the point of view of Boston,
that did full justice, however, to Margaret's morals. But
the tone of the discussions was seldom local. The topics
were usually those that were agitating the modern mind,
heredity, peace and war, the freedom of women, coöperation, hygiene, Darwinism. Was science antagonistic to
religion, in spite of all that John Fiske could say? Now
and then, a spell descended on the company, and one of
the members suggested a silent meeting. Those who best
construed, in the long years to come, the ideals of the
older reformers were Thomas Wentworth Higginson and
Julia Ward Howe. Colonel Higginson, living at Newport, often appeared in Boston, before he settled at last
in his birthplace, Cambridge. Mrs. Howe, with Dr. Howe,
had left "Green Peace," their home on Dorchester Bay,
near the Perkins Institution; but when they were not at
Newport they were always somewhere on Beacon Hill.
Mrs. Howe never lacked the courage to rise in her seat
and say, "Mr. B., you are uttering falsehoods."

Wherever the Howes lived was a cosmopolitan centre,
for the "Cadmus of the blind" attracted to his Institution whatever curious foreigners still came to Boston.

"Green Peace" had swarmed with refugees, Greeks, Hungarians, Poles and dwellers in Mesopotamia, some of them learned men like Count Adam Gurowski. Dr. Howe found employment for them, for the one English word they knew was "lessons." When this word was uttered, they beamed with joy, like the Russian, the Turk and the Spaniard in *The Peterkin Papers,* who had all come to Boston to give lessons but who could not explain themselves till the Lady from Philadelphia divined their purpose. They taught Dr. Howe's children, and the five little Howes could scarcely remember a time when they had not known half the tongues of Europe.* But Boston abounded with Agamemnons and Solomon Johns, who were eager for all their wares, beginning with Sanskrit.† It was a privilege to receive an exile,—so Elizabeth Peabody felt, and the Howes agreed.‡ Kossuth and many others had once stayed at "Green Peace." The rambling old house, a farmer's cottage, with two or three modern additions, was full of odd turns and crooked stairways. On the green hattree in the entry, Byron's helmet hung, with its floating plume, and the walls of the great square dining-room were covered with old masters, from "Uncle Sam" Ward's New York collection, the "Boar Hunt" of Snyders, the Domenichino, the Rembrandt that nobody ques-

---

* All the five Howe children later wrote books.

† "Mr. Peterkin suggested they should each take a separate language. If they went abroad this would prove a great convenience. Elizabeth Eliza could talk French with the Parisians; Agamemnon, German with the Germans; Solomon John, Italian with the Italians; Mrs. Peterkin, Spanish in Spain; and perhaps he would himself master all the Eastern languages and Russian . . . Mr. Peterkin made some enquiries about the Oriental languages. He was told that Sanskrit was at the root of all. So he proposed they should all begin with Sanskrit. They would thus require but one teacher, and could branch out into the other languages afterward.

"Mrs. Peterkin was afraid it would be like the Tower of Babel, and hoped it was all right."—Lucretia Hale, *The Peterkin Papers.*

‡ "Western Europe was civilized by the exiled Greeks . . . Why should not our citizens form such noble friendships as Lorenzo de' Medici and the rival princes of Italy formed with the learned Greeks?"—Elizabeth Peabody.

tioned, the Poussin that no one had to question. There lay the Gobelin carpet from the Bonaparte house at Bordentown. From the slope, with the terraced garden and the little classical temple that Dr. Howe used as a seed-house, one had seen the Cunarders steaming into Boston. The grand old doctor-cavalier had ridden about on his black horse, directing the work and play of the Institution, while Mrs. Howe conducted her "Hôtel de Rambouillet," which she carried on wherever she was, in Boston or at Newport in the summer season.

A Bostonized New Yorker, who had grown up in a banker's family, addicted to the world and Paris fashions, Mrs. Howe supplied the link, missing hitherto, between the somewhat hostile rival cities. She filled this role in a way of her own that scarcely fitted at the edges, for she was too earnest to please New York, too earnest even for social Boston, and she had her own frivolities,— to make the case a little odd,—that sometimes offended the reformers. But Mrs. Howe went her way serenely, plucking the golden fruit of all these gardens. As a young girl in New York, who was singularly pretty, she had learned Italian at sixteen, as later, living in Rome, she had studied Hebrew. Later still, she mastered Greek at fifty. Her special joy was German thought; and, when she was not running downstairs for "fun," she was often upstairs reading Kant and Hegel. "I have followed the great masters with my heart" was Mrs. Howe's motto, and she loved Goethe, Schiller, Aristophanes and Dickens and had also studied Catherine Beecher's cook-book.

> My practised hand the loaf can mould,
>   with careful touch and swift,

Mrs. Howe wrote in one of her poems, for she had a high regard for the household arts. A poet on all occasions, an *improvisatrice,* of the good old Italian type and

manner, she had written the *Battle Hymn* in a moment of
genius. This genius never burned again, either in *Passion
Flowers* or in *Later Lyrics*,—poems of summer nights
and lofty causes, or in the plays she wrote with small
success; * but Mrs. Howe's ambition was not exacting.
She faithfully strummed her lyre for fifty years. In many
of her poems she seemed to be rebuking the remnants
of Eve in herself, the vanities of the wicked world for
which she had retained a lingering fancy.

As Dr. Howe's companion, she had roamed over Europe, collecting funds and talking with other reformers,
not without moments of joy in the pomps of the flesh. A
deeply religious nature, she had sat at the feet of Theodore Parker, who had been interested in her early verses.
He had urged her to appear on the lecture-platform.
Theodore Parker's brain reposed in a box in a closet at
the Perkins Institution. It had been sent to Dr. Howe by
Parker's Italian physician, when the great preacher died
and was buried in Florence. The Howes regarded the box
with horror, not knowing what to do with this fearful
relic; but Parker's mind lived on in Mrs. Howe. She lectured in Unitarian pulpits, she preached in a Negro chapel
in San Domingo. She was quite as ready to preach to
the worldlings at Newport, whose hearts were set on
diamonds and yachts. She reproved the worship of wealth
and the vulgar aesthetics of luxury. Never more at home
than in "the chair," promoting another cause or another
hero,—the Armenian cause, Stepniak, Russian freedom,
—she founded clubs as Agassiz founded museums. Study-
circles rose in her path, peace associations and women's
unions,. as she scratched her furrows and dropped the
seed, ready to wait for results till the Day of Judgment.
She established a club in New Orleans; she reminded the

* Mrs. Howe's play, *Hippolytus,* written for Edwin Booth and Charlotte
Cushman, was first performed after her death by Walter Hampden and
Margaret Anglin.

ladies of Athens that "women are people," as Lucy Stone had recently remarked.* If, in her philosophical writings, character masqueraded as intellect, the character at least was real and potent. In her drawing-room, she delighted in contrasts. She confronted all the worlds with one another. When nothing else availed, she would set her guests to work translating Mother Goose into Greek and German.

At the Radical Club and elsewhere, Thomas Wentworth Higginson was Mrs. Howe's associate in all these causes, peace, universal suffrage, Russian freedom, the higher education of women; for even the Digger Indians, whom he had seen in the West, had not destroyed his faith in human nature. A true disciple of Channing, a liberal Unitarian, who had lived through the period of the "Newness," Higginson had grown up in Cambridge. His father, the bursar of the college, had planted the elms in the Yard, and all his early memories were connected with Harvard. At dancing-school, at the Nortons' house, he had cut off little Charlie's front hair. His nurse had married Longfellow's "village blacksmith." In the days of Brook Farm, when Thoreau was living at Walden, he had planned as his own experiment the cultivation of peaches. The only true free man, he thought, was he who could "live on a little." † Then he had entered the ministry, at Newburyport and Worcester, and become involved in the cause of the fugitive slaves. An active Abolitionist and a lover of nature, he had walked and talked with Thoreau, who praised his essay, *Snow*, in *The Atlantic;* and at Worcester he had lived near Harrison G. O. Blake, Thoreau's correspondent who had later become his executor. Higginson was one of the neigh-

---

* On her third triumphant visit to Greece, after Dr. Howe's death. Mrs. Howe founded the Women's Peace Association in London, 1872.

† Ellery Channing told Higginson that the Hawthornes lived in Concord on $300 a year. The rent of the Manse was $75 a year, which they paid from the apple-crop.

bours who gathered round the breakfast-table when Blake
received a letter from his friend in Concord, and he recognized bits of these letters when they appeared in *Walden*. In Kansas, he had shared in the Free-Soil struggle,
standing on real stumps to make his speeches; and, after
the war broke out, he had organized a regiment of
Negroes and fought in South Carolina for two or three
years. His friends were reminded of Cromwell's days
when this minister descended from his pulpit, drew on
his jackboots and rode off to the war. In 1864, the fighting colonel had been invalided to Newport, where he
lived as a simple man of letters. He had published a
translation of Epictetus, a rebuke to the new ideas of
luxurious living. He wished to remind the world that
slaves had been philosophers. He recalled that Epictetus,
his fellow-stoic, was also Toussaint L'Ouverture's favourite reading.

Colonel Higginson still bore, indeed he bore for life,
the scar of a sabre on his chin. It was a souvenir of the
day when he and Dr. Howe had forced their way into the
Boston court-house, in their attempt to rescue Anthony
Burns. A generous, valorous, hopeful soul, he was always
ready to write or speak on subjects suggested by the
zeitgeist,—the function of culture, the manners of tourists, the future of country towns, domestic service. He
had produced one book of permanent interest, *Army Life
in a Black Regiment,* a first-rate human document of the
Civil War. This was the story of the "military picnic"
of the First South Carolina Volunteers. Higginson had
looked for the arming of the Negroes for six years before the war began, ever since the days of the Kansas
troubles, and he had already raised a Massachusetts company when he was placed in command of the camp at
Beaufort. His mind was filled with military matters, but
the training of eight hundred slaves,—the first Southern
regiment of Negroes, as Colonel Shaw's, in Boston, was

the first in the North,—might well have taxed the skill
of Grant or Sherman. They felt they were fighting with
ropes about their necks, for the officers and soldiers of
all the Negro regiments suffered a felon's death when
they were captured. Higginson kept a diary in camp, as
Dana had kept a diary on the "Pilgrim," and the story
of this "gospel army," fighting for its freedom, had much
of the spirit and charm of Dana's book. It was filled
with grotesque and dramatic adventures, like those of
Marion's band in the Revolution, when the "old swamp
fox" eluded his foes in these same forest-paths of Carolina, in the pine-barrens and muddy creeks, embosomed
in blossoming shrubs, where the mocking-birds sang in the
magnolias. There were foraging expeditions up the rivers,
—up the Edisto, for one, to destroy the bridge on the
railroad,—where the cotton-fields were white with fleecy
buds and the air was full of hyacinthine odours. Never
could one forget the fascination of these nocturnal ascents
of unknown streams, leading far into the enemy's country, as one slipped in the moonlight through the meadows,
passing the picket-fires on the silent banks,—the rippling
water, the veiled lights, the anxious watch, the whispered
orders, while the reed-birds wailed overhead and one
heard the yelp of a dog on some distant plantation. Nor
could one forget the nights on picket, under the live-oak
branches with their trailing moss, among the wax-myrtles
and the oleanders, the japonicas, oranges, lemons, the
date-palms and fig-trees, in the endless bridle-paths of
the flowery forests.

In retrospect, the colonel saw himself adrift on a
horse's back in a sea of roses. He had spent scores of
nights in the saddle, in the starlight, in a mist or densest
blackness, while the chuck-will's-widow droned above and
the great Southern fireflies rose to the treetops or hovered
close to the ground, till the horse raised his hoofs to
avoid them, riding through pine-woods and cypress-

swamps, or past sullen brooks and clustered tents, or the
dimly seen huts of sleeping Negroes. He had spent a
whole night swimming in one of the rivers, alert for
every sound on the glimmering shore; and often, returning from rides on the plover-haunted barrens, he had
silently entered the camp in the midst of a "shout." The
dusky figures about the fire moved to the rhythm of the
dance,—the kind of scene that Winslow Homer loved,—
chanting, sometimes harshly, but always in the most perfect time, a monotonous refrain, *Bound to Go* or *When
the War is Over.* Higginson loved the Border ballads
that Child was collecting in Cambridge. He had always
envied Scott the delight of tracing them out and writing
them down; and here was a kindred world of unwritten
songs, as indigenous and simple as those of the Scotsmen,
usually more plaintive, almost always touching and often
as essentially poetic. He listened to these spirituals,
*Wrestling Jacob, Hold Your Light, My Army Cross
Over, One More River,* and jotted down the words, as
best he could, and carried them to his tent, like captured
birds or insects, to study them and print them at his
leisure. Had Europe or America seen an army so religious
since Higginson's own forbears fought with Cromwell?
The fatherly colonel thought of the Negroes as the
world's perpetual children, docile, lovable and gay. The
regular troops were mundane and rough beside them.

In later years, Higginson never rose again to the literary heights of some of these chapters, the superb *Up
the Edisto* and *A Night on the Water.* He had written
one of those rare books that recall a passage of history
as the works of the formal historians cannot recall them.*

---

* Army Life in a Black Regiment deserved to be remembered with
Stephen Crane's *The Red Badge of Courage.* Higginson later recognized
at once the "extraordinary freshness and vigour" of Crane, whom he
described as second only to Tolstoy in his pictures of war. See Higginson's
Book and Heart.

Meanwhile, he had thrown himself into miscellaneous writing and was one of the chief supports of *The Atlantic*. A linguist and an excellent scholar, he had never known a moment of boredom, nor could he imagine such a thing while there was still a language or science to learn. He remembered a time when a prison-cell would have looked rather alluring to him if he had had a copy of Laplace to read. He wrote historical essays, papers describing Newport,—*Oldport Days*,—a romance called *Malbone*, rather feeble, and pleas for literature and culture that were tonic in their effect on younger writers.* In *A Charge with Prince Rupert* and *Mademoiselle's Campaigns*, he was almost as good as Carlyle in a similar vein; and he followed Thoreau in his essays on birds and flowers. But the interests of women were his special study, as befitted a friend of Margaret Fuller who had spent days on the Rhine visiting the scenes that recalled Bettina and the spot where Günderode died. *Ought Women to Learn the Alphabet?* was one of his essays; and in *Saints and Their Bodies* he preached the gospel of out-door life, quoting Catherine Beecher's remark that in all the vast acquaintance of the Beechers there were not a dozen healthy women. He formed a collection of books on the status of women, the Galatea collection, which he left to the Public Library in Boston.

Mrs. Howe and Higginson were voices of a Boston epoch that might have been described as a "second growth." This feminizing Boston, this Boston that followed the war, wished to believe in itself rather than did so. But Mrs. Howe and Higginson still believed, with the faith of old and some of the force, in this resembling also Dr. Hale; and, if the faith had waned a little and lost its old effectiveness, it was full of generosity and

---

* It was one of these papers of Colonel Higginson that caused Emily Dickinson to write and ask if he would be her "master."

goodness.* For the rest, one of Higginson's hobbies was discovering talent. He had offered a prize at Newburyport, the bait that caught Harriet Prescott Spofford. He was one of the earliest friends of Celia Thaxter. It was he who sent Elizabeth Stuart Phelps her first letter of praise. He called upon Rose Terry Cooke at Hartford, when she was still unknown, living in a sort of moated grange, a mile out of town, an old brick house with an air of decay, where she dwelt with an old grey father. He discovered Emily Dickinson. He encouraged "H. H.," later known as Helen Hunt Jackson, Emily Dickinson's friend as a child at Amherst, who was Higginson's neighbour at Newport.† If the new age of writers was largely an age of women writers, Higginson was the first to find them and read them.

As for the elder Henry James, who had moved with his family to Cambridge, the Radical Club had no more faithful member; for, although this wandering New Yorker was a stranger in Boston, he had many friends among the old reformers. Besides, he was not wholly a stranger there. He had run away to Boston and supported himself as a proof-reader, while he was still a student at Union College. He had quarrelled with his father, a rich Albany merchant, of the straitest sect of Presbyterians, who disapproved of his wild habits, his love of cigars and oysters, and perhaps his friendship with an actor. For the young man abounded in animal spirits. But he had returned to college and had studied theology at Princeton, where he had met George Ripley as a fellow-student; and he had become a Fourierist in the days of

---

* Higginson said of Mrs. Howe, in words that might be applied to them both, barring his best book and her best poem: "Generally she feels about her editorials as if she were a pair of tongs that could not quite reach the fire. This she said to me and it well describes them."—*Letters and Journals of Thomas Wentworth Higginson.*

† Higginson also discovered George Edward Woodberry, whom he recommended to Lowell.

the "Newness" and a lecturer on this new philosophy. As a friend of most of the Brook Farmers, he shared their socialistic aspirations, agreeing with Fourier that men should follow their natures and that natural appetites and passions were meant to be enjoyed. He was convinced that property was not a final fact of history, since men were ashamed of the deference they paid it; and he dreamed of a new social order, a new church, a new world that would spring from the reconciliation of spirit and flesh. He was full of an impulsive love of humankind. He had met Thoreau and Alcott in New York, and Emerson had visited him often and admired him greatly, describing this New York friend as a "sub-soil plower." When William James was born, his eldest son, Emerson bent over the cradle and gave him a blessing. This was at the Astor House, the infant philosopher's birthplace; for hotels were a constant element in the life of the Jameses. The family had large means, and the elder Henry James preferred a detached existence on behalf of his children. He was vaguely opposed to their going to college, opposed to their forming any attachments that might perhaps lead to their undoing; for so many of his brothers and cousins had come to grief that he was afraid of America, or afraid of New York, as a nursery for the younger generation. Generally speaking, however, he adored his country; and although, in America, he often longed for Europe, he longed much more for America as soon as he got there. In his youth, he had visited England with the great Joseph Henry, who had filled him with a permanent interest in science; and there he had undergone a religious conversion. Fear had come upon him, and a trembling in his bones; and he felt that the writings of Swedenborg had saved his reason. Much in England rejoiced him, its ease and convenience, and the charm of which he sometimes spoke with rapture; but he felt that American disorder was sweet beside European order,—it was, as he said, so full of promise. He could not abide the class-distinctions that fossilized the English mind and caused his own heart to dance with glee, as he recalled his Nazareth across the Atlantic; * for the hope of mankind, as he saw it, was the hope of social equality, and, feeling the weight of the past in Europe, he pined for the land of the future. Emerson had given him a letter to Carlyle, who impressed him as a "literary desperado." † The sage of Chelsea ridiculed reformers and talked "as if the temple of his friendship were a hospital, and all its inmates were scrofulous or paralytic." His scorn for humankind disgusted James, who later wrote an essay on "cantankerous Thomas." ‡ For James was a mystical democrat. He once remarked that a crowded horse-car was the nearest approach on earth to the joys of heaven. Like Whitman, he preferred the company of stage-drivers to that of "our" literary men, the "vain, conceited nobodies" whom he knew in New York. As for the family, before they arrived in New England, they had roamed for several years all over Europe, with a faded set of Swedenborg as a part of their luggage; for the elder James, like Howells's father, was faithful to Swedenborg, though in this, as in everything else, he remained a dissenter.

In a few short years, the Jameses had settled into the

* "I venture to say that no average American resides a year in England without getting a sense so acute and stifling of its hideous class-distinctions . . . as makes the manners of Choctaws and Potawatomies sweet and Christian, and gives to a log-cabin in Oregon the charm of comparative dignity and peace."—Henry James.

† "Carlyle is the same old sausage, fizzing and sputtering in his own grease . . . He names God frequently, and alludes to the highest things as if they were realities; but it almost looks as if he did it only for a picturesque effect, so completely does he seem to regard them as habitually circumvented and set at naught by the politicians."—Letter to Emerson, 1856.

‡ "He"—Carlyle—"was Mother Eve's own darling cantankerous Thomas, the child of her dreariest, most melancholy old age; and he used to bury his worn, dejected face in her penurious lap, in a way so determined as forever to shut out all sight of God's new and better creation."—Henry James, *Recollections of Carlyle*.

Boston world as if it had been theirs from the beginning.
The two younger brothers, Robertson and Wilkinson, had
gone to Frank B. Sanborn's school in Concord. They had
enlisted and fought through the war, while William and
Henry, as invalids, were too frail for this. Alice, the sister, was also an invalid; indeed, she remained the victim
of a nervous disorder. Later, she lived in England near
Henry the younger, and her journal revealed a literary
gift as marked in its way as that of her father and
brothers.* Henry, who had spent a year at the Law
School, was known already as a writer. He reviewed
novels for *The Nation*. Norton had encouraged him to
work for the *North American* also, and Howells, on *The
Atlantic*, welcomed his stories. When William, who had
gone to Germany to study, returned in 1869, Henry went
to Europe for a year, the first of the several journeys
that took him across the Atlantic before he made up his
mind to live abroad. William had gone through the Scientific School, and later the Medical School. His bent was
all for science, and he had passed from chemistry to the
biological sciences, with a voracious interest in other
studies, literature, philosophy, history and art. He was

* "Henry, by the way, has embodied in his pages many jewels fallen
from my lips, which he steals in the most unblushing way, saying, simply,
that he knew they had been said by the family, so it did not matter."—
From Alice James's journal in England.

Alice James died in England in 1892. So strong was the literary habit
of the family that she was revising her journal during the hours of delirium that preceded her death. This journal abounds in fine passages, as,
for example, the following: "She . . . told me that she was going to my
land,—whilst my highest privilege, shrivelled and rickety, was to go to
bed in hers! What a tide of homesickness swept me under for a moment!
What a longing to see a shaft of sunshine shimmering through the pines,
breathe in the resinous air, and throw my withered body upon my native
earth, bury my face in the coarse grass, worshipping all that the ugly,
raw emptiness of the blessed land stands for,—the embodiment of a huge
chance for hemmed-in humanity; its flexible conditions stretching and
lending themselves to all sizes of men; pallid and naked of necessity; undraped by the illusions and mystery of a moss-grown, cobwebby past, but
overflowing with a divine good-humour and benignancy, a helping hand
for the faltering, an indulgent thought for the discredited, a heart of hope
for every outcast of tradition."—*Alice James, Her Brothers, Her Journal*,
edited by Anna Robeson Burr.

turning to psychology, which soon became his main field, but he had studied physiology in Germany, where he had seen much of Hermann Grimm. Emerson, with an avuncular fondness for the sons of his old friend Henry James, had given William a letter to his German translator, and he followed William's development and that of the younger Henry with an anxious pride and joy in their gifts and their progress. William was also reviewing for *The Nation,* but he was living at home in Cambridge in a desperate state of neurasthenia. He passed from crisis to crisis, suffering from insomnia, digestive disorders, mental paralysis, eye-strain, panic fear. He was consumed with a sense of futility, and this suicidal melancholia continued for three or four years before it left him. Meanwhile, he had interrupted his medical course to go to Brazil with Agassiz, the most exciting of all his Harvard teachers. Agassiz wished to explore the Amazon and conquer it for science, and the Emperor, Dom Pedro, rejoiced in his coming; for this Portuguese Harun-al-Rashid, who had liberated the slaves in Brazil, admired the New England scientists and poets.* Dom Pedro enthusiastically advanced the plan. Agassiz had organized a travelling school of science as Sherman organized his army: he divided his assistants into groups, some to explore the interior, others the coast, and he lectured on the downward voyage, preparing them for the work to come. All day long, on deck, with his joyous gusto, he talked about the Gulf Stream and its seaweeds, the South American fishes, the wonders of the world they were to see; and one moonlight night on the river, as they swung in ·their hammocks, Agassiz turned and whispered, "James, are you awake? *I* cannot sleep. I am too happy. I keep thinking of these glorious plans." William James learned

* Dom Pedro translated into Portuguese a number of poems of Longfellow and Whittier. He visited New England in 1876 to study its educational and scientific institutions. There are interesting accounts of this visit in the authorized biographies of Agassiz, Whittier and Longfellow.

much from this expedition. The collecting and geologizing bored him. He was not cut out for a field-naturalist,
much as he enjoyed pure adventure; but Agassiz's loving
eye and outdoor instinct and his sympathy with living
nature left lasting traces in James's mind. They taught
him the importance of "concrete fullness" as opposed to
what he called "abstractionism." This was the leading
trait in all his writings.*

During these years, the elder James brooded over his
children's problems, for he was a parent, perhaps, above
everything else. He was one of those uncrystallized
geniuses who are often the parents of real geniuses, with
a largeness and power of nature that everyone felt; and
if, in the autumn of his days, he had come to Boston, it
was mainly for the welfare of his offspring, much as he
enjoyed himself the Radical Club and the Saturday Club
and the chance to abound in his own humour. He had
reacted against a Presbyterian father who tried to crush,
as he felt, his natural instincts, and he diligently fostered
these instincts in his children as what he considered
divine educational forces. That one should obey these
instincts, as Emerson said, was the first of his articles
of faith. He was an absolute libertarian for whom all
evil was "fossil," the result of diseased institutions and
the pride of selfhood, the conceit of his moral endow-
ments that led the individual to feel he was not as other
men. His pet aversion was "flagrant morality," or any
sort of conscious virtue. He preferred the sinner to the
prig, and giving the Sabbath a "black eye" was one of
his favourite amusements. He liked nothing better than
to whip the "pusillanimous" clergy, whose narrowness

---

* "Behind the minute anatomists and the physiologists with their metallic
instruments, there have always stood the outdoor naturalists with their
eyes and love of outdoor nature. The former call the latter superficial, but
there is something wrong about your laboratory-biologist who has no
sympathy with living nature. In psychology there is a similar distinction."
—William James, *Memories and Studies.*

afflicted him like charcoal-vapour.* It was not because he took religion lightly. Religion was the theme of all the books to the writing of which he devoted his passionate thought. By social reform, by destroying selfhood, by abandoning the existing sects, the way would be opened, he felt, for the great consummation, the establishing of the true relation between mankind and its Creator, the revelation and presence of God on earth.

* See his letter to the Swedenborgian editor: "The old sects are notoriously bad enough, but your sect compares with these very much as a heap of dried cod on Long Wharf in Boston compares with the same fish while still enjoying the freedom of the Atlantic Ocean . . . Your mature men have an air of childishness and your young men have the aspect of old women . . . [As for your paper] I really know nothing so sad and spectral in the shape of literature . . . It cannot but prove very unwholesome to you spiritually to be so nearly connected with all that sadness and silence, where nothing more musical is heard than the occasional jostling of bone by bone. Do come out of it before you wither as an autumn leaf, which no longer rustles in full-veined life on the pliant bough, but rattles instead with emptiness upon the frozen melancholy earth."

CHAPTER VII

AESTHETIC BOSTON

WHILE the cause of reform in Boston languished, another symptom soon appeared that characterized the coming generation. This was a recrudescence of the old colonial feeling towards Europe that had seemed to be utterly extinguished. New England had lost its political leadership, and many of the New England men had lost their old connection with the soil. They were uprooted and adrift in a world they did not understand and found more and more uncongenial, and even some of the older men who had been ardent patriots were uncertain of their moorings and their bearings. They felt as if the labours of their fathers had been mocked, as if their country had been wrested from them;* and they looked across the sea again, despairing of a nation that had passed beyond their powers of comprehension. In their breasts rose once more a hankering for the ancient homeland, as if three generations of history had gone for nothing.

Scores of Southern families shared this feeling. Many of the Charleston Huguenots returned to France.† Embittered by the war, discouraged by the new regime, they abandoned their country forever and flocked to Paris; and they tried to grope their way back to the heart of the old French culture from which they had been weaned for generations. Others returned as suppliants to Eng-

---

* "The Land of Promise?" said Lowell. "The Land of Broken Promise." See also Lowell's *Letter to George William Curtis.*
† See the Probert family in Henry James's *The Reverberator.*

land. This movement resembled the Russian hegira that also occurred in the sixties, after the emancipation of the serfs, when many disgusted aristocrats withdrew from their estates and cast themselves adrift in western Europe.* The movement was widespread along the Eastern seaboard, in the class that had once so largely controlled the country; and it was strongest in Boston, perhaps, where the leading families felt most keenly the loss of their old political power and prestige. This power and prestige had shifted into Western hands, and Boston was left high and dry; and, moreover, the state of mind of the post-war years was bewildering to cultivated people. They could not understand the vast, shambling new republic, with its scandals, its corruption and its greed. To minds that were formed on the ancient plan, intellect and character were the ends of existence, and many troubled observers noted that intellect and character, with the shattering of the older culture, were no longer respected. The decline of political life was marked and shocking. The maggoty lobbyists of the "special interests" bribed their way all over it and destroyed its fibre, and a new tradition rose in which it was a merit not to know that politics existed. The respectable classes conspired to ignore them, as Godkin had observed with indignation. They even ceased to vote, in many cases. As the years went on, scores of novels deprecated this turn of affairs, urging good men to enter public life or showing how hopeless it was for them to do so;† but, except in so far as they kept the conscience of thousands awake, these novels were ineffective, like the writings of Godkin. Nothing availed to turn the tide, and the general mind, averted from politics, immersed itself in private affairs alone.

* These were the exiles described in Turgenev's *Smoke*.
† Among New England novels, or novels about New England, concerned with this theme, were John W. De Forest's *Honest John Vane*, Henry Adams's *Democracy*, F. Marion Crawford's *An American Politician* and Winston Churchill's *Coniston* and *Mr. Crewe's Career*.

Men drove further into business, with less regard for the public welfare. Their old sectional pride was broken, their national pride was still unformed; and they had little left to be proud of, aside from their success in money-making.

To many of the older Americans, in Boston and in the South especially, this national frame of mind was repugnant and alien. Proud of their country once, they were doubtful now; and some were ashamed of their country. Even Mrs. Stowe could have said no longer what she had said in the fifties, that the world looked hopefully towards America as a nation especially raised by God to advance the cause of liberty and religion. The day had gone by when New England ambassadors plumed themselves in foreign courts on the virtue of American institutions. Bancroft's salutary impudence was a relic of the past; * and, as for American institutions, many a Boston ear was open to the worst that English travellers said about them. Godkin's abhorrence of the West was shared by "stuck-up Boston folks" † who withdrew in proud reserve from their countrypeople, a reserve that was more and more jealous the more it was challenged; ‡ and

* When Bancroft was minister to Berlin, the British ambassador asked him why American ministers appeared at court "all dressed in black, like so many undertakers." Bancroft replied that they represented "the burial of monarchy."

† "Ohio people are sensitive about 'stuck-up Boston folks.' "—*Letters of Mrs. Henry Adams.*

"Such is the tendency of democracy to a general mingling of elements, that this frigidity is deemed necessary by these good souls to prevent the commonalty from being attracted to them, and sticking to them, as straws and bits of paper do to amber. But more generally the true-blue old families are simple and urbane in their manners; and their pretensions are, as Miss Edgeworth says, presented rather intaglio than in cameo."—Harriet Beecher Stowe, *Pink and White Tyranny.*

‡ "I think Americans who are jealous of their reserve are even more so than Englishmen,—perhaps because in a democracy it is a more conscious prize and has to be fought for."—*New Letters of James Russell Lowell.*

"A line of respectable connections, being the harder to preserve where there is nothing in the laws to defend it, is therefore the more precious when we have it really to boast of."—Redclyffe, in Hawthorne's *Dr. Grimshawe's Secret.*

meanwhile America ceased to interest many Americans, who closed their minds to their country and all its problems. The "best people" did not talk about it, as travelling foreigners noticed in the flesh and in fiction; or they only referred to their country to abuse their country. They preferred to talk about Europe, and especially England.* For they agreed with Matthew Arnold that America was not "interesting" and that for lovers of "elevation" the sky there was of brass and iron.† This verdict was unworthy of a thinker, although they did not see this; for, if every country should interest a thinker, what should one say of a country about which hordes of travellers were writing books? ‡ American conditions,

* "This not talking of America at all," or talking only to abuse, was a puzzle to many Europeans. "Very curious," says Lord Rainford, in Howells's *A Woman's Reason*, "I can't get the people I meet to say a good word for their country. They all seem ashamed of it, and abuse it, no end . . . I find your people, your best people, I suppose they are,—very nice, very intelligent, very pleasant,—only talk about Europe. They talk about London, and about Paris, and about Rome; there seems to be quite a passion for Italy; but they don't seem interested in their own country. I can't make it out. It isn't as if they were cosmopolitan; that isn't quite the impression, though—excuse my saying so—they try to give it. They always seem to have been reading *The Fortnightly*, and *The Saturday Review*, and *The Spectator*, and the *Revue des Deux Mondes*, and the last French and English books. It's very odd, upon my word, at one dinner the Americans got to talking to one another about some question of local finance in pounds, shillings and pence . . . I don't understand it."

See also the remark of the journalist Ford in Howells's *The Undiscovered Country*: "If I went to this lady's house . . . I should have to be just arrived from Europe, or just going . . . My talk should be of London and Paris and Rome . . . of English politics and society; my own country should exist for me on sufferance through a compassionate curiosity, half repulsion; I ought to have recently dined at Newport with poor Lord and Lady Scamperton, who are finding the climate so terrible . . . You see that's quite beyond me."

† "And so I say that, in America, he who craves for the *interesting* in civilization, he who requires from what surrounds him satisfaction for his sense of beauty, his sense of elevation, will feel the sky over his head to be of brass and iron."—Matthew Arnold, *Civilization in the United States*.

"The trouble about Matthew which sets so many against him is the entirely needless priggishness of his tone . . . His ultimate heads of classification, too, are lamentable. Think of 'interesting' used as an absolute term!"—William James, Letter of 1888.

‡ Some of these books were discerning. A few, like James Bryce's *The American Commonwealth*, were more than discerning. Most of them de-

American institutions were matters of burning concern
to most of these writers. Almost every liner brought some
Englishman or Frenchman who was bent upon solving
the puzzle and threading the maze; and, if Arnold's sense
of the interesting did not include what interested them,
what was one obliged to think of Arnold? And, as for
"elevation," those who had heard the Gettysburg speech
were on fairly intimate terms with this emotion. As for
the "sense of beauty," they agreed with Arnold. They
agreed when he called attention to their Briggsvilles and
Higginsvilles, those remnants of their too "Hebraic"
past. In this sphere, all he said was salutary, and Americans heard him gladly, young and old. But regarding
"elevation" they had their doubts. They had little to
learn in this respect from travelling rhetoricians, especially one who gravitated, as if by a natural instinct, to
Barnum and Andrew Carnegie, a few years later.* They
felt they knew more about this than their British advisers; for many besides the Adamses were shocked by
the low tone of British politics. There were nice old
ladies who pitied Thomas Arnold in his heavenly mansion
for begetting this impudent Matthew. But the confidence
of others had been shaken. They did not wish to parry
Arnold's charges. They were interested in Europe, and
Europe alone.

It was useless, in these circles, to quote Emerson's ob-
jurgations against their attitude of mind, their "mendi-
cant, curious, peering" ways, itinerant and imitative,
studious of other countries and ignoring their own. Emer-

served Josiah Quincy's phrase about Basil Hall and Mrs. Trollope:
"These birds of passage have skimmed over this country like vultures
over the surface of the Carolinas, pouncing upon whatever is corrupt,
and passing by whatever is sound or healthful, as adapted neither to
their taste or scent."

* Matthew Arnold was the standing illustration of Bromfield Corey's
generalization, in Howells's *The Rise of Silas Lapham,* regarding the
travelling Englishmen, that they are "more curious about the great new
millionaires than about anyone else, and they respect them more."

son could not share their feeling, indeed he was scarcely
aware of their feeling, rapt as he was in his dream of
America's future; * and most of the older writers, such
as Longfellow and Holmes, were as firmly rooted as
Emerson in the soil of the country. Longfellow had just
returned from his final visit to Europe, and "Holmes,
sweet Holmes," as the students called him in England,
was soon to make his last triumphal journey, with a day
at the Derby and a day measuring Tennyson's elms and
days with four generations of London beauties. Longfellow had visited at Windsor Castle, and, in Rome, Liszt
set to music, in his convent rooms, a part of *The Golden
Legend*. There Longfellow was crowned as a shepherd of
Arcadia. These two old poets were lifelong lovers of
Europe, but to them the new colonialism, the recrudes-
cent Anglomania, with its disregard of America, was
utterly foreign. Their minds went back too far for this.
They remembered the growing days of the young republic, and they had always seen themselves as builders of a
great, new, hopeful western civilization. They did not
measure themselves by other countries, for they felt they
had their own sufficient centre; and the younger men
whose interests were all in the country continued to feel
as their fathers and grandsires had felt. It was other-

* "The young men in America at this moment take little thought of what
men in England are thinking or doing. That is the point which decides the
welfare of a people, *which way does it look?* If to any other people, it is
not well with them. If occupied in its own affairs and thoughts and men,
with a heat which excludes almost the notice of any other people,—as the
Jews, the Greeks, the Persians, the Romans, the Arabians, the French, the
English, at their best times have done,—they are sublime; and we know
that in this abstraction they are executing excellent work. Amidst the calamities which war has brought on our country this one benefit has accrued,
—that our eyes are withdrawn from England, withdrawn from France,
and look homeward. We have come to feel that 'by ourselves our safety
must be bought,' to know the vast resources of the continent, the good-will
that is in the people, their conviction of the great moral advantages of
freedom, social equality, education, and religious culture, and their determination to hold these fast, and, by them, to hold fast the country and
penetrate every square mile of it with this American civilization."—Emerson, *Letters and Social Aims*.

wise with younger men whose local attachments were not deep. It was otherwise with Motley, Lowell and Norton, who were more disposed to feel the degradation of public life because their political interests had always been strong. They were lovers of New England whose hearts had scarcely embraced the nation and who loved New England less in its decline; and, as the immigrant races began to rival the Anglo-Saxon, they were drawn to an Anglo-Saxon England. Boston, for the rest, was closer to Europe than other American cities. There appeared *Every Saturday* and *Littell's Living Age,* compiled from European papers, and the French and English magazines were staples of conversation at every dinner-table and in all the clubs. "Boston is very well up in all things European," Henry Adams noted in 1873, "but it is no place for American news;" and, as the interest in things American rapidly dropped away, the relish for the old world grew apace. The return of the colonial feeling was a part of this.

In later years, Henry James exemplified this feeling more fully than anyone else, before or since; but James's curious Anglicism was only comprehensible in the light of the social context in which it arose. His sponsors abroad were Lowell and Norton, who introduced him to English society, and Lowell and Norton, with Motley, were members of the New England group that was most disaffected at home. They were acutely sensitive to the sudden drop of the national prestige and more or less abashed by their country, and they gravitated towards England in this frame of mind. Motley settled there and never returned to America, where he had been discredited and hurt. He became an Anglophile of a type his country had never known in the days when it gave scope to seasoned statesmen. Save in his technical allegiance, Motley became wholly English, and almost as completely the author of *The Biglow Papers* reverted to the pattern of English culture. Lowell, who had said, "We are worth nothing except so far as we have disinfected ourselves of Anglicism," * was the first to be reinfected as time went on. Socially and personally, he fell in love with everything English; and, after he had lived in England, he went back every year, and he formed closer ties there than he ever formed again at home. He never returned to his old simplicities of costume, manner and voice, and the "defiant Americanism" for which he was noted in England was the protest of his nature against his taste. Norton, who had left America to spend five years abroad, returned to fight it out at home; but his constant tone of exasperation showed how far, in doing so, he violated his taste and his inclinations. All these men found in England "the perfection of human society," Motley's phrase for the London dinner-table and the English country-house; and Henry James met this society under the wing of these men, in a state of mind that was influenced by their example. They were disappointed in their country, smarting from its disrepute, and inclined to apologize for themselves as Yankees; and they were disposed to see the English as somehow larger than life, the more they saw their countrymen as somehow smaller. If they did not feel inferior, this was because, as eminent men, they could always fall back on their achievements; although, for the matter of that, their self-esteem was involved in their esteem for their country. Younger men, like Henry James, had nothing to fall back upon and shared their mortification and chagrin. Of course, James felt, shall we say, uneasy, as everyone is bound to feel who cannot believe that his country possesses a standard. He may have felt that Americans were morally better than Europeans, but in other respects he felt that his country was "negative"

* *On a Certain Condescension in Foreigners.*

or nugatory.* This was to have strange consequences in James's writings.

*

*   *

Meanwhile, in Boston the interest grew in things aesthetic. The Museum of Fine Arts was founded in 1870, the symbol and crystallization of this movement of feeling; and half the domestic walls of Boston blossomed with Fra Angelico angels, with photographs or prints of Mona Lisa, or perhaps The Last Communion of Saint Jerome. Lounges appeared in houses that were studies in colour, hung with purple curtains, with rooms that were harmonies in green or melodies in blue; and even the Roman nose that had flourished in Boston was losing its severity of outline. On all sides, the question rose, What place was art to have in the satisfactory human life that Boston was trying to realize? Already a species of art-cant, as sharp observers called it, was displacing the commoner cant of religion and culture, and one heard on every hand the phrase, "He is a true artist," or "She has not the feeling of an artist." Everything was "artistic" or "inartistic." The great question "Love or Art?" filled many a youthful imagination that had fed upon Mrs. Browning's *Aurora Leigh*. While Aurora found that "love is more," she was desperately certain that "art is much;" and in this there were many Bostonians who agreed with Aurora.

The outburst of aesthetic feeling that expressed itself in the new museum was part of a wider movement of emotional growth. One saw this in religion, in all the fields of social habit; one saw it in the changing names of children. A generation of Mauds and Enids, of Alices, Daisys and Daphnes, of Isabels, Mariannes, Elaines and Graces

* "When one approached her [London] from the alien positive places (I don't speak of the American, in those days too negative to be related at all)."—Henry James, *The Middle Years*.

was growing in the garden where once the fresh New
England flowers had borne such names as Abigail and
Hannah. The new age was Hellenistic as it was also Ten-
nysonian: it scarcely required an Arnold to spread this
taste. Steeped as it was in all the poets, Greek, German,
French and English, it was losing the Hebraic flair, although it preserved the Hebrew names when these were
euphonious also. Esther, Ruth and Eva vied with Penelope and Imogene in the parental fancy. One observed
a similar change in the country districts, where the Hebraistic imagery was dying also. The country-people had
vaguer standards, but they too longed for something
pretty and were not concerned to scrutinize its source and
value. They sometimes invented names that struck them
as having associations with the classical world or the world
of the poets and romancers. In these less critical regions,
one encountered such names as Liverius, Lurella and Lu-
cina, Levina, Zepheretta, Loretta, Zerrilla.*

This indicated a tendency that was equally marked in
the sphere of religion. With the breakdown of the old
theology, the rural churches only flourished by meeting
the mundane demands of the congregations. The spiritual
element was generally submerged in the social, humanitarian, aesthetic, in music, dancing, lectures and oyster
suppers. It was held in effect that salvation must not be
made to appear depressing or the young would lose all
interest in their souls; and the ministers, for whom the
ancient faith had lost its outlines and its dogmas, preached
about "flowers, stars, love and crystal springs." † They
floated in a mist that was vaguely romantic and vaguely
poetic. In the more conscious classes, the growth of Epis-

---

* "Where the Puritanism has gone out of the people in spots, there's
the rankest growth of all sorts of crazy heresies; and the old scriptural
nomenclature has given place to something compounded of the fancifulness
of story-paper romance and the gibberish of spiritualism."—Howells, *The
Lady of the Aroostook.*
† Rose Terry Cooke, *The Sphinx's Children.*

copalianism corresponded to this development in the
simpler people. All the "best families," it was sometimes
said, were either Unitarian or Episcopalian. Dr. Holmes
had remarked in *Elsie Venner* that they were "expected
to be," a phrase that offended some of his readers; and it
was Dr. Holmes who explained the decay of his own
faith, of which the Episcopal Church was the advancing
rival.* The dignity of man and the beauty of virtue had
ceased to excite the thrills of old, and the religion of reason had starved the senses: it could not compete any
longer with the rapidly rising Catholic Church and the
Anglican Church that stole the Roman thunder with its
choirs and illuminations, its colour and music. No use to
protest that rites and forms were shallow, where the feminine mind especially had grown so strong.† They appealed to the aesthetic depths, they appealed to other
emotional depths which the old New England faiths had
left unsounded; and it only required a preacher of genius,
who appeared at once in Phillips Brooks, to establish the
Episcopal Church in the heart of Boston.‡ What Channing had once been, Phillips Brooks became, the typical
divine of an epoch; for this fuller-blooded Channing, this
muscular Christian, exuberant, robust and cultivated, had
all the traits that made the Boston leader. A kinsman of
Wendell Phillips, he revived the moribund art of the

* " 'The beauty of virtue' got to be an old story at last. 'The moral dignity of human nature' ceased to excite a thrill of satisfaction after some
hundred repetitions."—Holmes, *Elsie Venner.*
† "Something in its favour"—in favour of the Episcopal Church,—"is the
influence that every ritualized faith has with women. If they apprehend
these mysteries, more subtly than we, such a preference of theirs must mean
a good deal. Yes; the other Protestant systems are men's systems. Women
must have form. They don't care for freedom."—The Rev. Mr. Waters, in
Howells's *Indian Summer.*
  It was symptomatic of this moment in New England that Hawthorne's
daughters entered religious orders. Many others followed Una Hawthorne,
who became an Anglican nun. Rose Hawthorne later became a Catholic
nun and was famous later still as Mother Alphonsa.
‡ Phillips Brooks became the rector of Trinity Church in 1869, the year
in which Grant became President and Eliot became president of Harvard.

orator in a world that was less concerned for social reform and more concerned for science, art and travel. He
spoke for an age that was saturated with Tennyson and
Browning, with the gospel of *In Memoriam* and "the
larger hope."

If, in all these ways, the New England mind had cut its
ancient moorings, it was also drifting literally in the paths
of travel. The time had long since passed when a voyage
to Europe was like a voyage in Charon's ferry-boat, when
friends and families gathered with sobs and tears to speed
the adventurous wanderer and letters from across the
sea were like angels' visits. Where handfuls had followed
once in the footsteps of Byron, seeking out the conse-
crated sites and dilating with appropriate emotions, thousands were accustomed now to "hopping backwards and
forwards over the Atlantic," as Matthew Arnold's "Boston informant" put it. Travel-books no longer began by
telling why one took the journey and how it felt to be
rocked by the ocean waves. They no longer described the
condition of Shakespeare's tomb, or the busts in Westminster Abbey, or the Bay of Naples. These were old
stories to the new generation of travellers,* who were
often familiar with Syria, ·Egypt and Greece. Others
roamed over America, exploring the Florida scene and
straying to Quebec and Montreal, which had begun to
seem as historic as Europe; for Irving had made the Hudson classic ground and Parkman was garlanding Canada
with associations. They roved through Evangeline's country and the village of Grand Pré. Naturalists like Wilson
Flagg sought for birds in Tennessee, and Saint Augustine
and Summerville, as rising winter resorts, vied with the
Campobello of July and August. It is true, there were
certain Bostonians, like Howells's Mr. Arbuton, who were

---

* A new American type, after the Civil War, was the travelling-companion, hitherto not unknown but certainly rare. Louisa Alcott went abroad
in 1865 as a travelling-companion.

not convinced that America was entitled to legends. It struck them as presumptuous for this raw country to assume the prerogatives of Europe; and, as for the exaggerations of American nature, were they not in rather bad taste? Were not the cliffs of the Saguenay excessively high as a feature of river scenery? In a world of such well-bred streams as the Thames and the Tiber, they felt they had to snub the Mississippi, to maintain the Bostonian sense of proportion and fitness; and travel in Europe was growing so common that many felt obliged to snub the ingenuous souls who "did" the standard sights. But, sooner or later, one and all, however disdainfully, went the rounds from the scenes of *The Belfry of Bruges* to the Mer de Glace, from St. Ursula's church at Cologne and the Lion of Lucerne to the tomb of San Carlo Borromeo. They read *Hyperion* on the Rhine, they read *The Marble Faun* in Rome, and in Florence they quoted Longfellow's sonnet about the Ponte Vecchio, with the twisting dragon of the Arno underneath it. They strolled through the Via de' Bardi, where Romola lived, and they visited the grave of Theodore Parker, who resembled Savonarola in certain respects. They rowed into the Blue Grotto, climbed Vesuvius, drove to Amalfi; they were punctual at St. Peter's on Palm Sunday. They spent a day at Fontainebleau, a day at Rambouillet, an hour in front of Rubens's Descent from the Cross, and perhaps a week at Vevey or Baden-Baden; and they lingered at Gibbon's house in Lausanne and the Iron Virgin of Nuremberg and the organs of Freiburg and Haarlem. They snuffed the fog of Johnson's London and visited Chester and Coventry, where they faithfully murmured Tennyson on the bridge, rejoicing in the random corners and the feasts of crookedness that satisfied their passion for the picturesque.* The

* "If the picturesque were banished from the face of the earth, I think the idea would survive in some typical American breast."—Henry James, *Transatlantic Sketches.*

English lawns, the castle towers, the woods, the village churches brought tears of recognition to their eyes, as of the previous state that Plato spoke of; and, eager as they might be to improve conditions at home, there were no such tories—in Europe—as travelling Yankees. They longed for the picturesque at any price, regardless of dampness, injustice or any abuses.* But most of them, after a year or a summer, also longed for the keen air, the active life, the stimulus of home; and they came back laden with table-tops and paper-weights, with Psyches and Hebes and Graces in alabaster, and with caskets, lockets, picture-frames and laces. It was only a question of time before they also brought home façades of Venetian palaces and castles in boxes.

For this vogue of travel went hand in hand with the ever-growing rage for art that characterized the younger generation. Young men of means roamed over Italy, inspired with a wish to see sincerely, the fruit of their reading of Ruskin. They copied Roman inscriptions in their pocket notebooks. They studied Siennese architecture and Tuscan sculpture; and they went to Verona to examine the Lombardic pillars, often with a mounting scorn of all things modern. As they sat in Santa Maria Novella, they pored over *Mornings in Florence,* wondering how far they should follow the hectoring Ruskin. Most of the younger American artists were turning away from Italy,

---

* "The American who, in his own country, is in feverish haste to improve conditions, when he sets foot in Europe, becomes the fanatical foe of progress. The old world, in his judgment, ought to look old. He longs to hear the clatter of wooden shoes. If he had his way he would have laws enacted forbidding peasant folk to change their ancient costumes. He would preserve every relic of feudalism. He bitterly laments the division of great estates . . . He is enchanted with thatched cottages which look damp and picturesque. He detests the model dwellings which are built with a too-obvious regard for sanitation. He seeks narrow and ill-smelling streets . . . He frequents scenes of old murders, and places where bandits once did congregate . . . A heath ought to be lonely, and fens ought to be preserved from drainage . . . The religious pilgrim does not expect to find the old prophets, but he has a pious hope of finding the abuses which the prophets denounced."—Samuel M. Crothers, *The Toryism of Travellers.*

and those who travelled abroad to study now more often
went to Düsseldorf or Paris; but remnants of the circle
described in *The Marble Faun* still basked in the golden
air of Rome and Florence, where Powers died in 1873.
One still found sculptors working on allegorical figures,—
perhaps "The Pacific Slope," for San Francisco,—and
painters for whom Venetian priests and peasants remained the last word in picturesqueness. They were
mostly happy and innocent souls and fervently American,
however dim and vague about their country, using the
slang of the pre-war days, mingled with Italian phrases,
dim and vague as they were about Italy also. Most of
them were poor and driven, for their statues and their
pictures had little appeal for the new generation of tourists. William Wetmore Story lingered on in Rome, where
Charles C. Perkins, who had returned to Boston, had
given his musical soirées in the days of Mazzini. Story
had left the studio that Hawthorne pictured as Kenyon's.
Still living in the Palazzo Barbarini, he had built a larger
workshop, with a garden full of trees, flowers and vines,
strewn with broken statues and fragments of friezes; but,
although his ambition grew and his work increased, the
day was already passing for literary sculpture. Harriet
Hosmer's "Clasped Hands of the Brownings" retained a
sentimental interest, but Story's sculptures seemed like
bad translations; and the Sibyls and Cleopatras that had
charmed the eye of an earlier age more often aroused an
unkind mirth at present.* Meanwhile, two American boys,
both born in Italy, who were later to be known in art and
letters, were growing up more or less in Story's circle.
John Singer Sargent, whose father had come from
Gloucester, was carried as a child all over Europe, to

* "We went to Mr. Story's studio, and oh! how he does spoil nice blocks
of white marble. Nothing but sibyls on all sides, sitting, standing, legs
crossed, legs uncrossed, and all with the same expression as if they smelt
something wrong. Call him a genius! I don't see it."—*Letters of Mrs. Henry
Adams,* 1873.

Spain, France, Germany and England; but the family
lived in Florence, Sargent's birthplace. Francis Marion
Crawford was the son of Thomas Crawford, Story's associate and rival as a sculptor in Rome.*

This Italianate circle was closely connected with Boston, and there the rage for art was all-engrossing. Days
that had once been merely misty were described now as
"Corot days," and Giotto and Cimabue, as themes of conversation, vied with castled crags and historic landscapes.
The copies of Guido and Carlo Dolci, the fruit of earlier
grand tours, were displaced by the sort of pictures that
Ruskin approved of,—a Turner, perhaps, that was sold
upside down, and "no one found it out," as Miss Alcott
remarked. All these pictures were eagerly discussed. Their
merits and authenticity were as carefully canvassed as the
qualifications of new professors at Harvard, although
sometimes the most meritorious were the most disturbing. One heard of a little girl who remarked, as she
looked at Correggio's Magdalen,—a copy, in this instance, to be sure, "Why, that lady is dawdling! She is
reading a book when she ought to be dressing." Others
were troubled by Rembrandt's coarseness: his heads were
so un-Emersonian that one shuddered at them. But the
taste for art had come to stay, and Elizabeth Stuart
Phelps, in *The Story of Avis,* advanced the thorny problem of the woman artist. Avis had studied painting in
Florence, in a bare little studio-attic, like Hilda, in *The
Marble Faun,* among her doves, and had won Couture's
praise in Paris. Then her career was wrecked by an invalid husband. Should woman artists marry? Should Avis
have married? The question reverberated in many a
feminine breast in Boston; and many a reader rejoiced
in Miss Phelps's conclusion. Avis's daughter, please God,

* Marion Crawford was born at Bagni di Lucca, 1854. Sargent, born in
Florence in 1856, began his career in Paris, 1874, as a pupil of Carolus
Duran.

should be only an artist! One found this zest for art on the humblest levels. Young girls, obliged to earn their living, no longer took up teaching as a matter of course. They painted hollywood boxes, fans and vases, or, like the dutiful Ruth Felton, in Harriet Prescott Spofford's *Azarian,* they searched the rhodora marshes for flowers to paint, while their fancy roved in Italy and Greece. Mrs. Spofford's romances and tales expressed this lowlier phase of Boston. *The Amber Gods, Sir Rohan's Ghost, Desert Sands, In a Cellar,* were day-dreams that struck her readers as new and daring, for they dealt with artists who lived in Paris, cellars stocked with wondrous wines, ladies in gowns of Genoa velvet with peacocks' feathers of green and gold and painters who longed for the languors and heats of the desert. Their fanciful, airy style was full of a kind of aesthetic feeling, kindled by Keats and Tennyson, Browning and Hawthorne; and their high-flown phrases and recklessly chosen exotic words, "chatoyant" eyes and "sprinkles" and "spatters of splendour," were protests against the bare, the cold, the rigid. In two tales, *In a Cellar* and *Circumstance,* especially, Mrs. Spofford emerged from her flowery mist. *In a Cellar* suggested Poe, but *Circumstance* was all her own and a highly original story, though perhaps too long. This tale of the pioneer woman, in the wilderness of Maine, who saved herself from the lynx by singing to it,—for she had heard that music charms wild beasts,—was singularly real and thrilling. The idea was fresh and brilliant, and Emily Dickinson in Amherst was struck by this story.* In her

---

* "The only thing I ever read," Miss Dickinson wrote in a letter, "that I didn't think I could have imagined myself! Send me everything she writes." There were phrases and images in other stories by Mrs. Spofford that seem to have left their traces in Emily Dickinson's mind,—"A daintiness of morning costume but recently indulged . . . The solicited events of centuries transpired unnoticed beside him . . . On the soft soil of the avenue, the sound ferried the silence" (*Sir Rohan's Ghost*). These stories of Mrs. Spofford's were the rage in the sixties, according to Howells, and *Sir Rohan's Ghost* appeared in *The Atlantic,* which Miss Dickinson read religiously. Is it an illusion that one catches in these turns of speech the

general mood of romantic extravagance, Mrs. Spofford showed how far the New England mind was starving for colour and splendour.

As if in response to this demand, a group of remarkable artists appeared, two or three of whom were men of genius. Winslow Homer, George Fuller and Albert Pinkham Ryder were born in Massachusetts, one and all, and an artist of another type, Frederick Law Olmsted, was already at work in landscape architecture. Homer, a Boston boy who had grown up in Cambridge, had gone to the Civil War as an illustrator. Later, he had settled in New York, whence he returned in the eighties to the coast of New England to paint the Gloucester fishermen, the rocks and the waves with a magisterial grandeur of touch and feeling. As long ago as the Brook Farm days, Homer, who lived near the Washington elm, in a house that overlooked the Cambridge Common, had fished in Fresh Pond at four in the morning, and his drawings of barefoot boys and berry-pickers, of corn-huskings and barn-dances were as full of New England feeling as Whittier's poems. His first oil-paintings were campaign sketches, based on his powerful drawings for *Harper's Weekly*, and he knew the Virginia Negroes and the war-time camp-life as well as the northern woods and rivers, the sailors and the fishermen, the loggers and the deer-stalkers and even the idlers and girls at the summer-resorts who appeared in the novels of Howells. Like Howells, he knew that little things mattered, and he saw the details of army life that professional military painters had never noticed. Again, like Colonel Higginson, he

peculiar Emily Dickinson stamp and ring? One of Mrs. Spofford's heroines had "sherry-coloured eyes" before Miss Dickinson discovered that her eyes were "like the sherry in the glass that the guest leaves."

In her later stories, Harriet Prescott Spofford followed the tendency to realistic writing. The short pieces in the volume called *A Scarlet Poppy*, largely dealing with conflicts of husbands and wives, were among the best of the delicate sketches, sufficiently real but of no great moment, that were common in New England in the nineties.

was drawn to the Negroes, and his Caribbean water-
colours, with their Negro figures, recalled to many observers Whitman's line, "I behold the picturesque giant
and love him." As for his early paintings, fine as they
were, in their somewhat harsh veracity and candour, they
were only dim presentiments of the later Homer, the
great prose-painter as Ryder and Fuller were poets. Fuller was an itinerant portrait-painter who had gone into
practical farming to save his ancestral acres in the village
of Deerfield. There, with his own hands, he reclaimed a
tract of swamp-meadow, exchanging the plough for the
brush whenever he could, developing the unique style that
suggested the figures and scenes of Hawthorne, with its
veils of ambiguity and haze of distance, its Indian summer mists and depth of tone. Fuller was the painter of
October afternoons in the fertile harvest-lands of the
interior valleys. Ryder's world was midnight on the sea,
where lonely ships challenged the watery abysses and
ragged storm-clouds sped across the moon. Ryder, like
Winslow Homer, had gone to New York, where he lived
for the rest of his life, but his chosen scenes were those
of his native New Bedford, where Melville stopped before he set forth on his whale-hunt; and he spent many
summers in the Cape Cod harbours, "soaking in the moonlight," as he said. The impulse that was flagging in the
poets seemed to have been reborn in these three painters;
and meanwhile Olmsted also symbolized the times and
the rise of aesthetic feeling in the towns and cities. Olmsted, a Hartford man, had been one of Godkin's advisers
in the founding of *The Nation.* He had written three
studies of the South, in its economic and social aspects,
that Godkin had used as guides on a horseback journey.*
Godkin thought these books far surpassed Arthur Young's

* *A Journey in the Seaboard Slave States, A Journey in Texas* and *A
Journey Through the Back Country.* The best parts of these three books
were later combined in *The Cotton Kingdom.*

for vivid actuality in travel-writing; and Olmsted, in fact, was a first-rate observer who left a permanent record for historical students. As pictures of the old South, his books were irreplaceable: no one else had examined the scene so shrewdly. At that time, Olmsted was just beginning his great career as a landscape-architect. At a moment when the younger men were flocking to the cities, abandoning the soil and the farms, Olmsted's career was symptomatic. It was a reaction against the decline of rural life in the conscious cultivation of parks and gardens. An adventurous boy, the son of a prosperous merchant, who had wandered all over New England, hunting and fishing, and who had sailed to China before the mast, Olmsted had studied chemistry at Yale and become a Connecticut farmer and nurseryman. Then he had taken up landscape-gardening, for which his observations had prepared him, for on walking-trips and drives with his father, up the Connecticut valley and through New Hampshire, he had made a careful study of scenery. He had observed the dells and slopes, the grouping of trees and the vistas, the aspect and position of the homesteads, the arrangement of buildings, the relation of copses and woodlands to ponds, streams, meadows, rocks and mountains; and in Europe, where others haunted museums, he had spent his time in parks, till he knew their every aspect in London and Dublin, in Paris, Brussels, Berlin, Vienna and Rome. He was widely known as a writer on agriculture and scenery before he put his knowledge to the test in designing the park for New York. Central Park was the first of many, for the great Connecticut landscape-architect designed sixteen other parks, from Brooklyn to Stanford University. He made the name of his art a household word. Olmsted kept alive in a world of cities the values and associations of rural life.

The founding of the museum and the rise of art-schools were natural effects of the moment. So were the activities of a number of writers on art and music who appeared in the sixties and seventies, chiefly in Boston, "Tom" Appleton, Charles C. Perkins, William Morris Hunt and William Rimmer. During these years, the consul at Trieste, Alexander Wheelock Thayer, who was born at South Natick, was writing his *Life of Beethoven*. No doubt, Hunt stirred aesthetic Boston more than anyone else with his *Talks on Art*, but he shared the field, as a talker and teacher, with Rimmer, whose art-school was the first in New England.* This reserved and elusive physician, who had been a village shoemaker and was later a doctor at Quincy, where he worked among the quarrymen, had taken up sculpture and used the Quincy granite, with which he had made a remarkable head of St. Stephen. A self-instructed artist, who never went abroad, he produced the grand figure of Hamilton, vaguely suggesting a figure-head, that stood in Commonwealth Avenue, overlooking the Common. A draughtsman of great power, as one saw in his beautiful Blake-like drawings, he lectured on art-anatomy, the subject of his ablest book; and he had among his pupils John La Farge and Daniel Chester French, the Concord sculptor. A solitary, proud and silent man, Rimmer had none of the traits that made the magnetic Hunt a Boston favourite, though his influence was scarcely less important.† These two together led the Boston art-world. Hunt was an artist with a mission. That the present was a great artistic epoch, that Americans, who were poets, should also be painters,—this was "what Hunt said" on all occasions. If some of his other

---

* So it was said in the circular announcing the school, 1864. The Yale School of the Fine Arts, the first of its kind attached to a university, was founded in the same year.

† Rimmer was a man of mystery whose father, a French immigrant, had assumed this name. See Truman H. Bartlett, *The Art-Life of William Rimmer*.

The character of Dr. Bhaer, in Louisa Alcott's *Little Women*, is said to have been drawn from Dr. Rimmer, with whom May Alcott studied anatomical drawing.

sayings, which passed from mouth to mouth, were far from complimentary to Boston, they nevertheless expressed his faith that every place was another Hymettus when people looked for the honey in the flower that grows.

Hunt, before settling in Newport and Boston, had lived for many years abroad and had once been Couture's favourite pupil. Then he discovered Millet, who was still unknown, and went to live in Barbizon beside him. For two years he wore a blouse and sabots and walked in the afternoons in the fields with Millet, who showed him how to look at a cart by the roadside. They would stand for hours before this cart, observing how it sagged or how the light fell on the wheels, or perhaps they discussed the Bible, which they knew by heart. One might have thought that no one had ever read it as one heard this French peasant declaiming its phrases. "Now the famine was great throughout all the land,"—what a description, that, what breadth, said Millet. He saw the book of Ruth from a painter's standpoint. The story went about that an English collector was buying up all Millet's pictures, and the dealers in Paris began to be interested in him; but Hunt was the man who bought them, when no one would have "The Sower" for $60, as he also bought Barye's unknown bronzes and persuaded his American friends to buy them. It was Hunt who had since made Boston,— where Millet's brother Pierre was living, the brother who served as a model for the figure in "The Angelus,"—a focus for all the artists of the Barbizon school. There seemed to be an occult relation between these men and the Yankee mind. No doubt, the New England poets had prepared the ground, with their love of landscape, nature and the Bible.

A rangy, spare, muscular man, with a bony nose and flashing eyes, Hunt looked like Don Quixote or an Arab. He had kept his own horses in Paris, tall hunters and fast trotters, and every day at Newport he had galloped on the sands, with the air of a Moorish sheik in a Fromentin picture; or one saw him spinning along in a racing-buggy, with velvet jacket and scarlet sash, and a beard like a fountain in the wind. In Boston, with his art-classes, he stirred up a rage for charcoal-drawing, especially portrait-heads and cat-tails; and he liked nothing better than to tease the Boston people, whose niggling conscientiousness annoyed him. He would set his soup-plate on his head at restaurants, to save the waiters trouble, or throw his arms about some pompous lawyer, who had never seen a man like Hunt before. An actor, a mimic, a fiddler, whose violin had belonged to Balzac, he would meet an organ-grinder on the street, seize the organ and play it and collect the money, while the forlorn Italian stood by astonished; and he said he always voted for the politicians whose figures looked best on the beach. When one of the Boston critics wrote an attack on Barye, he ran out at night on the Common and stormed around it several times. These people did not deserve to see his Millets,—"Their dry eyes would burn holes right through them;" and, lonely as he was, with no one to look up to, he welcomed other artists who returned from Europe, eagerly bought their pictures and gave them exhibitions. The tenderest and most delicate things, he said, were snubbed out of the world; for art was like jelly in this, it was only recognized when it was cold. He had no use for the lectures on art that his Boston pupils enjoyed so much,—one might as well try to smell music or eat a cook-book; and he peppered them with Taine and Hazlitt and begged them to "paint for fun," regardless of their success or the New England conscience. Draw fearlessly, avoid the kind of finish that rats give to cheese,—that hide-bound air, that look of goneness, that unmistakably empty look which a house presents when the family has left for the country.

Hunt's *Talks on Art,* with their gibes at Boston, harrowed the ground for many seeds.* Meanwhile, Appleton, who had known Hunt in Europe, encouraged the taste for French art that his friend had introduced and that characterized the coming generation.† Appleton, the Boston wit, Dr. Holmes's rival, had crossed the ocean forty times before the Civil War and the deepest of his tastes was for painters and painting. He had studied in Italy and copied in the galleries there, as one of the passing members of Story's circle. His little talent had petered out in a passion for painting pebbles, which he gave his friends to use as paper-weights; for Appleton was like Bromfield Corey in *The Rise of Silas Lapham,*—"It was absurd for him to paint portraits for pay, and ridiculous to paint them for nothing, so he did not paint them at all." But his failure increased his sympathy for other struggling American artists, who were frequent beneficiaries of his sudden fancies. He would see a poor student copying in the Louvre and tap him on the back and say,

* The two series of Hunt's *Talks on Art* were compiled at the suggestion of the English painter, G. Lowes Dickinson, the father of the author of this name. The superintendent of the class stepped behind a screen and rapidly jotted down Hunt's remarks. They were printed in this impromptu form. The following are among Hunt's sayings:
"Boston is a great place for receipts.
"When anybody in Boston sees a picture he likes, instead of buying it, he goes home and tries to paint one like it.
" 'Why didn't you like Cambridge?' . . . Because I love art. Cambridge is like Kaulbach's pictures. It is all literature.
"The mouth is not a slit. It is shaped like a trumpet.
"People go to Europe and bring home second-hand 'old masters.' Get them cheap, and there's a cry over them. But if one of those old painters were living in Boston today, not one of his works would they buy . . . No, they go about whining because we have 'no art in this country,' and 'we never shall paint like Titian'! . . . Such people are logs across the track.
"If you have painted a sketch in two hours, don't tell of it. If you do, people will say it is horrid. They like the look of work that takes weeks and months. Just as in society you'll hear a lady say, 'See my beautiful embroidered handkerchief. The girl who worked it made herself blind. Isn't it lovely?' 'Oh!' 'Ah!' etc."
† "As our physicians gave up the training of England for that of Paris, so a kind of distaste even of English methods of art, and the keenest enjoyment of that of the best French school, has of late come about."— Appleton, *A Sheaf of Papers,* 1875.

"Come to Egypt with me;" for he had a special feeling
for Egypt and wrote a charming book about it.* He told
the Italian picture-dealers to cheat him as much as they
could, well knowing that he himself knew more than they
did.

A poet on occasion, Appleton was an essayist, abounding in good sense and shrewd ideas. It was he who said,
"Good Americans, when they die, go to Paris." He suggested tying a shorn lamb at a certain corner in Boston, to
temper the wind. He was a gourmet, and some of his best
essays dealt with the virtues of mutton, trout and white-
fish and the horrors of Puritan cooking. He was chiefly
interested, however, in the cause of advancing art in Boston, along with his fellow-founder of the museum, Charles
C. Perkins. Appleton gave the museum a collection of
Tanagra figures.† Perkins worked devotedly over all the
collections. A nephew of Colonel Perkins, who had given
the Athenæum its collection of casts and one of whose
other uncles had discovered Rimmer, he had lived for
many years in Rome and Paris, where he had studied
painting with Ary Scheffer; but he had surrendered this
ambition to become an art-historian and had published
Tuscan Sculptors in 1864. This first of Perkins's several
books, with its technical knowledge and charming style,
and its illustrations etched from the author's drawings,
had become an authority at once. It was followed by
Italian Sculptors, dealing with other than Tuscan subjects, by *Raphael and Michael Angelo* and the later *Historical Handbook of Italian Sculpture.* Perkins's last
book, *Ghiberti et son école,* was written in French. A
writer far superior to James Jackson Jarves, though with-

* *A Nile Journal.* See also the beautifully printed book by another Boston
art-lover, Martin Brimmer's *Egypt.* Brimmer, like Appleton and Perkins,
was one of the founders of the museum.

† See Appleton's charming story-essay, *The Artist of Tanagra,* in
Checquer-Work. It was Appleton who said of the museum,—the building
replaced in 1908,—that, if architecture was "frozen music," this was
"frozen Yankee Doodle."

out the provocative opinions that made Jarves exciting,—
for his work was descriptive rather than critical,—Perkins was one of a family of minds that included Symonds
and Pater in England. His *Tuscan Sculptors* ranked with
Norton's *Church Building* and Henry Adams's *Mont-
Saint-Michel and Chartres.*

Meanwhile, the interest in music was rapidly growing
in the home of Jonas Chickering, Oliver Ditson and the.
Mason and Hamlin piano; for John Sullivan Dwight and
his *Journal of Music* had had a profound effect on the
Boston mind. Perkins was involved in this development
also. He had studied music in Germany, like Henry Lee
Higginson, and he wrote the history of the Handel and
Haydn Society, of which he was conductor for a time. It
was he who had given the music-hall Crawford's statue of
Beethoven, the first statue of any artist erected in the
country. The Beethoven cult dated from the forties, when
the young Brook Farmers had walked in to Boston to
listen to the "Emerson of music;" * and during all these
years the more or less Bostonian Thayer was at work on
his life of the composer. The effect of all these influences
on the younger generation was almost as marked as that
of science.

It is true that Thayer's biography appeared in English
when most of this generation was dead and gone. But the
first volume was published in German in 1866, and the
work was a characteristic product of the Yankee mind of

* Beethoven and Emerson were closely associated in the young New
England mind of the eighteen-forties.
Two incidents connected Beethoven with Boston. In 1822, the Handel
and Haydn Society commissioned the composer to write an oratorio for it.
Beethoven referred to this in one of his letters: "If God gives me back my
health, which has at least improved somewhat, I shall yet be able to com-
ply with all the requests which have come from all parts of Europe, and
even from North Ameriea, and I might yet feather my nest."—Thayer,
Life of Beethoven, III, 87-88. One of Beethoven's last requests, when he
was dying, was to see the full report of Channing's address of December
12, 1826, of which he had read or heard an abstract.—Thayer, *Beethoven,*
III, 283.

an earlier decade when the cult of hero-worship flourished
in Boston. Alexander Wheelock Thayer had conceived his
passion for Beethoven while still at Harvard. All the existing accounts of the composer were a tissue of romantic
tales and errors, and Thayer resolved at once to write
the great biography, the first of all authorities on its subject. He went abroad in 1849 and spent two years in re-
searches in Bonn, Berlin, Prague and Vienna, and this
was the beginning of the forty years of labour and poverty at the end of which he left the task unfinished. He
acted for a while as Motley's private secretary, when
Motley was engaged in his Austrian mission, and then
for thirty years he was consul at Trieste, where he was
Hildreth's successor. From this convenient base he carried on his exploring tours with a single-minded zest and
perseverance. He roamed over the continent, examining
archives and libraries and talking with all the composer's
surviving friends, whether among the musicians or the
"princely rabble." He interviewed Grillparzer; he had
many conversations with Bettina von Arnim; he visited
Sir George Smart in England, who gave him his journal
to transcribe. In Paris he saw Thalberg, and he studied
the correspondence of Prince Galitzen. He called on old
violinists and singing-teachers who had known and remembered the composer, gathering anecdotes and records. He found some of Beethoven's letters in a London
music-publishing house and others in the hands of auto-
graph-dealers, and he made transcriptions of Beethoven's
conversation-books, deciphering the scrawls and hiero-
glyphics. At last he finished the first volume. He could not
afford to go home to oversee the printing of it, and he
knew it was not the custom at home to publish books in
parts; so he gave it to Dr. Hermann Deiters, the musical
court councillor at Bonn, who translated it and published
it in German. The appearance of this first volume roused

many other students, for he had opened up lines of research and pointed out subjects for special study. Old
men gave up their memories and hundreds of other documents came to light, and Thayer in the end had enough
materials to spend the rest of his life arranging and sift-
ing. Long before he died, in 1897, he had finished three
volumes of the work; but the old Yankee consul with the
patriarchal beard found himself unable to complete it.
It weighed on his mind like an incubus, while the musical
world pursued him, eager for the results of his final studies; but an hour or two of thought on the subject brought
on a racking headache and he had to stop. He turned for
distraction to other themes and wrote a book on the Jews
in Egypt, and another against the Bacon-Shakespeare
theory, with various essays and tales for children, while
others, using his papers, concluded the work for which
Thayer himself never received a penny.*

Aside from a handful of friends and students, this
grand old scholar's careless country knew little about his
work and never saw it. Thayer's *Life of Beethoven* had
long been a German classic when it first appeared in
America in 1920. The author had been dead for twenty-
three years, but the guild of musicians had not forgotten
him, and the story of this publication suggested the devotion with which the work itself was conceived and written.
Thayer, with his calm and logical mind, scrupulous, magnanimous and spacious, was a scholar of the other dispen-
sation. He had set out to describe for posterity the great

---

* The final German edition of Thayer's *Life of Beethoven* was issued
in five volumes in 1908–1911. It is said to have involved the labours of
more than eighty men, who were stimulated by Thayer's investigations.
The American edition, the first in English, was published in three volumes,
1920–1921, by the Beethoven Association of New York, A group of American musicians devoted to this purpose the proceeds of a winter's season.
The editor was H. E. Krehbiel, who revised and completed the work from
Thayer's papers. Thayer had known Krehbiel through his own connection
with the New York *Tribune,* on the staff of which he had worked in
Greeley's day.

man as he was and lived, as Cromwell had wished to be painted with all his warts; and his patient realism and all but inexhaustible industry had created an irreplaceable and masterly portrait.

CHAPTER VIII

FRANCIS PARKMAN

DURING these years, Francis Parkman was at work in his Boston study. He was a lonely man, detached from his time and place and their interests and causes. A classmate of Hunt, with whom he had travelled in Italy, he was also an old friend of Norton, who had helped him with the proofs of *The Oregon Trail*. He was indifferent to painting and sculpture, however, and European opinion meant nothing to him. He was still more remote from everything Higginson represented, or all but his admiration for Epictetus and his love of out-door life. Parkman detested reformers, though he also detested the worship of money. He despised the "morality of commerce," and he had made common cause with Godkin in his efforts to save the republic. He had no use for "flintlock business men." He was a soldier in all his instincts,·although fate had made him something else, a writer, and one of the greatest of his age and country. The state of his health had prevented him from taking part in the Civil War, and for him the post-war years were so ignoble that he wished for no part or lot in their concerns. He was only at home in his own mind, where he lived with explorers, borderers, adventurers and woodsmen.

Some years before the war, Parkman had published a novel bearing the name of the hero, *Vassall Morton*. This Morton was a rich young man with a preference for young ladies who were wild and lawless. He did not admire the tamer virtues that prevailed in his little Boston world. He refused any fixed and stated calling. Ardent and energetic, a lover of hardship, with a mind formed for action, he planned to devote his life to the study of primitive races, resolving to gain his ends at any cost. In this he succeeded, the reader was led to suppose, but only after encountering incredible odds and disasters. He spent four years in an Austrian dungeon, and he was condemned to die and imprisoned again, a "death in life," a "slow-consuming horror." But he hardened his heart, in this inferno, against himself and his own troubles; and, when he escaped at last and returned to Boston, he felt he was proof against all further woes. With a mind that had ripened in solitude and suffering, he was ready to face the future with golden hopes.

The novel was one of those still-born books that no one reads but the friends of the author. When the author is a man of genius who has put his worst foot forward, these books are always interesting, however; and Parkman's friends saw at once that he had pictured himself in Morton.* This impetuous young man, who had learned to be patient,—strenuous, eager, proud, confident, manly, —was certainly the son of Dr. Parkman, the minister, the friend of Dr. Channing, who had lived in a spacious old house in Bowdoin Square. It was Dr. Parkman's brother, the physician, who had been murdered by Professor Webster in the laboratory of the Harvard Medical School. In college, Francis Parkman, the grandson of a rich old merchant, had constantly read Cooper, Scott and Byron. He had "Injuns on the brain," his friends remembered, and he had crossed the plains, on the Oregon Trail, when it was as dangerous to do so as ever it was for Columbus

---

* It may be noted that Morton is also the name of the hero of Motley's first novel. Perhaps in both cases this name was suggested by that of the rebel of "Merry Mount," who disliked the ways of the Puritans as much as Parkman and Motley. These two Mortons were totally different, but both were rough self-portraits of men who found their vocation in historical writing.

to cross the Atlantic. The book he had written about his adventures was boyishly vigorous, fresh and frank, and he wrote as if he rather wished his pen had been a sword. One saw in Morton all these traits of Parkman, with his ethnological interests and his plans for historical writing. Parkman had published *The Conspiracy of Pontiac* five years before he wrote the novel. But even his friends might have been puzzled by some of the scenes in *Vassall Morton*. If the picture of the Tyrolese woods and mountains was highly circumstantial, they were aware that Parkman knew the Alps. He had visited the wilder Alpine regions, which recalled to him at once the American woods. No forester knew these woods better than Parkman. But what about Morton's anguish in the Austrian dungeon? What gave these prison-scenes their unmistakable air of reality? Had the writer of this novel been in prison? Or was the dungeon a symbol of something else? One could only say, though one said it with conviction, "Eccovi, this child has been in hell."

It was true. Parkman had lived in hell, and his life, at best, remained a purgatory. As a delicate, sensitive boy, with a passion for adventure, he had lived in a state of constant tension. Fascinated by Cooper's heroes and Byron's wanderers and outlaws, he was bent on surpassing the Indians in strength and endurance. He had spent all his summers in the woods, with his rifle, "Satan," riding the wildest horses without saddle or stirrups. He had tried to crush, in the Indian fashion, every personal weakness; and, while his will and energy were super-normal, his constitution could not bear the strain. He had broken down at one point,—overtaxed his heart,—then at another and another. His eyes had given way from excessive reading. To rest his eyes, while studying Indian life, he had undertaken the Oregon journey. This had destroyed his digestion and given him chronic insomnia. Arthritis attacked his knee and left him crippled, and, finally, a

nervous disorder engulfed his mind. At any attempt to
think or write, he felt an iron band about his head that
seemed to contract with force. He could not enlist in the
Civil War, the bitterest disappointment of his life, and
the doctor he consulted in Paris threatened him with insanity if he ever tried to use his brain again. He was reduced to the kind of inaction that men of his type can
least endure; for, while he exulted in danger and almost
exulted in suffering, he could not bear stagnation and confinement. For two long periods, one lasting four years, he
could not use his mind for any purpose; and at best he
was able to work two hours a day. Two or three hours,
of the twenty-four, was the most he ever slept. He could
not read continuously for more than five minutes, and he
usually read a minute at a time. "Prescott could see a
little," he wrote in one of his early letters; "confound
him, he could even look over his proofs, but I am no
better off than an owl in the twilight." He had composed his first books, *The Oregon Trail* and *Pontiac,* pacing back and forth in the garret of the old colonial house
in Bowdoin Square. Sometimes he sat in the dark, with
bandaged eyes and drawn curtains, memorizing his work,
chapter by chapter, dictating or using his writing-machine;
for he had what he called a "gridiron," like Prescott's
noctograph, a wooden frame with horizontal wires, with
which he could write in pencil,—at an average of six lines
a day,—when he could not even see to write his name.
Then, for fourteen years, he published nothing, or nothing but the novel, *Vassall Morton,* which showed, at
least, his gift for story-telling. His mind ran riot in the
darkness.

Not until 1865, when Parkman was forty-two, was he
able to resume his historical writing. Then appeared *The
Pioneers of France in the New World,* the first, or the
first but one, of his great series. He had published *Pon-*

tiac, the last of the series,—in chronological order,—as if he feared he could never round out the subject; and he had been preparing ever since, when he was able to work, for the other volumes. He collected his books and documents and had them read aloud to him. He jotted down his notes, which were later deciphered and read to him again till he knew them by heart. It was wonderful to follow his dictation, to watch the scenes unfold and the persons come to life out of the crabbed notes that he held in his hand. Although he could scarcely see these notes, he had lived them, in a sense, from his earliest boyhood; and he had formed a plan for his life during his student-years at Harvard. This plan was to write what he called the "history of the American forest,"—the history of the "old French war,"—the contest of the Indians, the French and the English for the control of the continent. He had met with little encouragement. No one seemed to care about this old French war, a dim and squalid struggle, as people supposed it, between savages and bushrangers, with nothing but a wilderness as the stake; and even *The Conspiracy of Pontiac* had aroused little interest in it.* But this war had decided the fate of the continent, and Parkman knew how important it was. Moreover, he knew that he had a chance, the last and only chance, to picture, in the Indians, who were disappearing, —at least, in their primitive form,—authentic American men of the Stone Age, the forbears of civilization. No

---

* In spite of the success of Bancroft's American history, the reading public long remained indifferent to the subject of it. John Fiske referred to an incident, in this connection, that occurred about 1875: "A gentleman in a small New England town was asked if some lectures of mine on 'America's Place in History' would be likely to find a good audience there. He reflected a moment, then shook his head gravely. 'The subject,' he said, 'is one which would interest very few people.' In the state of mind thus indicated there is something so bewildering that I believe I have not yet recovered from it."—John Fiske, *Essays Historical and Literary,* II, 126.

"The preferences of sentient creatures are what *create* the importance of topics."—William James.

one could have been better prepared to carry out this project, nor was any project ever achieved with a more tenacious will.

From his earliest childhood, Parkman's tastes and interests had converged to form this will. For, while he was a man of the world, he was a woodsman born. As a little boy, he had caught horned pouts in the Frog Pond,— a stone's-throw from Prescott's later dwelling,—and broiled them over a fire in his father's garden. At eight, he was taken to live on his grandfather's farm at Medford, in the woods of the Middlesex Fells, with their cliffs, ravines, marshes, streams and lakes, a patch of primitive wilderness that still remained within eight miles of Boston. He had four years of freedom in the fields and forest, riding, shooting, trapping, fishing, camping. He carried snakes in his pockets, he botanized; he even raised silkworms for a while. He knew all the animals and imitated their calls. In Boston, he was observed, on a Sunday morning, following his father and mother on their way to church, carrying by the tail a rat which he meant to take home and stuff. Then one day Cooper's novels came alive in Boston: a party of Sacs and Foxes, in deerskins and feathers, performed a war-dance on the Common. His college rooms at Harvard were the rooms of a sportsman. He spent all his summer vacations tramping through New England, western Massachusetts, New Hampshire and Maine, crossing the Canadian border, following the Indian trails, tracing the routes of the French and the *coureurs de bois*. He kept careful diaries on all these journeys.

He was highly systematic, though not by nature. With his temperamental zest for adventure, he found research repulsive.* He despised "emasculate" scholarship all his

---

* In this he resembled Prescott and Motley. The tension created by this repulsion is characteristic of first-rate minds. No good writer has ever liked drudgery, nor has any good writer ever permitted anyone else to do his drudgery for him.

days. But he forced his tastes to gain his ends. He was
ferociously accurate and savagely thorough. No one was
ever more reckless, as *The Oregon Trail* showed, and no
one was more methodical in pursuing an object. He
directed his travels and reading like a Jesuit novice. He
divided his time in college between rhetoric, history and
gymnastics; and when he was sent abroad, at nineteen,
to spend some months in Italy, for the sake of his health,
he stayed for several weeks at a convent of the Passion-
ists, near the Coliseum in Rome. The monks did their
best to convert him, but Parkman was intractable. Neither
then nor later was his positive mind open to religious
exaltations. He had an extreme distaste for the clergy at
home, in spite of his excellent father. He had fallen away
from the faith of Channing, although he was drawn to
Theodore Parker, with whom he climbed Vesuvius and
talked in Rome. Parker was a muscular man, who preached
a robust religion, while Channing had always been Parkman's special aversion,—because he was frail and small
and his habits were too sedentary and he preached the
superiority of mind over muscle. Parkman thought the
clergy as a class were soft, gushing, vague and spoiled by
women. He liked to describe them as "vermin;" and,
having small use for the Puritans, he had still less for
the Catholics. He was an agnostic, somewhat harsh in
temper. Then why did he visit these amiable monks and
get himself presented to the Pope? Because he wished to
carry out his plan. He haunted the churches and monasteries, in Italy and Sicily, because to write his history, as
he knew, he had to understand the Church, the methods
of the missionaries, the ecclesiastical system, from top to
bottom. He wished to live in a monastery and see it from
the inside, as later he wished to live in an Indian lodge.

   In the same systematic way, he studied human nature,
to learn what he called the springs of emotion and action.
His journal bristled with accurate sketches of soldiers,

sailors, farmers, priests and scholars. He went through
the Law School, not for the sake of the law, but to study
history and statesmanship and, still more, human character; and in Boston, after his breakdown, when he could
not sleep, he rose and prowled all night in the open,
watching the tramps on the Common. Just so, he had
watched the reformers in the days of the "Newness." The
Chardon Street Chapel, the haunt of the "Friends of
Reform," had once been the Parkmans' family stable,
and Dr. Parkman, who disliked reformers quite as much
as his son, always spoke of the chapel as "my mother's
barn." Parkman abhorred these eccentric people,—he
called the Brook Farmers the "she-philosophers,"—but
he went to their meetings just the same. He had no shred
of sympathy with their causes, but they were types to
examine. Visionaries, idealists, fanatics,—they were all
one to Parkman,—had played a part in Canadian history,
and he took pains to observe them. He had a contempt
for physical weakness that grew with his own infirmities
and suggested the "hard-boiled" mind of a later epoch.
"How I hate 'em!" he would say, referring to men who
were frail or sickly; but he noted their manners and motives, and their conversation, and set them all down
among the rest. What he really hated was the weakness
in himself, in this resembling all the "hard-boiled" writers.
Of Thoreau, in later years, he spoke with respect, for
Thoreau had known the Indians as he knew the woods;
but he was too self-conscious and introspective to please
this Boston Spartan. Wordsworth he could not abide.
Everything that savoured of speculation, the dreamy, the
sentimental, the philanthropic,—philosophy, metaphysics,
the inward eye,—was antipathetic to Parkman. He disliked the words "culture" and "refinement" because they
suggested the artificial. What he called the "improved
savage" was Parkman's favourite type, delicate in his

feelings and decent in behaviour and also virile, natural, resourceful and strong.

Such was this lover of action, this literary soldier who was to picture himself in describing his heroes, Frontenac, La Salle, Lord Howe and Wolfe. His element was the Border, and the life of the Border, where the primitive and the civilized were in conflict, where civilization prevailed, but only by means of the primitive virtues, and human nature appeared in its utmost starkness. In Italy, on Lake Como, he had written, "Give me Lake George, and the smell of the pine and fir!" He had preferred Vesuvius to all the ruined temples; and in England, with its smooth green hills and hedges, he had longed for the shaggy mountains, the cedars and the scrub-oak, the "fiery glare of the sun . . . its wild and ruddy light." In Scotland and Switzerland alone, among the crags and cataracts, he had felt at home. No one knew better than he the depths of the forest, dim and silent as a cavern, the cedar-bordered streams of the northern lakes, with their water-girdled rocks and verdurous islets, where the muskrats swam and plunged, the rock-maples rearing their shadowy masses, the sombre balsam-firs, the coves where the wild ducks dived beneath the alders, and the moose, neck-deep in water to escape the flies, vanished among the trees with clumsy trot. Many a time, on Lake Champlain, as the sun set behind the western mountains, piled in mist along the sky, he had watched some dead pine stretching its arms athwart the burning heaven, with a crow perched on its top like an image carved in jet. He had observed the night-hawk, circling in its flight, pitching through the air, on whirling wing, for the unseen prey that flew beneath it. To the farthest outposts of Canada, to the Rocky Mountains, Parkman knew the wilderness, the savage forests and the open woodlands, the mighty rivers and the lakes and prairies; and he knew the inhabitants of all these regions, the Indians, the half-breeds and the traders, the settlers, soldiers, trappers and pioneers. Before he was twenty-three, he had seen most of the Indian tribes from Maine to Colorado and Nevada and had visited many of the spots he described in his books. He had explored the sites of the Indian towns and villages, measured the ruined forts and talked with the oldest settlers. He had gathered from survivors of the tribes the legends of the Ojibways and the Mohawks, the Iroquois, the Foxes and the Hurons. An ancient brave at Old Town, Maine, patching his canoe, had described the attacks of the Mohawks, as the tribe recalled them: they had roasted the children on forked sticks like apples. He had heard fireside tales and wild recitals of necromancy and witchcraft, tales of the magic drums of the conjurors, of grisly weendigoes and bloodless geebi, of evil manitoes in the dens of the woods and malignant sorcerers dwelling on lonely islands, in lakes they had bound with spells. He had heard of pygmy champions, mighty in soul, who had subdued the monsters of the wilds, and heroes who had achieved marvellous triumphs over the brute force of their assailants. He knew the secret places of the woods where the Indians had held their councils; and he read the signs of the forest himself, the whistle of a bird that stood for danger, the rustle of a leaf that stood for death. In the perilous depths of the mountains, he had lodged with lonely trappers, in time-worn buckskins, gripping their rifles in sinewy hands, sleeping on the rough earth, with dried meat and water for their food and drink. The wild, hard life of these pioneers had for him a resistless charm. He had even found *coureurs de bois,* still dwelling beyond the solitudes of the northern lakes, unchanged in life and character since the far-off days when the Sun-king claimed this cheerless empire.

By the time he was able to write again, Parkman was

almost ready to carry out his whole ambitious plan,—for all his historical writings, taken together, were to form a single work in eleven volumes. Now and then he went abroad, to extend his investigations, for his studies were based on original manuscript sources. He made four visits to Paris. He had to take a secretary into the libraries with him and listen while the documents were read aloud; and all the income from his books scarcely paid for the copyists who collected manuscripts for him in Paris and London. But most of his notes were assembled in 1865, and he was already prepared for his double task: to picture the forest and its history and drama and to "realize a certain ideal of manhood,—a little mediæval," as he called it. He had been all the better fitted to live the story that he wrote because, like La Salle, he was a "man of thought, trained amid arts and letters." * Meanwhile, unable to use his eyes, and threatened with insanity, he turned aside for a while into horticulture. He took refuge in his garden at Jamaica Plain; and there, confined to his wheel-chair, he rapidly moved about, sowing seeds, raking and weeding, planting and cutting his borders and splitting wood. Active and methodical, as elsewhere, he studied the art of gardening. He even served for a year as professor of horticulture at the Bussey Institute. He developed the "Parkman lily" and brought out new varieties of larkspur, phlox and poppy. He was a famous grower of roses, like Bancroft and Prescott before him, and like John Fiske and Henry Adams and Henry Cabot Lodge.

* "The pioneer of western pioneers was no rude son of toil, but a man of thought, trained amid arts and letters."—*La Salle and the Discovery of the Great West.*
Parkman observed in a note appended to this: "A Rocky Mountain trapper, being complimented on the hardihood of himself and his companions, once said to the writer, 'That's so; but a gentleman of the right sort will stand hardship better than anybody else.' The history of Arctic and African travel, and the military records of all time, are a standing evidence that a trained and developed mind is not the enemy, but the active and powerful ally, of constitutional hardihood. The culture that enervates instead of strengthening is always a false or partial one."

He had a thousand varieties of roses. He even wrote a handbook on this flower of historians, describing its groups and families, its cultivation and propagation. Parkman was severe with roses as with men, an aristocrat in horticulture, an aristocrat in human culture. He would have liked to subject his race to the methods that governed the growing of flowers. If it was good for roses, why not for men? He expressed his social faith in *The Book of Roses*.*

Thenceforward, at 50 Chestnut Street, where he always spent his winters, one might have seen Parkman forever at work in the shadow of his third-floor study. Two of the walls were covered with books; the others were hung with portrait-engravings. The light from the north windows was subdued. A few Indian relics stood on the mantel, with statuettes of animals by Barye, whom Hunt, his friend, had more or less discovered. One saw two or three photographs of the statue of Colleoni, which he kept for the sake of the subject, not for the sculpture. Colleoni was never out of his eye or mind. Solitary and silent mostly, usually sleepless, often in pain, stoical as an Indian struck by an arrow, he could be amusing with his daughters,—his wife and son were dead,—who knew he had a capital sense of humour. He appeared on the streets, at a rapid gait, a tall, slender figure in a long grey coat, with the fur cap that rose in winter over the prow-like chin. But he was obliged to restrain his passion for action, and he who could so ill endure confinement, and who studied as it were against

* "The art of horticulture is no leveller. Its triumphs are achieved by rigid systems of selection and rejection, founded always on the broad basis of intrinsic worth. The good cultivator propagates no plants but the best. He carefully chooses those marked out by conspicuous merit; protects them from the pollen of inferior sorts, intermarries them, perhaps, with other varieties of equal vigour and beauty; saves the seed and raises from it another generation. . . . Thus the rose and other plants are brought slowly to their perfect development. . . . We cultivate the parent, and look for our reward in the offspring."—*The Book of Roses,* 95-98.

the grain, could not relax indeed but had to sit. Or, rather, he rode his chair as if it were a saddle. He had to sublimate his love of danger, he had to repress his energy to save his nerves. His mind was like a bow, too tightly strung; and this tension appeared in his work, in its frequent speed and picturesqueness. One felt the virile force of the writer, his pleasure in the savage and the vast, while his eagerness, transformed into patience, made him thorough and accurate.* One felt his impetuosity in the drive of his writing. With his cordial dislike of Puritanism, which he thought narrow and bookish, he retained its passionate fervour and its rigorous tenseness. No doubt, the isolation and strain of his life intensified his natural harshness. He loved hard truth, and he neither gave nor expected praise or pity; but this, with his positive mind, his New England practicality and liking for the useful, limited his sympathies and imagination. Of all the figures in his books, the one he most resembled was La Salle, the stern and self-reliant Roman Frenchman, masterful, martial, serious, austere and shy. For all his distaste for priests, he admired the courage and heroism of the Jesuit martyrs, and he followed the priestly model in his own career. The heir of a long line of divines, like many of the New England writers of the previous age, he shared their sacerdotal temper and all their pride of learning and pride of power. Parkman was a Brahmin of the Brahmins.

This mediæval strain of the priest and soldier, marked in Parkman's nature, fitted him for the theme that filled his life. He had something in common with all the types, English, French and Indian, that appeared in the drama, and the drama itself was mediæval, or, rather, it covered

* See, however, the strictures of Charles Francis Adams the second on Parkman's account of the capture of Quebec, a matter in which, according to Adams, no one could have been right who had not actually taken part in military operations.—C. F. Adams, *Lee at Appomattox and Other Papers*, 347-354.

the whole age, from Champlain to Montcalm and Wolfe, during which the mediæval became the modern. It was a conflict, as Parkman revealed it, between the past and the future, the old and the new, between feudalism and monarchism, an autocratic Church and State, and the democratic freedom that replaced them. That all the fervour of the Middle Ages revived in the enterprise of Montreal, with the spirit of Godfrey de Bouillon, that the settlement was another crusade,—a movement of faith that became a political movement, as the economic motive grew in power,—Parkman was the first to show, in any conclusive fashion, while he showed the meaning of the old French war as a cause of the American Revolution. He understood the protagonists, French and English, who had shared his romantic feeling and his feeling for action, and his imagination failed him only with the Indians, whose virtues, for the rest, he admired and knew. His Indians were visibly real. They were not operatic, like Prescott's, or the noble savages of Cooper. Parkman had lived with them, and his Indian scenes and portraits were drawn from life. But he had preconceived ideas about them, and he took no pains to keep up with later investigations and observations. Ethnology scarcely existed at the time when he began to write, and the Indians he had known best were the Sioux, at the very worst period to judge them. He had approached them, moreover, as a young New England man whose mind was filled with legends of Haverhill and Deerfield. He saw them as Miles Standish might have seen them, with his inelastic nature, from the outside only. His ungenerous treatment of Pontiac was a case in point. He had made up his mind in regard to racial and moral questions and he never expanded or changed it. He had no feeling whatever for evolution. But as, volume by volume, his work advanced till the series came to an end in the early nineties, everyone became aware that he was a great historian, the greatest perhaps who had ever appeared in the country. While *The Conquest of Mexico* was finer than any of Parkman's books, as a masterpiece of historical story-telling, he was more original than Prescott or Motley, for he had established the taste by which he was read.* He had made Champlain and La Salle historic figures like Charlemagne, Peter the Great and Robert Bruce. Until he wrote, students who thought the Tudors all-important saw nothing in the conflict in the forest that had made the American nation what it was; and Parkman, who had discovered his theme, or first perceived its real significance, created a form that matched his theme in grandeur.

* According to John Eglinton *(Irish Literary Portraits),* the question, "Is Prescott or Motley the better writer?" was one that George Moore liked to spring on his friends in Dublin. Parkman was never included in this question, in Ireland or anywhere else in Europe. This was because Europeans were not interested in his subject-matter. They did not care for American themes and persons.

To a large extent, their subject-matter determines the vogue of novelists also. Granting that Henry James was greater than Howells, the all but total oblivion that befell the latter after his death could only be explained on these grounds. The English did not care to read about Americans in their natural state, and "sophisticated" Americans of a later time did not care to read about their forbears. They were apt to prefer Anthony Trollope, not because he was infinitely better than Howells but because they were fascinated by Trollope's people.

CHAPTER IX

THE YOUNGER GENERATION OF 1870

THE young men were scattering in all directions. Their imagination was caught by the West, and scores who might have been writers in the days of *The Dial* were seeking their fortunes in railroads, mines and oil-wells. During the war, as Emerson noted, in every house and shop, a map of America had been unrolled and studiêd, and thousands for whom the country had once been as vague as Australia were well-informed about its means and prospects. The colleges, meanwhile, were pouring out new types to meet the new conditions, mining engineers and railroad experts, geologists and technicians. Most of these young men, born for action, lived undivided lives. What was remarkable, in the new generation, was the number whose lives were divided and sometimes ruined.

"Boston seemed to offer," as Henry Adams said, "no market for educated labour." To many young men for whom it was a centre the future offered nothing there but idleness and slow defeat. They were dispersing in exile, cattle-raising in Colorado, sheep-ranching in California, farming or growing cotton in the South. Two of Henry James's sons took up an orange-grove in Florida. Henry Lee Higginson, who founded the Boston Symphony later, had settled in Georgia for a time before he turned his mind to Western oil-wells. He and George Bancroft's son had planned to live in Virginia and cultivate the vine and the olive.* Edward Simmons joined an oil-firm in Pittsburgh before he went to Paris to study painting. Julian Hawthorne entered engineering. Edward Rowland Sill, the young Yale poet, had gone to California round the Horn. He worked as a postal clerk at Sacramento, as a ranchman, as a bank-clerk, as a teacher. Later he returned as professor of English at the new university in Berkeley, where Josiah Royce acted as his assistant. Others threw themselves into Western railroads. For westward lay the world of riches and adventures, as once, for young Bostonians, it had lain in China; † and Agassiz's son Alexander, the son who was born in Switzerland, had made a fortune in the West before he returned to Harvard and science. As a young engineer, he had gone out to Michigan, and there he had organized the Calumet and Hecla mines. In many ways, his life was like Pumpelly's, although, in making his fortune, he had ruined his health. As an oceanographer later, and one of the greatest, an authority on deep-sea fauna, he was said to have done more permanent work than his father. Alexander Agassiz, Henry Adams wrote, was "the only one of my generation whom I would have liked to envy." For the rest, the Agassizes, father and son, marked all the difference between the generations. Eminent, both, in science, and competent writers,‡ and lovers of writers and artists, they had scarcely another trait in common. To the reckless, exuberant father, warm-hearted and open-handed, utterly indifferent to money, innocently vain, with a hearty love of popularity and a great Humboldtian zest for life,

---

* Higginson and the younger Bancroft conceived this plan as a result of reading Olmsted's books, *A Journey in the Seaboard Slave States,* etc.

† "The West is the place for a young fellow of spirit to pick up a fortune, simply pick it up; it's lying round loose there . . . The richest land on God Almighty's footstool . . . If I had my capital free, I could plant it for millions."

"To the young American . . . the paths to fortune are innumerable and all open; there is invitation in the air and success in all his wide horizon." —Mark Twain, *The Gilded Age.*

‡ See Alexander Agassiz's *Three Cruises of the Blake.*

optimistic, liberal, unexacting, the dark, spare, tall son, retiring and reserved, was a singular contrast. Scrupulous in details, introverted, realistic, he detested notoriety, as his father loved it. He hated the teaching his father enjoyed, preferring a life of quiet research; and yet as a man he was far more essentially worldly.* One saw this contrast repeated in many other fathers and sons, the two Henry Jameses, for example, as the older generation, rooted in the soil, or at least in the popular life,— genial, emotionally profound, unconscious,—yielded to the younger generation.† Alexander Agassiz was restless, like all the unanchored men of his time. He spent half his life, another Pumpelly, wandering over the seven seas, and died at last on shipboard.

The type of all these restless men was a graduate of Yale, Clarence King. A Newport boy, of a merchant family, whose father had died in China, King was a geologist and a mining engineer who had studied with Louis Agassiz and Whitney. He was a born mountaineer who had rambled as a boy in Vermont, and in time he became the first director of the National Geological Survey. A brilliant, a "radiant" creature, as Henry Adams called him, with a quick step and a charm of person that made him irresistible, he had crossed the plains on horseback, in 1863, and shared in the survey of the Rockies. It was he who surveyed the Yosemite Valley and first defined its boundaries. He named Mount Tyndall and Mount Whitney, after two of his masters, and he might have named a mountain after Ruskin, whose descriptions of Alpine

* "I remember being shocked by a story told me by a lady who had sat next to Alexander Agassiz at a lunch party . . . Agassiz had said to the lady, 'Why, if it were a question of bribing a State Legislature, I should regard it in the same light as the removal of a bank of sand.' "—John Jay Chapman, in M. A. De Wolfe Howe's *John Jay Chapman and His Letters.*

† In one way or another, with variations, one saw this contrast in the Adamses, father and sons, in the Danas, the Hawthornes, etc. Turgenev's *Fathers and Sons,* a novel much read at the time, marked a parallel change in Russia.

scenery affected his own. His *Systematic Geology* ranked as a contribution to science with the younger Agassiz's work on deep-sea fauna; and his *Mountaineering in the Sierra Nevadas* was as fine as *The Oregon Trail* or *Before the Mast*. Neither Parkman's book nor Dana's had anything better in it than King's sketches of mountain characters, the Newty family, the Digger Indians, the "Pacific Slope Bonheur," or the spirited chapter, *Kaweah's Run,* in which he described his escape from the Mexican bandits. What made the book unique, however, as Parkman's and Dana's in their fields,—one for the plains, one for the ocean,—was its special feeling for the mountains. John Muir alone in later years approached in veracity and splendour King's pictures of the ice-fields and the gorges, the granite corridors filled with the tumult of water, the arrowy rushing of brooks and the grandeur of snow-storms, the cold, still peaks and the lake-basins, silent and black at night, like the void into which Dante looked through the bottomless gulf of Dis. King had a painter's eye,—he "fitted into the ways of thinking of artists," as John La Farge said later. He had rejoiced in the sapphire sky of the stark and glaring desert; and he never tired of gazing down long vistas where the shafts of pine stood in stately groups, each with its own tinting and finish, its feathery branches waving, while broad streams of light poured in, gilding the columns of purple and red and falling in bright paths along the floor. Above the spires of golden green, as through the dark, cool alleys, he saw the winding roadways of the Sierras; and the mountains, observed from a summit, shaped themselves like the ruins of Gothic cathedrals. There he perceived the sharp roof-ridges, the buttresses and pinnacles and statues, the receding doorways with pointed arches carved into blank façades of granite, doors that were never to be opened, cruciform peaks. He could not doubt that the Alps had furnished the models for the early Gothic builders.

In after years, to many observers, the brilliant, mercurial Clarence King was the symbol of his American generation. When Henry Adams met him, in 1871, at the
door of a Colorado cabin, he fell into King's arms, he
said. Adams had known Lyell in England, and he had reviewed Lyell's *Geology*. He shared King's interest in this
subject and had gone West with a field-party; but, quite
aside from this, he was drawn to King,—they might have
been friends in the Stone Age. In his wit and his bubbling
energy, his youth and his charm, Clarence King suggested
Alexander, all-conquering and to conquer.* He seemed
the "ideal American" that all his friends wished to be,
the "richest and most many-sided genius of his day," as
Adams wrote later in his memoirs. They all agreed in
this, La Farge, John Hay, for whom King was the "best
and brightest" of his generation. They were ready to
drop all other plans to go with King to the ends of the
earth; and, in fact, he was always "going," like most of
the others, to London or Paris, to buy pictures,† to Spain,
to find the helmet of Malbrino,—Don Quixote's barber's
basin, which he found, or liked to think he found, and
about which he wrote an amusing story,—to Mexico, the

* "King had everything to interest and delight Adams. He knew more
than Adams did of art and poetry; he knew America, especially west of
the hundredth meridian, better than anyone else; he knew the professor
by heart, and he knew the congressman better than he did the professor.
He knew even women; even the American woman; even the New York
woman, which is saying much . . . King's abnormal energy had already
won him great success. None of his contemporaries had done so much,
single-handed, or were likely to leave so deep a trail."—*The Education of
Henry Adams.*

† John Hay took King, in Paris, to the studio of Gustave Doré. King
disliked Doré's sensational effects, but "in five minutes" the two "were
brothers and were planning an excursion to Arizona to sketch the war-
dances of the Apaches." Hay also related how King made the acquaintance
of Ruskin at an auction in London. The two were standing side by side
and King, not knowing to whom he was talking, argued on a number of
subtle points. Ruskin, who was delighted with him, invited him to Coniston
and offered him his choice of two fine Turners. King always gave and
took with equal generosity, and the story is that he said, "One good
Turner deserves another," whereupon Ruskin gave him both.—See
Memorial of Clarence King.

Windward Islands, Cuba. It seemed to Henry Adams, his companion in Cuba, that he knew the whole population, the Spaniards, the Indians, the planters, the Negroes, with whom he spent his nights at Voodoo dances. He fraternized with the revolutionists, and his special friends were the old Negresses, whom he liked "because they were not academic." He sat with them for days in their cabins, drinking coffee and talking the Negro-Cuban dialect with them. When Adams joined him for this journey, —years later, in 1894,—King had been discharged from an asylum. He had made and lost fortunes and wrecked his health; and at last, alone and uncared for, he died in an Arizona tavern.

If King's life had a moral, as all his friends seemed to feel, if it was symptomatic and symbolic, of what was it the symbol? The waste of the brightest faculties unemployed by civilization, the *zeitgeist,* the time and the country. Henry Adams, in later years, drew this moral for all to see, Adams, who knew his age from the beginning and had foreseen its tendencies. A civilization that could not employ such men as Clarence King,—except for a dozen years as technical experts,—that allowed their capability and god-like reason to fust in them unused, or used so little, challenged the critical mind; and the critical mind itself failed and fainted in the want of a living air to bear it up. The old culture had broken down, the old causes were dead and forgotten, and no new ideal had arisen to rally the minds of the younger men; and, while many turned westward, almost as many turned towards Europe, in despair of the civilization they saw before them. Of these, the younger Henry James was the great exemplar in years to come; but there were numbers of others, from New England and elsewhere, who also sought for haunts of ancient peace. Most of them travelled in the spirit of Montaigne, from a "lack of relation to the present conditions of our country;" and most of

them were interested in art. Many collected pictures, like
Clarence King and Henry Adams, Alexander Agassiz,
John La Farge, like Pumpelly, Perkins, Appleton, Jarves
and Norton. A few, like Henry James's Rowland Mallet,
"looking round for something to do," and having ample
means with which to do it, went abroad with plans to buy
old masters and provide their native towns with art museums. Naturally, the artists themselves, the painters,
sculptors and architects, were those who felt most pow-
erfully the attraction of Europe. Sixty years before, after
the War of 1812, the painters who had lived abroad had
mostly returned to America. Vanderlyn, Morse and Trumbull, Peale and Allston had been full of hope for a life at
home and a country that had established its independence;
and their portraits, at least, were full of native character,
while some of their genre painting abounded in it. Their
impulse in returning home was justified in this, although
otherwise their lives were often thwarted; but after the
Civil War the artists flocked abroad again. At a time
when even the farms and villages, which had lost their
old political interests, were awakening to the appeal of
art and science,—brought in, as often as not, by the
"summer people,"—this was only natural; and it was also
natural that a cosmopolitan point of view should have
governed the minds and hands of migrating artists. The
element of "native character" that had given strength to
the earlier artists and that strengthened the home-grown
artists of the age to come had little weight for Whistler,
for instance, and Sargent, predestined cosmopolitans, like
Henry James. Sargent, who was born in Italy, saw America first at twenty; and Whistler, who had been taken to
Russia when he was nine years old, was at home as a boy
in England also, where his sister had married Seymour
Haden. Both these artists, however, like James, were
American in their inmost fibre, and both had connections
with New England. Sargent had grown up in a wander-

ing household that preserved its New England traits through all its travels. The legend of the American navy was as much a part of Sargent's childhood as the legend of West Point was a part of Whistler's; and Whistler, who "wouldn't" be born at Lowell, had lived at Stonington, Pomfret and Springfield, following his father's appointments as an engineer. In this first great age of American painting, Whistler and Sargent, like Henry James, achieved preëminence even in Europe as masters of technical processes. It was as if the virtue of the old Yankee craftsmen, the men who had built the clipper-ships, had passed into them, to reappear in new forms, just when the clipper-ships were disappearing. The brilliance of these artists no one questioned, and for many this virtuosity was all-sufficient. For others, it was insufficient, either then or later; they saw that Whistler and Sargent, like James, were light-armed soldiers of art, who travelled so far and so fast for an obvious reason. Relieved of the impedimenta that burdened the heavy-armed soldiers, who had their "native character" to deal with, they could turn their whole attention to technical questions. It was natural that Whistler, Sargent and James should have excelled in technique all but the greatest of the Frenchmen. But the French were always a step ahead of all the cosmopolitans, for they kept their "native character" as well.

This became poignantly evident as one followed ·the life of Henry James, for whom the "drama of Europe in American breasts" remained for fifty years the central problem. For most of the other sentient New Englanders of the generation of 1870, this problem, if not central, was important. Europe meant much to Howells also, to William James and Henry Adams, all of whom, like most of their friends, had lived there.* For most of them,

* "In old times I used to notice every window, door-handle and smell as having a peculiar and exotic charm, every old street and house as filled with historic life and mystery."—*The Letters of William James.*

for most writers, the question of facing the new America, with its worship of "bigness" and numbers, seemed overwhelming. The lesson of *The Man Without a Country* had served well in time of war, when the national mind was focussed on a single object. But the national mind was dispersed at the moment. It was clearly focussed only on the things of Mammon; and nothing was more difficult than to comprehend the country,—enough to create aesthetic patterns from it. How could a novelist handle this chaos? How could a philosopher synthesize it? How could a young political thinker, with all political thought behind him, cope with a public life that suggested the Stone Age? Henry Adams, an "estray" already, a "flotsam or jetsam of wreckage," was facing this problem; and the others were to meet it, one by one. Godkin predisposed them all,—all, that is, but Howells,—to look with suspicion on the West; and, in any case, the West was a menace for *les délicats,*—Ernest Renan's phrase for the tender-minded. The tough-minded throve there and returned with treasures of gold and oil; but for sensitive intellectuals, like Clarence King and the younger Agassiz, the reckless life which the West implied, its hardships and fever of speculation, meant ruined health and broken souls and madness. Was not Francis Parkman an earlier case in point? Even Charles Francis Adams,—Henry's tougher older brother, who was soon to win all the prizes which the West could give,—was to turn in the end in disgust from his life of money-making with the feeling that he had wasted his existence.* Certainly, for all these men, who were all at home in the modern languages,—for whom French and German, at least, and often Italian, were almost as native as English,—Europe might well have been a refuge. There was something else, moreover,

* "I should have settled myself systematically down on the development of my aptitude,—the art of literary expression."—*Autobiography of Charles Francis Adams.*

that made it seem so. Writers, as a class, follow the aristocratic pattern, follow it, that is, when they do not create it,—for they follow the "free will" that makes all patterns,—and the aristocratic American mind, disturbed and disrupted after the war, had reopened the trail to Europe for artists and writers. What held most of the young men back was their essential Americanism, with all that this implied in regard to Europe. It implied a divided life for them, almost as much as the West; and deeper than all this was the general feeling that America, at its lowest reach, was better than Europe. Howells and Mark Twain, the Western writers, were those who took this feeling most for granted; but even Henry James confusedly shared it. Sargent shared it also, and so did Whistler, who remained, with all his blague, a "West Point man." The faith of these men who had chosen Europe was very often shaken, and often their conscious minds denied this faith; for they had exposed themselves to conditions that shook it, and they were not well-armoured like the men at home. But in the depths of their souls they believed that the "real right thing," the essentially noble thing, was an American secret. For William James, with his "two souls," it was an open secret; and in even Henry Adams, a generation later, an ember of the faith still glowed under the polar ice. For Howells, as for Emerson and Whitman, the fact was as plain as the sun or the moon. Merely to picture his people was to show it.

These problems, the West and Europe, confronted all the younger minds, although most of them soon arrived at practical conclusions. New England, or the East, might be the frying-pan, but at least it was better than the fire. It was better than either fire, the West or Europe. The question of the West was further settled by the ablest of the younger Western writers, who were settling in the East, like Howells, as the price of survival. Mark Twain

was living in Hartford, where he could break the bread
and eat the salt of hospitality without any interference
in his opinions.* John Hay had joined *The Tribune* in
New York, where Bret Harte also lived before going
abroad. As for the question of Europe, the painters settled this most easily. They enjoyed the immunity of painters,—they did not have to think the question out. They
followed the still small voice that governs painters. Those
who were not deeply attached to the country, and whose
interest was primarily in technique, sailed for Europe at
once without doubts or regrets. Those for whom technical problems were of secondary interest, and whose local
attachments were deep, remained without regrets or
doubts at home. The painters, unlike the writers, were
not obliged to argue with the still small voice, and no one
was more indifferent to Europe than Homer, Fuller and
Ryder, who had scarcely seen it. They felt that whatever
painters gained in Europe was less than what they lost by
living there,—what all the American painters had lost
since Copley lost his edge in England, the grim force of
the native character that vanished under his later bra-
vura.† It was true that the conditions with which these
artists had to deal destroyed the weaker men and crippled the strongest. They were unable to profit by the
great growth of art-schools that followed the Centennial
of 1876; and they were obliged to live divided lives, as
shoe-makers and sign-painters, village doctors and practical farmers, tobacco-growers, cartoonists in popular
papers. They suffered and struggled alone, neglected and
poor. It took two generations for Americans to see that
they were the primary painters and always had been, these

---

* "Fortunately a good deal of experience of men enabled me to choose
my residence wisely. I live in the freest corner of the country."—Mark
Twain, 1876, Letter to a Western friend.

† "Don't you know how many New York and Boston artists have gone to
Europe and hermetically sealed themselves up somewhere to ferment into
greatness like a jug of cider turning into vinegar in a farmer's cellar?"—
Arlo Bates, *The Pagans*.

deep, unworldly souls who loved the scenes they painted, while Sargent and Whistler carried the world before them.

It was those who remained in the frying-pan and paid the full price of their courage that later times revered as noble grandsires. For great works are great not, first of all, for technical reasons, but because they express the ethos of the race behind them. The great technique only confirms the greatness; and this becomes apparent when an age of manifold snobberies is followed by an age that seeks the real. *Noblesse oblige* was never truer than it was with men like Homer and Ryder, who cast their bread upon the waters, who gave their country bread in return for stones. They accepted the local conditions and built upon them; and in this they were like two other men of the generation of 1870, the founders of American architecture. For Richardson and Sullivan well deserved this phrase: it distinguished them from the earlier architects, whose work was almost wholly derivative. H. H. Richardson, a Harvard Louisianian, who had returned from Paris at the close of the war and later came to Boston from New York, was creating a style of his own that suggested his person. It was florid, luxuriant and massive, reflecting the bold, exuberant Southerner, the teacher of Charles McKim and Stanford White. Exotic as his style was, what made this man important was that he faced the problems of the world he lived in. For instance, for an age of travel, he designed railway stations that made it a positive pleasure to wait for a train. In this respect, Louis Sullivan, a Boston boy born and bred,—one of the first fine shoots of the Boston Irish,—was to go far beyond Richardson, as the teacher of Frank Lloyd Wright and the father of an organic architecture.* Studying first in

* Louis Sullivan, born in Boston, was the son of an Irish dancing-master. One of the exciting causes of his career was a series of lectures on botany by Asa Gray. His *Autobiography of an Idea,* a sort of Whitmanian rhapsody, was written in the third person, perhaps on the model of *The Educa-*

Boston and later in Paris, he found his field in Chicago, where he met the conditions of a crowded business-district by developing the steel-framed skyscraper. These men and their followers soon met most of the local conditions, the conditions of a democratic world. They undertook to solve the problem of erecting banks and office-buildings, warehouses, ice-plants, factories and garages. They were builders in the line of Emerson and Whitman, who had established the principles on which they built; and they too were ancestors rather than descendants, like the mediæval and classical architects who created most of the public buildings. They showed that a native integrity was better than any borrowed nobility, the triumphs of which, if more obvious, were far more facile; and one might add that the generation of 1870 provided the country with ancestors also in music. There were abler composers than John Knowles Paine, the first professor of music at Harvard, in the years that followed his appearance; but Paine at least established a tradition for native composers to react against.* In 1881, Henry Lee Higginson, —Colonel Higginson's cousin,—founded the Boston Symphony orchestra. This banker whose imagination always remained his dominant trait had longed to devote himself to music, which he had studied in Germany. A patron of many good causes, he was also a forbear of modern America, for the orchestra that he founded and led, in all but the literal sense, was the parent of all the American orchestras later.

So much for the men who remained in the frying-pan,

---

tion of Henry Adams. Fanciful, emotional, mystical, rhetorical,—call it what you will,—it was incoherent; but it was written when Sullivan was a broken man, and it suggests the original mind of its author.

* Paine's oratorio, *St. Peter,* the first composed in the country, was performed at his birthplace, Portland, Maine, in 1873. John Fiske, himself a composer and a competent judge, said that at that time the Portland Choral Society was "the most thoroughly disciplined choral society in this country." The Bethlehem Choral Union was organized in 1882, the Bethlehem Bach Choir in 1900.

who faced the national problems and strove to solve them.
So much, that is, for those who preferred the state of
their minds to the state of their fortunes, in Richard
Steele's phrase; for even Major Higginson, the banker,
was always more concerned for the state of his mind.
Those who preferred the state of their fortunes sailed
before the wind. But even men of this type, when they
are young and tender, rejoice in the pattern-maker who
points the way, and Harvard, prolific in leaders, provided
them with a pattern-maker in the Unitarian minister,
Horatio Alger. As a young man, Alger, who had lived in
Paris, had tutored boys in Greek and French in Cambridge. He had organized them into a boy-scout group
that was known as "Alger's army of up-and-comings." He
moved to New York in 1866. The streets swarmed with
drummer-boys who had run away to the war and wished,
after the war, to see the city, where they were blacking
boots and selling papers. Their centre was the Newsboys'
Lodging-house, and Alger went to live there, secretly visiting Chinatown, when he was bored with the boys,
on errands that were far from edifying.* At Harvard,
he had read *Moby Dick,* which seems to have inspired
him to take up writing, and he soon set to work on his
Luck and Pluck series, to show Ragged Dick and Tat-
tered Tom how easily they might rise to fame and fortune. For many who began their lives as bootblacks and
newsboys, by sweeping out the store or by carrying par-
cels, and who rose to be captains of industry, the Horatio
Alger theme was a joy and a solace. It showed that a
young man who was too good to be true was also bound

* The life of this strange creature, who was born in Revere, Massachusetts, where his father brought him up to be a "spiritual leader," has
been written by H. R. Mayes,—*Horatio Alger, a Biography Without a
Hero.* Alger kept a diary in which he took delight in recording his prudish
amours and furtive orgies. He had his first taste of the literary life in
Paris. He related how, sitting in a café with his mistress, he was told of
the death of Murger, the author of the *Vie de Bohême.* This news caused
his face to be "stained with tears."

to be successful, a moral that history vindicated in the eighties and nineties. Alger was one of the men who all but effaced the New England tradition, for he vulgarized Emerson's *Self-Reliance* and turned into a laughing-stock Longfellow's *Excelsior* and *The Psalm of Life*. He made virtue and purity odious for thousands of the following age, who, having been taught to "swim," preferred to "sink." How good customs corrupt the world was the moral of his work, for he was the lineal heir of Jacob Abbott; and he spoiled the Rollo-philosophy by adjusting his mind to conditions that turned the Rollo-philosophy inside out. Where Abbott had written for country boys whose central motive was self-improvement, and who wished to advance, indeed, but as excellent men, Alger wrote for city boys whose only motive was self-advancement and whose "excellence" was hypocrisy and humbug. In adapting the Yankee morality to a motive essentially vulgar, he made the morality itself a reproach and a byword.

Meanwhile, the younger thinking men, who disdained the "bitch-goddess Success," and who never knew the name of Horatio Alger, were confronted with difficult problems. The *tempo* of their age was all against them. The *tempo* of the age favoured other types, the business man, the practical man and the scientific man of a practical turn who served the interests of business. Whatever ideality lurked in the country,—and it lurked, in fact, in almost every corner,—was hidden from all eyes but the most perceptive. Politics were a closed door,—only the toughest-minded could push it open; and the young men felt there was nothing to hold them up. There were no expressed ideals for them to cling to, and even the heroes had failed them, for Lincoln, whom everyone worshipped, was dead, and Grant, who might well have been a hero, had lent himself to every defamation. He had further corrupted good manners by appearing at the Boston Jubi-

lee as the guest of the gaudy Jim Fisk. Only the older
writers whose prestige was passing remembered Mazzini
and Kossuth and the patriot fathers; and even the women
had ceased to praise the men who "got up insurrections,"
who had once been so dear to Mrs. Stowe, or other recklessly chivalrous types of living.* Those who, like the
Adamses, were born to rebuff the prince of darkness, and
his minions in State Street and Wall Street, found their
consciences moving in an empty chamber: there was
nothing for them to resist. No one denied that the times
were evil; the times had never been so evil. Everyone cheer-
fully said so, and no one cared.†

No wonder the younger men were baffled. No wonder
they felt themselves at sea. It was all very well, in these
conditions, to repeat the word of the forties, "Be true to
the dream of thy youth." What was the dream of youth,
what could it be, in a day that had witnessed nothing but
war and destruction and the sordid scramble for money
that followed the war? The commercialization of life had
thinned the emotional atmosphere. It had almost destroyed the disposition to quarrel with public wrongs; ‡
and one of the new developments that Parkman observed
in the country was a mixture of cool emotions and excit-

* "How do you account for it," said Anne, "that the best-developed and
finest specimens of men have been those that have got up insurrections in
Italy, Austria and Hungary?"—Harriet Beecher Stowe, *Dred,* 1856.

† "Society was not disposed to defend itself from criticism or attack.
Indeed, the most fatal part of the situation for the poet in revolt, the par-
alyzing drug that made him helpless, was that society no longer seemed
sincerely to believe in itself or anything else; it resented nothing, not even
praise. The young poet grew up without being able to find an enemy."—
Henry Adams, *Life of George Cabot Lodge.* Adams was writing here of
Boston in the nineties, but he might have been writing of the seventies
just as well.

‡ "When I think of the versatile and accommodating habits of America,
it seems like a land without thunder-storms. In proportion as man grows
commercial, does he also become dispassionate and incapable of electric
emotions? . . . On the whole, I . . . find myself surmising whether a people
who, like the Americans, put up quietly with all sorts of petty personal
impositions and injustices, will not at length find it too great a bore to
quarrel with great public wrongs."—Lowell, *Literary Essays.*

able brains. In the past, the men with the calmest minds
had been those who possessed the deepest feelings, while
the younger men, compared with them, were shallow and
hypersusceptible.* No doubt, in addition to the war, the
change from country living to city living had much to do
with this, for almost all the younger men were born to an
urban civilization and had lost the sanitary influences of
rural life. The older writers, like Dr. Holmes, felt as if
to be too urban was an all but ignominious state of mind,
and most of the men of his generation had loved their
country places, where they kept in close touch with the
population. Many of them were bred on the Greek and
Roman authors, who abounded in sweet and genial pictures of rural life and the rural people. But the prestige
of the country had passed, as the balance of power had
also passed from agriculture to industry and business, and
the younger men no longer read the Greek and Roman
authors, who had once afforded the models that stirred
the young. They read, along with works of science, the
new French novelists and playwrights, who pictured city
life as the only life for ambitious men and described the
life of the province as dull and silly. This change in reading habits was decisive; for, while those who had known
their Plutarch and Virgil had grown up to spacious lives
in villages, in hamlets and on farms, as the older statesmen and writers abundantly proved, the young men,
steeped in modern books, were almost all uprooted before
they read them. This reading confirmed their habits as
déracinés. They could no longer feel that "the mind is its
own place," when the place where the mind existed was
the country or the village. Indeed, they feared the "local
habitation," which meant for them obscurity and worse;
and Emerson's noble saying, "Make much of your own
place," became for them a menace and a byword. Thrown
back upon themselves, they lost the inherited ties that

* Compare, e.g., Josiah Quincy with Henry Cabot Lodge.

bound them to the rest of the population; and, inasmuch as the population was urbanizing, like themselves, and was filled with strange, new elements of every kind, they did not even wish to know it. Parson Wilbur and Hosea Biglow were brothers under their skins, but what was one to make of a city proletariat, with its alien racial strains and unknown ways? The young men of 1870, bred in an Anglo-Saxon world, could scarcely have read the riddle of immigration. They would have had to know the tongues of Babel, in addition to their Dante and their Goethe; and, moreover, the urbanized Yankees were a difficult problem. For these Yankees had ceased to be the men one knew on their farms and their ships. Many were turning into Cornplows and Babbitts,—they were Philistines, in Matthew Arnold's phrase. What had once been "plain" was growing "common," as often happens when simple folk who have thriven in simple conditions are subjected to complex conditions that cheapen their minds,—for they cannot live up to these conditions, to which they are not accustomed, without discarding some of their moral ballast. The people were changing as much as the writers, and the writers regarded the people with a hostile eye; and thus arose the mood of the modern intellectuals, and their motto, "No compromise with the public taste." To recognize a rift between writer and public became almost the corner-stone of their self-respect. Inevitably, the writers were far less "young" than the young men of the previous age, which had given young men the openings that youth demands,—causes that aroused their faith, dreams of bettering humankind, adventures that stirred their souls and made them men. Having no roots in the popular life, they were restless, cynical, sceptical, doubtful, self-conscious, apprehensive and torn by scruples, the scruples that devour a mind which has no large impersonal interests or any instinctive connection with primary things.

Such was the general character of the younger writers of 1870, and such were the conditions that produced it. Henry Adams knew what the writers needed, as he knew that, at the moment, it was out of the question. "What we need is a *school*," he had written to his brother. "We want a national set of young men, like ourselves or better, to start new influences not only in politics, but in literature, in law, in society, and throughout the whole social organism of the country,—a national school of our own generation. And that is what America has no power to create. In England the universities centralize ability and London gives a field. So in France. Paris encourages and combines these influences. But with us, we should need at least six perfect geniuses placed, or rather, spotted over the country and all working together; whereas our generation as yet has not produced one nor the promise of one. It's all random, insulated work, for special and temporary and personal purposes, and we have no means, power or hope of combined action for any unselfish end." *
Was not this indeed foreordained? The school that Adams had in mind, in the nebulous state of the nation, was a daydream and a castle in the air; for the West was too busy at primitive tasks to lend itself to such a plan and the times were unpropitious in the older regions. The South was broken and hostile, New York was given over to money-making, New England was lastingly weakened. A "national set of young men to start new influences" was in fact an impossibility under these conditions, though the dream had been partially realized in 1865 when Godkin established *The Nation*. No wonder the young men were apprehensive. They knew they were doomed to fight their fights alone,† in a world that was more than likely to divide and destroy them. Some, like Henry Adams,

* 1862, *A Cycle of Adams Letters.*
† "Somehow the men of my generation never seemed to get acquainted with one another."—*Letters of George E. Woodberry.*

were all but born discouraged. Others, like Henry James, were to spend ten years trying to solve the question where to live. William James was also to pass ten years consumed with a sense of futility, although in the end he developed a faith like his father's. William James and Howells, who had come from the West, retained the buoyant mood of the early republic; but most of the others were cautious and conservative, cool and disillusioned on the surface, with the knowing air of men who expect to be swindled, who cannot trust the society in which they live. They were guarded, for they were surrounded with pitfalls. They had to struggle for their integrity in an age that was littered with failures. In conscious revolt against all things romantic, as young men always are in post-war years, they were as much concerned to react against the world about them as they were to coin the metal in themselves. To coöperate with this world was almost out of the question for them. If many of the younger minds that led the age seemed often morbidly scrupulous and over-refined, one had to remember how far the popular personalities were governed by numbers and money. In reaction against a public life that had grown corrupt and vulgar, they cultivated the "private life" and deliberately sought the unpopular. They exaggerated the "little" to shame the "big." These were a few of the traits that characterized the generation, producing its anomalous effects.

CHAPTER X

HOWELLS IN CAMBRIDGE

TO HOWELLS, living in Cambridge, absorbed in his writing, the new age, dawning in the country, was one of peace, prosperity and content. The scandals of public life, the abuses of business were remote from the little world in which he dwelt. Coming from the West, he had found a haven in Cambridge and Boston when the young men who had grown up in this region were most inclined to feel its limitations. Others might hanker for Paris and London: for him the New England capital was all-sufficient. Besides, he had known much more of America than most of the young New England men and had more reason to think it essentially sound. He knew New York and the Hudson river, Ohio and the Mississippi. He had seen Quebec and Montreal. His four years in Europe were incidental. As a child of the Western Reserve, he had shared the old political faith that Emerson and Whitman serenely embodied; and the atmosphere of his family had shaped his mind. His Quaker and Swedenborgian forbears had never questioned the "inner light." He was predisposed to be unaware of evil.

Howells was a happy man. The others were restless and anxious: he was tranquil. Even the Civil War was vaguer in his mind than it was in the minds of Boston men who had seen its woes at close range. In his Venetian consulate, he had caught only rumours of it; and, while he felt responsible for having missed the war,* it was like a

---

* "Every loyal American who went abroad during the first years of our great war felt bound to make himself some excuse for turning his back on his country in the hour of her trouble."—Howells, *A Fearful Responsibility.*

dream for him, as for some who had fought.* Moreover, while most of the other young men were groping for a foothold, Howells had found his vocation and was launched upon it. How could he not have been happy? He was prepared to accept the "true American gospel," that everything was coming right in time.† Years later Howells questioned this gospel. He awoke to the evils of his day far more than Henry James or Henry Adams, who had seen these evils at once; and he really faced the problem, which few of his generation faced,—what was a good American to do about them? Howells, happy, was also honest; his moral perception was deep and real. But he was predisposed to trust his country, and he rejoiced in the lull that followed the war. He rejoiced in his work, he rejoiced in his countrypeople, he rejoiced in the noble realities he found about him. Were not the poets and scholars as real as Wall Street? The Cambridge air was kind to the flowers of thought: it carried its burden of pollen from mind to mind. Sufficient unto the day were his misgivings. As the wife said in Tennyson's *Sea Dreams,* "Let all evil sleep." He felt as if the troubles of the world were settled.

In the house he had built on Concord Avenue, with the Eastlake tiles and the book-lined study, he carried on his work for *The Atlantic.* His travel-papers, reviews and stories were giving place to novels, slight at first, expanded sketches, then gradually more and more ambitious. Meanwhile, he explored New England in the summer season. With his manuscripts and his magazine-proofs, he went for a month or more to the sea or the

---

* "Of all things of the past a battle is the least conceivable. I have heard men who fought in many battles say that the recollection was like a dream to them."—Howells, *Their Wedding Journey.*

† " 'Ah,' said the old man gently, 'it will all come right in time.'
   " 'You preach the true American gospel,' said Colville.
   " 'Of course; there is no other gospel. That *is* the gospel.' "
                                   —Mr. Waters, in Howells's *Indian Summer*

mountains, to Kennebunkport, Conanicut, Bethlehem, Jaffrey, to the farm boarding-houses and the summer hotels that were rising all over the region. One spring he spent at Lexington, where the fathers of the village, who were proud to have an author in their midst, gave him the town-hall to use as a study. He spent a few days at Campobello, and he passed one summer at Nahant. There he rented an old place with a forsaken garden and a belvedere that overhung the sea, a relic of the romantic days, half ruined, that watched the tides crawl over the shining sand. Once he stayed at Shirley among the Shakers and went to meeting there with the brothers and sisters, dressed in their neat, white kerchiefs and clean, stiff caps and their Quakerish coats and shoes of 1780. One of the brothers wrote mystical tracts, such as Howells's father had also written; another had a system of musical notation, which he employed in hymns of the angelic life. Elder Fraser cultivated his grapevines and blackberries, and others made baskets, palm-leaf hats and rugs. There was much in this Yankee communism that appealed to Howells. It reminded him of his father's ideas. It confirmed his deep belief in equality as the guiding ideal of American life. The Shakers soon began to appear in his stories.

Indeed, the scenes of all these wanderings soon appeared in Howells's stories, the harvest of an all-perceiving eye. At the beaches, he observed the ladies, with their needlework beside them, sitting and talking in rows on the long piazzas. Sometimes they sat in the shelter of a cliff, and one of them read aloud while the others knitted, —*Felix Holt* or *Middlemarch* or the *Evening Transcript*. Occasionally, one of the ladies rose and trailed her shawl behind her, perhaps to pick up a spool that had fallen from her lap. Pursuing the spool, she dropped her scissors and thimble. Then all rose at once and scattered, for the time had come to lie down. While the older ladies were lying down, the young ladies were most in evidence, perhaps on the croquet-ground in front of the hotel or out in the rowboats on the river; for all these summer re- sorts abounded in loverless maidens, enough to provide a novelist with heroines forever. There were hammocks strung between the birches with young ladies in them, reading novels. They were always doing something to their hair, and all of them seemed to be prepared for what were called "attentions." They were the summer girls of the summer hotels, and it always seemed to be summer in Howells's stories. At the hotels in the moun- tains, the table-girls were school-teachers, who were add- ing to their income in vacation, and sometimes, in the afternoon, in their fresh, bright dresses, they played the piano in the parlour. The clerks were usually college boys, and often young men from the hill-towns, with their girls in the buggies beside them, drove over for supper. Now and then, a landscape-painter appeared with his easel and colours,—he was making studies of goldenrod and gran- ite and spread them about in the parlour for the guests to see. The great event of the day was the hop in the eve- ning. When a Boston family arrived, or a bride and groom, the plot began to thicken. The waitresses straight- ened their hair, the ladies looked up from their knitting, and everyone knew that something was about to happen. What happened was a Howells story. It had to occur be- fore it was written, but the chances were that, next summer, the young ladies in their hammocks were read- ing this. For the chances were that Howells had seen what happened. It might have been invisible to others, or nothing more than a breath or a ripple, the sort of thing that novelists seldom noticed. To Howells, who no- ticed everything and who seemed to be ubiquitous, this "nothing" that happened—for others—was the best of all. That he made something out of this nothing was the marvel of his mind and art; and moreover the something in question was highly important. It was love, in its American phases, love in the American form; and what, for American readers, was more important?

Sometimes, in his wanderings, Howells stopped at Hartford, a halfway house on the road to New York, where Mark Twain lived, near Mrs. Stowe. Howells had first met Clemens in Boston, when the latter's lecturing-headquarters were at Redpath's office. He had reviewed *The Innocents Abroad* and Clemens had called to thank him; and since then the two ex-printers, both of whom had pilot forbears and who had much else in common in their Western boyhood, had struck up a lasting friendship. Howells had introduced Clemens to the readers of *The Atlantic* and was publishing his stories and sketches; and Clemens, convinced that he lived at last in "the freest corner of the country," liked Boston better than New York.* His cronies there, besides Howells, were Fields and Aldrich. He would storm into Cambridge in his great sealskin coat, with his tousled red hair and wild moustache, and fall asleep in a bed at Howells's with a lighted cigar in his mouth. Once he took a room at Parker's and left the gas burning for two or three days, while he wandered about in his evening clothes, muffled in his overcoat. Most of the Cambridge circle looked at him askance, while another Western genius from San Francisco, who had burst on the world at the same moment, was received with open arms in Cambridge and Boston. Bret Harte was entertained by Longfellow, Lowell, Agassiz, Fields. He was as much of a lion as Dickens, who had reappeared in 1868,—when Howells and the younger Henry James had met him; and Harte disrupted dinner-parties and arrived as late as he chose at luncheons and seemed to be all the more popular the more he did so. But Howells gloried in

* See Howells, *My Mark Twain.* Referring to *The Atlantic*, Clemens wrote to Howells in 1874: "It is the only audience that I sit down before in perfect serenity (for the simple reason that it doesn't require a 'humorist' to paint himself striped and stand on his head every fifteen minutes)."

Mark Twain, and Norton and Child shared Howells's pleasure in him.* Later the two friends wrote a play together,—or, rather, they tried to do so,—on the story of Colonel Sellers from *The Gilded Age*. This novel, which Mark Twain composed with Charles Dudley Warner,— his neighbour, who was editing the *Hartford Courant,*— was only redeemed by its leading character. Sellers was a great creation of American folklore, while the book was otherwise without form and void, although Warner's hero, Philip Sterling, was a more or less lifelike sketch of the type of young New England men who were going West to seek their fortunes. Howells, visiting Hartford, sometimes stayed with Warner also. This son of a Massachusetts farmer had practised law in Chicago before he returned to New England and began to write. He had made a name for himself as a commentator on rural life in his weekly contributions to the *Courant*. In *My Summer in a Garden,* with woodcuts by Darley, followed by *Back-Log Studies* and *Being a Boy,* he described the repose and the happier aspects of the old New England country scene in a charming, natural style that suggested Irving's. He had known all the Indian trails in western Massachusetts in the days when the gate of the sea was at Boston and the gate of the West was at Albany; and, passing through the Western gate, he had lived for a while in Missouri, where he had worked as a surveyor. There he had had a chance to observe the "land and railroad operations" that he and Clemens described in *The Gilded Age,* and he well understood the ambitious young Yankees for whom every Western path was a path of fortune. He had seen Philip Sterlings by the dozen in Chicago, but his own ambition

---

* At the time of the Whittier birthday dinner, Child wrote to Mark Twain, praising his well-known speech as "the richest piece of humour in the world." Norton's admiration may also have been spontaneous. It seems more likely, however, rather more in character, that Norton was drawn to the work of this far from Nortonian author by his friend Charles Darwin's delight in Clemens. At the time when Norton was seeing much of Darwin, Mark Twain was the latter's favourite bedside reading.

was all for a life of letters, and he spoke in his earlier
books for the interest in farming and gardening that
Olmsted was reviving in his parks. His *Being a Boy* followed Mark Twain's *Tom Sawyer*. It was full of the
aromatic scents of the hill-pasture and green meadow and
the joys of the farmhouse attic on rainy days. Later,
Warner was better known for his mildly critical social
essays, in defence of high thinking and plain living, together with his useful compilations; * but he had already
appeared as a second Bayard Taylor, the author of a
series of books of travel. *My Winter on the Nile* was perhaps the best. These somewhat literal records, packed
with information, were tokens of this first great age of
tourists, when Americans were swarming abroad, hungry
for every crumb of knowledge, and the "beaten path"
was still a wild adventure.

Warner and Mark Twain,—ardent, optimistic men,
with an all-American vision like Howells's own,—were
comrades-in-arms, with him, in a great crusade. The war,
in breaking down the sections, had rendered a unified nation possible. The sectional schools of writing had passed
or were passing,—the New England school, the Knickerbocker school, the South Carolina school and others,—
and the Middle West and the Far West were finding
voices in Hay and Harte that suggested an all-American
point of view.† Howells, Warner and Mark Twain, who
had lived all over the country, were at one in their desire
to promote this movement; but, while this bond was deep
and real, the three had little in common otherwise. The
irony of Warner's fate lay in his having worked with
Clemens,—the man of talent collaborated with the man
of genius. The result was that this excellent writer, this
competent, ready, industrious craftsman, was only re-

---

* Warner edited the *Library of the World's Best Literature* and the
American Men of Letters series.

† Sectionalism reappeared in the new form of Regionalism in the American literature of the 1930's.

called in later years for the weakest work he ever did.
The Gilded Age, in fact, was a failure for both, although
its name survived as the name of an epoch; and Warner's
failure was remembered because Mark Twain was connected with it. As for Mark Twain, he knew that Colonel
Sellers was the only strong figure in the book, and he
wished to revive this figure and give him a separate existence. It was to help him in this that he called upon
Howells, a far more skillful craftsman than himself. In
the end, he succeeded alone with his play, when Howells,
unlike Warner, found that he could not work with Clemens,—a proof of the independence of Howells's talent. It
was as if Vermeer had tried to work with Rubens, as if
Jane Austen and Henry Fielding had attempted to write
a novel together. But the incident was important for both
these writers. While it threw Mark Twain back on his
own resources, Howells had not wasted his energy. At
this very moment, he was writing plays himself, and the
failure of his attempts to work with Clemens undoubtedly
cleared his mind. One only understands oneself by learning what one cannot do. Howells tried his hand at plays,
as if to make sure of his proper form before he committed himself to novel-writing. He had tested himself,
just so, as a poet and critic, and he carried on all these
lines to the end of his life. He knew they were minor
lines, but he was competent in them all, and no doubt his
experience with them enriched his mind. As for his plays,
they were comedies, and the best were farces.* Like his
own Maxwell, in *The Story of a Play,* he disliked the the-

---

* Howells's one fine comedy was *A Counterfeit Presentment,* the story of
a girl whose heart is broken by an unworthy lover but who is cured by
falling in love with his double. The situation in *Out of the Question,* another of Howells's comedies, might well have been suggested by Mark
Twain's marriage. It is "out of the question" for the young girl to marry
the Western steamboat-mechanic until the mechanic himself, by proving
himself a natural gentleman, makes it "out of the question" for her to re-
fuse him.

atre as much as he liked the drama.* The conditions of
the stage were repugnant to him. This indicated that
Howells was not a playwright born; but he had a gift for
private theatricals,—dramatic chamber-music, as one
might call them. In *The Elevator, The Register, The
Parlour-Car, The Sleeping-Car,* he exploited the possi-
bilities of these inventions. One overheard conversations
through registers, and strange things happened when
elevators refused to budge between the sixth and seventh
floors. Parlour-cars and sleeping-cars lent themselves to
situations. In after years, Howells's farces recalled a moment of history when all these modern toys were excit-
ingly new.

Howells's friendship with Mark Twain had various
repercussions, for each served the other as a foil. Each
became better aware of his quality in contrast with the
other mind, as always happens when men of high talent
meet. They defined themselves in this relation, and, while
both were pliable up to a point, each learned something
from the other. Mark Twain confirmed Howells's American consciousness, which might otherwise have been over-
borne by Boston; and his scorn for all things European
precluded any danger that Howells would follow the
course of Henry James. On the other hand, Mark Twain
deferred to Howells in matters of form and style. In this
he profited greatly, for his feeling for aesthetic values
was uncertain and weak. Howells's delicate taste and skill
checked his genius of improvization, which was always
running wild in absurd caprices. But Mark Twain also fell
a victim to Howells's limitations, for he seldom questioned
the right of his friend to censor and alter his work.

These curious limitations of Howells, his tendency to
the namby-pamby, his prudery and his timorous over-
niceness, were partly temperamental and partly due to

* Howells's attitude towards the theatre was much like Henry James's,
who was similarly repelled by the "sawdust and orange-peel business."

circumstances, his editorship, his marriage, the place and the moment. With a taste for the "cleanly respectabilities," he had avoided "abhorrent contacts," * while still a reporter in Columbus, the contacts with police-stations, saloon-keepers and ward-politicians who represented the seamy side of life. He had a morbid horror of the sordid and ugly; † and this squeamishness had grown on the tender-minded Howells with his life in Venice and later in Cambridge and Boston. In Venice, alone with his wife, he had known few men; and, in fact, Mrs. Howells was more and more a nervous invalid who required, if she did not exact, his continual devotion. He wrote much more for her than for anyone else, and his mind was unconsciously governed by her distaste for all that was disagreeable and unpleasant. He had whimsically complained to Norton that he suffered from "too much female society;" ‡ and, for all his literary friendships, he

* Howells, *Years of My Youth.*

† Edmund Gosse related that in 1882 Howells was planning a novel with scenes laid partly in Hong-Kong. As he bewailed his ignorance of China, Gosse, with much trouble, procured and sent him a detailed report on night-life in Hong-Kong. Howells did not acknowledge this. Later he admitted that he had received it but was so disturbed and horrified that he had burned the report. He dropped all thought of writing about Hong-Kong.

This, however, is not the whole story. Howells, in any case, on second thought, would probably have dropped the idea of writing about China. He never wrote well of things he had not seen. The most incongruous episode in all his fiction is the description of Fenton, in *A Woman's Reason,* cast away on a South Sea island. This was so unreal that it must have taught Howells never to stray again from his chosen world. Similarly, he always failed in verisimilitude when he departed too far from the middle ranks of society. The general feeling was that he failed in his portraits of Boston patricians, as he failed in his portraits of tramps *(Out of the Question)* and Boston working-girls *(A Minister's Charge).*

As for Howells's squeamishness, see his statement about Mark Twain's "Elizabethan breadth of parlance." He would hide away in holes and corners letters from his friend that he could not bear to burn yet could not bear to look at. While he exercised in many ways a beneficent influence over Mark Twain, he was undoubtedly prudish in toning Clemens's language down to the taste of a feminized public.

‡ "I think my state is partly attributable to too much female society; and what becomes of literary men in Paynim lands, where wives, nurses and grandmothers are indefinitely multiplied in households, I couldn't in my enfeebled condition guess."—Letter to Norton, 1868.

was never thrown closely with men. To see the world through the eyes of women, to humour them, to share their interests, to avoid whatever shocked their prepossessions, this was an instinct and a tendency in Howells that his life on *The Atlantic* had confirmed. He had been an editor before he began to write novels, and his mind was further shaped by this ordeal; for the new age of readers was mainly an age of women readers, and his mind was naturally in harmony with this obvious condition.* As an outsider, as one who revered *The Atlantic* and was anxious to forward its interests, he was eager to be so. Thus the editorial habit, with its feeling for the prospective reader, determined the novelist's mind as it were in advance.

All this qualified Howells's realism. His view of life was severely limited, although he was scarcely aware of these limitations. "Nuns fret not at their convent's narrow room;" and there was something nunlike in Howells's Quakerish innocence and simplicity of heart. A deeply truthful nature, both honest and courageous, he shared the

---

* "The man of letters must make up his mind that in the United States the fate of a book is in the hands of the women. It is the women with us who have the most leisure, and they read the most books. They are far better educated, for the most part, than our men, and their tastes, if not their minds, are more cultivated. Our men read the newspapers, but our women read the books."—Howells, *Literature and Life.*

See also the remark of Fulkerson, the promoter of *Every Other Week,* in *A Hazard of New Fortunes:* "We've got to recognize that women form three-fourths of the reading public in this country, and go for their tastes and their sensibilities and their sex-piety along the whole line."

Henry Adams agreed with Howells in his description of the reading public. "I suspect that women are the only readers—five to one—and that one's audience must be created among them. As I see the American man here, he is a negligible quantity. If a *dix-neuvième* is to be built up for America, it must be for—or by—the women."—*Letters of Henry Adams,* 1892–1918.

"It"—*Mont-Saint-Michel and Chartres*—"was meant only for nieces and women, for men no longer read at all, and I've given only to men who asked for it. Indeed I've not given it even to my brothers or nephews. They borrow it from their women-folk if they want it."—Henry Adams, Letter of 1905.

romantic American worship of women.* This did not prevent him from deriding their foibles, but to accept their
"sex-piety," as the editor Fulkerson called it, was second
nature with him as a man and a writer.† His mind was
bathed in a feminine atmosphere, and the air of his stories was sometimes close. He was singularly preoccupied
with domestic matters,‡ and he had a tendency to fuss,
to make too much of trifles, that was also characteristic
of Henry James. The tendency to fuss had always been a
New England trait,§ and the decay of its larger public interests had revived in the Yankee mind this spinsterish
habit. Howells was obliged to reflect it, but he often
seemed to humour the trait. He lent himself to the point
of view of people who magnified scruples and quibbles
into problems of conscience, who thought for days about
some peccadillo that a larger mind would settle and dis-
miss at once. Could a young man offer himself in the waiting-room of a railway station? Was it not wicked to go
driving with a girl one did not "quite respect"? Misunderstandings over such trifles abounded in Howells's
weaker novels, and often formed the substance of the
story. In some of his moral-obstacle races, the obstacles
were cobwebs that a breath of common sense would have
blown away.

Howells's mind, for all this, was large, alert, observant

* "They were Americans, and they knew how to worship a woman."—
Howells, *The Lady of the Aroostook.*

† How honest and courageous Howells was he showed in 1887 in his agitation on behalf of the "Chicago anarchists." This may be contrasted with
his action at the time of the notorious Gorky dinner. He had instinctively
accepted the taboo regarding sexual matters that characterized the mores of
the time, but he was reckless of consequences when he clearly recognized
a call for courage.

‡ There was something indescribably feminine in Howells's burning interest in domestic arrangements and comforts. See the innumerable pages
in *A Hazard of New Fortunes* devoted to the problems of apartment-
hunting, etc. *Their Silver Wedding Journey* abounds in the wildest ex-
cesses of domesticity.

§ Ever since John Cotton set all Massachusetts agog over the question
whether women should wear veils.

and witty, and the world that appeared in his novels was a revelation. For here was the real American scene, reflected in a burnished mirror, as no American eye had ever perceived it. This was not the romanticized scene of Cooper, or Hawthorne's crepuscular world, or the rudely drawn reality of Mrs. Stowe, still less the distorted scene of the ordinary novels, those formless, artificial, sentimental inventions that passed, in 1870, as reflections of life. There were no heroes or heroines here "dying for each other," no turgid flights of fancy or exaggerations, but a manifold assemblage of Yankees, New Yorkers, Southerners, Westerners, all in their habits as they were, going about their business in the morning sunlight. Aware as Howells was of Europe, which often appeared in these novels, he saw his people in terms of themselves and their country, moving in their own orbit, under their own American sky, in all the actuality of their daily existence; for he had followed Emerson's counsel, not seeking the great, the remote, the romantic, but sitting at the feet of the low and familiar. His work was an ample reply to those for whom America was not sufficiently rich and complex in its types to provide a novelist with subject-matter. In range and variety, his portrait-gallery was second to none; and so truthfully drawn were all his people that every reader exclaimed at once, Yes, this is right, how well I know them! They all assumed flesh and blood at once. For Howells's eye for detail in their costume and appearance was as subtle as his knowledge of their motives. And how natural were his conversations, what an ear he had for shades of distinction in tone between regions and classes, the rustic and the urban, the Western, the Virginian, three or four kinds of Bostonians and the people of Maine! Add to this Howells's style, so limpid and precise, so animated, gay, adroit and fresh, and one could understand the joy with which his American readers acclaimed this panorama of their charms and their foibles.

While New England, for a number of years, was Howells's central *mise en scène,* his mind from the first was
continental. If he had a purpose, this was to reconcile sections and classes in a broadly democratic feeling for life;
and, in order to bring them together, he often presented
his people as travellers, who meet in hotels, in stations, on
trains, on steamboats. One gathered from his novels that
Americans were always moving, always going or coming,
abroad or at home; and, in fact, in this respect, these
novels reflected the post-war years and Howells's own
habit as a constant tourist. In one of his tales, the girl was
married in a storage-warehouse. She had been meeting
the young man there for years, for the families had been
twenty times "in and out of storage." But how, except as
travellers, in a country so diversified, could Howells have
assembled so many varieties of people? Where could
Kitty Ellison of Eriecreek, New York, have met Mr.
Arbuton of Boston except on a Saint Lawrence river-
boat? Where, save on the "Aroostook," could Lydia
Blood have fallen in with Staniford and Dunham? Only
in Venice could Lily Mayhew have told the Austrian officer that her home was in Patmos, New York; and only in
a station or a summer hotel could the South have encountered the West in the casual, natural fashion of Howells's
novels. Accordingly, for settings, he liked these fortuitous
meeting-places, where his fellow-Americans gathered on
a neutral ground; and he shared all their pleasure in the
bustle of travel, in the chaos of docks and wharves, in the
rattle of baggage, in the jolting of stages and coaches, in
the views from the trains. How charming, as one sped
past, the sight of a woodcutter's shanty, losing itself
among the shadows in a solitude of the hills! How amusing to sit in a waiting-room and establish fanciful relations with people whom one saw for half a minute!
Howells delighted in these adventures, in the hissing and
coughing of locomotives under the flaring gas-jets of *

station at night, in the odour of paint and carpet that prevailed on the steamboats, in the tinkle of the ice-water
pitchers, in the cinders on the trains, in the Negro waiters, the porters, the conductors, the drummers, whom he
viewed with Walt Whitman's benevolent eye. What joy,
as he conveyed it, to receive your stateroom-key an hour
before departure on the Albany night-boat, well knowing
it would be light enough until you reached West Point to
see the best scenery on the river! How pleasant, on a
summer evening, on the Nantasket boat, as you sat on
your camp-stool on the deck, to feel the air freshening,
while you watched the gay life of the harbour, while the
islands of the bay waxed and waned and Boston slowly
vanished in the hazy distance! Was there ever such up-
holstery and music as one found on the Fall River boat!
Such gorgeously carpeted cabins, such a glitter of glass,
such a multitude of plush chairs and sofas! Or such mirrors as one found in the great hotels in Portland and
Boston, such tessellated floors and marble mantels, such
acres of Brussels carpet and glossy paint, so many var-
nished tables and fluted pillars! Howells's people moved
about their world in the perpetual presence of these mild
marvels, with a chorus of customs officials and conde-
scending hotel-clerks, stewardesses, cabin-boys and consuls.

This was the "young country" that Europeans talked
about, and the moon that overlooked it was of lucent
honey. In the foreground of every American landscape
one saw a bridal pair, at Mount Desert or Niagara, on
the Florida keys; and Howells was an accomplice of all
the lovers. Was not this country a larger Arcady? It struck
him so, at moments, in the presence of all these shepherdesses and shepherds. Wherever he looked there were
brides and brides, charmingly dressed, with ravishing toi-
lets. How small their gloves were, how high the heels of
their little boots, over which the snowy skirts electrically
fluttered! Howells was a born match-maker; he delighted

in a pretty woman; he had an eye for every touch of style, and he liked to show how naturally the simplest American village girl assumed the grace and elegance of the world of fashion. All his "young ladies" were "stylish," wherever they came from, whether the Lapham girls or Helen Harkness, with her vividly birdlike mobility, or Lydia, from South Bradfield, where the village seamstress had studied the paper patterns and *Harper's Bazar,* while she observed the costumes of the summer boarders; and Howells shrewdly noted the trifles of behaviour that so often carried the day in his game of love. A girl ran up the steps of a house with the loop of her train in her hand, or she wore the special "light hat" that settled the question, or she poked with her parasol a shaving on the pavement which the young man was holding with his foot. She changed the bow at her throat from scarlet to crimson, or perhaps she laughed at everything, not because she was amused but because she was happy. She always knew just how she looked; she always knew, like Howells, what she was doing. The parents often stood in awe of these phantoms of delight, deferring to their knowledge of the world; and Howells shared all their tender solicitude for them. He loved to see them piloted into safe harbours. With what distress he hovered over Helen Harkness, when she lost father, house and money and helplessly floundered in Boston to keep afloat! With what anxious care he followed Egeria, in *The Undiscovered Country,* drifting about the roads with the visionary doctor, until she found a haven with the Vardley Shakers!— and he liked to picture Lydia as the idol of the ship, with its pride and chivalrous sentiment revolving round her. When Lydia boards the "Aroostook," what pleasure the fatherly captain takes in making her feel at home in the little white cabin, with the rug that his wife has hooked and the gimcracks left by the girls and all as snug and tidy as a farmhouse kitchen.

Howells's world was a paradise of lovers, though the centre of his picture was not love. He was in reaction against the old romancers who saw love in a monstrous disproportion to the other relations of life. But his earlier novels especially abounded in love-scenes,—love in a blueberry-patch, in a sailboat, a rowboat,—and some of these were exquisitely felt. Such was the scene in *The Undiscovered Country* when the journalist Ford and Egeria, on opposite sides of the grapevine, find each other. No word of love passes between them, and yet, across the screen of vines, as they catch occasional glimpses through the leaves and the tendrils, they establish a perfect understanding. Howells excelled in these idyllic moments, and it was not from any fault of his if a life of endless holidays did not lie beyond them. He knew how often marriages failed,—in *A Modern Instance* he pictured a failure,—but, if he had had his way, the course of love would always have run smooth. Romeo would have saved his Juliet, and somehow Hamlet would have regained Ophelia. In fact, his people were usually happy. His nature obliged him to see them so, as he naturally saw human beings doing the decent, honest thing. His world was one of mutual trust, and Dr. Boynton's faith in people, when this Alcott who never found his Concord set forth on the road without a penny, confident that doors would open for him, was reflected in Howells's general view of life. His Dr. Ellisons abounded in self-respecting candour, his Kittys never imagined themselves misprized for anything but a fault. His policemen were kind and obliging; and if, in his New England, you went out for a walk, and the rain overtook you in the country, you could borrow a waterproof at the nearest schoolhouse. You could leave the waterproof with the station-master, knowing that the stage-driver would safely return it. Howells's Americans were all a natural family, and family loyalty was his favourite theme. His novels were full of loyal

households, the Maverings, and the Coreys, the Gay-
lords, the Laphams, and Howells delighted in testing the
bonds that held them together, conjugal, maternal, paternal and filial. With what pleasure he showed how Dan
Mavering, the young man in *April Hopes,* awoke to his
father's intellectual interests! How proud the Laphams
were of one another, the more they plumbed the probity
in each! Howells grieved over the inequalities that kept
his worthy people apart, and he liked to show how trifling
their differences were. Staniford quickly penetrated beneath Lydia's rustic phrases. Mr. Corey was ready to find
that the bull-headed Lapham was the soul of honour.
Howells resented only those who broke this law of trust
that bound his Americans together,—the arrogant, the
vulgar, the pretentious. He liked to show how far from
vulgar the apparently vulgar could be, how the poetry of
Lapham's paint redeemed him; but he could not abide
presumption, pretension or sham. Profoundly anti-aristo-
cratic, he treated his real patricians, the Bellinghams and
the Coreys, with understanding; but he was merciless to
those who presumed on their caste. With what cold scorn
he pictured Mr. Arbuton, the little Boston prig in *A
Chance Acquaintance,* who slighted the charming, imaginative Western girl! This was the poor young man who
felt that he honoured the farm in Quebec by saying it was
just like Normandy and "expected the cows to be grate-
ful." With what zest Basil March rallied his wife, who
was a bitter aristocrat at heart, when she took for a foreign nobleman the haughty commercial traveller with the
stare that indicated his long descent! It was notable that
Howells's blackguards were often newspaper-men, like
Bittredge, in *The Kentons,* and Bartley Hubbard, who
broke his law of mutual trust with their prying disregard
of human dignity and rights. Like Henry James and
Henry Adams, he detested these glib young journalists
who represented the new publicity. As an old newspaper-

man, he disliked to see this new type pushing aside the journalist with a feeling for letters.

As Howells advanced, his more serious novels reflected, one by one, the changing conditions and phases of American life. *The Undiscovered Country* described the rise of spiritualism at the time when Mrs. Eddy was settling in Boston, the queer streets where the mediums lived, with "Madam" on their door-plates, and the air was full of astral manifestations. Egeria and Dr. Boynton were types of the moment, as Marcia Gaylord was in *A Modern Instance;* for the growth of divorce was another sign of the times. *The Rise of Silas Lapham* was the best of all the pictures of the new self-made millionaires, and *A Woman's Reason* presented another type of the eighties, the girl setting out to make a living in open competition with the world of men. Through decade after decade, Howells followed the life of the nation, and he caught so many of its phases that as a social historian he had no equal. No doubt, he was most at home in domestic relations. His portraits of women perhaps were the best of all, and he aroused a passion of protest with his realistic record of their foibles and their instinct for manœuvre. An age of "feminization" was not prepared for this particular aspect of the Howells mirror, for these women with their strategic headaches, these mothers who feed on their daughters, who carry on a system of strikes and lock-outs and whose cabins, when they travel, are smugglers' dens. But Howells's portrait-gallery was varied and large. He knew the town and the village, the farm and the city, the factory, the business-office and the lumber-camp, the artisan, the idler, the preacher, the teacher; and he pictured artists and editors, shop-girls and students, American scholars in Italy, professors at home, religious impostors, philanthropists, helpless parents, manufacturers, scientists, journalists, country squires, hotel-keepers, lawyers, sterile dilettanti,

the hare-brained villager and the village fool. All these
people were admirably real, and they recalled in later
times a prosperous, buoyant American age when everyone
"got on" and most were happy. If there were other stories, these were true also; and Howells himself told some
of the other stories. His vision darkened as he advanced
in life. But, while he lacked a certain intensity, his writing
never lost the charm of a truthful, candid, cheerful, hopeful temper. Howells was the most winning of American
writers.

CHAPTER XI

HOWELLS AND JAMES

THE JAMESES had settled in Cambridge a few
months after the Howellses, and Howells and the
younger Henry James had soon become intimate friends.
James was six years the junior,—he was born in 1843;
but he had already published several stories when Howells, who was struck by his *Poor Richard,* encouraged him
to write for *The Atlantic.* James abashed Howells a little
with his air of worldly maturity, but the two had almost
everything in common.

For a good part of nine years, while James lived in
Cambridge,—he was absent for two or three years on
journeys abroad,—the friends had been constantly together.* They walked together at all hours, perhaps to
the Botanical Garden, where they sat and talked in the
sun on the edge of the hotbeds, pushing their walking-
sticks into the sandy path when the talk grew too exciting. On Sunday afternoons, they sometimes strolled to
Fresh Pond, where, as they rowed about on the placid
water, they discussed the stories they were writing. They
rambled at night all over Cambridge, debating methods
of fiction, and James told Howells, in the interest of art,
the picturesque tale of his uncles and cousins. They read
their work to one another under the kerosene lamp at
Howells's, where James ate nothing at dinner, or only
crumbled a biscuit; for he was a constant sufferer from

* Henry James was in Cambridge during the years 1866–1869, 1870–
1872, 1874–1875. He came back again in 1881 and 1882, returning to England in 1883. Thereafter he did not visit America until 1904.

indigestion.* Both were planning American novels, and
their European sympathies were closely related. Howells
was under the spell of Italy, and James loved Italy also,
though his literary predilections were all for France.

While the Jameses had come to live in New England,
they were even more alien there than Howells, whose
mind had been largely formed on the Yankee writers.
Henry James, as a boy in New York, had caught the New
England atmosphere in one or two of his playmates who
had come from this region, a suggestion of apples, nuts
and cheese, of doughnuts and personal toughness, a hardihood that went with Bible-reading; but he had not even
read Hawthorne when he came to Newport,—except for
The Wonder-Book and the *Twice-Told Tales,*—and he
had been moved about so much, in the wandering life of
his family, that he was almost as alien on the banks of the
Hudson. As a child, he had met his father's circle, the
New York illuminati and a few from Boston, Washington Irving, Sumner, Curtis, Ripley. But his "huge queer
country" in general was a puzzle to him. The family had
few associations with the roots of American history. If
their forbears whipped the redcoats in the good old days,
the Jameses apparently never heard it mentioned. Had
they ever heard discussions of Yorktown and Valley
Forge, Mount Vernon, the Tripoli pirates or Lake Erie,
the sort of discussions that flourished in most American
households with a long transmitted interest in the country? There was no evidence of it in the writings of the
Jameses; and they had few rural associations that connect
the mind with the soul of the country,—their Albany
counted for something, but not much. The elder James

* At this time Henry and William James were both semi-invalids. "The
unpublished parts of the correspondence between William and Henry
James are very largely composed of hygienic, symptomatic and therapeutic
details. Their interest in one another's condition of health was equalled
only by their faith in their own remedies."—Ralph Barton Perry, *The
Thought and Character of William James.*

was inveterately urban and was even obliged to live in
towns, for, having lost one of his legs, he depended on
cabs and adequate pavements. Moreover, the Jameses,—
"hotel children," floating vaguely about the world,—
knew nothing of politics or business, the primary occupations of their sex. The historical instinct of the country
was scarcely in them, though the elder James was American through and through.* In later years, William James
adjusted himself to this condition; he over-adjusted himself, in fact, a little. For was not his "plunge into the
muddy stream of things" a more or less conscious reaction against this detachment? He might have been described as more American than the Americans, as Henry
James was less, or, rather, different,—he became more
English than the English. Both had to fight for a local
foothold, and both were constrained to overdo it. Meanwhile, Henry was "at sea" about his "native land" and all
it represented for a story-teller.†

When he arrived in Cambridge, therefore, James's
mind was torn already by a problem that he never really
solved. He was bent on becoming a novelist, but novelists
always had "native lands:" this was the most obvious fact
about them. He recognized this fact in his critical writings,‡ and that he was aware of what it meant in regard

---

* It should be added that Henry James was deeply impressed by the
Civil War, from which two of his brothers, who fought, returned with
broken health. See the account of his hour of "consecration," after a visit
to the camp of wounded soldiers at Portsmouth Grove, near Newport.
Thenceforward he thought of the literary life as "something definitely and
firmly parallel to action in the tented field."—*Notes of a Son and Brother,*
317-8.

† "It was a joke, polished by much use, that I was dreadfully at sea
about my native land."—Henry James, *Essays in London.*

In *Notes of a Son and Brother,* James described himself as "a young
person reaching the age of twenty in well-nigh grotesque unawareness of
the properties of the atmosphere in which he but wanted to claim that he
had been nourished."

‡ E.g., apropos of Turgenev: "[His] works savour strongly of his native
soil, like those of all great novelists, and give one who has read them all
a strange sense of having had a prolonged experience of Russia."—*French
Poets and Novelists.*

to his own ambitions one saw in his hesitation to leave the country.* Hawthorne had shown him that one might be an American novelist without "going outside" about it.† Indeed, when Hawthorne went outside and wrote about the Roman scene he seemed to be divested of half his virtue: he "forfeited a precious advantage in ceasing to tread his native soil," as James observed later in his life of Hawthorne. This showed that the "American matter" was vital·to the "American hand," as the English, French, Russian or whatever matter was vital to the hands he most admired; while, as for himself, vague as he was about America, he felt he could scarcely endure an American existence. He had been struck too deeply by the "outland dart," he had absorbed the "European virus." ‡ As a boy in New York, he had missed no contributive image that went to form a picture of Washington Square,§ and his later impressions of Boston were equally sharp; but

* This problem was obviously central in James's mind during all the years that he lived uneasily in Cambridge. It remained central in his mind long after he had settled abroad. "I know what I am about, and I have always my eyes on my native land."—Letter to William James, 1878.

† Notes of a Son and Brother.

‡ "A return to America"—in 1870—"was to drag with it . . . the torment of losses and regrets. The repatriated victim of that unrest was, beyond doubt, acutely conscious of his case: the fifteen months just spent in Europe had absolutely determined his situation. The nostalgic poison had been distilled for him, the future presented to him but as a single intense question: was he to spend it in brooding exile, or might he somehow come into his 'own'?—as I liked betimes to put it for a romantic analogy with the state of dispossessed princes and wandering heirs."—Preface to The Reverberator.

§ Washington Square remained to the end of James's life his closest point of attachment to the land of his forbears. There was a touch of poetry in all his allusions to it, in spite of the "inexpensive ailanthus" that garnished the square in his novel about it. It is in lower Fifth Avenue that Bernard Longueville, in Confidence, scatters the dry autumn leaves. "He tossed them with his stick as he passed; they rustled and murmured with the motion, and it reminded him of the way he used to kick them in front of him over these same pavements in his riotous infancy." This image and situation recur in James's writings, early and late. Where, in his childhood, an American has first shuffled his autumn leaves, that is where his heart lies, there he belongs. James always thought of himself as a New Yorker, and he called his collected edition the "New York Edition."

he had heard his parents sighing for Piccadilly, Windsor
and Kew, and far more real to him than the scenes about
him were those he found in *Punch,* in Leech's drawings,
in Thackeray, Dickens and Trollope. Before he happened upon Hawthorne, these English writers had filled
his mind, and he knew the names of the London streets
as he never knew the streets of New York,—Drury Lane,
the Row, Kensington Gardens, with the little boys in
Eton jackets, the costermongers, the bathing-machines
and all the familiar images of the English picture. At
twelve, with infant memories of an earlier visit, he had
been taken abroad for four more years. In Switzerland,
France and England, drifting from school to school and
from pension to pension, he had learned languages, read
novels and especially gathered impressions that made a
return to his country look like failure. America, for him,
afforded no objects of interest to compare with this European "fantastication."

The problem in question remained on James's hands
unsolved during all the years that he was to spend in
Cambridge. By the nature of the case, he could not solve
it. He met it, as he met all his problems, just as his
brother did, by "pragmatizing," by acting as if they were
solved when he could not solve them. Years later, when
William James explained this "way of thinking," he saw
how far he had lived in accordance with it,*—how he
had let the problem drop, in the hope that it would solve
itself, after trying and failing to solve it by direct attack.
That he tried hard to solve it one saw in his earlier stories, in which he showed with what determination he
strove to meet the exactions of the "native soil," to become an American novelist, a successor of Hawthorne.
For, as to his being a novelist, this question was settled,

* "I was lost in the wonder of the extent to which all my life I have
(like M. Jourdain) unconsciously pragmatized."—Letter to William James,
on the appearance of *Pragmatism,* 1907.

whatever the conditions might be. No one had ever possessed a clearer vocation, and his mind was an inexhaustible well of stories. He could find, not sermons, but stories in stones, if the native soil, or the foreign, was beyond his grasp; and it might have been presumed that, if he could not grasp his own, the soil of other countries would elude him. He could always count on a fund of stories, and, as for the art of telling them, this was the joy of his life and always had been. He had been studying fiction almost before he attempted to write it. That he "read too many novels" was the burden of the complaint against him, in so far as his family circle indulged in complaints, and that one should *not* do as one chose, not exercise one's absolute liberty, was the only real ground of complaint in the house of the Jameses. No one was better aware than he of the efflorescence of French fiction that marked the years when his mind was coming of age. One of his early tutors was the son of Töpffer, who told him tales of literary Paris, and John La Farge at Newport had amplified the picture with his personal recollections of the later writers. If John La Farge had not known Balzac, he had met, at his cousin's house in Paris, Flaubert, Gautier, Daudet, the Goncourts and others who had since become the objects of James's study. Moreover, James had met Thackeray, his father's friend in Paris, who had called upon the family in New York. He had met Dickens at Norton's house, as Howells had met him at Longfellow's; and he had seen George Eliot on a visit to England, along with Tennyson, Ruskin and William Morris. He might have felt that he too was a link in the "apostolic succession," especially as some of these eminences admired his work.* He spoke with an authority in

* James's early work immediately impressed numbers of the distinguished older writers on both sides of the Atlantic. Lowell reviewed him with high praise. William James reported to him in 1869 a remark of Emerson's son that his father "does nothing but talk of your letters,"—James's travel-letters in *The Nation.* In *The Middle Years,* describing his visit to

his earliest reviews, which were followed by other notes on travel and painting, that showed an extraordinary knowledge of the art of fiction. He also wrote on Swinburne, Whitman, Browning, Morris and Matthew Arnold. His first "consecration to letters" had occurred in 1864, in the golden brown study at "Shady Hill;" and he had been taken up at once by the circle of editorial friends, Norton, Lowell, Fields, Godkin, Howells. James and Howells met as aspirants for American fiction and as students and followers of realism, the great new movement. For realism was coming in, along with "scientific history," as one of the marks of an age that was governed by science.

A mediator between these friends was Thomas Sergeant Perry, who was also deeply interested in the art of fiction. Like others in the Cambridge circle and elsewhere in New England,—the younger women as well as the younger men,—he had seen at once that realism was the art of the future. Perry, a grandson of Commodore Perry,—the "Lake Erie" commodore whose brother had opened Japan,—had known the Jameses well in their boyhood at Newport, where his older sister married John La Farge. He had rambled with Henry James along the beaches and over the Paradise Rocks, discussing Fourier's plan for redeeming the world,—one of the favourite themes of Henry's father; or, as more often happened, painting and fiction. Once Henry, who had been reading Ruskin, carefully copied a leaf with his pencil, and he made a faithful drawing of a rock. Now and again, they had put off in a sailboat, well-stocked for an all-day trip

Tennyson, James records that Tennyson "superlatively commended" one of his tales. Ruskin, who was delighted with a paper of James on Tintoretto, afterwards reprinted in *Transatlantic Sketches,* told Norton that henceforward he would "count Harry among the men for whom he should especially work."

with their chosen authors, Balzac, Victor Cherbuliez or Alfred de Musset. Perry had gone to Germany with William James and lived with him at Berlin as a fellow-student, at a time when the Americans at this German university outnumbered all other foreigners put together. There the mercurial William James had ranged over medicine, chemistry, languages, literature, public affairs and the traits of nations, and nothing stirred his mind more than the French and German novels,—the new realistic novels,—which he read with zest. He drew deep draughts of human nature from them. He even reviewed them for *The Nation;* and, from this German vantage-point, while Henry was in Cambridge, he sent his brother suggestions that he thought might please him, urging him to write essays on Balzac and George Sand, which Henry was already contemplating, and especially to read Gautier's travel-sketches. In all this, Perry was William James's comrade-in-arms, for Perry was roaming through literature as William James roamed through life. Perry was an omnivorous reader, as Howells saw at once, when Henry James brought the two together. For William James and his literary comrade had soon returned to Cambridge, where Perry became a tutor in French and German.

Thus Henry James and Howells, deep in the problems of novel-writing, formed a triumvirate with Perry, who was better-informed than either of them. For instance, he had discovered Turgenev at a moment when few writers of English were aware of such a thing as a Russian novel. A first-rate classical scholar, he also taught Sanskrit, and he was scarcely less interested in painting and science. In later years, in France, where he had known Turgenev, Perry became an intimate friend of Monet, and he knew John Fiske as well as James and Howells. His last book was a life of Fiske, and he followed the evolutionary method in his critical writings. He was all but universally curious, and his studies in three literatures were admirable in substance and in style.* Alike in his talk and his writing, he abounded in brilliant *obiter dicta,* and his feeling for modern fiction was clairvoyant. He was the chief reviewer of novels for *The Nation,* and he wrote for *The Atlantic* for several years all its reviews and notices of foreign books. His supple mind, rarely intuitive, divined the currents of modern thought, and he seemed to know the significant works of writers almost before they appeared,—his recognition of them was prompt and final. Howells and Perry, acting together, kept *The Atlantic* well abreast of all the new developments in the world of letters, and Perry wrote articles on Turgenev, Auerbach, Fritz Reuter, Cherbuliez, Victor Hugo, George Sand and others.† He translated several of Turgenev's novels, beginning with *Virgin Soil.*‡ He introduced Turgenev to James and Howells, both of whom, as novelists, were influenced by him as much as by anyone else, native or for-

---

* Perry's most important work was *A History of Greek Literature,* 1890. On a scale slightly smaller, it was incomparably finer in literary feeling than Ticknor's *History of Spanish Literature.* Less useful as a work of reference, it revealed a remarkable breadth of sympathy in regard to art and science and most of the major literatures, ancient and modern. The author's use of the evolutionary method was well shown in the treatment of the Greek drama. Perry's *English Literature in the Eighteenth Century* was rather a discursive essay than a history proper. *From Opitz to Lessing* was a good sketch of German literature in the formative years that preceded its efflorescence. Perry edited with Howells *The Library of Adventure by Sea and Land.*

† Between the years 1868–1883,—roughly, the years of Howells's editorship,—*The Atlantic* also published papers on Stendhal, Dostoievsky, the Goncourts, Flaubert, Zola (three articles), Mérimée, Mistral, Alfred de Musset, Baudelaire, Gautier, Björnson, Bourget, Renan, Sainte-Beuve, Scribe, Dumas the elder, etc. Among the writers of these papers, besides Howells, James and Perry, were Brander Matthews and Eugene Benson, the New York painter.

‡ From the French and German versions. Perry learned Russian later in the days when other New Englanders, Isabel S. Hapgood and Nathan Haskell Dole, were translating Turgenev and Tolstoy directly from it.

eign.* The vogue of Turgenev spread rapidly;† there seemed to be an occult connection between the Russian novelist and the young post-war Americans, both men and women. Nourished, in his far-off Russia, on English authors, Turgenev had grown up in a great wooden manorhouse, like an American Southerner on a primitive plantation. In his student days, he was called "the American," because he admired the Western republic, and, although he was not a reformer in temper, his writings had served the cause of reform: his *Sportsman's Sketches,* published in the same year as *Uncle Tom's Cabin,* had paralleled the American book as an agent of emancipation.‡ He had followed the growth of American literature, and by 1873 he had read Hawthorne, Whitman, Bret Harte and Howells.§ Disheartened by the turmoil of his country, he had settled in western Europe, as many of the new Americans were settling there, because they too were lost in the transition from an old regime to a new; although, far from losing touch with Russia, he brooded over all its problems, so like the American problems in various ways. One of these resemblances, in the younger generation, lay in the relation of the sexes. In the disorganized state of

* In *My Literary Passions,* Howells says that he read Turgenev over and over, more than anyone else. "The man who has set the standard for the novel of the future is Turgenev."—Letter of Howells, 1877. Turgenev, in turn, greatly admired Howells. See the letter of President Hayes in Howells's *Letters,* I, 280. James paid countless tributes to the "beautiful genius."

† See, in Howells's *April Hopes,* chapter XIII, the conversation on Turgenev among the ladies on the hotel-piazza at Campobello. There is another conversation on Turgenev in Howells's *Indian Summer,* Chapter V.

‡ "You may imagine how Turgenev's eyes stood out of his head on the day when he met Mrs. Harriet Beecher Stowe . . . who was introduced to him as being the heroine that had made the chains to fall from the limbs of the slaves of a continent . . . He said that she seemed to him to be a modest and sensible person . . . Perhaps the reader will think out for himself all that that amazing meeting signified."—Ford Madox Ford, *Portraits from Life.*

§ See Yarmolinsky, *Turgenev, the Man, his Art and his Age,* 330-331. It may be added that Emerson and Cooper are among the authors mentioned by the young intelligentsia in Turgenev's *Fathers and Sons.*

Russia, the young men were bewildered. They were ineffectual, divided, hesitant, weak, with all their good intentions, for their function in the body politic was obscure.
They were debarred from public life, much as the young
Americans were,—for somewhat different reasons, to be
sure,—and they were unmanned by this, their morale was
low; while the young Russian women, calm, steadfast,
passionate, eager for danger and hardship in the name of
love, were strong and complete beside them. So it appeared at least in Turgenev's vision, and a similar condition prevailed in America in these days of the "reign of
womanhood" and all it stood for. Were not James's and
Howells's novels the proof of this? In James more than
in Howells, but largely in both, the younger women
eclipsed the younger men. Howells's older men were sufficiently potent, but how many of his younger men were
light and vague, amateur artists or amateurs in life,—
like James's,—irresolute, indecisive, often flimsy, hovering about the girls in hotels or on shipboard, with an air
of apologizing for their want of purpose! They seemed
to be waiting for a breeze, their sails were flapping, and
the women supplied the breeze, for, with all their "tastes,"
they seldom had any masculine force or motive. In both
these writers, the masculine sex appeared to exist, even in
England, in order to fall in love with American girls.*
The young American men were the victims of conditions
that resembled in part the conditions of Turgenev's Russia. There was nothing to hold them up, they were all at
sea; and "the sex that discriminates most finely" † had all
the honours in American fiction and art as it had in life.
The sovereign charm of the young women was the one triumphant fact of an age and a civilization that had little
to boast of; and even Henry Adams's Virgin of Chartres

* See Lord Rainford in Howells's *A Woman's Reason* and countless
other instances in both Howells and James.
† Henry James, *Portraits of Places*.

was as much an American girl in essence * as the heroines
of James and Howells and Saint-Gaudens's Diana. The
American man was a "failure," Henry Adams thought,
and Turgenev's Russian man was a failure also; and Turgenev's enchanting young girls, ardent, shy, all of a piece,
seemed much like American girls to American readers.
The pages of *The Atlantic* were thronged with letters on
these Mariannes and Natalies and Lisas. For the rest,
how American were the traits of the Russians in *Smoke*,
their tall talk, their liking for new ideas, political, psychological and social, their recentness and the vastness of
their country! In 1874, Henry James the elder wrote to
Turgenev at Carlsbad, when the younger Henry had published an essay on him. This letter was both charming and
discerning. The old man wished to say with what un-
feigned delight their Cambridge circle had read Turgenev's novels, what multitudes of Americans read him
and how they talked about him often, in the evening, on
the piazza, facing the sunset. If ever he crossed the
ocean, he must come to Cambridge. Between the fumes of
his pipe, he could tell them what his eye divined, either of
promise or menace, in their civilization. Turgenev, who
was touched, replied that, although he did not smoke, he
would enjoy a quiet evening with them.

Turgenev left long traces in American letters. Perry
left traces, too, below the surface. An unambitious man,
self-effacing and wholly indifferent to fame, he was one of
many writers in this epoch who felt no special incentive
to continue at work. He produced three or four fine
books; then he serenely cultivated his garden in silence.
This man of rare intelligence was the friend of many

---

* "She was still a woman, who loved grace, beauty, ornament . . . and
liked both light and colour . . . She was extremely sensitive to neglect, to
disagreeable impressions, to want of intelligence in her surroundings . . .
Her taste was infallible," etc.—Henry Adams, *Mont-Saint-Michel and
Chartres*. Adams's Virgin of Chartres suggests in many ways such Henry
James heroines as Isabel Archer.

eminent scholars, and he taught for a while in a Japanese
university, as professor of English literature, like Lafcadio Hearn. At seventy, enthralled by Chekhov, he mastered Russian. He visited Russia, to see the Moscow Art
Theatre, and he ranged with zest afterwards over the
whole of Russian literature. He read with his finger-tips.
His apprehension was so quick that, while he was cutting
the pages of books, he felt obliged to hold them upside
down, so as not to absorb them all before he read them.
Fifty years after these early Cambridge days, he was
alert for new and fine creations.* His insight was prophetic.† But of all his manifold services to American
letters none bore better fruit than his influence as a student of fiction on James and Howells.

This widespread interest in fiction, in the new mode of
realism, was a natural effect of the moment. Just as in
Greece, in the days of Euripides, when the age of the interest in heroes had passed, the popular mind was drawn
away from the contemplation of grandeurs and mysteries
to the careful observation of human traits. Human nature
in all its complexity became a sufficient field of interest,
and minds that had once been concerned with principles
and lofty teachings devoted themselves with zest to the
study of manners. This inevitable tendency of all post-
heroic ages was reinforced at present by the spread of science, which attracted the mind away from itself to the
world of outer experience and all the wondrous fruits of
observation. Science revealed the importance of environment, the power of material conditions over the psyche,
and the half-romantic Balzac and his realistic French successors gradually brought the novel to terms with science:
they proposed to exhibit the types and classes of men as
zoology and botany exhibited plants and animals. This

* Edwin Arlington Robinson, who edited Perry's *Letters,* called him
"one of the great appreciators, without whom there would be no great
writers, or artists of any sort."
† See this remarkable statement, written in 1887, in Perry's *The Evolu-*

notion of fiction as one of the branches of natural history removed all the mystery from life: whatever was romantic, heroic, distinguished was revealed as an effect of natural causes, and more and more the novel devoted itself to picturing life as ordinary people lived it. As with the naturalist, so with the novelist, who also called himself a naturalist soon, the "document," the "fact" was all-sufficient; and a somewhat sober and literal style replaced the styles of the older writers, as if the facts of life were too important to be hidden under literary splendours. Realism, naturalism, the child of science and positivism, was allied with the democratic movement, and it flew the banner of "truth" on its forward march. Let the truth prevail, abolish all the mysteries: the facts of life revealed were the whole of life. Such was the art of fiction, as "history" and as "nature," that an age of science demanded, achieved and worshipped.

This realistic method arose in all the Western countries, spontaneously, inevitably, following similar general causes. No one invented it: it came. Howells was a realist before he ever heard the word,—he had written realistic sketches as a boy in Ohio, sketches "as natural as the tooth-ache," his father called them. Realism was only relatively new. In England, Defoe was a realist, and even Jane Austen. Howells, who knew these writers well, was also impressed by Goldoni, whose realistic plays, of the late eighteenth century, had struck his imagination when he saw them in Venice. Howells had developed his own realistic method, and Turgenev rather confirmed than de-

tion of the Snob: "It should be said that if *le monde s'américanise,* as desponding European writers are prone to say, it will alter slowly, for one peculiarly American quality is its intense conservatism: it adheres with, on the whole, wonderful tenacity to what has won the approval of Europe. These questions, it seems, will rather be decided by the Russians, who appear to be destined to take the place long held by the French; that, namely, of becoming the Greeks of modern times,—in other words, the people who shall carry out their ideas in action, who put their theories into practice."

termined this method: he confirmed it with his plotless
novels and his grouping of three or four persons whose
interwoven fates alone concerned him. Turgenev charmed
Howells and James with his poetry and his reticence; but
Howells's own personality ordained his method. By temperament anti-romantic, he was also highly susceptible to
changes of literary weather; and the realistic view of
life, which he drew as it were out of the air, appealed to
his democratic instinct. He did not believe in heroes and
extraordinary people. But science had intensified the realistic impulse, and the Yankee mind in general was prepared for this movement. It had produced realistic stories
before Howells and James appeared, in fact. Mrs. Stowe
had established her pattern before the Civil War, when
Mrs. Cooke had also begun to write, and Elizabeth Stoddard's *The Morgesons, Two Men* and *Temple House*
had appeared by 1867. These three precursors of Miss
Jewett and Miss Wilkins were all realistic, more or less,
although Mrs. Stowe was mainly historical,—she pictured a world that was past or passing,—and Mrs.
Cooke's tales were too often factitious, and Elizabeth
Stoddard's novels were all too dim. This Massachusetts
girl who had gone to New York, as the wife of the poet
Stoddard, had written and published her books during
the war-years. Hawthorne had mildly praised *The Morgesons,* and indeed, in all these cluttered novels, formless
and overcrowded with irrelevant details, one felt the
glow of an ardent nature and a notable gift of observation. In effect, they were pallid imitations of the Brontës,
through which the New England setting glimmered
faintly. But, with Mrs. Cooke's work and Mrs. Stowe's,
they marked a change of feeling, none the less. One of the
clearest symptoms of this change of feeling was Mrs.
Stowe's attack on Byron, which advanced the cause of
realism indirectly. Lady Byron's death in 1860 had re-
newed the discussions of her marriage: she was denounced

for having ruined her husband's life, and Mrs. Stowe, to
whom she had told her story, had poured the story out in
defence of her friend. The scandal had rocked *The Atlantic,* in which it appeared. It almost wrecked the magazine,
for it alienated hundreds of readers. But Howells had rejoiced in the incident: it put an end, he felt, to the glamour of Byron. That it marked a turning-point in the feeling of New England, where Byron, for all his errors, had
been a hero, this, to be sure, was accidental; but it showed
how the wind was blowing. Henceforward, the romantic
spirit, which had actuated all the poets, was regarded
with distrust and suspicion.

New England, meanwhile, had produced another
writer whose novels foreshadowed the work of James
and Howells. John W. De Forest, who lived in New
Haven, had served in the war as a captain, and Howells,
who greatly admired his writing, published three of his
novels as serials. *Kate Beaumont, Honest John Vane* and
Irene the Missionary all appeared first in *The Atlantic,*
although much finer than these was *Miss Ravenel's Conversion,* which had attracted Howells to De Forest.* As
a young man this writer had spent much of his life
abroad, in Paris, Florence and Beirut, where his brother
had a missionary school; and his first works were travel-
books, one of them picturing life in Syria. When the war
broke out, he was living in Charleston, but he returned
to New Haven and recruited a company there. Later, for
a year, after the war, he was stationed in South Carolina.
The settings of his novels,—two had appeared before
the war,—reflected the various scenes in which he had
lived. He wrote them in rapid succession, a dozen or

---

* This was a first-rate novel of the Civil War, published in 1867. It was
admirable in its scenes and characterizations. De Forest described himself
in Captain Colburne and his adventures in Louisiana and the Shenandoah.
    De Forest had read Balzac and Stendhal during his years in Paris, and
in Florence he had translated into Italian Hawthorne's *The House of the
Seven Gables.*

more. Then, like Thomas Sergeant Perry, he relapsed into silence.

Why De Forest ceased to write was a question that greatly troubled Howells, who tried to find an audience for this interesting author. If the answer was that nobody read him, this added to the mystery; for De Forest's work was remarkable, beyond a doubt. His touch, though sometimes crude, was strong, and he pictured American scenes and manners, in Connecticut, New York, the South, the West, with a breadth of understanding and a truth to actuality that were certainly unique at the moment. While he sometimes lapsed into melodrama, as in the Western novel *Overland,* the story of the Santa Fe trail, with its all-too-wicked Mexican cousins of the all-too-lovely American heroine and its lurid world of badmen and Apaches, he was usually veracious and observant. He skillfully chose subjects that were typical of the national life. As a picture of Washington politics and their corruption, *Honest John Vane* had few rivals. In a day when foreign missions were of general interest, *Irene the Missionary* gave its readers a lively account of a mission, with a story that brought its elements all together. De Forest knew the Americans in Syria, the wandering archæologists, the consuls, the learned and fatherly missionaries and their younger assistants, who taught the children to read English in Irving's *Life of Columbus,* as he knew the Washington lobbyists for whom the republic was the creature and servant of money; and, although he knew best of all the Connecticut Yankees at home, his two South Carolina novels, *The Bloody Chasm* and *Kate Beaumont,* showed that he also understood the South. As a man of imagination who had served in the war, he was eager to reconcile the discordant sections. He had suggested this wish in *Miss Ravenel's Conversion,* in which the Southern heroine lives in New Haven, and that he himself was at home in Charleston his other novels proved,—his portraits of South Carolinians, General Hilton, Colonel Beaumont and the knightly, simple, sensible Colonel Kershaw, were singularly keen and sympathetic. De Forest excelled in portraits of men, and he liked to picture reconciliations: one of his best scenes was the meeting of Beaumont and Judge McAlister, the chiefs of the rival Carolinian clans. In *The Bloody Chasm,* the North and South were reunited in a way that shed honour upon all.

In John De Forest, a writer had appeared with a panoramic eye for American manners. His scenes were vividly realized, the streets of New York, the Southern plantation-houses, the country-seats he loved in his own Connecticut landscape, overlooking the Sound,—a Parthenon on a rocky bluff or a low, wide-spreading house with pointed gables, perched on a turfy hillock with lawns below and parlours hung with portraits and spoils of travel; and, with his marked regard for the world that was passing, the "old-time society" and its patriarchal types, he recognized the new types and filled his novels with them. Side by side with Colonel Kershaw, the "white rose of Southern chivalry," and the Puritan Judge Wetherel, the Connecticut magnate, with his old-fashioned courtesy, unworldly in diction and feeling for all his wealth,* he

---

*The "master of Sea Lodge," in *The Wetherel Affair,* was one of De Forest's finest portraits. As a specimen of the old New England rural aristocracy, he enabled one to understand the power of the missionaries who founded schools and colleges all over Asia. Judge Wetherel is so steeped in the Bible that whenever he feels strongly his language is naturally biblical. With no suggestion of cant in his patriarchal simplicity, he represents the grand style of the Puritan tradition. See his words of welcome to the missionary's daughter who has come to Sea Lodge as a guest: "The child of God's apostle to his ancient church in the Kurdish mountains shall be a member of my family as long as she chooses to be." A dictatorial soul, grimly authoritative under a consciousness of duty, he is invariably courteous and gentle with the gentle. See, especially, the chapter, "The Judge's Manners and Customs."

De Forest's pictures of the old patriarchal life of America, both in New England and in the South, strangely resemble, in spite of every difference, Aksakov's pictures of the old Russian life in *A Russian Gentleman* and *Years of Childhood.*

described the girls who were "crazy for Newport," the foreigners with titles, often bogus, who were pursuing these girls, the rascally politicians of the post-war years, the Gallicized Americans in Europe, the young men who were going into chemistry and metallurgy, geologizing in California, developing phosphate-beds in the South; and, while his people had a way of meeting in Europe or on shipboard, as in Howells's novels and James's,* their interests were strongly American and characteristic. They were drawn with great vitality and directness. All in all, De Forest's work was a record of his time and country that should have aroused a more than passing interest.

So Howells felt, but the case was hopeless. De Forest did not appeal to women: this seemed to be the reason for his failure and silence. Men had largely ceased to read, and De Forest was a man's writer. His detached, ironical tone was masculine; so were his broad and general interests. If he had been a Bostonian, if the war had not appeared in so much of his work, he might have attracted more attention. But people wished to forget the war, and the larger American scene had little charm at present for women readers. Besides, he aroused the hostility of women readers. With a soldier's taste for dashing young ladies, he was rather disdainfully blunt with the rest of the sex. He had a pitiless eye for their foibles, and he liked to describe superannuated flirts and silly, extravagant wives who wreck their husbands. In a world in which women decided the fate of books, the odds were all against this virile writer.

The literary case of John De Forest was a sign of the place and the moment. While New England was ready for realism, as Mrs. Stowe had amply shown, De Forest

---

* "In society the mass of people have few startling topics in common, and still fewer interests; but among heroic ruins, solemnizing cathedrals, revered works of art and life-pictures of strange peoples, sensations rapidly sympathize, and thoughts become charmingly interchangeable."—De Forest's *Seacliff*.

showed the kind that New England was *not* ready for. The impalpably masculine character of his whole performance was the very thing that damned it,—which defined the type that readers were prepared to welcome; and what else could have been looked for, in the place, at the moment? The tastes and interests of women determined this type. Wherever realism appeared, in whatever region or nation, the regional mind remodelled it along the lines of its own conditions. French realism differed from Russian, and Russian from Spanish, and Spanish again from Norwegian, as Björnson showed it. American realism differed from these others, and New England had its special variation. To reject this latter, one had to begin by rejecting New England. Each to his own taste, —why not? But the realism itself could "do no other." The case was merely a repetition of the case of the previous age, in which romantic poetry was the dominant art in all the other regions *and* New England; and the dominance of Howells and James in the coming decades was a proof of the power of realism as the art of the moment. The delicate, limited mode of these writers, who were in New England, if not of it,—and they largely wrote in relation to New England readers,—was peculiarly sympathetic to the feminized public; and most of the women writers were realistic, although they were even more limited and severely conditioned. Howells and James transcended the others because of their centrality of vision, the unity of their style and tone and their all-American subject-matter. For the rest, what poetry had been, the novel was to be,—the novel or the story,—as a focus of interest. If the short story proved to be the form in which the local art of fiction triumphed, this was because it was better adapted to women with narrow horizons.

These tendencies were already current when Howells and James had begun to write. They were all in the ambient air of the post-war Yankees. In the novels of Har-

riet Waters Preston,* one read the minds of the younger
women who were largely to form the audience of James
and Howells. It was they, or other young women like
them, who were soon to write the New England stories,
and, while their horizons were certainly narrow, one had
to say it with qualifications. Their lives were restricted,
their experiences were circumscribed; and this determined
the range of their acts and their writings. But their feelings were far from narrow or shallow; indeed, they were
intense and deep, and, tested by the standard of "aware-
ness," these Claras, with their aesthetic teas, these Zoes
who had outlived their follies outrivalled many a damsel
of the years that followed. At times, in fact, in certain
ways, they made the bacchantes of Greenwich Village
look like rustic nursery-girls or milkmaids; and, if there
was something nun-like in them, it was not for want of
positive traits,—they had merely made their peace with
fate and fortune. Some of these girls, advancing in years,
were music-teachers in college towns; others dwelt together in the country; others carried on romances, perhaps in New Hampshire boarding-houses or in literary
circles in Worcester or Boston. Their over-active brains
at times were combined with over-sensitive consciences,
and they sometimes contracted their brows a little too
much and cultivated the "strong" way of speaking. But
all of them, whatever their age, as they read the scientific
monthlies and often went to church in their brown shade-
hats, were wonderfully well aware of the world they lived
in. They canvassed the modern novel from end to end.
They discussed the relations of labour and capital. They
touched upon the "woman question," quoting George

* Especially *Aspendale* and *Love in the Nineteenth Century*. These early
realistic novels resembled in their pallor and thinness the poems that preceded the outburst of the forties. They represented the faint beginnings of
a type that rapidly grew in strength. Weak enough as novels, they have
their special interest as revealing the state of mind of the younger people,
especially the young women of this epoch.

Sand and Mill; and they knew their Darwin as they read
their Huxley. They threshed out all the problems of love
and marriage. Was it ever, ever, "folly to be wise"?
They shared the light of Sainte-Beuve's exemplary ladies.*
How did Madame Swetchine regard these matters? What
did Madame Récamier think about them? If Madame de
Sévigné were living, how would she feel? Were they not
the heirs of twenty more ages than Plato? They knew
Rossetti's diluted Botticelli; and, as for French poetry
and fiction, it was all on the tip of their tongues. Matthew
Arnold led the rest in the matter of moulding their taste,
although even regarding Arnold they were still judicious.
For good sense abounded in their minds, and they were
Emersonian first of all. Was "the temper to which truth
is revealed" as fastidious or as desperate as the super-
cilious Arnold appeared to think it? They asked themselves
selves if "culture" and "anarchy" were not somehow one,
as shame and fame were all the same to Brahma. If they
were "Hebraists," they certainly had to be "Hellenists,"
and they shared James's joy in Arnold's phrases,—his
contempt for that bane of mankind, *das Gemeine*, the
common, his scorn of the "Philistine" and the "provincial." But, unlike James, they were rather inclined to take
the phrases with grains of salt; for James was much more
credulous than these Yankee maidens, some of whom took
him with grains of salt in the days when they had all

---

* See *The Library of Exemplary Women*, published in Boston about
1873. In addition to writing her novels and poems, Harriet W. Preston
translated three volumes of Sainte-Beuve. Miss Preston's special field, however, was Provençal literature. See her *Troubadours and Trouvères* and
her well-known translation of Mistral's *Mirèio.*
  Miss Wormeley, the translator of Balzac, also translated Sainte-Beuve.
Miss Grace Norton, Charles Eliot Norton's sister, discussed Sainte-Beuve's
women in her Cambridge classes. Miss Norton later published three volumes of essays on Montaigne, papers on his style, his reading, his friends,
his travels, etc. A veritable great lady, as John Jay Chapman recalled her,
she was usually, but not always, "boisterously frank." . . . "Grace gave
Mabel Quincy, as a wedding present, a copy of Montaigne with the
'naughty' pages gummed together. Could there be anything more deliciously droll?"—*Journal of Alice James.*

grown old together. Whatever their limitations were, they formed a critical audience,—if the audience had to be feminine,—for writers of novels; and they promised a new order of things in fiction when they, and other women, seized their pens.* As for Henry James himself, he never forgot the day when Matthew Arnold swam into his ken. He had only just arrived in Boston, and Fields had lent him the manuscript of Arnold's *Essays,* with its classic pages smirched by the printer. All day long, as he lay on the sofa,—for he had injured his back, the injury that prevented his enlisting,—his fancy followed the magic lines that carried him to Heine's Germany, to Oxford, to Paris and to Greece. Henceforth, the Arnoldian categories, the common, the provincial, the Philistine, distinction, the cult of the shade, were invested in his mind with a singular world of overtones that eventually led him far from primary facts.

As for realism, both Howells and James, in later years, qualified their strict adherence to it. Howells developed a vein of fantasy, and James's final phase was remote indeed, in effect, from the note of his prime. Moreover, some of James's first stories were exuberantly romantic in their feeling, *Gabrielle de Bergerac,* for instance. But he soon accepted the realistic method, which he and Howells professed to the end of their lives; and one of the last of James's utterances,—the lecture, *The Lesson of Balzac,*—reiterated the views of his earlier essays. Balzac was still, for him, the "father of us all," to whom every road still came back, as the beginning and end of the novel was the art of representation, based upon observa-

---

* "If ever we *do* come alongside of you, Mr. Journalist, in artistic and dramatic ability, there will be a new order of things in fiction . . . Is it not generally allowed that women read character more readily than men? . . . Dependence has made them very acute. All dependents are acute. How well your servants know you! And besides, women have had only individuals to deal with and think of and plan for . . . but men have had masses, and such as were quite indifferent to them."—Harriet W. Preston, *Love in the Nineteenth Century.*

tion of actual life. That the novelist was a social historian was always James's doctrine, and therefore the question of a terrain was one that he could not ignore. If he could not represent America, what could he represent? Could he ever understand another country?

Later, James told a friend that before he settled in Europe he had given his own country a "good trial." It was true; but his imagination was so Europeanized that he could only look for a Europe at home. He had seen his Cambridge boarding-house in terms of Balzac's Maison Vauquer, and he saw all America in terms of his reading, just as his cousin Robert Temple, newly returned from Europe, seemed to him a character "in the sense in which 'people in books' were characters, and other people, roundabout us, were somehow not." As America failed to stir his interest on its own account, he could only recreate it in accordance with patterns drawn from George Sand, Thackeray, Mérimée or Balzac. Thus, in *Poor Richard,* the young New England farmer kisses Gertrude's hand whenever he meets her, while she, a homespun Yankee, maintains in her parlour the ritual of an English country-house. In *De Grey: A Romance,* the American Mrs. De Grey keeps a priest in the house to serve as her confessor. In *Crawford's Consistency,* the young girl is brought up "in the manner of an Italian princess" in a "high-hedged old garden" in Orange, New Jersey. The hero of *Eugene Pickering* has been pledged in marriage to the unseen daughter of his father's friend. The family curse that hangs over some of these households is very different in accent from Hawthorne's curse, the good old convincing curse of Salem. It is a Frenchified curse, as the young men are Frenchified; for they always say *J'ai vécu* and *Nous verrons,* when even a travelling Frenchman would have said "We shall see." James shared Mrs. Follanbee's weakness: he had "a sort of indefinite faith in French

phrases for mending all the broken places in life." * But*
he did his best to follow American models, or the only
American model that he felt as germane. The influence of
Hawthorne was marked in his stories,† and perhaps if
there had existed a great American realist to show the
way for him and interpret the scene,—during his formative years,—James's whole career might have been different. As it was, he could make nothing of the country.
"I believe I should be a good patriot if I could sketch my
native town," one of his characters remarks, in *The Impressions of a Cousin*. "But I can't make a picture of the
brown-stone steps in the Fifth Avenue, or the platform
of the elevated railway in the Sixth . . . I can sketch the
palazzo and can do nothing with the uptown residence."
This was the situation of Henry James.

Long afterwards, living in England, James was to find
that he knew America,—or knew, at least, certain aspects
of it,—as he had never supposed when he lived at home.
He was to produce, in *Washington Square* and *The Bostonians*, brilliantly veracious pictures of it. But, during
these years of indecision, with his alienated mind, he was
wholly out of touch with the life of the country. Politics
and business, the forces that were shaping it, lay outside
his horizon, and he sought for it in places like Newport
and like Saratoga, where almost every thought was of
Paris and London. All that was not European repelled

---

* "You don't know, *mignonne,* how perfectly *ravissante* these apartments
are!" etc.—Mrs. Follanbee, in Harriet Beecher Stowe's *Pink and White
Tyranny*.

† *The Last of the Valerii, The Romance of Certain Old Clothes, A Passionate Pilgrim, The Madonna of the Future* (based on a story of Balzac),
etc.

"It also tickled my national feeling not a little to note the resemblance of
Hawthorne's style to yours and Howells's. . . . That you and Howells with
all the models in English literature to follow should needs involuntarily
have imitated (as it were) this American, seems to point to the existence
of some real American mental quality."—Letter of William James, 1870.

As for Howells, the influence of Hawthorne is most marked in *The Undiscovered Country. The Blithedale Romance* affected Howells most, as
James was especially affected by *The Marble Faun*.

and bored him. He liked to be reminded of old-world drawing-rooms, ambassadors, luxuries and splendours, and he found harsh lights and hard lines, a cold, vacant, undraped scene, without shade, without composition, as one said of pictures.* "I shall freeze after this sun," Albrecht Dürer said, returning to Germany from Venice, and this was James's feeling whenever he turned homeward after one of his visits to Italy or England. The Beacon Street windows were "terrible" to him. Like the baroness in *The Europeans,* after a year in America, he felt the annoyance of a swimmer "who, on nearing shore, to land, finds a smooth, straight wall of rock" instead of a "clean, firm beach." He could not scale this wall, and America was too big and too vague! He felt that his only safety lay in flight.

---

* "It is very hard, very cold, very vacant. I think of your warm, rich Paris . . . I had no idea how little form there was. I don't know what I shall do; I feel so undraped, so uncurtained, so uncushioned; I feel as if I were sitting in the centre of a mighty 'reflector.' A terrible crude glare is over everything; the earth seems peeled and excoriated; the raw heavens seem to bleed with the quick, hard light . . . When things are so ugly, they should not be so definite; and they are terribly ugly here. There is no mystery in the corners; there is no light and shade in the types. The people are haggard and joyless; they look as if they had no passions, no tastes, no senses . . . I want my little corner of Paris; I want the rich, the deep, the dark old world; I want to be out of this horrible place."—Louis Leverett, in James's *The Point of View* and *A Bundle of Letters.*

CHAPTER XII

HENRY ADAMS

IN 1873, Charles Eliot Norton, after spending five
years in Europe, had returned to Cambridge. Having
settled his summer home on the farm at Ashfield, to bind
himself more closely to the country, he had yielded to the
attraction of England, much in the manner of Motley and
Lowell, and had gone abroad, as it seemed at first, to
stay. With his well-known aptitude for friendship, he resumed his old relations with Ruskin and Dickens and was
soon on intimate terms with Carlyle and Darwin, whose
son married Mrs. Norton's sister. At the end of three or
four years, he seemed to be an established part of the
English literary landscape; and, if he had followed his
tastes, he might well have become so. But Norton personified conscience. The tough moral instinct of the old
Puritan first families, with its train of responsibilities,
possessed his mind. His political sense was strong. He had
shared in the anti-slavery movement; he had met the
problems of immigration by agitating for model lodging-
houses. He could not abandon his country to its own devices. He was convinced that America was on the road to
ruin, and its new developments horrified all his feelings.
All the more, for this reason, America needed a Jeremiah,
and Norton returned with the consciousness of a role to
play.

Thus began, at Harvard, in his chair of the history of
art, Norton's long career as a teacher and prophet, as a
scholar, a censor, a sage. To lay down the law was his

nature. He had laid it down to Ruskin in the matter of his unsteady habits, and he set to work at once to regenerate Harvard; for his cousin, President Eliot, was destroying the college, from the point of view that Norton represented, by embracing the abominations of the road to ruin, the materialistic practicalities through which the nation was losing its grasp of all that was noble and worthy in its own tradition. The delicate Norton, a semi-invalid, spoke for the "royal priesthood" that his forbear, John Norton, had once proclaimed; for, although he had ceased to believe in God, he felt that he spoke the word of God. Authority was authority, and the law was the law. He was an agnostic, like Clough and Leslie Stephen, his intimate English friends of the past and the present, and he even considered that Christianity, with its system of rewards and punishments, was debasing. He felt that Protestantism was an utter failure. But the mood of the Puritan clerical caste survived in his tenacious mind, as the mood of the old French priesthood survived in Renan. Norton remained a priest, with a mission; and since art, along with science, was the new religion, and Norton cared little for science, the nature of his mission was aesthetic. His aesthetic feeling was weak and derivative, but his scholarly feeling was strong, while his ethical feeling dominated all the others; and Ruskin had taught him that art had an ethical basis. To preach art as ethics was thus the soul of Norton's mission, and to preach the scholarly virtues as the soul of art. If the modern world was ugly, the modern world was also base: its baseness and its ugliness went together. Taste alone could redeem it, and taste was therefore Norton's gospel. He preached it as his forbears preached salvation.

He had prepared himself in Italy and England, in constant association with Ruskin's friends, Burne-Jones, Morris and Rossetti; and Carlyle's dictatorial temper had strengthened his own. He had spent long afternoons with

the sage of Chelsea, walking or smoking with him in his
study, while the old prophet, Emerson's friend, who took
a special fancy to Norton, told him the story of his youth.
Carlyle gave Norton his mask of Cromwell, and, through
him, he later gave to Harvard the books he had used in
writing his *Cromwell* and *Frederick*. He had grown to
feel that he was mistaken in his views about the Civil
War,—which had destroyed his authority in America
forever,*—and he wished to express his gratitude to the
friends in New England who had formed so large a part
of his early readers. Like Ruskin, his family appointed
Norton his literary executor; and Norton was confirmed
by these two masters in his own contumelious, cavilling
habit of mind. In Italy, meanwhile, he had carried on the
investigations that he had begun long since in his work on
Dante. He spent two years there, preparing for his admirable *Historical Studies of Church-Building in the Middle Ages*. This dealt with the cathedrals of Venice, Siena
and Florence. In all these cities, as well as in Rome, Norton worked in the archives, studying the political and
social conditions under which the cathedrals arose. He
was frail and easily tired, and he felt that his task was
rather to teach than to write. He bought Greek vases and
bits of Pisan sculpture for Ruskin and helped him in the
revision of *Modern Painters;* and in Italy, when Ruskin
joined him, he introduced his friend to the *Fioretti* and
the other Franciscan writings. Immersed in Italian chron-
icles and *trecento* lives and letters, Norton, as one later

* "Each oracle denies his predecessor, each magician breaks the wand of
the one who went before him. There were Americans enough ready to
swear by Carlyle until he broke his staff in meddling with our anti-slavery
conflict, and buried it so many fathoms deep that it could never be fished
up again. It is rather singular that Johnson and Carlyle should each of
them have shipwrecked his sagacity and shown a terrible leak in his moral
sensibilities on coming in contact with American rocks and currents."—
Oliver Wendell Holmes, *Our Hundred Days in Europe.*
    "The proof that a philosopher does not know what he is talking about is
apt to sadden his followers before it reacts on himself."—*The Education
of Henry Adams.*

saw in his further translations of Dante, was a master of
mediæval studies.

It was a mediævalist, therefore, who preached from
the pulpit at Harvard, where the youthful Henry Adams
was established already as professor of mediæval history.
For Adams, at a loose end after his foray in Washington, had accepted President Eliot's invitation. He was
deep in the study of Viollet-le-Duc and the architecture
of the Middle Ages. Norton, as a mediævalist, followed
Ruskin, for whom the age of Giotto was the golden age,
a reproof, a sublime example for a world of machines
and money-madness, a paradise of art and social justice.
If Ruskin had known more of economic history,—which
no one knew when he began to write,—he would have
discovered that the modern system he despised had already begun its career in Giotto's Florence. He would
have discovered that Giotto was a usurer, who rented
looms himself at exorbitant rates, and that the Florentine
guildsmen, the most ruthless exploiters in Europe, were
already destroying the life of the handicraft-system. In
Venice, built on the slave-trade, and Florence, the manu-
facturing centre, the modern age was beginning,—just
there and just then; and Ruskin's Utopia was itself the
fountain-head of all the modern evils he condemned. In
order to prove that great art expressed a good society,
Ruskin chose an example that was far from apt; for Man-
chester sprang from Florence as the flower from the
bud.* But this did not alter the fact that art is related to
social conditions. It did not impugn the art of the age of
Giotto!—and Norton, who advanced the study of this
art, while he railed at existing conditions, was a useful
teacher. His temper, to be sure, was that of an archæolo-
gist; he had small feeling for art as a living process. But
no one aroused the country more to a sense of its general

* See Miriam Beard, *A History of the Business Man,*—statements drawn
in part from Davidsohn's *Geschichte von Florenz.*

ugliness and a will to create a beautiful civilization. As an enemy of "numbers" * and "President Grant architecture," as a lover of perfection in details and of every craftsman, as the friend of Olmsted, the maker of parks, as the founder of schools and museums,† Norton deserved his fame as a mentor and leader. Henry James was only one of a series of younger men for whom the great brown study at "Shady Hill," with its manuscripts and paintings, its books and medals, was the scene of their consecration to art or letters.‡

A number of younger Cambridge men, more or less in Norton's circle, shared his aesthetic interests in one form or another. William James, who was teaching psychology, never lost his love of painting; and Oliver Wendell Holmes, the jurist of the future, who was lecturing at present in the Law School, had studied art before he went in for law. This Holmes,—the "second edition,"—had attempted etching and had only given it up when he felt that his etchings had no merit. As for the short, bald, bearded Henry Adams, with his multifarious interests, his interest in art was eager, universal and lasting. The first of Adams's lessons was the lesson of colour: he remembered a yellow kitchen floor on which, at the age of three, he had sat in the sunlight. He never forgot the

* When his classes grew so large that his lectures had to be given in Sanders Theatre, Norton observed, as he looked over the throng of students,—who had come, as he knew, for no good purpose,—"This is a sad sight."
Cf. Henry Adams: "I am much disgusted at this"—the size of his classes —"and have become foul and abusive in my language to them, hoping to drive them away."—Letter of 1876.
† Norton founded the Archæological Institute of America, the parent of the American School at Athens and the School of Classical Studies at Rome. The Fogg Museum in Cambridge, with its school of museum-directors, was largely an outgrowth of Norton's presence and teaching.
‡ Among the many eminent students whom Norton greatly influenced were George E. Woodberry, Bernhard Berenson and James Loeb, the founder of the Loeb Classical Library. Mrs. "Jack" Gardner went to Norton's classes, beginning in 1878. Norton and Henry Adams made purchases for Mrs. Gardner's collection, which was chiefly formed by Berenson, Norton's pupil.

greens, reds, blues and purples that haloed his childhood at Quincy; and later, in his student years, at Dresden, he had learned the gallery by heart. He had passed a whole day at Nuremberg, in two of the churches, lying on the altar-steps and looking at the stained glass windows with their glorious colours. He had even studied the theory of painting; he had planned a work on art "to smash the Greeks;" and, during his years in London, he had often run over to Paris for a talk with H. H. Richardson, his friend in college, who was studying architecture at the Beaux-Arts. This early taste of Adams was to find a splendid expression later,—he was a collector at the moment; and, in fact, in aesthetic perception and feeling, Adams excelled the scholarly Norton. So, for the matter of that, did James and Holmes.* But art was only one of their many interests. What their central interest was, the interest of the younger men,—whether history, philosophy, science, art or letters,—it might have been hard to say. Taking "mental photographs," perhaps. This was Chauncey Wright's favourite game, which he played with the Cambridge young ladies till 2 A.M., leaving them entranced, amid their "shivers of sleepiness," with the words, "I see you keep the same late hours." These psychological questionnaires struck the note of the place and the moment,† the note of James's lectures and his brother's stories; and, though Henry Adams found Cambridge a "social desert," ‡ it flowed with intellectual milk and

* "Talk about a green thought in a green shade. Dante's paradise is white on white on white—like a dish of certain tulips in the spring."—From a letter of Justice Holmes.

† "Does Mrs. Saintsbury like me?" asked Dan. "Well, she's awfully nice. Don't you think she's awfully fond of formulating people?"
"Oh, everybody in Cambridge does that. They don't gossip; they merely accumulate materials for the formulation of character."—Howells, *April Hopes.*

‡ "Several score of the best-educated, most agreeable, and personally the most sociable people in America united in Cambridge to make a social desert that would have starved a polar bear . . . Society was a faculty-meeting without business."—*The Education of Henry Adams.*

honey. Adams who had spent his youth in the social oases
of London and Paris, at court balls and royal garden-
parties, would have found Oxford as much of a desert as
Cambridge; and Henry James, whose mind was full of
the same oases, was taking steps to leave it, for this reason. "Poor nudified and staring Cambridge" was not for
him.* Even William James complained of the "buttoned-up
Boston respectable character," the "middle-aged tone"
of the club he had formed with his friends. The Cambridge manner was certainly staid, uncomfortably for the
older man,† absurdly for the younger and more vivacious.‡ Cambridge was not a social oasis, but the older
men, assembled there, had made it a preëminent centre
for thinkers; § and the younger men vied with the older.
Howells, Thomas Sergeant Perry and Henry James, at
intervals, appeared at William James's club, with Henry
Adams, John Fiske, Alexander Agassiz, Chauncey Wright,
Charles S. Peirce and Holmes. The subject of one of the
evenings was John Fiske's *Cosmic Philosophy,* and the
author, who was present with his friends, quietly went to
sleep under their noses. Once, at a livelier meeting, Charles
Peirce announced the name and the doctrine of pragmatism. The principle of this new philosophy lay unnoticed
for many years until William James exposed it for all
to see.

* "Life here in Cambridge—or in this house, at least—is about as lively
as the inner sepulchre . . . [Social relaxation] is not to be obtained in
Cambridge—or only a ghastly simulacrum of it. There are no 'distractions'
here . . . Likewise 'calling.' Upon whom?"—Letter of Henry to William
James, 1867.

† "Dr. Palfrey remarked at Cambridge, when we talked of the manners
of Wordsworth and Coleridge, that there seemed to be no such thing as a
conventional manner among the eminent men of England, for these people
lived in the best society, yet each indulged the strongest individual peculi-
arities."—Emerson's *Journals.*

‡ See Henry Adams's comment on his meeting with Swinburne: "One felt
the horror of Longfellow and Emerson, the doubts of Lowell and the
humour of Holmes at the wild Walpurgis-night of Swinburne's talk."

§ "Mr. Charles Darwin once said in a letter that he thought there were
clustered round Harvard University enough minds of ability to furnish
forth all England's universities."—T. G. Appleton, *Checquer-Work.*

As for William James, who was living with his parents, he developed much more slowly than his brother Henry. More vividly bright, as people said, and prompter in his human responses, he had too many sympathies and interests to be able to focus his mind at once. He had emerged from his long depression, the suicidal state of panic fear in which he had lived for a lustrum. His temperament was psychopathic; he was always subject to nervous breakdowns; he was neurasthenic, at intervals, for the rest of his life. This organization and all it entailed, in the way of experience and insight, opened his mind to the souls of abnormal people. It deepened his moral perception,— *The Varieties of Religious Experience* bore witness to this; * and psychology, in the meantime, gave him a footing. He was already advancing on a firm foundation. He was publishing valuable papers. Years were to pass before he produced a major work, and all his major work, in fact, appeared at a time when he supposed his career was over. He had reason to believe in the "energies of men," the latent powers that one so seldom uses,—it took so long for him to find his own. But all his traits were clearly marked already. Chivalrous, curious, courageous, he was eager and also unstable and easily bored. He seemed to be "born fresh every morning," as Alice James noted in her journal, but he could not stick to things "for the sake of sticking." Impulsive and spontaneous, he was keenly ready for everything new, a lover of adventure, risks and hazards; and, with his tough and sinewy mind, he was quick in his feelings and deeply compassionate.

* "When a superior intellect and a psychopathic temperament coalesce . . . in the same individual, we have the best possible condition for the kind of effective genius that gets into the biographical dictionaries . . . In the psychopathic temperament we have the emotionality which is the *sine qua non* of moral perception; we have the intensity and tendency to emphasis which are the essence of practical moral vigour; and we have the love of metaphysics and mysticism which carry one's interests below the surface of the sensible world."—William James, *The Varieties of Religious Experience.*

As he stooped over a poor dog, strapped on a board for vivisection, he felt that he must pay something back to life for every jet of pain that he was causing. All the dogs were under-dogs to James. He liked to run his own risks. He liked to use himself as a *corpus vile*, experimenting with mescal and nitrous-oxide gas as readily as with Yoga and mental healing. His delight in human nature was acute and unending, and all his doors and windows opened outwards, as he said of the house at Chocorua that he built in the eighties. In his boyhood, Mayne Reid's tales of out-of-door adventure had impressed him with the virtue of field-observers. To Reid, the "closet-naturalists," the collectors and the classifiers, the handlers of skeletons and skins, were contemptible beside the men who observed the ways of living animals; and James, as a psychologist, followed Reid. He had thought, as a child, that a "closet-naturalist" must be the vilest kind of wretch, and Agassiz had confirmed this fixed impression. So James was wary of generalizations, abstractions, preconceived ideas,* and sought for facts voraciously, the tame and the "wild." He sought them in the highways, he sought them in the byways and even in shady corners where conventional thinkers would not have believed their eyes if they had found them. He had a passion for physiognomy. He collected portraits of interesting men, as he praised his friends in proportion as they differed from him. This suppleness and catholicity, joined with his cosmopolitan outlook, were to make him a prince of psychologists, as time went on. Meanwhile, at the core of his being, James was religious. He had a poet's feeling for the marvel of existence, and he had hours of rapture akin to Whitman's. In the woods, in the fields, on the rocks at Magnolia, with the perfume of the laurels

---

* "One must know concrete instances first; for, as Professor Agassiz used to say, one can see no farther into a generalization than just so far as one's previous acquaintance with particulars enables one to take it in."—William James, *The Varieties of Religious Experience.*

and the roses, with the breath of the pines in his lungs and the surf in his ears, he felt, in the beautiful wash of light, the mystical union with Deity that still filled Emerson also with awe and courage.

At the moment, William James had scarcely begun to climb his ladder. Holmes was two or three rungs beyond him, and, as for Chauncey Wright, he had scaled his ladder to the summit. Chauncey Wright's short life was all but over. These novices and friends had much in common. It was William James's hope that philosophers might come to grips, as closely as realistic novelists, with the facts of life. This was Holmes's hope in regard to the law, for Holmes was a realist also; and nothing existed for Chauncey Wright,—the "great mind of a village," as James described him in a later essay,—but facts, facts, facts. The balder and barer the better! He had no use for metaphysics: experiment and description, for him, were the whole of thinking. All three agreed in distrusting abstractions; they all suspected general terms.* Holmes was already preparing his great work, *The Common Law,* in which he described the life of the law as experience, not logic. This idea of jurisprudence,—once a self-sufficient science, with traditions handed down as it were from Sinai,—was to make Holmes later, as John Morley said, "the greatest judge of the English-speaking world." The need of "thinking things rather than words" was the essence of Holmes's teaching, as of James's also, —although Holmes's words, for the rest, were bright new coins. He had been encouraged to mint them in his earliest childhood. His father, the Autocrat, had made it a rule at the breakfast-table to reward a well-phrased observation with an extra helping of marmalade; and Holmes, for ninety years, had things to say, on literature, philosophy, art and science, that were better than almost anything said by others. Chauncey Wright was a

* "No generalization is wholly true, not even this one."—Justice Holmes.

brilliant talker also.* He was famous for his Socratic
sessions with William James and the elder Henry, and
he fascinated the younger Henry James with his searching characterizations of people. A poor young man from
Northampton, Wright was a bosom-friend of the Jameses
and the Nortons and a local sage and character who was
second to none. A tutor and a lecturer, he wrote in the
North American, but he supported himself by computing
for the *Nautical Almanac,* compiled in Cambridge. He
devised new ways of computing, for he was a mathematical genius, and he forced the work of a year into two
strained months. No one saw him then, and he saw neither
sunlight nor moonlight; but he emerged from his cave
with time to burn. He walked and talked for weeks at
Mount Desert; he philosophized all over the Franconia
mountains. Once he went abroad for a visit to Darwin,
who had brought out one of his essays as a pamphlet in
England; and he remarked that "Paris was as good as
Cambridge,"—perhaps to annoy Henry James. A big
man, with mild blue eyes, somewhat sluggish and inert,
he was remote, slow, melancholy, but not unfriended; he
was shy, but he was serene; he was simple and frugal,
and his freedom from all cares and wants, material and
mental, reminded the Cambridge circle of the antique
sages. Like them, and like Emerson, he slighted books
and reading; indeed, as he never read, the wonder grew,
—he seemed to know much more than if he had. This
lonely soliloquizer, with his corncob pipe, excelled by the
sheer, bleak power of unaided thought. But he was a lover
of children, and, like Thoreau, he delighted in entertaining them with magic and juggling. He was a master at

* "A lad is a boy with a man's hand on his head." This is almost the
only surviving relic of Chauncey Wright's conversation, which reminded
the Cambridge circle of De Quincey and Coleridge. His phrase "cosmical
weather" also survives. Chauncey Wright's *Letters* suggest, better perhaps
than anything else, the intellectual atmosphere of Cambridge in the early
seventies. His philosophical essays were collected and published by Charles
Eliot Norton.

sleight-of-hand, and he used his mathematical genius to invent and exhibit all manner of puzzles and games. There were no Christmas parties like those of the Nortons at "Shady Hill," where Chauncey Wright was busy with his marvels and Child and his three little girls performed old ballads, which they turned into Robin Hood plays with their gestures and costumes.

Once Wright and John Fiske tired the moon with talking, as they strolled from each other's lodgings, back and forth. A dozen times they made the double journey, till the sun rose over their discourse. Fiske was turning from philosophy to history, as history was also turning from art to science. He was already beginning his historical studies. Indeed, he had begun them years before, and it was Henry Adams's post that he had hoped to have when Eliot dropped Fiske in favour of Adams. Fiske was too "'irreligious" to please the college, and no one knew that Adams was ten times more so.* As for the new historical mode, it harmonized with the Cambridge mind in novel-writing, psychology, philosophy, law. The day of the Prescotts and Motleys and Parkmans was passing. Parkman continued to write, and better than ever, in the shadowy Boston study where he rode his chair. He pursued his Canadian history, volume by volume, and his method, so realistic and so solid, compelled the regard of all. The more one insisted on "documents," the more one had to bow to him, and his thoroughness put the scientists on their mettle. He had six thousand folio pages carefully copied for one of his volumes,—from the French archives alone, not to speak of the English. While all this was true, he had no feeling for evolution; and he had a romantic belief in the "great man theory." He was a lover of heroes, and the kind of heroes,—adventurers,

---

* Like George Strong, in his novel *Esther*,—the geologist who was drawn from Clarence King,—Adams "looked at churches very much as he would have looked at a layer of extinct oysters in a buried mud-bank."

soldiers of fortune,—for whom an age of prose had little use. He, in turn, despised his age, an emasculate generation of policemen and bankers,—but the line of Scott and Byron could go no further. The bankers, the policemen and the younger intellectuals were bored by sieges, marches and clashes of arms. Spencer had destroyed the "great man theory," as John Fiske, for one, rejoiced to say.* To understand conspicuous men was not to understand their times, and "decisive battles" had ceased to seem decisive. Meanwhile, Comte had established the notion of the "laws of historical development," along the lines of any other science. The environment, the mass-psyche, the mores of the group seemed more important now than the intrigues of courts, and the new generation of students found the turning-points of history in the cumulative action of causes minute but incessant. They examined social institutions, legal theory, public law, and they took the whole of society as their field and their subject. In temper, they resembled the realistic novelists,— they were sober, objective collectors and arrangers of facts. They shrank from generalizations as much as William James or Holmes; they distrusted and avoided moral judgments. They looked at questions from every side. They scrutinized their witnesses. They tried to divest themselves of the party spirit, political, economic or religious. It was their aspiration to let the "sources" speak for themselves, to present a neutral mind to the past and its persons. They were to mirror reality in their placid pages. In short, they approached the phenomena of history as biologists and physicists approached their fields. It scarcely occurred to historians for a long generation that they were not, completely, men of science.

This was the note of historical studies when John Fiske and Henry Adams began their career as historians

* See Fiske's essay, *Sociology and Hero-Worship*, written in reply to William James's *Great Men and Their Environment*, 1880.

in the Cambridge setting. That history, if not an exact
science, might in time become so,—such was the current
belief, such was the programme. Years later, Henry
Adams thought the laws of history paralleled the laws
of physics, obviously and strictly. He even identified history with thermo-dynamics,—he believed he had the
science "in his ink-stand." Just then, for various reasons,
this theory exploded; and, in fact, neither Adams nor
Fiske, in their actual writings,—as historians, not theorists
on the subject,—paid any special regard to these fanciful
laws. Fiske, as an evolutionist, saw in American history
a chance to illustrate his favourite doctrine; and this, although he profited by the "scientific" method, was his only
major tribute to historical "science." Fiske's opportunity
sprang from his present labours. As one of the Harvard
librarians, he catalogued the books and pamphlets that
dealt with American history, an immense collection. With
his zeal for order, he worked wonders for the library and
incidentally read the books and pamphlets. He found
himself in possession of a theme forever. In 1878, to enlarge his income, he began to give public lectures in the
Old South Church; and henceforth writing American history and lecturing about it became the central interest of
his life. As a lecturer, the genial Fiske, the hirsute, be-
spectacled mammoth with his hearty manner, with his
gift for elucidation, was a master-performer. Spencer
said he had never heard such "glorious" lectures as
Fiske's, when he spoke, under Huxley's auspices, in London;* and the "Fiske season" rivalled Barnum's, in the
years to come, when he tumbled all over the country, as
far as Denver. He aroused in the population a zest for
American history, which the Centennial celebrations had
already awakened. The public had lost its interest in the

* Huxley, always generous and often just, said that Fiske's first lecture
on American Poliucal Ideas was the best lecture he had ever heard at the
Royal Institution.

long, close-woven, detailed studies of the writers of the older generation. It averred that what it lacked was the time to read them, though what it really lacked was pride in the country,—it had lost all interest in the past. The vogue of historical writing had vanished. The prevailing indifference to Parkman proved it; for Parkman's histories appeared in small editions, as small as seven hundred copies, where Prescott had had his tens of thousands of readers, and Henry Adams was soon to find how small the public was for works on a scale that Parkman took for granted. Adams's history, all but ignored by the press, never achieved even a second edition. John Fiske was the exception that proved the rule: he found as many readers as Prescott or Motley. For his books were broad surveys that simplified his subjects; and, with his light, attractive, flowing style, he was an unexampled popularizer. He was a relief after the Bancrofts and Hildreths and much more literary than the men who followed, James Ford Rhodes and Edward Channing. Readable, approachable, variously learned, he placed his country in relation to the history of the world, for he knew more than his predecessors about its earliest origins in the primitive life of the continent and the life of Europe. He traced the growth of American institutions as Darwin traced the origin of species. For the rest, his works were episodic, and they followed the exigencies of the lecture-platform. They were written piecemeal in the course of a rough-and-tumble career that left small time or energy for research or thinking. Fiske was unable to carry out his plan for a monumental work to cover American history from end to end; but one of his books, at least, *The Discovery of America,* possessed the weight and scope of a major creation.

All this lay in the future. Fiske had not yet begun his historical writing, and Henry Adams had written only occasional papers when he took up his teaching at Harvard. Five years passed before Adams turned to American history; and he spent only seven years in Cambridge and Boston. Then he returned to Washington to live for the rest of his life and to write the books that made him famous later. Meanwhile, he established the German historical method, and the so-called seminar method, in his classes at Harvard. He had studied law in Germany,— he had even planned to be a lawyer,—and he stressed the legal aspect of the Middle Ages, the early German, Norman and Anglo-Saxon institutions, along with domestic life and architecture. His course, beginning with primitive man, continued through the Salic Franks to the Norman English. In order to arouse his students, he rode roughshod over their prejudices and fixed ideas, and he gave them special subjects, well-chosen for each, to follow and examine for themselves. In 1875–6, he offered a course in American history. In 1877, he resigned. That Adams was a great teacher all his pupils affirmed later, and Henry Cabot Lodge, afterwards the senator, never forgot the stormy careers of the great German emperors and the struggles of papacy and empire. Henry Adams had burned them into his mind. Lodge was one of the pupils who became historians, under the tutelage of Adams; and, although he soon dropped history for politics, he produced a number of competent books.* Adams, who had married in the meantime, continued to pursue his other interests. He travelled, he geologized, he collected,—Palgrave and Woolner in London had encour-

* Henry Cabot Lodge's chief works were *A Short History of the English Colonies in America* and lives of Washington, Hamilton and Webster. He edited the nine volumes of Hamilton's writings. As a devoted Hamiltonian, he carried on the line of the Federalists of an earlier Boston. Shortly after opening his political career, he campaigned against "Ben" Butler's governorship. As Bishop Lawrence said, Lodge was the David who fought on the side of "all the powers of respectability and virtue" and slew this Goliath. Compare with this the later opinion of Adams, who was Lodge's life-long friend: "The true type of successful cant, which rests on no belief at all, is Cabot, who grabs everything, and talks pure rot to order." —*Letters of Henry Adams, 1892–1918.*

aged this taste. He was a tireless purchaser of water-
colours, drawings, Greek terra-cottas, bronzes, Spanish
leather. As for geology, Agassiz's lectures had aroused
this interest in him, and Lyell, a friend of his family, had
confirmed it in England. He spent days and nights geologizing; and this led him to Colorado in 1871, where he
met his friend Clarence King. As for travel, his wandering habits of later years were established in this earlier
time at Harvard.* But politics transcended these other
interests. All the Adams idols had been statesmen, and
this was a family inheritance that he could not escape.
He had grown up in the shadow of presidents; he had
visited the White House at twelve; he had lived among
politicians all his life, whether in Washington or London.
He had read, as a child, for proof-correction, the writings of John Adams, which his father had been editing
for publication; and winter after winter, every day, as he
worked at his Latin grammar in his father's study, he
had heard the elder Adams, with Dana, Sumner and Palfrey, discussing anti-slavery politics. He had copied his
father's speeches for the press, and Sumner and Seward
might have been his uncles. He had lived on comradely
terms with half of President Johnson's cabinet, and
Bright and Cobden in England were familiars of his
household. No other young American, except perhaps another Adams, had ever been so steeped in politics, and
some sort of connection with politics was inevitable for
him. He had received, with his Harvard appointment,
the editorship of the *North American,* which had become
with time a family trust of the younger patrician Bostonians; and, with Lodge as assistant editor, he found
himself deeper in politics than ever before. He even tried
to arrange to buy the Boston *Advertiser,* to start an

* As early as 1873, Adams referred in a letter to his "fifteen years of
knocking about the world, in every city and nearly every wilderness between Salt Lake City and the Second Cataract of the Nile."

independent-liberal party. His "vast and ambitious projects for the future" took him to New York and Washington often. The reformer was still strong in him, and his
first foray in Washington had not convinced him that his
case was hopeless. Indeed, he had high hopes of political
success.* He wished to attack the caucus-system, the heart
of party-organization, as the source of the worst corruption in the existing parties. His was a party of no-party,
representing the nation over the sections, defending free-
trade against the bankers and civil-service reform against
the machines. It was a continuation of the Adams programme. Henry Adams and his friends chose Carl Schurz
to lead this party, but the mores of the time were all
against them. Schurz left them in the lurch and returned
to the Republicans, and Adams recoiled from political
action forever.

Such was Adams's outer life, during these years at
Harvard. The historical writings that followed were out-
growths of it; or, rather, American history was in Adams's
bones, as Puss in Boots, Bluebeard and Cinderella were
bred in the bones of other children. Part of it was Adams
history and most that was not Adams had reached him
through a thousand early channels. His happiest hours
in childhood, in the farmhouse at Quincy, were passed as
he lay, in summer, reading Scott, on a heap of congres-
sional documents,—he day-dreamed on musty documents
as others on hay. Along with the materials, he had the
models. His father's shelves were stocked with historians,
and none of the Adamses ever forgot the haircloth
rocking-chair in the house in Boston where they pored
over Gibbon and Macaulay by the fire in the grate. Henry
and his brothers, Charles Francis and Brooks, had all
read history more than anything else. When, therefore,

* "I look forward to the day when we shall be in power again as not far
distant ... We will play for high stakes."—Letters of Henry Adams, 1870,
1875.

in 1877, the year of Adams's resignation, the papers of Albert Gallatin were placed in his hands, the retiring professor knew how to use them well. His life of the statesman-financier was published in 1879, together with three volumes of Gallatin's writings. He found this father of American ethnology, who had once been instructor in French at Harvard, a highly sympathetic subject; but he made no reparation to the hero of his following book, a brilliant ancient enemy of the house of Adams. The bitter *John Randolph* appeared in 1882, when Adams was already preparing for his magnum opus, the *History of the United States* * that occupied his mind until it was published at last at the turn of the nineties. After leaving Harvard, he had gone abroad to work in the archives of London, Madrid and Paris, studying the diplomatic aspect of American history of the years 1800–1812. He had a desk, in Washington, at the Department of State, with access to its documents and records. At about this time, George Bancroft, the patriarch of American history, had also returned to Washington for the evening of his days. It was at Bancroft's table in Berlin that Adams had met Mommsen and Curtius; and the old man, retired from diplomacy, though he plodded away at his history still, rejoiced in his vote of admission to the floor of the Senate. Bancroft's position was unique in the capital: he was the only private citizen at whose house the President dined. At eighty, as at eighty-eight, he worked fourteen hours a day; and this tough old survivor of Jackson's times set the pace for other and tenderer Yankees. He was an example to less dedicated spirits,—Henry Adams, for one, whose energy flagged.† Adams, meanwhile, hobnobbed freely with senators, generals, ambassadors, in

* During the administrations of Jefferson and Madison, 1801–1817; nine volumes, 1889–1891.

† One of Adams's friends said later that she had stirred him into a spasm of activity by telling him how many candles Bancroft used while writing before breakfast.

whose hands the political history of the present lay. He
was at home in Washington as never in Boston. The
Adamses had always been at war with Boston; they had
always preferred all-American relations and contacts,
and Henry Adams had never felt that he was a true Bostonian,—Boston, for him, was a "bore." He had liked
the Virginians at Harvard: a son of General Lee was
his special friend there. Besides, he had always liked
Washington,—even his father had felt its singular charm.
The summer alone had reconciled him to Quincy in his
childhood, the smell of the hot pine-woods and the new-
mown hay, the peaches, the lilacs, the syringas, the taste
of the pennyroyal and the flagroot, the sweet-fern in the
scorching summer noon. At Washington, the Potomac
squandered beauty, and he loved the soft, full outlines of
the landscape, the sunshine and shadow in May and the
heavy odours, the catalpa, the azalea, the laurel, the
chestnuts. He was at home in the brooding heat of the
profligate vegetation, sensual, animal, elemental, the indolence of the Negro population, the looseness and lazi-
ness and the Southern drawl, the want of barriers and
forms, the absence of pavements, women with bandanas,
pigs in the streets. The freedom and the swagger of nature and man captivated his Yankee imagination. As the
men to whom he was drawn through life were the happy,
unconscious, objective types, men like Clarence King and
"Roony" Lee, as he was drawn, above all and through
all, to women,—to those who did not reason and think
about themselves, who were not introspective like himself,—so he was always and everywhere at home in the
tropics.* He had affirmed in 1860, "I shall make up my
bed in Washington;" and in 1868 he had repeated that
he was settled in Washington "perhaps for life." It was

---

* "A good, rotten tropical Spanish island, like Cuba, with no roads and
no drainage, but plenty of bananas and brigands, never bores me."—Letter
of 1894.

natural for him to return there, "as stable-companion to statesmen." But he did not break his tie with Massachusetts. As long as his wife lived, he spent the summer in Beverly, where the Adamses had a cottage among the pines. Every day at noon, when he rose from his work there, a few more beautiful pages lay on his desk; for his handwriting was really beautiful,—the letters were carved and interlaced, as in some manuscript of the Middle Ages. In the afternoon, with his wife, he went off riding through the woods. Three terriers tumbled about the feet of the horses.

So much for Adams's outer life. He found history "wildly interesting," and he seemed to be a happy and successful author. Behind this mask, however, another life went on. Adams was deeply dissatisfied. He had not wished to be a professor,* and even historical writing, which he enjoyed for a time, soon palled upon him. His history was a masterly performance. With its easy and confident style, its wealth of portraits, its singularly unprejudiced point of view, with its long historical perspective and its rigorous standards, this monumental work was beyond all praise; or, rather, its only drawback was that the subject,—a passage of sixteen years,—was not sufficiently large for the abundance of the treatment. But Adams wearied of the task before it was finished. Later he explained this lapse of interest by saying that he could "make life work" no longer,† which meant that his life

* "He broke his life in halves again in order to begin a new education, on lines he had not chosen, in subjects for which he cared less than nothing, in a place he did not love, and before a future which repelled."— *The Education of Henry Adams.*
"My engagement [as professor] is for five years, but I don't expect to remain so long."—Letter of 1870.
† "You find my last two volumes more critical—deliberately fault finding?—than the earlier ones. They were written chiefly within the last five or six years, and in a very different frame of mind from that in which the work was begun. I found it hard to pretend either sympathy or interest in my subject. If you compare the tone of my first volume—even toned down, as it is, from the original—with that of the ninth when it appears, you

was not in writing, that he was not a historian as Parkman was; for nothing, neither ill-health, personal tragedy, popular failure, ever destroyed in Parkman the zest of the artist. It was true that Adams continued to write; in fact, in his desultory way, he wrote better than ever. He wrote his best two books towards the end of his life. If he could not "make life work," it was not as a writer. And yet he described himself and his life as a failure. Evidently, to write fine books was not to be a "success," for him. What was his standard, then? What did he wish?

What Adams desired was power, like Mrs. Lightfoot Lee, in *Democracy*,* a very different ambition from that of the artist. The Adamses had possessed power, and the will-to-power was a family trait that governed Henry Adams's every instinct. He had taken the White House for granted as a boy. Did he wish for office? He sometimes said so.† But, generally speaking, what he desired was to rule from behind the scenes; and this was his motive in writing,—it had always been so. Although he liked to write, and had early thought of history and fiction,‡ he had never thought of writing as an end in itself. Liter-

will feel that the light has gone out. I am not to blame. As long as I could make life work, I stood by it, and swore by it as though it was my god, as indeed it was."—Letter of 1891.

* "What she wanted was Power . . . It was the feeling of a passenger on an ocean steamer whose mind will not give him rest until he has been in the engine-room and talked with the engineer. She wanted to see with her own eyes the action of primary forces; to touch with her own hand the massive machinery of society; to measure with her own mind the capacity of the motive power. She was bent upon getting to the heart of the great American mystery of democracy and government."—Henry Adams, *Democracy*. Mrs. Lee did not wish merely to understand these things. She wished to have her hand "on the lever."

† "They [Hay's letters] are interesting to me—more so than my own *Education;* for he did what I set out to do, only I could never have done it."—Letter of 1907.

‡ "But how of greater literary works? Could I write a history, do you think, or a novel?"—Letter of 1859.

ature, beside politics, was small beer for Adams;* he
wished to exercise influence and govern opinion.† Not to
be a power, not to live up to the family pattern,‡ this
was ashes in his mouth; for in all his fantasies, whimsical
or otherwise, he always saw himself as the cock of the
walk. If he dreamed of being a monk, then he was the
abbot; § and he felt that a cardinal's hat might well have
become him.‖ He wrote for "prizes," ¶ he wrote to "win a
place" for himself.** "If he worked at all, it was for social
consideration," and this he even supposed was the motive
of artists,—as if Emerson and Winslow Homer, Ryder
and Emily Dickinson "found their return in the pride
of their social superiority"! *** That one could work

---

* "Of *Atlantic Monthly* and *Putnam* and *Harper* and the men who write
for money in them, my opinion is short. Rather than do nothing but that, or
make that an object in life, I'd die here in Europe."—Letter of 1858.
    See also his later remark in London: "So I am happy and contented to
think that at all events I am not bored by Andrew Lang, and Gosse and
Sidney Colvin."—Letter of 1892. Compare this with his interest in politicians. Every minnow of a politician, economist or diplomat unfailingly
interested Adams.
    † He "began what he meant for a permanent series of annual political
reviews which he hoped to make, in time, a political authority . . . Whether
the newspapers liked it or not, they would have to reckon with him; for
such a power, once established, was more effective than all the speeches in
Congress or reports to the President that could be crammed into the government presses."—*The Education of Henry Adams.*
    ‡ "Were you intoxicated when you wrote that I am to 'combine in myself
the qualities of Seward, Greeley and Everett'?"—Letter to his brother,
1858.
    § "If we lived a thousand years ago instead of now, I should have be-
come a monk and would have got hold as abbot of one of those lovely little
monasteries which I used to admire so much among the hills in Italy."—
Letter of 1863.
    ‖ "The only thing I wanted in life was to be made a cardinal, and in
Rome I sounded delicately the pontifical ocean to ascertain the bearings of
my hat."—Letter of 1899.
    ¶ "I am satisfied that literature offers higher prizes than politics."—Letter
of 1877.
    ** "His object was literary. He wanted to win a place on the staff of the
Edinburgh Review, under the vast shadow of Lord Macaulay; and, to a
young American in 1868, such rank seemed colossal—the highest in the
literary world . . . The position . . . flattered vanity."—*The Education of
Henry Adams.*
    *** "Thus far, no one had made a suggestion of pay for any work that
Adams had done or would do; if he worked at all, it was for social con-

for anything but "reputation," even in public life, he could scarcely imagine;* and in dealing with his pupils he had urged this motive.† Such was his standard, and, measured by this, of course he himself was a failure. He had failed as a king-maker. He failed as a writer, for his publications attracted little attention. Was this not why he could not "make life work"?

Vanity, in short, was Henry Adams's governing motive,‡ as one saw in the anonymity to which he resorted. If he could not have fame at once, he would not play. He had failed in politics because he would not stoop to conquer. He refused to accept the terms of political action. He wished for "a career in which social position had value," and without this impossible advantage he refused to fight. "He wanted it handed to him on a silver plate,"§

sideration, and social pleasure was his pay. For this he was willing to go on working, as an artist goes on painting when no one buys his pictures. Artists have done it from the beginning of time, and will do it after time has expired, since they cannot help themselves, and they find their return in the pride of their social superiority as they feel it."—*The Education of Henry Adams.*

* Length of service has much to do with future reputation, and if you did not take office for reputation, what the deuce did you take it for?"— Letter to John Hay, 1899.

† "The question is whether the historico-literary line is practically worth following, not whether it will amuse or improve you. Can you make it *pay?* either in money, reputation, or any other solid value . . . Now if you will think for a moment of the most respectable and respected products of our town of Boston, I think you will see at once that this profession does pay. No one has done better and won more in any business or pursuit, than has been acquired by men like Prescott, Motley, Frank Parkman, Bancroft, and so on in historical writing. . . . Further, there is a great opening here at this time. Boston is running dry of literary authorities. Any one who has the ability can enthrone himself here as a species of literary lion with ease, for there is no rival to contest the throne. With it, comes social dignity, European reputation, and a foreign mission to close."—Letter to Henry Cabot Lodge, 1872.

‡ "For I am, as you have often truly said, a mass of affectation and vanity."—Letter to his brother Charles. This may have been said in irony,—it was certainly true.

§ "I think of [Justice] Holmes as mostly keeping the doors of his sympathy open, and of Adams as mostly keeping them shut.

" 'If the country had put him on a pedestal,' said Holmes to me once, 'I

without descending into the rough-and-tumble; and, similarly, when publication failed to yield the longed-for prize, Adams ceased to write for publication. He had refused to write anonymously as long as he thought his name might count,* but all his later work was written so, or, if it was not anonymous, it was privately printed; † and that his motive was not indifference one saw in the curiosity with which he watched the sales of his two novels. He was immensely elated by the success of *Democracy,* much as he professed to despise the public,‡ and regarded its wholesale piracy as the triumph of his life.§ One saw the same inverted pride in his attitude towards honours, which he invariably refused in later years. Only a man who cared for them excessively could have found such ingenious reasons for declining these honours. President Eliot understood him well.||

Writing for Adams was therefore a makeshift, and yet the thing that he was born for. What else could he have

think that Henry Adams with his gifts could have rendered distinguished public service.'
" 'What was the matter with Henry Adams?' I asked.
" 'He wanted it handed to him on a silver plate,' said Holmes.
"Now Holmes had gone after 'it' tooth and nail."
—Owen Wister, *Roosevelt, the Story of a Friendship.*

* "I will not go down into the rough-and-tumble, nor mix with the crowd, nor write anonymously, except for mere literary practice."—Letter of 1869.

† "As you may have noticed, I have not published anything since 1890 . . . I have privately printed, but never published."—Letter of 1916. His novel *Democracy* was published anonymously. *Esther* was published under the pseudonym Frances Snow Compton. *The Memoirs of Arii Taimai* were privately printed under his Tahitian name. In the *Life of George Cabot Lodge,* his name was printed on the fly-leaf but not on the title-page. The *Education* and *Mont-Saint-Michel and Chartres* were privately printed in very small editions for his friends.

‡ "I hate publishing, and do not want reputation. There are not more than a score of people in America whose praise I want."—Letter of 1893.

§ "As for piracy, I love to be pirated. It is the greatest compliment an author can have. The wholesale piracy of *Democracy* was the single real triumph of my life."—Letter of 1905.

|| When he refused an honorary degree at Harvard, President Eliot wrote to Adams: "To decline it would require a thousand explanations—to accept it is natural and modest."

done? What could he have been? Certainly not a statesman. He was not aggressive enough for this. Nor was he
in temper a reformer. He had no zest for the role of an
oppositionist; and, disliking the tendencies of the age he
lived in, he still enjoyed their fruits too much to fight
them. He had too deep a stake in the welfare of banks
and stock-exchanges, he was too fond of "luxury as a
steady business;" * and, while he abhorred the politics of
John Hay and Cabot Lodge, these two remained his constant companions and friends. In fact, he developed a
hatred of reformers, and he could scarcely find words to
express his contempt for those who tried to carry out in
action the ideals he had represented in earlier days. Were
not Theodore Roosevelt, La Follette and Woodrow Wilson attempting, in terms of their day, what he had tried
to do in 1870? He regarded them all as bores, insane and
dishonest. But, feeling that he should have been a statesman, that he ought to have been a reformer, that he
ought to have carried on the Adams line, he could not
feel that writing justified him. Writing amused him, and,
because he had a first-rate mind and the pride of an excellent craftsman, he wrote admirable books. But in motive
he was always a dilettante.

* "I am not so easy about the coal-strike and labour-troubles in Europe,
because they may bother me. I keep my eye fixed on the stock-exchange,"
etc. . . . "After all, I do like luxury as a steady business . . . As a man of
sense I am a gold-bug and support a gold-bug government and a gold-bug
society."—From letters of Henry Adams.

CHAPTER XIII

HENRY JAMES

HENRY JAMES had crossed and recrossed the Atlantic, trying to solve his great dilemma, whether to live at home or to live in Europe. In 1875, he settled in Paris, and it seemed at first that he meant to remain there forever. The writers he most admired were living there, and Paris was the best of meeting-places in which to view his countrymen abroad. He had concluded that the "international novel" was the type that he was qualified to write;* and where were the auspices happier for a writer of novels?

So, for a twelvemonth, Henry James lived in Paris, in constant association with La Farge's friends, the novelists whom he had studied with rapture at home. Howells had agreed with his comments on the English novel, which had everything to learn in the matter of handling, of artistic treatment and form;† and James had all but worshipped these French writers, with their instinct for

---

* This "conclusion," practical if not deliberate, was a natural outgrowth of James's childhood and the atmosphere of the James family. The patriotic father "overflowed with the bravest sort of contradictions," and, while he disdained what he called "this fumbling in the cadaver of the old world," he encouraged the comparison of different European countries and of them all with America. Louis Leverett, in Henry James's *A Bundle of Letters,* spoke for both Henry and William when he said, "I am much interested in the study of national types, in comparing, contrasting, seizing the strong points, the weak points, the point of view of each."

† "The novel, as largely practised in England, is the perfect paradise of the loose end."—James, preface to *The Awkward Age.* Compare Howells's remarks on Thackeray, Dickens, etc., in his *Criticism and Fiction.*

The Irish writer, George Moore, who had also lived in Paris and who shared James's admiration for the French art of the novel, carried on through life a quarrel with English fiction that was similar to James's. He

settings and details, their gift for analyzing the reports of their senses. Art, he had always felt, lives on discussion, the interchange of views, the comparison of standpoints; and in Paris the Goncourts, Flaubert, Turgenev and Zola gave him a place in their circle. He spent mornings at Auteuil, in Edmond de Goncourt's study, and rainy afternoons with Turgenev, whom he always left with excitement, leaping over gutters lightly and stopping to look in shop-windows,—with an air of being struck,—for no reason at all. He felt that all manner of secrets had been placed in his keeping. He dined with Renan, the hideous and charming, and at Madame Viardot's Sunday afternoons he often saw Turgenev again, sometimes on all fours, in a mask and shawl, in some extravagant charade that reminded him of historical games at Concord. The best of these occasions were Flaubert's Sunday afternoons, when the old master, in his Arab blouse, discoursed with his younger disciples, one of whom was Guy de Maupassant. Flaubert was annoyed with James because he spoke with disrespect of Prosper Mérimée's style; but James had never dreamed of such conversation, such confidences about plans and ambitions, such counsels of perfection that spoke of an intense artistic life. The talk was all of logic, lucidity, the clear image, precise observation, the inevitable word,

complained of the English "lack of seriousness;" he felt that the great English novelists had scarcely a trace of discipline, unity or artistic direction, and he went to London with the hope of winning "freedom" for English fiction by remodelling it in the style of the great French writers.

While both James and Moore added much to the English art of fiction, both remained unreconciled to the English genius. They were unwilling to accord the English the right to the sort of novels that the English liked. James was as indifferent as Moore to what John Eglinton calls *(Irish Literary Portraits)* the "vitality and good spirits" of the English novel, "its incomparable sense of romance, its thoughtfulness, its gift of humour, its affiliation to drama and poetry rather than to the arts of painting and drawing."

It may be added that Moore's uneasy relations with Ireland were much like James's uneasy relations with America. Both were always going home to find themselves disillusioned again, and both remained essentially foreigners in London.

grace and felicity, lightness and shapeliness, design, style, manner, the virtues of form. The intelligence of these writers was truly infernal.

All this confirmed James's resolution to carry his art of the novel to a pitch of perfection. How deep this resolution was one saw in his work and his prefaces later, but the themes of many of his stories also showed it. He was passionately concerned with self-education, although the concern of his characters was to educate others. "I believe in you," said Rowland Mallett to Roderick Hudson, as they set out for Europe, "if you are prepared to work and to wait and to struggle and to exercise a great many virtues." Rowland Mallett's hope was to make a great artist of Roderick, and this was Sherringham's object in *The Tragic Muse,* in connection with Miriam Rooth; while Gabriel Nash conceived it as his function to serve as a conscience for Nick Dormer. The theme of *The Bostonians* was the tutelage of Verena Tarrant,— who was to exercise it, Ransome or Olive?—and James's early novel, *Watch and Ward,* described the bringing up of a little waif by her future husband, Roger Lawrence. In the continual recurrence of this motive one saw how much his own development occupied James's mind; * and

* James's austerity of purpose was reflected in many of his young men, the youthful Roderick, Rowland Mallett, Longueville, in *Confidence,* and Longmore, in *Madame de Mauves,* who, "like many spirits of the same stock, had in his composition a lurking principle of asceticism to whose authority he had ever paid an 'unquestioning respect." Compare this passage about Longueville: "It was annoyance that he had passed out of his own control—that he had obeyed a force which he was unable to measure at the time . . . In spite of a great momentary appearance of frankness and a lively relish of any conjunction of agreeable circumstances exerting a pressure to which one could respond, Bernard had really little taste for giving himself up, and he never did so without very soon wishing to take himself back." Compare also these passages from *Roderick Hudson:* " 'I believe that a man of genius owes as much deference to his passions as any other man, but not a particle more, and I confess I have a strong conviction that the artist is better for leading a quiet life.' . . . There was in all dissipation . . . a vulgarity which would disqualify it for Roderick's favour . . . The young sculptor was a man to regard all things in the light of his art, to hand over his passions to his genius to be dealt with, and to find that he could live largely enough without exceeding the circle of pure delights."

there were other motives that drove him forward. He
felt that he had to make up for missing the war; and he
felt the "Higginsonian fangs" behind him.* He had to
justify his expatriation;† and he had to counterbalance
his American birth. For James believed that art was a
European secret: he had much more to learn than a
European. Did he not feel, at times,—he later implied it,
when he said the tale was "documentary,"—as the painter
Theobald felt, in *The Madonna of the Future?*—"We
are condemned to be superficial. We are excluded from
the magic circle. The soil of American perception is a
poor little barren, artificial deposit. Yes, we are wedded
to imperfection. An American, to excel, has just ten times
as much to learn as a European. We lack the deeper
sense; we have neither taste, nor tact, nor force. How
should we have them? Our crude and garish climate, our
silent past, our deafening present, the constant pressure
about us of unlovely circumstance, are as void of all that

* "The truth is that Mr. James's cosmopolitanism is, after all, limited;
to be really cosmopolitan, a man must be at home even in his own country."—Thomas Wentworth Higginson.
† James's will and pride were undoubtedly piqued by the numerous gibes
at his expatriation. Typical of these is the following passage from *Rollo's
Journey to Cambridge,* which appeared in the *Harvard Lampoon,* 1879–
1880:
"Now it happened, while this scene was taking place, a foreigner had
got into the car. In his coat-pocket there was a red 'Guide to New England.' He was reading de Tocqueville on America, and had asked Benny
whether Jarvis Field was a prairie, and whether buffaloes (bisons) were
still shot in Cambridge. This gentleman was Mr. Henry James.
"As soon as he saw Dovey, he began to take notes of her with a polyglot
pencil on analytic paper. When the proctor saw this, he fled incontinently.
"Mr. James then enquired of Mr. George, with a strong foreign accent,
whether the lady, his *vis-à-vis,* was *de ses amies.* Mr. George emphatically
disclaimed her acquaintance, though admitting she had been of service to
him the day before.
" 'The gentleman, her *compagnon de voyage,* is I fancy her husband?'
queried Mr. James. 'A most unhappy *ménage.'*
" 'I do not believe it,' said Mr. George.
" '*Tiens!* and can it be the custom in this country for young ladies to
travel unattended, or, still worse, in the company of a young man, from
Cambridge to East Cambridge? I must remember this in my forthcoming
work on the American girl.' "
Turgenev was similarly lampooned in Russia.

nourishes and prompts and inspires the artist as my sad heart is void of bitterness in saying so." He certainly felt this at moments; and nothing more actively spurred him on to prove that his misgivings were not true. The great craftsman that he became was the product of all these motives, and he finished his apprenticeship in Paris. He had been stirred to a passion of emulation, a "rage of determination to *do,* and triumph."

At the end of a year, however, James moved to London. He had wearied of the company of these French writers. Much as he had gained from them, he had not found them congenial: they sometimes reminded him of a pirates' cave. Aside from their craft, they had no interests, and they struck him as brutal, exclusive, corrupt and complacent. They had no vision, no humanity, no taste for the intangible; and, besides, he could not endure their Bohemian ways. They often shocked Turgenev, the gentle Russian giant, and they shocked this young American ten times more so. He felt, for the rest, an outsider in Paris. He felt that he could not establish relations in France; and to know the great world of Europe, to penetrate its secrets,—this had been James's object in coming abroad. He had tried Italy before he went to Paris and found that he could not pierce behind the scenes. "I feel forever how Europe keeps holding one at arm's length," he wrote in one of his letters, "and condemning one to a meagre scraping of the surface." And again: "What is the meaning of this destiny of desolate exile—this dreary necessity of having month after month to do without our friends for the sake of this arrogant old Europe which so little befriends us?" On the continent he could not hope for any initiation,* although he felt he had grasped in

* James undoubtedly expressed his own feelings in the story, *At Isella,* referring to the old burgher mansions in a Swiss town through which the narrator is passing: "I wondered of course who lived in them, and how they lived, and what was society in Altdorf, longing plaintively, in the manner of roaming Americans, for a few stray crumbs from the native

Italy "what might be meant by the life of art." In *Trans-atlantic Sketches,* he had pictured his rambles through Tuscany, with a volume of Stendhal in his pocket, his rides on the Campagna and his starlit nights in Venice, amid the accumulations of the festal past; and he often returned to Italy later for its "tonic picturesqueness" and all its "mellowed harmonies of tint and contour." * There he had found the remnants of Story's circle, "much broken up," or "broken down;" and there he had written some of his earlier stories, among them *The Madonna of the Future.* Suggested by Balzac's *Le Chef-d'œuvre inconnu,* this also suggested the life of Washington Allston, be-fore whose unfinished "Belshazzar's Feast," over which the painter had toiled at home, James had lingered long, with sad misgivings. He had "lived it over," the painter's nostalgia, the "grim synthetic fact of Cambridgeport," where Allston's beautiful talent had wasted away. He had also partly written in Florence the first of his im-portant novels, the story of the sculptor, Roderick Hud-son; and it was in Florence that he met Sargent, who gave him the idea of *The Aspern Papers.* Sargent had known Claire Clairmont, who had died in Florence, the mother of Byron's Allegra and the friend of Shelley. In the same house with old Miss Clairmont and her middle-aged niece

social board, with my fancy vainly beating its wings against the great blank wall, behind which, in travel-haunted Europe, all gentle private in-terests nestle away from intrusion. Here, as elsewhere, I was struck with the mere surface-relation of the Western tourist to the soil he treads. He filters and trickles through the dense social body in every possible direc-tion, and issues forth at last the same virginal water-drop. 'Go your way,' these antique houses seemed to say, from their quiet courts and gardens; 'the road is yours and welcome, but the land is ours. You may pass and stare and wonder, but you may never know us!' "

* "I have come on a pilgrimage," I said. "To understand what I mean, you must have lived, as I have lived, in a land beyond the seas, barren of romance and grace . . . Here I sit for the first time in the enchanted air in which love and faith and art and knowledge are warranted to become deeper passions than in my own chilly clime . . . The air has a perfume; everything that enters my soul, at every sense, is a suggestion, a promise, a performance."—James, *Travelling Companions.*

there had lived an ardent collector of Shelleyana, an American, Captain Silsbee of Salem, who longed to procure from Miss Clairmont her jealously guarded collection of Shelley papers. Silsbee, who happened to be in America when Miss Clairmont died, rushed back at once to secure the papers, which the old-maid niece agreed to give him if he would accept herself as part of the bargain. Thereupon Silsbee fled, and lost the treasure. Such was the germ of one of James's finest stories, as he received it from Sargent.*

Meanwhile, James had been drawn to London as one of the many "American claimants" for whom it was a paradise as well as a world. He approached it in a spirit of reverence and awe that somewhat suggested Howells's at the gates of Boston.† Had he not shared all the emotions of his "passionate pilgrim," who felt that England should have been his home?‡ Could it be his home? Could he understand it? These were questions for the future. At present, so far as introductions went,—James was under the wing of Lowell and Norton,—he was soon in the centre of the picture. He shared the prerogatives of travelling Americans in realms that native writers seldom entered.§ As for the rest, he applied himself to the

* *John Sargent,* by Evan Charteris. Captain Edward Silsbee bequeathed his collection of Shelleyana in equal parts to Harvard and to Oxford.

† "He was always the great figure of London, and I was for no small time, as the years followed, to be kept at my awe-struck distance for taking him on that sort of trust."—James, *The Middle Years.*

‡ "I was born with a soul for the picturesque . . . I found it nowhere. I found a world all hard lines and harsh lights, without shade, without composition, as they say of pictures, without the lovely mystery of colour . . . Sitting here, in this old park, I feel—I feel that I hover on the misty verge of what might have been! I should have been born here and not there."—Searle, in James's *A Passionate Pilgrim.*

"I had taken . . . the adventure of my twenty-sixth year 'hard,' as *A Passionate Pilgrim* quite sufficiently attests."—Later preface.

§ "The position of the American of some resources and of leisure was, in European society of the nineteenth century, one of a singular felicity. Without, or almost without, letters of introduction or social passports of any kind, the American 'went everywhere,' everywhere in the world—into the courts of the Emperors of Austria or into the bosom of English county

study of English ways and types with his usual assiduity
and firmness of purpose. Hawthorne in Rome had seemed
to him to prove that a novelist could not "project himself into an atmosphere in which he had not a transmitted
and inherited property." But what could not be done by
observation? It was the doctrine of his friends in Paris
that one could "get up" any subject, that one could master any field or world, provided one lived sufficiently in
one's ears and one's eyes. Zola had recently got up Rome
with a Baedeker and a visit of four or five weeks. If
Hawthorne had been more observant, he might have done
so,—and what could not a novelist do with a lifetime?
James submitted himself to the "Londonizing process."
He dined out almost every evening; by day and by night
he roamed the streets. He "went everywhere," shy, sedate,
grave and watchful, with his guarded, formal manner
and his dark brown beard. He had a flat in Kensington,
but he moved about the country freely. One of his favourite retreats was an inn at Torquay, and once he worked
for a while on the Irish coast; and he stayed on the
Normandy coast, at Bayonne, at Dover. He spent a summer at Broadway with Sargent, Abbey and Millet, the
American painters, and he usually went to Paris for a
month each year. In 1881–82, he returned for a year to
America, and he wandered over the continent between
whiles. *A Little Tour in France,* the best of his earlier
books of travel, was the fruit of a jaunt through Balzac's
country.

Meanwhile, in a rapid succession of novels and stories,
James pictured the world of wanderers that he knew so

families. To know, or to admit an American into your family circle appeared to commit you to nothing. There was the whole immense Herring
Pond between yourself and their homes and you just accepted the strange
and generally quiet creatures on their face values, without any question as
to their origins and taking their comfortable wealths for granted. Thus
Mr. James could really get to 'know' people in a way that would be absolutely sealed to any European young writer whether he were Honoré de
Balzac or Charles Dickens."—Ford Madox Ford, *Henry James.*

well, the Americans in Europe whom he had watched as
a child and whom he was encountering in his peregrina-
tions. Who were these Americans, and what were the
motives that drew them abroad? Most of them were
products of the post-war years. There had always been
Gallophiles in Paris and Anglophiles in London, and
James pictured these older American types as well, along
with the "aesthetic" colonists in Rome and Florence. But
the sudden growth of wealth at home accounted for most
of the travellers, together with the spread of a feeling
for culture.* The drop of the national thermometer had
alienated many, who had lost interest in their country;
and the absorption of men in business had provided their
families with money to spend and driven them abroad
for romance or amusement. While the vast majority lived
at home, just as Howells pictured them, hordes were governed by these motives. They felt they had no function at
home any longer. The men, who existed to make money,
had ceased to care for the public good, and the women
were bored by business and knew nothing about it. They
were no longer required to be mothers of homesteads;
they had been largely absolved from their ancient duties;
and, with leisure on their hands, in a world that made no
provision for leisure, they were drawn to Europe, where
leisure was an art. Middle-class women had always felt
that they had a right to be warriors' wives; they had
wept over romances of knights and princes and followed
the patterns of aristocratic ladies. With their instinctive
love of valour, these women could not be content with a
drab and grubby world of business men; and the more
the American male was absorbed in this, the more the

* In Matthew Arnold's sense of the word. "To care only for the best! To
do the best, to know the best,—to have, to desire, to recognize only the
best. That's what I have always done, in my quiet little way. I have gone
through Europe on my devoted little errand, seeking, seeing, heeding only
the best. And it has not been for myself alone; it has been for my daughter. My daughter had had the best. We are not rich, but I can say that."—
Mrs. Church, in James's *The Pension Beaurepas.*

women dreamed of castles and titles and a brilliant life of social adventure elsewhere. There were thousands of Madame Bovarys in New York and in Boston, as in San Francisco, Milwaukee, Chicago and Denver, and they played in fancy with a frequent theme of the French novel, the story of the young wife, tired of domestic monotony, who exchanges the dullest of husbands for the gayest of lovers. The American men had given up their chance of aristocracy, for they had withdrawn from politics and war; and where were the women to find it, since they had a natural craving for it? Where could they find the elegance they also dreamed of?—which existed at home, to be sure, but in no such measure. America had always had its aristocracy, but this had not evolved in native forms. Its forms had remained European,* and for this reason, and because it was without prescriptive rights, European aristocrats, who embodied the source of all these forms, possessed in American society a special glamour; † and now, with the decay of European aristocracy, together with the growth of American wealth, Europe offered an open field for American social ambition. Was not the example of the Empress Eugénie, the little Spanish girl with the Yankee grandsire, one that all the American girls might follow? The international marriage was one of the striking facts of the moment; ‡ and

* "We haven't socially evolved from ourselves; we've evolved from the Europeans, from the English. I don't think you'll find a single society rite with us now that had its origin in our peculiar national life, if we have a peculiar national life."—The "facetious gentleman," in Howells's *Through the Eye of the Needle.*

† Henry Adams said that his father was "one of the exceedingly small number of Americans to whom an English duke or duchess seemed to be indifferent, and royalty itself nothing more than a slightly inconvenient person."

‡ ". . . The great truth that the star of matrimony, for the American girl, was now shining in the East,—in England and France and Italy. They had only to look round anywhere to see it; what did they hear of every day in the week but the engagement of one of their own compeers to some count or some lord?"—James, *The Reverberator.*
The marriage of Miss Jennie Jerome to Lord Randolph Churchill, 1874, was sometimes described as the "entering wedge."

the American magazines swarmed with stories of girls
who had caught sham nobles, and sometimes real ones,
though more often than not to their sorrow.* For they
were usually pictured as leading a life of domestic misery;
they were often abandoned penniless on some foreign
strand. During the years of the Second Empire, Paris
had had all the prestige.† Americans had praised everything French and were rather inclined to slight everything
English. The Napoleon III moustache blossomed on
countless American faces, and the happy dream of countless women was to appear at a ball at the Tuileries. Paris
abounded with families like the Follanbees;‡ and the
young girls, as Mrs. Stowe remarked, longed to be "à la
everything Frenchy and pretty," everything "gay and
glistening," like the Empress herself, with their hoops
and puffs and pinkings and ruffles and bows. No one
denied that they succeeded. The legend had arisen that
all American women were charming and that their men
were always plain, awkward and dull. Meanwhile, with
the downfall of Napoleon and Eugénie, the prestige of
London had risen as the centre of fashion. Many of the
American suppliants were flocking thither. Add to this
the romance of Europe, all the more alluring as American life seemed to grow drabber and drabber, add the
rising hunger and thirst for culture, which had become
so largely the province of women, and one could under-

* The grim stay-at-homes retaliated by inventing such comic characters
as Count No-account, Count Screwloose of Toulouse, etc.
† This was the moment of T. G. Appleton's phrase, "All good Americans, when they die, go to Paris."
‡ In Harriet Beecher Stowe's *Pink and White Tyranny*. Mrs. Follanbee
"felt that a residence near the court, at a time when everything good and
decent in France was hiding in obscure corners, and everything parvenu
was wide awake and active, entitled her to speak with authority about
French manners and customs." Mr. Follanbee,—a pedlar who had risen to
untold wealth,—"was one of the class of returned travellers who always
speak condescendingly of everything American, as 'so-so,' or 'tolerable,'
or 'pretty fair,'—a considerateness which goes a long way towards keeping
up the spirits of the country."

stand the great hegira that afforded Henry James the theme of his lifetime.

For this was James's chosen world, the world for which he was foreordained; and he returned to this world in his last long novels. He had even followed the general movement by moving from Paris to London himself, and he pictured Americans in Italy and France before he pictured them in England. Later, when he had largely relinquished his hope of describing English society, he found in this earlier theme a recourse and a refuge, although, just as he attempted to picture the English among themselves, so, in three or four of the novels of his prime, he presented his Americans at home. *The Bostonians* and *Washington Square* were two of his brilliant achievements; and possibly *Washington Square* was the best of them all. The scene of his earliest memories returned to his mind, after he had lived for a while in London, and nothing that he ever wrote was more hauntingly truthful and final than the story of Catherine Sloper, her father, her lover and her aunt Lavinia Penniman of Poughkeepsie. This perfect little novel was an American classic, surely, an irreplaceable picture of old New York, with its sights and its sounds and its odours; and was not *The Bostonians* almost as much so? James had known these phases of his "huge, queer country," with his Cambridge, his Cape Cod, his Central Park, and with Dr. Tarrant, Verena and Basil Ransome, Miss Birdseye, Olive Chancellor and so many others. It was true that outside these circles, and even within them, he sometimes failed in verisimilitude; * and his Boston was the unlove-

* Thomas Wentworth Higginson observed that James opened *The Europeans* with horse-cars on the Boston streets ten years before they were introduced; and it was generally noted that it was impossible for such a girl as Gertrude Wentworth never to have seen an artist. Lowell objected that no Boston household like the Wentworths could have been so amazed by the sight of Europeans. "In the new story, when you reprint it, soften Mr. Wentworth's ignorance of European phrases and things a bit . . . I must have known many Harvard graduates of the class of 1809 and I assure

liest of all the Bostons. His American scene was severely
limited, and his American novels were singularly cold
beside the warmth and glow of his pictures of Europe.
It was in their longing for Europe that he sympathized
with his countrypeople; and the ardour with which they
shared this motive quickened them in James's mind. "In
Boston one can't *live* . . . One can't live aesthetically;"
and "the great thing is to *live*, you know." What Louis
Leverett said, in *A Bundle of Letters*, Strether repeated
in *The Ambassadors* later; and living, for James and his
people, meant going abroad.*

What happened to these people? What was the nature
of their adventures? And, first of all, who were they?
There were dozens of types, and they came from all over
America, Washington, Boston, Schenectady, Northampton, San Diego, and one saw them in Florence, in Paris,
at Homburg, at Vevey, in Baden-Baden, Geneva, in
Rome or in London. There were business men who had
made their pile and were out for entertainment.† There
were odious society reporters like Mr. Flack. There were
broken-down husbands who tagged along with their wives
and daughters.‡ There were patient American citizens

you they knew Europe pretty well. You boys fancy that nobody went
thither before the Cunarders began to ply in 1837. In most respects Europe
was better known then than now."—Letter of Lowell to James, 1878, referring to *The Europeans*.

* "The city of Boston be damned!" Ransome said in *The Bostonians*.
The violence with which Ransome rescued his Andromeda was certainly a
reflection of James's feelings. Was not the story a symbol of James, escap-
ing from America with his art?

† "I want the biggest kind of entertainment a man can get . . . I want to
see the tallest mountains, and the bluest lakes, and the finest pictures, and
the handsomest churches, and the most celebrated men, and the most beautiful women."—Christopher Newman, in *The American*.

‡ "Mr. Ruck is a broken down man of business. He is broken down in
health, and I suspect he is broken down in fortune. He has spent his whole
life in buying and selling; he knows how to do nothing else. His wife and
daughter have spent their lives, not in selling, but in buying; and they, on
their side, know how to do nothing else. To get something in a shop that
they can put on their backs,—that is their only idea; they haven't another
in their heads."—*The Pension Beaurepas*.

who were bored by Europe.* There were old American
Francophiles, who worshipped privacy and good manners, and others who said "Mount Blank," "Amurica"
and "Parus;" and there were earnest young men who
had rushed abroad to save some charming creature from
a French deceiver. There were young men, sketching in
Italy, who had not found at home "a great deal to take
hold of," and who, after going back "to see how it
looks," hit upon some plan for returning to Europe.
There were ministers, on summer vacations, with Mrs.
Jameson in their luggage, and young men, passionless,
subtle and knowing, who were always comparing nationalities, contrasting their manners and customs, with a
special regard to the ways of the "baronial class." These
young men sometimes liked to think that they were "as
particular as any Englishman could be;" and they were
as eager to know the geography of other countries as
they were vague about their own. They were analytical;
they went into the "reasons of things," and they were
always trying to get visual impressions. Of what did the
"character" of objects and persons consist? They were as
fastidious about furniture and bric-a-brac as James himself and some of James's women; and this is saying much,
for some of these women were always collecting bric-a-
brac, material and human. They went in for snuff-boxes,
Dresden tea-cups, altar-lace and occasionally some "rather
good old damask;" and sometimes they were satisfied
with members of the other sex whose resemblance to good
old damask was their principal charm.† These women
usually cared a great deal about money, although they

* "Bored, patient, helpless; pathetically dependent on his wife and
daughters; indulgent to excess; mostly a modest, decent, excellent, valuable
citizen; the American was to be met at every railway station in Europe,
carefully explaining to every listener that the happiest day of his life would
be the day he should land on the pier at New York."—*The Education of
Henry Adams.*
† Gilbert Osmond, in *The Portrait of a Lady.*

disdained the men who made it, who were lacking in "social drapery," more often than not; * and, if they returned to America, it was to look after their investments, for they felt that their country existed to provide them with money. Some spent money with implacable persistence. Others travelled in order to economize. They had an inexhaustible knowledge of hotels and pensions, and their rooms became dwellings over-night, with the books they spread about, the flowers and the draperies; for they had the housekeeping habits of inveterate nomads. There were some who hoped to "get into society," like Mrs. Headway of San Diego; others, born for society, were trying to find it; others carried their Murray in their laps, even when they went to the tailor; others again were marked by a passion for knowledge. There were American women in Paris who smiled at the "big-footed" English, and there were American wives in London who were better tories than their husbands, and there were others who spent hours looking out of their London windows, longing to "see something of the life." There were small boys, like Randolph Miller, who could not find any candy in Italy,—they usually had pale complexions and sharp little features; and especially there were young girls who were variously enchanting,—there was always some young man who found them so. A few of these young girls were plain: they had been brought up on "nature." † Others were travelling for culture,‡

---

* "Isabel hesitated a little. 'I think I value everything that is valuable. I care very much for money, and that is why I wish Mr. Osmond to have some' . . . She cared nothing about [Goodwood's] cotton-mill, and the Goodwood patent left her imagination absolutely cold."—*The Portrait of a Lady.*

† "She had been brought up to think a great deal of 'nature' and nature's innocent laws, but now Rowland had talked to her ingeniously of culture; her fresh imagination had responded, and she was pursuing this mysterious object into retreats where the need for some intellectual effort gave her an air of charming tension."—*Roderick Hudson.*

‡ "I always have my answer ready: 'For general culture,' to acquire the languages, and to see Europe for myself."—The young girl in *A Bundle of Letters.*

and others for fun. Others again had "modelling" and a
large infusion of colour and mystery; some were brilliant
and dashing; some were flirts. There were prettily innocent Daisy Millers who lived in a round of dressing and
dancing. They had found at Vevey a better Saratoga, and
they flitted hither and thither in their muslin flounces,
with their knots of pale-coloured ribbon and their thin,
gay voices. How light their figures were, how quick their
glances, how rapid were their gliding steps, how coquet-
tish their hats! Their profiles were delicate, their tone
was full of mockery; and the more discreet Americans
wondered where these uncultivated children got their
taste.* For others were chaperoned, well-bred and well-
conducted, often in the care of mothers who knew their
world. Perhaps they had come abroad to learn the art
of wearing a train, present a cup of tea and compose a
bouquet. Sometimes they nursed a secret dream of marrying a son of the Crusaders. There were Francie Dossons,
Bessie Aldens, Pandora Days and Linda Pallants, and
Isabel Archers who moved in a realm of light; and they
were invariably idols of their fathers and mothers, their
lovers and masculine cousins, or their uncles and aunts.
A chorus of Europeans danced attendance on them, English lords, French counts, Italian guides. There was often
some German baroness to forward their matches; and
occasionally some stalwart American male became involved with Bellegardes who "pouted at" the Empire.
But the delightful American girls were the cynosure of
every eye. The world of James, as of Howells, revolved
around them.

Such were James's *dramatis personae*, and dozens
of others surrounded these principal persons, Henrietta
Stackpole, Casper Goodwood, General Packard in Paris,

* "She has that charming look that they all have. I can't think where they
pick it up; and she dresses in perfection . . . I can't think where they get
their taste."—Winterbourne's aunt, in *Daisy Miller*.

Miss Flora Finch, old Mr. Touchett, the American
banker in England,—but how could one begin to name
them all? This American world in Europe was almost as
wide as Howells's world and pictured with a more distinguished art; for, while James's sympathies were nar-
rower than Howells's, the quality of his mind was more
intense. And what befell these people? In many cases,
nothing, or something so intangible that only James could
make it count. They drifted about in isolated groups,
satisfied merely to bask in the sunlight of Europe. They
explored their own minds; they studied one another; they
lived in a "passionate consciousness" of their situation.
They met at tea on the lovely lawns of beautiful English
country-houses; they revelled in Italian palaces and
French chateaus. They watched from the outside the
gaiety of Baden-Baden, or they surveyed the riders in
Rotten Row, the shining procession of English beauty
and fashion; or they sat submissive in cafés or on rows
of chairs in the Champs Elysées. They floated on the
edges and surfaces of things. Some were initiated, some
were detached, some were disposed to treat Europe as a
holiday toy, to be thrown away at the dawn of another
convenience; but just to be in Europe, in many cases, made
their drama, and most of them wished, in one way or
another, to merge their lives with the life of Europe. If
they were not bewildered by Europe, they were beguiled
and charmed by Europe. They were charmed and then
they were beguiled; for they were usually innocent creatures, virginal, upright and open-hearted, and in almost
every case they came to grief. The unsuspecting Christopher Newman was trapped and betrayed by the Bellegardes. Daisy Miller was misprized and died. Isabel
Archer was led astray, like Roderick Hudson and so many
others,—for innocence wronged was the theme of James's
work. And this innocence was American innocence at the

mercy of the dark old world that so charmed it, deceived
it, destroyed it and cast it away.

Now, what James suggested in all these stories was
that his fellow-Americans were morally superior to Europeans. The magnanimous Christopher Newman was the
type of them all, the chivalrous, honest, candid soul who
submitted his fate to the hands of the Bellegardes and
suffered through their cruelty and tortuous behaviour.
This was the story of Maggie Verver, this was the story
of Milly Theale, in James's last long novels; and he
seemed to feel, from first to last, that the world into
which they were drawn, the great world of Europe, and
especially England, was arrogant, base, corrupt, insolent
and greedy. This indeed was James's feeling about the
English upper class, as he expressed it in one of his letters to Norton; * yet this was the world that fascinated
James, as it charmed and beguiled his American characters. Had he not "roamed and wandered and yearned,"
like his own Hyacinth Robinson, watching the great company of London fashion, longing for an identification
with it that letters of introduction could never supply? †
Had he not watched like Lucien de Rubempré in Paris,
like all those young men in his own stories whose imagination wistfully wandered, as Hyacinth Robinson's did,
"among the haunts of the aristocracy?" His American
characters might be nobler, but, if the old world was cor-

---

* "The English upper class . . . The condition of that body seems to me
to be in many ways very much the same rotten and collapsible one as that
of the French aristocracy before the Revolution—minus cleverness and
conversation; or perhaps it's more like the heavy, congested and depraved
Roman world upon which the barbarians came down . . . Much of English
life is grossly materialistic and wants blood-letting."—Letter to Norton,
1886.

† "I arrived so at the history of little Hyacinth Robinson—he sprang up
for me out of the London pavement. To find his possible adventure interesting I had only to conceive his watching the same public show, the same
innumerable appearances I had watched myself, and of his watching very
much as I had watched."—Preface to *The Princess Casamassima.*

rupt, its glamour outweighed its corruption in James's
mind; and, while he upheld his moral standard, the
glamour filled his imagination, regardless of all the baseness that might lie beneath it. He admired it socially more
than he condemned it morally, and this led to a confusion
in his sense of values, so that he later pictured people, actually base, whom he described as eminent, noble and
great. Was there not something in it that was "better than
a good conscience," as Longmore, envying the baron's
manner, felt in *Madame de Mauves*? * All of James's
characters were drawn by this glamour, which struck
them as mystically superior, whether noble or base. They
turned away from other people who represented probity,
and whom James usually described as banal or prosaic,
and were captivated, by Europeans, or Europeanized
Americans, although they were often aware that the latter were base. So Roderick Hudson turned from Mary
Garland in order to pursue Christina Light, a thoroughly
perverse little baggage, and so Isabel Archer turned
from Warburton and Goodwood, attracted by the ignoble Gilbert Osmond; and these choices were not presented as matters of passion but as somehow indicating
a higher discernment. What seemed to James really important was not morals but manners, which would not
have compromised his work if he had not professed to
stand for morals; and it was inevitable that, worshipping
manners, he should have lost interest in his countrypeople.
For they were least interesting in the sphere of manners.
In his heart he had always felt that they were scarcely
worth writing about, in comparison with Europeans, if
one could grasp them; for they were, by definition, provin-

---

* "Something he had, however, which Longmore vaguely envied—a kind
of superb positiveness—a manner rounded and polished by the traditions
of centuries—an amenity exercised for his own sake and not his neighbour's—which seemed the result of something better than a good conscience
—of a vigorous and unscrupulous temperament. The baron was plainly not
a moral man, and poor Longmore, who was, would have been glad to
learn the secret of his luxurious serenity."—James, *Madame de Mauves*.

cial for James,* and he felt that "luxurious aristocracies" were superior as subjects.† This was a pity, for his relation to the latter was always artificial and factitious, while he possessed his Americans as extensions of himself; and who cares what race or class a novelist pictures, so long as he is at home with his world and its types?

* "I don't at all agree with you in thinking that 'if it is not provincial for an Englishman to be English, a Frenchman French, etc., so it is not provincial for an American to be American.' So it is not provincial for a Russian . . . a Portuguese, a Dane . . . to savour of their respective countries: that would be where the argument would lead you. I think it is extremely provincial for a Russian to be very Russian . . . Certain national types are essentially and intrinsically provincial."—Letter to Howells, 1880.

Everything American, whether literary or social, was provincial for James. Thus he described Hawthorne as "consistently provincial" and Thoreau as "worse than provincial—he was parochial;" and he said of Poe's essays that they were "probably the most complete and exquisite specimen of provincialism ever prepared for the edification of man."

† Thus he said to Mrs. Wharton, contrasting Tolstoy with *Madame Bovary,* "Ah, but one paints the fierce passions of a luxurious aristocracy; the other deals with the petty miseries of a little bourgeoise in a provincial town."

CHAPTER XIV

ALDRICH AND HIS CIRCLE

IN THE pages of the "Contributors' Club," at the back of *The Atlantic,* the youngest generation aired its problems. This literary confessional hummed with its comments on the grimness of country life and the struggles, earnings and interests of aspiring authors. It abounded in suggestions for translators, discussions of Americanisms, a matter of concern for story-tellers who were eager for verisimilitude, defences of the Boston speech against the vulgar forms of English actors. But the chief preoccupation of these letter-writers, their all-absorbing interest, was the art of fiction. The day had passed when Godkin, in 1867, referring to the production of novels,—about two a week in England,—could speak of it as a "vicious fecundity." The "coming novel," as people called it, the "great American novel," was a matter of urgent importance to scores of writers.*

This interest filled the contributors' letters with questions and reflections. What constituted an "interesting" character? What were the pros and cons of the autobiographical form in fiction? Why should not the American novel develop the dramatic form? One writer said that story-tellers should vary their situations more, for one knew in advance, by heart, what was going to happen. The contributors bristled with comments on Hawthorne and Henry James, whose novels, along with Howells's, were running in *The Atlantic.* If Hawthorne had not been a

* See the "Contributors' Club" during the years 1877–1881. Howells had established this department in the magazine.

story-teller, he might have been a famous chemist, for he
was a mental chemist in his method of handling emotions
and passions.* Henry James's stories and people were
the most exciting topics. Was *Daisy Miller* a loyal service—or was it not—to American girlhood? Should the
hero of *The American* have accepted defeat? Was Newman's character really consistent? His idea of equality
ought to have triumphed. No, said another contributor,
James was right. A third took issue with a critic in *The
Nation* who said that James should not have created
Newman,—he was "not aesthetically attractive." How
César Birotteau must have shocked this critic, or Frey-
tag's *Soll und Haben!* A fourth enquired how it was that
James's novels had such charm, with so little life, motion
or progression. The answer lay in the delicate care of his
brush-strokes. A fifth objected that James saw only the
ludicrous points of his simpler people, such as Mr. Brand's
large feet and his passion for home-made cake. Was he
fair, moreover, in *The Europeans,* in picturing *first* the
blemishes of the baroness's features? He was following
Turgenev, of course; but was it fair?

While James led all the rest, as a theme for discussion,
with Howells, who remained in the background,—for the
editor selected the letters, and Howells was modest,—the
writers ranged far and wide over the field of modern fiction. Howells and James themselves had largely aroused
this interest, and their vogue was a stimulus also. They
were appearing together in the Tauchnitz series, and one
read them on summer tours in Europe, on the plush-
covered seats of the railway-carriages or in tea-gardens
and beer-gardens, where Baedeker lay on the table and
the Lion of Lucerne looked on. It was delightful, in such
surroundings, to turn the little square leaves, while Howells and James young men and women strolled among the

* Similarly, a well-known living critic has described James Joyce as an
"engineer," because of his marvellous feats of "engineering" in style.

plane-trees. One had only to watch one's fellow-travellers to see how deftly these two writers caught their turns of phrase and their characteristics; and then it was a pleasure to send *The Atlantic* a line of corroboration or objection. James was appearing in German,—he was the "fashionable darling" of the Teuton public, according to the Leipsic prospectus. But for all this charm of James and Howells, the "Contributors' Club" teemed with comments on other novelists, English and continental. Trollope was a frequent theme, and it was noted that English writers dwelt more and more on the charms of American women, —even Matthew Arnold had given them a C+ in his general examination of human types.* George Eliot was much discussed. Was she not too severe with her pretty girls? How many of her Dorotheas had one met? Was Deronda's friendship with Gwendolen true to life? The critics who denied this were obviously men: only women could understand this kind of relation between the sexes. But could any woman really like Deronda? Was Gwendolen meant to be "fast"? So voluble was this discussion that a lively contributor soon proposed the founding of a Deronda chair at Harvard, with a chemical laboratory adjoining the lecture-room to assist in establishing habits of analysis.† The cult of Turgenev continued to rage. To

---

* "Almost everyone acknowledges that there is a charm in American women,—a charm which you find in almost all of them, wherever you go. It is the charm of a natural manner, a manner not self-conscious, artificial or constrained. It may not be a beautiful manner always, but it is almost always a natural manner, a free and happy manner; and this gives pleasure."—Matthew Arnold, *Civilization in the United States.*

† This was perhaps suggested by the lectures on George Eliot that Elizabeth Stuart Phelps was delivering at Boston University. For other echoes of this rage, see Henry James's *Partial Portraits,*—the dialogue of the young women on *Daniel Deronda,*—and the discussion of *Middlemarch* in Howells's *The Rise of Silas Lapham,* chapter IX.

See also Alice James's comment on George Eliot's *Letters and Journal:* "Whether it is that her dank, moaning features haunt and pursue me through the book or not, she makes the impression, morally and physically, of mildew or some morbid growth,—a fungus of a pendulous shape, or as of something damp to the touch."—Anna Robeson Burr, *Alice James, Her Brothers, Her Journal.*

one writer, Turgenev's stories suggested an unfinished frieze with charming figures painted here and there, in cool greys, blues and whites, with harsh tints and unformed shapes between. Meanwhile, *The Atlantic* published papers on virtually all the modern novelists, French, Norwegian, Russian, English, German. These articles abounded in discriminating comments on the methods and themes of the writers in question, their close observation, rich in shades, their delicacies, veracities, refinements. Even Zola's *L'Assommoir,* with all its washing of dirty linen, was recognized as a stout piece of work. The energy with which the author followed his own straight line was certainly highly respectable.

This lively interest in modern fiction undoubtedly quickened the minds of the novelists.* Each new work of Howells and James was debated through the press as the Waverley novels had been in the eighteen-twenties, and all their characters were as eagerly discussed as if they had been living souls and models. The writers and their public were on intimate terms with one another, as in all the healthy epochs of production; and one could understand the dismay of Henry James when he found that he had lost this public later. Realism had come to stay, in a form that Americans found congenial, and even the older generation, which protested against more intransigent forms, acclaimed and rejoiced in the writings of James and Howells. While realism progressed, however, there were always exceptional cases in which the romantic spirit reappeared. In the early eighties, Marion Craw· ford began to write; and William Henry Bishop and Julian Hawthorne were producing somewhat colourless romances, with settings in Germany, Italy and France that reflected the current passion for travel, with persons of all nationalities and sometimes their own. Bishop's

---

* In 1889, there was a summer school at Deerfield, organized for a "general discussion" of "the novel."

The House of the Merchant Prince, a sprightly picture
of New York, in the post-war years of trade and fashion,
was perhaps the best work of either author. The "rather
romantic novel with realistic characters" was Bishop's
definition of his work; * and this described the work of
Arthur Sherburne Hardy, the author of *The Wind of
Destiny* and *But Yet a Woman.* These novels might have
been described as just about as good as almost-good
French novels, but, when the fashion passed and people
continued to read French novels, written by the French
about the French, who cared to read about people "just
like" the French in novels that were "just about" as good?
Neither Hardy, Bishop nor Julian Hawthorne compared
with Marion Crawford, whose formula was much the same
as theirs, or with Helen Hunt Jackson, the author of *Ramona,* which appeared in 1884. The impulsive, attractive,
clever woman who called herself "H. H.," the protégée
of Higginson at Newport who was also Emily Dickinson's early friend,† had long been a popular author when
she wrote this book, her only work that later times remembered. She had lived at army posts with her officer
husband and wandered at home and abroad; and she
rivalled Gail Hamilton, as a lively woman journalist,
with her "bits" of domesticity and travel. She was universally known as the leading American woman poet in a
world that had never heard of her friend in Amherst,
and her fluent and fanciful poems were sometimes good.
But her prose and her verse were alike undistinguished
till she happened on a theme that stirred her to the depths

---

* Bishop was sufficiently interested in the realistic movement in fiction to
call upon Galdos, Valdes and Juan Valera during a visit in Spain. In
A House-Hunter in Europe, he gives an amusing description of these three
writers, whom Howells introduced in America.

† The heroine of her novel, *Mercy Philbrick's Choice,* seems to have
been suggested by Emily Dickinson. The "unique and incalculable" Mercy,
with the "orchid-like face," is a morbidly diffident young woman who has
had an unhappy love affair and secretly writes poems that she will not
publish.

and electrified her talent for a moment. She had gone to
Colorado, in search of health, and the state of the Indians there excited her pity. As she studied their history,
the relations of the races, the conquest of the Indians by
the whites, the old crusading zeal of the Yankee Abolitionists awoke in this mind of a later, indifferent New
England. While the plight of the Indians was more tragic
than that of the Negro slaves had been, since they were
virtually outlaws and without protection, the public took
no interest in their condition. They who had once been
feared were now ignored; and even Mrs. Jackson's *A
Century of Dishonour,* a documented history of the Indian question, had no effect on this general apathy. She
thereupon determined to write the romance that paralleled *Uncle Tom's Cabin,* the book that roused the popular mind to the sorry state of the conquered race and led
to a change of policy in dealing with it. *Ramona* thus became a part of American history, as Mrs. Stowe's book
had been before it, though it lacked the crude power of
Uncle Tom's Cabin and was far more sentimental and
melodramatic. With all its faults, however, its excessively
simple psychology and theatrical setting, it remained,
with its high vitality, a popular classic. "H. H." excelled
as a bold and effective story-teller; and this brilliantly
coloured romance of the Indian girl and the old California hacienda, the Mexicans, mission priests and American settlers, took its place, as time went on, in the folklore of the West and the nation.

Meanwhile, Marion Crawford had appeared in New
England, where he wrote his first romances at the turn of
the eighties. A nephew of Julia Ward Howe, he had been
born in Italy, the son of Thomas Crawford, Thorwald-
sen's pupil, the New York sculptor of the fifties whose
circle Hawthorne pictured in *The Marble Faun.* He had
lived as a child in this circle in Rome, where many of his
later stories had their setting; and every day he had

walked past Constantine's basilica, the Capitol, the Forum, the Coliseum, with the pageant of Roman history spread out before him. Towards the end of his life, he returned to this theme in his *Ave Roma Immortalis*. He had been sent to America to school and had studied at three universities, in England, in Germany, at Rome, where he took up Sanskrit; and at twenty-five he had gone to India and stayed there for two years, as editor of the *Indian Herald* at Allahabad. He had joined the Catholic church in India, and, tiger-hunting there and playing polo, he had studied the Zend-Avesta with a Parsee priest and developed his gift as a linguist. He kept his diary in Urdu, and in time he spoke sixteen languages, five or six of which he knew already. At a loose end, in his late twenties, he had returned to America, not knowing what to do but with burning ambitions. He thought of entering politics, he longed to be an opera-singer, he saw himself already as a conquering hero. Handsome, arrogant, clever and young, the centre of an adoring circle of aunts and cousins, he seemed to be universally informed and gifted. He drew, he modelled, he studied singing with George Henschel, who led the new orchestra in Boston; and he was already a journalist with an excellent training. So he began to write for the press, on any and every subject, from Buddhism to politics and railroads.

He was living in Boston, at Mrs. Howe's on Beacon Street, when he was not in New York to be near his uncle, the well-known "king of the lobby," Samuel Ward; but he wrote his first novel at Newport, in Mrs. Howe's "green parlour," the rustic, open-air study under the Norway firs where his aunt communed so often with Spinoza and Hegel. He had made an instant impression as a storyteller. When he had first appeared in Boston, Longfellow and Holmes were enthralled by his tales and anecdotes of Indian life. One of these tales was about a Persian diamond-merchant, a sort of Sir Basil Zaharoff whose name

was Jacobs and whom Crawford had known in India, in
the mountains, at Simla. This Jacobs had told him the
story of his life, an Arabian Nights entertainment in
modern conditions, and Crawford wrote the story out
and called it *Mr. Isaacs* and found himself instantly
famous. Gladstone spoke of the tale as a "literary marvel," and the name of Marion Crawford went round the
world. He had anticipated Kipling with his bold pictures
of Indian life, and his burst of fame was much like Kipling's later. Still at his aunt's house, in the study facing
Beacon Street, he wrote *Dr. Claudius* and *A Roman
Singer*. The story of *Dr. Claudius,* a Swedish professor
at Heidelberg, who inherits an American fortune and
comes to Newport, suggested the philosophical discussions in which Mrs. Howe rejoiced at Lawton's Valley;
while *A Roman Singer* was the fruit of Crawford's defeated ambition to conquer the world as an opera-singer
himself. For all these first romances were largely transcribed from his own experience. *An American Politician,*
a Boston novel, reflecting his political ambitions, pictured
the drawing-room of Mrs. Jack Gardner, where Crawford spent much of his time, and the conversations there
on finance and Dante. *The Three Fates,* again, was a
good description of his struggles as a writer in New York,
when, toiling away at articles, in a little hall-bedroom, he
suddenly struck the vein that made him famous. The hero
of this novel inherited a fortune also; and Crawford's
own struggling-time was brief. Three years after his first
appearance in Boston, he went abroad again in a blaze of
success. This was in 1884, when Crawford was thirty.
He spent a winter at Constantinople, where he was presently married, in a cloud of ambassadors, admirals, generals and princes. Then he settled at Sorrento, where he
lived for the rest of his life, in the villa that overlooked
the Isles of the Sirens.

Thus opened the career of the deft, ingenious story-

teller who was known for twenty-five years as the Prince
of Sorrento. For he lived there in princely style. He liked
an atmosphere of grandeur, with trains of servants and
sailors in Sorrentine dress, with gay masquerades and
parties on the loggia and a cosmopolitan troop of friends
and guests. One of his romances, *With the Immortals,*
suggested the conversation at his dinner-parties, which
ranged over literature, politics and art from the days of
Pliny and Horace to those of King Humbert. The Englishman in the story had bought a villa like his own, a
half-ruined castle on the cliffs, and he invented an electri-
cal device that produced an immense eruption under the
sea. This suddenly caused the reappearance of seven or
eight immortals, Caesar, Leonardo, Pascal, Heine, Chopin and two or three others, who emerged from the mist
after the storm and wandered about the grounds and
joined in the conversation at the castle. For seclusion,
Crawford leased a tower on the Calabrian coast, San
Niccola, a stronghold built as a refuge in the Saracen
times, on a cliff that overhung a little bay, with a dungeon
lashed by the waves in stormy weather; and there he
wrote many of his novels. In his lateen-rigged felucca,
with four sailors, he explored the Mediterranean, sailing
from island to island and along the coast, sometimes with
the youthful Norman Douglas, who obtained the idea of
his first novel from a priest on the island of Elba during
one of these cruises. Later, in a larger yacht, he crossed
the Atlantic. This was in the days when he went to America every year for lecturing tours and winters in New
York, where he turned out hasty novels that no one mentioned seriously to maintain his magnificence at home.

    In fact, between this later work and the novels he
wrote in the eighties there was little difference in quality,
in type or in style. He was an improvisator, a story-teller,
natural, nonchalant, easy, and the art of the novel was
always the last of his cares. Personally brilliant, he was

anything but a brilliant writer, and problems of technique
and social problems, which occupied the minds of James
and Howells, were far from his intellectually simpler
world. His fresh, brisk style was in no way distinguished,
and his characterizations were general and somewhat
blurred. His people were puppets in what he called a
"pocket theatre," and one scarcely recalled their traits
when the curtain fell. But his narrative gift was astonish-
ing, and his interest in life was eager and inexhaustible,
wide and observant. In his historical novels, about ancient
Arabia and Persia, the Crusades or the Spain of Philip II,
in his novels of modern life in many countries, Germany,
Turkey, Bohemia, America, England, in the Saracinesca
series, most of all, describing the Roman nobility in the
decades after 1860,—the social world he had known from
his earliest boyhood,—he seemed to possess in every case
the special and accurate knowledge that created a perfect
illusion of the *mise en scène*. He could tell you how life
on the Bosphorus differed from life in Pera. He knew
every street and shop in Constantinople. He could tell
you about glass-blowing in the glass-works at Murano
and how cigarettes are made in a factory at Munich, how
silversmiths conduct their trade and how the Baden tailors
are able to make their clothes at a moment's notice. He
could take you on a duke's yacht at Newport, or as readily introduce you behind the scenes at an embassy in
Petersburg or Paris, a cardinal's apartment in Rome or
a rectory in England; or it might be the court of Darius,
a tiger-hunt in India, a German professor's household, an
Italian castle. He could take you through a duel in all its
phases. He knew the cry of the trumpeter swans when
they pass overhead in the early morning in Iceland; he
knew how a Cossack feels on a bench in exile, and he had
at his tongue's end the proverbs and untranslatable phrases
of Italians, Russians, Czechs, Arabs and Spaniards. Add
to this versatility, which was truly astounding, his lucidity,

his energy, his dash and the zest and the masculine charm
that informed his writing, and one understood the vogue
of Marion Crawford, with his tone of a clever, accomplished man of the world. He was the perfect romancer
of the Tauchnitz series, born to be read on trains and in
Swiss hotels, as one contemplated raids on Munich or
Venice, on Prague, Rome, Heidelberg, Naples or Constantinople. Wherever one proposed to go, Marion Crawford had been there first and had written a charming
story on the scenes in question, a story that gave a third
dimension to Baedeker's dry notations and enabled one's
fancy to share in the life of the people.

With Marion Crawford and "H. H.," following
Howells and James, the interest in fiction steadily grew
in the eighties. Meanwhile, the interest in poetry lapsed,
perhaps because, as Godkin said, the spread of science
"killed the imagination." The poets seemed to be disappearing, as the wild flowers had disappeared, in the
regions where the poets had thriven of old. The arethusa,
the gentian, the cardinal-flower that had bloomed near
Agassiz's museum, the rhodora that lurked in West Cambridge, the Watertown yellow violets and the ginseng of
Brookline had retired before civilization. They had not
even waited for the coming of the suburban streets; they
seemed to feel the danger miles away. They had followed
the Indians into oblivion, and the poets were following
the flowers; for no new poets of equal scope had appeared in the train of the older poets, who were gradually falling silent, one by one. It was true that Emily
Dickinson, in her hermitage at Amherst, excelled in her
special intensity all but the greatest; but Miss Dickinson
throve in conditions that throttled the rest. The great social causes and the spiritual causes that had stirred the
romantic poets of the earlier time, the faiths and the
adorations all were gone; and poetry was left high and

dry in a world that had ceased to nourish poets, who remained as idle singers of empty days.

The best of all these idle singers was Thomas Bailey Aldrich,—for poetry of a kind abounded still. This alert little man, blond, erect, ruddy and jaunty, had arrived in Boston as recently as Howells. Born in Portsmouth, he described himself as Boston-plated because he had lived in New York in his formative years, in the well-known Bohemian circle; and he wore a waxed moustache, a symbol of his mundane tastes, in the style of Napoleon III, the Paris-plated. A journalist, an assistant of Willis, he had gone to the front in Virginia, like Winslow Homer. He had reported the war, as Homer sketched it;* and he had returned to New England in 1866 as an editor under the same roof with Howells. His magazine, *Every Saturday,* reprinted selections from foreign papers, reflecting the new cosmopolitan interests of Boston. It was "eclectic," to use a word that was much in vogue, and Aldrich's own mind was eclectic also,—it borrowed freely from every source that appealed to a roving fancy. A wit as well as a poet, Aldrich had had an early success, in this, and in other ways, resembling Lowell; for, along with his exotic themes, he shared the pure New England feeling that Lowell expressed in his poems about birds and springtime. He was a lesser Lowell, more deft than his master. He was already a "household poet" in 1866; and Howells, in his Western remoteness, had thought of Aldrich as one of the reigning stars of the Boston circle. Aldrich had a cottage in the village of Ponkapog, overlooking the Neponset marshes, south of Boston.

By 1881, when he took the place of Howells, who had resigned from *The Atlantic,* Aldrich's best-known work had already appeared. He was popularly respected as a

* Later, Winslow Homer contributed full-page drawings to Aldrich's magazine, *Every Saturday.*

poet and a story-teller whose writing was always accomplished and sometimes brilliant. In his cool and polished prose and verse, he revealed himself as a notable craftsman; and he said he would "rather be censured in pure English than praised in bad,"—which was not true, of course, but let that pass. His writing was undoubtedly distinguished. It was lucid, skillful, crisp and fresh; and the neat-handed Aldrich, who was very seldom commonplace, always knew when to stop, an unusual virtue. The fluent elder poets had not possessed it; and Aldrich's flute-like note was exceedingly pleasant in a world that was used to poets who went on and on. Moreover, he was adroit as well as brief. Dr. Holmes had warned him against verbal epicureanism and his liking for vanilla-flavoured words, the end of which was "rhythmical gout," as the hardy doctor knew, and "incurable poetical disorder." Aldrich scarcely needed this admonition. He was more consciously an artist than Holmes or Lowell, though he lacked their moral force and their wealth of perception, and he soon outgrew his early faults of style. Even his travel-writing, *From Ponkapog to Pesth,* was clear and witty: where most of his travelling friends,—for instance, Warner,—when it came to their "days in Tangier," could never find words enough to convey their impressions, Aldrich's care was not to say too much. These literary virtues marked his stories, *Majorie Daw, A Midnight Fantasy,* the little tales of *Two Bites at a Cherry* and his three short novels or romances. Fanciful or whimsical, realistic now and then, these tales ranged widely in their themes and persons: they dealt with Western gold-seekers, returned soldiers and human oddities, yachtsmen, strikers, misers and insane young women who recover their wits at appropriate moments. Sometimes they were Hawthornesque, sometimes they were arch or coy, sometimes they were impossibly melodramatic; but their touch was almost invariably expert and clever. *Mar-*

jorie Daw, the cleverest, was the novelist's dream of the perfect reader, in a day when the novelist's readers were mostly young ladies. For Marjorie was incredibly lovely; and what was she doing under thè trees, lying in her hammock, swaying like a pond-lily? Reading,—and what but a novel?—and a novel by whom? Would not Howells and Henry James have liked to know? While *Marjorie Daw,* of all these tales, was the most original invention, *The Story of a Bad Boy,* the most sincere and natural, was destined, on all accounts, for the longest life. This picture of Aldrich's childhood at Portsmouth was the first of the series of books about boys that his friends of Mark Twain's circle were soon to write. For Aldrich was intimate with Clemens, as with Howells ánd Warner, and even had something in common with this friend from the West. As a child who had lived in New Orleans, before he returned to Portsmouth, he remembered the steamboat-life on the Mississippi. *The Story of a Bad Boy* started the train of associations that led to the similar books of all these authors, Warner's *Being a Boy,* Howells's *A Boy's Town* and Clemens's *Tom Sawyer* and *Huckleberry Finn.* In this somewhat inglorious post-war epoch, boyhood seemed better than manhood. At least, the leading authors wrote about it with a relish they seldom brought to the rest of life. Aldrich's book was happier than Warner's as an evocation of childhood in the older New England.

For the rest, there was more of New York than Boston in the temper of Aldrich's prose and verse, for all it owed to Longfellow, Hawthorne and Lowell. Aldrich's "surprise endings" reflected the love of effects that was always said to characterize New Yorkers, and his taste for the Second Empire savoured of Broadway. He was a tireless reader of the light French novels that everyone discussed on the banks of the Hudson, and the studio-talk of the New York painters had left long traces in his mind. Many of these painters imitated Isabey, Gérôme,

Fortuny and their scenes of Algeria, Arabia, Spain and Tunis, with odalisques and dancing-girls, snake-charmers and Moorish models, brocaded hangings, minarets and mosques. These pictures reappeared in the verses of Aldrich, which also reproduced their skillful brush-work. He shared the taste for bric-a-brac, for the picturesque at any price that characterized this age of collecting and travel, for knick-knacks and what-nots, Persian carpets, Spanish leather, Turkish brass, vases and German silver, sandalwood, cloisonné, lacquer. His poems were as full of these trappings as the studios and parlours of the eighties.* He carried in his head and transferred to paper what others brought home from Europe in their trunks and boxes.† As for his songs and epigrams, they were fresh and charming. He excelled in the light verse that English writers were also producing in this evening of the greater English poets.

Round Aldrich, as an editor, clustered most of the other poets who spoke for this twilit world of the later New England. One of his protégés was George Edward Woodberry, whom Higginson had introduced to Lowell. Woodberry, the Beverly boy, had catalogued Lowell's library, when he was a student at Harvard. He was one of Henry Adams's pupils and had also studied with Norton; and his first book, *A History of Wood Engraving*, was one of the many products of Norton's teaching. Half

---

* For an account of this phase of household art in Boston, see Harriet Prescott Spofford's *Art Decoration Applied to Furniture*, 1878.

No one in the eighties passed for an artist whose studio was not crammed with objets d'art and such articles of virtu, to use the current phrase, as bits of armour, cups of ruby glass, giant altar-candles, old silver altar-lamps, tall brass flambeau-stands, stuffs from Algeria, weapons from Tripoli and Tunis, musical instruments from Egypt and Spain and pottery from every known land. Most of these objects appear in Aldrich's poems. This was the age, alike in Boston and Moscow, in which Tolstoy was regarded as a saint because, as Lewis Mumford says, his bedroom was "unfurnished."

† "I have come back chock-full of mental intaglios and Venetian glass and literary bric-a-brac generally."—Letter of Aldrich, on returning from Europe, 1875.

its illustrations were from Norton's collection. The remarkable efflorescence of American wood-engraving had suggested this excellent book; but Woodberry was already a poet, and Norton and Lowell considered him the most promising of the rising generation. He had reviewed for *The Atlantic* under Howells, but Aldrich gave him an opening as a regular writer; and Edward Rowland Sill, the Connecticut poet, was another of Aldrich's favourites. Both these men were living at a distance. Woodberry was teaching in Nebraska, and Sill was in California, a professor of English. A more immediate member of Aldrich's circle was John Boyle O'Reilly, who edited the Boston Catholic weekly, *The Pilot*. This romantic Irishman, a schoolmaster's son, had been a trooper in the British army. Imprisoned for republican agitation, he had escaped from Dartmoor and had been recaptured and transported to the Australian penal colony, where he wrote patriotic poems on the walls of his cells. Thence, in 1869, he had escaped again by the aid of a New Bedford whaling captain; and, reaching America, he had come to Boston as the literary centre of the country. Visitors in his Boston study observed a track across the room where he had worn the carpet threadbare. He had been used to pacing up and down his cell and had not lost the habit after years of freedom. A floridly handsome, black-eyed man, warm-hearted, virile and winning, he belonged to the "tempest class," as Whitman said; but he did more than anyone else, as editor of *The Pilot,* to reconcile the Catholics and Protestants in Boston. He was a highly magnetic reciter and speaker. His passion for freedom, which sprang from his love of the Irish cause, enabled him to bring to American causes the libertarian feeling of the pre-war times; and one of his closest friends was Wendell Phillips. Listening to this Irish orator, one felt as if one lived again in the days of the Abolitionists and the Yankee crusaders. He brought back life and fire to the languid eighties. Most of his work recalled the older Irish political poets, with their fluent versification and flowery diction. But he wrote a few songs and lyrics,—*A White Rose* and *The Useless Ones,*—that were lovely and lasting reminders of his delicate feeling.

Edward Rowland Sill shared with Aldrich, although the two had nothing else in common, the leading place among these lesser poets. A slight, shy, diffident man, a graduate of Yale, Sill had gone to California in 1861, where he spent five years in various occupations. Returning to Connecticut, his birthplace, intending to study theology, he went to the Harvard Divinity School for a year. But, finding that he was too sceptical to continue his studies, he soon went West again, with memories of Agassiz's lectures on science and the Boston music-hall that later found expression in his verses. He taught for a while in Ohio, but the greater part of his later life,—he died in 1887, not yet fifty,—was passed in California, at Berkeley, where he left a deep impression as professor of English. Aldrich heard of this "teacher who occasionally wrote verses," as the unassuming Sill described himself, and gave him a free hand in *The Atlantic,* where Sill, who shrank from publicity and preferred to appear anonymously, often signed his poems with a pen-name. In person, he resembled Amiel, and he shared Amiel's mental habits. He was introspective, and the bent of his mind was generally ethical. He was obsessed with the conflict of religion and science, and most of his delicate verses were concerned with this conflict, with doubt and disbelief, a somewhat vague aspiration and a wistful, post-Emersonian nature-worship. At their worst, they were marred by an adolescent mawkishness, and Sill was a poet of low vitality always; but his finest poem, *The Venus of Milo,* with its evocation of Greek serenity, and some of his fables and field-notes were graceful and moving. *The Clocks of Gnoster-Town,* Browningesque in form, was an admirable illustration of Emersonism. Sill's rather fragile essays were often charming, with their notes on humming-birds and the redwood forests where he rode for weeks on horseback in the high Sierras. He translated some of Sully-Prudhomme's sonnets. But his work, as a whole, was pallidly reflective and rather a matrix of poetry than poetry itself. There was scarcely a distinguished line or phrase, or any suggestion of magic, in his flowing verses. He lacked the intensity of another obscure New England poet who was scarcely known at all during his lifetime. Frederick Goddard Tuckerman, born in Boston, a classmate of Higginson at Harvard, who had retired in early life to Greenfield, had died in 1873. Emerson had praised his one book of sonnets, and Tennyson, whom he visited in England, and who gave him the manuscript of *Locksley Hall,* was drawn to the youthful poet and recalled him fondly. But Tuckerman, the shyest of recluses, after the death of his wife, withdrawing to western Massachusetts, had made no further attempts to interest readers. He passed his days in botanical studies and amateur astronomy, adding from time to time to his series of sonnets. It was not until 1931, sixty years after his death, that he found his belated place in American letters. The poet Witter Bynner republished the sonnets of Tuckerman. Admirable in craftsmanship, firm, fresh and clear, these sonnets were memorable expressions of tragic feeling.

Meanwhile, side by side with Aldrich, Louise Chandler Moulton presided over the poets who remained in Boston. This somewhat gushing lady, as Whitman called her, had appeared in the days of the gift-books as "Ellen Louise." A Connecticut girl, she had gone to school, in the village of Pomfret, with Whistler, who had given her some of his drawings. She was a cousin of Stedman and had married a Boston editor, and she wrote Boston let-

ters for the New York papers; then, forming a regular
habit of going abroad in the summer, she introduced to
American readers many of the newer poets of France
and England.* A good-hearted, sympathetic literary go-
between, sincerely devoted to poetry, she collected poets
as others collected old masters; and she passed from
Mallarmé's circle to Lord Houghton's in London, discovering, acclaiming, acquiring and sharing her treasures.
She was eager to rescue and forward unfortunate poets.
Chief among these was Philip Bourke Marston, blind
and beset with calamities, who left her his manuscripts
to publish; and she also assembled the poems of his
brother-in-law, the afflicted Arthur O'Shaughnessy, who
died in his thirties. William Sharp wrote many sonnets
for her. As for her own poems, they were of the facile
kind that several New England women produced in the
eighties, for most of the women novelists were poets
also.† This poetry of women, by women, for women, as
it might well have been called, was a *réchauffé* of Tennyson and Browning, sometimes accomplished, usually flaccid, stereotyped and vague, abounding in hackneyed
phrases and threadbare conceptions. While it occasionally suggested depths of feeling, as in Rose Terry Cooke
and Elizabeth Phelps, it was often sicklied over with the
palest thought and very seldom fresh, direct or vital. All
too literary, it was mostly second-hand; and the characteristic note of the earlier poets, through whom the American scene had found expression, was lost in its general
reversion to English models. The lark and the night-
ingale reappeared in Mrs. Moulton, as if the American

---

* Two of the latter she introduced were William Watson and John
Davidson.
† Among the New England women novelists who published volumes of
verse were Helen Hunt Jackson, Elizabeth Stuart Phelps, Rose Terry
Cooke, Harriet W. Preston and Harriet Prescott Spofford. Of these, "H. H."
was by far the best poet, but most of the others occasionally wrote good
poems, as, e.g., E. S. Phelps's *Gloucester Harbour.*

landscape and its birds and flowers had never been won for poetry. These singers were the "caged warblers" whom Amy Lowell silenced, in her effort to revivify poetry thirty years later; and indeed, their weary verse, as Miss Lowell called it, devitalized, nebulous, dim, slipping along the path of least resistance, invited, and even demanded, a bold reaction. Meanwhile, in Amherst, another woman poet was preparing the way for this vigorous movement later.

CHAPTER XV

EMILY DICKINSON

THE Dickinsons lived in the principal house in Amherst. A large, square, red-brick mansion that stood behind a hemlock hedge, with three gates accurately closed, it was a symbol of rural propriety and all the substantialities of western New England. Edward Dickinson, the lawyer, had always had his office in the village, and four times a day, in his broadcloth coat and beaver hat, with a gold-headed cane in his hand, he had passed through one of the gates, going or coming. A thin, severe, punctilious man who had once been a member of Congress, a friend of Daniel Webster in his youth, a Calvinist of the strictest persuasion, he was a pillar of Amherst College until his death in 1874. The college had been founded, largely by his father, to check the sort of errors that were spreading from Harvard, and he never abated his rigour in the interests of pleasure. He was said to have laughed on one occasion, but usually he was as cold and still as the white marble mantel in his parlour. The story was told in Amherst, however, that once he had rung the church-bell, as if to summon the people to a fire. The whole town came running, for he rang the bell excitedly. He wished to call attention to the sunset.

Next door, behind the hemlock hedge, another ample dwelling stood, suggesting in its style an Italian villa. Here lived the Squire's son Austin, once his partner, who kept open house for the college. While the Dickinson mansion was somewhat forbidding, with the stamp of the

Squire's grim ways and his invalid wife, the villa was a centre of Hampshire hospitality that shared its rolling lawns and charming garden. Olmsted had visited there, when he was planning Central Park, to examine the shrubs and trees, the plants and flowers, and distinguished guests at the college commencements and lecturers during the winter season were received and welcomed there as nowhere else. Emerson, Phillips, Beecher and Curtis had stayed in this house next door, and Samuel Bowles of the *Springfield Republican* was an intimate friend of all the Dickinsons. In an age when the newspaper was largely taking the place of the pulpit, Samuel Bowles was known all over the country as one who fought for honest politics. He had joined with Carl Schurz in the movement for reform that was also the cause of Henry Adams. The *Republican* was a school for journalists, known far and wide, and travellers,—Dickens and Kingsley among them,—constantly stopped at Springfield in order to have a chat with Samuel Bowles. His paper was a sovereign authority in Amherst, and he often drove over for a call at the villa or the mansion, sometimes bringing manuscripts by well-known authors to show the Dickinson daughters before they were published. His favourite was Emily, who was older than Lavinia, but Emily usually "elfed it" when visitors came. She was always in the act of disappearing. Through the blinds of her western windows, overlooking the garden, she observed the hospitalities of the villa, and snatches of whatever was current in the books and talk of a college town, in the politics and thought of the moment, reached her when the guests had gone away. But even her oldest friends seldom saw her. While sometimes, in the evening, she flitted across the garden, she never left the place by day or night. To have caught a fleeting glimpse of her was something to boast of, and a young girl across the way who watched at night for a light at her window was thrilled if Miss Emily's shadow appeared for a moment. There were nurse-maids who thought she was a witch. They frightened the children by uttering her name, as if there were something malign in Miss Dickinson's queerness.

While her friends seldom saw her, and almost never face to face,—for she spoke from the shadows of the hallway, as they sat in the parlour, or sometimes down the stairs,—they were used to receiving little letters from her. These letters were also peculiar. Miss Dickinson rarely addressed the envelopes. Some other hand, perhaps her sister's, performed this office for her. More often the names of the person and town had been clipped from a printed paper and pasted together, as if it were a sort of violation to expose the strokes of her pen to the touch of the postman. The letters themselves were brief and cryptic, usually only a line or two: "Do you look out tonight?" for example. "The moon rides like a girl through a topaz town." Or "The frogs sing sweet today —they have such pretty, lazy times—how nice to be a frog." Or "Tonight the crimson children are playing in the West." Or "The lawn is full of south and the odours tangle, and I hear today for the first the river in the tree." Now and again, some fine phrase emerged from the silvery spray of words,—"Not what the stars have done, but what they are to do, is what detains the sky." Sometimes her notes had a humorous touch: "Father steps like Cromwell when he gets the kindlings," or "Mrs. S. gets bigger, and rolls down the lane to church like a reverend marble." But her messages often contained no words at all. She would lower baskets of goodies out of the window to children waiting below. At times, instead of a letter, she sent a poem, an odd little fragment of three or four lines, with a box of chocolate caramels or frosted cakes and a flower or a sprig of pine on top, heliotrope, perhaps, or an oleander blossom or a dande-

lion tied with a scarlet ribbon. Her letters were rhythmical, they scanned like the poems, and they were congested with images,—every phrase was an image; and
the poems themselves suggested nursery-rhymes or Dr.
Watts's hymns, broken up and filled with a strange new
content. They might have struck unsympathetic readers
as a sort of transcendental baby-talk. It was evident that
Miss Dickinson had lost the art of communication, as
the circle of her school-friends understood it. She vibrated
towards them, she put forth shy, impalpable tentacles,
she instantly signalized with a verse or a note every event
in their lives. But she did not speak the language of the
world outside her, and one gathered that she did not wish
to touch it. She was rapt in a private world of sensations and thoughts. It was even observed that her handwriting went through three distinct phases and that towards the end the letters never touched. Each character,
separately formed, stood quite alone.

She had been a recluse since the early sixties, and her
family surmised the reason. She had fallen in love with
a married man, a Philadelphia clergyman, and had buried
herself at home by way of refuge. When her supposed
lover supposedly pursued her there, her sister dashed
across to the house next door and exclaimed to their
brother Austin's wife, "Sue, come! That man is here.
Father and mother are away, and I am afraid Emily will
go away with him." Such was the family legend, which
may have been apocryphal. Undoubtedly, the clergyman
came to see her, but probably only to call. Was he in love
with Emily? Probably not. In any case, she did not go
away. She withdrew from all activities outside the household, and her mind turned in upon itself. She had hitherto
been eminently social, or as much so as her little world
permitted. Born in 1830, in the red-brick mansion, she
had grown up a lively girl who was always a centre of
attention. She was a capital mimic. She travestied the

young-lady pieces, the "Battle of Prague" and others, which she played on the mahogany piano, and her odd and funny stories enthralled her friends. Later they remembered that she placed bouquets of flowers in the pews of those she liked best, at church. Helen Hunt Jackson, now a well-known writer, had been her favourite playmate in early childhood. Dancing and card-playing were not allowed in Amherst, but Noah Webster's granddaughter, who lived there, evaded the prohibition on behalf of her circle. She held "P.O.M." meetings for the Poetry of Motion, and Emily Dickinson excelled in this branch of learning. She joined in picnics and walks over the Amherst hills with groups of boys and girls from the town and the college. They had "sugaring-off" parties and valentine parties, and they often climbed Mount Norwottuck where they found ferns and lady-slippers; and sometimes they met at a brookside in the woods, where the boys went fishing and the girls made chowder. Emily was an ardent botanist. She knew the haunts of all the wild flowers in the region, and sometimes she scrambled alone through the forest, perhaps with her big dog Carlo. She was an expert cook. At home she baked the bread and boiled her father's puddings, but her father was difficult to please. He read "lonely and rigorous books," she said, on Sunday afternoons, fearing that anything else might "joggle the mind;" and Shakespeare, the Bible and Dr. Watts's hymns were the reading that he chose for his daughter. He did not like her to work in the garden, or to make visits without him, and when she was too witty he left the table. At fifteen she could not tell the time: her father supposed he had taught her, but she had not understood him, and she did not dare to ask him again or ask anyone else who might have told him. Now and again, she rebelled. She smashed a plate or a tea-cup, and her friends and her brother found ways to provide her with books, hiding them in the box-bush that stood beside the front door or on the parlour piano, under the cover. In one way or another, she contrived to read most of the current authors, especially the Brontës and the Brownings, with Hawthorne, Coleridge, Irving, Keats and Ruskin. One of her special favourites was Sir Thomas Browne, and she loved the drollery of Dickens. For the rest, she read Heine in German and Emerson's poems, and Frank B. Sanborn's letters in the *Springfield Republican* kept her in the literary current. She was by no means passive in this house of duty. Once, at a funeral in Hadley, whither she had gone with her father in the family barouche, she ran away for several hours with a young cousin from Worcester and drove back to Amherst in his buggy. At school, she declared her independence. She had been sent as a boarding-pupil to Mary Lyon's seminary, where she had written her themes on the nature of sin. She had listened to lectures on total depravity as if, like most of the other girls, she had meant to be a missionary's wife; but when, one day, Miss Lyon asked all the girls to rise, all who wished to be Christians, Emily alone refused to do so. She had found that she could not share the orthodox faith. Otherwise her life went on, with a few journeys here and there, like that of any country lawyer's daughter. As a young girl, she had visited Boston. She remembered the concerts and Bunker Hill, the Chinese Museum and Mount Auburn; and later, on two occasions, she stayed in Cambridge, to receive some treatment for her eyes. When her father was serving his term in Congress, in 1854, she spent seven weeks in Washington with him. Her father's friends were struck by her charm and her wit. It was on her way home that she stopped at Philadelphia and received the sudden shock that had changed her life.

This was the whole of Miss Dickinson's story, so far as outward events were concerned, when Thomas Wentworth Higginson entered the picture. Higginson had written an appeal in *The Atlantic*, addressed to the rising generation. Remembering the days of *The Dial*, when the hazel wand, waved over New England, had indicated hidden springs of talent in many a country town, he said that to find a "new genius" was an editor's greatest privilege. If any such existed who read *The Atlantic*, let him court the editor,—"draw near him with soft approaches and mild persuasions." Higginson added a number of admonitions: "Charge your style with life . . . Tolerate no superfluities . . . There may be years of crowded passion in a word, and half a life in a sentence." This appeal was anonymous, but many of the Amherst people knew who wrote the articles in *The Atlantic*, for Sanborn's literary gossip kept them posted; and presently Colonel Higginson, who was living in Worcester, received an odd little letter. The letter was unsigned, but the writer sent four poems, and she placed in a separate envelope the signature "Emily Dickinson." She begged this distant friend to be her "master." The poems puzzled Higginson. While he felt a curious power in them, he was not prepared for a "new genius" who broke so many rules as this lady in Amherst, who punctuated with dashes only and seemed to have small use for rhyme and merely wished to know if she was "clear." She did not ask him to publish the poems, and he did not pass them on to the editor, but he wrote her a sympathetic letter that was followed by a long correspondence. She continued to send him poems at intervals, signing her notes "your gnome" and "your scholar," but, although she asked him again if he would be her "preceptor," and he offered her a number of suggestions, she never changed a line or a word to please him. In one note she said, "If I read a book and it makes my whole body so cold no fire can ever warm me, I know that is poetry. If I feel physically as if the top of my head were taken off, I know that is poetry. These are the only ways I know it. Is there any

other way?" And once she replied, when he asked her
for a photograph, "I had no portrait now, but am small,
like the wren; and my hair is bold, like the chestnut burr;
and my eyes like the sherry in the glass that the guest
leaves." This feminine mystification piqued the colonel.
He wrote, "You enshroud yourself in this fiery mist and
I cannot reach you, but only rejoice in the rare sparkles
of light." When she told him that her companions were
the hills and the sundown, he replied that she ought to
come to Boston: she would find herself at home at Mrs.
Sargent's. At last, in 1870, he went to Amherst. After a
brief delay, while he waited in the parlour, he heard a
faint footstep in the hallway and a shy, little childlike
creature glided in. She carried two day-lilies, which she
placed in his hand, saying, in a soft, breathless voice,
"These are my introduction," adding in a whisper, "Forgive me if I am frightened. I never see strangers and
hardly know what to say." She spoke of her household
occupations and said that "people must have puddings,"
and she added a few detached, enigmatic remarks. She
seemed to the amiable Higginson as unique and remote
as Undine or Mignon or Thekla. But he was disturbed by
the tension in the air and was glad he did not live too
near this lady. There was something abnormal about her,
he felt. He had never met anyone before who drained
his nerve-power so much.

At that time, Miss Dickinson was forty years old and
had long since withdrawn from the world; and the
friends who came to see her sister were used to the "hur-
rying whiteness" that was always just going through a
door. She sometimes swept into the parlour, bowed and
touched a hand or two, poised over the flowered Brussels carpet, and vanished like a ghost or an exhalation;
but even these appearances had grown rarer and rarer.
Only the neighbours' children really saw her. She had
given up wearing colours and was always dressed in

diaphanous white, with a cameo pin that held the ruching together. She was decisive in manner, anything but frail. Her complexion was velvety white, her lips were red. Her hair was bound with a chestnut-coloured snood, and when it was chilly she wore a little shoulder-cape crocheted of soft white worsted run through with a ribbon. She often had a flower in her hand. She moved about in a sort of revery, flitting "as quick as a trout" when she was disturbed. This was one of her sister Lavinia's phrases. The children knew her "high, surprised voice." They knew her dramatic way of throwing up her hands as she ended one of the stories she liked to tell them. She made them her fellow-conspirators. They followed her upstairs and heard her comments on the guests she had left in the parlour. She would say, with finger on lip, as feminine callers left, "Listen! Hear them kiss, the traitors!" Or, peeping down the stairs, she would say of some man, "Look, dear, his face is as pretty as a cloth pink," or "His face is as handsome and meaningless as the full moon." She remarked, apropos of some scholarly person, "He has the facts, but not the phosphorescence of learning." She said that her own ideal caller was always just going out of sight, and that it made her shiver to hear people talk as if they were "taking all the clothes off their souls." She called herself the "cow-lily," because of the orange lights in her hair and her eyes, and she observed that the housemaid moved about "in a calico sarcophagus." Once she said to her little niece, who was puzzled by her shy ways, "No one could ever punish a Dickinson by shutting her up alone." Meanwhile, her life went on with her flowers and her sister. She had a small conservatory, opening out of the dining-room, a diminutive glass chamber with shelves around it; and there she grouped the ferns and the jasmine, the lilies and the heliotrope and the oxalis plants in their hanging baskets. She had a little watering-pot, with a long, slender spout

that was like the antenna of an insect, and she sat up all
night at times in winter to keep her flowers from freezing. The garden was her special care, and occasionally
one saw her at dusk through the gate fluttering about the
porch like a moth in the moonlight. When it was damp,
she knelt on an old red army blanket that she had thrown
on the ground, to reach the flowers. Usually, on summer
evenings, she sat for a while with Lavinia on the side
piazza, overlooking the flagged path that led to the
villa. There stood the giant daphne odora, moved out
from the conservatory, and the two small oleanders in
their tubs.

Meanwhile, since 1862, Miss Dickinson had been writing poems, although there were very few of her friends
who knew it. They all knew the little rhymes she sent
them with arbutus buds, but they did not know how seriously she pursued her writing, at night, beside the Franklin stove, in the upstairs corner bedroom, in the light that
often glimmered over the snow. From her window she
had caught suggestions that gave her a picture, a fancy,
an image. Perhaps a boy passed whistling, or a neighbour
on her way to church, or a dog with feet "like intermit-
tent plush;" or perhaps she knew that a travelling circus
was going to pass in the early morning, and she sat up to
watch the "Algerian procession." A dead fly on the win-
dow-pane stirred her imagination, and once in the glare
of a fire at night she saw a caterpillar measuring a leaf
far down in the orchard. She saw the bluebirds darting
round "with little dodging feet,"

> The motions of the dipping birds,
> The lightning's jointed road;

and all these observations went into her verses. She wrote
on sheets of note-paper, which she sewed together, rolling and tying the bundles with a thread or a ribbon and

tucking them away in the drawers of her bureau; although sometimes the back of an envelope served her as well, or a scrap of the *Springfield Republican*. But, casual in this, she was anything but casual,—she was a cunning workman,—in her composition. Poetry was her solitaire and, so to speak, her journal, for, like Thoreau in Concord, she watched the motions of her mind, recording its ebbs and flows and the gleams that shot through it; and she laboured over her phrases to make them right. Were they all her own? Were there echoes in them, or anything of the conventional, the rhetorical, the fat? Were they clear, were they exact, were they compact? She liked the common hymn-metres, and the metres of nursery-jingles, which had been deeply ingrained in her mind as a child, and she seemed to take a rebellious joy in violating all their rules, fulfilling the traditional patterns while she also broke them. She was always experimenting with her rhymes and her rhythms, sometimes adding extra syllables to break up their monotony, sometimes deliberately twisting a rhyme, as Emerson did, for the sake of harshness, to escape the mellifluous effect of conventional poems. Many of her pieces were like parodies of hymns, whose gentle glow in her mind had become heat-lightning. For Emily Dickinson's light was quick. It was sudden, sharp and evanescent; and this light was the dry light that is closest to fire.*

The visible setting of these poems was the New England countryside, the village, the garden, the household that she knew so well, a scene, the only scene she knew, that she invested with magic, so that the familiar objects

---

* Why did not Miss Dickinson publish her poems? This question is insoluble and idle. One can only say that, if she had published them, the poems would have been quite different in their total effect. If she had seen her work in proof, she would have arranged the poems in some reasonable order, she would have rectified the punctuation, etc. Her work would have seemed less arbitrary and less eccentric. The poems as they stand abound in misprints; and Miss Dickinson's collected work consists of serious poems, fragments and trivialities confusedly shuffled together.

became portents and symbols. Here were the hills, the changing seasons, the winter light, the light of spring, the bee, the mouse, the humming-bird, the cricket, the lonely houses off the road, the village inn, the lamp-post that became, in the play of her fancy, sublime or droll; and with what gifts of observation she caught the traits of her birds and insects, of everything that crept or ran or flew, —the snake "unbraiding in the sun," the robin's eyes, "like frightened beads," the umbrella of the bat that was "quaintly halved." She often seemed a little girl, amusing herself with childish whimsies, and, in fact, as the ward of her father, she remained in some ways adolescent; and, as she dressed to the end in the fashion of her early youth, so she retained the imagery of the child in the household. But her whimsies sometimes turned into bold ideas that expressed an all but fathomless insight or wisdom. She saw the mountain, like her father, sitting "in his eternal chair;" her ocean had a "basement," like the house in Amherst, and her wind and snow swept the road like the brooms that she had been taught to use,—the brooms of the breeze swept vale and tree and hill. A journey to the Day of Judgment struck her as a "buggy-ride," and she saw a "schoolroom" in the sky. She domesticated the universe and read her own experience into the motions of nature and the world she observed. The sun rose in the East for her "a ribbon at a time," and the "housewife in the evening West" came back to "dust the pond." Clouds for her were "millinery," mountains wore bonnets, shawls and sandals, eternity "rambled" with her, like her dog Carlo; the wind had fingers and combed the sky, and March walked boldly up and knocked like a neighbour. Volcanoes purred for her like cats, and she saw the planets "frisking about," and her Providence kept a store on the village street, and she thought of death as coming with a broom and a dustpan. The moon slid down the stairs for her "to see who's there," and the grave for her

was a little cottage where she could "lay the marble tea."
One could not "fold a flood," she said, and "put it in a
drawer," but she rolled up the months in moth-balls and
laid them away, as she had swept up the heart and put
away love; and she saw hope, fear, time, future and past
as persons to rally, tease, flee, welcome, mock or play
with.

The turns of fancy that marked these poems were
sharp and unpredictable, and yet they were singularly natural,—nothing was forced. Miss Dickinson lived in a
world of paradox, for, while her eye was microscopic, her
imagination dwelt with mysteries and grandeurs. Ribbons
and immortality were mingled in her mind, which passed
from one to the other with the speed of lightning, though
she sometimes took a mischievous pleasure in extravagant
combinations of thought, uniting the droll and the sublime, the trivial and the grand. There was in this an element of the characteristic American humour that liked to
play with incongruities, and Miss Dickinson maintained
in the poems of her later years the fun-loving spirit she
had shown as a schoolgirl. To juxtapose the great and the
small, in unexpected ways, had been one of her prime
amusements as the wit of her circle, and this, like the la-
conic speech that also marked the Yankee, had remained
an essential note of her style as a poet. "Shorter than a
snake's delay," her poems were packed with meaning;
and, swiftly as her images changed, they were scarcely
able to keep the pace with which her mind veered from
mood to mood, from faith to mockery, from mysticism to
rationalism, through ecstasy, disillusion, anguish, joy.
These poems were fairylike in their shimmer and lightness, they moved like bees upon a raft of air; and yet one
felt behind them an energy of mind and spirit that only
the rarest poets ever possessed. Was not Emily Dickinson's idiom the final proof that she possessed it? Her
style, her stamp, her form were completely her own.

Such were the games of solitaire that Miss Dickinson played in the silent room, as lonely as Jane Eyre, in her red-curtained alcove, dreaming over the book with its pictures of the arctic wastes and the rock that stood up in the sea of billow and spray. Miss Dickinson had only this "acre of a rock," and yet what a harvest it yielded of grape and maize. Having but a crumb, she was sovereign of them all, as she said quite truly; for her constant theme was deprivation, the "banquet of abstemiousness," and this sharpened as nothing else her perception of values. When the well's dry, we know the worth of water, and she felt that she knew victory because she knew defeat, she felt that she knew love because she had lost it; and certainly for all she missed she made up in intensity. Where others merely glowed, she was incandescent.

CHAPTER XVI

INDIAN SUMMER

IN THE mild air of the early eighties, a haze of Indian
summer hung over New England. The heats and the
rigours of the past were long forgotten, the passions of
the war, the old crusades, and a mood of reminiscence
possessed the people, for whom the present offered few
excitements. Society had lost its vital interests, and the
Boston mind was indolent and flaccid, as if the struggle
for existence had passed it by. Its ambition seemed to be
atrophied, except on the practical plane, and this was
equally true in the rural regions. Many a clock had gone
dead in hamlets that had hummed with life, where the
men, it was often remarked, were torpid and listless; and
farmers sat in the village stores, wagging their beards all
day, chewing and whittling, as shiftless as Canada thistles.
The old strain was wearing out, or so the Boston people
said; but the region was tranquil and mellow, at least on
the surface. In the absence of motives, its mind was be-
calmed; and Thomas Wentworth Higginson, with his
nose for causes, could find no shield on which to break a
lance. So he jogged about the country with a horse and
buggy. Sometimes he collected ferns. Sometimes he ransacked the farms for spinning-wheels and colonial chairs
and tables.

For the vogue of antiques had begun, both in people
and objects. The story-tellers looked for types, as if the
race were truly dying and one had to gather the relics before they vanished. Others gathered the shells it had left
or was leaving, the grandfather's clocks and the claw-

footed furniture, the pewter plates, the latches, the knock-
ers, the lanterns. They picked up Sheraton highboys and
Hepplewhite lowboys; they even collected wax flowers
and funeral wreaths. The country was becoming a museum or a vast antique-shop; and the sense of the past
was omnipresent, with a feeling of decay and desolation.
Had the Yankee mind really lost its vigour and its hold
on the bounding modern world? It was certainly losing
some of its characteristics. All manner of strange religions
were taking root in Boston, where novel forms of spiritual
dissipation seemed to be the order of the day. The seeress,
Mrs. Eddy, had opened her Christian Science church, and
swamis and mystics from Persia began to appear in drawing-rooms in a town that was ready for everything and
amused by all. It was amused by Mrs. Jack Gardner, who
walked down Tremont Street with a lion in leash, who
hired locomotives when coaches were not fast enough and
appeared at balls with a page to bear her train. The Anglo-
Catholic church had risen, following Phillips Brooks's
rise, and marking the gradual return of the colonial feeling. The new Back Bay streets and apartment-houses also
reflected this change: the names that most of them bore
were notably English, Clarendon, Wellington, Hereford.
In schools like Groton and Saint Paul's, the tendency to
revert to England in educational methods, in sports and
in manners denoted the secession of the fashionable
classes from the democratic forms of the old republic.
The Anglo-Catholic movement had repercussions in literature soon, and it concurred with the growth of aesthetic
feeling, the most recent symbol of which was Trinity
Church. Richardson had built this church in 1877, with
the aid of John La Farge and Stanford White and the
Franco-Irish-American sculptor Saint-Gaudens. Burne-
Jones and William Morris had made windows for it. In
its colour and splendour, it indicated forcibly the break
of the Boston mind with its Puritan past.

Boston was prepared to see itself as others saw it, in this hour of elasticity and relaxation. Its days of storm and stress were past. It was ready to laugh at itself and its oddities and foibles, and Edward Everett Hale's vivacious sister, the witty, the sprightly Lucretia, improved the occasion at once with *The Peterkin Papers*. This book was an amicable satire on the well-known culture that was everywhere associated with the name of Boston, and the Peterkins suggested the literary families that also abounded in Boston and its learned suburbs. They might have been drawn from the Alcotts, the Howes or the Hales. With their innocent pedantry, their breezy gullibility, their high-minded faith in life and utter lack of common sense, they carried the traits of these families to a pitch of the absurd. Their "educational breakfasts" were one of the notes of a nonsense-Boston that might have been conceived by Edward Lear. Their bent for self-improvement, their conundrums at picnics, their zest for the acquisition of Sanskrit and Turkish, their joy in making life an object-lesson,—studying the butter at table and including the cow,—could only have been possible in a world that had known Elizabeth Peabody and the candours of transcendental Concord. But the book that recounted their adventures could only have been written when the day was already passing for these candours and joys.

In Concord itself one found the note of Indian summer, an afterglow of Transcendentalism. Emerson's early dream of a new university had had a late fulfillment at the Hillside Chapel. Alcott, on his lecturing-tours, had met in the West numbers of students for whom the little town was a loadstar and who were flocking thither in the summer, along with their New England condisciples, to sit at the feet of the Yankee worthies and sages. The redoubtable William T. Harris was one of these students, a Connecticut man, like Alcott, who lived in Saint Louis, where he edited the *Journal of Speculative Philosophy.** Alcott and Harris joined hands, and the Concord School of Philosophy came into being. It was founded to counteract the materialistic tendencies of the current scientific thought, and there the Hegelian categories, introduced by Harris, mingled in the lectures and conversations with the modes of thought and speech of the days of the "Newness." The omnibus, the "Blue Plato," rumbled through the town, astir with Hypatias in muslin and straw-hatted Kants; and, sooner or later, two thousand neophytes sat on the rustic settees or gathered on the grassy stretches outside the chapel. The trees brushed the open windows, through which the murmuring summer sounds mingled with the voices of the speakers.

The school was Alcott's triumph. It had sprung from a conversation at Orchard House, beside which the Hillside Chapel stood, with its Gothic doors and windows, and the hardy old philosopher was the dean and leader. Under his elms stood the academy, the river was his Ilyssus now; for Emerson, who remained as a presence, was fading out. One saw Emerson, slightly stooping, with a shawl about his shoulders, patiently standing in line at the post-office wicket. He sometimes appeared at the school, and a reverential student now and then joined him for a stroll to Sleepy Hollow, perhaps with Elizabeth Peabody and Ellery Channing. As these ancient luminaries stopped for discourse at the foot of an oak, or moved from gravestone to gravestone, they always forgot their portfolios, their sticks and their hats. The outlines of Emerson's personality remained firm and clear, but the details grew dimmer and dimmer as his memory waned; while Alcott, at eighty, was beginning a new career as a poet with a series of excellent sonnets addressed to his friends, the past or pass-

---

* In this first journal in the English language devoted exclusively to philosophy appeared the first philosophical essays of Charles Peirce, William James, Josiah Royce and John Dewey.

ing worthies of New England, Garrison, Dr. Channing, Thoreau and Hawthorne, Whittier, Phillips, Emerson and his daughter Louisa, who decked the Hillside Chapel with flowers and branches. These sonnets, noble and touching, had an unmistakable ring of authority, unlike the skillful exercises of most of the current sonneteers. Sometimes Miss Peabody presided at the sessions, sometimes Mrs. Howe, who was always at home in the "chair;" but the younger intelligentsia joined with the older, and the school was a lively parade of American thought. It lingered on through nine idyllic summers. There were courses on Goethe, Emerson, Dante and Plato, on Buddhism, Homer and Milton; and among the speakers were Dr. McCosh of Princeton and President Porter of Yale, Higginson, Frank B. Sanborn, Charles Peirce and Stedman. Harrison G. O. Blake read from Thoreau's unpublished journals. William James and John Fiske, representing Cambridge, lectured on psychology and religion, and Julian Hawthorne spoke on novel-writing. Thomas Davidson scandalized some of the students by comparing Zola with Christ.*

Thus, for a season, once again, Concord swarmed with earnest thinkers, as forty years before at the time of *The Dial*. Young men and maidens, aging sibyls who sometimes wore their skirts inside out, white-haired reformers and prophets with a gleam in their eye threaded the winding woodpaths, and the glens and hills reëchoed with their talk. They hovered about the Manse, they visited the battlefield by moonlight, and they added their stones to the cairn on the site of Thoreau's hut, while, unconscious of all observers, Emerson's daughter Ellen ambled about the roads on her large grey donkey, with her full skirts billowing in the summer breeze. If they strolled, by chance, to Walden on a Sunday, they found themselves in the

* Similarly an eminent critic of our day has compared D. H. Lawrence with Christ.

midst of another assemblage, remote from the austerities
of Concord, that was yet not unrelated to the Concord
scene. There, in the grove by the pond, the spiritualists
held camp-meetings, and trance-speakers addressed the
crowd, gathered from buggies and carryalls tied to the
trees, inviting them to "come to spirit-land." Mediums
gave exhibitions of self-expansion and self-compression,
and mesmerists and faith-healers waved their wands and
cast their spells. The connection may have been tenuous,
but still it existed, between this new religion and Emerson's doctrines, which denied the reality of matter, or
seemed to deny it, while they taught the omnipotence of
mind. Had not Emerson said, "Never name sickness"?
Was it not his idea that, since man was divine, evil could
scarcely have any real existence? Alcott had shown an
active interest in Mary Baker Glover,—Mrs. Eddy, as
she was known in Boston,—for whom pain, disease, old
age and death were "errors." Alcott had been struck by
her *Science and Health* and had visited her classes in
Lynn and lectured before them. There was a deep relation
between the Concord point of view and the mind-cure that
was raging through New England; and, beside this cult
and the spiritualism that flourished in the Walden grove,
the School of Philosophy seemed a mere survival.

There was nothing essentially new in this interest in
the "spirit-land" and these other allied phenomena that
excited New England, phrenology, astrology, galvanism,
hypnotism and the study of manifestations and astral
forms; but since the war their vogue had grown immensely. They had thriven from early times in this land
of the Shakers, whose founder, Mother Ann Lee, the
"Woman of the Apocalypse," had lived in the hills near
Mrs. Eddy's birthplace. The founder of phrenology had
died in Boston: it somehow seemed natural that Spurz-
heim should have found a grave in Mount Auburn. Hawthorne had pictured a medium in *The Blithedale Romance;*

Orestes Brownson had written about spirit-rappers; Epes
Sargent continued the theme in his novel *Planchette*.*
But what had been a casual interest in the fuller days before the war was a much more serious matter in the post-
war years. The decay of the old religion had left the religious instinct unsatisfied, and the Yankee mind was lost
without the causes that had given it an outlet and a focus.
These psychical mysteries filled a void; and, if this was
true among thinking people, was it not truer still in a village world that abounded in ailing women and empty
houses? Many of the New England authors were interested in spiritualism, from Shepherd Tom Hazard in
Rhode Island to Celia Thaxter on the Isles of Shoals.
Mrs. Thaxter acted as a medium herself, and even Tom
Appleton in Boston was caught by this fashion: he wrote
a charming story about Lavater, and no one was more
curious than he in all these matters. Mrs. Stowe was addicted to planchette, and she and Whittier sat up many a
night discussing manifestations and table-rappings.† For
some of these worthies, who had lived through great excitements and who found themselves in a world that was
dull and empty, spiritualism afforded new sensations; and
life was duller still for the village people. The building
days were long past, with all their compensations, their
ambitions and interests, the tasks that had filled the present with zest and meaning. The men who had gone to the
war and returned to their farms were often idle, slack and
discontented; and the hope of a future life seemed vaguer
and vaguer. In these stranded villages and lonely home-

* William James's review of this book is included in his *Collected Essays and Reviews*. Epes Sargent was a cousin of the painter Sargent.
† Whittier's closing years were attended with "manifestations," in which
he always took a lively interest. On the last night of his life, he was dining
at Hampton Falls College. There were thirteen at the table, and twice
newcomers appeared and guests left the table to break the spell. As he said
"Good night" and left the room, the old clock struck one. The clock had
not been wound for years, and no one had ever heard it strike, and it could
not be made to strike again.

steads, one found countless queer and stricken women, brooding on death and disease, obsessed with their complaints and their troubles and symptoms. If they had "complications" in addition to troubles, they aroused a special interest in their families and neighbours, and many a young girl had tantrums and conniption-fits when she could not attract attention by other methods. Hysteria in all its forms, the fruit of isolation and repression, throve in these regions, and one heard all manner of rumours of miraculous cures. Mediums appeared and conducted séances, mesmerists and men who "pulled out tooth-aches," like the hero of Henry James's *Professor Fargo*. One of these mental healers was Dr. Quimby, who cured Mrs. Eddy at Portland and died of an "erroneous" tumor shortly after. Partly because the people were sickly and partly for want of other excitements, they amused themselves with leaps in the dark. They played with automatic writing, communing with ghosts in default of friends, they tried to exert magnetic influences, and they talked about clairvoyance and antagonization; and many who seldom spoke aloud rejoiced in the spread of mental telepathy, a new and more entertaining form of silence. These border-line activities, which were neither religion nor science, partook of both; and Mrs. Eddy's rising fortunes showed how far they answered a deep, insistent need of the population. It was riddled with nervous disorders. It was also bored.

The dusky genius of Mrs. Eddy was therefore a sign of the times, a portent of the race, the place, the moment; for only a time of declining vitality, only a region at ebb-tide could have given birth to the cult of Christian Science. It presupposed hysteria as the normal condition; for health is the centre of religion only for the sick. More closely connected with Concord was the school of remarkable naturalists who rose with the reputation of the dead Thoreau. While Wilson Flagg perhaps owed little to

this, Bradford Torrey edited Thoreau's journals; and
Frank Bolles made a famous journey up the Concord
river with his fellow-Cantabrigian, William Brewster,
whose Concord home was called "October Farm." Wilson
Flagg, the first of these excellent writers, was a Beverly
boy, like Woodberry, who lived in Cambridge. His interest in natural history was awakened at eight, on a driving-
tour from Beverly to lower New Hampshire, through the
"Dark Plains," a tract of sandy country that was covered
with a primitive growth of pines and hemlocks, such as
later existed only in northern Maine. The music of these
woods, their darkness and silence, their echoes and their
solitude and vastness caused in the boy what he called a
religious conversion, and for many years this doctor who
never practised medicine rambled whenever he could in
the depths of the forest, in Tennessee and Virginia as well
as New England, observing the foraging habits of birds,
sharing the diet of the squirrels, listening to the log-cock,
the red-headed woodpecker and the song, unheard by
others, of the lonely veery. *A Year Among the Trees,
Studies in the Field and Forest* and *The Birds and Seasons of New England* assembled his notes in a fine though
somewhat formal style, unlike the familiar manner of the
later writers. Torrey also roamed through Tennessee and
studied the birds in Florida and North Carolina, as well
as Maine, New Hampshire and Vermont. He carried on
with Celia Thaxter a correspondence about their habits,
and he counted seventy-three species of plants in bloom
in Massachusetts in November. His essays in *A Rambler's
Lease, Birds in the Bush, The Clerk of the Woods* were
fresher and more deft than Flagg's, if also slighter. Both
these writers maintained the Cambridge tradition of Nut-
tall and Gray, although both were more literary than scientific; and they owed their vogue to the interest Thoreau
aroused, in ever widening circles, as the years went on.
      A more vigorous writer than either of these was the

secretary of Harvard College, the tall, rugged, bearded
Frank Bolles. Bradford Torrey first met Bolles in the
great swamp in Cambridge. In the dark, they could not
see each other's faces, but both had come on the same
errand, to watch the aerial evolutions of the April snipe.
Bolles, who haunted the Belmont meadows, the Bussey
woods and the Waverley oaks, whenever he could escape
from his Cambridge office, had tracked dove-prints in the
snow in Boston, on Rowe's Wharf and in Crab Alley, and
studied the whistler ducks and the gulls in the harbour.
He had a "wren orchard" near Cambridge, and one of his
favourite resorts was the Middlesex Fells, where Parkman had lived as a boy; but his Walden was Lake Chocorua in New Hampshire. At the tip of this heart-shaped
lake he built a cottage, and there he learned the secrets of
the wilder creatures that flitted about his abode on foot
or wing, the muskrat and the fox, the mink, the bittern.
He also roamed in Nova Scotia,—*The Land of the Lingering Snow*. He studied the birds of Cape Breton and
recorded in *From Blomidon to Smoky* his ascents of the
northern summits. But this lake with its oaks in New
Hampshire was his permanent centre. There he kept his
captive owls, eleven of various species, and perhaps the
finest of all his papers was *A Night Alone on Chocorua,*
the horn-like peak that rose above his cottage. He knew
the secret places of the mountains, and once when the
time for meteors came round in August he proposed to
count his meteors from the loftiest point. Clarence King
never excelled his report of the mountain thunder-storm,
when the peaks seemed to fall in noisy ruin, when the
sounds striking here and there on misty promontories
gave out their softened booms and waning rumbles and
the ghost-like clouds slipped over the black abysses. His
canoe-voyage up the Concord with William Brewster recalled the well-known journey of Thoreau's *Week*. Brewster, the ornithologist, had grown up in Cambridge when

farms existed still on Brattle Street, or at least large barns with horses, cows and poultry. He had first visited Concord in 1872, to hear a woodcock sing, and he found woodcocks' nests at Walden. Then he had bought a tract of woodland at Ball's Hill, near the river, a favourite haunt of Thoreau; and he carried on his observations at his eighteenth-century farmhouse and recorded them in journals like his master's. He made annual trips up the river with Daniel Chester French, the Concord sculptor, who had begun his career with the statue of the minute-man and a seated figure of Emerson, which remained in the town. It was Brewster who made the first collection of North American birds, and the journals that he kept with loving care abounded in excellent descriptions. He sometimes spent an afternoon perfecting a sentence, in order to do full justice to some furry battle, perhaps be-tween a mouse and a shrike, or the strange behaviour of a muskrat or a snapping turtle.*

This interest in wild life steadily rose in the eighties, as the cities encroached on the country and destroyed its beauty. Norton was only one of many who deplored the dirt and the smoke in the sky, the denuding of the hills, the cluttering of the seashore, the converting of mountain streams into factory-sewers. At Ashfield, his summer home, Norton established an annual festival to combat these abominations and all the others that were eating away the roots of American life. He restored the ruined

---

* Two posthumous volumes, *Concord River* and *October Farm,* have been drawn from William Brewster's journals.

A writer far greater than any of these, W. H. Hudson, the author of *Green Mansions,* might also be claimed for New England. Although he was born in the Argentine and never set foot in America, his father was a Maine man and his mother was of the oldest New England descent. Hud-son settled in London in the early eighties, as much of a stranger there as Hawthorne had been. For several years he made his living as a genealo-gist, searching out pedigrees for Americans of English descent.

In connection with these naturalists it might be added that Luther Bur-bank was born at Lancaster, Massachusetts, in 1849. He perfected at Lunenberg the "Red rose" potato. Burbank moved to California in 1875.

Ashfield academy, and for twenty-five years his "academy
dinners" threw light on most of the current American
problems. The village band marched up the road, and the
maples glimmered with lanterns on these occasions, and
the wagons thronged the little town with neighbours who
came from far and wide to hear the speeches. Norton
strove to arouse their interest in civil-service and tariff reform,—the causes that were also dear to Godkin,—anti-
imperialism, Negro education and the preservation of
nature and the beauties of landscape. George William
Curtis, Lowell, Howells, Woodberry and Booker Washington were among the speakers. It was Norton who
largely saved Niagara Falls. Meanwhile, as Olmsted's
parks spread over the country, bird sanctuaries arose on
abandoned farms; and Higginson, collecting ferns, sought
eagerly for native plants that were dying out in eastern
Massachusetts. He found at Worcester two or three that
had vanished on the seaboard. Others, already rare at
Worcester, flourished further inland; while the country
abounded with importations,—the dandelion, the butter-
cup, the celandine, burdock, mullein, chickweed and yar-
row,—that had never known the tread of Miles Standish's
foot. New England swarmed with foreigners, botanical
and human, while the native races ebbed and shrank away.
In the botanical sphere, Higginson observed that the ex-
otics were coarser than the indigenous flowers. The children instinctively recognized this and were apt to over-
look them, when gathering the more delicate native
blossoms of the woods.* In his nostalgia, the colonel re-

---

* T. W. Higginson, *The Procession of the Flowers.*
In the human sphere, New Englanders made the same distinction. In
this they resembled the natives of all long-settled regions where a strong
folk-feeling has developed with time. Families from other counties remained "aliens,"—there were said to be people in Concord who considered the Emersons aliens. How much more alien were families that had
one foreign forbear, how infinitely more if they had three! See Kate
Douglas Wiggin, *Rebecca of Sunnybrook Farm:* "The Randalls were
aliens. They had not been born in Riverboro nor even in York County.
Miranda would have allowed, on compulsion, that in the nature of things

gretted the day when every Yankee boy could give intimate details of out-door life from observation. The current nature-poetry was sentimental because it was di-
vorced from the rustic living that had lain behind the
work of the older poets. For the rest, another symptom
of an urbanizing world was the growing charm of the
wilderness for the men of the eighties. The "Philosophers' Camp" of the fifties had been almost unique; and
Emerson, Lowell and Agassiz were pioneers for the rest
of their circle when they shared the unbroken forest with
the bears and the wolves and lived for a while as woodsmen at Follansbee Lake. The simple life had been everyone's heritage, but roughing it was the fashion now, and
life in the Adirondacks was a kind of salvation for William James and other younger men. James had spent his
honeymoon there in 1878, and for many years the farmhouse in Keene Valley, converted into a camp, remained
an inspiration and a refuge for him. There he could enjoy
the "wild animal personal relations" with nature that
were necessary, he found, for his mind and body; and
there later Thomas Davidson, the peripatetic philosopher, conducted the well-known school in which James
rejoiced. Others, like Tom Appleton, whose nerves were
Europeanized, regained their American consciousness in
the Adirondacks. An Adirondack literature soon appeared. One of its first and best books was Warner's *In
the Wilderness,* with an essay on hunting from the deer's

a large number of persons must necessarily be born outside this sacred
precinct; but she had her opinion of them, and it was not a flattering one
. . . 'They used to say' (a villager remarks) 'that one o' the Randalls married a Spanish woman . . . Lorenzo was dark complected, you remember;
and this child is too. Well, I don't know as Spanish blood is any real disgrace, not if it's a good ways back and the woman was respectable.' "
    All this would be taken for granted in Ireland, Denmark, etc. In con-
nection with New England and the South, it strikes Americans as comic
because the American mind in general is not used to the mental habits of
long-settled regions.

point of view. Another was Philander Deming's *Adirondack Stories.**

Meanwhile, the "summer people," in quest of the odd and picturesque, invaded the remotest hamlets with their strange, new customs; and painters interpreted the landscape, while story-tellers explained the "natives" for city-dwelling folk who did not know them. William Morris Hunt, who had turned away from portrait-painting, had built a painter's van for sketching-tours. In this gypsy-wagon, with its team of horses, its bunks and compartments for provisions and canvases and easels, he had wandered all over the region, developing a new career as a landscape-artist. Hunt, despondent, had drowned himself on the Isles of Shoals, in the pond where Celia Thaxter found his body; but, three or four years before, he had discovered George Fuller in the village of Deerfield. It was the generous Hunt who persuaded Fuller to go to Boston and organized an exposition for him; and there the Deerfield genius, with his great ruddy head, enjoyed a late success with his glows and mists. For two or three years, he lived at Belmont, where Howells was one of his neighbours.† At Dublin, Abbott Thayer had begun to paint Monadnock; and at Gloucester, where Elizabeth Stuart Phelps had a summer cottage, Winslow Homer studied the fisher-folk, the Grand Banks fishermen who frequented the harbour. There tales of ancient mariners abounded, and flocks of pleasure-sails possessed his eye, with lumber-schooners from Machias and coal-barks bound for Boston and fishing-sloops headed for New-

---

* These vivid little sketches of the lonely mountain and forest folk were published in 1880.

It was at Saranac, in 1887, on a fine, frosty night of stars, "sweet with the purity of forests," that Stevenson conceived *The Master of Ballantrae,* which he wrote in this Adirondack village.

† See the fine biographical sketch that Howells wrote of the painter in *George Fuller: His Life and Works.*

foundland. Homer, the solitary, with all of Thoreau's love for the tough and the pungent in men, rejoiced in Gloucester; and his great pictures, "Eight Bells," "Kissing the Moon," "The Fog Warning," with their oilskins and sou'westers and towering waves, were full of the feeling that Kipling partially caught in *Captains Courageous* after he had visited these scenes. Homer had settled at Prout's Neck in lower Maine, where he built a cottage-studio overlooking the ocean. He had a painting-hut on runners, for cold or stormy weather, and he moved it from spot to spot, where he wished to paint, observing through the big plate-glass window the tumult of the surf and the lights on the rocks. Thence he set out for the northern woods, to sketch deer-stalkers and lumbermen, as later he went to the Barbadoes to study the Caribbean and the Gulf Stream. Miss Phelps wrote at Gloucester *The Madonna of the Tubs* and other stories of the fishing-people. The humanitarian note in these ran too much to the sentimental; but Miss Phelps jealously guarded the self-respect of the natives, who were sometimes patronized by the summer people.

For the summer people were a problem. They were often as odd as the natives, and troublesome also; and, although they were of many types, they had one trait in common,—they seldom understood the country-people. Numbers had forgotten their rustic antecedents, others had no forbears in the country, and the villagers were as strange to them as the roaming Indians who sold their sweet-grass baskets in the hotel parlours. There were others who came in a reverential mood, the Western pilgrims, for instance, who returned in the summer to visit ancestral homesteads and scenes of the past. These pilgrims, who swarmed at the Concord School, were strangers like the rest, though at least there was no vulgarity in their attitude and feeling. There were some who had lost all memory of the land of their fathers, as the Yan-

kees had lost their memory of the mother-country; while
in others this homesickness had mounted with the years,
so that the scene was touched for them with magic. They
sought out the sacred objects, familiar by name in their
childhood, of which they had read in Whittier, the "neighbourhood" poet, the lighthouses, the old schoolhouses,
the beaches, more fabulous yet to many who had never
seen the ocean; and often they ransacked some family attic, with its old hoopskirts and broken chairs, relics of the
"hand-made" days and the days of the war, shells from
battlefields, haversacks and bayonets, spinning-wheels,
wrecked portraits and rusty muskets. All this was natural
and touching, and so was the hunger for beauty that was
bred in the city, the eagerness of the summer people for
every tidbit of sea and landscape and all that was quaint
or charming in the ways of the natives, the clambakes and
the fishing-parties, the latticework flakes and the lobster-
pots, the gulls and the flags and the fog and the general
freshness,—lobsters just out of the pot, corn from the
field, eggs from the visible hen, milk from the cow and
chickens half an hour out of their feathers. The girls who
wove rag-rugs were interesting to city-people who were
hearing about handicrafts again;* and who could resist
the charm of the Maine boat-builders, in their airy shops
on sunny wharves, where the children played with the
sweet-scented shavings and the work always ended in
something graceful and useful? The villagers were glad
to share their pleasures. They were proud when some
fellow-native, a great man in the West, turned up again
and spoke at the little red schoolhouse,—the hero of Dis-

* There was a marked revival of interest in the arts and crafts, in tex-
tiles, pottery, etc., in the years round 1880. This reaction against machine-
methods was further stimulated by the visit of Oscar Wilde in 1882. Longfellow's *Keramos,* 1877, appeared when the interest in ceramics was
reviving. The poem sprang from Longfellow's memories of an old pottery
near Deering's Woods at Portland. There the poet had stopped as a boy to
watch a potter making bowls and pitchers at his wheel in the shadow of a
thorn-tree.

trict Number Four; and they did not object when the summer people set their bean-pots on the floor and filled them with clematis and woodbine. Aware that they had neglected the graces, they did not object too much when the summer people covered their houses with vines, though the vines attracted spiders and were bad for the paint; and they permitted their tenants to open the parlour blinds, though the sunlight was sure to fade the carpets. But the summer people did not stop at this. They painted the old grey clapboards of the mouldering houses, they rooted up the bushes by the wayside, they smartened the village greens and remodelled the churches, they straightened the winding lanes that were better before.* In short, they improved the country, a doubtful blessing, while they looted the furniture and china. The natives could scarcely protest against this, however they might resent it,—but the visitors went on to improve the natives, an apple off another tree indeed. They gave Browning readings to widen their "spheres." They disapproved of the food that was eaten at picnics. They flaunted their silks in the morning and abashed the women, who guarded their one black silk as if it were cloth of gold.† It was bad enough to have strangers come to play for fun at the sort of life they lived in sober earnest all year round.‡ It was worse when the strangers tampered with the village good-for-nothings and turned these bribable souls into lackeys and swindlers. But, worst of all, they arrogantly "studied" the natives, as if natives were curiosities like hoopskirts and muskets. They regarded selectmen as "types." This was all very well with Neapolitan *lazzaroni,* but whoever assumed this attitude with a sovereign Yankee deserved

* "Improvement makes straight roads, but the crooked roads, without improvement, are roads of genius."—Blake, *The Marriage of Heaven and Hell.*

† Mary E. Wilkins, *The Jamesons.*

‡ "People don't like to have what is practical to them patronized as amusement by others. It cheapens it in their own eyes."—Edward Bellamy, *Six to One: a Nantucket Idyl.*

the contempt and hostility he won for his pains. The result of the confrontation of summer people and country-
people was a kind of covert warfare, a real class-war,
though the friction never resulted in violence or blood-
shed; and the country-people usually triumphed, except in
the fashionable colonies where the lackeys abounded, because, as often as not, the summer people, with their city
cheapness, were the true grotesques. If this warfare sub-
sided in time, it was largely because of the writers who
acted as interpreters and filled the breach. Howells was
one of these. With his knowledge of city and country
alike, and his perception and charity, he brought together
all sorts and conditions of men; and Sarah Orne Jewett,
who knew her Howells,* and also knew the natives as a
native, established for other interpreters a scale and a
standard. Like Howells, she knew the world as she knew
the village; and, as an admirable artist, she saw the village
in the light of the "scale of mankind." † Her vision was
certainly limited. It scarcely embraced the world of men,
and the vigorous, masculine life of towns like Gloucester,
astir with Yankee enterprise and bustle, lay quite outside

* A passage in Howells's *A Chance Acquaintance* might well have been
the germ of Miss Jewett's stories. It expresses a fancy of Kitty Ellison as
she strolls with Mr. Arbuton about Quebec. "'Why, it's Hilda in her
tower,' said Kitty. 'Of course! And this is just the kind of street for such a
girl to look down into. It doesn't seem like a street in real life, does it?
The people all look as if they had stepped out of stories, and might step
back any moment; and these queer little houses; they're the very places for
things to happen in! . . . I suppose there's a pleasure in finding out the
small graces and beauties of the poverty-stricken subjects, that they
wouldn't have in better ones, isn't there?' asked Kitty. 'At any rate, if I
were to write a story, I should want to take the slightest sort of plot, and
lay the scene in the dullest kind of place, and then bring out all the possi-
bilities. I'll tell you a book after my own heart: *Details,*—just the history
of a week in the life of some young people who happen together in an old
New England country-house; nothing extraordinary, little, every-day things
told so exquisitely, and all fading naturally away without any particular
result, only the full meaning of everything brought out.'"
One can hardly doubt that Miss Jewett was struck by this passage when
she read it in *The Atlantic* in 1873. She had already published one of her
stories, but the *Details* that Howells mentions is a sketch in advance of
Miss Jewett's first book, *Deephaven,* published four years later in 1877.
† Dostoievsky.

her province and point of view. She spoke for a phase of
New England, a scene that was fading and dying, the
special scene her experience presented to her. But her people were genuine Yankees and stood for the rest. They all
reflected her own transcendent self-respect and put the
summer people in their places.

Miss Jewett lived at South Berwick in Maine, up the
Piscataqua, twelve miles from Portsmouth. She was "one
of the doctor's girls," as people called her. Born in 1849,
the daughter of Dr. Jewett, who had once been a professor at Bowdoin College, she had grown up with grand-
parents and great-aunts and uncles in a world of square,
white houses, picket fences,—some of them ornamental,
with high posts and urns,—and yards overflowing with
larkspurs, petunias and asters, with hollyhocks and borders of box. When the fences were torn down, and the old
reserve went with them, she felt that she belonged to an
age that was passing; for she had shared in imagination
the lives of all these older people who recalled the brisker
days when the town was growing. Once an inland port,
with a few old mansions, Berwick had carried on a busy
trade, bartering timber for rum and West Indian molasses. Its ships had sailed to Russia for iron and cordage.
John Paul Jones had recruited his men from the Berwick
farms,* and later French prisoners of war had appeared
on the river. In those days, ships from many countries had
struggled up the channel, and even now two gundalows,
fitted for lateen sails, were rotting by the wharf near the
sawmill. But one felt as if all the clocks in the town had
stopped, and as if the population had stopped with them.
The gravestones outnumbered the people, and for those
who were left the brooks no longer ran as they used to
run, and the snow was not nearly so deep. There were cer-

* Miss Jewett's historical novel, *The Tory Lover,* dealt with John Paul
Jones and his time at Berwick and the men he assembled for the "Ranger."

tainly no such drifts on the schoolhouse steps as the older
folk remembered.

Such was the atmosphere, reflected in many a town and
village, that enveloped Miss Jewett in her childhood. Her
grandfather had owned the ships the names of which she
knew as if they had been members of the household, and
everything in the Jewett house, an ample, formal colonial
dwelling, spoke of a time, once full, that was full no
longer. The carving in the hallway was the work of three
ships' carpenters, and the mirrors and the tables had been
brought from England. The playroom was a chamber in
the barn at the rear with a foresail from some old vessel
spread over the floor; and whenever, as a little girl, Miss
Jewett had wandered along the river, which separated
Maine from New Hampshire, she found herself in abandoned mill-yards, dark-red, weathered ruins and haunted
houses where cries were heard at night. The attics were
full of yellowing letters, and the houses looked as if they
said, "Good heavens, the things that we remember!"
The little girl was eager for impressions. She mounted the
teams and listened to the talk of the drivers. She scrambled up the great white oaks, swinging from branch to
branch and from tree to tree. Once she climbed to the top
of Agamenticus, five or six miles away, and saw the White
Mountains in the distance. Later, on her horse, she
roamed beyond, exploring the woodpaths and clearings,
the cellar-holes and abandoned graveyards, the hollows
where the lilacs bloomed in Maytime. She found forsaken
orchards, with gnarled and tangled apple-trees spreading
their shrivelled arms abroad; and often, at the end of
some dim trail, she discovered the ghost of a garden, with
honeysuckle, sweet marjoram, lilies and mallows. Sometimes, in a clearing, she happened on a lonely dwelling
where an old woman sat on the doorstep, or she saw two
sisters spinning yarn, stepping back and forth at their big

wheels. But many of the houses were deserted and empty, with floors that creaked as she crossed them, and the windows shook in their loosened frames or lay in the grass below. She would build a fire in the crumbling hearth and imagine the life that had once been lived there. She liked these silent, long-lost places, with a few bits of bright colour relieving the green of the woods or the white of the snow. She seemed to die out of the world in this forest quiet, where everything was merged in the life of nature.

When she was not alone, she was often with her father, who liked to take her with him on his rounds. The doctor drove along the country byways, through the low, straggling woods of spruce and fir, stopping here and there at some high hill-farm or some little house, blackened by rain, with its tangle of roses. His daughter, his favourite companion, sat beside him, and he told her the stories of his patients. She heard the secrets of these dwellings, grey as boulders and silent as the mounds in the graveyards, with their front doors locked and guarded by lilac-bushes and every blind shut tight. Secrets, hidden away from curious eyes, that no one knew but Dr. Jewett. She joined him in the smoke-browned kitchens and the darkened parlours, where a whale's tooth stood on the mantel with a ship drawn on it; or she waited behind the horse till the call was over, at the corner of the dooryard fence. Then, as they drove along, they discussed the household, or the doctor described some incident in the family's life. Perhaps the "last of the Jeffreys," a sterile old scholar, was supported by his sister's little shop. Perhaps a lover had gone to sea, forty years before, and had come back as a tramp and no one knew him. Perhaps an old man, as he lay dying, had insisted that the grass in the yard should be cut, so that all this good hay would not be wasted when the folks came to the funeral and trod upon it. A will had been lost, perhaps: the house had gone to the cousins and the true heir, who had gone away to

Boston and made his fortune, had found the will by chance and torn it up. Here was a lonely old woman who thought of herself as the queen's twin, because she had been born on the same day as Queen Victoria and had seen the queen once on a voyage to London; and here a mysterious stranger had appeared at the corners, a man who wore gaudy shirts and liked a dinner of boiled fowl and went every day to the graveyard, or a grey man who never smiled and who cast a chill over his neighbours whenever he softly opened the kitchen door. The doctor was a local historian, although he never recorded these stories, and his daughter might well have been a doctor. She debated his remedies with him, and she read his medical books and his diaries. When later she wrote *A Country Doctor,* describing her father's character, she imagined herself as the daughter who became a physician and greatly shocked the town by doing so. For women doctors were appearing in the country, and Howells and Miss Phelps wrote novels about them, *Dr. Breen's Practice* and *Doctor Zay,* who lived in a Maine village, like Miss Jewett, and cured the young Bostonian, Waldo Yorke. Miss Jewett used her knowledge in other ways. It helped her to understand her people better, and to understand her people was all she wished. For Miss Jewett was a natural story-teller. She saw stories on every side,—in a funny old man in a linen duster on a station platform, in an old country-woman on the train, with her basket and bundle-handkerchief, who had lost her farm, in a poor old soul who had run away from an almshouse. Growing up in Berwick, with music-lessons and German lessons, and with *Cranford* and *Pride and Prejudice* as her favourite stories, she had read *The Pearl of Orr's Island;* and this novel about Maine people living in a decaying harbour had suddenly opened her eyes to the world she lived in. *The Atlantic* accepted one of her sketches when she was not yet twenty, and eight years later, in 1877, she published her first little volume. This book, called *Deep-haven*, was the story of two Boston girls who came to spend the summer in a town like Berwick. They opened the long-closed Brandon house and rediscovered their family past in the relics and bundles of letters in the drawers of the desks, in the neighbours who made braided rugs, in sea-chests filled with forgotten treasures, in the church where the flute and the violin were played in the gallery still. Miss Jewett found her own world in the persons of these Boston girls, and Howells caught, in the delicate fancy that marked this youthful book, the note of a rare new talent.

This little corner of Maine, with the islands northward, was Sarah Orne Jewett's peculiar realm. She travelled early and late,—as a girl to Wisconsin, and three or four times abroad, as far as Athens,—but she always returned to Berwick and the house and garden where she had lived as a child and where she died. Her closest friend was Mrs. Fields in Boston, with whom she formed the habit of passing her winters, and she visited Celia Thaxter on the Isles of Shoals. When Mrs. Thaxter came to Berwick, the great event was a drive in the woods and a glimpse of a hermit thrush, if the friends were lucky, or a winter drive in the basket-phaeton to Witch Trot or along a ridge where the bare branches stood out clear against a cloud or a yellow sunset. Miss Jewett spent long days on the river in a rowboat, or, driving perhaps to York or Wells, she rambled about the narrow alleys where buildings stood cornerwise or had their back doors where the front should have been, where the roofs had windows in them and the streets were cobble-stoned and the grey, rough-shingled warehouses were covered with lichen. She knew the fishermen's cottages as well as she knew the farmer-folk, and she talked with the old sea-captains who basked on the wharves like drowsy flies that had crawled from their cracks in the spring, as worn as

the driftwood and the ship-timber and rusty iron that
were rotting away beside them. Sometimes she went to
Tenant's Harbour, where, in the summer, she hired the
schoolhouse for fifty cents a week and strolled to her
morning's work through a bayberry pasture. In this
"country of the pointed firs," with its long frost-whitened
ledges and its barren slopes where flocks of sheep moved
slowly, she found the Dunnet shepherdess and Mrs. Todd,
the herbalist, and many of the scenes and persons of her
finest stories,—stories, or sketches, rather, light as smoke
or wisps of sea-fog, charged with the odours of mint, wild
roses and balsam. There, in the low, unpainted houses,
mourners watched with the dead, and sometimes a funeral
train wound over the hills, like a company of Druid worshippers or strange, northern priests with their people;
or, looking seaward, one saw perhaps an island funeral,
a coffin in a rowboat, covered with its black pall, and a
line of little boats close behind it. On the shore, old sailors
baited their trawls whose eyes had looked upon far-away
ports, who had seen the splendours of the Eastern world
and painted South Sea savages. They spent their idle
times carving ship-models or a model of Solomon's temple, following the Scripture measurements. As for the
scattered islands, each had its story. One had its king,
like Celia Thaxter's father, who had vowed he would
never set foot on the mainland again. On another dwelt
two families, divided by a feud, who had not exchanged
a word for three generations. A hermit-woman occupied
another, who thought she had committed the unpardon-
able sin. But most of the people were like the trees that
grew in the cracks of the rocks and kept their tops green
in the driest summer. Miss Jewett knew where to find
their living springs. No one since Hawthorne had pictured
this New England world with such exquisite freshness of
feeling.

CHAPTER XVII

THE WANDERINGS OF HENRY ADAMS

HENRY ADAMS built a big red house in Washington. His friend, John Hay, at work on the life of Lincoln, built an adjoining house in a similar style. Richardson had raised the standing of all American architects, and Adams, who was an old hand at architectural studies, had commissioned this vigorous friend of his Harvard days. Most of the larger American cities had one or more of Richardson's buildings, which had spread across the country like Olmsted's parks. The houses he built for Adams and Hay in 1884 suggested his Sever Hall in Cambridge, the architectural masterpiece whose floors in later years were watered by the tears of countless freshmen.

The sunny rooms of the great red house were hung with Adams's pictures, the English water-colours and Italian drawings, with the Chinese bronzes, the Turner landscape and Blake's Nebuchadnezzar, crawling on his knees and eating grass. The chairs and the sofas were made very low, to fit the diminutive legs of the bearded master. In the greenhouse roses grew, the flower of all the historians, Bancroft, Parkman, Fiske and Cabot Lodge. Here Adams had hoped to finish his history, and his friends were to have a centre here, whenever they found themselves in Washington; for the Adams circle was unique in the capital,—the embassies and the White House were dull beside it. Richardson and John La Farge and Alexander Agassiz occasionally joined the Adams circle, and Henry James, when he happened to be in the country. The nucleus of the circle was the "Five of Hearts,"—the Adamses, the Hays and Clarence King. It was for the "Five of Hearts" that Adams had written *Democracy,* the first of his two little novels. The friends debated it, chapter by chapter, and, when it was published anonymously, the rumour went about, and lingered long, that King was the author of this novel. But King's brief writing days were over, and he flitted hither and thither in pursuit of the fortune that eluded him more and more as time went on. King was a bird of passage. Hay was Adams's constant crony. Every afternoon, when their work was finished, the two set out for a walk, the little, dark, brooding Adams and Hay, who was also a little man, but for whom a generation that blighted his friend had brought, and was to bring, success and fame. They were both deep in American history, and they had been more or less intimate since they had met in Washington at the close of the war, as Minister Adams's secretary and President Lincoln's secretary; and Hay had advanced from triumph to triumph, as a popular author in prose and verse, as a diplomat in Austria, France and Spain, as editor of *The Tribune* and assistant in the Department of State, and finally as the writer of the life of Lincoln. A Western man, untroubled by memories or traditions, he had sailed before the wind with the party in power, while his friend, the saturnine Adams, whom he called "Oom Hendrik," fought against the political stars in their courses.

Adams, who had longed for power, had known for several years that he could not hope to exercise power directly. But he liked the feeling that he was near it * and even exerting it indirectly as the confidant and friend of men in office. Ambassadors came to consult him, and

---

* "Socially speaking, we are very near most of the powerful people, either as enemies or as friends."—Letter of 1882.

they sometimes followed his advice; and later, when Hay and Cabot Lodge were running the foreign affairs of the country, they had a way of running them in his house. It was even rumoured that Henry Adams wrote some of Theodore Roosevelt's state papers. Meanwhile, he had written his two novels, *Democracy* and *Esther,* before he moved into the great red house,—the first expressing his disgust with politics as he found them, the second bidding farewell to traditional religion. Nimble in style and light in tone, these novels resembled in many ways the earlier works of Henry James and Howells, and in both, as so often in James and Howells, the leading figures were women, who presented Henry Adams's point of view. The charming Mrs. Lightfoot Lee, the heroine of *Democracy,* who had come to live in Washington, was bent upon learning what went on behind the political curtain and taking a hand in reforming public abuses. She was disillusioned much as Adams was. Esther Dudley, the heroine of the other novel, was equally disillusioned with the Church. She fell in love with a clergyman, vaguely suggesting Phillips Brooks, who stood for her as a symbol of modern religion, and found that she was incapable of sharing his faith. The characters in *Esther* were drawn from Henry Adams's friends. The geologist, George Strong, was Clarence King, and there was much of La Farge in the artist Wharton. The story suggested the building of Trinity Church in Boston, which occurred when Henry Adams was teaching at Harvard. He had shared in the discussions of church-arrangement and decoration, matters in which his clergyman, Hazard, was learned. Hazard, in this aspect, was clearly a portrait of Phillips Brooks, as Wharton at work on his murals was inspired by La Farge.

Suddenly, a blow fell from which Henry Adams never recovered. His wife committed suicide one Sunday morning, while he was out for a walk. The mainspring of his life, he felt, was broken; and, moving into the new house on Lafayette Square, he could not bear to live in it alone. He burned his diaries, and his notes and correspondence, and he commissioned Saint-Gaudens to design the Rock Creek monument that was to stand henceforth on the unmarked grave. He seemed to himself as dead as a ghost or a mummy. Meanwhile, like Mrs. Lightfoot Lee, he longed for the oblivion of Egypt. Mrs. Lee's nerves had also been shaken by Washington politics. She also felt her life had gone awry, and her final word expressed Adams's thought: "Oh, what a rest it would be to live in the Great Pyramid and look out forever at the polar star!"

Thus began for Henry Adams a life of restless wandering that carried him round the world for twenty years. In time he returned to Washington, and later he finished his history at Quincy, where his forbears had eaten out their hearts in disgust and disappointment at the turns of fortune; but the work had lost its vital meaning for him. He was ready to join any friend for any sort of expedition, Hay for a camping trip in the Yellowstone, King for a visit to Trinidad, a casual English acquaintance exploring the West. Sometimes he went alone, when friends were lacking, perhaps to South Carolina, perhaps to Vancouver. He wandered over Mexico on muleback, wearing a sugar-loaf hat and a leather jacket, living with the Indians in their mud-cabins, intimate with their pigs, hens, burros and babies. King was the friend he joined most happily. Geology, he found, was tranquillizing. It carried one's thoughts away from time, and the reckless, active, adventurous King, unsicklied by analysis, was the crony he needed.* With King he visited Dos Bocas, a Cuban

* "As for Strong,"—Clarence King,—"he was always in good spirits. Within the memory of man, well or ill, on sea or shore, in peril or safety, Strong had never been seen unhappy or depressed. He had the faculty of interesting himself without an effort in the doings of his neighbours."— Henry Adams, *Esther.*

plantation, rising with the sun and rambling over the hills, geologizing. Adams had a theory there: if they could get down deep enough into the Archæan rocks, they would find President Eliot and all the professors of Harvard College. But he was drawn especially to the lands of Buddha. He felt that longing for the East which proud people often share, when, as Kinglake said, they are "goaded by sorrow." * On the first of his expeditions,† in fact, he went to Japan with La Farge, who had his own reasons for wishing to see it.

This longing for the East was a symptom of the moment, especially marked in New England. Numbers of Boston and Harvard men were going to Japan and China in a spirit that was new and full of meaning. Oriental art was the vogue among Bostonians, and they were filling the region with their great collections. Alexander Agassiz was an early and ardent collector. So was Raphael Pumpelly, for whose first book La Farge had written an essay on Japanese art. Mrs. Henry Adams's brother collected Chinese paintings. Edward S. Morse, the Salem zoologist, ‡ who made three journeys to Japan, collected Japanese pottery; Ernest Fenollosa, the son of a Salem musician, made a great collection of Japanese pictures, and William Sturgis Bigelow brought back from Japan twenty-six thousand objects of Japanese art.§ Some of these col-

---

* Kinglake, *Eothen.*

† 1886.

‡ Edward S. Morse, a pupil of Agassiz, went to Japan in 1877 to study the brachiopods in Japanese waters. He made two subsequent visits and became professor of zoology in the Imperial University of Tokio. His published journal, *Japan Day by Day,* was filled with careful observations of Japanese life and manners, accompanied by amusing pen-and-ink sketches. His great collection of Japanese pottery was bought by the Boston museum.

§ Morse wrote as follows, regarding his journey through the southern provinces, 1882, in the company of Bigelow and Fenollosa: "We shall see a little of the life of old Japan; I shall add a great many specimens to my collection of pottery; Dr. Bigelow will secure many forms of swords, guards, and lacquer; and Mr. Fenollosa will increase his remarkable collection of pictures, so that we shall have in the vicinity of Boston by far the largest collection of Japanese art in the world."—*Japan Day by Day.* This prophecy proved to be true.

lectors were detached observers. Morse had no interest in Japanese religion; neither had Thomas Sergeant Perry, whose grandfather's brother, the Commodore, had opened Japan and who spent three years as a professor at one of the Japanese universities.* But others were enthralled by Oriental thought; they were seekers of salvation in the Buddhist way. Henry Adams was not the only one who turned to the East for Nirvana, which was "out of season" in Omaha but not in Boston.† This word fascinated Boston, and even Tom Appleton named one of his yachts "Nirvana,"—he who enjoyed the world so heartily. Japan, for these minds, was a loadstone, and in several cases its influence was profound and lasting. Fenollosa became a Buddhist, and so did Sturgis Bigelow, whose *Buddhism and Immortality,*—his only book, a lecture,—was a relic of the interest he aroused. Bigelow, a student of medicine who had worked with Pasteur, had gone to Japan with Fenollosa and studied seven years with a friendly abbot. He was received into the Buddhist communion. Three or four decades later, dying in Boston, he summoned a Catholic priest and besought him to annihilate his soul. He could not forgive the priest for refusing to do so. He left directions to have his ashes carried to Japan, where they lie beside Fenollosa's on the shore of Lake Biwa.

When Adams was drawn to the East, it was thus with a motive that other New Englanders shared, and for similar reasons. Still others continued to go as missionaries, who never had a doubt regarding their own possession of the true religion. But the day had passed when the great scholars shared this faith and acted on it,—the men

* Thomas Sergeant Perry was professor of English literature at Keiogijiku University, 1897–1900.
† "At Omaha a young reporter got the better of us; for when in reply to his inquiry as to our purpose in visiting Japan, La Farge beamed through his spectacles the answer that we were in search of Nirvana, the youth looked up like a meteor, and rejoined, 'It's out of season!' "—Letter of Henry Adams, 1886.

who had once translated the Bible into the tongues of Asia and boldly disputed with the brahmins and the mandarins. The Tamil and Burmese and Chinese dictionaries, written by New England men, to convert the Asiatics through the Scriptures, were the work of an earlier generation. The scholarly mind of New England was torn with doubts, and when Sturgis Bigelow returned to Boston he found an open field for his message. This was something else than the teaching of Concord, in which even the Buddhist texts had been applied to magnify and stimulate the will. It was a message of resignation, peace, passivity, inactivity that appealed to the tired minds of this later New England. In the Unitarian form, the Christian faith had lost its positive content, and the sons of those who had hoped to convert the Asiatics were wondering if the truth was not in Asia. The old Unitarian hope had failed, and for many New England itself was a failure. Boston had grown complex, with the coming of alien races, and the feverish activity of the rest of the country seemed senseless to these hurt, bewildered minds. The optimism that John Fiske and William James maintained in Cambridge was foreign to their mood and offended their taste. It justified the restless striving that had lost all meaning for them. They longed for quiet, solace and escape. Sad and fatalistic, feeling that life was empty, they found a natural haven in the teachings of Buddha. Blessed for them was Nirvana, where illusion ceased, where the trials, the expiations and the whirlwind of life were calmed and silenced and ended in absolute truth.*

One of these students of Japanese thought was a young

* The character of Dr. Peter Alden, in Santayana's *The Last Puritan,* may well have been suggested partially by Sturgis Bigelow. Dr. Alden, a man of means who never practised medicine, had wandered in his youth through Japan and China, collecting ivory carvings for the Boston museum. Driven by a "hunger for something less disconsolate," the hypochondriac Alden roamed the seas in his yacht, the "Black Swan," with two gilded Buddhas in the cabin, and at last in his own way found Nirvana.

man of fashion, Percival Lowell. This grandson of the poet's cousin, a well-known polo-player, had gone to Japan three years before Henry Adams. He had arrived in Tokio in 1883, drawn by a wish to study the language and people. As a boy, he had gone in for astronomy, and later he remembered seeing the white snow-caps of Mars crowning a globe that was spread with many colours. He returned to astronomy afterwards at Flagstaff, Arizona, and became world-famous as "the Martian," with his theories about life on this favourite planet; but for ten years Japan was his chief intellectual interest, and he wrote three fine books about it. He hired a house in Tokio and set up an establishment, where he lived like a Japanese prince; but at first he stayed for a while in Korea, as a governmental counsellor and guest. His official position gave him a chance to see the Hermit Kingdom as no one from the outside world had ever seen it; and he described, in *Chosön,* the life of the court and the nobles, as well as the arts and the ways of the streets and the people. This picturesque and solid book was unique and permanent, for Japan was soon to destroy the old Korea; but Lowell's *The Soul of the Far East,* slighter in form and more theoretical, was the book that gave the author his reputation. This study of the Japanese mind, its impersonal nature, in family life, in language, art, religion, in which individuality was a transient illusion, attracted many readers who were ready for the message, " 'Tis something better not to be." This impersonality was painful to Lowell. He was not in search of Nirvana, however he ministered to other seekers, and he had before him a strenuous life such as even Theodore Roosevelt might have envied; but he made Lafcadio Hearn in America feel "like John of Patmos." Percival Lowell's little work, "precise, fine, beautifully worded," as Hearn described it in a letter, had much to do with sending to Japan the greatest writer of English who ever lived there. Lowell, moreover, wrote two other books that ranked with Lafcadio Hearn's for perception and beauty. He had made a special study of the Shinto trances, the subject of *Occult Japan;* while *Noto* was a simple book of travel. Only one foreigner before him had explored the mysterious peninsula that bore its name. This isolated region, with its deep-bosomed bays and headlands, stood out to the west of Tokio, a striking outline. It had long caught Lowell's fancy before he undertook the journey that carried him into this world of primeval Japan.

Later, Amy Lowell,—Percival Lowell's sister,—shared in the multifarious fruit of these travels. Amy Lowell, a roly-poly little girl, was twenty years younger than her brother. Not long ago, as a baby in a basket, she had been brought by her father to the Saturday Club; and there she was passed around the table, so that the aging poets might beam upon her. As for fairies, those she knew were fox-sprites and spider-demons, of which she was always hearing from her brother in Japan. He sent her long letters on decorated note-paper, and he told her about these pixies during his visits to Boston. She was already familiar with the two-sworded nobles and the camellia-trees that appeared in her poems. Meanwhile, a more serious student than Lowell who had gone to Japan five years before him was living there when Adams and La Farge arrived. Ernest Fenollosa had settled in Tokio in 1878. He was already engaged in a work that was to mark an epoch in Japanese culture.

This half-Yankee son of a Spanish musician had grown up in Salem, his birthplace. His father, a musical prodigy who had led the cathedral choir in Malaga, had toured the American cities as a member of a marine band and finally settled in Salem as a teacher of music. George Peabody had attracted him there with his great collection of musical instruments, and the elder Fenollosa had married one of his pupils, the daughter of a Salem shipping magnate. The son, at Harvard, was influenced by Herbert Spencer, whose teachings John Fiske was popularizing, and, when the University of Tokio was opened, he was appointed professor of philosophy. Fenollosa felt at home in Japan at once, and he had among his pupils so many future statesmen that he acquired a name which meant "Teacher of Great Men." But his interest shifted away from philosophy. He had always been a lover of music and painting, and, as Oriental art more and more became his central study, he was soon involved, as a sympathetic foreigner, in the Japanese aesthetic revival. The moment was one of confusion. The feudal system had passed away, and the Japanese, who were adopting the European dress and customs, were disregarding their own traditions and methods. In the schools they were teaching American drawing and studying under Italian instructors, and the great Japanese works of art, rejected and despised, were disappearing. Many belonged to daimios who, reduced to poverty, left these treasures to their servants, through whom they reached the pawnshops; and collections of paintings and porcelains, lacquers and bronzes were scattered and sold for next to nothing. The "foreignists" were burning them as rubbish. Fenollosa found one of the greatest paintings in the Osaka market, and he picked out of an ash-barrel a great ceramic head of Buddha. This was part of a statue destroyed in an earthquake, the pride of an ancient monastery, and the monks, tired of keeping the fragment, which they no longer valued, had thrown it away. Fenollosa's moment in Japan was like James Jackson Jarves's in Florence, when, thirty years before, Jarves had collected the primitives that nobody wanted. The Japanese nobles and priests who had owned these works for centuries seemed to have lost all feeling for their national past.

But the Yankee-Spanish Fenollosa was not a mere collector. He had become a Buddhist and cast in his lot with

Japan, and he became the centre of a movement to save this ancient art. He bitterly reproached the Japanese for throwing away their birthright. He established an artists' club, over which he presided, and he helped to form the "Art Club of Nobles," to interest the ruling class in this great cause. Largely as a result of his insistence, the Japanese methods of art-instruction were soon restored in the schools; and he was appointed, in 1886, Commissioner of Fine Arts for the empire. He was the first director of the Tokio Academy and the Imperial Museum. He was asked to register all the art-treasures of the country and draw up laws regarding the restoration and exporting of works of art. He was authorized to inspect the godowns and open long-closed shrines. For two hundred years, in certain cases, these shrines had never been unlocked, and the priests, who thought it a sacrilege, tried to prevent him. The greatest of all his discoveries was the standing Buddha of Horiuji, a figure of wonderful beauty that was wrapped in swathing bands of cotton, covered with the dust of centuries. For weeks he lived in monasteries with the kindly priests, studying the great scroll-paintings and other treasures, haunting the sanded courts with their mossy stones and their banks of ancient shrubs and irregular slabs. He sat before the stupendous rolls, in the light, cool, beautiful rooms, to the murmur of trickling water, with tears in his eyes. While he studied these pictures, he studied the Noh-plays, which had risen from the Buddhist and Shinto rites. Umewaka Minoru, Fenollosa's teacher, had revived the plays in 1871. This scholar and poet had found an old daimio's stage and set it up and trained his sons as actors. He collected costumes and re-established the ancient drama, with its masks and choruses and sacred dances. For twenty years, Fenollosa worked with Minoru, studying Noh, acting and singing, and he recorded the traditions of this drama, which resembled in certain ways the plays of the Greeks and the English morality-plays. He prepared translations of about fifty texts. Some of these Noh-plays were remodelled later, from Fenollosa's notes, by Ezra Pound. As *Certain Noble Plays of Japan,* with their art of gesture, dancing and chanting, they influenced the Western theatre, especially through the poet Yeats.* Fenollosa had foreseen this influence. He knew that he lived in what he called a "weak transitional period" in the poetic life of America and Europe and that Japanese and Chinese forms, with their subtlety and condensed power, were bound to affect the work of the Western poets.

In his later years, Fenollosa returned to Boston. The emperor said to him then: "You have taught my people to know their own art." His collection was bought by the Boston museum, where he acted for a while as curator. He lectured all over America, went back to Japan for three more years and died at last in London in 1906. In the summer of that year, in a New York apartment, he made a pencil draught of his one great book. This *Epochs of Chinese and Japanese Art,* compiled after his death, was full of errors, for he had no opportunity to revise it; but it remained as a monument and landmark in the study of Oriental culture. Fenollosa's purpose was to break down the old idea that Chinese civilization had been static by showing the special beauties of all its epochs, along with the relations of the Chinese and Japanese as interlocking phases of one great movement. With his "vistas of strange futures of world-embracing cultures half-weaned from Europe," Fenollosa later seemed a prophet, the somewhat cloudy symbol of a day when East and West were merging for ends unknown. But in his earlier time, as a scholar and awakener, his object was distinct and his work specific; and Fenollosa was in full

---

* See Yeats's preface to the Irish edition of this book, 1916. The translations from the Chinese in Ezra Pound's *Cathay* were also based upon Fenollosa's notes.

career when Adams and La Farge reached Japan, where his ashes were to lie, like Bigelow's, in one of the temples. With the shy, retiring Bigelow, who acted as their courier, he received the wandering students and took them in hand. They had brought no books and meant to read none, for they wished to come "innocently," as La Farge described it; and the strict Fenollosa, for whom all true art had ended with the advent of the shoguns, taught them to discriminate between the classic forms and the modern imitations and degradations.

La Farge had definite reasons for visiting Japan. He was planning his fresco for the Church of the Ascension,* and he hoped to find "certain conditions of line in the mountains," as he wrote in his *Artist's Letters from Japan,* that would help him for the background of this picture. He kept this in mind, and he found a space of mountain, with rocks and clouds, that exactly fulfilled his intention. He sketched it many times, and he used it later in his fresco. But, more than this, the atmosphere suggested the miraculous. One could imagine there the ascension of Christ and feel it in relation to the setting, for ascensions and disappearances of pilgrim saints were normal events in Buddhist history, and Buddhism joined with the earthly faith in attaching religious value to mountain heights and solitary places. Sacredness dwelt in the Japanese mountains, and nature lent itself to miraculous events, to moods in which the edges of all things blended and man and the outside world passed into each other. Nature was not separate, as it seemed in the West, although nature had never seemed separate to Emerson in Concord. As Emerson had felt, La Farge felt here,—how little plants and flowers, grasses, mountains, the clouds that rose from the water, the drops of water, begotten by nature absolute, great and small, might all become the godhead. And

* In New York.

then, after years of wilful energy, it was a relief to be
guided by the "inner light" of Tao. It was good to try
again the freshness of the springs, to see if one was capable of the new impressions that had once been so common
in childhood.

So La Farge had reasoned, or so, at least, he felt; for
he left the reasoning to his companion. "Adams, you reason too much," he said one night. He dreamed, after one
of their arguments, that he heard the mind of Adams
making a great clatter in the room. He awoke,—it was
only a rat. They had taken a little house at Nikko, overlooking a temple and garden, with the Japanese mountains in the distance; and, while La Farge sketched,
Adams read Dante's *Paradiso* or walked or rode on
pack-horses over the hills. Sometimes he took photographs, or he sat cross-legged on the verandah, overhaul-
ing bales of stuffs and lacquers, mounds of books and
tons of bronzes, with Bigelow and Fenollosa to guide his
choice. The friends rejoiced in the sacred groves, where
the god Pan might still be living, the holy trees and stones,
the little shrines, the old roads between the walls, broken
by turrets and bridges. Here were the "soul-informed
rocks" of the Greeks and a world that associated spirits
with every visible form of the earthly dwelling. The bare-
ness and coldness of the Japanese interiors, which insisted
on the idea of doing with little,—a noble one, certainly,
—pleased La Farge: the highest care in workmanship
was all that adorned the emperor's palace at Kioto. How
civilized, this emptiness, after the accumulations of Western houses! La Farge was in high feather. He discovered
in the figures in field and street reminders of the antique
world, so dear to the artist. The distinctly rigid muscles
of the legs and thighs, the ripplings and swellings of the
backs revived his old excitement as a draughtsman. For a
painter, Japan was a godsend; while, as for Adams, he

found in the statue of Kwannon the image of his quest.
Here was Nirvana indeed, achieved in eternal calm, with
eternal compassion.

The travels of La Farge and Adams, soon to be continued, left traces in the lives and work of both. Adams's
"historic sense," La Farge said, "amounted to poetry,"
and even Adams's reasoning was full of suggestion. His
deductions set La Farge's mind sailing into new channels,
and the *Artist's Letters from Japan* owed much to Adams.
For his part, Adams developed new faculties under La
Farge's influence. He had left the world of public affairs
behind him. The author of the *History* underwent a transformation, and the Adams who wrote *Mont-Saint-Michel*
and Chartres was, in a measure, at least, La Farge's creation. Adams had always been drawn to art; as a student
of things mediæval, he had been drawn especially to architecture; he had had an early passion for stained-glass windows. He had collected pictures, terra-cottas, bronzes.
But this was all rather external: his aesthetic feelings
were buried under other interests. He was prepared for
the spell of La Farge only when the political world had
lost for him,—for the moment,—its stirring appeal; and
the "spectacled and animated prism," as he called his
friend, led him to feel from within the meaning of colour.
La Farge had lived in Paris at the time of the battle-
royal between the pupils of Ingres and Delacroix. Ingres
had held that the first motive in colour-decoration was
line, while for Delacroix the great point was colour,—
colour, wherever one chose to place it, colour, however
one wished to use it, if one's lions had to be pink and
one's camels green. So all the French artists had felt in
their great days of stained glass, and La Farge, who was
trying to work in glass like a twelfth-century artist, was a
partisan of Delacroix from the first. He was always talking glass and talking colour, and the feeling that Adams
showed for glass and colour, when he came to write *Mont-*

Saint-Michel and Chartres, was largely a result of these conversations. The friends even worked together. During their second journey, to Samoa and Tahiti, Adams tried his own hand at painting.

Between his various expeditions, Adams reopened his Washington house. He returned, he said, "as a horse goes back to its stable." There he remained alone, for he never dined out any longer, while the world ran by with spectre-like silence. He finished his history, volume by volume, but he could not believe it would interest anyone: he did not even send it to his friends. He wandered out to Rock Creek and lurked in the evergreens and holly that surrounded Saint-Gaudens's Nirvana, as he sometimes called it. In his absence, the hooded figure had become a fad of tourists, and he found an ironical pleasure in listening to their comments. Occasionally, he mingled with them, knowing that he was himself unknown, and the resentment that clergymen showed at this figure of denial, —as they saw it,—filled him with a bitter satisfaction. He had lost his own faith in life; but what was their faith and security if a graven image could so provoke and wound them? A faith that could not ignore this challenge was no great loss for him, he felt. They were no more secure than himself, for all their professions.

When La Farge suggested another journey, Adams longed for the East again. He would have liked to sleep forever in the trade-winds under the southern stars, in the void of the dark purple ocean. But once again La Farge had a positive purpose. He was eager to paint the South Sea islands, and Clarence King's phrase about Hawaii and the "old-gold girls tumbling down waterfalls" captivated the fancy of both the friends. For the greater part of a year, they wandered from island to island, La Farge with his paint-box and Adams as La Farge's pupil; and again it was La Farge who wrote the book. *Reminiscences of the South Seas,* suggested partly by Adams's talk, related their common adventures. The dances and the native feasts delighted La Farge and amused his companion, who described them at length in his letters; and both were enthralled by this new world of colour, which they tried to capture with their brushes. There were the old-gold girls, like nymphs of streams, swimming and hiding in the vines, with faces and arms glancing out of the branches, while the men were a deep red beside them. There was the velvet-green of the mountains, streaked by long white threads of waterfalls; and the ferns grew thick on the dripping banks, and the sea glowed blue through the pandanus leaves. The shores were fringes of gold and green, and the palm-trees glistened in the moonlight, with their long arms waving and rustling; and Adams and La Farge went swimming in the purple light. Adams watched La Farge at work, intoxicated himself with the broad bands of orange and green in the sunsets, the strong blues, the soft violets, the shifting tints of the ocean, the glow of the mountains. There was an endless charm in the colour and light of every visible hour in these tropical islands. La Farge splashed in deep purples over dark greens till the paper was soaked into a shapeless daub, and yet the next day, with a few touches, it all came out a brilliant mass. He would see sixteen shades of red in a sky that was cobalt to Adams; and Adams wondered vainly how he did it. But he mixed his own colours by the dozen and splashed away. The results were certainly feeble, but one could never tell: next time, perhaps, the miracle might happen. He felt as he had felt as a boy about fishing. There was always a chance of getting a bite tomorrow.

With this education of the senses, Adams recovered his feeling for history. He had long powwows with the Samoan nobles. These great chiefs, immense, with heavy arms, who sat with spaces between them, majestic, indifferent, as if for a decoration on a frieze, suggested

Agamemnon or Ajax. Their bodies expressed reserve, and they were as sacred as demigods, intermediaries with heaven. They reduced to the level of stable-boys the aristocrats of Europe: so Adams felt in their presence. But they accepted him as a great man also. The American frigate "Adams" had voyaged through these seas and left his name behind it. He discussed their laws of property and kinship with them, questions he had studied in connection with the Anglo-Saxons and early Germans. In Tahiti, his interest in history returned in full measure. The old chiefess Arii Taimai adopted him into her family, and Henry Adams became Tauraatua. He was named for a forbear of the queen who had once been enamoured of a maiden called Marae-ura, and songs about these lovers still survived. As one of the Tauras, with all the ancestral privileges, he became the heir of an estate of six orange-trees and a mango, and he took investiture of his duchy in the shape of an orange. From this relationship grew in time one of Henry Adams's books, the *Memoirs of Arii Taimai;** for he persuaded the chiefess to relate her family history to him, and he retold it, with his own investigations, as if she herself had composed the story. At certain hours every day he repaired to a cottage behind her palace, shut in by trees that filled the little garden. Then, from some inner apartment, the queen appeared and repeated her legends and songs. Betweenwhiles, with her sister Manihinihi, she prepared the material for these conversations; and sometimes, in the early evening, the sisters walked down to the shore and answered Adams's questions about the past. They sat on the rocks under the palms, in the light of the afterglow, with the blue ocean far away and the shadows moving over the water. The great heights of Aorai appeared and vanished behind the clouds, and nothing broke the stillness

* One hundred copies of this book were privately printed in Paris in 1901. It was signed only by Adams's Tahitian name, Tauraatua I Amo.

but the rustle of the surf. The musical voices of the sisters mingled with the murmur of the ripples, into which Manihinihi thrust her bare foot. It might have been a Puvis de Chavannes! Genealogy, in Tahiti, was a science. It ranked with the intellectual work of Europe, and the tale of the Tauras was the tale of Tahiti. Adams brought his historian's skill to the task. He knew the writings of all the travellers who had visited the islands, and he disentangled the complex threads of rumour, legend and fact. But only a few reflections and a few quotations from French and English authors disturbed the reader's illusion that the queen herself had written this charming book.

Meanwhile, La Farge and Adams continued their journey. This took them to Ceylon, where, seated like priests or deities in a sacred ox-cart, on chairs upholstered in red, they were dragged through the woods to Anuradhapura. There, among the stone doorways standing in the jungle, monkeys jumped from branch to branch; and Adams sat for half an hour under the shoot of Buddha's bo-tree. Where else could he ever hope to find Nirvana?

CHAPTER XVIII

HOWELLS IN NEW YORK

ONE by one, the older writers were gathered to their fathers. Emerson, Longfellow, Motley and Dana were gone. In 1886, Emily Dickinson died at Amherst in the red-brick house where she was born. Fifty-six years old, she had been for a while an invalid and more invisible than ever; but one of her pleasures had been to listen while a younger neighbour played the piano for her in the empty parlour. Miss Dickinson hovered in the hallway, a glimmering whiteness. In her isolation, she had never heard Beethoven, Bach or Scarlatti; and she always sent in to the player a glass of wine on a silver salver, with a cake, a flower and a poem, a flash of the moment. At the funeral, Colonel Higginson read *No Coward Soul is Mine,* and Emily Brontë's unknown fellow-poet was carried to the grave by labourers on her father's land.

This youngest of the older writers passed obscurely, while the public fame of the others was in everyone's mouth. She had left word to have her poems burned. She had kept them in envelopes and boxes in her desk and her bureau, rolled like parchment in bundles bound with ribbons. Her sister destroyed her papers; then, struck by the poems, she saved them, in a fever of excitement. She turned them over to Higginson and the friend who had played for Miss Dickinson, and four years later they began to appear in the series of volumes that announced a unique and original American poet. Meanwhile, of the earlier writers a few survived. At Hartford, Mrs. Stowe, who had lost her mind, roamed about her grounds in the

care of a muscular Irishwoman, drifting in and out of
Mark Twain's house. Now and again, on slippered foot,
she stole behind some sleeper and roused him with a sudden Indian war-whoop, or she wandered into Warner's
house and sat at the piano, playing some weird refrain or
quavery hymn. To those who spoke of *Uncle Tom's
Cabin*, she often said, "God wrote it." Whittier had retired to Danvers, where he lived at "Oak Knoll" with his
spinster cousins. There he had revived his old skill in
horticulture and busied himself with flowers, plants and
trees; and there a visitor found him once playing croquet
against himself among the many-coloured autumn leaves.
A vessel built on the Merrimac bore his name, and the
governor and his staff went out to Danvers to celebrate
his eightieth birthday. In Boston, the half-blind Francis
Parkman pursued his Canadian history in his shadowy
study. One met Parkman out of doors, with a walking-
stick in either hand, hobbling at a run along the pavement, then throwing himself, to breathe, against a wall;
for, although he could scarcely support himself, neither
could he saunter. In his mind, for all his crippled body,
he was still on the Oregon trail. Pale, with his desperate
energy and his black-rimmed glasses, moving as if a demon
drove him forward, he frightened the children who came
upon him suddenly, lying in wait on a doorstep. But Parkman's health and eyesight had improved with age, and
he wrote his finest book, *Montcalm and Wolfe*, with his
own hand, in pencil. Howells was only one of an army of
readers for whom Parkman had made Quebec and Montreal "the beautiful inheritance of all dreamers." The
birthdays of most of these aging worthies were com-
memorated throughout the country, and their visages
were almost as familiar as those of the national heroes
on coins and stamps. In the game of "Authors," the
heads of historians and poets eternally rested from their
labours, brow on hand. Dr. Holmes felt like Nestor rec-

ollecting his ancient comrades, Theseus, Polyphemus and the rest; for the Saturday "club" was only a walking-stick now. As a wholesale talker, the doctor kept his end up, and he still presented his keyboard of nerve-pulps, not yet tanned or ossified, to the finger-touch of everything outside him. But the days of the conversational dogmatist, on the imperial scale, were gone forever. Johnsons and Popes were impossible in an age of science. For the rest, the veteran harper of Boston often attuned his strings now to birthdays that foretold a vacant future.

About this time, an English authoress, at a Boston dinner-table, said, "Isn't it a pity, don't you think, that all the really interesting Americans are dead?" The remark might have been phrased more happily, but, after all, this lady expressed what many of the Bostonians were thinking. Their classic age was past, or passing. The "second growth" of New England authors scarcely rivalled the first, and that "interesting" Americans might still be living elsewhere was no great consolation to the men of Boston. Besides, could they be really interesting if they were not Bostonians?* In other fields than literature, in science and philosophy, New England was certainly advancing. William James had long been at work on the *Principles of Psychology,* which was to appear in 1890, and Josiah Royce had been called from Berkeley to Harvard. In California he had been the "solitary philosopher between Behring's Strait and Tierra del Fuego." † Royce, whose head suggested the world poised on the body of the tortoise, was one of those "extraordinary men, too eminent for praise," as his colleague, George Herbert

---

* When someone mentioned the proposal to publish *Who's Who in America,* Edmund Quincy is said to have asked, "Wouldn't the Harvard Quinquennial Catalogue answer every purpose?"

† "There is no philosophy in California from Siskiyou to Fort Yuma, and from the Golden Gate to the summit of the Sierras."—Royce to James, 1879.—"Your wail as the solitary philosopher between Behring's Strait and Tierra del Fuego has a grand lonesome picturesqueness about it."—James to Royce.

Palmer, called him, who were forming the great philosophical department in Cambridge. These men were new centres of agitation in the intellectual life of Boston, and as long as Holmes and Lowell survived, with Parkman and two or three others, its literary prestige was secure. Writers from afar still came to Boston with veneration and curiosity. A case in point at the moment was Hamlin Garland. When he took the "back trail" from Dakota, reversing the pioneer law of development, even as Royce had reversed it, Boston attracted Garland, not New York. He had come with a feeling like Howells's, twenty-five years before, and was living there on forty cents a day, reading John Fiske at the Public Library, along with Spencer, Taine and Whitman, while his tan melted away with his corn-fed muscle. He lived in Boston several years, studying, lecturing, teaching, and he wrote *Main-Travelled Roads* at Jamaica Plain, where Parkman continued his history in the summer season. He haunted the streets with as firm a conviction that he was at the centre of the world as Henry James felt in the streets of London. But, for all this, the American centre had shifted to New York,—or was rapidly shifting, at least,— and Boston knew it. The literary leaders of the younger generation, Howells and the "Boston-plated" Aldrich, were half outsiders. They were loyal to the Boston genius, but not to Boston without the genius; and Howells had grown restive, although literary Boston had heaped him with all its honours and crowned him with laurels. The town that he adored was dying, the other Boston was none of his, and the young men were growing up dispirited and listless there.* A Harvard student, John Jay Chapman, lay awake at night, "wondering what was the

* "The young men of the seventies were told that there was no health in them; that Boston's classic age was gone; and Howells and Aldrich were perhaps none too loath to believe it, and that they were the only successors. They never really liked Boston. Lowell remarked once that Howells always wrote 'as if some swell had failed to bow to him on Beacon Street.' "— Frederic J. Stimson. *My United States.*

matter"—as he put it—"with Boston." Another acute observer explained it later. That Boston had "filled up" was H. G. Wells's diagnosis. Its capacity was just sufficient to comprehend the whole achievement, up to a certain year, of the human mind. About 1875, it had reached an equilibrium. Its finality was a proof of the laws of physics.*

This was partly true, at least, sufficiently so for Howells, who felt an insistent need for pastures new. Boston had been kind to him, and he held a unique position there as the confidant of writers old and young. When Longfellow died, it was Howells who was asked to look over his posthumous poems and make a last selection for publication. When Whittier cast about for someone to write his official biography, Howells was the first to whom he turned. Later, Norton asked him to write the official life of Lowell, who had offered him the Smith professorship. Cambridge could no further go than to add the name of Howells to those of Ticknor, Longfellow and Lowell, or, rather, to suggest this honour, which Howells refused; and, when the Boston writers and artists wished to establish the Tavern Club, he was invited to form it and lead the meetings. Just under fifty, he had vindicated Holmes's joke,—the apostolic succession was in his hands; but he had lost his feeling for New England, as New England was losing itself in the rest of the country. *The North American Review* had moved to New York; so had Edwin Booth, Parkman's neighbour, who had lived so long in the town. Boston had ceased to represent the widest American interests, and the younger American writers were ceasing to come there: they were drawn to New York much more in their

* "The finality of Boston is a quantitative consequence. The capacity of Boston, it would seem, was just sufficient, but no more than sufficient, to comprehend the whole achievement of the human intellect up, let us say, to the year 1875 A.D. Then an equilibrium was established. At or about that year, Boston filled up."—H. G. Wells, *The Future in America.*

dreams of careers, and they carried the widest American interests with them. The Boston writers were local writers, more and more, as the years went on, as the law of metropolitan attraction gradually lost its force there. The centre of poets and thinkers had become the centre of tutors and scholars and followed the path of a greater and earlier Athens. Dr. Holmes was touchy on the subject, and the question mildly raged in the Boston press. It was observed that, whenever a Boston author died, New York at once became the American London. The Bostonians, as Aldrich said, were not thin-skinned about it. They had no skin at all.

Howells had moved from Cambridge to Belmont, and at last into Boston itself. There he had bought a house on "the water side of Beacon Street." In this house he had written *The Rise of Silas Lapham*, and the story of the house that Lapham built was drawn from his own experience here and at Belmont. For Howells cared deeply for architecture.* He had an instinctive feeling for all the plastic arts, and he invariably saw with the eye of a painter.† But he had had his "twenty years of Boston," and the basis of his New England life was

---

* At the time of Howells's eightieth birthday, Cass Gilbert wrote that he had done more to cultivate good taste in architecture than any American architect then living. This architect added: "A single sentence in *Silas Lapham* about black walnut changed the entire trend of thought and made it possible for the architects of the time to stem the turbid tide of brownstone and black walnut then so dear to the heart of the American millionaire."

Howells's Belmont house was designed by his brother-in-law, William Rutherford Mead, of the firm of McKim, Mead and White. John Mead Howells, the architect, was Howells's son.

† "Mrs. Alderling . . . was leaning against one of the slender fluted pine columns like some rich, blond caryatid just off duty, with the blue of her dress and the red of her hair showing deliciously against the background of white house-wall."—*Questionable Shapes.*

See also his portrait of Mrs. Bowen in *Indian Summer:* "There was reason in Mrs. Bowen's carrying in the hollow of her left arm the Indian shawl sacque she had taken off and hung there; the deep cherry silk lining gave life to the sombre tints prevailing in her dress, which its removal left free to express all the grace of her extremely lady-like person . . . She

broken. He was· disturbed and unsettled. He had gone
abroad for a year and seen his country once more in perspective. Boston, from the point of view of Florence,—
of the English and Americans there,—was much the same
as Denver, Chicago, St. Louis;* and this was the feeling,
rapidly growing again in Howells, that every excursion
from Boston served to confirm. He went for a winter to
Buffalo; he thought for a time that he might live perhaps
in Washington. Meanwhile, he arranged with the Har-
pers to publish his books and was writing in *The Century*
and *Scribner's,* the New York rivals of *The Atlantic.* He
withdrew from New England reluctantly and slowly. He
sometimes returned to Boston for a year or a season,
and many of his later summers were passed in Maine.
But henceforth New York was his centre. The world was
still full of novelty and interest for him, and he liked the
huge, kind, noisy, sprawling city.† As an all-American

had, with all her flexibility, a certain charming stiffness, like the stiffness
of a very tall feather."
    This might be a picture by Alfred Stevens or any of a dozen American
painters of the time.
    Here Howells sees Mrs. Bowen as she sees herself, as a psychologist sees
her, and also, very notably, as a painter would see her. This is characteristic of Howells's portraits.
    Howells's aesthetic feeling,—congenital, of course,—attracted him to art-
ists from the outset. The sculptor J. Q. A. Ward was one of his early
friends in Ohio. But this instinct grew with his open sympathies and his
friendship with artists. His essay on George Fuller memorialized one of
these many friendships. It was not an accident that one of Saint-Gaudens's
finest works was the large relief of Howells and his daughter.
    * "Some geographical distinctions which are fading at home had quite
disappeared in Florence . . . He found in Mrs. Bowen's house people from
Denver, Chicago, St. Louis, Boston, New York and Baltimore, all meeting
as of apparently the same civilization . . . The English spoke with the
same vague respect of Buffalo and of Philadelphia."—Howells, *Indian
Summer.*
    † "March could not release himself from a sense of complicity with it, no
matter what whimsical, or alien, or critical attitude he took . . . She"—
Mrs. March—"lamented the literary peace, the intellectual refinement of
the life they had left behind them; and he owned it was very pretty, but
he said it was not life,—it was death-in-life."—Howells, *A Hazard of
New Fortunes.* Mr. and Mrs. Basil March were scarcely veiled representations of Howells and his wife. These characters, who first appeared in
Their Wedding Journey, reappeared in *Their Silver Wedding Journey.*

mind, sensitive to national changes, he wished to be in touch with the younger writers; and he was forever in search of new types for his work and ready for new points of view.* There were various other reasons for his change. One was the rapid growth of his sociological interests. Another was his desire for a simpler life, for Boston had lost the simple intensity that once had been its charm for him and had grown more reactionary also.† In all this he showed the influence of Tolstoy, who, as he often said, remade his mind.

For Howells was deep in Tolstoy. Eagerly interested in all the new novelists, whom he was introducing to American readers,‡ he was drawn to the author of *Anna Karenina,* as formerly Turgenev had drawn him. In this latter case, it was not merely the artist that drew him. Tolstoy's Christian socialism appealed to him still more and had a profound effect on his life and writings. Howells was prepared for this doctrine. Essentially, it

* From Mark Twain to Robert Frost, over a stretch of fifty years, there was scarcely a good new American writer whom Howells was not the first to acclaim. The list of these authors about whom he wrote is virtually coincidental with the literature of two generations. It includes Hamlin Garland, Stephen Crane, Frank Norris, Mary E. Wilkins, Robert Herrick, Edith Wharton, John Oliver Hobbes, etc.

† "Elinor and I both no longer care for the world's life, and would like to be settled somewhere very humbly and simply, where we could be socially identified with the principles of progress and sympathy for the struggling mass."—Howells, Letter of 1887.

To his wife, in 1906, he wrote of their early days in Cambridge: "The phrase for our life there is, *Intense and simple.*"

‡ "I read everything of Zola's that I can lay hands on."—Letter of 1882.

Among the European novelists and dramatists about whom Howells wrote,—in addition to Tolstoy and Zola,—were Galdos, Palacio Valdés, Björnstjerne Björnson, Thomas Hardy, Ibsen, etc.

Howells knew Björnson well in Cambridge, where the latter spent the winter of 1880 in the house of Mrs. Ole Bull. Björnson, an ardent republican, was in disgrace in Norway because he had described the king as a donkey.

It may be added that George Gissing,—also in disgrace, at home, for less creditable reasons,—spent several months in Boston in 1876. There he supported himself by tutoring. Later he drifted to Chicago, where he contributed stories to the Chicago *Tribune.* He returned to England in the fall of 1877.

was not new to him: it was a reformulation, startling in
its power, of thoughts that were familiar in his childhood. He had always believed in human equality. His
father had nourished this faith in him, and he had grown
up in an atmosphere that brought before him every day
the ideal of coöperation as a way of living. He believed
in the public ends that make men "a family, as private
property never does;" * and he desired the good society,
as what he loved was personal goodness,—he called himself a socialist because he was one. He had found in the
Shakers an emblem of the good society, for all their
sometimes squalid limitations. Their primitive Christian-
socialist brotherhood held his imagination,† much as he
also rejoiced in the world as it was; and, while he never
lost this zest,—this delight in the play of human relations,—his conscience laid the train that Tolstoy fired.
He was alarmed by the growing division of classes, the
rift between poverty and wealth. The popular ideal had
once been political greatness, while the modern Web-
sters and Clays were the millionaires; and the older
America, which had seemed to be tending towards equality, was yielding to another social order. Along with the
millionaire, the tramp had appeared on the scene, and the
streets were full of beggars and hungry workmen, while
the papers recounted the scandals and rascalities of business. Meantime, the trial of the Chicago anarchists
proved that Americans could be killed for unpopular
opinions.‡ Howells brooded over this case. For two
months it filled his mind, as the Sacco-Vanzetti case, in a

* Howells, *A Boy's Town.*
† Howells's mind was haunted by the simple, communal life of the
Shakers. They appeared in four of his novels, *The Undiscovered Country,
A Parting and a Meeting, The Day of the Wedding* and *The Vacation of
the Kelwyns.* See also, in *Three Villages,* his description of the community
at Shirley, Mass.
‡ "The historical perspective is that this free Republic has killed five
men for their opinions."—Letter of Howells, 1887.

later decade, occupied the minds of other writers; and he
cared nothing about the risks he ran, defending the
anarchists after their unfair trial. His horror and heart-
sickness, the more he dwelt on this, "indefinitely wid-
ened" his horizons; * but he felt he could no longer trust
his country.† Was America a republic still? ‡ His optimism had been mistaken. Socialism alone could save the
nation. All his major views passed through a sea-change,
and even his own success smote his conscience.§ He felt
that writers and artists should ally themselves with the
toilers of shop and field. They had no part or lot in the
secular world; ‖ and they had to confront the "ugly

* Letter of 1887.
† "I should hardly like to trust pen and ink with all the audacity of my
social ideas; but after fifty years of optimistic contact with 'civilization'
and its ability to come out all right in the end, I now abhor it, and feel
that it is coming out all wrong in the end, unless it bases itself anew on a
real equality."—Letter to Henry James, 1888.
‡ See his letter to Mark Twain, 1889, at the time of the downfall of the
Brazilian empire: "I have just heated myself up with your righteous wrath
about our indifference to the Brazilian republic. But it seems to me that
you ignore the real reason for it which is that there is no longer an American Republic, but an aristocracy-loving oligarchy in place of it. Why
should our money-bags rejoice in the explosion of a wind-bag? They
know at the bottom of the hole where their souls ought to be that if such
an event finally means anything it means their ruin next; and so they
don't rejoice; and as they mostly inspire the people's voice, the press, the
voice is dumb."
§ "He felt the self-reproach to which the man who rises without raising
with him all those dear to him is destined in some measure all his life. His
interests and associations are separated from theirs, but if he is not an
ignoble spirit, the ties of affection remain unweakened; he cares for them
with a kind of indignant tenderness, and calls himself to account before
them in the midst of pleasures which they cannot share, or even imagine."
This instinctive *noblesse oblige,* attributed to Lemuel Barker in *The
Minister's Charge,* characterized Howells through life. It marked his relations with his Ohio family, as with all who were less fortunate than
himself.
‖ "In the social world, as well as in the business world, the artist is
anomalous, in the actual conditions, and he is perhaps a little ridiculous
. . . Perhaps he will never be at home anywhere in the world as long as
there are masses whom he ought to consort with, and classes whom he cannot consort with. The prospect is not brilliant for any artist now living,
but perhaps the artist of the future will see in the flesh the accomplishment
of that human equality of which the instinct has been divinely planted in
the human soul."—Howells, *Literature and Life.*

realities" also.* The old Howells lived on, the sunny, cheerful, happy man who believed in his countrypeople as much as ever. But the new Howells continued to live with the old. His social consciousness never deserted him. It remained the burden of much of his work, alike in verse † and in prose.

This change,—or this resurgence of Howells's original feeling,—was part of a widespread movement of the eighteen-eighties. Projects of reform were in the air, and the Western plan of Henry George arose with the Massachusetts plan that sprang from Edward Bellamy's *Looking Backward.* Literary Boston was more and more reactionary. As the town had lost its adventurousness and guarded its spoils,—the spoils of the adventures of its forbears,—it returned to the Federalist views of the faraway past; and Aldrich followed Lowell ‡ in this direction. Aldrich was hostile to every movement of social reform. His mind reverted to the French Revolution, and he saw the struggling workers as the "lazy *canaille.*" §

* "It is not ill, but it is very well to be confronted with the ugly realities, the surviving savageries, that the smug hypocrisy of civilization denies; for till we recognize them we shall not abate them, or even try to do so."—Howells, *Heroines of Fiction.*

† "Yes, I suppose it is well to make some sort of exclusion,
Well to put up the bars, under whatever pretence:
Only be careful, be very careful, lest in the confusion
You should shut yourself on the wrong side of the fence."
—Howells, *Stops of Various Quills.*

‡ Lowell did not "think straight," as William James remarked, but his general political tendency was sufficiently clear. This did not prevent him from saying, in *Democracy:* "Socialism means, or wishes to mean, coöperation and community of interests, sympathy, the giving to the hands not so large a share as to the brains, but a larger share than hitherto in the wealth they must combine to produce—means, in short, the practical application of Christianity to life, and has in it the secret of an orderly and benign reconstruction."

§ "We shall have bloody work in this country some of these days, when the lazy *canaille* get organized. They are the spawn of Santerre and Fouquier-Tinville."—Letter of Aldrich.

This feeling is reflected in Aldrich's stories. Nothing could be more sinister than the union of the marble-cutters in *The Stillwater Tragedy.* In *Shew's Folly,* the retired business man who builds a model tenement is swindled for his pains. Everything happens in life, but an author reveals his tendency in his habitual choice of the things that happen.

All this contributed to Howells's alienation from Boston, though even there the radical movements throve. Boston was the scene of *Looking Backward,* and Tolstoy made a deep impression there.* A Tolstoy Club was organized, largely by Edward Everett Hale, whose "Lend-a-Hand" clubs were spreading through the country. Hale lent a hand to every effort to christianize civilization, and he had a memorable talk with Howells on Tolstoy;† and Thomas Wentworth Higginson, who was called a socialist, said the name was "a feeler in the right direction." ‡ Both Higginson and Hale, meanwhile, favoured Edward Bellamy's movement, with Howells and his friend Mark Twain. § Howells wrote a preface for Bellamy's *The Blindman's World,* and he and this country editor had much in common; for, while Bellamy was a villager,—he lived at Chicopee Falls,—he. had seen enough of the world to horrify him. He had spent a year as a student in Germany, and the slums and hovels of

* There was much translating of Tolstoy in Boston and Cambridge or by New Englanders elsewhere. The first English version of *Anna Karenina* was that of Nathan Haskell Dole, 1886, who translated many other works of Tolstoy. In the same year, the Bostonian Isabel S. Hapgood translated *Childhood, Boyhood and Youth.* Miss Hapgood also translated Gogol, Turgenev and Gorky and various Dutch, Polish, Italian and Spanish authors. While the standard English version of Tolstoy is that of Aylmer Maude, the most nearly complete edition, up to 1902, was that of Professor Leo Wiener of Harvard.

It may be added that Tolstoy often expressed his admiration for Howells.

† On a train in 1887. Hale wrote to his wife, regarding this talk with Howells: "You know how deep he is in Tolstoy. Tolstoy has really troubled him, because he does not know but he ought to be ploughing and reaping . . . I dare not begin to write down what he said and I, I went nearer the depths than perhaps I have ever done with anyone but you . . . Howells is a loyal Christian, and hates to have anybody say that Jesus made plans or demanded things that are impossible."—*Life and Letters of Edward Everett Hale.*

‡ At this time, Higginson said later, Harvard was almost the only college where even the word could be mentioned.

§ Mark Twain was fascinated by *Looking Backward* and welcomed a visit from Bellamy at Hartford. He sympathized strongly with the organization of labour and regarded the unions as the workmen's only hope of standing up against the power of money. See Howells's *My Mark Twain.*

In his preface to *The Blindman's World,* Howells said that Bellamy moved the nation "more than any other American author who has lived."

Europe haunted his mind. He had never known that such misery existed, though he found it, on his return, in New York and Boston. He was convinced that America was going the way of the old world and losing its democratic hope and basis. With a deep distrust of city-life, he saw the villages drifting towards it. He saw the future steadily growing darker. Within a few years, he had written *Looking Backward,* with his plan for a better system of human relations. A new political party sprang from his teachings.

Bellamy had a fresher mind than even this book suggested, although he began to write as a follower of Hawthorne. He liked to play with the sort of fancies that were always running through Hawthorne's head,—stories about homeless ghosts and queer old doctors and young men who fall in love with portraits.* The atmosphere of all these tales reflected the Yankee village life that Bellamy knew so well in the seventies and eighties. This was Mrs. Eddy's world, a world of lonely people who had lost their vital interests and were bored and ailing; and Bellamy's tales mirrored this boredom, as they also mirrored the shifts by which the villagers tried to escape it. In trances, through mediums, the characters sought to retrace the past, or they tried as hard to penetrate the future. The two old souls in *A Summer Evening's Dream* convinced themselves that they were young again; and the boys and girls in *The Old Folks Party* masqueraded as their future selves, as what they expected to be when they were old. This scarcely implied that the present was

---

* Of his earlier novels, only one suggested the socialist Bellamy. This was *The Duke of Stockbridge,* a historical romance about Shays's Rebellion, the revolt of the debtor-farmers and ex-soldiers after the Revolution. In Bellamy's own Berkshire region, the seeds of all the present miseries had been sown at the dawn of the Republic. After this romance appeared, in the Great Barrington paper, Bellamy withheld it from book-publication. He wished to develop his political ideas, and he meant *The Duke of Stockbridge* to serve as an illustration of them. It did not appear as a book until after his death.

very exciting; and anything but reality here and now was
the moral of most of these stories. The old maid in *Miss
Ludington's Sister* preferred to build a town for ghosts
rather than dwell any longer in the living Hilton.

In all this, Bellamy, like various other New England
writers,* was merely reproducing Hawthorne's dream-
world. In doing so, however, he soon struck out a line that
was followed by H. G. Wells a decade later. In the small
towns of which he wrote, with all their interest in pseudo-
science, there was an interest in actual science also. John
Fiske's friend Youmans found an eager audience there,
and the *Popular Science Monthly* was a staple of reading. For the Yankees were a race of inventors, and the
marvels of applied science, with its labour-saving devices,
appealed to them deeply. They were prepared to understand the wonderful hints of coming discoveries and
even try them out in their sheds and workshops. In the
cluttered, laborious life of the farm and the village, the
material delights of the cities, with their ease and convenience, possessed a charm that city-people, who took
these things for granted, never dreamed of. † Science
stood for rest and comfort, anodynes for aching bones,
peace for the heavy-laden, hope for all. The heaven pic-

* Aldrich, Julian Hawthorne, Barrett Wendell, etc. Aldrich's "Mr. Jaffrey" is an old bachelor who *makes real* the son he has not had. "To such
a man," says the author, "brooding forever on what might have been and
dwelling wholly in the realms of his fancies, the actual world might indeed
become as a dream, and nothing seem real but his illusions." In Julian
Hawthorne's *The Professor's Sister,* the German characters reflected the
New England interest in galvanism, materializations, astral forms, unexpected awakenings, etc. See also Barrett Wendell's *The Duchess Emilia,* a
novel of metempsychosis, and some of Henry James's later stories.

† This explains the vogue of *Looking Backward,* in which Utopia is
cluttered with modern inventions, among the simpler people of the country.
More aesthetic readers, Howells said, were shocked that nothing better
could be imagined than the futile luxury of their own lives; and later, in
fact, when these inventions were realized and widely spread, Utopia was
as far away as ever. With no disrespect for machinery, it may be said that
Hawthorne showed a more enlightened instinct when, in his *Hall of Fantasy,* he satirized this machinery-worship. He knew well how little, beyond
a certain point, machinery could ever mean to man.

tured in the hymns which the country-people knew by heart was a place where the burdens of farm-life were gently eased from their shoulders. It was an infinite and endless Pasadena, and science seemed to promise this on earth. Bellamy's stories also reflected this interest. They mirrored this feeling for science, with its vistas of the future and the worlds of speculation to which it led, in astronomy, psychology, mechanics and physics. *At Pinney's Ranch* is the story of a man who recovers his wife by mental telepathy. The dreamer in *The Cold Snap* enters interstellar space and experiences the ineffable cold that prevails there. The astronomer in *The Blindman's World* passes into a state of mind in which he is independent of his body. His consciousness visits Mars and finds that the Martians have developed beyond the earth-people: they literally possess foresight and know the future. In the islands of the mind-readers, in *To Whom This May Come,* the people do not need to use their tongues. They live by direct mental vision. In *With the Eyes Shut,* the people do not need to see. Their books are phonographed and their clocks talk,—the ear performs the functions of the eye. The physician in *Dr. Heidenhoff's Process* invents a galvanic-mesmeric device that extirpates unhappy recollections. Patients whose lives have been wrecked by the past can have their obnoxious thoughts removed and live as if the past had never existed. The unhappy young girl who undergoes this prefiguration of psycho-analysis sleeps and wakes again with a happy mind.

Ten years after Bellamy, H. G. Wells began to write similar stories. Wells, a student of science in London, was full of the same ideas. He imagined time-machines and visits to Mars and trances from which the sleeper wakes in a world that has changed beyond all recognition. With Wells, as with Bellamy earlier, these fantasies led to Utopia-building, for both were obsessed with the miseries of the social system and science seemed to both to point the way to a just and sensible order of things. All one required was a plastic human nature, willing to accept the means of its own salvation; but that human nature was not plastic, or not sufficiently so, had always been the obstacle in Utopia-building. Wells, at first, was unaware of this, and Bellamy died too soon to be disillusioned; or, rather, he shared the American faith in the will, which has never counted costs or consequences, and he saw men as infinitely plastic.* For him, as for Emerson, nothing was fixed in human nature, everything lent itself to transformation; men were naturally good, the will was able to work miracles, and, if mankind desired a reasonable world, why should it not obtain one overnight? This American faith, which outlived Bellamy, had actuated the Brook Farmers. All the revivalists shared it,—sudden changes, for them, were a matter of course; and it sprang from the age-old belief in the millennium that had always lurked in the depths of the Yankee mind. Bellamy mirrored this mind at a moment when the nation was changing so rapidly that everything seemed possible tomorrow.

For Howells, the realist, who knew his human nature, these Alice-in-Wonderland methods were beside the question; but he sympathized with Bellamy and also, largely, with Henry George, to whom Hamlin Garland introduced him. Garland had reviewed his Tolstoyan novel, *The*

---

* To reconstruct a town or a world, to restore the past or build the future, is as simple as saying Jack Robinson to Bellamy's people. Miss Ludington, the rich old maid, who does not like the "march of improvement," thinks nothing of building a town to suit herself. She reproduces the Hilton of her childhood, complete with its country roads and grassy borders, schoolhouse, meeting-house and all. Such things really happen in America. Henry Ford realized this fantasy in Dearborn.

The plasticity of human nature is the theme of many of Bellamy's stories, which are always ingenious and plausible. The young man in *Pott's Painless Cure*, who has made the young girl love him, devises a method of making her un-love him. In *A Love Story Reversed*, the roles of the lovers are inverted with excellent results.

Minister's Charge, and discussed with him the West and its problems. He was writing his own first stories, under Henry George's influence, and, also impressed by Taine, he reminded Howells of the "local colour" movement in the West, the need for writers in every section to deal with the life they knew and the conditions peculiar to their scene and climate. All this weaned Howells further away from the narrowing life of Boston. In New York he was in touch with all these writers; and *A Hazard of New Fortunes* showed how much the metropolitan scene amused and stirred him. He rambled about the East Side, where the streets were picturesque, the docks, with steamers arriving from Spain and France, the Chinese quarter in Mott Street, a paradise for painters, the Bowery, where one still met ballad-sellers. The turmoil of the cars and trucks, the web of the elevated railways pleased his eye, the fields and cellar-holes and old farm-fences one found on rocky hill-sides near the park, where low sheds jostled huge apartment-houses, and goats and hens wandered in and out. He shared Walt Whitman's pleasure in the beaches, in the dime-museums, horse-shows, circuses and theatres, which he had so rarely seen in Boston; and, as he sat on benches in Washington Square and haunted Italian restaurants, he felt once more his old delight in travel. He rejoiced in the touch-and-go quality of the metropolitan life, after his intense identification with Boston; and a whole world of the new types for which he was always in search crossed his path in offices, in the streets, in the shops,—clerks and bankers, promoters, editors, newspaperwomen and shop-girls, publishers, art-students, visiting Southerners, self-made men from the West. This multitudinous life of the city appeared in *A Hazard of New Fortunes,* which caught the note of New York as *Silas Lapham* conveyed the feeling of Boston. But now he saw on every hand poverty and misery. Suffering was lurking everywhere. He grieved over the slum-children, the old women sleeping on door-steps, the hungry workmen searching in the gutters. The world that had seemed to him so full of pretty and pleasant things was overcast with sadness, death, injustice; and he thought of his older America now as a dream of his youth that had passed. That race of shepherds and shepherdesses no longer existed. He had himself grown older, and America had changed; but, more than all, Tolstoy had altered his vision.

For a number of years, in a series of novels, the question of social reform overshadowed everything else in Howells's work. Then his expression of this question grew less and less direct, as the movement of reform waned in the country. With his temperamental optimism, a fruit of the older America, he felt that all was coming right in time,* though he never ceased to share, as a man, in the fight for social justice, and the theme of social injustice recurred in his books. He watched with anxiety the growing of class lines and barriers and the rising power of ruthless business men, establishing inequalities, as it seemed, forever. The earlier types, the Silas Laphams, scrupulous, honest and liberal, seemed to be giving place to more sinister figures, as industry also gave place to gambling in stocks; and he pictured in Dryfoos, in *A Hazard of New Fortunes,* the new kind of despot-financier. Gerrish, in *Annie Kilburn,* was a similar portrait; and the defaulter Northwick, in *The Quality of Mercy,* was a type he saw on every hand. The rascally manufacturer in *The Son of Royal Langbrith,* who had gone through life as the hero of the town, was another proof of Howells's distrust of business; and this novel, which appeared in 1904, was one of many proofs that

---

* "In America, life is yet a joke with us, even when it is grotesque and shameful, as it so often is, for we think we can make it right when we choose."—Howells, *Their Silver Wedding Journey.*
There were "oceanic depths of ingenuous affirmation" in Howells's nature, as Newton Arvin said of Walt Whitman.

Howells's mind responded to every change in the mood of the nation. For Langbrith's disillusioned son, who had idolized his father, was a type of these early twentieth-century years, when the younger generation, bathed in a false idealism, perceived how much hypocrisy lay behind it. Howells was sensitive to all the currents of thought and feeling that passed, for two-score years, through the mind of the country; and, while his novels of social reform were far from being his best, they caught the leading note of the eighties and nineties. With what delicate perception he showed, in *Annie Kilburn,* the growth of a quiet old New England village into a sprawling modern American town, losing its humaneness and its heritage of freedom as the factory-system rose and gained control. Looking back at Boston, Howells saw its sordid aspects, as he had never seen them in happier years, as Lemuel Barker saw them, in *The Minister's Charge,* when this country boy arrived from Willoughby Pastures. He saw the wretched restaurants where the poor forgathered, the "Misfit Parlours" where they bought their clothes, the confidence-men who robbed them, the benches where they slept at night, the lodging-houses, hospitals and jails. He saw how little official religion was able to grasp their problem, out of touch as it was with the humbler classes, and he saw how pharisaical the upper classes were, beating down their workpeople's wages, while they carried flowers to hospitals and took up subscriptions. Lemuel was the touchstone by which Howells tried Boston, from the point of view of Tolstoy's Christian doctrine; and the minister in *Annie Kilburn* gave up his church and went to Fall River to live with the mill-workers as they lived, to help them as a teacher while sharing their life. But these novels were too evidently prompted by conscience. They were strained and unreal and wanting in verisimilitude. Howells's mind was driven by his will into regions where it never felt at home.

A Traveller from Altruria was therefore the best of
his socialist novels, for it made no attempt to be realistic.
It was a fantasy, one of the few he undertook, in the vein
of William Morris's *News from Nowhere*. Mr. Homos
had come from Altruria, an early-Christian republic; and
he "felt like a sort of bad conscience," as one of the characters said. He was Howells's conscience embodied, wandering over Howells's world, holding Socratic conversations with ministers, bankers, professors and lawyers,
while he surveyed the scenes that Howells had pictured.
He visited a summer hotel, where the ladies were always
resting, wondering what it was they rested from, and with
his air of innocence he challenged the assumptions of the
"most advanced country of its time." Its assumptions
were those of his own Altruria; its reality was a squalid
struggle in which the shrewd was valued more than the
noble, in which personal worth had small recognition and
the man who needed a dinner was never asked to dine. In
the irony of these indolent sketches, Howells, speaking
through Mr. Homos, tested the sincerity of American
professions; and he was happier here than he was in the
novels in which he tried to present the war of the classes.
Deep as his convictions were, his nature was too passive
to comprehend profound antagonisms. He could not convey the feeling of groups in conflict, and his imagination
too generally failed him when he strayed outside the middle class. But of all his later portraits there were none
more sympathetic than those of David Hughes, the old
Brook Farmer, who saw mankind as "the family," in *The
World of Chance*, and Lindau in *A Hazard of New Fortunes*. Lindau was drawn from an old German immigrant
through whom he had heard of socialism as a boy in the
West.

As he passed into this later phase, Howells's style lost
much of its sparkle, the gaiety, brilliance and wit of his
earlier novels; and the novels themselves all but lost their

old compactness, the perfection of organization they had once possessed. He had become suspicious of conscious style and conscious art, in this again reflecting the teaching of Tolstoy. His longer novels had scarcely any structure. They were aesthetically flaccid; though, occasionally, in some briefer novel,—*Miss Bellard's Inspiration,* for example,—he recovered the verve and form of his earlier years. In these briefer novels there were beautiful pages, —*Fennel and Rue, New Leaf Mills,* in which he returned to the forest scenes of his childhood; and in some of his short stories, *Questionable Shapes,* Howells achieved his utmost in mastery and ripeness. These tales, indeed, were beyond all praise in their effortless movement and quiet grace, the rewards of exact observation and scrupulous candour. His zest for new phases of life remained fresh to the end; and he caught the feeling of all the various groups he entered, the realm of the magazine in *A Hazard of New Fortunes,* the realm of writing and publishing in *The World of Chance,* and, in *The Coast of Bohemia,* the realm of the artists. He saw New York through the eyes of Shelley Ray, the young Western novelist who had come to the city in a mood so like his own of an earlier time. He saw it through the eyes of the young art-student who, in *The Coast of Bohemia,* had come from Ohio; and the New York types of the nineties thronged in these novels, drawn with the subtlest feeling for the place and the moment. Here were the "light" New Yorkers, so different from Bostonians, with all the levity of their old Dutch blood, and, among countless others, the impressionist Ludlow, the painter who had just returned from Paris, eager to report the native American world on canvas and draw as much pathos out of the farm-folk as Millet had ever drawn from the Barbizon peasants. Sometimes the scene shifted, and Howells returned to a summer hotel,—in *The Landlord at Lion's Head,* for instance,—or the grassy-bordered street of a

Shaker village, or Saratoga, now bereft of fashion. There, sitting on a bench, he had watched the country-people who had come to "get acquainted" at the great hotels, where the wooden courts and parlours and piazzas buzzed with ingenuous flirtations and the "Washington Post March" blared over all. Howells, who had for-sworn his old delight in match-making, remained the incorrigible Santa Claus of youthful lovers; while, with his open sympathies and devouring eyes, he had followed every phase of the life of the country. In his conversations one traced its interests, from the days of Turgenev and Rossetti to those of Ibsen, Maeterlinck, Lombroso and Hauptmann; and William James's "will to believe" and his explorations of psychical mysteries were reflected at once in Howells's "border-line" stories. These tales of eidolons and hallucinations, presentiments, metaphantasmia, *Between the Dark and the Daylight, Questionable Shapes,* bespoke in Howells a mystical afflatus that carried one back to the poetry of his early life. They were touched with an exquisite spirituality; and, indeed, this lover of all things human, truthful and benign, was always a poet. Was he shallow? Was he narrow? Here and there, undoubtedly; and he never sounded the depths of the minds that are oceans. He was rather like some great fresh-water lake. If these lakes have their shallows, they are transparent, and, if they have their narrows, they are also large; and all manner of living things forgather in them, as they forgathered in Howells.

CHAPTER XIX

HENRY JAMES IN ENGLAND

HENRY JAMES had remained a stranger in England. Shortly after his arrival, he had met a German who had also come to make his home there. "I know nothing of the English," this man said. "I have lived here too long—twenty years. The first year I really knew a great deal. But I have lost it." So it was, in a measure, with Henry James. Deeply as he had submitted himself to the "Londonizing process," had he become an "insider," except in "that limited sense," as he called it, "in which an American can ever do so"? His earlier impressions had been so sharp that he felt he knew the English character as if he had "invented it," he said. But so it often is with an alien's impressions: after the novelty passes and the first sensations have worn away he perceives that he has scarcely crossed the threshold. James had become with time,—in the phrases of two of his friends,—an "old-established colonist," but a "homeless man." That he had failed to root himself in England was more and more evident every day in his work.

This was the outstanding fact that explained the events of his middle years, the vague anxieties that weighed upon him, the nature of his later work and the strange hiatus in his career in which he abandoned the novel and turned to the theatre. America had faded from him, and he was "deadly weary of the whole 'international' state of mind."* It was clear to him that he must "do England in

* "So that I *ache,* at times, with fatigue at the way it is constantly forced upon me as a sort of virtue or obligation."—Letter to William James, 1888.

fiction;"* and he had attempted to do it in two long
novels; and how solidly real were the English characters,
—the fruits of his early impressions,—in *The Princess
Casamassima* and *The Tragic Muse*. Miss Pynsent, the
seamstress, Mr. Vetch, the old violinist, Lady Aurora,
the socialist aristocrat, the young revolutionist, Paul
Muniment, and Millicent Henning, the Cockney girl, were
as clearly alive as Newman or Daisy Miller. So were Captain Sholto, Mrs. Dallow and Nick Dormer and Mr.
Carteret, the old politician. Not in vain had Henry James
met John Bright and Gladstone, some of whose traits appeared in this fine portrait. But these were his only long
novels, except *The Awkward Age,* in which the scenes and
the characters were predominantly English; and James
returned thereafter to the international theme of which
he had grown so "deadly weary." † The stone rejected by
the builder once more became his headstone; and would
this have occurred if he had felt that he could really "do
England"? For James never relinquished his faith that
the novelist is a "patient historian, the living painter of
his living time," and therefore, if he returned to American
subjects when they had faded from him, it was obviously
because England had eluded his grasp. Was this not evident in his later English characters, who behaved in a
most un-English way? ‡ James felt he had fallen between

* "One thing only is clear, that henceforth I must do, or half do, England in fiction—as the place I see most today, and, in a sort of way, know
best. I have at least more acquired notions of it, on the whole, than of any
other world, and it will serve as well as any other. It has been growing
distincter that America fades from me, and as she never trusted me at
best, I can trust *her,* for effect, no longer."—Letter to Howells, 1890.

† "The 'international' is very presumably indeed, and in fact quite inevitably, what I am *chronically* booked for."—Letter of 1904.

‡ As many critics have observed. Thus Ford Madox Ford, who based his
claim for James's greatness on his being a "historian," showed that the
Gereths, in *The Spoils of Poynton,* if they had been English, would cer-
tainly have gone to law. Ford, for this reason, described James as an "un-
Americanized American" who was also the "least naturalized of all the
English."

two worlds. He was "troubled about many things." * He had ceased to speak the language of his army of readers; and he turned for a while to shorter stories and plunged into the theatre, with results that were calamitous and futile.

It was after this hiatus that James emerged with the "later manner" in which he seemed to abandon the objective role. He never did so consciously; he never meant to do so; he believed he was quite as much the historian as ever. He still observed the world around him, eager for "revelations, confidences, guesses," † for "anything that others could give him from their personal lives . . . food for his ruminating fancy." ‡ To the last, as Hugh Walpole said, he was "unconsciously using his notebooks;" but, if he had mastered his English world, would he have craved in later years for the "vivid and solid *material*" that he felt a return to his country might give him? Charmed as he was by England, he had too little in common with it. Politics meant nothing to him, professional life, the love of the country, sport, school or college, riding, hunting; and, if the tastes of English men were mostly beyond his horizon, he was scarcely more in rapport with the English women whom he had chosen to study. Their interests were much like those of the men; and what did these women care for art? That they did not

* "I am troubled about many things, about many of which you could give me, I think (or rather I am sure) advice and direction. I have entered upon evil days—but this is for your most private ear. It sounds portentous, but it only means that I am still staggering a good deal under the mysterious and (to me) inexplicable injury wrought—apparently—upon my situation by my last two novels, *The Bostonians* and *The Princess*, from which I expected so much and derived so little. They have reduced the desire, and the demand, for my productions to *zero*."—Letter to Howells, 1888.

† Edmund Gosse.

‡ "He was insatiable for anything that others could give him from their personal lives . . . He welcomed any grain of reality, any speck of significance around which his imagination could pile its rings. It was very noticeable how promptly and eagerly he would reach out to such things, as they floated by in talk."—Percy Lubbock, *The Letters of Henry James.*

care for art at all was the principal thing he noticed in
them. He had not been obliged to share the interests of
his countrymen to understand his countrymen themselves.
By a deep racial instinct he had comprehended Christopher Newman, Isabel Archer, Roderick, Rowland Mallet; and up to a certain point, by observation, he had penetrated the English mind as well. He had had every chance
to penetrate it, and English acquaintances told him things,
because he was American, which they did not confide to
one another. But what, in the end, was the sum of his
knowledge beyond the talk of dinner-tables, anecdotes,
gossip, rumour and tittle-tattle? He was lost, as he said,
in the "fathomless depths of English equivocation."
Hovering about the English mind, circling round and
round it, hankering for some deeper initiation, he was
perpetually baffled, like the people in his later novels who
hovered about one another with the same effect of strained
curiosity. Did they not hover because he had hovered?
Was not this posture of James's people the result of his
own frame of mind? At the same time, in this alien world,
with which his relations were so tenuous, he drifted further and further from life itself. He lost his feeling for
the "vital facts of human nature," as his brother William
said. And William James was not for nothing the greatest psychologist living. He knew whereof he spoke, and
he was right.

Were not these the essential facts that lay behind the
"later manner" in which James triumphed as a craftsman? He triumphed by substituting for his old interest in
character an interest in predicaments and situations, an
interest that he had developed in his work for the stage,
in which the situation was all-important. "Saturation" and
all it implied, a living sense of objective reality, this had
slipped from his grasp, and he was reduced to the "grain
of suggestion," the "tiny air-blown particle" of which his
later novels were amplifications. Did he not say that *The*

Sacred Fount, The Spoils of Poynton, What Maisie Knew
"grew by a rank force of their own" from the short
stories that he had planned?—and what he called the
"long-windedness" of *The Wings of the Dove* and the
"vague verbosity" of *The Golden Bowl* were fruits of the
same kind of unnatural expansion. There was scarcely
enough substance of life in these great ghosts of novels to
fill the novelette in which he excelled; but what concerned
him now was form, almost regardless of content, the
problems of calculation and construction, and he who had
once been unable to think of a situation that did not depend for its interest on the nature of the persons had begun to think of his persons as pawns in a game. Did they
"compose" together? Were they sufficiently foreshortened? The day had not yet come when he forgot the
names of his characters, when, in his scenarios, he referred to "the girl" and "Aurora What's-her-name," or
perhaps to "my first young man" and "my second young
man," to persons who concerned him only as to their size
and weight in the structure he was building. But it was
significant that *The Spoils of Poynton,* the first of his
later novels, was a story of "things." His persons were to
grow dimmer and dimmer, like flames of an exhausted
lamp, while his technical virtuosity worked its wonders.

This technical virtuosity was the "figure in the carpet"
of which Hugh Vereker spoke in one of his stories. It was
the particular thing that Vereker wrote his books most
for, the secret buried in them that no one observed. It
was James's "well in the desert," the something he had
found that he felt was a compensation for all he had lost;
and he was entitled to the pride with which it filled him,
for what novelist had ever revealed such prodigies of
skill? He had taken up the gauntlet that Europe had
flung at the feet of America, as he had seen it in his youth,
he had accepted his handicap, as he also saw it, and
striven with faith and force. He had waked and toiled

while others slept, and the indifference of his readers had
only served to toughen his will the more. Only difficulty
interested him now, as he said in a letter, the problems
of organization, the "secrets of the kitchen," and it was
by this concentration that he developed the method which
remained as a model for novelists in days to come.* The
details of this method were explained in the prefaces that
were collected later in *The Art of Fiction.* There one saw
the conjuror at work with his puppets; and who had ever
devised such arch-refinements or such supersubtleties as
his? But was not this absorption in technique the proof
that James's themes had lost interest for him?

He had emerged as a passionate mathematician of art,
or, shall one say, a huge arachnid, pouncing on the tiny
air-blown particle and wrapping it round and round. For
a new prodigy had appeared, the later style of Henry
James, the style that was the man he had become. He had
remodelled his personality. He had outgrown his American self and largely grown to be the type he loved. He
had disliked the American "thinness" and "paleness," the
something "meagre" about the American type. Its line
and composition had seemed to him wanting in roundness
and richness,† while the English had a "fatter, damper"
nature. He had desired the rich and the round, the fatter,
the damper, the resonant, and he had developed these
traits, or their appearance; for had he not become, in a
sense, an actor, a curiously artificial being who seemed to

---

* But only, or mainly, for those who resembled James in the paucity
and tenuity of their subject-matter. In expounding his doctrine that the
novel is to be judged by its oneness, he admitted that Tolstoy and Balzac
could never have followed his method. "The promiscuous shiftings of
standpoint and centre of Tolstoy and Balzac for instance . . . are the inevitable result of the *quantity of presenting* their genius launches them in . . .
With the complexity they pile up they *can* get no clearness without trying
again and again for new centres."—Letter to Mrs. Humphry Ward, 1899.

† "We are *thin,* my dear Howard; we are pale, we are sharp. There is
something meagre about us; our line is wanting in roundness, our composition in richness."—*A Bundle of Letters.* Did not James speak in his own
person here?

have borrowed a mantle and to wear a mask? One heard
reverberations when one tapped this shell. But James's
sensibility had grown with all it fed on, and the fabrics
upon which his eyes had feasted, the colours that he loved,
the soft sounds, the delicate scents had surely left their
stamp on the house of his spirit. This house was Henry
James's style, and it threw out "extensions and protru-
sions," as he somewhere called them, "indulging even, all
recklessly, in gables and pinnacles and battlements, things
that had transformed the unpretending place into a veritable palace, an extravagant, bristling, flag-flying structure that had quite as much to do with the air as with the
earth." His senses had been nourished by the collation of
types and tones, of signs and aspects and items, the comparison of beautiful objects and degrees of finish; and
type and object and form had moulded his style. Wonderful metaphors blossomed in his pages, like air-plants from
the tropics.

But other things appeared in this style, the evasiveness
and hesitancy of a man who was habitually embarrassed.
The cautious ceremoniousness, the baffled curiosity, the
nervousness and constant self-communion,—these traits
of the self-conscious guest in the house where he was not
at home had gone to fashion his personality also. And
why the atmosphere of uncertainty that hovered over all
these novels, the conscious cultivation of indirectness?
Why all those "crooked corridors" and "antechambers"
in which he seemed to delight in eluding his readers? Was
he not, in reality, hiding from them, as the cuttlefish hides
from the pursuer by ejecting the black fluid that assures
his escape? All these devices of James, in which he rejoiced as a craftsman, served him as a smoke-screen behind which to vanish; for had he not always been fleeing
from something, the American self that he deprecated and
that he longed to lose in the European? Then, too, America had always lacked "mystery" for him. It had seemed

to him "undraped" and "uncurtained." He had disliked
its glare of daylight and its "harsh, hard" lines; and were
not his circuitousness and his veils of ambiguity the result of a lifelong desire to escape from these? Perhaps a
childhood in hotels had increased the morbid love of privacy that caused him to shrink with horror from any ex-
posure; and, meanwhile, all these crooked corridors enabled his mind to evade the presentation of moments of
emotional stress. After his long association with people
who merely glimmered for him, in the museum-world in
which he lived, he was no longer equal to this because he
was out of touch with life, with the vital facts of human
action and passion. Did his stories correspond to the "life
without rearrangement" that had always been his standard for the novel? He presented his people as "eminent,"
as "wonderful," "noble" and "great," and most of their
actions belied his professions for them. Thus, in *The
Wings of the Dove,* a "gentleman, generally sound and
generally pleasant," presently appeared as a potential
murderer, without any adequate explanation. The countess
in *The Ambassadors,* supposed to be a great lady, used
her daughter as a scapegoat. The exquisite young girl in
The Spoils of Poynton ridiculed her hostess behind her
back. The "pure, passionate, pledged" radical, the young
man in *Covering End,* married the girl he disliked and
went back on his party in order to retain possession of his
family estate. The guests in the country-house in *The
Sacred Fount* solemnly devoted themselves for days to
"nosing" out the secret of one of the ladies. The two
young men in *The Ivory Tower* refused to read the will,
which they had a perfect right to open, in order to discuss
for hours what it probably contained. Other young men,
supposed to be in love, were presented as admirable beings because they preferred a house to the girl of their
choice; and one of them broke his engagement to devote
his life to discovering an author's "intention." One man

procured as a private preserve an altar in a Catholic
church; and a great author died in a country-house, under
the roof of a lady who did not respect him, fearing that
he would offend her if he went home. Was not this author
rather a goose than a lion? All these people acted out of
character, or against the nature of things, or in violation
of James's description of them; for how could one respect
the lover who preferred his furniture to his mistress, how
regard as honourable the politician who betrayed his own
convictions to save his house? James's "noble" characters
peeped through keyholes, and his "perfectly splendid"
beauties lied and schemed; many of his "fine" souls behaved like monkeys, and his "eminent" beings were eminent for inquisitiveness only. Was not this odd derange-
ment of values the fruit of a mind that worked in a void,
without any clear sense of human cause and effect?

Thus James's world was remote from reality. It was a
subjective world, peopled by dim projections of the author's fancy; and more and more these characters spoke
with the voice of James himself.* He had become the
victim of his own personality. He said, "We take for
granted a primary author . . . We forget him in proportion as he works upon us, and he works upon us most in
fact by making us forget him." Certainly no one had ever
been conscious of James in contemplating the world of
his earlier novels. There the illusion was complete: one
saw the people, knew them, felt them. But who could
forget the manipulator in this vague later world, in which
one scarcely remembered the names of the people? James
himself filled the foreground; he stood between the reader

---

* How far James had lost the sense of his early characters one saw in
his revision of *The American*, for instance. There the frank, shrewd
Christopher Newman, emotionally direct and simple, assumed the sophis-
tications of the later James. Thus he was made to remark, in the spirit of
a connoisseur, as his final reflection on love, "Fancy this being to be had
and—with my general need—my not having it!" All of James's later people took one back to James himself. They spoke with one generalized voice,
the voice of their author.

and life; and one might almost say that he made the substance of his art out of his failure to grasp the materials of it. For where the primary novelist begins by possessing his people, whom he then presents in action, James, without possessing them, presented them merely in the act of discovering one another. They formed little groups, detached from all life beyond their circle, and their ruling passion was curiosity. They tried to discover what went on in one another's minds and remained in the end as mystified as they were in the beginning. Nor did the reader know them any better, after all this psychological exploration. One was scarcely conscious of anything but an avid eye, fixed on a human spectacle that barred it out. Everyone watched in James's novels, watched himself, watched the others, "nosed about" for relations, sniffed and pried, and the people were without consistency,—one seldom knew what to expect from them,—they were apt to destroy one's impressions of them at almost any moment. They spun webs about themselves, and, in fact, they were ghosts without interests or attributes, without passions, ambitions, convictions, hearts or vitals; and they drifted about in a curious limbo as insubstantial as themselves. They were made, as William James remarked, "wholly out of impalpable materials, air, and the prismatic interferences of light, ingeniously focussed by mirrors upon empty space."

Was it not largely true, then, as Middleton Murry expressed it, that James "yearned after the fullness of European life, which he could not rejoin again, and had to satisfy his impulse of asceticism in the impassioned formalism of an art without content"? This was only partly true because, with his imagination, as an extraordinary artist and man of genius, James was not wholly dependent on the world outside him. He could turn everything into art. His own perplexities served him well; and, if his people were ghosts, he could make ghosts people. He could make atmospheres palpable. The short stories and novelettes that he poured forth so abundantly were marvellous evocations of their kind; and, playing his labyrinthine games, James remained a happy man, with a sense that, if he was a mystagogue, he was a master. He knew he was teaching novelists in times to come to look for the half-resolutions, the nuances of motive, the velleities, disinclinations, misgivings, obsessions that also govern the mind, along with the decisions and rejections that make for action. For them he extended the sphere of human consciousness, even as he added greatly to the novelist's craft. But a psychologist is not a novelist,—psychology is not the same as character;* and did not James feel that he had somehow missed his way, that he had paid too much for his expatriation? Why otherwise should he have bewailed his "thin, starved, lonely, defeated, beaten prospect"? Why should he have said of Edith Wharton, "She *must* be tethered in native pastures, even if it reduces her to a back-yard in New York"? How much was implied in the letter to Howells in which, looking back on their two careers, he said that Howells had always had the advantage of breathing an air that suited and nourished him, sitting up to the neck amid the sources of his inspiration.† In one of his last, unfinished novels, James was still pondering the question what living in America might make of a man; ‡ and to more than one younger American writer who saw him in his later years

* "The writer must be a psychologist, but a secret one; he must sense and know the roots of phenomena, but offer only the phenomena themselves, as they blossom or wither."—Turgenev, quoted in Yarmolinsky, *Turgenev, the Man, his Art and his Age.*

† "For you have had the advantage, after all, of breathing an air that has suited and nourished you; of sitting up to your neck, as I may say—or at least up to your waist—amid the sources of your inspiration . . . I can only feel and speak for those conditions in which, as 'quiet observers,' as careful painters, as sincere artists, we could still, in our native, our human and social element, know more or less where we were and feel more or less what we had hold of."—Letter to Howells, 1912.

‡ *The Sense of the Past.*

he bitterly regretted the road he had taken. "Don't make my mistake," he said to Amy Lowell. "I have cut myself off from America, where I belonged." He had cut himself off from the culture that had produced him and failed to attain the culture he had tried to acquire. He had come to feel that his work was a "tangle of temporal and local differences that revealed, after all, nothing of the depths, references as fleeting as O. Henry's slang, flavours mistaken for essences, split hairs, not dissected anatomies." * This was in 1913, three years before he died. Fourteen years before, he had uttered the same regrets to Hamlin Garland.†

Certainly, he somehow felt that he had been deluded, like the American characters in so many of his stories. Was this not evident in his tales of the disappointed author, of the "poor sensitive gentleman" who is "too fine for his rough fate"? These tales, among the best he wrote, poured from his pen in the nineties and after, and they presented the plight of the writer in a fashionable world which he has followed in good faith and which utterly fails to understand him. The exquisite artists in *The Next Time, Broken Wings, The Velvet Glove, The Middle Years* and others are all of them "badgered and bothered on the pretext of being applauded," while they are treated as cat's-paws, ignored and misused by people who have no imagination. No one has any conception of what they are trying for. No one knows what they are talking about; and they are driven by their genius to produce hopelessly beautiful books that nobody has in the house and nobody reads. People lose their manuscripts and only the

* S. Foster Damon, *Amy Lowell.*

† "He became very much in earnest at last . . . 'If I were to live my life over again,' he said in a low voice, and fixing upon me a sombre glance, 'I would be an American. I would steep myself in America, I would know no other land. I would study its beautiful side. The mixture of Europe and America which you see in me has proved disastrous. It has made of me a man who is neither American nor European. I have lost touch with my own people, and I live here alone.' "—Hamlin Garland, *Roadside Meetings.*

"crazy" admire them, while the authors of the latest shockers have all the honours. All their readers care about is vulgar personal gossip about them. In the world to which they are drawn they have no place. All these exquisite artists, Neil Paraday, John Berridge, Hugh Vereker, Mark Ambient, Ralph Limbert rose, James said in one of his prefaces, from the depths of his own experience, and they were indications of his own disenchantment. And in how many of his other stories some child or some innocent creature was victimized by a callous and malevolent world! Innocence and good will exploited and abused remained James's theme to the end of the chapter. Was it not the story of the Puritan child in himself who had toiled up the slope of the British Olympus and found that the gods had turned into "cats and monkeys"?

In the generation after he died, James's later novels were praised at the expense of his early writings. Their vogue was immense in a world of cosmopolitan aesthetes who saw themselves dimly reflected in James's people, functionless people, like themselves, without objective interests, who spun webs of thought about one another, who analyzed themselves, for want of other occupation, while they collected bric-a-brac, material and human. The great work of James's prime was forgotten or ignored, as he had sometimes seemed to wish himself, the work in which he had celebrated an actual historic drama, the nostalgia of the American for his ancestral home in Europe. All his great novels had dealt with Americans at a time when he had understood them, when he was at home with himself in his own domain, alert, witty, tender, benevolent, freely at play with a world that he saw from above and behind, from without and within. This was his major work, although he remained to the end an artist of extraordinary power and a lover of perfection, with an inexhaustible fund of ideas and subjects and a style that was often magnificent; and those for whom his later novels were grey webs of speculation, peopled with phantoms in a fog, could always rejoice in his shorter tales. There, in *The Pupil* and *Brooksmith*, in *The Author of Beltraffio* and *The Beast in the Jungle*, in *The Turn of the Screw, Glasses* and *The Great Good Place*, flawless and full in their tone and structure, with their softly flowing outlines, one saw him in his clearest autumnal beauty.

CHAPTER XX

BOSTON IN THE NINETIES

WITH the advance of the nineties, the New England mind was steeped in disappointment and chagrin. The impulse that had characterized it seemed to be exhausted, and its mood was sad, relaxed and reminiscent. Boston, absorbing its suburbs, had grown larger and larger; but this huge and cosmopolitan population had little to distinguish it from others. If the old race was not actually dying, if the old culture was not extinguished, there were many who felt it was merely a question of time. The Boston mind, once so cheerful, was full of the sense of last things, as if it hoped for no resuscitation. The older writers were all but gone, as the squirrels were disappearing on the Common; and Barrett Wendell, the Harvard professor, expressed a general feeling that the days of the Yankee folk were numbered. "We are vanishing into provincial obscurity," he wrote in 1893. "America has swept from our grasp. The future is beyond us."

In one way or another, many New England men of letters echoed and amplified this note of Wendell's. Henry Adams, George E. Woodberry, George Cabot Lodge,— the son of Senator Lodge, Adams's friend,—were only a few of these prophets of doom and destruction. For Godkin, always close to the mind of Cambridge, the whole American enterprise had ended in failure; Parkman more or less agreed with Godkin; and Norton, for whom New England had meant so much, was struck by the waste and futility of all its effort. In the face of the foreign inrush, how apparently ineffective were the labours of the earlier

generations! Others were cheerful and hopeful as ever,—
perhaps they were also the wisest; but the evidence seemed
to be against them. William James looked forward calmly.
John Fiske had few doubts. President Eliot serenely confronted the future. The Emersonian Eliot believed in the
future: he had no tears to waste on the past in regrets.
For Howells, as for Justice Holmes, so open in their sympathies, the good could never lose its sporting chance;
and one found no ear for tales of woe on the part of Miss
Sarah Palfrey, the historian's daughter, who, every morning, at the age of seventy-five, took a spin on her tricycle
round Fresh Pond before breakfast. The older were the
bolder in Boston, as elsewhere; and the older and bolder
they were the less inclined to think the world was going to
the dogs. They were tough enough to know that the good
was tough; and, like all true aristocrats, they believed in
their country, if only because their country included themselves. Those who had fought and bled in freedom's
cause, like Justice Holmes and Colonel Higginson, were
prepared to take long views of these ultimate questions;
and so was Edward Everett Hale, the "grand old man
of Boston," and Julia Ward Howe, the romantic old
sibyl. These magnanimous worthies, these generous natures, for whom nothing had ever existed that was common or mean, were destined to see mankind as forever
triumphant. They ignored the signs of the times and lived
above them, as Emerson had lived all his life. But for
those who lived close to the ground the signs of the times
were anything but roseate or auspicious. It was easy for
William James and Howells, John Fiske and President
Eliot to take long views of the future. They were sufficiently realistic, but they were not New Englanders merely.
Howells was not a Yankee at all, James was a Yankee
only by courtesy, and the consciousness of Eliot and Fiske
embraced the nation. Their ships were heavily ballasted
and sailed on broad bottoms. The true-blue Yankees who

were only imperfectly also American sailed in skiffs and found the water shallow. Most of their birds of the hour were of evil omen.

Was the Yankee race really dying? Barrett Wendell felt so, not without grounds for his feeling, both inward and outward.* George Cabot Lodge, who agreed with Wendell, broadened the base of the question. He felt that the whole old American race was dying.† That the Yankee stock which had leavened the nation was somehow wearing thin one saw in Mary E. Wilkins's remarkable stories. If the strength of the flower of Boston sprang from its roots, what was the meaning of these stories, which had begun to appear at the turn of the nineties? What light did they throw on the human soil of the region? Mary E. Wilkins was only one of a number of writers whose minds were preoccupied with the ends of things, families running out, forlorn old women, ramshackle dwellings, lone eccentrics. The almshouse and the village pensioner figured largely in these stories. In Elizabeth Stuart Phelps's *Jonathan and David,* the man had only a dog to share his world; and dogs and cats, the children of the childless, ranked with men and women as *dramatis personae.* All these authors took fag-ends for granted. Their theme was desolation doing its best, or so at least it seemed to Boston readers; and up and down the scale, from roots to flowers, the New England mind repeated its tale of exhaustion. Had Hawthorne perhaps been right when he said to Howells that the apparent coldness of the Yankees was real, that the suppression of emotion for long generations would extinguish emotion at last in the soul of New England?

* "I feel that we Yankees are as much things of the past as any race can be."—Barrett Wendell, Letter of 1893.

† "We are a dying race, as every race must be of which the men are, as men and not accumulators, third-rate."—*The Life of George Cabot Lodge,* by Henry Adams. Lodge's argument was based on biological grounds. It followed the line of Theodore Roosevelt, apropos of "race-suicide."

The Boston mind appeared to have lost its force. It was yielding, inch by inch, to the Catholic Irish; and the time was approaching when a Catholic Irish mayor of Boston was to say that the New England of the Puritans was as dead as Caesar. It was the Irish, he added, who had made Massachusetts a "fit place to live in,"—the Irish had had letters and learning when the forbears of New England were savages living in hyperborean· forests. This last remark was largely true; but still it was an unkind cut for the makers of New England. The Puritans who had conquered the Indians had not been so unkind. They had not poured scorn on the red men for their forest-existence, although, it must be added, the Puritans were not rhetoricians,—they were not compelled to assert themselves by means of these floral displays. There were cuts on both sides. The Bostonians resented the Irish, though the case already had its compensations, —the conquerors were bearing gifts for the joy of the conquered. John Boyle O'Reilly was one of these gifts; another, just emerging, was the lovely spirit of Louise Imogen Guiney, the essayist and poet. Miss Guiney was the daughter of an Irish lawyer who had commanded a regiment in the Civil War. Brevetted a brigadier-general, like Charles Francis Adams,—as gallant as all the Irish fighters were,*—he had been hopelessly wounded; and one day in Boston, twelve years later, he suddenly stopped in the street, removed his hat, knelt, crossed himself and died. Miss Guiney's spirit rode forward in her father's stirrups. None of this was lost upon the city of the Puritans. The Bostonians knew a soldier, as they knew a poet. What they had seen in O'Reilly they saw in the Guineys; and the Irish, in the Protestant form, had given them Godkin and both the Henry Jameses and William James. Heaven only knew what future gifts the conquerors had

* "In all the records of the Civil War there was no such thing as an Irish coward."—Thomas Wentworth Higginson.

in store for a later New England; and the Yankees were
not ungrateful to them. Some of Miss Jewett's best stories
were tributes to them, and certainly Miss Jewett knew
the Irish,—she had spent the greater part of a year
among them, once, at Bantry Bay. It was in the nature of
things that the Yankees resented the Irish, but they resented their own impuissance more. They could present
no equal counterforce; they could not hold their end up
any longer. They saw their glory vanishing before the
invaders.

The old New England was slipping away. The rock-
bound coast was stern no longer: its villas, lawns and
gardens suggested the Hudson river or the Isle of Wight.
The Reef of Norman's Woe was merely a rock. The old
public spirit was fading, along with the old religious
spirit, as they had faded away in an earlier Athens. Senator Lodge, the "scholar in politics," the first New England statesman who had played a national role for many
years, the conscious heir of all his predecessors, seemed
oddly small and shrunken in their light. This David who
had slain Goliath Butler and who had been the hope of
the younger Yankees traduced the spirit of his forbears,
though he wore their mask. As virtually a nephew of
Sumner, Motley, Parkman and Holmes, who had called
him "Cabot" from the cradle, he was the scion of all
the old patricians. He owned and worked on Bancroft's
writing-table, he followed Bancroft and Parkman as a
grower of roses; and his speech alone had style, as they
said in the Senate,—he led his fellow-Senators away from
bombast "towards reality and forceful expression." * It
was Lodge who brought about the copyright-bill, deserv-
ing, as he won, the praise of authors. In these and other
ways, he carried on the old line, and he went through
all the motions of the older statesmen. But he had none
of their breadth of soul and vision. Sectional interests

* Elihu Root.

and caste-interests really governed his motives, while he stood as a defender of the nation; and he was merely the lawyer in his international policies, with none of the understanding of the life of nations that illumined the men of the past.* The older statesmen had found their models in Plutarch, while he found his in the busts of the older statesmen. He was the victim of a day of small things, and one felt in him the end of a spent tradition.

The religious tradition seemed equally all but exhausted. There was little to withstand the Catholic power, except the dubious faith of Christian Science,† and within a few years the most prominent objects in Boston were the Catholic cathedral, the dome of the Synagogue and the dome of Mrs. Eddy's Mother Church. The prevailing religion was comfort, with accessories, which varied from mind-cure and easy-going optimism to cults that gave aesthetic satisfaction; and the leading doctrine of Boston was not to offend, in the shade of which conviction turned to dust. The faith-healer had won the day, and invalids frequented practitioners who silently thought benevolent things about them. The miracles of mind-cure were naturally numerous, although Fletcherism flourished as a rival; and people solemnly chewed their food very fine and slowly to be slender enough to pass through the eye of the needle. A modish high-Anglicanism led the other cults, together with drawing-room faiths from Arabia and Persia; and young men who, in Channing's day, would have proselytized the West enjoyed a romantic destiny as high-church monks. The ethical caprices of Boston could

* "When working at the language of a treaty, he thought of it as a document and did not allow his mind to wander far into the country, habits and religions of the people on the other side of the treaty."—William Lawrence, *Henry Cabot Lodge.*

† "I can't bring myself . . . to blink the evil out of life . . . It's as real as the good, and if it is denied, good must be denied too. It must be accepted and hated, and resisted while there's breath in our bodies."—Letter of William James.

scarcely have been numbered.* They rivalled those of
Los Angeles in a day to come; and anything but Protestantism, anything else than the Puritan past,—this was
their common emblem and their watchword. Anything,
in fact, that was not Boston,—for Boston had its forms
for all these faiths and was bent on rejecting the forms
because it had them. In the Episcopal faith, it possessed
a genius in Phillips Brooks, who had reconciled Anglican-
ism with its inmost fibre; and what, with their beards
and robes, did the Eastern mystics have to say that Channing and Emerson had not said before them in a form
that sprang straight out of the soul of New England?
But Boston, as strangers gathered, no longer wished to
believe in itself, and robes and incense † now made all
the difference. What came from Pusey's Oxford and
somebody's Persia seemed necessarily better than anyone's Boston,—which meant that Boston really believed
in nothing, or so, at least, Bostonians occasionally said.‡
In short, the Bostonians were lost, as a family, in this
resembling the Peterkins, as in other respects; § and they
had no Lady from Philadelphia to tell them to meet at
the Sphinx.‖ Whether they could have found the Sphinx

* "We are the children of the Puritans and have inherited a twist toward the ethical and the supernatural so strong that we have to have
these things served up even in our amusements."—Arlo Bates, *The
Puritans.*

† "I am too old to hear religion, I am too old to see religion. But I can
still smell religion."—Mrs. Bell, Rufus Choate's daughter, who, in her later
years, occasionally went to the Church of the Advent.

‡ "As some reactionary backslider has said, the spiritual history of this
region from Channing's day to ours may be summarized as that of a theological progress from certainty concerning what the devil is to uncertainty
concerning what the devil anything is."—Barrett Wendell, *Liberty, Union
and Democracy.*

This moment was appropriate for the founding of the Ingersoll Lectures
on Immortality, 1897. Few indeed believed any longer in immortality, but
there was a general interest in hearing what could be said for it.

§ " 'This time,' Elizabeth Eliza said, 'it is not our trunks that were lost—'
" 'But we, as a family,' said Mrs. Peterkin."

—Lucretia Hale, *The Peterkin Papers.*

‖ *The Last of the Peterkins.*

and what the Sphinx might have had to say were questions which they scarcely dared to ask.

All this had happened in Athens as it happened in Boston, though in Athens, when the great days passed, literature remained. Then, in Athens, literature vanished also. Was it vanishing in Boston already? The Bostonians felt so. The bells tolled every year for a great man gone: Lowell in 1891, Whittier in 1892, in 1893 Francis Parkman. Holmes, who died in 1894, had lived to "sing the swan-song for the choir." These were "pitch-pine" Yankees of the stoutest timber. They had withstood the storms that battered down the lesser men, and the second growth had yielded few equals or rivals. Parkman alone perhaps was built for another millennium, but all had produced their planks for the house of the future; and whether their eminence was relative or absolute, this, after all, mattered little. Lowell as a sage was not impressive,* but *The Biglow Papers* counted for much and long; so did a few of his literary essays, and his speech on Coleridge in Westminster Abbey might have made the fame of another man. His wit was as genuine as Holmes's, and this said much. As for Holmes himself, most of his verse had had its day, but his "high-bred amicability,"—Goethe's phrase on Molière,—was a lasting possession. He had permanently enriched the Yankee scene with his genius of good sense and his gaiety and vigour. Green was the golden bough of life for him. At eighty-five, at Beverly Farms, he had found a mammoth elm that was finer than all his other favourites; and the charming little old man in his open carriage, holding his minikin sunshade, perhaps with Mrs. Bell on the seat beside him, had used his amicability to diffuse the sun in

---

* "They"—Americans generally—"are right in feeling that way about Lowell here too,—as a political teacher and wiseacre he surely ought not to be very seriously taken. Doesn't 'think straight,' etc. Charles· Norton ditto! with his 'culture,' never forgetting that it is not vulgarity."—Letter of William James, 1888.

corners, unlike his, that were damp and dark. Mrs. Bell,
Rufus Choate's daughter, whose mind was also of the
kind one spoke, spoke it often and well, as well as he.*
Whittier, too, stood lastingly for the gods of New England, the passion for goodness and justice and the
household lares; and Parkman, who never drew morals,
lived the moral that all his books conveyed. These men
had fought good fights in one way or another, and all of
them had won the Promethean prize. They had carried
their lamps unextinguished to the end of the race.

There were plenty of Bostonians who were never willing to say die, but who was to take the place of these
men that had gone? The future echoed the question.
There was no reply. That the fortunate bloom of Athens
was only a question of fifty years, that Spain's great hour
was brief, this mattered little. How long were any of
these "heats and genial periods"?—Emerson's phrase
for the "high tides" of the spirit. The morning after was
always grey and sad; and Boston for twenty years
counted its survivors before it reluctantly said, This is
the last. It was too chagrined to observe the new generation that was rising in its presence, all unknown. Those
who remained to recall the times that people called
"heroic" or "Augustan," chips of the older block indeed, were smaller. They were the equals in character of
those who had passed, but as writers they were subordinate and mostly humble. On Cornhill, at the Athenæum,
in the Old Corner Bookstore, one met these lingering
worthies when the sun came out, Edward Everett Hale,
Mrs. Howe or the sweetly, sadly beaming little Norton,

---

* "I do not believe Henry James is so silly as to pompously announce
that he is no longer an American. He probably said it was a pleasant day
in such a roundabout way that no one knew what he was driving at."—
Mrs. Bell, at the time of James's naturalization in England. Mrs. Bell, the
complete Bostonian, did not like the country. She said to a friend who was
setting out for the woods and fields, "Well, kick a tree for me." When a
dray passed her house, filled with jangling rails, she said to her sister,
"Never mind, it might have been a bird."

with his habit of shaking his head as he smiled and sighed; or it might have been Colonel Higginson, on his high-wheeled bicycle, bolt upright, scorching at five miles an hour through the streets of Cambridge. The great-grandmotherly Mrs. Howe, never at a loss for causes, appeared in her lace hood at every meeting. No meeting could have deserved the name unless she recited the *Battle Hymn,* in her flowered silk cloak and lilac satin. She was never too old to appear at the State House to plead for justice or mercy,—no day without its cause was her constant motto; and, as Holmes had celebrated birthdays, she celebrated centenaries, from Bryant's and Margaret Fuller's to Abraham Lincoln's. As a national institution, Dr. Hale was her only rival. The rough-and-ready Hale, like Mrs. Howe, had kept the faith and gusto of the early republic. With his air of an untidy Pilgrim father, he seemed to say that Gilead still had its balm. Every child in Boston had sat on his knee, from Beacon Street to the byways and lost alleys where he searched for the lame in body and the maimed in spirit; and, more-over, this hardy old Christian, who loved adventure, and who knew all the world as he knew his country, had kept the statesmanly instinct of the ministers of old. "Cradled in the sheets of the Boston *Advertiser,*" he had known most of the statesmen of America and England, and he who was soon to become the chaplain of the national Senate * was one who had not been discouraged by the post-war years. No one knew politics better. No one knew the founders of the country better; † and it was in their name that he took, at the age of eighty-one, the line that others followed in after decades. In his daily edi-

---

* "Do you pray for the Senators, Dr. Hale?" someone asked the chaplain. "No, I look at the Senators and pray for the country."

† After *The Man Without a Country,* Hale's most substantial work was his *Franklin in France,* two volumes, 1888. This was based on unpublished documents and letters. He was an unpretentious journalist in most of his other writings.

torials, he defended the Rochdale coöperative system, the
government ownership of coal-mines, old-age pensions,
and he asked why all these measures were regarded as
novel. Did not the people own the roads, the canals,
aqueducts, schoolhouses, lighthouses? Did they not own
the libraries, reservoirs, churches? Was not the word
"commonwealth" first used by Winthrop for a political
organization? Had not the American genius always run
in the line of the "government ownership of the essen-
tials"? Was the "ownership of wealth in common" anything so odd? * John Quincy Adams had asked, in his
way, a similar question; and Hale, who was not "without a country," knew that the best way to possess a
country was to follow the path of justice for the greatest
number. Dr. Hale and Mrs. Howe were living illustrations of the truth that New England perhaps was created
to show,—that character was what Emerson had called
it; and one felt this in Colonel Higginson's presence as
one saw the sabre-scar on his chin, a souvenir of the fight
for Anthony Burns. Norton, too, had character, though
not so simply. When, attacking the war with Spain as
"inglorious" and "criminal," he was called a traitor for
his pains,† Norton sighed perhaps but he shrugged his
shoulders. He had heard all this before, with Lowell and
Dana, when the Mexicans instead of the Spaniards were
the bone of contention. If Norton lacked the moral sweep
of Higginson and Hale, this was because his sympathies
were far less open; and for this reason his teaching, fine
as it was, was very far from what it might have been.
Like his sympathies, his imagination was imperfectly developed, a fact that was all the more glaring because his

* *We, the People,* 1903.
† Among men of letters, Howells, Higginson, William James, Mark
Twain, Aldrich and William Graham Sumner equally opposed the Span-
ish War. "Don't yelp with the pack," William James said to his classes.
The Anti-Imperialist League was organized in Boston in 1898 to oppose
the annexation of the Philippines, etc.

field was of imagination all compact. So he left the "art"
out of art, just as, in following Ruskin, he left out the
heart of Ruskin's teaching,—for was not Ruskin a socialist, like Dr. Hale? Strange as it might have appeared, the
chaplain of the Senate had more in common with Ruskin
than the exquisite Norton.* Norton, perhaps, was not
the "real thing." William James was certain that he was
not; † and the popular phrase about Norton that, entering heaven, he exclaimed, "Oh, oh! So overdone! So Renaissance!" expressed a general feeling that was true and
just. Always an invalid, he had carried his fastidiousness
to a point that was all but absurd and unsound as well.
As with many dons who glory in their donnishness, his
alienated taste was over-ripe; and many an equal of Norton's in culture whose sympathies were open out-smiled
the smiling sage at his expense. John Jay Chapman ‡ and
Santayana § were only two of these; and indeed there

* "He was a kind of angel gone astray; meant for the thirteenth century,
he got delayed on the way, and when he finally arrived was a white-
winged anachronism."—Norton's comment on Ruskin at the time of his
death. This was a fine phrase but far from true. No man was less an
anachronism than the author of *Unto This Last.*

† "Charles Norton, I see, receives the bequest of Lowell's manuscripts,
etc. The way that man gets his name stuck to every greatness is fabulous,
—Dante, Goethe, Carlyle, Ruskin, FitzGerald, Chauncey Wright, and now
Lowell! His name will dominate all the literary history of this epoch. 100
years hence, the *Revue des Deux Mondes* will publish an article entitled
'La Vie de l'esprit aux Etats-Unis vers du XIXme siècle; étude sur Charles
Norton.' He is our *foyer de lumières;* and the worst of it is that he does
all the chores therewith connected, and practically fills the position rather
better, than if he were the genuine article."—Letter of William James to
Alice James, 1891.

‡ "The great business of Bostonians was to place values upon everything
in the world, with conscientious accuracy. Professor Norton once said to
me on the steps of Sanders Theatre, after a performance of Beethoven's
'Eroica Symphony,' that, after all, the 'sentiment' of the funeral march was
a little 'forced.' This was charming, too. Of course, it is not great or of
the great world. . . . It was Boston's foible to set metes and bounds to everything."—John Jay Chapman, *Memories and Milestones.*

§ "Old Harvard men will remember the sweet sadness of Professor Norton. He would tell his classes, shaking his head with a slight sigh, that the
Greeks did not play football."—Santayana, *The Genteel Tradition at Bay.*
There were also professors who told their classes that the Greeks did
nothing but play football.

was something preposterous in this winning old pundit, with his "note as sweet as an eighteenth-century organ." * Howells had shown the right perception when, years before, Norton had first returned to teach in Cambridge. He had said that Norton's standard was "dreadfully high," by which he did not mean that it should have been laxer, and that the apple-blossoms were worth all the past of which Norton sighed "to find us disinherited." † This might have seemed an exaggeration in 1874, but one saw what Howells meant in 1890, observing the contentment with which Norton told his classes that they too might have been happy, on one condition,—not to have been born at all in the age they lived in.‡ There had always been something wrong with a standard that led to this denial of life, a denial that was sterile and complacent. The "apple-blossoms" taught a better lesson, and so did the genuine pessimists, unhappy themselves, who denied life in order to affirm it.§ But those who said that Norton was precious also said he was powerful, a teacher "in the mystical and personal sense" ‖ who was all but unique in his time; and his translation of Dante in masterly prose,—he felt this befitted the temper of the age more fully,—was a proof that his scholarship was vital. This was more important than Norton's writings. For scholarship and character one never had to look far in New England, character with salt and scholarship with wit and poetry. But poetry and wit themselves were an-

* John Jay Chapman.
† Letter of Howells, 1874.
‡ "Professor Norton lectured in Italian 4 this afternoon. The dear old man looks so mildly happy and benignant while he regrets everything in the age and the country—so contented, while he gently tells us it were better for us had we never been born in this degenerate and unlovely age . . . I wonder if these dear and reverend people realize what an impression they give the younger ones when they beg them to believe that there is nothing high and lovely in this country or this age."—*Diary and Letters of Josephine Preston Peabody*.
§ "If way to the Better there be, it exacts a full look at the Worst."—Thomas Hardy, *In Tenebris*.
‖ John Jay Chapman.

other matter. Literature proper was evaporating, surely. In Gautier's verses, the bust outlived the city, but in Boston the bust had also outlived the poem.

The Bostonians were convinced of this, whether it was true or not, and those who called the moment Alexandrian knew their history well. On its smaller scale, New England was repeating the conditions of the classical age that bore this name. The Alexandrians could return no longer to their homogeneous early Athenian life. The gods of the State and the household were diminished in stature. Indeed, they ceased to be gods, they were even as men; and men no longer reverenced the temples in their own breasts,—they respected their mundane interests more than their feelings. The bonds that had held them together had fallen apart, and persons were merely persons without the attachments that had given them significance and value. Idiosyncrasies flourished without rhyme or reason, and women assumed the tasks in which men had failed. As in Greece, so in Boston, the logic of cause and effect worked itself out in literature, as in all things human. Literature became merely literary,—to use the phrase of the hour,—because it had lost its native impulse. It was driven to follow models more abjectly than ever, and models that were also arbitrary, unlike the co-ordinated models of the earlier writers, who had borne an organic relation to the men they followed. Learning took the place that poetry had held in a day when men shared heroic passions; and no one better than Bostonians knew what this implied, however their prosperity had grown. They were all Agamemnons and Solomon Johns, when it came to reading encyclopædias, and they knew that these compendiums, which represented human standards, contained a hundred poets for every banker. To be able to compete with Detroit was no great prospect when they had been, uniquely and potently, Boston. If New England was to rise again, it would have to rise on another basis; and what this basis was few men could see. It was certain that the pitcher of the past was broken at the fountain. Cambridge might have its worthies to the end of the chapter, like old John Holmes, the Autocrat's brother, whose sole occupation had been friendship. John Holmes, blind now, had to put up with an attendant, who led him out to the Common and left him on a bench. There he sat alone, basking in the sun, murmuring Homer. Cambridge, Boston, Worcester, Hartford might long have their John Holmeses; but when would another mayor of a factory-town, stirred by another Yankee poet's death, utter a funeral oration in the manner of Athens? *

Boston was left to gather up its relics, with a feeling that its forbears had had "all the fun." † The New Yorkers laughed when Oliver Herford characterized New England as "the abandoned farm of literature." The Bostonians did not laugh,—the barb struck home. The *North American Review* had gone to New York, and the *Atlantic Monthly* was doing its best to forget that it represented Boston. Last things were in order now,‡ and all the Boston men could do,—or all they thought they could do,—was to bury the dead. Mount Auburn was becoming over-crowded. Every other Boston book was somebody's *Retrospections,* and *Yesterdays,* cheerful or other-

---

* "To honour the memory of the great, the wise and the good by suitable expression has at all times and under all conditions of civilization been a criterion by which to judge of the degree of intelligence, morality and refinement attained. In their ideals we may measure their aspirations and ambitions . . . In a city preëminent for its devotion to business, this audience is assembled to honour the memory of one the aim of whose life was higher than the ambition to accumulate wealth. Here may we be reminded that man is most honoured, not by that which a city may do for him, but by that which he has done for the city."—From the speech of the Mayor of Haverhill at the funeral of Whittier, 1892.

† Thomas Sergeant Perry.

‡ Even Dr. Hale wrote a sketch called *The Last Shake,* commemorating the last man with a hand-cart who was ever allowed to shake carpets on Boston Common.

wise, flooded the book-shops. Doing the Pharaohs up in
spices, in Dr. Holmes's phrase, was the central occupation of the literati. Dr. Holmes's own life was written
by John T. Morse, Jr.,—almost as salty as his subject,—
the veteran who edited the *American Statesman Series*
and ran like a sugar-maple with wit and wisdom till he
died at the age of ninety-six. M. A. De Wolfe Howe, the
Boston historiographer, also began at this moment the
long career that united the liberality of the old New England with the sunniness and fullness of New England culture. As a Rhode Islander, Mark Howe, so-called universally, saw Boston with an edge of difference; and this,
no doubt, was the reason why, having so much in common
with it, he was able to reveal to others its potent charm.
He performed a historical function in so far as Boston
was itself a historical city; for he was to live through all
the decades in which the country turned against it, and
more than anyone else, in his own person, he led the
country back. Mark Howe possessed the secret that puzzled the burghers, like other Pied Pipers before him. The
biographer of Phillips Brooks, Bancroft, Norton, Moorfield Storey, and later of Wendell, Holmes and John Jay
Chapman, was a poet all the time; and that is why, in
Mark Howe's books, the Pharaohs came to life again, as
they died again in other "lives and letters." He shared in
whatever was human because it was human, so that all
his heroes abounded in their own sense. Most of the other
biographers were dazzled by their heroes, or they were
humdrum themselves; and they so swathed the mummies
of the Pharaohs that it took a generation to unwrap
them.

This mood of retrospection, so closely allied to the
moods of regret and defeat, expressed itself most fully
in Barrett Wendell. He shared Norton's feeling,—he
was born too late in a world too old; and he could not

find his way back to the earlier Boston.* Where was Boston, the Boston of the springtime twenties? He whipped his horse about the roads in vain. For Wendell was Peter Rugg incarnate, and the image of this old man in the yellow-wheeled chaise, who was forever asking, "Where is Boston?" haunted many in these bewildered years. Miss Guiney and Amy Lowell wrote poems about Peter Rugg, who had stepped out of a story and become a folk-figure.† He stood for the seekers of lost trails who abounded in Boston, for those who felt their world had gone awry and who tried to grope their way back to an earlier time when life had been vigorous and hopeful. There were many of these besides Wendell, and, like him, they sorted their family papers, as if in these yellowing documents they might possibly find the secret of the life which they had missed. Might not the virtue flow into them again if they touched these relics of their forbears that spoke of a large and active life in the past? ‡ This sorting of family papers seemed to them a public service, though in certain cases the families had scarcely been public and had never played a part in the larger world that called for any general interest in them. In other cases, anxious descendants who longed to live up to a family tradition continued to go through the motions of a pub-

---

* "The very pleasantest little oasis of space and time was that of New England from about the beginning of the century to about 1825."—Charles Eliot Norton.

"At this moment, very often, I feel a certain regret that I had not the fortune to be born fifty years earlier. Then I could eagerly have joined in the expression of faith in the future which made New England literature promise something. Now I find my temper doubtful, reactionary. Such moods as mine are not things that literature demands."—Barrett Wendell, 1893.

† See Amy Lowell's *Before the Storm* and Louise Imogen Guiney's *Peter Rugg, the Bostonian.*

‡ The well-known Boston malady, "grandfather on the brain,"—so called by Harriet Preston in *Aspendale,*—reached its crisis in the nineties. This malady, or this mood, spread through the country. It was during these years that the Colonial Dames, the D.A.R., etc., were organized, to restore the fading racial faith and to assert the prestige of the original stock, threatened by the waves of immigration.

lic life on the small private scale that was open to them. If they could not promote bills in Congress, they could write letters to the *Transcript,* declaring war on the sparrows, instead of the British, and urging the protection of the squirrels on the ground that they sucked the sparrows' eggs. The contrast between their inherited tone and the trivial field their world afforded was a fruitful cause of satire, both then and later. Robert Grant's *The Chippendales* anticipated by thirty years the delicate, but sharper satire of *The Late George Apley.**

Barrett Wendell, like so many others, wished he had lived in the great good time when things were a-doing in Boston. He shrank from the "bewildering surge" of a world that seemed "sadly bound nowhither," † and cherished his Harvard memories of a world that was gone. But, if he had lived in the days he longed for, would he have shared in the "faith that made New England literature promise something"? He felt so. He wished to believe it. He was surely mistaken. For the tender-minded Wendell, who likened himself to "a Federalist in Jefferson's time, a sound Whig in Jackson's, or an honest Southerner in Lincoln's," could never have had the root of the matter in him. The "last of the tories," as he also called himself, would have been a tory all the time; but, glorying in this, as he was certainly free to do, how could he have shared the springtime faith? He was hostile to all its premises and all its results. Deploring the French Revolution,‡ he deplored the American Revolu-

---

* By John P. Marquand. The pathos of this Boston type is illustrated best in Bliss Perry's life of Richard Henry Dana III. When Dana was baptised, as an infant, in 1851, the clergyman exclaimed, "May there ever be a Richard Henry Dana to stand before the Lord!" Having, with small capacity, to live up to this,—to live up to the family tradition of sacrifice and service,—Dana spent his life in bewildered efforts to find some way of being useful. As in the case of George Apley, he had the patrician's pattern of mind in a world that had ceased to afford scope for patricians.

† Letter of Barrett Wendell.

‡ Of the results of the French Revolution he said, in *The France of To-day,* "More than a little philanthropic purpose was accomplished, they say."

tion,* which had divided the English-speaking world; and, missing the significance of all the Revolution stood for, he had missed the meaning of his country. Indeed, he scarcely pretended to be loyal to the country; † and yet the paradoxical Barrett Wendell saw in himself a defender of "American traditions" ! ‡ By American traditions, he meant a number of things, no doubt, but mainly that good old families had good old glass, Heppelwhite chairs and good Madeira; and he meant that they had been English and should have remained so. Meanwhile, the important traditions were beyond his horizon, for Wendell, travelling over the country, wining and dining at Harvard clubs and sharing in "our funny local life," had certainly never experienced the American present; and only those who experienced the American present were able to comprehend the American past. Had he undergone any experience, for the matter of that, the vital kind of experience that affords one a key either to the past or to the present? The wistful Wendell, who had always yearned for "peace," § had never known, he said, the "stress of life;" and did he know what experience was? What did he mean by the word? Nothing that concerned the spiritual depths; for he observed that the Saviour died too young to have the sort of experience he

* "The American Revolution, then, disuniting the English-speaking world, has had on history an effect which those who cherish the moral and political heritage of our language may well grow to feel in some sense tragic." —Wendell, *Literary History of America.*

† "The virtue of loyalty has been denied me by a fate which has hardly ever afforded me a sovereign to whom I could conscientiously be loyal."— Letter of 1915.

‡ "I remember . . . how disappointed he became in a certain young man who, presuming to be his follower, said to him, 'But we Americans have no traditions.' If the sense of the remark had been to the effect that Americans should not respect traditions, that he could have borne. The offence of the young man lay in his failure to realize that no man can help having traditions, and also in the indirect affront cast at the quality of American traditions."—Daniel Sargent, *Essays in Memory of Barrett Wendell.*

§ "Peace I have always yearned for. Four or five of my earlier books purposely ended with the word."—Letter of 1919.

knew and valued.* He meant a certain mundane sophisti-
cation; and, when he said that American literature was a
record of "national inexperience," † this was the standard
that lurked in the depths of his mind. The real experience of the country, which found a voice in literature,
was vague and repugnant to Wendell; and naturally he was
half-hearted, therefore, even about its greatest writers,
even in his own New England, to say nothing of the rest.
The defender of American traditions gave them away.

Thus the past, in Wendell's mind, as in others that
shrank from the present, was a sort of phantasmal entity
without life or substance. And not the American past
alone. The remoter past was phantasmal also, as one
saw in his efforts to recreate it; ‡ and it was phantasmal
for an obvious reason, because tradition, like charity, begins at home. One can only reach the background through

* "Historically considered, the Gospels tell the story of a remarkable man
who lived under extremely fixed earthly circumstances, remote from any
we know, and died before he was old enough to have much experience."—
Letter of 1919.
This seems to suggest that all would have been well if the Saviour had
had a taste of London and Paris.

† "In the flush of its waking, [America] strove to express the meaning
of life; and the meaning of its life was the story of what two hundred
years of national inexperience had wrought for a race of Elizabethan
Puritans. Its utterances may well prove lacking in scope, in greatness; the
days to come may well prove them of little lasting potence . . . We used to
believe them,"—Thoreau, Hawthorne, Emerson, Whitman,—"heralds of the
future; already we begin to perceive that they were rather chroniclers of
times which shall be no more."—Wendell, *Literary History of America*.
The impression that readers will get from this book, Howells observed
in reviewing it, "is that American literature is not worth the attention of
people meaning to be really critical."

‡ In *The Traditions of European Literature*. A comparison of this with
Emerson's *Representative Men* marks all the difference between crescent
and senescent Boston. Emerson, who professed to despise tradition, chose
six great historical figures and made them live for his contemporaries.
Wendell, who worshipped tradition, wished to make Plato and Dante live,
but he completely failed to do so. He represented them merely as manifestations of traditions, not as men who sought truth in their time. Emerson conveyed the substance of tradition, Wendell conveyed only its shells.
Which should a lover of tradition prefer,—one who "despises" tradition or
one who worships tradition for its own sake?
Wendell's leading thought was much the same as Henry Adams's,—that
the world had been steadily going to the dogs ever since the time of Dante.

the foreground; for what makes the past real except a vigorous present existence that reads itself into the records of times that are gone? It was no accident that the great New England histories appeared in the days when New England was a force and a power. Prescott, Motley and Parkman shared the pulse-beats of a great and developing nation, and their Spain, their Holland, their Canada lived through this. They were participants in the past, and recreators of it, because they were also participants in the age they lived in. That Parkman was a born explorer, like his Canadian heroes, that Motley was a diplomat and statesman, that Prescott had eagerly followed the Peninsular War,—all this counted for something; and one and all had grown up at a time when young New England men were ardently conscious members of a country in the building. No one thinks of defending tradition in days that are making tradition, when people feel the past as a force of the present, an auxiliary, a ministrant, a helpmate. One only defends tradition, one resorts to tradition to fill the void in oneself, when life runs low. And then one grasps only the forms of tradition. Only the husks of tradition remain in one's hands.

Boston, sorting its papers, like a man who is dying, anxious to arrange his affairs, was full of these forms. Its dominant mind was a dry sea-beach where all the creatures of history had deposited their shells. Its tone was elegiac. It abounded in praisers of times past who would never have known their Catullus, had he walked their way, and who savoured the "decencies of comfortable corruption" * while they fondled their costly bindings and their choice mementos. There brooded over the town, as a stranger noted, "an immense effect of finality," as if all intellectual movement had ceased there; † and a horrible

* Barrett Wendell.
† "There broods over the real Boston an immense effect of finality. One feels in Boston, as one feels in no other part of the States, that the intellectual movement has ceased."—H. G. Wells, *The Future in America,* 1906.

sense of conviction overcame this stranger, at a certain club of Boston bibliophiles. The mind of the world was dead, he said to himself; and this was a distribution of souvenirs! "I felt," H. G. Wells recalled, "that all the books had been written, all the pictures painted, all the thoughts said." Wells, dismayed, rushed from the room and roamed through the streets in the moonlight, till he caught the glimpse of a ray· in a bookseller's window; and there, in fresh covers, lay books that had just come out. The mind of the world was still alive!—in spite of the bibliophiles and in spite of Boston.

CHAPTER XXI

THE EPIGONI

WAS New England really dying? Or did it merely
wish to think so? Was it dead or simulating death?
All these questions puzzled the enquiring stranger. There
were evidences corroborating almost every possible view,
for the Yankee mind had grown to resemble the Sphinx,
the Sphinx of the desert as well as the Sphinx of the mountain. In some respects, it seemed certainly moribund, while
in others it maintained a state of suspended animation; but
now and then one asked oneself if there was not a hoax
at the bottom of it all. For if the Yankee mind was dead
it had the best of all excuses for no longer providing the
country with statesmen and poets.

Such were a few of the riddles the Yankee mind proposed to strangers, who were sometimes rash in their responses. But the Yankees were companionable. In this
they were unlike the Sphinx,—they were willing to discuss the riddles as well as to propose them. They even
had their vanities: they encouraged people to talk about
them. They welcomed all the unpleasant things that
strangers said about them, and even said them first and
rather better; and their most admired authors were those
whose constant burden now was that they were going to
the devil. The Yankees, sometimes vain, were proud.
They had stood for intellect and virtue. Even more than
the false, they had stood for the real; and, more than any
other strain, their strain had leavened the life of the
country. Their failure was not merely a failure of per-

sons; and it was not solely on their own behalf that they were filled with anxiety and chagrin. Suppose these authors of theirs were right, suppose their day was over, then much for which they stood was over also. However this might have been, it was not for strangers to smile at the lamentations at the wailing wall. If, as these authors believed, New England was a failure, New England was a tragic failure, truly. It had won the respect of mankind; and the willing suspension of disbelief,—that is, in this belief,—was the mood in order.

Henceforth, at least, for twenty years, the chief pursuit of the Yankee authors, and of most American authors concerned with New England,—was the game of pulling the skeletons out of the cupboards. There were plenty of skeletons in them to pull, for no one had ever done justice to the fund of evil that lurked in the soul of the region. The Yankee mind was beginning to pay for its somewhat cocky optimism, and even for Emerson's noble ignoring of pain. It had had perhaps too easy a victory over a virgin world of nature, where every prospect pleased and man was good; and its energy reverted now to the earlier Calvinistic view that narrowed and all but closed the eye of the needle. New England was searching its conscience, an unlovely task, but one that it had to perform. It was useless to dwell any longer, in the happy older fashion, on the blue-jays that bickered in the hedgerows, on the goldenrod with its splendid plumes, the gentians and the morning-glories and the purple asters nodding on the road-sides. These flowers that had filled the New England poems had once been the symbols of health and joy. They had burgeoned in the Yankee soul, pervading the mind with zest and vigour, in days when all the roads, with their fragrant borders, were roads of generosity, hope and purpose. Whither did the roads lead now? This ominous question shadowed the flowers and muted the songs of the birds, to such an extent that poets, concerned with this question, the more they were concerned to answer it, turned their backs the more on the flowers and the birds. For the ground of the literary mind was gradually shifting, and the writers of the future were destined for a season to reverse and even deny the writers of the past. Whither did the roads lead? Some led where they had always led, although fewer and fewer minds were disposed to see it. The day was approaching for Irving Babbitt to have his say, for Edwin Arlington Robinson, for Santayana, for Eugene O'Neill and T. S. Eliot, for Edna St. Vincent Millay and E. E. Cummings. It was true that in these writers,—in Robert Frost especially,— New England was to have another springtime. But, first of all, it had to dree its weird. It had to pass through the valley of the shadow. Only then was it ripe for these new revelations.

The nineties were not the day for revelations. They were a day of little faith, the day of the epigoni, the successors, in whom the nineteenth century went to seed. Poets abounded, novelists, critics, in several cases highly gifted, but most of them were discouraged or astray in blind alleys. Like all Alexandrians, they had lost touch with their own tradition, or they resumed this tradition in mechanical ways; and they sought to recover trails their forbears had abandoned or else to follow new trails that were blazed by others. The blazing of new trails was not for them. They symbolized the end of an epoch in which the strongest were incomplete; for, as numbers had withdrawn altogether from the struggle,—such men as Clarence King and T. S. Perry,—so William James never built the arch of his philosophy, John Fiske's historical plan remained abortive, and Henry James and Howells and Henry Adams, great as they were in their way, were somehow qualified successes. All required explanations. None swam free in the crystalline upper air of the genuine classics, however the Jameses and Howells and Adams produced a few books that were built to live. If this was true, of the greater writers, what was the natural fate of the lesser? Yet, of these epigoni, George Edward Woodberry, George Cabot Lodge, Trumbull Stickney, Louise Imogen Guiney and various others, all were symptomatic and all had their interest, either as writers proper or as Yankee types.

In the region of aesthetics, the Boston mind was clearly advancing, and all that was most vital in the nineties and after was associated with this advance. Arlo Bates's novel, *The Pagans,* spoke for a group of younger artists who were gifted, fiery and truthful and who really existed. They stood for sincerity in life, in art, in manners, against established formulas, conventions and shams. They opposed the spirit of imitation, and the golden gods of Philistia were not for them. Mrs. Helen Grayson, the heroine of this novel, might well have been Mrs. Whitman, the beautiful, generous creature who had appeared in Boston suddenly,—from "some savage town—Baltimore perhaps," * and who became the sun of the Boston artists. At Mrs. Whitman's salon, William James, Royce and Holmes abounded in the sense of the younger people who only required an eye to seek them out; and what could one say of such a woman, whose spiritual hospitality was this eye,—what more than Sainte-Beuve said apropos of Madame Récamier, with all that was implied in three French verbs? *Elle se sent, elle passe, elle apparait,* and in the presence of her gaiety, her joy of life, her tragic faith, her love of youth and promise, in the presence of these emotions everything changes! So it was with Mrs. Whitman. She was the Wingéd Victory that other Bostonians liked in casts, while others again preferred original statues; and the story of the MacMonnies

* John Jay Chapman, *Mrs. Whitman,* in *Memories and Milestones,*— Sarah Wyman Whitman, a very different sort of person from Sarah Helen Whitman, the betrothed of Poe. See also *Letters of Sarah Wyman Whitman.*

Bacchante, which caused so many blushes,—more than a few at the expense of Boston,—showed how seriously Boston could take a statue. It took the Shaw Memorial seriously, as it took Saint-Gaudens's Phillips Brooks, in which the Franco-Irish-American sculptor showed he was more American than French or Irish. Perhaps it took these things too seriously. At least, it was serious enough, which could not have been said of other cities. It prayed over the Florentine Library and Mrs. Jack Gardner's Venetian palace, and it even made Florence and Venice Bostonian somehow because of its regard for Italian culture. The fact that Boston girls grew up with Botticelli manners made Botticelli almost a Boston painter; and the Library seemed quite at home in a town where Italian studies, fostered by Norton and Longfellow, by Perkins and Lowell, were a part of the atmosphere that all men breathed. Dante,* Petrarch, Ruskin and Browning were Boston citizens in their way, although, for the good of all, they kept their distance; and handbooks on Italian art poured from the Boston presses, together with the reminiscences of New England worthies. Whistler was invited, along with Sargent and E. A. Abbey, not to speak of Puvis de Chavannes, to decorate the walls of the Library; and meanwhile the college settlements ministered to the arts and crafts, and the Copley prints appeared,

* The cult of Dante had woven itself into the fabric of Boston life. In 1881, Marion Crawford introduced Mrs. Gardner to Dante. They read the *Divine Comedy* together, and the two copies they had used were interleaved and bound by Tiffany, after a design by Crawford. Somewhat later, in an upper room of the Athenæum, John Jay Chapman read Dante with the half-Italian lady who became his wife.

It is recorded that Emerson translated the *Vita Nuova,* and that Ellery Channing rendered for him the sonnets and canzoni. This version was not published, nor was the translation of the *Inferno* made—of all people in the world—by President Calvin Coolidge in his youth.

The two chief New England continuers of Dante studies were Professor Charles H. Grandgent of Harvard (*Dante, The Ladies of Dante's Lyrics, Discourses on Dante,* etc.) and Professor Charles A. Dinsmore, later of Yale (*The Life of Dante, The Teachings of Dante, Aids to the Study of Dante,* etc.).

and *Poet-Lore.** There was a rage for poems about Titian's garden. The Symphony advanced from triumph to triumph, and the "sublime sweet evening star" of Wagner eclipsed for the moment Emerson's morning star. The clever Mrs. Gardner did the rest. This "gloom-dispeller, corpse-reviver and general chirker-up," as Sturgis Bigelow called her,—the rival collector,—this reckless, exuberant, witty woman whose motto was *C'est mon plaisir* was filling Fenway Court with the spoils of Europe. As a local Queen Elizabeth, she cut off heads right and left and stuck them on again if it pleased her to do so; and, when the Bostonians called her an upstart, she cut off their ancestral heads by proving that she belonged to the house of Stuart. Norton, her master, had bought Della Robbias for her, and Henry Adams had procured for her the best French window in the country. Meanwhile, Bernhard Berenson, whom she befriended at Harvard, became her regular adviser and expert-in-chief.

All this represented vitality. The question was, What kind of vitality? Did it not rather suggest the "museum of idols" that Mrs. Whitman found in Sargent's fresco, —"all the things without being the one thing," and rather an assemblage of objects than a composition? † The Bostonians were great collectors. They collected religions,‡

* There was also at this time a notable movement in Boston in behalf of fine printing and book-making. D. B. Updike established the Merrymount Press, which produced the magnificent *Humanists' Library,* works by Erasmus, Leonardo, Pico della Mirandola, Dürer, Sir Philip Sidney, etc. For an account of this, see Updike's delightful *Notes on the Merrymount Press and Its Work.* Bruce Rogers became, in 1895, the designer of the Riverside Press. Less distinguished in its work, the firm of Copeland and Day excelled in the production of beautiful books; nor should one forget the charming publications of Thomas B. Mosher of Portland, Maine.

† "It"—Sargent's fresco on the stairway of the Library,—"is all the things without being the one thing; clever, decorative, enormously so,—and rich in colour, yet not beautiful in colour; an assemblage of objects rather than a composition; a museum of idols rather than a picture of the world's religions. So it seemed to me."—*Letters of Sarah Wyman Whitman.*

‡ The history of religions was a favourite subject at Harvard.

along with these objects of art; and the archæological
manners of the Botticelli girls suggested an even more
intimate kind of collection. They also collected political
ideas; and, in their revolt from democracy and realism,*
their desire to expunge all remnants of the Puritan past,
they conceived a monarchist movement, a royalist movement, in which "King Charles his gentlemen" figured
largely. They never saw a purple king but always hoped
to see one, for the kings they contemplated were purple
indeed, and far from the "business kings" of the age they
lived in. They organized a local branch of the Jacobite
Society, the "Order of the White Rose," namely; and
they offered expiation on the feast of St. Charles, drank
seditious toasts on all occasions and even corresponded
with Queen Mary of Bavaria and also Don Carlos of
Spain, the Legitimist sovereigns. Ralph Adams Cram,
the archæological architect, who was bent upon reversing evolution, was the prior of the chapter.† This singular Boston royalism, with other admixtures of soberer
hue, reappeared in T. S. Eliot two decades later; and
meanwhile Mrs. Gardner, with King Charles on her family tree, scrubbed on Good Friday the altar-steps of the
Advent. Mrs. Gardner proudly wore religion as the best
gem upon her zone. For the rest, her eye, otherwise discriminating, ignored art when it blossomed in the fields

---

*The reaction against realism was marked in New England, as in al-
most every region in the nineties. It appeared in the most unexpected
quarters. Thus the old New Haven realist, John W. De Forest, reëmerged
after a long silence with a romantic novel, *A Lover's Revolt*, dealing with
Revolutionary Boston. Sarah Orne Jewett produced *A Tory Lover*, and
even Mary E. Wilkins wrote a cavalier romance, *The Heart's Highway*.

This romantic reaction, although short-lived, was completely romantic,
unlike the similar reaction in the eighteen-eighties. Marion Crawford, William Henry Bishop, Julian Hawthorne and Arthur Sherburne Hardy paid
tribute to the force of the realistic movement by mingling realism with
their romance. The later writers threw off all pretence of realism.

† "I still treasure my parchment as 'Prior' in those American territories
lying between the Canadian border and the Rio Grande."—Ralph Adams
Cram, *My Life in Architecture.*

around her. She saw Giorgione's finest points, as she saw the virtues of Sargent and Whistler, who blazed like meteors over the world of fashion. But she did not see the Yankee Giorgiones, Maurice Prendergast, Winslow Homer, Ryder. The innocent eyes that perceived these wore no veils.

What, then, was vital in all this connoisseurship, in the world of art, religion, politics, manners? It was the scholar's instinct, the historical sense that reënforced the instinct of the common collector; and even a little magnificence was good for Boston. For the rest, in an age when vulgarity reigned, when barbarians gambled in pictures as they gambled in stocks, when the passion for display glutted itself with castles and palaces and raided the department-store of Europe for million-dollar bargains in the basement, Boston had an advantage over other cities. Mrs. Gardner was vulgar enough. In the game of self-glorification, in the game of sensation, she outglittered even the magnates of Nob Hill; and similarly Cram's Gothic churches gave the village meeting-houses a dignity that even they had lost. There was something meretricious in all these manifestations, which were often sentimental and occasionally silly. Almost as much as Harry Lehr's Newport, they discredited religion, politics, art. Alas, for Mrs. Howe's old friendly Newport, where architects and priests were on their knees before the insane vulgarities of the world of fashion. There, where the old patricians had paid their way in manners, in kindness, in culture, there ladies supposedly great insulted their guests and daughters blackmailed their fathers, there savages told beads of jade, moving their lips in prayer while they hissed insults, and a President of the nation, surrounded by grooms, was forced to call his own carriage, while the grooms tittered.* Realities were

---

* See 'King Lehr' and the Gilded Age, by Elizabeth Drexel Lehr.

wrecked at Newport along with illusions. Mrs. Gardner's
Boston was allied with this Newport, but Boston was
never Mrs. Gardner's, and all that Mrs. Gardner stood
for had a certain dignity because it also stood for thought
and learning. Obliquely as it spoke, it uttered still the
tongue that Blaxton spoke, the learned settler, who had
heard the wolves howling on the site of the State House;
and the good name of Boston survived these orgies, the
name of the Boston of effort, of conscience, of schools.
This note emanated from the Fogg Museum, which was
spreading an influence that was almost despotic as a
school of museum-directors. It produced aesthetic valets
for barbarian collectors. It also gave whatever schools
can give,—and so much the worse for artists if they could
not withstand it, if they could not leave the chaff and
take the grain. Out of this milieu, moreover, the brilliant
and useful career of the expert, Bernhard Berenson, was
just emerging. A protégé of Mrs. Gardner, he had begun
at Harvard his long-continuing studies of Italian painting, and before the end of the nineties he had almost
completed the handbooks, at once profound and charming, that were later assembled in the single volume,
Italian Painters of the Renaissance. These handbooks, so
different from the anecdotal and fanciful writing of most
art-critics of the past, characterized precisely the work
of all the Italian schools in the light of a philosophy of
taste. Berenson had conquered a tendency to follow Pater
before he developed his theory of "tactile values." He
had stood for hours before the Mona Lisa, repeating
Pater's rhapsody over and over, until he perceived that
it had no objective sense. He was already known as one
of the modern students of art who applied the methods
of science in their connoisseurship; and at twenty-six, in
1891, he had expertized the pictures at Hampton Court,
which were hopelessly confused in their attributions. The

great Renaissance names, in all the museums, were sprin-
kled over paintings by later artists, and Berenson undertook the task of authenticating works and accrediting
them to the proper names and schools. While he lectured
to classes in museums, he deduced the history of artists
from a study of their works; and he also reconstructed
unknown artists, as paleontologists with a handful of
bones reconstructed the unknown animals to which they
belonged. Before the turn of the century, he had settled
in Florence, where James Jackson Jarves had lived before him. He was already consulted by museum-directors,
collectors and dealers; and the time was approaching
when the world of expertizing was divided between Berenson and Wilhelm von Bode.

Boston existed for education, Henry Adams said, and
its genius had triumphed again in the field of art. It was
collecting the documents of art as it had gathered historical documents. It was concerned, moreover, with
theories of art; and, while Berenson was writing his
handbooks, George Santayana was lecturing at Harvard
on aesthetics. This young Spanish colleague of William
James, Royce and Palmer had been brought to America
at the age of eight. Born in Madrid, he had grown up
in a Boston family, into which his mother had married,
a strange, alien, lonely child, a duckling, far from ugly,
in whom perceptive eyes foresaw the swan. Louise Imogen Guiney had seen him as a boy kneeling in a neighbouring pew in the Jesuit church; for he was brought up
as a Catholic, and he kept his Catholic habits of mind,
albeit Catholicism had become for him only a "theoretic
pose" or a "vista," as he said, "for the imagination." *
He lived in his imagination, with Greek myths and Latin
traditions, for he felt he had nothing in common with

* Santayana, *Soliloquies in England.*

the life about him; and he assumed a calm detachment
from this world, which seemed to him foreign and repulsive.* The literature of New England struck him as
"all a harvest of leaves;" its liberalism was alien to him,
and he scorned its humanitarian impulse. The "agonized
conscience" of Protestantism he felt was futile, and he
disliked its atmosphere of spiritual striving, its Emersons, Whitmans and Brownings, as if its will and energy
availed in the end. For was not progress merely the bab-
ble of dreamers? What mattered who ruled the land, or
what form of government one had to submit to? And
were not classes the normal order of nature? Were not
soldiers the natural leaders, with cardinals and engineers?
Why quarrel with conventions? Were the standards by
which one judged them any truer than they were? And
why should one quarrel with nature? Why not rather
welcome its fugitive beauties? Why not rejoice in its fair
outward ways, detached from the world without hostility to it? Were not repose and serenity the paramount
virtues? The Apollonian Santayana, with his "Epicurean
contentment," a pagan and a sceptic in his naturalism,
was launching into the great soliloquy in which he expressed his hedonism and all his wonder and pleasure in
the face of nature. Meanwhile, disliking the taste of academic straw, he preferred the wandering life of the mediæval student; and he usually went abroad in the summer
to Spain, France or England, where he lived in later years
before settling in Rome. In Cambridge, he wore a long,
picturesque cape; and, aloof as he was from the other
professors, he was charmed by some of the students.

* "You tax me several times with impertinence and superior airs. I wonder if you realize the years of suppressed irritation which I have passed in
the midst of an unintelligent, sanctimonious and often disingenuous Protestantism, which is thoroughly alien and repulsive to me, and the need I
have of joining hands with something far away from it and far above it."
—Santayana, Letter to William James, 1900.

Their "animal faith" was sympathetic to him. Amused and serene as he was, a poet, a writer of exquisite prose, with a style that was musical and happy, he suggested a Greek of Plato's time or an avatar of humanistic Florence. His lectures were published as *The Sense of Beauty*.

All these interests of Boston and Cambridge were vital for education, none more so than Santayana's lectures.* But they were only obliquely related to living art and poetry; and the ladies who listened to papers on Pico della Mirandola were not disposed to welcome the artists and authors who lived in an actual Boston, not a fanciful Florence. The culture of Boston was higher and dryer than ever. Having become a religion, it was dying as culture; and it regarded with a glassy eye the poor little efforts of poets who struggled beneath it. It identified itself with Dante, Browning, with Matthew Arnold, Ruskin, Walter Pater, and felt that because it somehow knew these authors it was entitled to regard with scorn the ingenuous beings who also tried to write. Did they think they could write as well as Browning? What nonsense, then, to try to write at all. It was true, the Bostonians were not Brownings; but if one has wrestled over the question, What does the Dark Tower mean? one feels one has a right to speak for Browning, and Boston, as everyone knew, was divided into Browning "sections" as other towns were divided into wards. It proved points by quotations from Browning, as once it had proved them by the Scriptures. Poems without Dark Towers could scarcely be poems; and, unless they lent themselves to explanations, they were hardly worth the attention of

* Daniel Gregory Mason's earlier books on music,—*From Grieg to Brahms, Beethoven and His Forerunners* and *The Romantic Composers,*—were written under the influence of Santayana.—See Mason's *Music in My Time.*

cultivated ladies. Such was the "readeress's" view of the "babes of Apollo," unless one chose to call it the "scholastic blight." * One had to be a Donne to bear the test.†
And why try to be a poet when it was greater not to try, and so much more refined to live one's works? ‡ Boston, congested with learning, was hypercritical,§ hyperæsthetic, cramped, self-conscious, tortured with notions and problems. Its conscience was always tripping it up, invading spheres where it scarcely belonged, for the mind had lost

* "To what a pass has the ascendant New England readeress brought the harmless babes of Apollo! She seeks to master all that is, and to raise a complacent creation out of its lowland wisdom to her own mountainous folly's level; she touches nothing that she does not adorn—with a problem; she approves of music and pictures whose reasonableness is believed to be not apparent to the common herd; she sheds scholastic blight . . . We lay it all to the ladies; for the old lazy unprovincialized world of men was never so astute and excruciating . . . There were no convenings for the purpose of illuminating the text of Dr. John Donne, although the provocation was unique. Poets were let alone, once upon a time; and all they did for their own pleasure and sowed broadcast for the pleasure of others failed not, somehow, to fulfil itself from the beginning unto the end . . . The man's attitude, even yet, towards a book of poetry which is tough to him is to drop it, even as the gods would have him do; the woman's is to smother it in a sauce of spurious explanation, and gulp it down."—Louise Imogen Guiney, *Patrins.*

† John Donne, a favourite of the Concord authors, Emerson, Alcott and Thoreau, who referred to him often in their writings, became in the nineties in Boston a fashionable poet. Lowell corrected extensively, in regard to punctuation, his own copy of Donne's poems, which had never been properly edited. The Grolier Club of New York published this edition in 1895. See also Norton's collection, *The Love Poems of John Donne.*

‡ "Berri says there are lots of people like that in Boston,—painters and writers and musicians who are really very great, but think it more refined just to 'live' their works."—C. M. Flandrau, *The Diary of a Freshman.*

§ "A remark made to me, last night, by a young woman, apropos of some amateur music at Dr. Wadsworth's, to which we were listening, 'It really seems as if we might develop in Boston, some day, a glimmer of talent.' Your good Bostonian is nothing if not critical, still speaking 'as if he were the Pope,' to quote Longfellow's journal."—*Journal of Thomas Russell Sullivan,* 1898.

Howells, in *Mrs. Farrell,* spoke of "those critical spirits, rather commoner in Boston than elsewhere, who analyze and refine and re-refine and shrink from a final impression, with a perseverance that leaves one in doubt whether they have any opinion about the matter."

the power of deciding simply;* and Boston was full of a sad sterility, the fruit of emotional desiccation, that masked itself in assumptions and sometimes in sneers. Senator Lodge, whose "mastery of the sneer" † was identified with Boston in other regions, where people were unaware of the kindness of Boston, had many followers both then and later. Literary or otherwise, they indulged in a savage contempt for America, which, though they hardly felt it, included themselves.‡

Thus the vitality of Boston turned against Boston. Its Culture-Philistinism sowed the wind; the creators of its culture reaped the whirlwind. The Boston authors, fed on Dead Sea apples, were hungry for nourishing pastures, —they longed to escape. Not all, to be sure, shared this feeling. Numbers remained in the town, and some who were good. Robert Grant, for one, the admirable novelist, was soon to produce *Unleavened Bread,* in which "American womanhood," so generally flattered, was asked to regard the abuses that sprang from its power. Robert Grant's American scene foreshadowed Sinclair Lewis, and his earlier novel, *An Average Man,* and *The Undercurrent,* reaffirmed his remarkable gift as a student of manners. The finest of his books, *The Chippendales,* remained the classic picture of this age of Boston, with all its futilities and foibles and tempests in teapots

* " 'Well, well, well!' said Joshua, coming to the door-step, and washing his hands and arms just outside, in a tin basin. 'I thought I see you set down a parcel of oysters—but there was sea-weed over 'em, and I don' know's I could have said they was oysters; but then, if the square question had been put to me, "Mr. Carr, be them oysters or be they not?" I s'pose I should have said they was; still, if they'd asked me how I knew?' " etc.—H. W. Chaplin, *Five Hundred Dollars and Other Stories.*

For "oysters" substitute "Cinquecento Painters" or "Metaphysical Poets" or whatever, and one has the mental pattern of many a New England magnum opus, emerging from learned descendants of Joshua Carrs.

† Owen Wister, *Roosevelt, the Story of a Friendship.*

‡ "I had a classmate at college who had never been far from South Boston, and one evening while dancing at the Dorchester assembly he slipped and fell to the ground. He arose at once with great aplomb, remarking, coldly, 'These cursed American floors!' "—John Jay Chapman, *Memories and Milestones.*

and all that was excellent and solid beneath and behind
them. Born and bred in this literary brier-patch, Robert
Grant and others held their own; while writers of a local
scope produced their deft little sketches and verses in
the manner of Thomas Bailey Aldrich. They wrote about
the summer people at Mount Desert and the North
Shore; and tales of Harvard class-days and adventurous
yachtsmen were interspersed with comedies of dinner-
tables. They abounded in problem-novels about troublesome children and lawyers who did not understand their
wives. The wives in question were usually goddesses, and
the children were often imps of perdition, which threw
more light on the authors than it threw on the subjects,
for most of the authors were women; and, as some of the
children were also authors,—or were to be in twenty
years,—one understood their wish to run away. Having
ceased to attract outsiders, Boston was repelling its own;
and the time was approaching when one might have said,
What shore is not filled with its labours save Boston only?
Anywhere, anywhere out of the world, the younger people said to themselves, anywhere, at least, out of Boston;
and, while some fled bodily, others retreated into their
minds, where they escaped to Greece or the Middle Ages.
Robert Herrick went to Chicago, and there, in years to
come,—as a novelist, a successor of Howells, bolder than
Howells and somewhat bitter,—he viewed the Western
scene from a New England standpoint. With much of
the old Yankee moral fervour, he wrote in terms of protest and revolt. Edwin Arlington Robinson had gone to
New York from Gardiner, Maine, though he lingered a
while in Cambridge to try it out. Robinson, who had acted
as President Eliot's secretary, had left Harvard early in
his course there. He had returned to Gardiner, where he
worked in his room all day till five, emerging with a fiddle to amuse the children. A silent man, always writing,
he spent a summer reading Hawthorne, whose shadowy

personality his resembled; and he liked to mingle after
dark with the outcasts on the water-front, who were soon
to appear in his poems. He had published a little book at
Gardiner, and New York eyes perceived his talent, which
no one recognized in Boston; but he had reappeared in
Cambridge, where he worked in a magazine-office while
he was writing *Captain Craig.* He was soon convinced
that New York was the place for him. All these writers
were lonely, but those who remained were as lonely as
candles in bottles.

George Cabot Lodge was extinguished in the bottle.
He died, like Trumbull Stickney and Philip Henry Sav-
age, in his early thirties, feeling he had lived in a void.*
This son of Senator Lodge had studied in Berlin and
Paris, where he met Trumbull Stickney, who, born in
Switzerland and brought up largely in Europe, later re-
turned to Harvard as instructor in Greek. Both felt that
they were Greeks born out of time. Stickney, whom Henry
Adams knew in Paris, and who studied six years at the
Sorbonne, was the first Anglo-Saxon who was ever awarded
a doctorate in literature there.† He wrote a Greek play,
Prometheus Pyrphoros, and most of his work was dis-
tinguished, although it resounded, like Lodge's, with
Victorian echoes. What, in the eighteen-nineties, could

---

* "The gap grew steadily wider . . . This consciousness of losing
ground . . . the growing fear that, beyond this narrow range, no friends
existed in the immense void of society . . . the suffocating sense of talking
and singing in a vacuum that allowed no echo to return, grew more and
more oppressive with each effort to overcome it."—Henry Adams, *The Life
of George Cabot Lodge.*

† "Well I remember the day when he was examined by the French professors, led by Croiset, the Dean, in the Great Hall of the Sorbonne, under
the scarlet picture of Richelieu. With what learning and subtlety he defended himself against their sleight of tongue! How they pricked and tore
and tossed his thesis! With his beautiful grey eyes and sad, bewildered
face he met them on his own ground and in their own tongue. How care-
lessly the Greek flowed from his lips, and with what unperturbed French
he met all their objections for hour after hour. When the strife was over
they were all polite congratulations . . . He was made a doctor of the
Sorbonne *cum summa laude.*"—Shane Leslie, *American Wonderland.*
Stickney died within a year after his return to America.

odes to Greek liberty mean except that one knew Walter Savage Landor? Lodge's work was also rhetorical, and his principal writings were long verse-plays, suggested rather by Swinburne than by Shelley or Byron. For Swinburne charmed the latter-day New England mind. He was "capable of passion," as Woodberry said; and his freedom and extravagance, which had cast a spell over Henry Adams, enchanted the souls of these other inhibited Yankees. Lodge's poems, *The Song of the Wave, The Song of the Sword, Ode to the Earth,* were exuberant exercises in Swinburnian rhythms, and they expressed the various moods of an ardent, adventurous, active young man who knew the Western plains and the sea at Nahant. Lodge served in the Spanish War as an ensign in the navy, and he longed to get into the tide of American existence; but his plays were as remote from this as they were from the plays of the Greeks, which had none of their solemnity and abounded with life. In these accumulations of declamatory dialogue, the poet rebelled against the world he lived in; but there was something autumnal and sad in Lodge's note and Trumbull Stickney's, too little native hue, too much pale thought. Lodge received from Sturgis Bigelow a tincture of Buddhistic thinking, and Schopenhauer, Lucretius and Leopardi left traces in the minds of both these friends. The poet Savage was also elegiac. All were alone against the world, and in all one felt the weariness of lives "little in joy, little in pain." *

* "An important element in the tragedy of Oliver (not in his personality, for he was no poet) is drawn from the fate of a whole string of Harvard poets in the 1880's and 1890's—Sanborn, Philip Savage, Hugh McCulloch, Trumbull Stickney and Cabot Lodge . . . Now, all those friends of mine, Stickney especially, of whom I was very fond, were visibly killed by the lack of air to breathe. People individually were kind and appreciative to them, as they were to me, but the system was deadly, and they hadn't any alternative tradition (as I had) to fall back upon; and of course, as I believe I said of Oliver in my letter, they hadn't the strength of a great intellectual hero who can stand alone."—Letter of Santayana to William Lyon Phelps, discussing *The Last Puritan.*—Phelps, *Autobiography with Letters.*

No less lonely was George Edward Woodberry, who lived in exile in New York. He felt that he was an exile, both in time and in place, an exile from the old humane New England for which, like Barrett Wendell, he was born too late. He did not belong in this "mastodon age of gold;" and he saw his life "going down in the sands of the desert like a river born on the wrong side of the mountains." * A Beverly boy of the oldest descent, he had been a pupil of Henry Adams, and he was also a favourite of Norton's at Harvard. He had been regarded there as a natural successor of Lowell and by far the most promising of the younger poets. Woodberry had often lectured at Norton's Ashfield festivals and had written for *The Nation* under Godkin; and he had gone as a teacher to Nebraska before he settled in New York. He was professor of English at Columbia University, where he carried on a work that paralleled Wendell's. This was to convey to a rootless generation a feeling for the tradition of English letters, and, more than this, a feeling for the race-mind in general, as it had found expression in other great writers. Woodberry, whose critical sense was incomparably finer than Wendell's, was also a magnetic and powerful teacher. With a touch of the old Emersonian fire, he appealed to the poet in his pupils, inviting them to share his exaltation; and he made them feel that literature was a torch they were to carry on, the light of the developing mind of the race. His general papers were often vague,—they suggested a Transcendentalism too far from its source; but this was not true of the critical studies he devoted to Virgil, Cervantes, Montaigne, and to various English poets, Marlowe, Milton, Gray, Scott, Byron, Matthew Arnold. Some of these were masterly essays, overflowing with fresh ideas, the best that America offered, after Lowell's. The only essays that ranked with them were those of Lewis E. Gates, whose two small

* Woodberry's *Letters.*

volumes were drawn from lectures at Harvard. Gates, an instructor in composition,* was a first-rate critical writer. He died too soon to give the measure of his fine analytical talent.

In later years, Woodberry drifted back to Beverly and wandered through the Mediterranean lands. A lost and bewildered romantic, he was filled with a nostalgia for worlds that he had missed, he knew not how. All that he cared for he felt was "dying out of us,"—kindness, the honour of literature, all were gone. The old ideals had vanished; nothing was left but the din of traffic; he had no part or lot in this modern nation.† The desert, he felt, was the only fit place for him; and perhaps his travel-papers, after all, were the best of Woodberry's writings. His mood of self-pity resembled Henry Adams's, and, like Adams's letters in similar scenes, *North Africa and the Desert,* with its charming impressions, glowed with a life of the senses too long denied. Woodberry's poetry, good as it was,—and so much better than good in poems like *Wild Eden,*—seemed rather a distillation of all the other Victorian poets than anything individual or new. It carried on the line of Lowell at one remove still further from Lowell's masters, Tennyson, Milton and Keats; and it suggested that Woodberry, who had lived in books so ardently, had never lived at all in his age or his country. His contemporaries scarcely existed for him. In his little volume, *America in Literature,* he spoke of American literature as dead and gone. It had passed its prime in 1860,—it lay "a generation, and more, behind us;" and, as for the "period of dubious fame" in which the writer himself had lived, he found few names even to mention in it. Had he heard of Emily Dickinson? Had he heard

* Frank Norris wrote much of *McTeague* in Lewis Gates's classes. Gates's two volumes were *Studies and Appreciations* and *Three Studies in Literature.* Perhaps his finest essay was *Newman as a Prose-Writer.*

† *"I am not of it,* I am unhappy here, and the country has not the least use for me, or my books, or for poetry at all."—Woodberry's *Letters.*

of Melville? He had small use for Whitman, and Mark Twain, Howells and James meant little to him. This literature had wholly "failed to establish an American tradition," and it had failed to produce a poet "even of the rank of Gray." *

With teachers like Woodberry, whose note was much the same as Wendell's, the writers who came to maturity twenty years later felt that they were men without a country.† They were the intellectual children of men who had ceased to believe in the country, who had no faith whatever in their place and their time. If this coming generation was rootless, there were certainly other reasons for it, but the nostalgia of its teachers was one of the reasons. Woodberry's mind, like Wendell's, harked back to other times and places in which their imagination felt at home; and especially, in their inmost hearts, they longed again for England, which had more and more resumed its sway over the Yankee mind. No books were more popular than Kate Douglas Wiggin's *Penelope's English Experiences* and *A Cathedral Courtship*. Tours of cathedral towns were more in vogue than ever; and Louise Imogen Guiney was only one of a number of pilgrims who tramped over England with a stick and a pack and an oak-leaf badge in their hats for King Charles the Second. Miss Guiney connected her father with the cavaliers of Stuart times, and felt she was a cavalier's daughter; and from this atavistic fancy, followed in all good faith, she drew the inspiration of her poems and her es-

---

* "It behooves us, especially, to be modest, for our magnificent America has never yet produced a poet even of the rank of Gray."—Woodberry, Essay on Gray.

† Wendell, in his best book, *English Composition*, invariably referred, in his illustrations, to English authors, never American. He chose De Quincey instead of Hawthorne, Carlyle instead of Emerson, Hazlitt instead of Thoreau, etc., although these American authors were equally classics. Woodberry followed consistently the same half-unconscious policy. It was natural that younger writers growing up under these teachers should have felt that they had no tradition, although Woodberry and Wendell talked tradition, in season and out.

says. She supported herself as postmistress at Auburn-
dale, where her friends bought postage-stamps in enormous numbers to make her position more secure; and
later she worked as a cataloguer in the Public Library,
where Philip Henry Savage had a post. Dr. Holmes had
been charmed by her poems and called her his "little
golden guinea," although he was dismayed by the two
huge Newfoundland dogs with which the pretty young
poetess invaded his study. These poems had a fragile
beauty that constantly verged on the false-archaic, and
her mannered little essays were very self-conscious. She
imitated cavalier poems and early Christian ballads,
sometimes with mediæval spelling, for her gift was ven-
triloquistic and intensely bookish. But sometimes her
poetic note was true, direct and fresh,* and the prose of
her later essays was precise and distinguished.† *A Little
English Gallery,* papers on Farquhar, Henry Vaughan,
Hazlitt and two or three other less-known figures,
abounded in curious learning. She lived in a dream of the
seventeenth century, with other Bostonians of her time,‡
who often shared her interest in the Oxford Movement.§

In 1901, Miss Guiney went to live in England. The
rest of her life she spent in Oxford, a friend of Lionel
Johnson and Alice Meynell, with whom she had much in

* See *When on the Marge of Evening* and especially *A Talisman.*

† "My old friend Lionel Johnson once wrote to me: 'When I'm dead, the
colon won't have a friend in the world but you.' "—*Letters of Louise
Imogen Guiney.*

‡ Among other seventeenth-century poets, besides John Donne, to whom
Bostonians paid special attention, were Robert Herrick and George Herbert, an old New England favourite. The Harvard philosopher, George
Herbert Palmer, was named after the latter,—"so that I might always
have a friend," as Palmer said in his autobiography. Palmer published an
elaborate edition of *The English Works of George Herbert,* 3 vols., 1905.
Robert Herrick was the favourite poet. of Thomas Bailey Aldrich, who
planned to write a life of him. Aldrich's best essay was a fragment of
this otherwise unwritten biography.
See also Austin Warren's fine later study, *Richard Crashaw.*

§ One of Miss Guiney's many books was a life of Hurrell Froude. She
also made an anthology of the Recusant Poets. This was published in 1939,
nineteen years after her death.

common both in mind and in style. She had an American bust of Keats set up in the Hampstead parish church, and she paced the crowded Poets' Corner, measuring the flagging and the wall, hoping that Keats's ashes might be moved there. She tried to arrange for the recutting of Drayton's epitaph, and she rescued the grave of Henry Vaughan. These pieties of the romantic American were much like Delia Bacon's, while they expressed a wish to make amends for all that religious New England had represented. Meantime, various other New Englanders, who were scarcely aware of America, were also writing in England during these years. Howard Sturgis and Pearl Craigie,—John Oliver Hobbes,—were hardly American at all by experience or birth, and yet in certain traits of mind they recalled their long New England inheritance, and they were as detached in England as Whistler or James. Whistler had made a virtue of his rootlessness. He said, in his *Ten o'Clock*, in *The Gentle Art of Making Enemies*, "The master stands in no relation to the moment at which he occurs." That the artist was not a product of any place or any time was the doctrine that he preached on all occasions, and this enabled him to turn his sitters into "arrangements" and "harmonies," which had no sort of connection with the world they lived in. Swinburne observed that Phidias thought of other things than "arrangements" in marble, even as Æschylus had something in mind besides "arrangements" in metre. But Whistler wished to justify an art that had no roots in life. Meanwhile, he kept his Yankee twang; and was not Whistler's butterfly,—the signature of all his later works,—a reminiscence of Hawthorne and his early New England? * Whistler was something more than detached in London. He was antagonistic to the

* "The butterfly came and hovered about his head, and reinspired him, as, indeed, this creature of the sunshine had always a mysterious mission for the artist—reinspired him with the former purpose of his life."—Hawthorne, *The Artist of the Beautiful*.

English mind. All England was a bull for him into which
he thrust his banderillas, the barbed little notes that
sprang from the quills on his table. John Oliver Hobbes
and Howard Sturgis, beside Whistler, were English of
the English, but one found in their work an alien touch
that almost as clearly suggested the world they came
from. Howard Sturgis, Santayana's "quasi-cousin," a
dilettante of genius, was born in England, the son of
Russell Sturgis, the Boston China merchant who had become a partner of Baring Brothers; while Pearl Craigie,
born in Boston, had been taken there to live as a child,—
her father was an American manufacturer in London.*
Sturgis, who wrote *Belchamber,* an admirable novel, might
have been one of Henry James's heroes. He lived near
Windsor, in a "nest of cushions, of wit, and of tenderness,".† surrounded by dogs and a swarm of friends and
relations; and Edith Wharton recalled him later lying on
a sofa, with a basket of bright silks beside him.‡ For
knitting and embroidering were his favourite amusements;
he would work for hours at his embroidery-frame. As for
Belchamber, the sensitive, lame young marquis, who rebelled against his class and its barbarism, suggested, in
his vision of universal brotherhood, the Unitarian note
of an earlier epoch; and there was a deep ascetic strain in
John Oliver Hobbes that savoured of New England quite
as strongly. This brilliant, beautiful, witty woman felt, in
the world she satirized, that she was "an alien and a
stranger," and the theme of her earlier novels was the
theme of James. It was the plight of the artist in the

---

* John Morgan Richards, who, for a while, owned *The Academy,* one of
the principal organs of the circle of *The Yellow Book,* with which his
daughter was more or less connected.

† "My inimitable friend and quasi-cousin, Howard Sturgis, host and
hostess in one, who held court in a soft nest of cushions, of wit, and of
tenderness, surrounded by a menagerie of outcast dogs, a swarm of friends
and relations, and all the luxuries of life."—Santayana, preface to *The
Last Puritan.* It was in Sturgis's garden that Santayana professed to have
met Mario Van de Weyer, the young man in this novel.

‡ Edith Wharton, *A Backward Glance.*

world of fashion; and while, with her "knack of uttering literature as though it were conversation," to quote her own phrase about Lord Locrine, she showed that she understood this world, she was "in the wrong paradise," she was not at home there. She felt like "an air-bird in the water."

CHAPTER XXII

COUNTRY PICTURES

WHILE so many minds were turning towards England, an English writer, Rudyard Kipling, turned his face the other way. Kipling, like Stevenson, had married an American and had come to live in Vermont, near Brattleboro. His wife was a sister of Wolcott Balestier, a friend of Henry James's who had gone to London, where this young American novelist died of typhoid fever, a victim of his love of the picturesque. He had clung to his mouldy old chambers until they killed him. Kipling had met Balestier on his triumphal return from India and had written with this friend a romance, *The Naulahka,* a sort of Marion Crawford novel after which he named the ship-shaped house he built when he came to Vermont. In this house, where he spent three years, he wrote the *Jungle Books* and *Many Inventions,* and he hauled the dirt and spread the phosphate over the farm where he dug the well and where he took Monadnock for his weather-prophet.

Meanwhile, he roved about the country, falling in with Henry Adams and forming a strange alliance with Norton in Cambridge. Norton, who hated imperialism and found few other things to please him, wrote with extraordinary praise of the young man's poems. He said that Kipling carried on "the royal line of English poets," —which may have had its grain of truth, indeed, but was yet a surprising statement, coming from Norton. That Kipling was a nephew of Burne-Jones by marriage may well have been the reason for this singular outburst, for a tendency had developed in Boston to find a writer interesting because he was somebody's grandson or nephew or cousin.* Kipling made one or two visits to Gloucester at the time of the celebrations of the men who were lost or drowned in the codfishing fleet. With a doctor who had served in the fleet, he wandered about the water-front, dining in the sailors' eating-houses, boarding the schooners, examining the compasses and studying the charts old and new. His head was full of the Grand Banks when he also visited the old T-Wharf in Boston. Then he wrote *Captains Courageous* in his house in Vermont, a prose transliteration of Winslow Homer that was meant especially for boys. He had his own long thoughts about the Vermonters. He was struck by the loneliness and the desolation that other outsiders felt and the Yankees bewailed.† What might have been attributes and powers were perverted there, it seemed to him, and strange faiths and cruelties flourished like lichen on sick bark.‡

What Kipling thought about the natives other writers

* The witty Mrs. Bell explained the matter otherwise. "Someone expressed surprise at the admiration of Professor Norton and his family for Rudyard Kipling's poems. 'Of course they like them,' said Mrs. Bell. 'They never heard a bad word in their lives.' "—*Mrs. Bell,* by Paulina C. Drown.

There was, at this time, in Boston a distinct reversion to the "vulgar Quarterly standard,"—as Lowell had described it, apropos of the critics of Keats,—"measuring genius by genealogies." This was one of Barrett Wendell's foibles.

† See the remark of the woman in the farmhouse on the next ridge. "Be ye the new lights 'crost the valley yonder? Ye don't know what a comfort they've been to me this winter. Ye aren't ever goin' to shroud 'em up—or *be* ye?"—Kipling, *Something of Myself.* The Kiplings kept the lights bright on that side.

‡ "The land was denuding itself of its accustomed inhabitants, and their places had not yet been taken by the wreckage of Eastern Europe or the wealthy city-folk who later bought 'pleasure-farms.' What might have become characters, powers and attributes perverted themselves in that desolation as cankered trees throw out branches akimbo, and strange faiths and cruelties, born of solitude to the edge of insanity, flourished like lichen on sick bark."—Kipling, *Something of Myself.*

Mary E. Wilkins's *Madelon,* the scene of which was laid in Vermont, prefigured the well-known Kipling feud.

were also thinking, as many a story and poem had begun
to show. For, whether in Vermont, in Maine or Massachusetts, this was the view that prevailed at the moment,
and later. Few were able to see any longer what Sarah
Orne Jewett saw at the ends of the grass-grown cart-
tracks, choked by alders. The lights that glimmered in
lonely windows suggested thoughts that were far from
hers, although her idyllic scenes were sufficiently truthful.
All that Miss Jewett saw was there, but how much that
was sinister and dark she had failed to see! It was not the
desiccation merely that struck the younger writers, but
the skeletons in the cupboards, the sombre secrets. They
could scarcely imagine a time when this world was alive.

That Vermont itself had been very much alive one saw
in Rowland E. Robinson's stories and essays. This blind
old man, who had grown up at Ferrisburgh, over by the
shore of Lake Champlain, was writing a series of books
in the eighties and nineties that recalled the earlier times
for the natives themselves. Outsiders found it difficult to
read these books,—they were written in the purest Ver-
montese. Robinson, who had gone to New York as an
illustrator after the war, had returned to Vermont with
failing eyesight; and, unable to draw any longer, he had
taken to writing down his memories, while he supported
himself by raising sheep. The best Sheffield shears had
once been called the "True Vermonter," because of the
fame of the wool that was grown in these hills. But most
of the sheep had vanished now, and the cows outnumbered the people, and Robinson pictured the days before
the cows came, the days when the pioneers had struggled
up the rivers, with a flintlock, an axe and an ox-cart, and
the valleys swarmed with bears, wolves and panthers. All
this had happened within fifty years in Robinson's childhood; he had known survivors of the time; and he had
followed the streams and tramped the pastures when the
covered bridges and tanneries and grist-mills were new.

Blind as he was, he rambled over the country still, led by one of his children, and he knew the signs of the forest like an Indian hunter. His sensitiveness to sounds, the gift of the blind, had caused him to observe the varieties of speech he recorded all too faithfully in his dialect stories.* *Uncle Lisha's Shop* was the best of his books, with its scenes of the hearty life of the old Vermonters. The cordwainer, Uncle Lisha, was a kind of Yankee Uncle Remus, at home with the trout and the kingfisher, the muskrats and foxes, and his little shop was the social centre of a world that drew no social lines save that between eaters of white bread and eaters of buckwheat. There, on rainy days, in slack times, on winter evenings, the brotherhood of axe and gun assembled, Sam Lovel, the master of woodcraft, Peletiah, Solon Briggs, Joseph Hill and Antoine, the ingenious Canuck, who saw the axe-helves in the hickory, the baskets in the ash, the planks in the pine and hemlock, before he cut them, as Michael Angelo had seen the statue that lay in the uncut block. They stumbled over the frozen roads and fought their way through blizzards for a chance to sit on Uncle Lisha's sap-tubs; and, while the old man mended their boots, they swapped their yarns of the week's adventure, tales of sugar-making and bears in cornfields. The walls of Uncle Lisha's shop resounded with many a wondrous exploit of the rod and the gun.

This high-hearted older life had followed the frontier westward. Even Uncle Lisha had gone to Wisconsin; and the Yankees with the "real, old-fashioned, downright rustle and razzle-dazzle," with "git up and git," like Kipling's Tarvin, were building towns in Iowa and Colorado. The West attracted the men of Vermont even more than

---

* There are said to be seventeen dialects distinctly recorded in Robinson's books, those of the Indians, Canucks, Quakers, Yankee woodsmen, etc. All the kinds of American speech that were heard in the Green Mountains appear in *A Danvis Pioneer, Danvis Folks, Uncle Lisha's Shop, Uncle Lisha's Outing,* etc.

the other Yankees, and the young philosopher, John
Dewey, who was almost a neighbour of Robinson,—he
was born at Burlington, where he went to college,—had
first gone to Michigan as professor of philosophy before
he established his School of Education in Chicago. For
all the decay of the region, there was life enough in the
Yankee breed. John Dewey alone was enough to prove
it, Dewey whose passion for social democracy sprang
straight out of this rural Vermont. Twenty years later,
the hardy Dewey outrivalled all other Americans as a
leader of thought; and others who were children now,
scattered all over New England, were to show what re-
serves of energy the region possessed. Conrad Aiken, a
shoot of the oldest Yankee stock, brought to New Bedford from Savannah, lived as a boy in a house overlooking the harbour. He saw the last whaler setting out on its
last adventure, and the scenes of Herman Melville mingled in his eye with the nocturnal images of Albert Ryder.
Eugene O'Neill lived in New London. The son of an
Irish-American actor, he read Dumas from end to end
and swam every day in the Sound in the dead of winter.
He saw that his father's art had been ruined by the old
romantic drama, and he was turning away from the life
of the mask. What lay behind the mask? It was this that
concerned him, and some of this he saw as a schoolboy at
Stamford. He saw still more as a New London reporter.
On the coast of Maine, at Rockport and Rockland, Edna
St. Vincent Millay climbed the waves. She lived in a world
of anchors and shells and ships, and well she knew

> the green piles groaning
> Under the windy wooden piers,

the bell in the fog, the reach of the winter ocean. She had
in her bones the marrow of the Maine sea-farers. Longfellow had had this also, and, as he expressed it in songs
that recalled the Vikings, the scalds and the gleemen, so

she was to revive, in *The King's Henchmen,* the throbbing pulse and breath of Beowulf. Later, too, on this coast of Maine, overlooking the cedar-grown islands, beside the northern winter sea, Elinor Wylie found she was a poet; and T. S. Eliot's poems bore traces of the New England capes and harbours, the grey rocks, the woodthrush calling through the fog. At present, all over the region, with the ascendant summer resorts, colonies of artists were appearing. Howells, with whom the summer hotel was always a favourite *mise en scène,*—it brought so many types of Americans together,—pictured in *A Ragged Lady* and *The Landlord at Lion's Head* the gaieties and diversions of the summer people. Here one found the rustic philosophers who took the ladies for walks and talks, or, as they were called, "Tramps Home to Nature," the picnics that ended with readings from Browning, the chafing-dish parties, the coaching parades at which miracles were performed with cheesecloth and bunting. A young girl swathed in flowers represented the "Spirit of Summer," and the coaches, decked with goldenrod and asters, filed under the flag-draped arch that rose in the street. As for the colonies, Saint-Gaudens had established one at Cornish in 1885. The "Spirit of Summer" appeared in Saint-Gaudens's work, in forms that offended the taste of the sensitive Howells.* Abbott Thayer was

* Was not Howells right? Saint-Gaudens, in turn, disliked the realism of Howells.

"Your father was then slowly and desultorily completing the equestrian Sherman, and showed me with particular interest the figure of the Victory, which he said was studied from a young Southern girl. I owned that I did not like the introduction of the ideal in that group and the Shaw monument, but he defended it strongly, and, I have no doubt, effectually.

"Apropos of my realism, he told me a dream he had had about me. We were on shipboard together, and a dispute rose between the passengers as to the distance of a certain brilliant planet in the sky. Some said it was millions of miles away, but I held that it was very near, and he related that I went down to my stateroom and came up with a shotgun, which I fired at the star. It came fluttering down, and I said, 'There! You see!' "—Letter of Howells to Homer Saint-Gaudens, in *The Reminiscences of Augustus Saint-Gaudens.*

the centre of a colony at Dublin; * and at Stowe, in Vermont, Edward Martin Taber, who had studied painting
with Thayer, lived and wrote. He sketched the plants on
Mount Mansfield and he kept a journal that appeared as
Stowe Notes after his death, a record of observations
that revealed a grave and beautiful mind, with something
of Hans Andersen's feeling for winter. Few poems of the
nineties were touched with the natural magic of these unpretentious notes of the short-lived painter, scenes of winter nights, effects of landscape, of evening stars quivering
over the snow, comments on the changing winds, on the
light of the sunset gleaming through icicles or perhaps the
glitter of moonlight on the head of an axe. At Shelburne,
New Hampshire, in the Androscoggin valley, there was
another colony, especially of writers. Paul Elmer More
was writing there the first of his *Shelburne Essays;* and
Vida D. Scudder and Florence Converse spent their summers in this village. Miss Scudder, born in India, a missionary's daughter,—she had grown up, like More, on
the *Bhagavad-Gita,*—was one- of the Boston mediæval-
ists, well-known in her later years for her devoted study
of the Franciscan writings.† Paul Elmer More had a

---

* The Winslow Homer of the New Hampshire mountains. Thayer, a
naturalist in a world of naturalists, originated the study of protective col-
oration. (See *Concealing-Coloration in the Animal Kingdom,* a summary
of Thayer's discoveries, by his son, Gerald H. Thayer.) The development
of camouflage in the first world-war was largely a result of the theories of
Thayer.
    Near Dublin, at Chocorua, the summer home of the naturalist Frank
Bolles and William James, lived Truman H. Bartlett, the sculptor-
philosopher, who wrote the life of William Rimmer. For an admirable
picture of Bartlett and his circle,—he was one of E. A. Robinson's triumphant failures,—see Daniel Gregory Mason's *Music in My Time.*
    † Vida D. Scudder, a follower of Ruskin, Morris and Tolstoy, had stud-
ied at Oxford in the eighties. She was one of the first two American
women to do so; and there she had formed her lifelong feeling that the
Middle Ages, rather than the nineteenth century, were her "natural home."
During the eighties and nineties, she shared in the ferment of thought in
Boston, excited by Edward Bellamy and the settlement-houses, that seemed
to revive the fading emotions of the era of Brook Farm and Abolition. As
an active socialist, she sought for a *via media* between the Catholic Church

cabin by the road, with an inscription in Sanskrit over the doorway. More had appeared at Harvard in 1892, and there he had met Irving Babbitt, his brother-in-arms in a future crusade, who had returned to Cambridge after studying in Paris. The two formed together the whole of an advanced class that Professor Charles R. Lanman conducted in Sanskrit,* and they had begun to develop in common an attitude towards literature that grew from this early study of religion and ethics. New shoots of intellectual life were emerging all over the region, and at Derry, in these mountains, Robert Frost established himself on a farm at the end of the nineties. Frost, who was born in San Francisco, had returned as a boy to the land of his fathers, of which he was to become the unrivalled spokesman. He had made shoes and taught school, with intervals at Dartmouth and Harvard, and had written and even published a handful of poems. Two decades were to pass before the public heard of Frost, while he lived the obscure existence of an upland farmer.

Later, Frost affirmed and proved, as no one else for many years, the depth and the vigour of life that subsisted in New England. But he knew how much was morbid in it, and his early poems reflected a world of dearth,

and the teachings of Marx. Miss Scudder's Franciscan writings included two romances, *The Disciple of a Saint* and *Brother John,* and the fine historical study, *The Franciscan Adventure.*

Most of Florence Converse's early books had a Shelburne setting. Miss Converse's best work perhaps was the romance *Long Will,* about Langland and the vision of the Ploughman.

* Another of Lanman's pupils was Arthur W. Ryder, later professor of Sanskrit at the University of California. A Yankee sage and scholar, in some ways like Thoreau, Ryder maintained the traditional bond between the New England mind and the wisdom of the East. As indifferent to renown as Edward FitzGerald, he had much of the literary power of this English translator, and he was widely known for his admirable versions of the *Panchatantra,* the *Bhagavad-Gita,* the poems of Kalidasa, etc. His translations of the *Sakuntala* and *The Little Clay Cart* have been frequently produced on the stage.

Marion Crawford and T. S. Eliot were also pupils of Lanman, whose career as a teacher spanned three generations.

decay and desiccation. What Kipling glimpsed in this
Yankee life, Robert Frost knew all too well. Edwin Arlington Robinson also knew it; and there were summer
visitors, like Edith Wharton, and children who were to
write, like Eugene O'Neill, in whom this desiccation left
lasting impressions. They wondered about the black old
tenantless houses, where the windows lay in the grass and
the roof had tumbled in, the houses, damp and cold, with
people in them, where the rain had rotted the shingles,
the barns with wooden cages in dark corners, the double
houses of brothers who never spoke, the thresholds that
had never been crossed since someone's death. They wondered about the Yankees who had shut out humanity,
like all those sinister characters in Hawthorne's tales, in
whom the force of the past, repressed and turned inward, reeked with suspicion, hypocrisy, hatred and poison. What lay behind the shutters of the white Greek
temples, with the dark shadow-pines beside the door?
What secrets lurked in the graveyards, under the head-
stones, whose inscriptions, for the rest, were sometimes
true? The Yankee sun had shone over the world. It was
time for the moon to have its say, and these younger
writers saw what the moon saw. There were colonies of
savages near Lenox, queer, degenerate clans that lived
"on the mountain," the descendants of prosperous farmers.* There were old women poisoners in lonely houses.
There were Lizzie Bordens of the village, heroines in reverse who served the devil. There were Draculas in the
northern hills and witch-women who lived in sheds, luna-
tics in attics and men whose coffins hung with their bodies
from rafters, who had thought they could escape the
grass that waited, lapping round the walls, to catch them
when the old barn fell. The Yankee power had spread
over the world. It had launched a thousand clipper-ships;
it had despatched the Mormons to conquer Utah; it had

* See Charity Royall's people in Edith Wharton's *Summer*.

transformed the South Seas with its missions and planted schools all over heathen Asia. Now, having lost its outlet in the Yankee homeland, this power, at last inverted, devoured itself. There were Yankees like Heine's gods in exile, the gods who became diabolic when they could no longer be divine.

How terrible this power could be, turned backward on itself, few readers were aware in the eighteen-nineties. Others had to wait till Eugene O'Neill wrote *Mourning Becomes Electra*.* But Mary E. Wilkins, if one read between her lines, revealed, if not its terribleness, at least its strength; and there was a certain truth in Louise Imogen Guiney's phrase,—she was "a sort of sordid Æschylus." There was something fierce and primitive in her view of life, and the Furies existed for her, and for her, in the laws of range sublime, there was a mighty god that grew not old. It was a pity that her later books obscured the stories of her prime. Tragic at first, they became pathetic and often sentimental,—because Miss Wilkins had a village mind. As long as she wrote in terms of the village, she possessed the village integrity and all the grand inheritance of the Puritan faith; and this gave her a profundity that made her point of view, at moments, all but universal. But when she attempted to write novels, for which she was not qualified, and when she dealt with other than village types, she lost her universality and, along with this, the integrity that sprang from her village birthright. She did not understand the types Miss Jewett understood so well, the more cultivated life of the "mansion-houses,"

* Edith Wharton's *Ethan Frome* and O'Neill's *Desire Under the Elms* were examples of this drama of the later New England and all that is "warped and twists and eats into itself and dies for a lifetime." The scene of *Mourning Becomes Electra* was laid at the close of the Civil War, but the author's mood was that of his own moment. This play will remain, no doubt, as the classic picture of a singular phase of New England.

Ethan Frome, good as it was, could not compare with the best of Miss Wilkins. Its plot was factitious, and it had the air of a superior person surveying the squalid affairs of these children of fate.

where the women wore "blue-lavender silk" instead of the calico dresses she knew, or instead of the "one black silk that stood alone." Her attitude towards all this was that of the other village women, resentful yet romantically dazzled; * and as, with success, she moved from her early position and outgrew her resentment of the rich, her romantic admiration of them took the upper hand and she lost her hold on the verities for which she had spoken. She became unreal and self-conscious in the presence of high life, regarding which she was driven to write too much, and she cut her people to fit the story instead of letting the story spring out of the people. But in some of her early tales, perhaps twenty or thirty,† she was an eminent artist, as eminent as Miss Jewett, and even more so, because of the depth of feeling that informed her art. In one sense, Miss Wilkins warranted all the laments of Boston. She revealed the desolation of the Yankee ebb-tide. But, better than anyone else, she also pictured the powers of last resistance in the Yankee soul. Was the Yankee soul at bay? At least, its lights were burning,— this was the fact at the heart of Miss Wilkins's tales. It was quick to fight for its self-respect, and even for perfection, whatever the odds might be and whatever its fate.

Although she had lived for a while in Vermont, Miss Wilkins was born in a Boston suburb, the daughter of a

* This attitude of the village women was reflected in *The Jamesons,* one of Miss Wilkins's longer stories. The Jamesons were city-people who settled in the village and tried to "improve" it. They were almost totally absurd, but Miss Wilkins only partially saw this. She saw that they overdid the "Browning readings," which were meant to enlarge the "sphere" of the village mind, but she could not stand up stoutly for the village. She shared its curiosity and resentment, and also all its dazzled admiration.

Mary E. Wilkins suggested Matilde Serao, as Henry James described this Italian writer: "Madame Serao is at her best almost in direct proportion as her characters are poor. By poor I mean literally the reverse of rich; for directly they *are* rich and begin, as the phrase is, to keep their carriage, her taste totters and lapses, her style approximates to that of the ladies who do the fashions and the letters from the watering-places in the society papers."—Henry James, *Notes on Novelists.*

† Mostly in *A Humble Romance, A New England Nun* and *People of Our Neighbourhood.*

carpenter in Randolph; and she had returned there in
1883, the year in which she published her first story.*
Randolph at that time was not a suburb. It was a fading
Yankee village, and this was the moribund village,—the
symbol of hundreds of others,—that appeared in her stories. In its dilapidated houses dwelt a race that seemed to
be dying, as shell-fish on a shoal that is seldom reached by
the tide wither and perish at last when deprived of water.
To begin with the shells, the houses, they were usually
mortgaged. Sometimes they had never been painted and
the shingles were falling off like scales, while the roof
sagged, with its holes, in a mossy hollow. If they had been
painted, only a few discoloured patches remained to prove
a fact one seldom guessed. The doors and windows were
often awry, and the doorsteps were sunk among the
grasses, as if the houses were settling into their graves.
The barns were generally deserted, and a few rusty tools
and the phantom of a sulky alone suggested that they had
ever been used. Most of the apple-trees were too aged
and sapless to blossom freely. They had deteriorated
along with the houses, and the apples were small, hard
and sour. Within, the houses breathed an "icy wind of
loneliness," a characteristic phrase of Miss Wilkins herself. The clock had often gone dead, and no one could
make it tick any longer. The parlour and the kitchen were
the only rooms that visitors saw; and the kitchen was the
scene of all the life,—that is, the social life,—which the
house admitted. The parlour was commonly used for
funerals only, and it sometimes had no carpet on the floor.

---

* Miss Wilkins disclaimed the influence of other writers, though, like
Miss Jewett, whom she had not read, she walked in her own way in the
footsteps of Howells. She had read Turgenev, and, like others of the nineties,—Stephen Crane and Hamlin Garland,—she felt the need of a realism
more drastic than Howells's. She said that she was afraid of reading. She
feared that other writers might blur her mental pictures, showing how
aware she was that her vein was thin. She knew that she might be over-
powered; and as, from other causes, this actually happened, she was right
for herself in regard to the cause in question.

There stood the shabby haircloth rocker and sofa, shabby
alike from age and excess of care; for the haircloth had
been house-cleaned through so many seasons that its holes
represented much besides its years. A clove-apple, a nau-
tilus shell shared the shelf with bits of china. Perhaps
there were two or three pieces with lavender sprigs, each
one an heirloom of incalculable value, as precious as a
rajah's ruby to the members of the household. Framed
coffin-plates hung on the walls, together with funeral-
wreaths that had sometimes been woven from the hair of
five generations. A great-grandsire's hair had provided
the acorns, a grandmother's curls had yielded the leaves,
and the lilies had come from the tresses of an aunt, which
had turned a greenish yellow in her last illness. Uncle
Abijah's hair had produced the poppies; the rosebuds
were souvenirs of Lois. On the mahogany table lay Mrs.
Hemans and Mrs. Sigourney, bound in red and gold, and
perhaps a photograph-album with views of the Holy
Land or pictures of uncles and cousins who had died or
gone West. Death pervaded the air, and what remained
of life seemed to have reached a state of fossilization.

Such was the setting, and the people were in harmony
with it. They were mostly old, and mostly women; and
their object in living seemed to be to keep out of the poor-
house and get safely settled in their graves. If they
avowed an object, this was to pay off the mortgage, an
effort that almost always proved to be hopeless. They
were content if they kept one hen that laid one egg a day.
They were village-bound, and they were house-bound. Beyond the horizon of the village, they had no thoughts;
and whether they had thoughts below the village was a
question that strangers asked as seldom as whether or not
they possibly had thoughts above it. As for a social life,
they scarcely knew the phrase existed, although they still
had quilting bees and apple-paring bees and sometimes
did housewifely jobs for more opulent neighbours that led

to an interchange of words. When one of these opulent neighbours sent them some lamb-broth, they responded with a gift of peas or turnips; for there were mansions in the village, two or three big square houses where a ghost of the old prosperity still existed. More often, even there, one found only a lone old maid, who hoarded her burial-money in the musty chambers. Perhaps she had a mania for asking folks to tea, which meant that she asked them once a fortnight. For the rest, the village women wove rag-carpets and braided rugs, and they knocked at one another's doors to borrow a pitcher of milk or return an egg. If one of them went to Boston, she was more than likely to make her will; for how could she count upon surviving a ten-miles' journey on the railroad? The young people, such as there were, had Christmas sings and annual picnics, usually on the Fourth of July; and the brisker girls were often called "fast quilters." But, as if to settle the social question, the secretaries were squarely shut, unless one had to find a will or a deed. Only the kitchen door ever stood open.

The village life was plainly dying. There were very few young men, and the young girls were delicate, ailing and fading. They seemed to be always "going down," condemned to an early death from nerves or consumption. They were often left alone to look after the house. They supported themselves by making shoes or doing the village fancy-work, contriving tidies or lambrequins in red worsted and beads or colouring prints of crosses twined with flowers. They had been taught to sew their square of patchwork or seed and pick over the raisins before their supper, and to knit lace edging for the store and get a reputation for it was the best way to keep them in bacon and butter. Sometimes the young men who had gone West came back after twenty years; and their notion of a pleasant walk was to visit Mr. Sims's grave and see what sort of flowers had been placed upon it. They carried on their courtships in the graveyard,—that is, when they were able to speak their minds; but more often they were the victims of misunderstandings. Occasionally, two lovers sat side by side on a haircloth sofa every Sabbath evening for eighteen years and never reached the point of raising the question. Perhaps they were "too terrible set;" or possibly, after eighteen years, the question of marriage had ceased to have any importance. Often they gave it up for a nervous whim. But now and then a woman waited thirty years for the letter that was always coming and never came,—she stopped the postman every day at noon. Most of the women settled into spinsterhood, and they turned their minds to substitutes for love. They hid their best chemise in the lowest bureau-drawer, where the neighbours could find it and use it to bury them in; and they filled their jars and sugar-bowls with rose-leaves, or they collected cats, or they expressed their thirst for action by changing the position of the books on the table. They shifted the views of the Holy Land from the right-hand corner to the left-hand corner or reversed the china cups with the lavender sprigs. The bony figures of aging spinsters dominated the village scene, where one might have supposed that the end of the world was at hand. Stiffnecked and tough-minded, they seemed to be fighting a losing battle against fire, mortgages and illness and almost as much against life as they fought against death. Beyond them stood the almshouse. Beyond the almshouse stood the graveyard. An air of winter twilight enveloped all.

This seemed to be the whole story. Strangers thought so, readers thought so, albeit a handful of readers received from Miss Wilkins another impression, and of another order. In what way was her picture "sordid"? Sometimes these women were driven to steal; and this had an air of the sordid,—they certainly felt so. They stole a loaf of bread, or a few toys for the children's

Christmas, or a glass or two of milk from a cow in the pasture. They thought this was sordid; but was it not true that they alone had the right to think it? They measured themselves by the highest standard of honour; and, pinched as they were, they drank of the water of life, however the buckets were rusty and the dippers were small. Socially, their days were nil, from the point of view of the city-people, and they clung to the cliff of existence with the tips of their fingers. They were suspicious, and they were superstitious; they were hard, inquisitive and odd, and their actions were often mechanical, or appeared to be so. They tucked pieces of camphor under the wings of stuffed canaries; they spent the whole spring cleaning house, and sometimes they had the boards of the parlour floor arranged so that they could be lifted and cleaned on the under-side. Much of this was morbid, and a boarder needed the help of heaven to survive amid these terrible exactions. But what did these exactions mean? What lay behind these morbid activities? Was it not because the men were absent that the women minded their households to this degree? Besides, these habits spoke of a thirst for perfection that could not command its field of action, or, rather, could command no larger field. The temperament that cleaned the under-side of floor-boards would have cleaned the under-side of a government also, if it had had the government instead of the parlour; and in any larger sphere,—the running of a homestead,—these habits would have had their normal sweep. Indeed, in former days, they had had their sweep. The forbears of these desperate women, two or three generations earlier, had been prosperous farmers, statesmen and mothers of households; and they, in their unmanned sphere, without enterprise or politics, were living up to the sphere in which they had thriven. The situation, not the persons, produced the morbid symp-

toms; and the women who had for their supper one-half
of a cold boiled potato and a spoonful of jelly and saved
their one egg for the morning were contending for something far more important than thrift. As they could not
alter conditions, they lived within them; and, living within
the conditions, they mastered the conditions and kept a
margin for their souls to grow in. Well, then, what a triumph to pay off the mortgage, to become as free once
more as their forbears had been; or, if they could not do
this, to have a black silk dress or a bonnet with black-
thread lace and a tuft of jet. This was really living, and
they lived with zest. To keep up with the neighbours was
to keep up with their forbears, or, one might rather say,
to keep up with themselves; and, if they resented the rich
and were dazzled by them, this implied no loss of self-
respect. It was merely the tribute to *savoir-faire* which
those who do not know the world inevitably pay to those
who do,—at the moment, for the period, of their confrontation; for, in the unsophisticated, this frame of mind
rapidly passes when they return to their sphere and resume their standards. As long as their sphere maintains
its integrity, they are safe, remaining in it. Only when
they lose it do they lose their values; then, emulating
others, they are lost indeed. They have had no prepara-
tion for the world. This happened, in some degree, with
Miss Wilkins; and it happened to countless other villagers who became, not sentimental, as she, but vulgar. For
the rest, their aesthetic sense betrayed them. It hankered
after a beauty it had scarcely earned; whereas, on its own
ground, this sense was firm. On its own ground, it throve
on two willow-ware dishes as in few of the tourists who
gaped through the rooms of the Louvre. Whitman understood the lilac in the dooryard, and readers of Miss
Wilkins soon discovered that a rhododendron-bush was a
sacred symbol, or an oleander-tree, pink with blossoms,

the only spot of colour in a shabby old house; and those
for whom these aging women seemed to be creating nothing might have changed their minds if they had seen what
lay behind the bush or the oleander. What lay behind the
yellow stand with its heliotropes and geraniums? In pos-
sibility, what did it represent? Or the lombardy poplar
that signified "company"? Or the blinds that one had always wished for? Or the window facing the road that one
did not have? They were all symbols of life for people
who were filled with a passion for life that was very seldom shared by city-dwellers; for those who prefer to
starve rather than say they are hungry are living as
the well-fed seldom live. All these villagers lived with a
vengeance; and, however the weft of their tapestry was
worn and thin, its warp was as sinewy and as firm as ever.
This may have been the grimmest of all the well-known
Yankee jokes. Both whimsical and grim, it was also grand.

Thus, underneath Miss Wilkins's village something
lurked that was still sublime, although it was true that
the village guarded its secret. It exacted from fate every
last penny of tribute. Those who, like many Bostonians,
were already disheartened found evidence in Miss Wilkins's dun-coloured stories to suppose that Yankeeland
had come to an end. Perhaps it had, on the old basis; and
there was always the chance that it could not react any
longer to new conditions. It may have been pushed to the
wall and beyond the wall. But is it not a law of life that,
the more it is repressed, the more intense the will to live
becomes,—provided it is able to survive at all,—and that
if, at last, it finds an outlet, it expresses itself in proportion to its former repression? What fate was in store for
New England? Were the Barrett Wendells right? Was
its prospect really as dark as Miss Wilkins seemed to
show it? In so far as writers counted, the prospect was
reassuring; for writers emerging all over the region were
to suggest before long that the Yankee stock was hale

and as virile as ever. They were a proof that the real New England was not to be found in the Barrett Wendells or in what Miss Wilkins's stories appeared to show. They proved that the reality was what Miss Wilkins really showed, in her plain, stark, factual tales.

CHAPTER XXIII

THE ADAMSES

THE heyday of the Boston historians had come to an
end with Parkman, but a number of other historical
writers carried on the school that Bancroft, Sparks and
Prescott had established. As a man of letters, only Henry
Adams compared with the great triumvirate, Prescott,
Motley and Parkman, although John Fiske's art of exposition almost amounted to genius. James Ford Rhodes
and Edward Channing were distinctly inferior to these.
What one missed in their work was the grand design of
the older men, the shaping imagination and the narrative power. Godkin's remark was largely true,—"science
killed the imagination;" for where Prescott, Motley and
Parkman had recreated the past, these later historians
could only describe and explain it.

There were few sparks of the artist in Channing. He
scarcely wished to be thought a writer. That history was
a form of literature seemed to him to mean that it could
not be a form of science, and his work, with all its dignity, was bald and humdrum. For the rest, in scope and
massiveness, his *History of the United States,** covered
its field better than any other. James Ford Rhodes had
come from Cleveland. There, in his early years, in the
coal and iron business, he had been Mark Hanna's partner. He had retired to Boston with a fortune, after study-

---

* From the beginning to 1865, six volumes. Edward Channing was the
son of Ellery Channing, the poet, the friend of Emerson and Thoreau in
Concord. He was also a nephew of Margaret Fuller. He had been one of
Henry Adams's pupils, and he had planned in college the work to which
he devoted the rest of his life.

ing in Paris and Berlin, and he carried on there for twenty
years the work that he had already begun in Ohio. His
History of the United States, in seven large volumes, covered the years from 1850 through the post-bellum period
of reconstruction. It was best in its account of the Civil
War, for Rhodes was too much the plain man of business, immersed in current politics and finance, to discuss
with imagination a country at peace. Nothing concerned
him deeply but questions of tariffs and panics, and his psychology was crude, and his style was a dignified news-
paperese. The decline of humanistic interests was notable
in these later historians, marked as it was in the audiences
for whom they wrote. Bancroft had written for statesmen and farmers, and Prescott, Motley and Parkman for
lovers of letters. Channing wrote for his graduate students, whose interests were special and technical, Rhodes
for men of business like himself.

Meanwhile, the Adams brothers, Brooks and Charles
Francis, were following Henry Adams in history-writing.
Charles Francis Adams had always felt that his real vocation was history, and he had retired, like Rhodes, from
business, to work over his father's papers. He planned a
diplomatic history of the Civil War, and, while this remained unwritten, he felt that any sort of historical writing was like coming "out of the darkness and into the
light." He became a local chronicler of the utmost distinction, for, working on a small canvas, he revealed an instinctive taste and skill that were never achieved by the
bolder Rhodes and Channing. He saw the men and events
of Massachusetts as he saw French or English men and
events, with the same realism and the same detachment,
and his picture of the bigotry of early New England,
which he compared with Spain, was a blow to conventional notions of ancestor-worship. He described as the
Massachusetts "ice-age" the period from 1637 to the
Boston renaissance of the eighteen-thirties; but, deplor-

ing its religious life, he showed how Massachusetts had advanced the cause of civil liberty. The finest of all his papers was the history of Quincy, which remained a model in its field.* "Otherwise-minded," like all the Adams brothers, he detested a civilization of business men; † and he was an anti-imperialist, who did not believe in the "white man's burden," for he felt that any self-government of the people involved was better than any government imposed from without. He regarded his education as a series of errors, in this, as in other ways, resembling Henry; ‡ but his historical writing was wholly concrete. He was not interested in the "laws" of history, and he contributed little to the well-known Adams philosophy that kindled so much interest in the years to come.

This Adams philosophy, bleakly fatalistic, expressed the dominant mood of the later New England. There the vision of Lucretius appealed to many minds as the only true one. They rejoiced in the vivid strokes with which he described the approach of death, lassitude in pleasure, the fatigue of the will and the final disposition of the atoms of the soul, lost in the universal flux.§ The only

* *A Study of Church and Town Government,* in *Three Episodes of Massachusetts History.* It seems safe to say that this is, by all odds, the finest history of an American town that has ever been written.

† "As I approach the end, I am more than a little puzzled to account for the instances I have seen of business success—money getting. It comes from a rather low instinct. Certainly, so far as my observation goes, it is rarely met with in combination with the finer or more interesting traits of character. I have known, and known tolerably well, a good many 'successful' men —'big' financially—men famous during the last half-century; and a less interesting crowd I do not care to encounter. Not one that I have ever known would I care to meet again, either in this world or the next; nor is one of them associated in my mind with the idea of humour, thought or refinement. A set of mere money-getters and traders, they were essentially unattractive and uninteresting."—*Autobiography of Charles Francis Adams.*

‡ Charles Francis Adams quoted with approval Lowell's remark, "The Adamses have a genius for saying even a gracious thing in an ungracious way."

§ Lucretius was constantly quoted during these decades in Boston. Santayana's essay, in *Three Philosophical Poets,* was only the finest of many utterances about him.

fact was force, irresistible, unchangeable, a conception
that spread through the world as the century waned; and
this doctrine had a special appeal in New England, where
faith in the will and in progress had once been so strong.
That the old aspirations were delusions was the teaching
of William Graham Sumner, the great Yale sociologist
who expressed the mood of the moment better than the
novelists and poets. This hard-headed realist, the son of
an English workingman, with a voice like a howitzer in
action, attacked every cause that New England had stood
for. He did not deny the doctrine of progress. He followed Herbert Spencer. He introduced Spencer at Yale,
fighting for the right to teach him there as John Fiske
had fought ten years before at Harvard. But he scouted
all the New England conceptions of progress. He ridiculed "ethical views of wealth," reform, popular education, the "absurd attempt to make the world over." Sumner, for good or ill, was one of the minds that formed the
future. He developed, in *Folkways,* the anthropological
view of ethics. There were no ethical forces in history, he
said, and good and evil had no reality except as expressions of the mores, the customs and habit-patterns of the
time and the place. As the father of all the "debunkers,"
Sumner exposed myths and legends. What· Ethan Allen
said at Ticonderoga was something very different, as he
conceived it, from what the wishful historians had always
reported. But, while he attacked cant, he undermined, as
no one else, the ancient humanitarian faith of the Yankees.
He was a preacher of force in a world of fate.

  Now, certainly this was very far from the point of
view of William James, a more influential American
thinker than Sumner, and William James also expressed
New England, or a large and living section of New England feeling. James's conception of life was the reverse of
Sumner's, and so was Josiah Royce's conception of life,
which differed in so many ways from James's and yet as-

serted quite as much the power of the individual as opposed to fate. Both were deeply religious natures and
ardent humanitarians, and James had quarrelled with
Spencer's fatalism, which lay behind William Graham
Sumner's and which ignored the patent fact that progress
is not automatic but that subjective interests govern it
also. As a psychologist, he had explored the range of
these subjective interests. No one had ever explored them
so thoroughly before; and James had remained an opti-
mist, a convinced free-willist who believed that the power
of the will could redeem the world. Through all the
changes of his time, William James had kept the buoyant
faith of Emerson and the old Brook Farmers; and he had
consistently preached the gospel of individual effort as a
means of achieving personal and social freedom. Detest-
ing every tyranny, the worship of power, the "bitch-
goddess Success," the omnipotence of science, he fought
them and believed in fighting them, believed that the
struggle availed,—fought for the Boers against the English, for the Filipinos against America, for the private
against the officer, for youth against age, and especially
for the new against the old. For he believed in the future
intensely, believed in the reign of peace and justice, believed that human effort could bring it about; and he
believed in the utmost of human variability. Was not the
least of God's creatures worthy of respect? And who was
to judge the value of another creature? Might not the
last prove to be the first? He sought to evoke the potential energies that people possessed without knowing it,
showing that these energies would grow with use; and he
attacked the bosom-vices of modern civilization, swin-
dling, adroitness and cant, and sang the praises of poverty, loyalty and honour. In all this, James was governed
by a passionate faith in human nature and its power to
mould, control and create the world.

James exerted over the country a more effective influ-

ence than any of these other New England thinkers. With
his wealth of imaginative sympathy, his sinewy mind, his
tolerance, spontaneity and magnetism, he threw into cir-
culation more general ideas than any American thinker
since Emerson, perhaps. His notion of the stream of consciousness fed the minds of novelists. His "moral equiva-
lent of war" was a memorable counsel. His antithesis of
the tough-minded and the tender-minded was one of the
fertile suggestions in which he abounded. In his Protean
imagination,* his feeling for concrete realities, for all varieties of experience, James was an artist; and he was a
"high-hearted freeman," †—one of his phrases,—who
imputed to others the power that he found in himself.
Moreover, James, who was more humane than any of the
Adamses, was quite as realistic as they or Sumner. But,
while he expressed the mood of the nation, they expressed
the regional mood, or what seemed to be this mood at the
end of an epoch.

That man could not control his world was the Adamses'
doctrine as well as Sumner's, although Sumner believed
that fate worked out for the good. For Brooks Adams,
Henry's younger brother, the "law of force and energy"
was the only law, and it foreboded no good in a visible
future. He had conceived a theory of history, partly
drawn from Marx, that in many ways anticipated Speng-
ler, for he saw civilization as proceeding in cycles, pro-
pelled by fear and greed, in which the individual counted

* "Can we realize for an instant what a cross-section of all existence at
a definite point of time would be? While I talk and the flies buzz, a sea-
gull catches a fish at the mouth of the Amazon, a tree falls in the Adirondack wilderness, a man sneezes in Germany, a horse dies in Tartary and
twins are born in France."—James, *The Principles of Psychology.*

† Sigmund Freud recalled a moment when he and James were walking
together, during Freud's visit to America in 1909,—James "stopped suddenly, handed me a bag he was carrying and asked me to walk on, saying
that he would catch me up as soon as he got through an attack of angina
pectoris which was just coming on. He died of that disease a year later,
and I have always wished that I might be as fearless as he was in the face
of approaching death."

for nothing. Fear gave birth to superstition, and this to religion, in turn, and religion produced an accelerated social movement that led to a civilization governed by greed. The instinct of greed supplanted the instinct of fear and gradually dissipated in war and trade the energy that religion had developed. Such were the oscillations between barbarism and civilization, in which the greatest men, like the floods and the whirlwinds, were merely natural forces. No use to regret the past or oppose these mighty revolutions, which were inevitable and automatic. Nations must float with the tide, and men must float with them. Society could never reach a permanent equilibrium, and only change was constant. But, regarding as futile all opposition to natural forces, Brooks Adams claimed the right to express his taste; and he could not forgive an age in which pig-iron was more important than poetry. The times that bred religion bred also the imaginative mind, and the artist and craftsman arose with the warrior and the priest. These were Brooks Adams's chosen ages, and the age of the French cathedrals led all the rest. For Brooks Adams shared his brother's interest in architecture and saw it as the highest expression of religious faith. As the bankers won the day over warrior, priest, craftsman and mystic, the emotional life and civilization withered; and Brooks Adams saw his world at the dying end of one of these cycles in *The Law of Civilization and Decay*.

This book was published in 1895, long before Henry Adams's *Education;* and Brooks had anticipated Henry in applying to history the laws of physics, of acceleration, retardation and mass. Henry adopted the second law of thermo-dynamics as explaining the world in which he lived, the law of the degradation of energy,—the universe was running down, it was losing its vital energy and was headed for death. Was it a universe? It seemed to

him a multiverse, a random manifestation of aimless
forces, of which man was as much the sport as the trees
and the rocks. He had discussed these theories with his
brother, who was living at the old house in Quincy during
his Washington years; and his mind had turned, like
Brooks's, to the age of the French cathedrals as one in
which he might have felt at home. For then, whatever the
universe was, man felt it was a universe, and he held the
highest idea of himself as an active participant in it.

What struck the reader in all this, when Adams printed
his *Education,* was rather his wish to believe it than the
theory itself. Could one apply to history the laws of physics? These laws, in the first place, were constantly changing, and the theory of relativity invalidated soon the laws
that Henry Adams accepted as final. All attempts to cor-
relate history with science were exploded as time went on,
as historians perceived that history, as it actually was, is
not and cannot be known.* Adams's conception, then, was
a vast and intricate rationalization. It was what he wished
to be true; and he evidently wished it in order to find an
excuse for the chaos and futility of his own existence. If
the world was chaotic and futile, it relieved him of all responsibility for the scattering of his own energies, his
defeated ambition, for the unresolved conflict between his
tastes and his inheritance, for the anarchy of the forces
that dwelt within him. Adams's soul was the "multiverse."
He was the chaos.†

For twenty years, Henry Adams, globe-trotting or sitting at home, had been gleefully watching the world going

* For the various reasons why history cannot be correlated with science,
see Charles A. Beard, *The Discussion of Human Affairs,* pp. 85-86.

† Admirably as he wrote on most occasions, there was no unity even in
Adams's style. Except for certain recurrent conceptions and phrases, the
history, the novels, the memoirs of the Queen of Tahiti, the *Education* and
Mont-Saint-Michel and Chartres might all have been written by different
hands.

to the devil.* Dead himself, as he liked to say, "stone coffin dead," landed, lost and forgotten, he lived alone in his Washington house, a "long-established ghost." One saw him on horseback, riding alone in Rock Creek Park, with his air of an emperor in exile, or out for his daily walk with Hay. At home he played solitaire, studied physics and read Byzantine books, gloating over the fall of the Roman Empire. He never dined out any longer, but ambassadors and statesmen thronged his house; and he saw himself as an old courtier, "sitting among the mighty, and sneering at them to their faces." † He had once thought of himself as a sort of American Horace Walpole, recording the manners of his time, and many of his letters, when they were published in after years, justified this one of his many ambitions. They abounded in sketches and flashes of the rarest insight. But this was not enough to satisfy him. He had "too much ego in his cosmos," like Kipling's Bimi. He winced when he saw himself mentioned as "the late Henry Adams," although for a dozen years he had covered his tracks. He was bitter when the cab-drivers pointed out his house as the residence of the late Charles Francis Adams. "He lives well that has lain well hidden," Abraham Cowley said; but this was not what Adams had really desired. The sense of his obscurity rankled in him, and he was still consumed with the "insanity of restlessness" that had filled him ever since the death of his wife. Wherever his friends

* "One revelled at will in the ruin of every society in the past, and rejoiced in proving the prospective overthrow of every society that seemed possible in the future."—*The Education of Henry Adams.*
"To me the crumbling of worlds is always fun."—Letter of 1914.
† "I am sitting here in Washington just as you left me ten years ago. I have grown so used to playing the spider, and squatting in silence in the middle of this Washington web, and I have seen so many flies and other insects caught and devoured in its meshes, that I have now a little the sense of being a sort of ugly, bloated, purplish-blue and highly venomous hairy tarantula which catches and devours Presidents, senators, diplomats, congressmen and cabinet-officers, and knows the flavour of every generation and every country in the civilized world."—Letter of 1899.

beckoned, there he went, to Egypt with the Hays, to Constantinople and Greece with the ambassador Rockhill,
with the Lodges to Caen and Coutances. It was in Paris
that he fell in with Trumbull Stickney, with whom he discussed Greek philosophy, and saw most of George Cabot
Lodge, whose life he wrote when this young poet died;
and it was during these years that he rediscovered the
twelfth century and made the preliminary studies for the
finest of his books. Saint-Gaudens took him to Amiens,
and La Farge to Chartres, where again they discussed
stained glass together; and Adams spent whole summers
in Champagne and Touraine, visiting parish churches,
"collecting spires," wandering through the streets of
Troyes with Joinville, till he felt he was a "twelfth-
centurian." He had begun to realize a prophecy of his
earlier years, that art was to give him his greatest advantage and pleasure.* His contempt for the present grew
with his love for the past. He wandered from desert to
desert and from Ritz to Ritz, "playing with the toys
of childhood, Ming porcelain, salons, operas, theatres,
beaux-arts;" and everywhere, "dead," but "gay as a rabbit," examining the great hall of Karnak, and the domes
of Justinian and Constantine, he saw the jackal creeping
down the ruin. England was "cardiacally diseased," Spain
was "extinct," Austria was "splayed," France was "rotten." Each year, his "beloved old senile wreck of Europe"
was more decrepit than ever.† It was at its last gasp;
and, as for his own country, nothing in it seemed to him
worth preserving. The illusions of young men occasionally touched him, and perhaps a remnant of faith still

* "After all, I shall get most pleasure and (I believe) advantage from
what never entered into my calculations, Art."—Letter of 1858.

† "The more I live here in western Europe, the more I am impressed
with the sense of decay,—not the graceful and dignified decay of an Oriental, but the vulgar and sordid decay of a bankrupt cotton-mill."—Letter
of 1898.

glimmered in his breast.* But, on the whole, for him, it was over and done with, and he was for forcing the pace and speeding the ruin.†

Now, certainly, in the pre-war years, much in Adams's view of the world was penetrating, truthful and prophetic. He felt the nightmare of those years. He sensed the impending calamity. He perceived that the old order was collapsing. He saw that Russia was "sailing straight into another French Revolution;" and he foresaw the collectivized world of the future. Although he did not like it, he knew that a socialist order was bound to follow the downfall of the one he had known; and, while he abused all the statesmen who were trying to bring it about, he even recommended a socialist system as the only one that could work in the given conditions.‡ He felt that even

* When Owen Wister called upon him in 1912, Adams said, "What do you think of the state of things in this country?"

"I shook my head," wrote Wister, "and said nothing.

"'Our old friend over there,' continued Henry Adams, with a wave towards the White House, where we had spent such unforgettable hours in the days of the Roosevelts, 'did his best. But whose best could save us?'

"'Oh, well. I don't feel as black as all that about it.

"'You don't? With that saturnalia going on up there?' And he waved in the direction of the Capitol.

"Again I shook my head.

"He continued to look at me with his most gimlet-like expression. Then, suddenly, his countenance softened. His eyes grew warm, he got out of his chair, came over and laid his hand on my arm, and in a voice quite changed said, 'Keep the faith!'"
—Owen Wister, *Roosevelt, the Story of a Friendship.*

† "Hating vindictively, as I do, our whole fabric and conception of society . . . I shall be glad to see the whole thing utterly destroyed and wiped away . . . My view of the case is always to encourage the big thieves and to force the pace. Let's get there quick! I'm for Morgan, McKinley and the Trusts! They will bring us to ruin quicker than we could do it ourselves."—Letters of 1893 and 1895.

‡ "The world is abjectly helpless. It is running a race to nowhere, only to beggar its neighbours. It must either abolish its nationalities, concentrate its governments and confiscate its monopolies for social economies, or it must . . . founder, at last, economically; while it will founder socially if it does not concentrate and economize."—Letter of 1898.

"All the same, I revert to my political platform of last year. The only possible political party must stand on a well-defined platform of State Socialism. Nothing else can reflect the social movement."—Letter of 1899.

"Society is ready for collectivism; it has no fight left in it; and our class is as defunct as the dodo."—Letter of 1910.

with communism he could exist.* His political divinations
were long to be quoted; and there was a certain grandeur
in Adams's tone as he dwelt on the collapse of the world
he lived in. He perceived it, he rejoiced in it, he feared
it. With his "nose in the champagne brut," cursing his
dyspepsia, he resembled other old men who sat in club-
windows, and there were times when it seemed that his
agony over the fall of the world was merely due to fear
for his investments. He imputed this motive to Brooks
Adams,† and he undoubtedly shared it.‡ But Henry
Adams's feeling was also spacious. There was a deep vein
of poetry in his sense of the ruins of empires. As a historian, he had looked down from the tops of the pyra-
mids over Alexander, Caesar, Napoleon and Lord Cro-
mer, seeing them foreshortened to the same plane, of the
same apparent scale and proportions; and, as a geologist,
he had felt the mutations of history and the insignificance
of the personal atom, lost in the awful vastness of time
and space. On mounds in deserts of the East, he had pondered on dead cities, generations gone and crumbling
kingdoms, and all this mingled in his mind with his feeling of the present and gave it a sombre magnificence. His
style abounded in grand figures, and his geological similes
sometimes imparted to it a majestic sweep. But why did
he rejoice in the downfall of worlds? And why did he entirely fail to see the signs of a new life all about him?
For, truly, he saw nothing, and he wished to see nothing;
and he uttered at the Paris exposition his ironical prayer

* "With a communism I could exist tolerable well, for the commune is
rather favourable to social consideration apart from wealth."—Letter of
1893.
† "He considers the world to be going to the devil with the greatest
rapidity quite apart from war; and I endeavour, as you know, to console
him by the assurance that it went there at least ten years ago . . . I am
sorry to say I really think his agony of mind [is] chiefly due to the approaching destruction of all values in the stock-market."—Letter of 1917.
‡ "The imminent peril of the finances of the world weighs on my mind
more than anything else."—Letter of 1904. He described himself during the
"money panic" of 1893 as "the scaredest man this side of the Milky Way."

to the dynamo because he found nothing else in his time to respect.* When the Irish republic was rising, he saw "energy" only in Ulster.† When France was purging itself in the Dreyfus case, he could see only "treason" in Zola.‡ And, as for literature, music, thought and art, he was certain they had vanished from the planet. Literature was "nil." There were "no new books," even in Paris. There were "no books, no pictures." History was "dead." There was "no thought," except in mathematics. There were "no plays,"—Shaw was a "howling" socialist orator,—although he had heard that the Russian ballet was good. There was "no music." There were "no beautiful women or witty men." § There was "hardly anyone living . . . worth writing for;" and, while the young men at the British embassy assured him that "never in history was so much beautiful work being done," he agreed with friends, readily found, for whom literature, art and poetry were as dead as Achilles. No doubt, these were difficult years for old men with settled tastes, and Adams's age in America was a relatively dull one; ‖ although, save for his little circle of friends, Adams had missed in his age the

* "Every afternoon, I went to the Exposition, and prayed to the dynamos. There was nothing else to respect."—Letter from Paris, 1900.

† "The most encouraging sign is Ulster. Those people still retain energy. It cannot last another generation, but it is a measure for us."—Letter of 1914.

‡ On the imprisonment of Zola: "If he did not deserve it for the special offence, he did for his novels; and on the whole I think he had better have joined his friend Dreyfus on the Devil's Island some time ago."—Letter of 1898.

§ "I hear of no books that need writing, or at least reading; no plays that need to be seen, no music that should be heard; no pictures that should be bought. I hear of no beautiful women or witty men . . . Paris is as flat as a flat-iron."—Letter of 1913.

His letters are peppered with similar phrases.

‖ "Nothing tries my lovely nature so much as the startling rapidity with which every form of thought or intellect has vanished in America. Neither science, art nor literature produces anything any longer. Since 1870 we have lived on our previous product, and there is little left. I cannot be mistaken."—Letter of 1896.

finest writers and artists that America produced. Had he heard of Emily Dickinson or Stephen Crane, Winslow Homer or Ryder? He never referred to them in his books or his letters. Had he bothered to read even James or Howells, except for a novel or two? He mentioned them only once or twice.* Convinced that he "knew everybody," that he was "wiser than anyone else," however ironically he said it,† he shrank from meeting even the lights of the Sorbonne, the great authorities on the Middle Ages, whose conversation might have unsettled his mind.‡ *Omne ignotum pro magnifico;* and he was without a rival companioned by nieces, by ladies with whom he went shopping and adoring young men. He closed his sympathies to every sign of life in the world because, if the world was alive, then he was wrong. If there were other men fulfilling their careers, he might have been to blame for missing his. But, no; and, if he was a failure, so must the world be. If Henry Adams was dead, the world must die.

Naturally, therefore, Adams could see in the world no hidden forces to appeal to, the sense of which buoyed his

* "Since the Civil War, I think we have produced not one figure that will be remembered a life-time . . . What is more curious, I think the figures have not existed. The men have not been born.

"If they had existed, I should have attached myself to them, for I needed them bad. As life has turned out, I am dying alone, without a twig to fall from. I might as well be a solitary woodchuck on our old Quincy hills as winter comes on."—Letter of 1911.

† "Between us we know everybody, and those we don't know, know us." —Letter of 1869.

"As you know our role in life has always been to be wiser than anyone else and the consciousness of that is the only reward we are likely to get from it."—Letter of 1917.

‡ "During all those summers spent in Paris, he never made friends or even bowing acquaintance with any of the lights of the Sorbonne or the Collège de France. He might have known Gaston Paris, Gebhart, Langlois . . . all great experts on the Middle Ages. He read all their books but would not meet them, preferring the society of his own little group, consisting almost entirely of Americans."—Mrs. Winthrop Chanler, *Roman Spring.*

friend La Farge.* He had felt the existence of these
forces until he was middle-aged, as long as he had faith
in his will and himself; but when he began to drift the
light went out. For what is our consciousness of the forces
in others, if it is not a sense of the forces in us? When
Mont-Saint-Michel and Chartres was published, Adams
was astonished to find himself a "leader of a popular
movement;" † and how much more surprised he would
have been if he had foreseen the success of the *Education.*
He had taken it for granted that no one could understand
these books, whereas they were just the books that the
moment called for. A younger generation had risen who
shared his despair of the present, and thousands who, like
him, had lost their faith were turning, as he turned, to
the Middle Ages. The hidden forces existed in society,
although he had failed to perceive them. The hidden
forces had even persisted in Adams!—who had simulated
death, and had really died in some respects, but who had
also remained "as gay as a rabbit." His sympathies had
died, but not his senses. He had lived and grown aesthetically with a vengeance; and he who had "yearned for
nothing so keenly," even in his earlier days, "as to feel at
home in a thirteenth-century abbey," had found in his
imagination a refuge and a drug for all the chagrins of
his existence. "Running madly through the centuries," he
had brought up at an age that he had known from the beginning and that had come to seem to him a symbol of the
believing community in which he might have lived to some
effect. Chartres was all that Washington ought to have

---

* "La Farge . . . seemed held up by an intuitive conviction that society
had hidden qualities which he could appeal to. He had the instinct of a
primitive cave-dweller, who painted hairy elephants on a cave's stone roof.
The God knew how good they were! I always broke down at the door.
After middle-age,—say fifty years of age,—I was satisfied that our society
contained no hidden qualities that artists could appeal to,—that it is really
what it appears on the surface."—Letter of 1911.

† "I, vastly to my surprise, find myself a leader of a popular movement,
with my Chartres as Evangel, and Ralph Adams Cram for St. John Bap-
tist."—Letter of 1912.

been! His old studies of Viollet-le-Duc, his studies of mediæval law were the basis upon which La Farge had wrought;* and he had "hunted windows like hares," he had lived at Chartres, Bourges and Le Mans,—from Quimper to Troyes and Vézelay he had ravaged France. He had lived with the pointed arch, the illuminated missal, the chanson and roman and pastorelle, and had groped his way into the presence of St. Thomas Aquinas, of Abélard and Francis of Assisi, Aucassin, Blanche of Castile and the Queen of Heaven. He had found forgotten treasures of French musicians, love-songs, spinning-songs, songs of crusaders, and had had them all transcribed into modern notation, so that his young nieces might sing them to him; and the age of the Crusades, the monks and abbots, the Courts of Love, the queens of France, the pilgrims had become more real to him than the age he lived in. For days, in the afternoon light, he had sat in Chartres cathedral, reading the open volumes of colour in the windows, till he could all but overhear the talk of the architects and priests who had built this shrine for the Virgin; and there, while the voices of the children chanted in the choir, while the music drowned his ears and his eyes were flooded,—one sense reacting on another until sensation reached the limit of its range,—he could feel a sense beyond the human ready to reveal a sense divine that would make the world once more intelligible. He almost felt the presence of the Virgin, in the depths of feeling that she showed here, in lines, vaults, chapels, colours, chants and legends; and he shared the life he had missed but might have had. He would have known what to do in an age of faith and youthful ardour, light-heartedness, candour, gaiety, simplicity, action.

Adams, as a writer, had verified another prediction,

* "The text of a charter of Edward the Confessor was uncommonly remote from a twelfth-century window. To clamber across the gap has needed many years of La Farge's closest instruction to me, on the use of eyes, not to say feet."—Letter of 1901.

made in his youth to his brother,—that he was going to "plunge under the stream" and "remain under water" and come up at last "with an oyster and a pearl." If the *Education* was the oyster, *Chartres* was the pearl. After so many deaths, Adams had triumphed. He had worked himself into the Middle Ages, grasping so many aspects of them that *Chartres* was destined to live as a history and a classic; and in the *Education* he had pictured his time with a force and a power of suggestion that were surely unique. Were his representations objectively true? Was the age of Chartres the "unity" that he wished to think it? Was his own age as hopeless as he thought? Would not Henry Adams have been Henry Adams in the days of Abélard as in the days of Grant? However one answered these questions, his Chartres was a symbol. It stood for all the believing communities,—New England had been one,—in which alone the human spirit thrives; and it said that men must have an object, men must have the common faith which the socialized mind of the young was already embracing. And was not Adams's Dynamo also a symbol, in a world in which blind power was running wild? The *Education,* with its acrid flavour, struck, during the war-years, the note of the moment. It appealed to the younger generation, who felt themselves adrift, and who were in revolt against their past, against puritanism and its restrictions, the sexlessness of American art, the power-house, the teacher, mechanics and business. Adams, for many, seemed an older brother, who had shared their disillusionments long before them; and, more permanently, the *Education* revealed a phase of American history with an unparalleled boldness and measure of truth. This was Adams's greatest achievement, this and the golden glow of *Chartres;* and they assured for the bored old man, with his cold, old heart, the length of days he had only desired for Nirvana.

CHAPTER XXIV

THE PRE-WAR YEARS

WITH Henry Adams, the New England mind seemed to have come full circle. It had passed through its springtime, its summer and Indian summer, and Edwin Arlington Robinson was not the only Yankee who saw

> A dreary, cold, unwholesome day,
>   Racked overhead,
> As if the world were turning the wrong way,
>   And the sun dead.

Had Charles Francis Adams's "ice-age" reappeared in this vigorous region, which had produced such abundant fruits of the spirit? The fatalism of Henry Adams was surely ten times darker than Calvin's fatalism had ever been. Was the tale of the Adamses symbolic? One thought of old John Adams, under his apple-tree at Quincy, rejoicing in the prospects of his "Christian Sparta;" and one thought of his great-grandson invoking Nirvana under the sickly shoot of Buddha's bo-tree. How much had waxed and waned in these four generations! Brooks Adams had only to look homeward to find an illustration that seemed to prove the truth of his theory of cycles.

Edwin Arlington Robinson personified winter. Abandoning New England, he had carried to New York an aura of blight, desolation, decay and defeat. His view of the world was wintry,—so was his life,—and his style and his personality were bleak and bare. Had there ever been a poet who loved life less or found so little joy in the turning of the seasons? In the down-east phrase, Robinson was "master chilly." There was something starved and cold about him, as if his clothes were too scanty and his blood were too thin, as if the Maine wind had invaded his marrow. He was like the stranger in his *Tasker Norcross* who confessed that he had "never yet been warm." Taciturn, shy as an owl, diffident, lonely, he could only establish relations with others by drinking; yet everyone confided in him, for he was the most sympathetic of men, as winning as he was aloof, and completely unworldly. Helpless in practical matters, naturally forlorn, he had the will to write but not to live; and he suffered himself to be rescued again and again and reverted again and again to a life in the shadow. Abjuring the "octopus of superficial self-respect," he haunted mean streets and sordid houses, for the only success that he recognized was failure in the eyes of men, and he saw even this as distorted and thwarted. He had become vaguely known as the "poet in the subway," in days when few were aware that he wrote or existed; for he had a post, in New York, in the newly-built underground railway, checking the loads of material that were dumped at the mouths. There, all day, in his long black coat and broad-brimmed hat, he paced the damp, dark tunnel, with its odour of gases. If he saw a light at the end of the tunnel, it was usually choked with mephitic mist: it was not so much a light as a murky glimmer. And this was like the light in Robinson's poems. He seemed to share at moments the old Emersonian faith, which he variously called the "gleam" and the "vision." But, in him, this faith was only a dim conjecture. More often he looked out upon "dark tideless floods of nothingness," where men escaped from their dungeons only to drown.

Robinson brought to the "Town Down the River" a view of life that was formed in "Tilbury Town." He saw

New York as he had seen Gardiner, Maine, in his youth in this moribund port on the Kennebec river. Gardiner, which had once been a thriving shipping-centre, had gone the way of other New England towns, and Robinson, whose father had been a prosperous timber-merchant, had witnessed in his own household the decay of the region. The family fortune, such as it was, had vanished, and Robinson's brothers had fallen on evil days; and Gardiner abounded in men who had once been important and who had no life any longer to shape to their code. Their minds had been formed for a large way of living. They had set the tone for their neighbours and headed their clans. But they had no clans to lead now, and the making of laws was not for them: they were left with the "dusty ruins of their fathers' dreams." They had lost their confidence, as the years went by, and they crept away into their houses and grew queerer and queerer. Eccentricities multiplied on humbler levels also, and misery walked patch-clad through the streets. There was never a more wintry world, as Robinson saw it. The sun rose dull there. Brown weeds grew through the floors of houses. Torn curtains flapped in broken windows. The trees were leafless, a ghostly band in cold array, and the thin leaves skipped on the stones with a freezing whisper. The streets were swept by an icy wind from the river, and the water was black under the piles of the docks. Spring never came there. At best, a late autumnal glimmer lingered by the river-side and warmed the bones of aging men. There were Archibalds and Isaacs on some of the farms, ripe and sweet as the cider they kept in their cellars. There were good old uncles who were good old liars. There were admirable doctors of billiards, "fallen from on high." But these were few beside the lonely men who wandered through the scene, disconsolate shadows. There were outcasts, in broken shoes, sleeping in doorways on Water Street, who

had once driven their span of horses; there were skirt-
crazed old reprobates, misers and spendthrifts; there
were men who had been wrecked by kinks, horrors who
had never lived, ruins ridden by fear and killed by terror.
There were creepers among catacombs, "whose occupation was to die," there were respected citizens who blew
their brains out; and one saw them straggling through
the town, stumbling over frozen ruts, in the cold white
shine of a dreary day. In short, this population was a
whole *Spoon River Anthology,* acting out its epitaphs in
the world of the living.

Such was Robinson's picture of Gardiner, where he had
seen his future life as a "long and foggy voyage;" and
through the cold fog, wherever he went, he saw the old
familiar faces. Sometimes the derelicts of Gardiner appeared in New York, and "queer fellows" drifted all over
the city. But why were they derelicts? Why were they
queer?—and were they not, in any case, more interesting
than men who were called successes? They interested
Robinson more, as they interested many another young
man who was living in New York at that moment and
who found a spokesman in Robinson, then or later. Robinson was always drawn to them. Most of his Gardiner
friends had been square pegs in round holes, a doctor, for
example, who had lost his standing, a disreputable tin-
smith, an outcast named Wash Benjamin who kept a mistress down the road. As long as the town did not respect
them, they were likely to find a friend in him,—and not at
all because he felt a failure. He had no interest in success; and he was quite content when a single suitcase contained all his possessions, including his books. Nor did his
kindness explain it, kind as he was: he made an intimate
friend of a lighthouse-keeper, largely because he had had
a foot wrenched off. He had, he said, a little of the hobo
in him; and he sought, by a natural impulse, the despised
and rejected, the lost, the maladjusted and the lonely be-

cause, in his time and his place, he was a poet.* Who
were the successful men, on the whole, in a world of business? One might have asked Sinclair Lewis, who was
young just then, and who was so soon to reply with *Main
Street* and *Babbitt*. Whether in New York, in Gardiner
or in Gopher Prairie, the "bitch-goddess Success" repelled
the young. It was noisome to the sensitive, as it had never
been before: even for Horatio Alger it had lacked the
glamour that failure as a symbol had for them. When
Henry van Dyke was a great man and Veblen was a nobody, the Veblens had for the young an extraordinary
charm; and one saw in every "queer fellow" a genius *in
posse,* if not *in esse,*—one knew that if they were geniuses
they had to be queer. To be adjusted to such a world, yet
not to be a Babbitt, implied an all but unprecedented
force of soul; and, as people had ceased to look for heroes
and the young could scarcely believe they existed, they
regarded maladjustment as a sign of grace. Five times
out of ten, in fact, it was so. Most of Robinson's "lost"
souls possessed some spirituality, and it was just for this
reason that they were "lost." The people who were queer
were the people who were real. Such was Robinson's message for an age of rebels.

Now, of course, there was nothing new in this. The
founders of all the religions had known where to look for
their apostles; and Hawthorne, in his *Feathertop,* had
pictured the successful man who had not been able to pass
through the eye of the needle. That successful men could
not pass through it, neither Christ nor Hawthorne said;
but a poet in a day like Robinson's could not dwell on exceptions. Poets had seldom dwelt on these exceptions, well

* Long after Robinson had himself become a "success," he gave up his
New York friends and music and went to live in Brooklyn in a dingy
apartment to care for two good friends who were said to have been
"failures." No one else apparently saw anything in them; but how much
more they undoubtedly gave this poet than New York dinner-tables could
ever have given!

knowing that successful men can look after themselves. In a day when success was the only visible goddess, a poet could only point out that it signified failure; and Robinson's successful men were Feathertops in every case, whited sepulchres full of dead men's bones. This, and its natural corollary, was the whole of his teaching. In all his long psychological poems, he stripped the emperors of their clothes,—what was false within always betrayed them; while he turned the tables on conventional opinion by showing goodness and genius walking in tatters. It was the Fernando Nashes and the Captain Craigs, the castaways who "went begging" that really "went giving;" and this, the oldest of morals for poets, had never ceased to be new. The novelty had always lain in the local application. Hawthorne had applied it, and Robinson applied it, each in his own place and time; and Robinson thus revealed a fact which Americans had almost forgotten, that poetry is always opportune. Emerson had restated this fact two generations before him, and only Emily Dickinson had revealed it since, in the line of the Yankee tradition; and Robinson carried on their line,—he was their natural heir,—just as he carried on the line of Hawthorne. And if, in him, the Yankee tradition seemed to be tapering off, this was characteristic of the moment. The scene that he pictured was moribund, and the Emersonian gleam that often appeared in his poems was shrouded and dim. He could not share the old assurance that life was part of a purposeful plan, much as he wished to share it and almost did so. A sad man in a withered world, he could not believe in the triumph of life, and the best of his real successes were scarred by their failure. They, too, all too often, were sterile fruit for the button-moulder, children of the abyss, impotent and vain.

In later years, after the war, when poets talked of a "renaissance," Robinson was called its prime precursor. At a time when American poetry had reached its lowest

ebb, he, in his obscurity, was real and vital; and the
"irony and pity" * with which he regarded his victims of
fate struck the new note of the novelists as well as the
poets. His probing, questioning, doubting mind was the
mind of the new generation; and his portraits, even his
sonnets, were novels in little. His longer psychological
poems continued the line of Howells and James; and his
technical development foreshadowed the poets that were
coming. He had cast off early the influence of Aldrich,
which dominated the magazine-verse of the moment, although, as if to train his hand, he had written his villa-
nelles and ballades. He had reacted against this facile
jingling. He had sought for the spoken phrase, for the
neat and plain; and, if his style was too prosaic, if it was
too bare and cold, it was hard, it was clear and it was
honest. Here again Robinson was in the line of Emerson,
who liked "dry light and hard clouds, hard expressions
and hard manners." Robinson eschewed the nebulous, the
blurred and the vague, as he abhorred the fatuous and
the stereotyped. In short, in a poetical world of baker's
bread and confectionery, Robinson brought forth real
bread again.

It might have been foreseen that, after this return to
nature, American poetry was destined for a liberation.
The "renaissance" that soon occurred was the result of
various causes, and Robinson was only one of these. But
his austere integrity and his tragic feeling were more than
a little influential and his style cleared the ground for
other growths; and the time was approaching when no
one who was concerned for poetry looked for this year's
birds in last year's nests. Robinson, a traditional poet,
carried on the New England tradition, together with the
classical tradition that lay behind it; but "last year's

* A phrase of Anatole France, much used and even abused in the post-
war years. " 'What's all this irony and pity?'—'What? Don't you know
about Irony and Pity?'—'No. Who got it up?'—'Everybody. They're mad
about it in New York.' "—Hemingway, *The Sun Also Rises.*

nests" in poetry, as the new poets saw them, were the nests of the romantic mind in its hour of decay. Romanticism had given birth to a verbal fatty degeneration that revealed the degeneration of the life it sprang from, in a world whose actual deity was the goddess Success; and younger minds reacted against such phrases as "reverence for life" and "quest for beauty," because of their sense of the false and the hollow behind them. The older poets, in all good faith, had used these phrases because they meant them. They really reverenced life, they sought for beauty; while the recent poets, the magazine-poets used them merely because the older poets had used them. They did not reverence life,—they only said so; and they sought for the pretty and the charming but not for beauty. The passions they claimed were not real passions; their heartbreaks never broke their hearts. They took in vain a language that had once been great. In short, they were "phonographs," as Amy Lowell presently said, or, as she might have said, ventriloquists, for their voice was not their own, it was alien to them, and they were either ordinary children of Mammon or wistful sentimentalists without strength. What had become of the great old life? What had become of the great old language? The bitch-goddess had them in her toils, and the "great words" had gone down with the great life-patterns.* It was no use to talk to the young about "sacred" and "glorious" things, especially when the war had traduced them further; and the more sacred one felt they were, the more one felt it was obscene to use the words or even think about them. The younger writers, growing up in this dying phase of

---

* "It is advertising that has been the death of words.
  The word 'Personal' now on an envelope means 'impersonal;'
  'Important,' 'unimportant.'
  'The Finest,' 'The Best,' 'The Purest'—what do they mean now?
  Something somebody wants to sell.
  We are a nation of word-killers: *hero, veteran, tragedy,*—
  Watch the great words go down."
      —Edna St. Vincent Millay, *Conversation at Midnight.*

the old society, knew that Robinson was right. Success in this civilization was inevitably failure, although failure might be success. The more honest these younger writers were, the less they believed in the world they lived in,— they were all rebels at the outset,—and the better they expressed their minds, the surer they were to express them in terms for which Robinson had prepared the way. For just as he had swept the house for all that was truthful and loyal in living, he had swept it for plain speaking, veracity and candour. As for poetry, he had broken up the "roof of heaven,"—the cotton-batting roof it had become,—and the "new forms" followed as a matter of course. The free verse, the new rhythms, the imagism, the realism, the characteristic forms of the coming decades,—and especially the classicism that was salient also, —expressed new states of mind and new ideas of which Robinson was one of the prophets.

These new American states of mind, the new ideas of the coming epoch, flourished, with unparalleled luxuriance, in New York. Robinson had found New York "the best town to live in," * as Howells had found it before him. It was the best town because it was the town of "life," as Howells had shown in *A Hazard of New Fortunes,* but the life of which Howells had written in the "age of innocence" had become the life of megalopolis. It was vital with a vengeance, and the vengeance and the vitality were equally marked; for, if there one saw the American eagle "mewing her mighty youth and kindling her undazzled eyes at the full midday beam," the eagle's brood were apt to forget their nest there. Most of the younger writers gathered there, from New England, the South and the West, because the currents of thought converged in New York that had formerly met in Boston

---

* "Boston is a good town to write in—perhaps the best, just as New York is the best town to live in . . . I can't feel at home anywhere else."—Letter of Robinson, 1905.

and spread from New England. They gathered, and they drank the heady waters, and some grew strong thereby, those in whom the eagle remained undazzled; but in many of the brood, from New England, the South and the West, the heady waters produced delirium tremens. They were constrained to feel provincial, and, feeling their provinciality, they lost their bearings; for never in modern history had any cosmopolitan town presented a more overwhelming chaos. Howells, the ripe old veteran, lived serene there; and Robinson, the tough Yankee, kept his head. His Pierian spring was unsullied by the river* of whiskey he drank; and Howells, with his open sympathies, rejoiced in the chaos. He saw it as life, multifarious life, full of hope and promise; and he was inoculated against the poisons, the virus that lurked in the chaos. He had long since taken the serums of Italy, Spain, Germany, Russia,—he had entered all their literatures by an inner line; and the beautiful travel-books that he was writing in his calm old age were a proof of the catholicity óf his understanding.* As an old socialist, he was an internationalist also, and for him the cosmopolitan had no poisons. There was nothing to disturb him, there was everything to feed him in the mixture of races in New York; and he who knew so well the American eagle knew it had room for all under its wing. He knew the young West as he knew the old New England; and he who was one of the first to review Robert Frost was the first to review Abraham Cahan. Moreover, this "linchpin" of Boston had linked the two ages of poetry, the old and the new; for he had recognized Emily Dickinson, whose star was about to rise to its zenith, and had passed her work on to Stephen Crane. He had fought for the publication of Crane's *Maggie,* and inviting the young man to dinner,

---

* As Howells had always been a first-rate travel-writer,—ever since his early *Venetian Life,*—so he excelled in the final fruits of his "mental kodak," *Familiar Spanish Travels, Hither and Thither in Germany, London Films,* etc. The vein of these books was psychological.

had read him Miss Dickinson's poems, which had just appeared; whereupon Crane wrote *The Black Riders,* the poems that carried her torch to the poets who followed. In fighting for *Maggie,* the candid Howells had fought for all the new novelists whose realism was paling the light of his own; and this suggested that if he had had the audience of these later writers he might have shared their drastic point of view. For men were beginning to read again, and women were casting off the old taboos; and the "young lady" standard that his time and his place imposed on Howells was going the way of Cooper's "young female" world. Howells was a "dead cult," * although this cult was to live again when the inverted prudery of Howells's successors had gone the way of Howells's prudery. The "he-men" were to follow the "she-women" into the abysm of time; and Howells's complex psychology and delicate art were to win new readers who loved the American scene. Meanwhile, all standards and values were at risk in New York; and, if this explained why Howells and Robinson liked it, still what was meat for them was poison for others. That life has laws to which death pays tribute the strong had always known and were always to know; and, knowing it, they had always rejoiced in life, and the more life the better. But few of the younger writers could afford this risk. The law of metropolitan attraction all but compelled them to take it, but most of them were too soft to bear the strain. They were heirs of the confusion of morals with which the nineteenth century ended, and, besides, they were uncertain about their country. There were some who had listened to teachers, like Woodberry and Wendell, in whom the American tradition had gone to seed; and all of them had seen their country whoring after the bitch-goddess,—they could not

* "I am comparatively a dead cult with my statues cut down and the grass growing over them in the pale moonlight."—Letter of Howells to Henry James, 1915.

believe in themselves as Americans any longer. So chaos
often overwhelmed them; for every brass tack contra-
dicted the feeble talk they heard about "ideals" and "inspiration," which was drowned by the Babel of voices
that rose in New York. Puritanism, once so grand, Vic-
torianism, once so potent, went down like houses of glass
at the impact of Freud, who had found incest in filial affection, guilt in generosity, malice in the tender feelings,
hatred in love. The facts that Freud revealed were pat-
ently present; and what modern ethic was there to defend
these feelings, whose substance of reality Freud never attacked? In those who could not meet him with a modern
ethic, or with a core of tradition, stoutly maintained,
Freud subverted religion and romantic love, which became for them a gloss over animal instincts; so that romantic young men and women,—and all Americans were
romantic,—were suddenly confused and deranged at the
roots of their being. Better to be honest animals than
dishonest men!—though, unhappily, the case was not so
simple, and many became dishonest animals also. That
Freud met no resistance was not his fault, and nothing
met resistance in New York, where the doctrines of all
the iconoclasts were sown broadcast. The brilliant journalist James Huneker spread before the younger minds
the writings of Shaw, Nietzsche, D'Annunzio, Strindberg,
Laforgue, Schnitzler, Wedekind, Anatole France, presenting them all on one level, as equally great, the boule-
vard-thinkers and drawing-room poets together with the
lonely seers who had wrestled with the deepest problems
in their cottages and attics. Each of these minds was a
logical outgrowth of some one national ethos, personified
in New York by an immigrant group, and they could only
have been really understood in relation to these groups
and their traditions. But the immigrant groups themselves had lost their keys. They had cut themselves adrift
from their own traditions and sought for an American

tradition to which to cling, which they could find nowhere in New York,—any more than Henry James could find his birthplace when, in 1905, he reappeared. As Henry James's birthplace had long since vanished, so all the native ideas seemed remote and dim beside this staggering onrush of new thoughts. These European authors floated in a vacuum. No critic related them to the native mind, and Huneker welcomed them all and passed them on with a sympathy and enthusiasm that knew no standards. Indeed, his impressionism, the prevailing doctrine, invalidated the very conception of standards; for it argued that taste and thought were subjective and thus destroyed all objectivity, whether of authority, precedent, scholarship or tradition. Its only standard of value was the reader's pleasure. This universal hedonism, the note of megalopolis, condoned all irresponsibilities; and it marked a disillusioned, urban, cosmopolitan people who had lost all sense of their former attachments. This was the note of the melting-pot whose contents failed to melt because there was no fire underneath it, no conscious native feeling to fuse its warring elements into a common ethos that all accepted.

Meanwhile, Boston was hostile to the world-ideas, the ideas of the coming age that congested New York. *The Atlantic* was the medium through which these new ideas had once been announced to America, more often than not, while Huneker was the medium now, and Huneker was anathema to the mind that had gradually come to prevail in Boston. The city remained, in its way, a city of readers, in a measure that astonished Arnold Bennett,* but it was also "finished," as Bennett said; and, while by "finished" he meant complete,—other cities "will be," Boston "is,"—this was a more fundamental comment. Its

---

* When Arnold Bennett visited Boston in 1912, he was amused and surprised to find in his room a catalogue of the hotel-library, one hundred and eighty-two pages.—See Arnold Bennett, *Your United States.*

completeness implied a certain complacency, as if, having reached its limit of growth, it had nothing to learn from other quarters; and the Watch and Ward Society was doing its best to prevent it from growing any further. Within a few years, the society prohibited sixty books that were generally accepted in the rest of the country as representing the life and ideas of the time. The Irish, the official rulers, had inherited the Puritanism that was no longer active in the true-blue Yankees; but the Yankees allowed them to have their way, for they had lost interest themselves in ideas that were novel and disturbing. The phrase "banned in Boston" was the novelist's dream of successful publicity, but Boston banned itself in excluding the world; and American writers generally now regarded it with a certain rancour as illiberal, sterile, indifferent, censorious and petty. They were prepared for the Adamses' gibes at Boston,* they shared Mencken's contempt for the "ashes of New England;" and certainly the New England critics, Woodberry and Wendell, had been singularly indifferent to American letters. Both depreciated what the country had done already, neither showed any interest in what it was doing; † and both appeared to wonder why Americans wrote at all or what they found in its life that was worth expressing. When they were not

---

* "This is the trouble with Boston—it is provincial. Including Cambridge, one finds there what might be called a very good society stock company . . . Socially, however, the trouble with Boston is that there is no current of fresh outside life everlastingly flowing in and passing out. It is, so to speak, stationary—a world, a Boston world, unto itself; and, like all things stationary, there is in it, as the years pass, a very perceptible lack of that variety and change which are the essence and spice of life; it tends to stagnate . . . In the course of my life I have tried Boston socially on all sides. I have summered it and wintered it, tried it drunk and tried it sober; and, drunk and sober, there's nothing in it—save Boston."—*Autobiography of Charles Francis Adams.*
"Boston is a curious place . . . When a society has reached this point, it acquires a self-complacency which is wildly exasperating. My fingers itch to puncture it; to do something which will sting it into impropriety."—*Letters of Henry Adams.*
† Wendell, who had glanced at Crane's *The Red Badge of Courage,* described it in one of his lectures as "sensational trash."

looking backward, they looked across the sea towards
Europe; but they were as oblivious of the new ideas that
were coming from Europe,—the ideas that were flowing
especially through Huneker's mind,—as they were of the
life beyond the Charles and the Hudson. They resembled
the Anglo-Irish critics in Dublin, Edward Dowden and
his school, who were equally indifferent, when they were
not hostile, to the literature that was coming to birth in
their country. Their necks were awry, their eyes were
twisted.* Hamlin Garland, speaking for the West, had
recently disowned, in *Crumbling Idols,* these critics who
ignored the American scene; † and Boston represented,
for the rest of the nation, the blight one felt behind them.
Boston was the schoolmarm, and the nation had grown
too big for her,—it was altogether out of hand; and the
schoolmarm herself had lost her humility and grown, with
the waning of her power, arrogant and peevish. The

* "There is a school of criticism in Ireland, a school that knows the
work of the finest critics in the world, and knows too, what is more
important, the finest literature in the world. This, when dealing with
literature in general, adds to the store of fine critical work. This at times
encourages and approves good original Irish work. I think it unfortunate,
however, that it should have grown with, or indeed before, the original
work. Dealing with the monuments of the older literatures,—English,
French and the like,—this criticism knows its place, its bearings, its conditions. Dealing with a naissant literature . . . it looks over its shoulder,
as it were. Its neck is awry. Its eyes are twisted round. Its feet turn from
their known way and stumble. When it does get a clear view of its object,
it misses the shapes and forms it saw in other lands and expresses its
disappointment.
"Ireland is not the only country that suffers so today. America also has
a full-grown criticism and a baby literature. Something of the same relation exists between the two there is in Ireland."—Thomas MacDonagh,
Literature in Ireland.
† "For fifty years the best writers of England and Europe have been
calling for the native utterance of American writers . . . and almost as
constantly have the conservative and narrow critics of Boston and New
York discouraged the truest, freest utterance of the American poet and
novelist . . . Upon the tender springing plant of American literature the
frost of conservative culture has fallen.
"It really comes down to a contest, not between the East and the West,
but between sterile culture and creative work, between mere scholarship and wisdom, between conservative criticism and native original
literary production."—Hamlin Garland, *Crumbling Idols,* 1894.

West would have none of her, and a rising generation
that saw itself reflected in Henry Adams, whose quarrel
had always been with his educators, found Boston its natural enemy. Why waste words on the definition of puritanism? The fact that it came from New England was
enough to damn it. Puritanism was Miss Ophelia, who
had reformed Dinah's kitchen; and Dinah had rebelled
and thrown her out. For was she not a shrew?—was
she not old?—like those two other symbols of Boston,
the sphinx-like Mrs. Eddy and the aged Mrs. Gardner,
swathed in white. These latter suggested, in their car-
riages, animated mummies. It was rumoured that Mrs.
Eddy was actually dead and had only a pretended existence in the person of a double.

Now, true it was that, all this while, and for all the
dry-rot on the surface, the Boston, the New England authors continued to write; and many of them wrote as well
as ever. The tough New England intellect and its still
tougher moral force were not to be downed by adverse
circumstances; and, while William James was at his zenith, the Spaniard-Yankee Santayana had finished his
great work, *The Life of Reason.* The Adamses were in
full career, Mark Howe was memorializing his New
England worthies, and, at Wellesley Hills, Gamaliel
Bradford wrote his *Lee, the American,* the first of his
long series of literary portraits. Samuel M. Crothers, a
follower of Dr. Holmes with a touch of Western "folksi-
ness," was writing his essays; and William Roscoe Thayer
produced his magnificent *Life and Times of Cavour,* the
fruit of a lifelong devotion to Italian studies. This theme
was as congenial to a good New England liberal as the
rise of the Dutch republic had been to Motley; and the
masterly composition of Thayer showed that for scholarly writing the New England intellect was as strong as
ever. Bliss Perry carried on at Harvard the noble Yankee humanism that Lounsbury and H. A. Beers main-

tained at Yale,—despite the militant philistinism of the
formidable Sumner,—its ethical delicacy and its tolerant
candour, together with its steadfast faith in the goodness
of men. With Lounsbury, Beers, Chauncey Tinker and
William Lyon Phelps, Yale had outgrown its earlier indifference to letters,—marked by the obscurity of John
De Forest, who had lived all his life in New Haven, invisible as a treetoad in an oak. De Forest died in 1903;
and in 1911 Wilbur L.Cross founded the *Yale Review,*—
after writing his memorable life of Sterne and before he
wrote the life of Fielding,—the quarterly that was to play
the part which the moribund *North American,* revived by
George Harvey, had largely relinquished. The breeze
that was blowing over literary Yale was to have its effect
on the new generation of writers, brilliant groups of
whom were at nurse there.* When it came to scholarly
writing, nothing could ever down New England, but in
poetry, fiction and drama it was also alive; and, while
Robert Frost pegged away on his New Hampshire farm
and Robinson pegged with him in New York, Amy Lowell was growing up in Boston. There Robert Grant was
publishing his finest book, *The Chippendales,* and Alice
Brown was continuing her admirable stories. *Meadow-
Grass* and *Tiverton Tales* lacked some of Miss Jewett's
poetry, as they lacked the full force of Miss Wilkins's
tragic feeling, but they certainly combined Miss Wilkins's
veracity with a very large part of Miss Jewett's charm.
Miss Jewett died in 1909, and Miss Wilkins had fallen a
prey to the sentimental; but James B. Connolly was writing his fine Gloucester tales and Vida D. Scudder her
Franciscan romances. Amy Lowell was still a beginner.

* Among the future authors who were students at Yale during the years
(roughly) 1900–1920 were Henry Seidel Canby, William Rose Benét,
Stephen Vincent Benét, Sinclair Lewis, Waldo Frank, Thomas Beer, Paul
Rosenfeld, Leonard Bacon, Chard Powers Smith, Robert M. Coates,
George Soule, Clarence Day, Philip Barry, Archibald MacLeish and Thorn-
ton Wilder.

The brilliant apparition of the future was scarcely indicated in her timid verses; but the little roly-poly girl had
turned into a tomboy, and the tomboy had become a redoubtable woman, and it only required the warmth of the
spring that was coming to reveal the flower in this portentous bud. As a child, she had browsed in the Athenæum, in a quiet nook aloft, gained by a "little painful
spiral stair." Her earliest love had been Keats, the favourite poet of her grandfather's first cousin, the preëminent Lowell; and she had lived with her usual verve
through the aesthetic nineties in Boston, absorbing Huys-
mans, Laforgue, Remy de Gourmont and other new
French writers already in vogue there. She had grown up
with her brother Percival's letters from his far-away
Japan, and she was steeped in the Boston Orientalism
that flourished with Sturgis Bigelow and Fenollosa. She
knew their Japanese and Chinese collections as she knew
Mrs. Gardner's Fenway Court; and all these exotic notes
were to appear in her later work. The reigning poet,
meanwhile, in Boston, was Josephine Preston Peabody,
whose fluent and graceful verses were admired to excess.
These verses, usually fervent but often insipid, expressed
the humanitarian mood and feeling that remained en-
demic in New England and that Vida D. Scudder and
Anna Hempstead Branch also expressed in their poems,
romances and plays. All these writers were in revolt
against a commercial civilization, as the rebels of the following decade were; but, unlike the later writers, they
reacted against the world they lived in by falling back on
mediæval themes. In her verse-plays, *The Piper, The
Wolf of Gubbio, Marlowe* and others,—all more intense
than her poems,—Miss Peabody dramatized the widespread interest in history that filled the New England
colleges during these years. Her plays, which ignored the
present, except by implication, offered escapes into moments that seemed nobler and richer; although Hamelin,

in *The Piper,* might have been Boston,—since the money-bag served it for a heart. This piper who led the children away was not the sinister creature of legend but the poet who saved them from the waste-land. *The Wolf of Gubbio* was a Franciscan play, suggesting Miss Scudder's romances. Anna Hempstead Branch, who lived in New York and New London, was also humanitarian and mediæval. Her work abounded in echoes of Coleridge and Wordsworth and especially in Pre-Raphaelite archaisms, with ballads and plays of court fools, princesses and pages that were popular in the colleges for women.* But her religious feeling was authentic, and she often wrote admirable verse.

Literary Yankeedom was quick enough, in short, however the rest of the country was disposed to ignore it;† and this was particularly true in the case of the drama. The first "little theatre" in the country was established in Boston, the Toy Theatre, 1911; and there, as nowhere else in America, the Elizabethans had come to life. The Elizabethan poets and playwrights had long been a central interest in Cambridge, where their plays were constantly revived; and most of the New England poets of the present and immediate future were full of Elizabethan conceptions and rhythms. Everyone was talking of Webster, Middleton, Beaumont and Fletcher, for whom Gamaliel Bradford had a passion; and Miss Peabody's *Marlowe* expressed a sympathy that Robinson also expressed in *Ben Jonson Meets a Man from Stratford.* This sympathy

---

* Edna St. Vincent Millay's early plays, *The Lamp and the Bell, Two Slatterns and a King,* etc., were in the vein of Anna Hempstead Branch.

† In the revolt against New England that marked the nation's coming of age, the New England authors were almost totally ignored. The Yankee classics were dethroned, and the critics scarcely mentioned such authors as Miss Guiney, Lodge and Stickney. These New England writers were at least as good as the secondary and tertiary precursors elsewhere. In 1925, Miss Peabody's excellent plays were completely forgotten, and Alice Brown and other living authors had passed into an undeserved eclipse. One had to pay for being a Yankee in these great formative years of the national mind.

later appeared in various forms in Edna St. Vincent Millay, Eliot and Cummings, who abounded in Elizabethan imagery. New England was undergoing a revival of the drama, which was marked by George Pierce Baker's Harvard "workshop," later transferred to Yale; and the Provincetown Theatre was foreshadowed in the Greek plays of Lodge and Stickney and the prose-plays of Robinson and Percy MacKaye.* But, while all this was promising, especially in the field of forms, the spirit of most of these writers was atavistic. Rebels as they were, like the writers who followed, Miss Peabody, Miss Branch and Miss Scudder were more like the "escapists" of the nineties, the seekers of lost trails who wandered back to the Middle Ages, or to a fanciful Greece or an actual England. They did not like the present, but they did not come to grips with it, as the writers of the future were obliged to do, although, by implication, they attacked the present,—and in this they were unlike the writers of the nineties.† They attacked the unlovely present with the weapons of the past, they used the weapons of the past to abuse the present, whereas the young writers who were growing up at Harvard were bent upon finding their weapons in the present also. The latter were realistic, however romantic they also were; and, disliking the present quite as much as any of the existing writers, they shared Robinson's frank obsession with it. They did not

---

*Robinson published two plays, *Van Zorn* and *The Porcupine*. Percy MacKaye's New England plays, like Eugene O'Neill's, were only a phase of his work. *The Scarecrow* was suggested by Hawthorne's *Feathertop*. *Yankee Fantasies*, 1912, were New England folk-plays, dealing with surprising variations of the Yankee psyche. See also Robert Frost's play, *A Way Out*, published in *The Seven Arts* magazine.

Josephine Preston Peabody's *The Piper* was produced at the Shakespeare Theatre in Stratford-on-Avon.

Among other more or less New England plays were Marion Crawford's *Francesca da Rimini*, produced by Sarah Bernhardt, Paris, 1902, and Thomas Bailey Aldrich's *Judith of Bethesda*, produced in 1904. One might also mention here the work of William Vaughn Moody, the Indiana poet who was closely connected with Cambridge and Boston.

† An exception should be made here of George Cabot Lodge.

wish to escape from the present, for they were of the present. To escape from the present was to escape from themselves, and this, as realists, they could not do. Moreover, they did not wish to abuse the present: they wished to understand it, unravel it, solve it and use it as a foundation for the building of the future. Such was the basis of many of the points of view that characterized the Harvard authors who were coming.

For Harvard, in these pre-war years, teemed with growing writers who were to show that geniuses are "ferments." * This was William James's word, and they were drawn to Harvard by its "persistently atomistic constitution." † Again, the phrase was James's, and the Harvard faculty had grown along the lines of James's department, in which the professors of philosophy were chosen to represent variety, first of all. It avoided inbreeding and aimed at diversity and thus promoted a critical attitude, while it encouraged every private bent; and it maintained, both above and below the various vital ideals it stood for, its own tradition and its "scale of value." A remarkable group of powerful teachers, with nothing in common but their humanity, presented the special subjects that attracted writers, philosophy, psychology, the literary languages, history, comparative literature and the best of

* Among the future writers who were students at Harvard during these pre-war years were Conrad Aiken, Heywood Broun, Witter Bynner, Stuart Chase, Malcolm Cowley, E. E. Cummings, S. Foster Damon, John Dos Passos, Walter Prichard Eaton, T. S. Eliot, Arthur Davison Ficke, John Gould Fletcher, Hermann Hagedorn, Robert Hillyer, Walter Lippmann, S. E. Morison, Charles Nordhoff, Eugene O'Neill, Lucien Price, John Reed, Edward Sheldon, Stuart P. Sherman, Lee Simonson, Harold Stearns, Wallace Stevens, Claude C. Washburn, John Hall Wheelock and John Brooks Wheelwright.

† Why did the "undisciplinables" go to Harvard, that "nursery for independent and lonely thinkers"? William James, considering this question, answered it as follows: "It is because they have heard of her persistently atomistic constitution, of her tolerance of exceptionality and eccentricity, of her devotion to the principles of individual vocation and choice. It is because you cannot make single one-ideaed regiments of her classes. It is because she cherishes so many vital ideals, yet makes a scale of value among them."—William James, *Memories and Studies.*

English; and one could trace in the later work of almost all the coming writers the influence of one or more of these.* William James's realism pervaded the atmosphere, together with all the romance that young men liked; and one gathered that the line of valour was to face the music, whether the music was Bach or whether it was jazz. Harvard was the *Dive Bouteille* of all the intellectual passions. Its motto was *Fais ce que vouldras* and take the risks; and, whether as novelists, poets or playwrights, historians, journalists, critics, as socialists, liberals, aesthetes or radical tories, the Harvard men were often disposed to do so. If they went up alleys of the past, these alleys could not be blind alleys, and, if they lived in the future, they did so with reason; and as moulders of forms and setters of fashions, and even as "movers and shakers," they played an unusual role in the times that were coming.

There were few of these young men at Harvard,—there were still fewer at Yale,—whose destinies were deeply involved with New England. But there were Yankees among them, and others who were partly Yankee, and these young men were in a special case; and this case was marked when they were tough-minded, as they were apt to be, for the Yankee mind was traditionally a mind of wrestlers. The Yankee mind, for hundreds of years, had been wrestling with angels and devils, and it could not take life lightly, in the New York fashion; and the tough-minded Yankees were still wrestlers. There were tender-minded Yankees, there were "white-pine Yankees,"—to abuse a shrewd distinction of Dr. Holmes,—† Yankees

---

* The Harvard teachers of the humanities included during these years the following: Irving Babbitt, George Pierce Baker, L. B. R. Briggs, Charles T. Copeland, Kuno Francke, Charles H. Grandgent, Charles H. Haskins, William James, George Lyman Kittredge, Charles R. Lanman, George Foot Moore, Hugo Münsterberg, William Allan Neilson, Bliss Perry, Edward Kennard Rand, Josiah Royce, George Santayana, Frederick J. Turner, Leo Wiener and Barrett Wendell.
† In *The Poet at the Breakfast-Table.*

of the softer grain, unlike the "pitch-pine Yankees," who were able to follow the line of least resistance. These white-pine Yankees saw nothing amiss with New England. They were not the wrestling kind, they were not concerned with angels and devils, and their comfort meant more to them than the state of their souls. They were easy-going traditionalists, and they were joined by outsiders who were prone to idealize New England in the Western way; for Westerners either hated New England or they loved it over-much, in this resembling Howells in his earlier phase. The literary life of Boston was largely composed in the future of these tender-minded natives and visitors from afar; and certainly it was a happy fact that Boston found appreciators when most of its tougher minds were turning against it. The tough minds were driven to turn against it; for, granting that one was born to wrestle, what was there to wrestle with?—what risks, in this latter-day Boston, were there to take? What was reality in Boston, since one had to face it? Harvard, with its realism, Harvard, with its gospel of risks, had spoiled these New England men for their region and their town. For Boston offered them no resistance, nothing to cut their teeth upon; and wrestlers must find their resistance or they cease to be wrestlers.

There was nothing essentially new in this, for, ever since the Civil War, the Boston mind had been growing softer and softer; and whatever drove the young men forth in the early twentieth century had driven Henry James and Henry Adams. Howells had been driven forth in a similar fashion. As long as the old nobility was dominant in the Boston mind there had remained a rock to cling to, but this had long ceased to be dominant, although it still existed, and much of what was left was Pharisaic; and those who took most seriously the old professions of Boston,—its moral dynamism and its faith in progress, its faith in the goodness of men,—were those who were most

disillusioned with the Boston of the present. For they saw
a Boston that had suffered itself to be betrayed and that
was on the way to betraying them. It seemed smug, flaccid, tepid, snobbish and priggish. It was fatuous in its pes-
simism, which consisted in throwing up sponges. It was
still more fatuous in its optimism; for it abounded in
"glad books," and the "Pollyanna philosophy" vied with
the sterile despair of the house of Adams.* The tribe of
the Pooh-Poohs, which Dr. Holmes had routed,† had reclaimed its ancestral totems in the town of Boston; and
everything new was "pseudo" there, from the point of
view of Irving Babbitt.‡ Everything new was pseudo to
Dr. Crothers. What Holmes would have welcomed as
vigorous and fresh, Crothers gently ridiculed in the name
of Sir Walter and the good old days that knew no modern science. Everything embryonic for him was pseudo,
and he threw out all the babies with the bath. The "new
biography," the "new poetry," the "new psychology" or
whatever were all so many bubbles for him to prick; and
nothing struck him as more absurd than keeping up with
the march of mind that New England had once been so
willing and eager to follow. For Irving Babbitt there was
no march of mind, and he virtually included all contem-

* Eleanor H. Porter's *Pollyanna,* 1912, was a characteristic expression of
the Boston of the moment.
† "The Pi-Utes and the Kickapoos of the wilderness are hard to reason
with. But there is another tribe of irreclaimables, living in much larger
wigwams and having all the look of civilized people, which is quite as
intractable to the teachings of a new philosophy that upsets their ancestral
totems. This is the tribe of the Pooh-Poohs, so called from the leading
expression of their vocabulary, which furnishes them a short and easy
method of disposing of all novel doctrines, discoveries and inventions of
a character to interfere with their preconceived notions. They may possibly serve a useful purpose, like other barbarous and semi-barbarous
human beings, by helping to keep down the too prolific family of noxious
and troublesome animals,—the thinking, or rather talking and writing
ones. Beyond this they are of small value; and they are always retreating
before the advance of knowledge, facing it, and moving backwards, still
opposing the leaders and the front rank with their inextinguishable war-
cry, Pooh-Pooh!"—Holmes, *Pages from an Old Volume of Life.*
‡ "I am sorry I need so many 'pseudos' in describing our modern activities."—Irving Babbitt, *The Masters of Modern French Criticism.*

porary tastes when he said, "There are tastes that deserve the cudgel." As for Boston, the old spirit of effort
and strife had long gone out of its Emersonianism, and
the sons of the patricians who had taxed themselves for
the great republic were bent upon nothing so much as
evading their taxes. To undo the labours of their fathers
was the chief of their cares. The old force had been sadly
dispersed, and the famous culture of Boston consisted of
vague generalities and empty intentions. So, at least,
the younger people saw it. The poets all wore "singing
robes," and they all had "mystic illuminations," which
meant anything or nothing: they were sentimentally mediæval or, as a rising poet soon said, compounded of
"marshmallows and tears." * The festering lilies of Boston smelt worse than weeds.

So it seemed to the younger writers who were growing
up at Harvard, especially T. S. Eliot and E. E. Cummings. Eliot had returned from St. Louis to the home of
his forbears, and Cummings was the son of a Boston and
Cambridge professor and minister, Dr. Hale's successor
at the South Church. Both felt as Henry Adams felt
about Boston, and there were many others who shared
their feeling. Their "fingers itched to puncture it," as
their poems were to show, to "sting it into impropriety."
It struck them as a "dreary place," a "target for disgust,"—as the ill-fated Harry Crosby presently called
it; † and they were irritated by the "Boston virgins . . .
with their flat-heeled shoes and tortoise-shell glasses," by
the "Cambridge ladies with permanent faces" who lived
in "furnished souls," ‡ by the worshippers of "Matthew

* Conrad Aiken.

† "A dreary place (dreary, drearier, dreariest) . . . No concentration
here, no stimulus, no inner centrality, no exploding into the Beyond, no
Sun. It is a City of Dreadful Night, a Target for Disgust."—*The Diary
of Henry Grew Crosby,* published in three volumes by the Black Sun
Press, Paris. For an account of Harry Crosby, see Malcolm Cowley's
Exile's Return.

‡ E. E. Cummings.

and Waldo." * Eliot's earlier poems, the fruit of the
years he spent at Harvard, were mostly gibes at Boston
states of mind, at Cousin Harriet's *Evening Transcript,*
Miss Helen Slingsby, the maiden aunt, the dowager Mrs.
Phlaccus and her palace and Prufrock's indecisions and
inhibitions; yet Eliot's mind was itself a compound of all
the tastes of this latter-day Boston, a scholarly "museum
of idols," like Sargent's fresco. There one saw the Boston
royalism, the Boston Anglo-Catholicism, the taste for
Donne, Laforgue and Remy de Gourmont, the interest in
Dante, Sanskrit, the *Bhagavad-Gita* and the Elizabethan
dramatists and poets, the classicism of Babbitt and Santayana. Eliot's mind was a mirror of Boston Alexandri-
anism, and its learned religiosity evoked in him later a
singular mode of Christianity,†—small faith, less hope,
no charity at all. Was it because he was deeply involved in
so much he despised that Eliot's characteristic note was a
sneer suggesting the cold east winds at the tip of Nahant?
However this may have been, he saw the "waste-land"
first in Boston before he ever described it in terms of
London. Here was the sterile and desolate country that
was ruled by an impotent king, the rats' alley full of stony
rubbish. This waste-land of all the modern cities, where
the dry stone gave no sound of water, was suggested to
Eliot by Boston when he was in college; and it amused
him to contrast its desiccated culture with Sweeney, whom
he found in a bar in South Boston. The present filled him
with cold aversion. He saw the reality of the modern
world in dingy furnished rooms and sawdust restaurants,
cocktail-smells in bars, cigarettes in hallways; and E. E.
Cummings too saw "putrid windows," disintegrating
cigar-stubs lying in gutters and the first star feebly
scratching the "sore of morning." Other young writers

---

* T. S. Eliot.

† "The spirit killeth, but the letter giveth life."—T. S. Eliot, *For Lance-
lot Andrewes.*

turned to low life, which may have been ignoble but was certainly real, unlike the feeble pretensions of the people of culture. Conrad Aiken was soon to picture, in *The House of Dust,* the seething life of the masses in the chaos of the city, and his mind was filled with images of Boston tailors and vaudeville jugglers dying among violins and paper roses; and John Dos Passos, who also haunted the slums, was struck by the lovely face of an Italian woman, suggesting Botticelli amid all the squalor. Sometimes these young men saw low life with compassion, sometimes they saw it with disgust, but they usually saw it as interesting, as actual, as real; and, as Stephen Crane had gone to the slums and found a heroine there in Maggie, so they sought for the primitive and, if need were, the brutal. Had not Synge said that poetry must learn to be brutal, in order once more to be human, as the teeth, after too much sugar, need flesh and gristle? Everywhere writers, in the decay of the old society, were seeking for the "salt in the mouth" and the "rough to the hand." Eugene O'Neill was already doing so; and all these writers, following Robinson, turned their backs on "success," as they turned them on "culture," and looked for life in its nakedness, however raw. What lay behind the "mask" was the object of their quest.

Now, in all this the young New Englanders were at one with the young of the rest of the world, who had generally lost faith in the world they lived in. In England, they were dethroning their Tennyson, and Victor Hugo fell in France, precisely as the Americans of the following decade dethroned their Emerson, Whittier, Longfellow and Bryant; and it only required the first world-war to crush the shams of this liberal culture, which seemed to have become a simulacrum. Was its idealism real, as Emerson had felt, or empty, as the young were constrained to feel it, a humbug that stank in their nostrils? For this idealism had been mouthed too long; it

was an abuse of Pharisees who evaded its tasks, while all
they really cared for was their own success, their pursuit
of dollars, francs, marks and shillings. What had become
a festering lily must have been a humbug always,—such
was the inference of the younger people, who had read
all the idol-smashers that Huneker spread through New
York and who knew the actualities behind the shams.
They were aware of the secrets that lurked behind the
prevailing comstockery, and they turned against their
elders, who seemed to have maintained a conspiracy of
silence about them; and in their need for frankness and
honesty they were impelled to tear down the false roof of
the house in which they had grown. The more, in their
hearts, they believed in progress, the more they denied
this travesty of it; the more sensitive they were, the more
embittered; and it was much the same in London as in
Boston, in Paris and Milan and Dublin. The culture of
the nineteenth century had gone to seed, and the young
were bent on destroying it, root and branch. It was futile,
it was incoherent, it was full of cant. It was so much sentimentality, priggishness and "slop." * Such was the mood
of the younger writers who were growing up in the pre-
war years and who were to find their voices in the years
that followed; and many a Yankee agreed with Eliot and
Cummings. They hated "cheerfulness, optimism and hope-
fulness." † They turned against "education" and ridiculed it.‡ They ridiculed patriotism and patriotic poetry; §

---

* "There is no standard of values in the modern world—it's mostly
slop, priggishness and sentimentality. One had much better be a wild man
in Borneo and at least have a clear and unabashed love for the sight of
blood."—Hart Crane.
† T. S. Eliot.
‡ "O Education: O
    thos cook & son."
            —E. E. Cummings.
§ "My country, 'tis of you, land of the Cluett Shirt," etc.
"Listen my children and you shall hear the true story of Mr. Do-
nothing," etc.
            —E. E. Cummings.

and they sometimes seemed to turn against humanity it-self. Many were convinced that society was too banal to write for. They scarcely even wished to communicate with it; and they cultivated an "esoteric literary art" such as Henry Adams had dreamed of in his isolation.* Mean-while, with showers of Parthian shots, they withdrew from Boston and launched into the chaos of the modern world.

* "As my experience leads me to think that no one any longer cares or even knows what is said or printed, and that one's audience in history and literature has shrunk to a mere band of survivors, not exceeding a thousand in the entire world, I am in hopes a kind of esoteric literary art may survive, the freer and happier for the sense of privacy and *abandon*." —Letter of Henry Adams, 1907.

CHAPTER XXV

SECOND MARCH

IN THE spring of 1915, Robert Frost returned from England, where he had been living for two or three years. He had published there *A Boy's Will* and *North of Boston,* which had been reviewed by Ezra Pound; and, as he left the pier, at the port of New York, he picked up a copy of *The New Republic.* It contained a review of the book by Amy Lowell. This liberal weekly was only six months old, and all these names were new to American readers, Amy Lowell, Ezra Pound and Frost; and it was symptomatic of a change in the country that Frost, who had gone to England obscure and discouraged, should have stepped off the ship a well-known man. America was undergoing a transformation. It was rousing itself like a strong man after sleep; and it was casting off its sloth of literary dullness,—eager, impressionable, receptive, it was vocal also. It had suddenly received a gift of tongues. The signs of a maturing life, self-scrutiny and discontent, that had characterized the confusion of the pre-war years, foreshadowed the revelations of the years that followed. It was generally felt that America was coming of age.

What this meant in the larger sphere the future was to show more clearly. It was certain that a new literature was coming to birth, a poetry more vigorous than had been seen for fifty years, a vital American theatre, a flowering of the novel. Criticism was in high feather, so was American architecture, so, at no distant date, was American painting; and for writers the most striking

change was that men had begun to read,—they had ceased
to regale themselves with newspapers only. The new generation of men actually talked about novels and poetry,
just as men before the Civil War had talked about Webster, Bancroft, Irving and Cooper, and just as in days
that were earlier still they had talked about Fielding
and Smollett, with the same enthusiasm and the same
directness. This was the greatest of possible changes, for
the new writers were in rapport with minds that were
frank, clear and virile; and the new women were almost
as direct as the men. They were almost as direct as
women could be; for the spread of education and popular
psychology had restored their old acquaintance with their
own instincts. Their entrance into professional life had
revived a sense of responsibility which they had lost in an
age of parasitism, and they moved in an open world with
open men. The mists of Victorian gentility were melting
away. It was the lack of masculine readers and feminine
readers with clear minds that had crippled the earlier
novelists, Howells and James; and was it not this that
had brought American poetry to its low estate? Poetry
had been on the way to something when men and women
both read Burns and Byron. For the rest, and this too
was essential, Americans were aware once more how radi-
cally they differed from Europeans. That they should
differ, to be themselves, while maintaining the general
traditions of the civilized races, few had ever questioned
in earlier times. But this realization also had been largely
forgotten. Americans, awake again, were rediscovering
their traditions, the deep, instinctive springs of their own
life. The day was approaching when the great nation was
to revolve as freely and confidently on its own axis as the
little nation had revolved in the days of Commodore
Perry and Andrew Jackson.

Literature reflected, as it had always reflected, more
swiftly than any other art, the temper of the nation. The

West and the South were expressing themselves through
novelists and poets who were singularly original, powerful and fresh; and the new poets appeared in the magazine *Poetry,* founded in Chicago by Harriet Monroe. For
a few years the claim was made, not without justification,
that Chicago was the literary centre of the country; and,
while it was true that Boston had forfeited this claim,
the claim of New York was not yet fully established. Perhaps it was never to be established, for no one felt at
home in New York. Not even the New Yorkers felt at
home there. Even the New Yorkers hankered after other
homelands, perhaps in old New York, perhaps in the
country; and no one from other regions or nations felt
that New York was finally home,—the longer one lived
there, the more one loved Vermont, or Kansas, or Tennessee, or Sicily, or Poland. It was the practical centre
merely, the centre of life but never of lives; and those
who were born to love New York loved it for its past or
future. For it had no present that one could love. It was
"permanently in transition," as Henry James remarked:
one could not halt one of its moments to call it fair. Nor
was it yet established as the practical centre, as the movements of the younger writers showed, and especially perhaps the writers who came from New England. For New
England, too, was finding expression, among the various
regions, with a new and vigorous chorus of notable poets.
It was not that these young writers remained in New
England, although, after their diaspora and as time went
on, they were prone to do so, more and more. And it was
not that they were "unreconstructed." They had no axes
to grind in favour of Boston, which they were disposed to
treat with disrespect. But, while a few remained in Boston, and others, like Robinson, went to New York, others
still found their way to London, not so much as returning
pilgrims, in the manner of Henry James, as because they
felt that London was still the centre. For the centre for

writers is where their life is most intense. It is the magnetic centre; and, as Boston had ceased to be the magnet, and New York was not the magnet yet, London seemed as magnetic as Paris seemed later. This was the spirit in which John Gould Fletcher, the Arkansas poet from Harvard, had gone to England; * Robert Frost had gone for a similar reason; and even T. S. Eliot had settled in London at the very moment when Frost returned to this country not so much in Henry James's spirit as because of the superior intensity of the literary life there. But Eliot was a special case. He had rejected America and the American tradition and soon abjured his formal connection with them.† Meanwhile, Conrad Aiken felt as John Gould Fletcher felt, and as Amy Lowell felt when she went to London and met there, among others, Pound and Fletcher. Miss Lowell was astonished that she had had to go so far to find two young Americans who cared so much for modern poetry. The literary life in London was more intense than it was in New York at the moment. As for these voyagers, Ezra Pound was the type of them all; and he was never more this type than when he soon abandoned London for Paris. For Paris later supplanted London for most of these American writers who sought for what they could not find at home, an intensity of literary living. Later still, for various reasons, most of them returned to America, and then New York became fully the practical centre. That New York could not be more than

* See John Gould Fletcher, *Life is My Song*. This book is by far the best yet written (1940) on certain important phases of the so-called "renascence of poetry" during these years.

† Eliot rejected the American tradition *in toto*,—the cause of the Roundheads in the English Civil War, the cause of the American Revolution, the consequences of the American Civil War ("The Civil War was certainly the greatest disaster in the whole of American history."—*After Strange Gods*). In *The Use of Poetry*, he spoke of Shelley's beliefs as "beliefs that excite my abhorrence." They seemed to him "childish;" yet these "catchwords of creeds outworn, tyrants and priests" were the basic ideas of the American Revolution. Eliot made good his position by causing himself to be naturalized in England.

a practical centre these writers showed themselves, for many of them returned to their own regions.

In 1915, this was a decade or more in the future, but what seemed to be on the horizon already was the ultimate regionalization of American writers. Not of all these writers. Other motives governed many,—for there are many mansions in the city of letters. But the tendency to regionalism was a natural effect of the size of the country; and Hawthorne had spoken for the South and the West as well as New England when he said, during the Civil War, "New England is quite as large a lump of earth as my heart can really take in." There were writers who felt this way in South Carolina, in New Orleans, in Virginia, in San Francisco; and, while there were always other writers, sometimes eminent, sometimes intense, for whom the *genius loci* scarcely existed, this local attachment was highly important for many. For writers are moved by love, though they often seem to be moved by hatred; and they learn to love the more by loving the less. They come to know the general by knowing the particular, and this particular is often the spot where they are at home with their own instincts; and there were no more American writers, and none more universal, than those who were Southerners, Westerners, New Englanders first. The widest American visions had been village visions, the visions of Concord, for instance, and the visions of Camden. The time was coming when all the regions were to have their flowering, when regions that had never flowered were to burst into bloom; and that another spring was breaking in New England anyone could see with half an eye. Within five years this spring declared itself in a region that for Barrett Wendell had been "virtually extinct." It had appeared with Robinson, and Frost was a decisive fact. Edna St. Vincent Millay, a student at Vassar, had written her *Renascence* in 1912. T. S. Eliot had appeared in *Poetry* with *The Love-Song*

of J. Alfred Prufrock; and Conrad Aiken, impressed by
Freud, was writing the nocturnes that recalled the haunted
old New Bedford of Melville and Ryder. E. E. Cummings had gone to New York to study painting,—he was
soon to write *The Enormous Room*; and presently Wallace Stevens of Hartford published the polychromatic
poems that suggested Henry Adams's old French windows. For, reading these poems, one felt as if a window
of Chartres had been shattered, and the lovely bits of
colour lay on the grass, and one forgot the picture, which
one could scarcely reconstruct, in the pleasure of letting these fragments fall through one's fingers. Gamaliel
Bradford appeared along with the younger writers, with
his impressive series of literary portraits; nor was Edward
J. O'Brien to be forgotten, an offshoot of the Boston
Irish, like Boyle O'Reilly and Louis Sullivan, with a mind
as mediæval as a gargoyle. This youthful avatar of the
old romantic Irish scholars was to be known later for his
"five-foot shelf," as the President Eliot of the "best short
stories;" and Samuel Eliot Morison was soon to revive,
if not the grand style of Prescott and Parkman, at least
their natural adventurousness and their masculine verve.
One felt on every page of his *Maritime History of Massachusetts* the man who was not the student merely. The
"abandoned farm of literature" was producing in these
writers a crop that all but rivalled the crop of the "Newness;" and this was more than a regional share of the
general crop of the moment, the national revival of letters. For, as Robinson was the precursor of all the new
poets, so also Amy Lowell was their militant leader. In
poetry, Miss Lowell was all that, in other fields, Elizabeth
Peabody and Susan B. Anthony had been. She crowned the
line of the puissant women of Boston.

Now, many of these writers were exiles from New
England. They were exiles from the wintry world in
which they had grown; and, while they might have lost

by this, they had gained more than they lost by attaching themselves whole-heartedly to the life of the country. Most of the tougher New Englanders were all-American minds, such as John Dewey, for example. Such was Gamaliel Bradford; and the Yankee historian Morison was to be another in his time. There was no more all-American mind than that of Robert Frost, who was born in California and named after Lee;* and Amy Lowell, who shared with Frost the intensest kind of Yankeeism, was quite as all-American as he was. But, wherever they went, wherever they lived, these writers carried their aura with them; and, if there were other writers who suffered from exile, there was reason to think that this need not occur in the future. For, behind their backs, new signs of life were appearing all over the region; and one gathered that another generation would find New England what it had formerly been, a sufficient homeland. These signs of life were marked and stirring. The Provincetown Players appeared in 1915 and soon transformed the sleepy fishing-village, which was already known, like Rockport and Gloucester, like Old Lyme and Ogunquit, as a centre of artists. They opened their theatre in a weathered fish-house, and there one saw the first plays of Eugene O'Neill, a lover of the sea who dwelt across the dunes in an old, abandoned coast-guard station. Edna St. Vincent Millay appeared on the boards there, and Robert Edmond Jones was the stage-designer, a New Hampshire boy who had grown up in a grim and lonely farmhouse, like the house in *Desire Under the Elms.* "Bobby" Jones introduced the stage-craft of Max Reinhardt; and soon wharves and barns all over New England blossomed as summer-theatres and concert-halls. Villages and ports that had seemed to be dying bustled with a new activity, and the

---

* It was significant that Gamaliel Bradford began his most serious work with a study of Robert E. Lee, about whom Charles Francis Adams wrote so well. This was an instance of the instinctive effort of the New England mind to nationalize itself at this critical moment.

old handicrafts were coming to life, and local printing-presses were appearing in Vermont, in New Hampshire, in Maine. There was a rapid spread of art-museums, at Andover, Hanover, Worcester, Hartford, Springfield; and the Pittsfield Musical Festivals, at the instigation of Arthur Whiting, were turning factory-hands and farmer-boys into fine musicians. The MacDowell Colony at Peterboro was a haven for writers. There Edwin Arlington Robinson came into his own; and there, as time went on, his life achieved the rhythm that had once been broken and sporadic. The "misfit" became the master-poet in the cabin in the woods that faced Monadnock; and the wintry mind of Robinson burst into summer in a passionate glorification of love and joy. He had his first popular success in *The Man Against the Sky,* which appeared as a part of the general chorus of poets; but who could have expected from the cold and ironical Robinson the vernal glow and emotional splendour of *Tristram*? It was true that one found in this poem, as in those that followed, the old obsession of frustration; and the light that had shone for a moment grew dimmer and dimmer in the long psychological poems that he wrote in the future. But Robinson had felt, if only for a day, that dust and ashes were not the whole of life.

There was more than a little symbolism in Robinson's later development, as if his repatriation in New England had somehow focussed his mind. If he had found himself, was it not significant that he had also found himself once more in living touch with the body and soul of his region? The most traditional of poets, he had been starved in his long exile in New York, which, for the rest, had been so good for him; and this belated spring in Robinson's life, in the presence of his own New England folk, was a part of the general spring of the region itself. For these signs of a new life were not merely aesthetic. The interest in art that was rising all over the country, where art-schools

and museums appeared on every hand, was marked in
New England by many such manifestations as the employment of Orozco by Dartmouth College. But, more
generally, the region was recovering its confidence with
new methods of industry, a new population and the currents of the wide world of thought and feeling that were
passing through the loneliest village and farmhouse. With
the telephone, the radio, the movie, the abandoned districts were on speaking terms with Washington, London
and Paris; and the mood of Eugene O'Neill's New England dramas was already beginning to pass when the
dramas appeared. *Desire Under the Elms* was a truthful
picture. *Mourning Becomes Electra* was both truthful
and great; and there were Cabot farmhouses still and
households like the Mannons, as any New England villager would have recognized at once. They had existed
for generations, especially since the Civil War, when the
ebb-tide of the old pioneering spirit had bred this legacy
of hatred and sadistic lust; and it only required a masculine genius to read this phase of New England in the
light of mythical Greece and its heroines and heroes. All
this was true indeed, but only those who contemned New
England fancied that the pictures of O'Neill were the
only truth. For them,—and there were many during these
years who wished to wreak vengeance on New England,
—a sort of stage New Englander walked the boards who
was comparable to the stage Irishman of the popular theatre. For them all the Yankees were Cabots and Mannons; whereas those who were familiar with the scene
knew that *Our Town* was also true, and that Thornton
Wilder's Grover's Corners, when it appeared on the
stage, was quite as real and typical as the purlieus of
O'Neill. Grover's Corners had always existed also. Presented with far less power, it was equally there; and the
force of O'Neill was not more potent than the force that
emanated from this quiet village, which seemed to be

nothing more than a "very nice town." * While this force was disguised by its mildness, what was this mildness but a calm and confident sense of its probity and health? Tragedies occurred there; the organ-master hanged himself; the graveyard figured largely in the minds of the people; and, while there had been no burglars yet, everyone knew there were burglars, and the people had taken to locking their doors at night. But in Grover's Corners the mortality and birth-rates were constant; nine-tenths of the high-school graduates wished to live there; the young men wished to be farmers, the young girls wished to be farm-wives, and love and youth were the centre and heart of the picture. There was even as much fresh paint in Grover's Corners as there had been a hundred years before; and one felt, as one saw the play, that if the New England village was moribund this was a moribundity that never meant death. Perhaps the force of the village was passive, perhaps it was a feminine force. It was a force of humility and under-statement; but it aroused the protective instinct,—it was sufficiently potent for this,— in those who were predisposed to feel its charm. Who would not fight, if need were, to save from destruction a civilization so winning and so worthy to live? Grover's Corners had always existed, and by 1938 the mood of the region had changed so that one could see it, as few had wished to see it seven years before when O'Neill produced *Mourning Becomes Electra*. And this change of mood followed a change of fact; for many another village, such as Mary E. Wilkins had written about, had recovered its equipoise and its confidence in life. Alice Brown's Bromley had climbed again "to a fair degree of prosperity." It had even ceased to have a poor-house,— "none of its people were, as of old, on the town." Alice

---

* "Grover's Corners isn't a very important place when you think of all New Hampshire, but I think it's a very nice town."—Thornton Wilder's *Our Town*.

Brown's development told the story. She had begun, in the manner of Miss Wilkins, with tales of lean-jawed widowers, lorn spinsters and poor-farms, and she had ended with novels that were scarcely less good in which these themes were all but forgotten. Alice Brown was a writer of integrity, and she reflected reality in its changes; and she knew that New England itself was outliving these themes. It was assuming a new lease of life.

This was a far cry from the mood of 1915, though the poems of Robert Frost were a forecast of it. In 1915, it looked as if New England had withered and floated away from the rest of the nation. It was a Wickford Point, sadly adrift from realities, whom there were few to love and less to praise. Its force seemed to have rotted away, it followed random impulses without the repressions that were natural when the force was focussed; it was like a clock that was running down, and those who loved it saw in it a vanity of effort, together with a certain "sadness of predestined failure." * Where was New England in New England? Was it not like Chekhov's Cherry Orchard, where there was nothing left but to put up the shutters, turn the key in the lock and go away? But those who felt this did not know the writers, in whom the prescient saw other signs of the times. For the Yankees were writing again with talent and vigour; and did this suggest that New England was really exhausted? Had they ever ceased to write with vigour? Had they ever ceased to write in the New England tradition? The clock of Wickford Point went on ticking; and the new Yankee writers, ap-

---

* "I can see that Wickford Point was like a floating island that once had been solidly attached to the mainland. I can see it being severed from realities when I was still very young, and drifting off, a self-contained entity, into a misty sea . . .

"The whole place was like a clock which was running down, an amazing sort of clock, now devoid of weights or springs or hands, yet ticking on through some ancient impetus on its own momentum. Always when you thought it was going to stop, it would continue ticking."—John P. Marquand, *Wickford Point*.

pearances notwithstanding, remained in the New England tradition which they seemed to flout. They sometimes thought they were outside it, they sometimes wished to be outside it, but unconsciously they were within it, which was more important; and was it not part of their tradition that they should flout tradition, even as the greatest of the Yankees had flouted it before them? That one should flout tradition was the first of laws for Emerson's heirs. Rebellion was of the essence of the Yankee tradition, which was always concerned for fresh affirmations of life; and the most obvious thing about the new rebels was that they rebelled in the Yankee way. If they derided New England, if they disliked a standardized world, if they opposed the rigidities of the times and the mores, were they not repeating the pattern of 1840, when the young had been rebels at the outset? They all ran true to type in one fashion or another. To invent a "new way of being alive," the motive of E. E. Cummings, was a new way of being Thoreau at Walden; and no one ever vibrated to the "iron string" more than this terrible child, who wrote on the lintels of his doorpost, Whim. The author of *The Enormous Room* was an Ellery Channing with genius; and to turn one's back on banalities, with Edna Millay's force of feeling, was not remote from Margaret Fuller's plan. Amy Lowell played a role that had many a Boston precedent; and Robert Frost revived, for a new generation, the part of the poet-seer of Emerson's day. These writers represented a high degree of intensity, and all the plays of their game were buoyant and fresh; but they were all tarred with the brush of the Yankee tradition. One saw this in the doggedness with which they pursued their careers; and they proved that the Yankee mind was brimming with life.

Amy Lowell's force of will, the secret of her success and failure, was her most markedly racial characteristic. For this was the Yankee will, and she won her victories

by it, and she largely failed by this will in her life as a
poet. Too much of her poetry sprang from the will, not
the poet. But there was no doubt about the will. She was
a Lowell and a Lawrence, and she liked to run things,
whether fleets of clipper-ships or colleges or towns; and,
having the taste, she had the capacity, as dozens of the
Lowells had. She ran right well whatever she chose to
run. She was a born promoter, as masterful as her forbears were, and the shrewdest of salesmen also, like the
old China traders; and, seeing that America was giving
birth to a first-rate product, she put her shoulder to the
wheel and pushed it on the market. The product was
American poetry, which was plainly on the rise again and
which she handled like any other "big business." Was it
good, bad or indifferent? What did it matter? It was
good in bulk, and that was the point. It was another
form of Standard Oil; and Miss Lowell set out to put it
"on the map," as others had put salvation or woman's
suffrage. Agassiz, in just this wholesale fashion, had put
natural science on the American map; and this required
perception, in his case as in hers. For Miss Lowell had
perception, just as her grandfather's cousin had had it
when he saw that American poetry was on the rise and
wrote his *Fable for Critics* in the eighteen-forties.* What
scorn she felt for those who did not have it!—for the
"caged warblers" and "phonograph" poets who thought
they still lived in Victorian times, for those whose work
was not their own but echoes, for those who cowered in
ivory towers and never looked out of the window, for
those who praised the glories of old New England and
could not see the genius of Masters and Sandburg. She

---

* With less concentration of energy, James Russell Lowell had performed a similar role as the impresario of this earlier movement. Amy
Lowell's *A Critical Fable* repeated her cousin's performance with about
the same measure of success. Her judgments were equally fresh and
shrewd, and the poem abounded in lucky hits, e.g., the portraits of herself and Vachel Lindsay.

scorned Henry Adams, who had thrown up the sponge. She scorned Henry James and other "traitors." * She scorned the lady-painters and performers of Chopin, with their "ghastly nights on cracked hotel-pianos." She was arrogant enough to impress occasional English observers, who were full of admiration for her because she reminded them of their own dear betters. She ran ocean liners and terrorized their orchestras by telling them to stop their outrageous noise; and she whizzed over the face of the earth in her claret-coloured motor, reorganizing hotels where she spent the night. Like Eliot's Cousin Nancy, she "strode across the hills and broke them;" and, if she was not bearded, she was full of oaths; and her bed had eighteen pillows, and she had ten thousand black cigars and seven megatherian sheep-dogs that mauled and all but murdered her visitors. This Daniela Webster was also an actress, whose earliest idol was Duse, and all her dramatic flair, with her verve and her gusto, went into the great pitched battle that she waged for the poets. She fought in the front rank, when occasion called for her, or, as less often happened, behind the lines, where she mustered her majors and colonels, her generals and lieutenants.

For literary soldiership, or literary statesmanship, America had never seen Miss Lowell's equal. Literary politicians had always abounded, but she was the prime minister of the republic of poets; and under her control this republic rose from the status of Haiti and became an imperial republic of the calibre of France. The poets had reason to thank their stars that they had a Lowell behind them, for whom editors and publishers were factory-hands and office-boys. Her telephone had the force of a dozen Big Berthas; and God might have picked up

---

* See her portraits of T. S. Eliot and Ezra Pound in *A Critical Fable.* Amy Lowell was one of those who felt that Henry James made a great mistake in detaching himself from the life of his countrypeople.

the fragments of those who opposed her,—there was
little left of them for men to bury. One could hear the
guns go off at the other end of Texas. But the Texans
and Nebraskans and the people of St. Paul crowded
the window-ledges of their halls to hear her; and the map
on which she had put poetry started and trembled under
her feet,—the map of poetry blossomed in purple and
red. She touched a fuse wherever she went, and fire-
works rose in the air; and there were no set-pieces more
brilliant than hers, no Catherine-wheels or girandoles or
fountains. There was no still, small voice in Amy Lowell.
Her bombs exploded with a bang and came down in a
shower of stars; and she whizzed and she whirred, and
she rustled and rumbled, and she glistened and sparkled
and blazed and blared. If, at the end, it seemed like the
Fourth of July, it was a famous victory, none the less,
though the fields and the trees were littered with the
sticks and the debris, with charred frames and burnt-
out cases.

Besides, much more was left than people felt on the
morning after. Miss Lowell was a pyrotechnist, but some
of her scenic effects were permanent; and when she was
not permanent she was salutary. Her theory of "externality" was undoubtedly fallacious, and much of her
work was factitious, the fruit of the will. As if poetry
could ever be "external"! Yet her actual externality was
good for the moment. It was a challenge to internality at
a time when the "internal" poets were so often sentimental, derivative and soft. When the *fond* was so corrupt
and weak, the way to sting it into life was to assert that
nothing was important but the *forme*; and all the new
poets made much of technique,—they sometimes talked
as if nothing else mattered. And what, in the end, did
this matter?—though the end perhaps might be long
in coming. The poets of the further future were to gain
by this immediate future, in which the false remnants of

the past were trampled out of sight and in which all
manner of new forms were placed at their disposal when
they developed the *fond* that was equally worthy. The
world could always wait for its poets, and this was a time
for tuning the instruments; and the free verse and poly-
phonic prose which Miss Lowell adapted and popular-
ized provided a whole new orchestra for the poets who
were coming. How good this audacity was after so much
futile indirectness! After so much weltering in borrowed
souls, how good it was to "live in the eye alone"! How
good was imagism to sharpen the perceptions, and all
this zest for seeing, reporting, recording, this joy in the
visible world, this picture-making, after so much wreath-
ing and writhing and fainting in coils. How good this
"religion of art," the note of the epoch, after so many
woolly abstractions and impotent emotions, so many
blurred conceptions and mouldy morals! This technical
virtuosity, so clean and fresh, this feeling for orchestral
colour and verbal music, and this all but morbid fear of
the obvious also! These poets reacted against bad technique by making technique an end in itself. What of it!
The poets of the future would redress the balance. And
they rightly threw out of the window the old New England classics, with all their Miltonic ideals and all their
Victorian nature-worship. No need to fear that they
would not come back. Were the Yankees really in danger
of losing their ethos? If the classics went out by the
window, they were sure to return by the door when the
noble mind had outlived the abuse of its virtues. The new
generation started with Poe, the first favourite of Frost
as of Robinson, with Emily Dickinson's novel perceptions
and Whitman, who had discarded the past. The new generation was also redressing a balance.

As a writer as well as a propagandist, Miss Lowell
was part of all this movement, so similar in France and
England in its causes and effects. For the whole Western

world was undergoing the same changes, and Boston was
a centre of this world,—as it had been in the eighteen-
forties. It had never ceased to be a centre, despite the
croakers and despite the dry-rot; and in the darkest hour
of Boston and Cambridge world-influences had emanated
from these twin cities in the persons of William James
and Mrs. Eddy. For all the reactionary forces that opposed new culture, they were still hungry for new culture;
and Amy Lowell was as hungry for the culture of this
morning as an Omaha woman's club was hungry for the
culture of the day before last. She made the Omaha
woman's club hungry for it,—and she begged it and
borrowed it, stole it, invented it, like all the writer-con-
querors, with a high hand and a high heart and the enterprise of a merchant-adventurer.* No doubt, her externality reflected her own extroversion. It was an escape
as well from a troubled psyche; for Miss Lowell's inner
life knew no repose. She had solved none of her vital
problems, and she remained the conventional child that
expressed itself in the first of her volumes of poems.†
Indeed, she was never a poet, properly speaking,—the
poet in her never struggled through,—so she seized on
the outsides of things as her only chance of effectuality,
and her dramatic instinct achieved the rest. She had awakened suddenly to modern painting and music, and she
pillaged them as she pillaged the Boston museums where
she had played as a child. Among her objets d'art she

---

* "My ship has tasted water in strange seas,
    And bartered goods at still uncharted isles.
    She's oft coquetted with a tropic breeze,
    And sheered off hurricanes with jaunty smiles."
        —The Dutch merchant, in Amy Lowell's *Sword Blades and Poppy
        Seed.*
    † *A Dome of Many-Coloured Glass,* 1912. This book was a curious
revelation of Amy Lowell's equipment as a poet in the proper sense. It
represented her work up to the age of thirty-eight, after which she
developed her "external" method. Conventional and weak in thought and
feeling, it was on the level of the writing of most of the current New
England poetasters.

was always the child, a Gargantuan child with the reach of a khan or a brigand; and she pillaged books,—she tore the entrails out of them,—and she used in the composition of her rockets and pin-wheels the *alchimie du verbe* of Rimbaud, Verhaeren, Mallarmé and heaven knew how many others. She wrote free verse after Debussy's piano-pieces; she stole the show at aquariums, with their "swirling, looping patterns of fish;" and every place she read about and every place she visited,— whether Mexico, China, Peru, Saint Louis or Charleston, —left in her hand some scrap of a rhythm or a picture. She found a mine in Keats, whom she admired for his fearlessness, straightforwardness, directness, for all he had in common with herself;* but everything served her purpose that gave her a little gold or brass, a beam of sandalwood or a bolt of silk, a flag, a trumpet, a tuba or a box of spices. And she toiled over her poems from midnight till dawn, not as one to whom the muses whispered, but as one who had to wrestle with them and force them to their knees in the sweat of her brow.

Well, was it all for show? Was it merely a night of the Fourth of July? Was it only a parade and swagger of Boston fashion? There was surely enough of the material in Miss Lowell's talent, too much noise, too much excitement; and yet how much remained that was new and crisp, what vividness of colour, what joy of action! One could say much for externals that enlivened the senses; and, when one had given up to time the bric-a-brac, the petals of Chinese flowers whose roots were somewhere else around the planet, one came back to Miss Lowell's story-telling. She was a story-teller, if not a

* Amy Lowell's *John Keats* was the master-work of a powerful mind that suffered from its author's limitations. Miss Lowell saw Keats as primarily a poet of colour. She was largely outside the subject, by the nature of things; but he only can throw stones at this magnificent tour de force who shares Miss Lowell's zest, her learning and patience, her knowledge of the world, her natural authority, her power of concentration and her feeling for truth.

poet, who had studied her art in Chaucer, in Keats and in Browning, and who, in some of her best tales, followed Miss Jewett and Miss Wilkins, when she was not touched by Robert Frost. Perhaps this deep Yankee in her was to live the longest, the Yankee whose tales in *East Wind* and the ballad of *Evelyn Ray* refurbished this old New England *genre* with a note of her own that was wholly fresh. Her colours here were browns and greys, but some of her blues and reds were fast; and, among other pieces, *Can Grande's Castle,* with its cinematographic style, remained her most characteristic. Perhaps its excess of vivacity wore one out. It was charged with enough electricity to burn one's hand off: it was like a third rail, it was like a power-line, and one had to touch the wires with circumspection. But there Amy Lowell exulted in her strength; and her feeling for ships and battles, for barbarism and heroism, for pageantry, pomp, dash and fanfaronade, for the theatre of history and the clash of peoples boiled up and bubbled over with a splendid brio. She was Lady Hamilton, she was Nelson, she was Commodore Perry in Japan, with his sailor-chanties; and no New England historian since the great days of Prescott and Motley had given the world such brilliant historical scenes.

If Amy Lowell was a Yankee of the Yankees, so were Cummings and Edna Millay, although both were in sharp reaction against New England. They delighted in turning topsy-turvy the house of the mind they had grown in,* as in decking their "amorous themes with the honester stenches." † Edna Millay was "the booth where folly holds her fair," and both had accepted the word of Blake, in face of their Yankee inheritance, "The road of excess leads to the palace of wisdom." It sometimes

---

* "Safe upon the solid rock the ugly houses stand:
  Come and see my shining palace built upon the sand."
  —Edna Millay, *A Few Figs from Thistles.*
† Edna Millay, *Conversation at Midnight.*

seemed as if Cummings's governing motive were to thumb
his nose at Cambridge and all it stood for, propriety, reg-
ularity, the neat and the tidy;* but what, at bottom, was
this motive if it was not the love of freedom that had
always marked the Yankee mind? This passion filled
The Enormous Room and constituted, in *Eimi*, the protest against the compulsions of Soviet Russia, a "joyless
experiment," as he saw it, "in force and fear;" and,
while a hatred of tyranny actuated both these books, they
were much more deeply actuated by a sense of the life
that tyranny "bossed and herded and bullied and insulted." For Cummings had a marvellous feeling for life
and for the "gods that come in low disguises;" † and he
turned away from the tyrants and humbugs to give himself with joyous zest to the wretched and beautiful people
whom they misprized. With what gallantry and tenderness he painted, in *The Enormous Room*, the portraits of Jean le Nègre, Mexique, the Zulu, magnificent
representations in the Rabelaisian vein that expressed his
high animal spirits and his love for men who could not be
pigeon-holed. With his burlesque-loving spirit, he saw the
world through a child's eyes. He liked, as he said, "shining things," he liked barber-poles and hurdy-gurdies; and
he liked to play the clown in the universal circus and
knock over ministers, veterans, policemen and bankers. ‡ He was an enemy of clichés, pomposity and cant;
and did he not play havoc with the English language as
a way of protesting against them? Behind his mockery
lay a sense of the infinite worth of the individual, coerced
and constrained and menaced by a standardized world;
and he showed that the Yankee mind, the more it

---

* "By being dirtier than usual, I was protesting in a (to me) very satis-
factory way against all that was neat and tidy and bigoted and solemn."
—E. E. Cummings, *The Enormous Room*.
† Emerson.
‡ See *By E. E. Cummings*.

changed, remained the more irrepressible and the more
the same.*

In Edna Millay's high lyrical talent, the Yankee note,
which one felt from the first, increased in depth and
clarity as time went on, as the flippancy of her earlier
verse,—its conscious naïveté mingled with wonder,—
yielded to profundity of feeling. She had begun with
fairy-tale fancies and travesties of nursery-rhymes, in
which she turned the moral inside out; but this mood of
an infantile mischief-maker had always been half-rap-
turous, and the rapture grew together with her force of
passion. An accomplished and disciplined craftsman, Miss
Millay was a learned poet, with the Yankee love of
Virgil, Catullus, Chaucer and especially the Elizabethans
whose vein she recaptured in her tragic sense of youth
and the brevity of life. She was direct and lucid because
her feeling was intense. So had been the feeling of the
ballad-makers whose forms she so generally followed;
and her gift of music was like theirs; so was her physical
perception, her sense of the miracle of consciousness and
the things of earth. Her poems were full of the odours
and flavours of New England, bayberry, hay, clover,
seaweed and sorrel, and the salt smell of the ocean in
them, of weedy mussels on rotting hulls, mingled with
the rustle of eel-grass in the cove and the tinkling of cow-
bells in stony pastures. Thoreau had never felt more
keenly the beauty of animal forms and movements, of
the buck that stood in the forest "with listening hoof;"
and all the old Yankee feeling for justice revived in the
cycle of verses which the Sacco-Vanzetti case evoked
from this poet.

That the Yankee tradition was still alive one saw in
all these poets almost as clearly as in the Yankee classics.

* Much of Cummings's symbolism suggested his New England inheritance. His play *Tom* was based upon *Uncle Tom's Cabin,* and *The Enormous Room* abounded in symbols from the *Pilgrim's Progress.*

Cynical as they sometimes seemed, they still maintained
the root-ideas that had always governed America and
governed New England, faith in the individual, the passion for justice, the sense of the potential in human nature
and its world, the love of life, the belief in its ultimate
goodness. These traits persisted in the Yankee mind in
a world that seemed to be losing all consciousness of
them; and in 1915 the day was coming when writers
from all the regions were to flock to New England, when
Connecticut farms and farms in Vermont were to house
recalcitrant souls from the South and the West who had
long made their peace with New England. They found
New England friendly, and they found it alive. One could
be regional there without being provincial; and one could
rejoice there in the "sweet American vaguenesses" * of
mountain, forest, lake and upland pasture. In those days,
even Boston, in the mind of the nation, had ceased to be
the city of Pharisees only. It had its Sacco-Vanzetti case;
but where were the liberals more in evidence? Where did
they picket a state-house with livelier zest? Where were
the old Abolitionists still more active in every new cause
of truth and freedom?—and, if O'Neill's *Strange Inter-
lude* was banned in Boston, was it not a triumphant success
in the suburb of Quincy? The most refractory Westerner
was willing to grant the old, proud boast of Massachusetts, that it had surpassed many empires in its contributions to progress and in its great men;† and the
nation could not forget New England, could not let the
subject drop,—Americans could do anything but leave it

---

* Henry James, in *The American Scene.*

The most embittered exiles sometimes longed, like Harry Crosby, "for
the sunbasking on Singing Beach, for the smell of the woods around
Essex, for the sunset at Coffin's Beach, for the friendⳡness of the apple-
trees . . . I would even like (for me tremendous admission) a small
farm near Annisquam, with a stone farmhouse looking out over flat
stretches of sand toward the sea."—*The Diary of Henry Grew Crosby.*

† "Massachusetts which, though but a small commonwealth, has since
1770 surpassed so many empires, in her contributions to human progress,
and in her great men."—*The Letters of William Roscoe Thayer.*

alone. They liked to tease New England, but they were never indifferent to it. They could not have enough of Henry Adams, Santayana's *The Last Puritan,* the novels of Marquand. New England haunted the minds of Americans, who tried to read its riddle, as if for their souls' good they must know what it meant. What was the truth about it?—and there were reasons for this obsession, for, generally speaking, Americans had a stake in New England. They were deeply implicated in it, as the seat of their deepest, their stoutest, their greatest tradition. Their blood was mixed perhaps with other strains, and perhaps they had long lived in other regions, but New England was their ark of the covenant still. How fared this ark? Into what hands had it fallen? Were these hands strong and good, so much the better. Were they good but weak, they must be supported. Were they strong but evil, they must be corrected. For it meant much to Americans that this old region should fare well, as their palladium of truth, justice, freedom and learning. They could not rest until they were reconciled to it, and until it was reconciled to them.

It was Robert Frost's function to mediate between New England and the mind of the rest of the nation, so sceptical of it, yet so solicitous also, eager for its welfare, willing to believe in it, but not without proofs of its probity, its sanity, its health. Robert Frost afforded these proofs. In him the region was born again,—it seemed never to have lost its morning vigour and freshness; and one felt behind his local scene the wide horizons of a man whose sympathies and experience were continental. He had himself discovered New England after a boyhood in California, and he had tramped through the Carolinas and wandered over the West; and he knew how to say that "Yankees are what they always were" in a way that commanded affection as well as respect. A true folk-mind, Frost was a mystical democrat, compassionately filled with a deep regard for the dignity of ordinary living; and he was an artist as well as a poet, a lover of goodness and wisdom, who found them, not by seeking them, but rather along the path of gaiety. At home, like Hawthorne's snow-image, in the frosty air of polar nights, he felt the wild and the strange in the low and familiar, and the stones in his walls were meteors, and the tamarack-swamps were playgrounds for his boreal fancy. He invested with his white magic the woodpile, the log-road, the blueberry-patch, the birch-tree, the barn and the orchard; and through his gnarled poems, twisted and tough, a still music ran, like the music Thoreau heard in the poles by the railroad. Sometimes this was like the music of a hidden brook, lost in the grasses of a pasture, or the whisper of the scythe, or the whir of the grindstone; and it bespoke a tranquil happiness, drawn from fathomless wells of living, more often tragic than otherwise, but jubilant and hardy. A boy and a sage at once, Frost carried with him an aura as of infinite space and time. Yet so paternal was he, and so human, that many a younger writer felt about him as Gorky felt about Tolstoy, "I am not an orphan on the earth as long as this man lives on it."

INDEX